THE KING NEVER SMILES

The King Never Smiles

A BIOGRAPHY OF THAILAND'S
BHUMIBOL ADULYADEJ

Paul M. Handley

Yale University Press ∾ New Haven and London

Printed in the United States of America.

Library of Congress Cataloging-in-Publication Data
Handley, Paul M., 1955–
The king never smiles : a biography of Thailand's Bhumibol Adulyadej / Paul M. Handley.
    p.   cm.
Includes bibliographical references and index.
ISBN-13: 978-0-300-10682-4 (cloth : alk. paper)
ISBN-10: 0-300-10682-3 (cloth : alk. paper)
1. Bhumibol Adulyadej, King of Thailand, 1927–   2. Thailand—Kings and rulers—Biography.
I. Title.
DS586.H36   2006
959.304'4092—dc22   2005033009

A catalogue record for this book is available from the British Library.

The paper in this book meets the guidelines for permanence and durability of the Committee on Production Guidelines for Book Longevity of the Council on Library Resources.

10 9 8 7

Pour mon petit Robin des bois

Contents ∾

Preface ∾

ANY JOURNALIST OR ACADEMIC who takes an interest in Thailand soon learns that one topic is off-limits: the modern monarchy. One is told variably that there is nothing more to say than the official palace accounts; that such matters are internal; that the subject is too sensitive and complex for palace outsiders to handle; or simply that it is dangerous, and one risks expulsion or jail for lèse-majesté.

Most people give in to these explanations with little argument. It is easy to do: nearly every Thai one meets expresses unquestioning praise for the king, or at least equivocates to the point of suggesting that there is really not much to be said: the history that is in the open is the whole of it. Palace insiders sometimes concede that there is indeed more to the story, but then demur to say that only real insiders, only Thais within the inner royal circle, can comprehend the mysteries of the king's reign.

The subject, then, hardly seems worth the trouble to dig into, and so as even the most curious succumb to Thailand's charm and King Bhumibol's carefully crafted image, the palace remains an enigma. The result, however, is a crucial gap in modern Thai history and political analysis. In many accounts of Thai politics after the overthrow of the absolute monarchy in 1932, the palace is almost nonexistent, an innocent bystander to the struggle for power. When it does appear, the throne is either a victim of a disrespectful politician or general, or else it is a momentary hero in a rare but successful intervention in a crisis. Most works acknowledge the king and his family only in passing for benign, inspirational leadership and minor good works.

After several years in Thailand as a foreign correspondent, I began to understand just how deeply the king and the institution of the monarchy were involved politically, and the great impact of this on Thailand's public affairs and social development. It became most evident when I covered, for the *Far Eastern Economic Review,* the pro-democracy uprising in May 1992. By his eleventh-hour intervention the king emerged from the bloody tragedy as the protector of democracy and the people's interest against a military-dominated government. But there were many other things before, during, and after the events that suggested a sharply different interpretation.

This was the main spark for this book, and over the years researching it I went through several sharp shifts in my view of Bhumibol and his lengthy reign. Some Thai readers will view my critical portrayal of their sovereign as a destructive attack. Yet in all I have never had any purpose but to satisfy my own curiosity and then to tell a more complete story of Bhumibol's life and tenure on the throne.

This book is in no way meant to be the definitive version of that story. Such a version awaits the day internal palace and government records regarding the monarchy are open to public scrutiny. Instead, my hope is to provide an initial perspective from which other Thailand specialists can work in the future. Moreover, I hope to offer for students of monarchy a case study of one kingship's confrontation with modernity and rationalism.

A note on names and spelling: there is no official system of romanization of Thai words and names, so I have tried to work with commonly accepted English spellings, and in the case of people's names I have tried to use the spelling preferred by the people themselves.

The highest hereditary royal ranks in Thailand are *chaofa* and *phra-ong chao,* both of which are typically given here as prince or princess. The princely ranks below these are designated by an honorific title before the name: M.C. (for *mom chao*), M.R. (*mom ratchawong*), and M.L. (*mom luang*). The palace also awarded peerage-like titles to commoners prior to 1932, including *chao phraya, phraya,* and *luang,* in descending order.

In the text I have shifted at times between the use of Siam and Thailand. The difficulty lies in the fact that the name of the country was changed twice between

1939 and 1949, a key period of the book. But generally Thailand is used to refer to the modern constitutional era (since 1932), and Siam to the period before that.

A lot of people helped me with my research, not always knowing the full aim of it. Several read and commented on the manuscript in immensely helpful ways. And far more people helped me over the years to learn about Thailand, its virtues and its problems. I cannot thank enough the certain few who especially taught me about Isan, the Thai northeast. Given the difficult atmosphere within the country on matters regarding the monarchy, rather than single any of these people out by name—possibly bringing trouble to them—I would just like to express my immense gratitude for their patience, knowledge, sharing, and encouragement when there was not much available.

A special acknowledgment is necessary for the underappreciated dissertation *Thailand: The Soteriological State in the 1970s* by anthropologist Christine Gray of the University of Chicago. As the only in-depth examination of the modern monarchy's image, Gray's work opened my eyes to the continuing significance of its mythology and rituals, and stood as a beacon of reassurance that Bhumibol's story was indeed worth telling.

Finally, as is necessary at the end of a preface—and I now understand deeply just why—I have to thank LN for not leaving me or murdering me while I was writing this book.

Introduction ໒ຯ

THE IMAGE WAS SCRATCHY, the sound poor, reminiscent of television 40 years before. Two men were prostrated on a thick carpet, one wearing the coarse indigo garb of a Thai peasant, the other a trim business suit. Legs tucked behind them submissively, they gazed up at a stern figure seated on a gilt-trimmed settee.

With aides crouched at his flanks, the figure in the chair addressed the men, and even though his voice was muffled, the image spoke loud and clear: a father calmly, but with utmost firmness and authority, scolding his sons for fighting, or some such transgression that requires public admonishment.

The two men were neither brothers nor children, however, and their infraction was hardly trivial. The man in the suit was Thailand's new prime minister, the corrupt, Machiavellian four-star general Suchinda Kraprayoon. The other man was the ascetic politician Chamlong Srimuang, who had led massive demonstrations against Suchinda for several weeks. Two days before, on May 18, 1992, Suchinda ordered combat troops to open fire on the demonstrators, killing scores and wounding hundreds. Just at that moment, Suchinda's troops were bearing down on a university where thousands of students were gathered for a new confrontation. Neither side showed signs of compromise.

The two men now knelt side by side, bowing to the fatherly figure seated in the middle, a man who held no political office, wielded no arms, and commanded no soldiers. He was Bhumibol Adulyadej, the ninth king of the Chakri Dynasty, a man who though little noticed outside Thailand had sat on his throne for 46 years, and would soon become the world's longest reigning living king.

As a television camera recorded the event, King Bhumibol softly reprimanded Suchinda and Chamlong for the damage wreaked by their personal rivalry and selfish desires. It was their moral and patriotic duty to stop, he said, before the entire kingdom was destroyed.

His halting words carried neither order nor demand. Yet within hours the violence ceased, soldiers and demonstrators returned home, and both Suchinda and Chamlong withdrew from politics. "Who will soon forget the remarkable picture of the military ruler and the opposition leader together on their knees before the king of Thailand?" the *Washington Post* said admiringly the next day.

Decades earlier, Bhumibol would have been brutally snubbed by someone like Suchinda. Indeed, just on the eve of his return to Thailand in December 1951 to fully assume the throne, venal generals had seized the government, slashed his official powers, and threatened to dethrone him unless he cooperated with them. Their coup cast a dark cloud over the young king's throne for many years.

Yet four decades later, with only minimal statutory powers, King Bhumibol had accrued the authority to summon the country's most powerful men to his feet and, with a few deliberately spoken words, expel them from politics and end the bloody fighting on the streets of his kingdom. Amid established institutions of law, a parliament, courts, and influential religious, social, and business leaders, only Bhumibol had the prestige and command required to rise above explosive chaos and restore peace and unity.

That evening in May 1992 was the culmination of a life's work for King Bhumibol. When he took the crown in 1946 following the mysterious shooting death of his elder brother, King Ananda Mahidol, the Thai monarchy was on a precipice. Weakened by the misrule of two previous kings and 14 years of de facto vacancy, the Chakri throne could easily have disappeared in the political landscape of the postwar era. At 18, Bhumibol was abruptly saddled with the task of not only reviving the throne but also modernizing it in a rapidly changing world.

As the events of May 1992 demonstrated, he went far beyond that. By his fifth decade on the throne, among his people King Bhumibol had become a sovereign of unmatchable virtue and sagacity, alone able to resolve their most intractable problems and disputes. For many worldwide he represented the enduring utility of sovereign monarchy amid the uncertainty of liberal democracy and capitalism. For some of his Thai subjects, he was much more: a bodhisattva, an earthbound incipient Buddha, like a living deity.

King Bhumibol Adulyadej's restoration of the power and prestige of the Thai monarchy is one of the great untold stories of the 20th century. Bhumibol was never even expected to become sovereign of Thailand. He was born in the United States, lost his father at age one, and was raised in Switzerland by his commoner mother, who reluctantly prepared his brother Ananda, just two years older, for a crown that might never be worn.

Due to greed, incompetence, and impotence, both physical and political, the throne's foundations had eroded steadily ever since the death in 1910 of Rama V, the great King Chulalongkorn, the boys' grandfather. By the time Bhumibol was born in Boston, Massachusetts, in 1927, the monarchy was well along on the path to extinction already taken by the kingships in neighboring Burma, Vietnam, and India. What was then called Siam was changing too rapidly for the tradition-bound court, and global political and economic pressures proved beyond the princes' ability to respond.

In 1932 an elite group of French-educated civil servants and soldiers overthrew the absolute monarchy of Bhumibol's uncle King Prajadhipok, Rama VII, and replaced it with a constitutional monarchy. Loosely following the British model, the king was made a symbol of state, and outside the palace, royal title and blood were no longer infused with power. After failing in a desperate fight to recover control of the government, the royal family and its court went into exile in England. The monarchy fell into abeyance, the throne occupied in name only. To symbolize the change in regimes, the new leadership dropped the name Siam, favored by the monarchists, for the more modern-sounding Thailand.

In 1935, the disenfranchised Prajadhipok abdicated the Chakri mantle to Ananda, who was only ten years old at the time, putting Bhumibol next in line. But it didn't seem likely that Ananda would ever sit atop the gilded octagonal throne in Bangkok. Power had collected in the hands of Field Marshal Phibun Songkhram, an admirer of Napoleon and the rising European fascists who kept a signed portrait of Mussolini hung over his desk.[1] Phibun hated all the princes, and he began supplanting royalism with a German- and Japanese-style modern militant nationalism.

Neither boy was a likely king. Ananda was born abroad as well, in Germany. Their celestial father, Prince Mahidol, died young, and they grew up with their mother, Sangwal, in Lausanne, Switzerland. Within the Siamese court, Sangwal's background as a commoner who was part Chinese left the two boys' blue-blood qualifications in question.

In Lausanne, Ananda and Bhumibol studied French, Latin, and German instead of Thai and Pali, the language of Buddhism. They hiked in the mountains and skied the snow-covered peaks while most Thai kids frolicked in steamy rice paddies with water buffaloes. As teenagers they were captivated by World War II battle exploits, fast cars, and American music. By the war's end, both were better suited for the life of well-heeled bon vivants in Europe than golden-robed, sacral princes in an impoverished tropical Asian state. Bhumibol was as likely to end up a footnote in his country's history as anything.

After Phibun's dismantling of royal culture, by the time he was ousted from power in 1944 there wasn't a whole lot of the court left. The king's powers and prerogatives were gone, and much of the throne's prestige had withered. The ranks of celestial princes were dangerously thin, and the crown's magnificent wealth had been stripped away. Still, in the postwar spirit of reconciliation, Ananda was invited back to assume the throne. The Mahidol family returned at the end of 1945 for a temporary stay; the two boys intended to return to Switzerland to finish university before assuming their celestial duties.

Days before their departure for Europe, however, on June 9, 1946, Ananda was found in his palace bed, dead from a single bullet in the head. The capital filled with rumors as to who had killed him—he himself, republican assassins, and even his brother were all mentioned. The case remains a mystery to this day. But the result was certain. Overnight, the happy-go-lucky, gangly, and thick-spectacled Bhumibol, 18 years old, became King Rama IX, holy and inviolate sovereign of a land whose language he spoke poorly, whose culture was alien to him, and whose people, compared with those of Switzerland, seemed crude and backward.

From the day of his brother's death, the story of Bhumibol's reign developed like a tale from mythology. After four more years in Europe studying, Bhumibol finally returned in 1950 for an opulent formal coronation. He married a vivacious blue-blooded princess, Sirikit, who would become world famous for her charm and beauty. They had four children, including one handsome boy to be heir and three daughters.

A figure of modernity in a feudal-like society stuck in the 1800s, the young king sailed, played jazz, ran his own radio station, painted expressionist oils, and frequented high-society parties. Whenever required he donned golden robes and multi-tiered crowns, like the costumes of the musical *The King and I*, which parodied his great-grandfather, to undertake the arcane rituals and ceremonies of traditional Buddhist kingship. He went into the monkhood as a novice, fasting as he studied ancient scripture for weeks. In his shaven head, saffron robes, and dark sunglasses, he appeared to the world like some cool, beat dharma bum from a Jack Kerouac novel.

The legend of his monarchy grew and grew. In the 1960s he and dazzling Queen Sirikit made triumphant tours abroad, honored by heads of state, received generously by Europe's royalty as brethren, and greeted by a grand tickertape parade in New York. At home, enthusiasm for the royal family turned into a great revival of royal culture. Thais seemed to desire a traditional moral leader amid the unruliness of Western-style secular government and the specter of communism sweeping through Indochina.

Increasingly, Bhumibol left behind his European-bred modernist persona to guide his kingdom in the millennium-old tradition of the *dhammaraja,* the selfless king who rules by the Buddhist code of *dhamma* (or dharma). By dhammic principles he directed Thailand's social and economic development, setting errant and corrupt governments and political leaders on the right path. In emergencies, like that in 1992, his decisive interventions rescued his kingdom from chaos.

At each juncture his power and influence increased, rooted in his silent charisma and prestige. Thais, who believe it is their land's fortune, their karma, to be blessed with such a king, saw a man who worked tirelessly for them without reward or pleasure. His sacrifice was readily visible: while Thais are known for their gracious smiles and bawdy humor, and a what-will-be fatalism, King Bhumibol alone is serious, gray, and almost tormented by the weighty matters of his realm. Ever since the day his brother mysteriously died, he seemed never to be seen smiling, instead displaying an apparent penitential pleasurelessness in the trappings and burdens of the throne.

For Thais, this was a sign of his spiritual greatness. In Buddhist culture, either a smile or a frown would indicate attachment to worldly pleasures or desires. Bhumibol's public visage was unfailingly one of kindly benevolence and impassivity. In his equanimity he resembled the greatest kings of the past, the dhammarajas of the 13th-century Sukhothai kingdom who were called *Chao Phaendin*, Lord of the Land, and *Chao Cheevit*, Lord of Life. Increasingly many Thais compared his noble sacrifice to the Buddha's own.

That is one view of the Ninth Reign. But there is another story, never before told. Bhumibol's restoration of the power and prestige of the throne was no accident of fate. It was the fruit of a plodding, determined, and sometimes ruthless effort by diehard princes to reclaim their birthright and avenge the 1932 revolution. And it was the product of Bhumibol's unquestioning commitment to the restoration under their tutelage.

Starting from the end of World War II, the remnant princes shrewdly and subtly recomposed the state and culture around the throne, just as in absolutist times. With Bhumibol as their tool, they made the throne's interests paramount over those of the state. Attacking not communism but the rise of liberal democracy, they entered alliances with anyone who would advance the palace's power, from brutal army bosses, drug dealers, and exploitative bankers and business monopolists to the U.S. government and the CIA.[2] Each in turn tapped the throne's support for its own ends.

To restore the strong monarchy, the princes seized tight administrative control over education, religion, and how history is recorded and interpreted, and they injected the idea of an indivisible trinity underpinning Thai society—known as *chart, sasana, phra mahakasat,* or nation, religion, and king—throughout everyday life. Monarchy was the central pillar of this trinity. Meanwhile, in schools, in history lessons and books, and throughout the broadcast media, competitors to royal prestige were excised. There were no politicians, prime ministers, or statesmen to remember for their accomplishments, only Chakri kings and princes. In society there were no selfless do-gooders, save the royals; all holidays were constructed to honor the monarchy, and social institutions, schools and hospitals especially, were named calculatedly to commemorate royals.

This was exceptionally effective in the Thai milieu. At the time Bhumibol acceded to the throne, the country was edging toward democracy. But some four-fifths of the 18 million Thais lived on meager farms or in forests, their lives centered on the village *wat,* or temple, and planned around seasonal Buddhist ritual and farm schedules. With little education or sense of the modern state, the people readily accepted the idea that their well-being rested on the figure of the virtuous and inviolate Buddhist king. From him came all good, from seasonal rainfall to disaster relief to scientific innovation and above all justice, rather than from the bureaucratic government or elected representatives or constitutional laws. These were only sources of misery.

Through disciplined training, astute image and news management, and above all dedication to an incessant regime of ritual, Bhumibol assumed this exalted role. Ritual imagery conveyed to the people that he had a unique sacrality, wisdom, and goodness. They saw proof in the way powerful generals, bankers, statesmen, and the most respected monks prostrated themselves before him—even though the law requiring prostrating before the king had supposedly been abolished a century before. And they saw proof in his dour countenance, exuding at the same time serenity and suffering. This was a calculated presentation of the king displaying one of the identifying qualities of an enlightened Buddhist, *uppeka,* or equanimity. Canny palace minders made sure no one published a photograph, or even a drawing, of King Bhumibol smiling.[3] All of this confirmed his unsurpassable virtue, his worthiness of worship, and the monarchy steadily rose to a position of paramountcy over the institutions of modern democracy, parliament, constitution, and rule of law.

Remarkably, along the way Bhumibol, American-born and raised and educated in rationalist Switzerland, himself became a strong believer in the idealized reign of the dhammaraja king. As he studied the great achievements of his ancestor kings, learned the arcane royal rituals, investigated Buddhist philosophy and deep meditation techniques under wise masters, and negotiated the cutthroat politics surrounding him, Bhumibol assimilated the idea that his position, and he himself, had accumulated matchless wisdom and insight into the ways of man and the cosmos. He believed that, by his training and his selfless commitment, he was the one best equipped to direct his people and kingdom.

In this confidence he went far beyond what his mentors of the ancien régime had hoped for. In the late 1960s, at the height of the Indochina wars, Bhumibol injected himself deeply into national politics, development planning, and military strategizing. From behind a protective screen of courtiers and powerful allies, he strove to set the direction of the government and the people, to the point of selecting the leadership. He joined in directing his army's counterinsurgency program, which took its lead from U.S. tactics in Vietnam. By the end of his third decade on the throne, in 1976, he was the most potent political force in Thailand. Among the world's constitutional monarchs he was perhaps the most politically active, regularly intervening in the affairs of government.

Bhumibol is deeply adored, often to the point of worship, by the Thai people. This is understandable, as few have heard any doubts about his greatness. In part it is because he is genuinely personable and desirous of helping his people. But this unquestioning adoration also arises from the toughly enforced law of lèse-majesté protecting his inviolateness. Embedded within national security statutes, the lèse-majesté law is applied to protect not only the person of the king and his immediate family but the institution of the monarchy itself, both current and historical. Maligning even a previous king can bring charges, conviction for which could bring over ten years' imprisonment. The result is that no one dares question the story of King Bhumibol, or his family, or the semi-deified kings of the entire dynasty. And after nearly six decades on the throne, Bhumibol's life and reign and impact on his kingdom remain wholly unexamined, outside palace-approved hagiographies.

In these official histories of the reign, Bhumibol's pursuit of a royal political ideal has engendered stability, fairness, and satisfaction from the king's subjects. Whenever conflicts erupted, like in May 1992, the king intervened openly to restore unity and direction.

But the consequences of King Bhumibol's revival and utilization of the throne's power were much less unequivocal and beneficial than his reputation would have it. Under the post-1932 constitutional regime, the king was to serve mainly as a unifying figurehead. Instead, his political activeness has often fomented conflict and cleaved deep fissures among his people. Although promoted as leading the way for pluralistic, liberal democracy, the palace instead became a boundary limiting it. Political, social, and economic activity were free as long as they remained within the narrow realm of the throne's needs and interests, within the king-focused ideology of nation, religion, and monarchy.

Bhumibol was taught by his monarchist uncles that his primary duty was to protect the monarchy itself, at all costs. From this foundation, over time he concluded that elected parliaments were self-serving and unrepresentative of the people's true needs. He decided that constitutional law in practice benefited the non-royal elite and didn't protect his subjects. Ultimately, he believed, European-style democracy, constitutionalism, and capitalism only divided the people, undermining the unifying and justice-dispensing role of the dhammaraja. In his alternative vision, the modern Thai state would be guided by the king and the laws of dhamma, and administered by virtuous, loyal, able, and also tough men, neo-princes found in the top ranks of the military and civil service who worked at their jobs under the king's guidance for the good of the whole.

To this end, Bhumibol partnered the palace with a series of army generals who pockmarked the Ninth Reign with military coups d'état and the serial abrogation of one constitution after another. Their brutal and corrupt administrations often exacerbated the social problems they were expected to solve, like the 1970s communist insurgency. Much of this, though not all, took place in the throne's name and with the palace's quiet nod, always under the rubric of nation, religion, and king. As long as the generals paid more respect and attention to the throne than to the constitution or parliament, and as long as the kingdom was orderly under their direction, Bhumibol accepted their hold on power.

Besides the nine successful coups and a greater number of aborted takeovers, this stance resulted in several tragic and deadly ruptures. These included perhaps the most savage episode of the century in Thailand, a massacre of students at Thammasat University in October 1976, carried out in the name of defending the throne.

May 1992 was another example. General Suchinda's deeply corrupt military clique had risen to power by virtue of the king's affinity for military leaders. Suchinda seized power in a coup in 1991 and received Bhumibol's sanction, which he used to segue into the premiership the following year. Confronted with mass peaceful protests over his power grab, Suchinda arrayed combat troops with machine guns trained on the demonstrators, declaring that they threatened the holy nation-Buddhism-monarchy trinity. The king held back from intervening, and all indications were that Suchinda had his support. It was only three days after the shooting that Bhumibol finally took action. In his televised scolding of the antagonists, his muffled words singled out not Suchinda but the protest leader, Chamlong, as most at fault.

As so often during his durable reign, King Bhumibol's eleventh-hour intervention that May was executed with masterly aplomb, sweeping aside the uncomfortable details to become yet another official milestone. For years after, the scene of the king upbraiding Suchinda and Chamlong was regularly reproduced on television, in movie theaters, and in books as a reminder to 60 million Thais that the sole source of the kingdom's harmony and democratic spirit is the Chakri throne.

As a constitutional monarch pursuing political power in competition with the modern elected government, King Bhumibol is something unique in the 20th century. Rather than accepting his position as simply a benign cultural object like the modern Japanese or British monarchs, Bhumibol made himself a full-fledged, dominant political actor. This achievement hasn't been without significant risk. Intervention for a constitutional monarch with limited official powers is a two-edged sword. Success fortifies royal prestige and the myth of royal infallibility. Failure wrecks both. Because prestige is the only real power of a modern constitutional sovereign, and it is difficult to construct, most modern kings and queens refrain from intervening as much as possible, especially in vulgar communal politics.

Bhumibol ignored this maxim with great regularity and, remarkably, always seemed to add triumphantly another layer to his munificent image. In virtually every crisis during his reign—excepting the 1976 Thammasat massacre—by a sort of mysterious royal alchemy he came out a hero, credited with expelling evil men and defending constitutionalism and democratic spirit. This feat is the brilliance of King Bhumibol's reign. By keeping his daily political involvement mostly out of the public eye and preventing it from being discussed, he maintained and enhanced his prestige and virtue even when caught deep in antinomial compromises. His intercessions often made the nation's political leaders appear brutal, foolish, and corrupt, rendering royal intervention even more desirable to the people.

To the Thai elite who themselves cooperate with and use the throne, this is a cynical act to protect an aristocratic, military, and business hierarchy. But Bhumibol recognizes and transcends their selfishness for a different conceit. He is a true believer in the state led by a traditional dhammaraja king, shaping policy according to his wise interpretations of dhamma. He understands that those around him use him without real commitment to the dhammic ideal. He also knows that his people, the peasants who are powerless in this hierarchy, implicitly trust him to represent them.

To be sure, for more than five decades Bhumibol has been genuinely dedicated to good works. He has tried to bring into Thai society the poor and marginalized. He quietly intervenes on behalf of those abused by Thai officialdom, and he has been a constant reminder against destructive greed. And all the time he—though certainly not his family—has shown little interest in the luxurious trappings that a bejeweled crown could bring. But that doesn't diminish the fact that, by the completion of his fifth decade on the throne in 1996, the Thai people were encouraged to celebrate Bhumibol as a semi-deity. Like a century before, Bhumibol's palace has done everything to give this impression.

Much of Thailand's course following World War II revolves around how Bhumibol and the princes surrounding him achieved such a feat. Yet, remarkably for such an enduring leader of the postwar and Cold War era, this story has never been written. Journalists and political scientists have universally shrunk from the issue. Virtually every history of Thailand from 1932 onward omits the palace as a political actor. Some are blinded by the romance of monarchism, and others are cowed by the archaic lèse-majesté statute. The result is an unchallenged mythology of a selfless, just, and apolitical king.

This work, then, seeks to portray just how and to what ends Bhumibol undertook his extraordinary restoration of the Chakri throne. Key to his achievement have been the power of traditional symbolism, the dynamics of the Cold War, the evolution of Bhumibol's own thought, the little-known world of the king's spirituality, and the palace's even less known capitalism. Also essential to this story are

Bhumibol's controversial and not uniformly popular family, including Queen Sirikit and their children and grandchildren. They are of crucial importance because ultimately, for all its success, the Bhumibol restoration must be judged on the sustainability of the monarchic institution and the royal family itself.

Monarchy is by definition a hereditary institution, and its power passes not to one of proven ability or public choice but most often simply to the highest-ranked prince of the next generation, usually the king's first son. Succession by primogeniture is notoriously fickle, an ever-present monarchic Achilles heel, overcome by neither divinity nor real political muscle. There is no guarantee that the talents of a sovereign will pass to the heir, and there is little protection against ending up with an incompetent or evil king.

When the crown fell to Bhumibol, this system proved a surprising, stunning success. But Bhumibol and Sirikit's one son and designated heir, Prince Vajiralongkorn, is nothing that his father is, and everything his father isn't. Like England's Prince Charles, ineluctably waiting year after year for the only job for which he has been prepared, Vajiralongkorn marks his time in volatile frustration. Even in this monarchy, where every blemish on the throne is kept secret, throughout city streets and countryside hamlets the prince is roundly feared and reviled.

Moreover, the kingdom he will inherit is nothing like that of young Bhumibol's. Today less than half the Thai people are farmers, most have a basic education, and many have lived or worked in more advanced countries in Asia and the West. The country's problems are much more complex, requiring more modern, open, professional government. Meanwhile the palace is losing its control over the media, and so over its own image.

There is little chance that Vajiralongkorn can fit his father's shoes, and most Thais fear his even trying to do so. At the peak of its success, then, the Thai monarchy is confronted with unnerving future prospects. The succession quandary has left both palace and government frozen, with no comforting solution but to keep promoting the throne as the nation's salvation. These issues raise broader questions about the Ninth Reign restoration itself. Has King Bhumibol really created a sustainable model of the meaningful monarchy in the age of liberal constitutional democracy? Or has his restoration wistfully, and maybe recklessly, taken the monarchy back to a time which can no longer exist, and perhaps never really did?

1 A Dhammaraja from America ◌

The situation which has led to the Tsar of Russia having to relinquish the throne was [brought about by himself]. He refused to adapt himself to progressive groups, which had become very vociferous, and to make timely concessions to them. One can not fight progressives. It might be asked why one should not listen to conservatives also, since they are there; the answer is that conservatives can never harm the king because it would be against their beliefs. Progressives are capable of anything, and therefore one has to consider them more than conservatives. Conflict between the two is normal, but conservatives have never prevailed and containment is only temporary; in the end it will be as desired by the progressives.

—PRINCE CHAKRABONGS *in a letter to Rama VI, April 1917*

BHUMIBOL WAS BORN ON A FRIGID DECEMBER 5, 1927, in Brookline, a prosperous suburb of Boston, Massachusetts, as far as one could get from the thick tropical air and gilded throne halls in Siam's capital, Bangkok. There his uncle, King Prajadhipok, was struggling against a tide of modernism for the very survival of the absolute monarchy.

Prajadhipok, also known by his Chakri Dynasty title, Rama VII, had recently inherited the throne after the disastrous 15-year rule of his brother Vajiravudh. The government's coffers were empty, and a simmering resentment of the royal family's monopoly on power permeated the emergent bourgeoisie. Prajadhipok justly feared a revolt like the ones that had already reduced the power of monarchies in Europe and eliminated the throne entirely in Russia and China.

For a moment, though, Prajadhipok had to divert his thoughts to the infant in faraway Boston. Only the king and his Brahman advisers could select the name of high-born royalty. After a week, it was declared by telegram: Bhumibol Adulyadej, or Strength of the Land, Incomparable Power. Bhumibol remains today the only king ever born in the American republic.

His father was Prince Mahidol, Prajadhipok's half brother. Mahidol was born in 1892 as the 69th son of the great King Chulalongkorn, Rama V, by the second of Chulalongkorn's three official queens, Sawang Vadhana. Such parentage made Mahidol a celestial, with royal blood pure enough to qualify for succession to the throne. But he ranked only sixth among heirs at the time, making him unlikely to ever be tapped for kingship. At 12, Mahidol was sent to England to attend Harrow, and after two years he transferred to military school in Germany. In 1914, four years after Chulalongkorn died following a 42-year reign, Mahidol earned his commission and returned home for a top position in the fledgling Siamese navy.

In 1917 he decided to study medicine at Harvard University. While there he fell in love with Sangwal, a Siamese nursing student. A commoner, part Chinese, Sangwal was born to poor parents in 1900 just across the Chaophraya River from the Grand Palace. Orphaned a few years later, at seven she was given into the palace to attend to, among others, Prince Mahidol's mother and sister, who eventually sent the clever girl to study at Boston's Simmons College. Meeting the prince while they were both in Boston was inevitable, but marrying him was not. The palace opposed formal marriages outside the royal bloodline. But because Sangwal had the favor of dowager queen Sawang, and because Mahidol was unlikely to figure in the succession, the marriage was officially blessed. She bore the low but respectable title *Mom* (Lady) Sangwal. After their wedding, in 1920, the couple traveled widely in the United States, Europe, the Middle East, and Asia for study, pleasure, and the occasional royal duty. Their first child was born in London in May 1923, a daughter named Galyani Vadhana.

Like most of his siblings, Mahidol was frequently ill. It was, some said, the fault of inbreeding: King Chulalongkorn's official queens were all his half sisters, and numerous of their offspring died in infancy. In 1925 the Mahidols moved to Heidelberg, Germany, where the prince took medical treatment. That September 20—auspiciously, Chulalongkorn's birthday—Sangwal gave birth to a son, Ananda Mahidol.

That event took on much greater significance two months later, when King Vajiravudh expired, leaving no male heir. In the previous five years, three of Mahidol's other celestial half brothers had died, all in their thirties. Because the new king, Prajadhipok, was likewise childless, Mahidol was suddenly next in line for the throne.

Kingship held little attraction for him, however. The prince had spent over half of his 33 years outside Siam, away from the intrigue and formality of the court. Mahidol was said to be privately critical of the tradition-bound monarchy and in favor of American-style democracy. He was believed willing to cede his slot to another half brother, the powerful and disciplined Prince Paripatra, Chulalong-korn's son by his third queen, Sukumala. After the coronation of Prajadhipok in 1926, Mahidol returned to Harvard to obtain an advanced medical degree. He wanted to bring modern medical treatment to his country.[1]

Mahidol and Sangwal loved the United States, with their large home in exclu-sive Brookline, a grand limousine, and nannies to handle the children and house-hold duties. Sangwal studied the modern arts of child raising and running a household. The family took drives around the New England countryside and was entertained at Martha's Vineyard on occasion by Francis Sayre, the throne's Ameri-can adviser and the son-in-law of President Woodrow Wilson.

Bhumibol was their third and last child. Despite Sangwal's commoner status, both Mahidol boys were bestowed the title of a high prince. In late 1927, Pra-jadhipok declared that all sons and future sons of his celestial brothers, half broth-ers, and uncles (those titled *somdej chaofa*), regardless of their mother's status, would be given the high princely designation *phra-ong chao,* just below celestial level, with the potential for further elevation. It was unorthodox, but the alchemic trick of turning impure blue blood to pure was imperative for dynastic survival. Mahidol's six brothers produced among them only two sons, neither fully Chakri-blooded. The late Prince Chakrabongs had left a son, Chula Chakrabongs, a half Thai with a Russian mother. And the late Prince Chutadhuj had left one son, Varananda Dhavaj, whose mother was a housemaid. To ensure dynastic regenera-tion, Prajadhipok's promotion created a pool of eleven phra-ong chao princes, including the Mahidol boys.

Still, Prince Mahidol kept a distance from the palace's whitewashed and crenel-lated walls. He didn't want his children hopelessly bound to ritual and treated as near-gods. When he fell direly ill in 1928, he implored Sayre to prevent either boy from being placed on the throne if he died.[2]

Mahidol lived to graduate from Harvard, and returned to Bangkok, where the streets filled with lively discussion of him as the heir apparent. He was called clever but erratic, and less politically adept than indecisive Prajadhipok. Others criticized his wife's pedigree. He was frequently ill and therefore likely to put the monarchy again at risk. And within royal and diplomatic circles it was said that he had republican sentiments, being enamored of American universal suffrage. Nevertheless, he had many supporters, in part out of fear of the alternative, Prince Paripatra, who controlled the Siamese military.

Mahidol hoped to practice as a doctor, but royal inviolability interfered at every step. Meetings with patients had to be carried out in the esoteric royal court language, which few outside the palace understood. As an incipient Lord of Life, as the king was called, Mahidol could touch only the uppermost, most sacral part of a patient's body, the head, if anything at all. To learn hands-on doctoring, Mahidol went north to Chiangmai, to an American-run hospital, in April 1929. After 24 days he fell ill, returned to Bangkok, and succumbed that September, only 37 years old.

The 1924 Palace Law of Succession was not clear about where the line would go: to Paripatra, as Chulalongkorn's last surviving celestial son, or to the newly orphaned Prince Ananda. There were lesser options too, and no decision was made right away. But four-year-old Ananda was immediately treated as a possible future king, placing the two-year-old Bhumibol at the foot of the throne as well. Widowed Sangwal was given a new title: Mom Sangwal Mahidol Na Ayutthaya, or Lady Mahidol, in the line descending from Ayutthaya. Protecting her royal status was the dowager queen Sawang, who was determined that her own family line should be perpetuated in the dynasty.

The family resided at Sawang's spacious Srapathum Palace, a recently built canalside teakwood mansion in a huge estate on the edge of Bangkok's center. Life involved the constant presence of dozens of nurses, servants, ladies-in-waiting, and foreign governesses and teachers. Influenced by modern American notions of child raising, Sangwal scrappily asserted herself over her children's upbringing. Ananda and Bhumibol were allowed to run about the Srapathum gardens with abandon, playing with toys from Europe and America, splashing about in the small home pool, and tumbling in the mud in their garden. They had cats and dogs and monkeys for pets. On birthdays there were grand garden parties for children and parents, both Thai and foreign, with games, horse rides, and fancy costumes.

The Mahidols enjoyed the most modern conveniences and ate as much Western as Thai food: cakes, sandwiches, and milk were standard fare for breakfast and lunch, instead of the noodles and rice that were Siamese staples. Like most of the Siamese elite they wore Western clothes and donned traditional Thai dress only for formal rituals and costume parties. The family took regular trips to the seaside, the zoo, and other sights, where the children were well cared for by officials who treated them as little future kings. To escape the hottest part of the year, they joined the aristocracy in the seaside resort Hua Hin. Schooling involved study groups at home with children their own age, both Thai and Western, with Thai, English, and American tutors. Sangwal was determined that they learn English. In 1930 Ananda was enrolled in the elite Catholic school Mater Dei; two years later Bhumibol followed him.

The socialization of Ananda as a possible future dhammaraja was not neglected, and Bhumibol was frequently at his side. The family partook in a few court ceremonies and rituals, and Sangwal taught the boys the basics of Siamese Buddhism, taking them to temples and relating Buddhist folk stories. On their birthdays they made merit by giving alms to monks and releasing captive birds and fish to their freedom. In 1932 Ananda began Buddhist studies with a leading monk, the future supreme patriarch. One of the lessons, his sister Galyani later recalled, was that it was a sin to kill even mosquitoes.

Ananda seemed unaware of his special position until one day in 1931 when he returned home from school to ask his mother, "Why does everyone call me *Ong Baed* ['the Eighth Royal One']?" When his mother explained that he might become the next king of Siam, Galyani said, Ananda became ill. In fact, he seemed to inherit the frailty of his father and uncles. He was often sick and bruised easily in play, missing school as a result. His doctor called it thin blood.

Life in the Srapathum Palace became increasingly difficult in 1931–32. Sangwal couldn't bear Bangkok's heat. Political tensions rose. Battered by the shockwaves of the U.S. financial collapse, the government began to run out of money. The high princes pressed new taxes onto the bourgeoisie while protecting their own fortunes. As Prajadhipok vacillated when faced with the complexity of global economic disorder, to little surprise and with minimal force a group of civilian and military bureaucrats overthrew the throne and introduced constitutional government, retaining a monarchy bereft of power.

Prajadhipok publicly acceded to the constitutional regime. But the princes around him refused to give up. As they plotted to restore the absolute monarchy, in April 1933 the Mahidols packed up and moved to Lausanne, Switzerland, for safekeeping. There they would stay until 1945, more than a decade after King Prajadhipok abdicated the throne to Ananda and established Bhumibol as first heir.

The 1932 revolt wasn't only a reaction to economic crisis and the selfish mismanagement by the princes. Prajadhipok had become king just at the time rationalist modernism confronted the traditions and mythologies that underpinned Chakri power. His immediate predecessor, King Vajiravudh, had tentatively turned the monarchy toward a European- or Japanese-style martial nationalism. But this approach foundered on Vajiravudh's own profligacy, along with the stiff resistance of the high princes. They clung tightly to the belief that the traditional Siamese Buddhist kingship was the very essence of the land, its culture, and its life. With them, Prajadhipok built his reign mostly on traditional terms of centralized power and sacralized royal privilege. In 1932, the global financial crisis steered the Chakri absolute throne head-on into a collision with modernism, and it finally gave way.

But tradition was hard to kill and replace with a modern state. Like the princes, the peasants in the countryside believed their ancient and holy cosmos could be securely balanced only with the throne occupied by a powerful, wise, and just Buddha-like king. It was this belief, and its skillful manipulation, that would serve as the basis for Bhumibol's restoration decades later.

The old model of a sacralized absolute monarchy that weighed so heavily on the shoulders of King Prajadhipok in 1932 was grounded in two traditions of kingship that developed from the complementary Indian cosmologies of Hindu-Brahmanism and Buddhism, which spread into mainland Southeast Asia as early as the third century CE. Both were based on a semidivine warrior-king, the *kasatriya* (in modern Thai, *kasat*), whose claim to absolute, dynastic power was justified, after military might, by his blood and pure practice. Although the two traditions have never existed separately from each other in Thailand, they have distinct features that are important to how the modern monarchy defines itself and projects itself.

Thailand identifies itself with the Theravada Buddhist tradition, which under state sponsorship became paramount beginning with the 12th-century state of Sukhothai. This tradition of governance focused on the idealized concept of the dhammaraja king. The Buddhist king could take power as a warrior. But to justify and sustain his rule, he had to conduct himself in accordance with dhamma (in Sanskrit, dharma), the cosmic law, natural law, an unmanifest phenomenon that nevertheless is the only thing in the cosmos having permanence. All else is transitory. Dhamma rules the world, not man. Humans only propel this law—in Buddhist parlance, they "roll the wheel of dhamma."

Because dhamma is coterminous with truth, pursuing it is pursuing pure virtue; the way it is pursued is through pure practice, living as the Buddha himself did. Principles of pure practice include renunciation and the acceptance of *anicca,* or impermanence; practicing *dana,* or almsgiving and merit-making; selflessness, piety, charity, mercy, and rectitude. The guidelines to pure practice are found in the *dhammasat,* the laws of dhamma.

Enlightenment is full knowledge and practice of dhamma. On this path, traditionally, one's karma accrues from one's virtuous actions and behavior. Accrued karmic energy, or accumulated merit from virtuous activity, takes one closer to the dhamma. Unvirtuous actions retard that progress. Lists of precepts for practitioners of Buddhism point the way for virtuous practice: there are five for laymen, and an additional three for novice monks and others more dedicated to pursuing dhamma; a more detailed list for the strictest, purest monks totals 227 precepts. Hierarchy in Buddhist society is then constructed upon levels of closeness to enlightenment, to the dhamma. Those more virtuous—who engage in more pure practice—are better suited to lead others. Their primary duty is to reveal the dhamma to others through their words and actions. By doing so they accumulate more merit and move ever nearer the great truth.

In Siamese Theravada Buddhism, accumulated karmic energy and merit can outlast mortal life, to be carried through to another life in the process of reincarnation. Thus rebirth, in improved conditions, is seen as a natural progression, even a reward, of virtuous behavior. And those born into more blessed conditions or roles carry the karma of virtuous previous lives. For the dhammaraja king, high birth in royal circumstances is proof of great karma and merit accumulated in earlier lives. As long as the king continues to live according to the dhammasat, he naturally rules from the basis of greater knowledge of the truth, making him a just and deserving king.

The king's only possible rivals at the top of the Theravadan hierarchy are the seniormost monks in the temples and the greatest wandering meditation monks. Often they are considered bodhisattvas, or incipient Buddhas. They are the greatest practitioners, protectors, and revealers of dhamma. Who is superior to whom? The monks adhere absolutely to more precepts every day, while, outside of special holy days, the dhammaraja practices only the layman's five. In principle it would seem that the monks are superior. Indeed, it is a primary stated duty of the king to protect the sangha, the Buddhist priesthood, not the other way around.

Whenever priests challenge the sacrality and virtue of sovereigns, the very foundation of the throne is tested. The dhammaraja overcomes questions of his superior virtue by following a code of behavior laid out specifically for the Buddhist king who, because of his weighty job, cannot live as a monk. This is the *thotsaphit rachatham,* the ten principles of "raja-dhamma," king's dhamma, otherwise known as the ten kingly virtues: charity, morality, sacrifice, integrity, gentleness, restraint (of senses and habits), avoidance of hatred, nonviolence, patience, and conciliation. These are parallel to the ten superior virtues, or *barami,* which the

Buddha perfected before attaining enlightenment. Barami is an expression of moral perfection, in both Buddhist and Hindu practice (in Sanskrit, *paramita*), and today is, in reference to the monarchy, often translated as "royal prestige." So royal barami, the following of the ten kingly virtues, is the source of the king's undisputed authority and sovereignty. Without making him absolutely superior— only the dhamma is superior—the thotsaphit rachatham represents the uniqueness of his sacrality, distinguishing him from the highest monks.

This construction doesn't square all the requisites of kingship. To be heredi-tary, and to avoid frequent physical battles for the throne, monarchy must con-struct a myth of blood purity. The people must believe that the sovereign's warrior talents, his infallibility, his sagacity, and his divinity exist biologically in his blood, so that his children enjoy the same inviolate character. In Buddhism, however, knowledge of dhamma is passed on not through blood or genes but through pure practice. The lowliest individual can attain enlightenment, or become a top monk or even a king, via virtuous practice, whoever his parents may be. A dhammaraja's transcendent merit and accumulated karma do not necessarily accrue to his off-spring, just as they did not come from his own parents.

The problem is solved by bringing into play the concept of proximity to dhamma. In popular belief, the students of a great monk absorb some of his purity by his transmission of the dhamma, automatically giving them a karmic boost over students of lesser monks. Through the proximity of teaching, great monks create dynasty-like lineages that carry their prestige through generations of students. Likewise, the sons and grandsons of a king are superior by their intimacy with their father's pure practice and teaching. They attend to him and learn from him, and his virtue naturally rubs off. It does not transfer through physical blood, through actual DNA, but blood ties make the transference of superior virtue happen. The king's offspring become more deserving of the throne, and by this means dynastic permanence can be established.

In the overlapping Hindu-Brahman culture of kingship, the Buddha is regarded as Brahma's ninth incarnation. But Hindu kingship, which took root in the Khmer Angkor empire, developed as a more straightforward and effective structure for absolute rule, in which the sovereign is a sacral *devaraja*, or god-king. Whereas in Buddhism there is no real deity, dhamma is the only reality, and knowledge of it is the highest plane of existence, Hindu thought is directed at the existence of a permanent self-strength, a deity of the self, known as *atman*. Within the self can be found both subjective reality and objective reality, which are then one and the same. So understanding the self, maximizing atman, leads to understanding all, or enlightenment. Dhamma, virtuous living, is only a means to this end.

If ultimate reality resides in the deity of the self, the self is then greater than all, and at its highest level it can be a manifestation of the gods, or *deva*, especially of Shiva and Vishnu. Those whose knowledge of atman is highest, whose practice is purest, can achieve divinity. So the Hindu king could be a god. Devaraja status allowed the king to be more forceful, more absolute, and the Khmer rulers were, though they still had to demonstrate virtue according to the interchangeable guidelines of barami and the thotsaphit rachatham.

Additionally, Hindu tradition allows that humans are born into a preexisting condition, or inclination, and into established social classes, the castes, which shape and limit the potential of pursuit of the self. Rebirth in a higher class, rather than simply pure practice, is the way to transcend these limits. Since they are born into the highest caste of all, the Hindu devaraja's offspring automatically carry superior self-knowledge in their blood, and primogeniture is justified in succession. There is an enduring, unchanging deity within the person of the sovereign, a pure godly substance which is passed on through his descendants.

Straightforward divinity could make the Hindu king much more effective than the Buddhist king, who was simply a leader by example, propelling the wheel of dhamma for his people. The Hindu devaraja laid out and enforced all the structures and rules of society, to establish the character, place, and rank of all things, of humanity and all life. He was protector of the earth and the cosmos. As an avatar of Shiva, he controlled the seasons and the weather, bringing rain when it was needed, giving fertility both to soil and to women. As the political scientist John Girling wrote: "The function of the ruler was to harmonize activities on earth with the cosmic forces of the universe. This was achieved by organizing the kingdom as a universe in miniature: the king's palace represented the sacred Mount Meru, city of the gods, while his four chief ministers corresponded to the guardian deities of the four cardinal points of the universe. The capital itself stood for the whole country: It was more than the nation's political and cultural center: it was the magic center of the universe."[3]

Shoring up the Hindu king's power was the high-ranking caste of Brahman priests. But there was no ambiguity about the sacral pecking order: the priests honored and worshipped the devaraja. Not allowed to govern, they could only be palace advisers, carrying out the rituals that served to identify the king with the gods. The Khmer kings established their divine presence by installing stone-carved siva-linga, simultaneously the essence of the god Shiva and the living king on earth, at road junctions, in cities, in temples, and on mountaintops. The siva-linga embodied the sovereignty and might of the Hindu god-kings.

In practice, the two traditions were blended and practiced amorphously together with older animist and Mahayana Buddhist beliefs in the Angkor Kingdom, and in the ethnic Tai and Mon states that sprang up in Siam proper as Angkor receded in the 13th century. These included the seminal kingdom of Sukhothai, which took shape at the top of the central plains. In establishing the case for their own hereditary power, the Chakris trace their roots directly to Sukhothai's third king, Ramkhamhaeng ("Rama the Bold," after the hero of the Hindu epic the *Ramayana*). Ruling from 1277 to 1317, he was a warrior who expanded the small fiefdom into a wealthy city-state. Sukhothai appears to have been built on the combined foundations of Hindu and Mahayana Buddhist culture. But, in a revolutionary shift, its early rulers adopted Theravada Buddhist practice, spread by Sri Lankan monks, forming the basis of modern Thai culture.

Ramkhamhaeng is said to have ruled by gentle example and persuasion, unifying his nation through Buddhist practice. The king constructed new temples, lavished support on the monkhood, and led merit-making rituals, such as the *kathin*, the ceremony in which monks and temples are presented gifts at the end of *phansa*, the Buddhist Lent. Ramkhamhaeng's style of rule is enunciated on a famous eponymous stone tablet purported to date from his reign:

> In the time of King Ramkhamhaeng this land of Sukhothai is thriving. There is fish in the water and rice in the fields. The lord of the realm does not levy toll on his subjects for traveling the roads; they lead their cattle to trade or ride their horses to sell; whoever wants to trade in elephants, does so; whoever wants to trade in horses, does so; whoever wants to trade in silver and gold, does so. . . . When commoners or men of rank differ and disagree, [the King] examines the case to get at the truth and then settles it justly for them. He does not connive with thieves or favor concealers [of stolen goods]. When he sees someone's rice he does not covet it; when he sees someone's wealth he does not get angry. . . . [H]e has hung a bell in the opening of the gate over there if any commoner in the land has a grievance. . . . King Ramkhamhaeng, the ruler of the kingdom, hears the call; he goes and questions them and examines the case, and decides it justly for him. So the people of this [city-state] of Sukhothai praise him.[4]

In modern terms, this translates into lenient autocratic rule with good government. Under the guidance of Buddhist principles and the ostensibly gentle culture of the Tai, the king was princely and fatherly, liberal and just, and as such the real source of the kingdom's economic and cultural wealth. King Bhumibol's palace has called Ramkhamhaeng the land's "first democrat," who launched a long tradition of "democratic kings" sustained through the Chakri Dynasty.[5]

Even so, the adoption of Theravadism threatened to weaken the Sukhothai hereditary throne, as it deemphasized Hindu principles of deific kingship. Responding to this conundrum, the Sukhothai monarchs reiterated and refined a cosmology of the state that justifies the king's dynastic authority under the principle of the dhammaraja. This was explicated in the lengthy *Trai Phum Phra Ruang*, or the Three Worlds According to Phra Ruang. Believed to have been composed by or for Ramkhamhaeng's descendant King Lithai (styled Mahathammaracha I, "the great dhammaraja"), the Trai Phum was a holistic Theravada view of the world from creation, which served as a soteriological directive on how people should live their lives. Most important, in its tale of the exemplary king Phra Ruang (suggesting both Sukhothai's kings and the Buddha) it sets out a framework for strong, hereditary kingship. *The Trai Phum*

The Trai Phum was not a new departure in Buddhist thought. It brought together many of the traditional ideas of Buddhist and Hindu folktales and parables known to the people. But through an elaboration of the principles of karma and the moral hierarchy that karma underpins, the Trai Phum established more firmly the basis of moral behavior in the world. The rule of monarchs is justified by their superior merit and dedication to the ten kingly virtues, the thotsaphit rachatham. The land they rule—Lithai's Sukhothai is implied—is the Buddha's chosen kingdom, the Buddha its first king. Thus all subsequent kings were his blood or spiritual heirs, by his teaching and the passed-down reservoirs of his unparalleled merit. In the absence of the Lord Buddha, in his place there was a great Cakkavati king—the king who rolls the wheel of dhamma. The Trai Phum says he "knows merit and dhamma, and teaches the people how to know the dhamma. It is just as if a Lord Buddha had been born and was teaching the people to live according to the dhamma." And so, "Neither the ogres, nor the evil spirits, nor any kind of beasts . . . harbor any evil intentions against the great Cakkavati king. The reason is that they stand in awe of the merit and the power of the great Cakkavati king."[6]

This was a very effective justification of monarchic rule. By equating the king with the Buddha, almost but not a divinity, the Trai Phum raised the king's sacral prestige above any other in the kingdom. By emphasizing the concepts of karma and merit, it laid down a framework for hierarchy and class: those with higher positions necessarily had greater merit. The Trai Phum was explicit that accumulated merit from a previous life explained those born into a better existence in the present. (It is possible, too, that placing such a high value on merit-making provided the ruler better access to the kingdom's assets, in particular surplus food production. The people were prodded to donate rice and other goods to both the temples and the dhammaraja ruler.)

Sukhothai rulers didn't eliminate Hindu devaraja mythology and ritual. These continued both out of tradition and for the extra sheen they put on the king's sacrality, further strengthening his rule and his family dynasty. Eventually Sukhothai was superseded by Ayutthaya, a state to the south, which similarly arose out of the Khmer retreat. Far more rich and powerful, over four centuries Ayutthaya grew steadily, establishing the basic geopolitical shape of modern Thailand. As a crossroads of the region's various cultures, in Ayutthaya Buddhist and Hindu traditions both contributed importantly to the construction of royal power, possibly with much less delineation than in Sukhothai.

Uthong, Ayutthaya's first recognized king, imported Brahman priests from India for his coronation ritual in 1351, which ascribed to him the attributes of a devaraja.[7] He named himself Ramathibodi, after King Rama in the Ramayana. But also, in pursuit of dhammaraja status like Sukhothai's Lithai, who ruled concurrently to the north, Uthong conspicuously patronized the Buddhist sangha, building new temples and undertaking Buddhist rituals.

The powerful mid-15th-century king Borommatrailokanat (or Trailok) is recognized by many historians for having ruled Ayutthaya through a strong, centralized, and very hierarchical court and society that had more in common with Angkor than Sukhothai. Yet, like Lithai, Trailok portrayed himself as the Buddha. He initiated a revision of the *Mahachat Kamluang,* the story of the Buddha's last life as the bodhisattva Vessantara before his enlightenment. The revised story reiterated key Trai Phum themes and said outright that Vessantara was reborn as Phra Borom Trailokanat, implying King Trailok himself. But Trailok did not permanently establish Buddhism as the foundation of kingship. Some historians believe that, in the early 1600s, the usurper king Prasat Thong undertook a more thorough revival of Khmer-style Hindu kingship to shore up his rule, though without casting out Buddhist cosmology.

Although spare, historical records seem to indicate that in Ayutthaya Hindu and Buddhist traditions of kingship both continued to underpin the throne's power and prestige, the balance of the two shifting according to the different needs or aspirations of each king. Buddhist cosmology remained the foundation of the king's sacrality as a dhammaraja adhering to the thotsaphit rachatham. Kings made regular alms sacrifices to Buddhist monks, performed the kathin ritual, and some like Trailok even joined the monkhood for a limited period. Across the far-flung kingdom, Buddhist practice helped manage the loyalty and production of the peasantry.

Hindu-based rituals meanwhile added a devaraja layer to the king's image, heightening the sense of awe and fear of the throne. Elaborate titles asserted the king's sacerdotal presence: he was lord of the land, and lord of life, owner of all things in his realm and holding divine power over life, weather, fertility, and wealth. Brahmanical taboos were enforced, such as prohibitions against looking on the face of members of the royal family. Violations could bring heavy punishment, even death. Court protocol and rituals were managed by Brahmans using an elitist language mix of Sanskrit and Khmer. It all served as a reminder of the blood superiority of the sovereign and his family, crucial to perpetuation of dynastic family rule.

The combination of the two traditions ultimately justified the absolute and hereditary king to different constituencies. The historian David Wyatt explains: "Buddhism, in its edification of an essentially Brahmanical cosmology, directed the moral authority of the kingship toward ends that were in harmony with the ethical tenets of Buddhism. The Brahmanical concept of the devaraja, the king as god, was modified to make the king the embodiment of the law, while the reign of Buddhist moral principles ensured that he should be measured against the law."[8]

Nevertheless, the real key to kingly power in Ayutthaya was control over the realm's wealth. Established on a large island in the middle of the Chaophraya River in the central plains, Ayutthaya's success lay in its position as an important Southeast Asian maritime trading entrepôt, drawing traders from China, Japan, India, Persia, and, from the late 16th century, Europe. The city was such a success that each king struggled with great difficulty to protect the royal trade monopolies and controls over lands and manpower. Numerous families, including even foreigners, built sizable fortunes and fashioned alliances across the aristocracy, which rivaled the throne's hold on wealth and power.

Consequently, in practice the Ayutthaya court was notoriously turbulent and bloody. In pursuit of the throne, murder in the palace was shockingly common— kings by princes and queens, princes by kings and queens, princes by princes. Over four centuries Ayutthaya had 35 kings, an average of one every 11 years. By contrast, since 1767 Bangkok's ten rulers averaged 24 years per reign.

Ayutthaya's fights for power were only barely contained within the realm of royal blood. There were several coups by non-royal pretenders, who to enhance their own legitimacy would take in marriage the wives, daughters, or sisters of the previous king. A clear lineage of succession to the throne could never be established.

Ultimately the kingdom was weakened by the incessant competition over power and wealth. After a year-long siege, in April 1767 invading Burmese forces overcame Ayutthaya's walls and moats and devastated the city, destroying virtually every palace, stupa, temple, and statue, and sending the population fleeing to the countryside. Ayutthaya ceased to exist.

2 From Pure Blood to Dynastic Failure ∾

IN SPITE OF ITS UTTER DESTRUCTION, Ayutthaya is credited with refining the social hierarchy and powerful central administration into shapes that held to the 20th century. Its successful kings were those who best assumed the principal attributes of absolute monarchs: the foremost warriors, possessing unsurpassed sacrality and wealth. What they lacked was the ability to refine that power into an accepted primary bloodline for orderly succession based on primogeniture.

This problem spilled into the new Chakri Dynasty, which arose in Bangkok in Ayutthaya's wake. To authenticate and consolidate their rule of the state that became Siam, the new rulers had to distance themselves from Ayutthaya's failure, which was difficult because they were themselves Ayutthaya aristocrats. To this end, the Chakris undertook to refashion the cosmology of kingship and the history of the land in a way that established them as the spiritual and actual blood heirs of an idealized Sukhothai and its benevolent dhammarajas, and not of bloody Ayutthaya.

They developed a narrative that Sukhothai represented true Siamese culture as an ethnically Tai state, characterized by an indigenous liberal Buddhist leadership that replaced despotic Hindu rule by Khmer foreigners. In popular etymology, the word "Tai" is said to mean "free," and is the basis for the modern names Thai and Thailand. In this version of history, the very gentleness and justice of the Sukhothai dhammarajas prevailed over the Khmer. By the late 19th century Sukhothai was being described as a huge empire, and by King Bhumibol's reign it was called the Golden Era of Siamese monarchy, where the kings adhered "exclusively to the Buddhist science of kingship."[1]

Ayutthaya, by contrast, is portrayed as Siam's Dark Ages. An official history from 1990 says that Sukhothai's paternalistic ideal "was at times lost during the long Ayutthaya period, when Khmer influence regarding kingship reappeared and the monarch became a lofty, inaccessible figure, rarely seen by most citizens."[2] Even so, the Chakris made neither a sudden nor by Bhumibol's time a complete departure from Ayutthaya. They retained many aspects of Hindu kingship, for the sublime devaraja implication remained crucial to the monarch's power. Blood and spiritual links to Ayutthaya royalty still carried some weight, especially with some of Ayutthaya's greater warrior kings.

Within three years of Ayutthaya's fall, the ethnic Chinese district governor Taksin assembled a body of troops and dislodged the Burmese. Establishing a new capital at Thonburi, on the western bank of the lower Chaophraya River, opposite modern Bangkok, in 1768 he named himself king. Through patronage and intermarriage, Taksin fashioned two different constituencies, the immigrant Chinese merchants of the area, and the surviving Ayutthaya nobility. To establish his virtue, he made lavish demonstrations of merit and built temples like Wat Arun, the famous Temple of Dawn on the Thonburi riverside. He sought dhammaraja credibility by putting the sangha under his own guidance.

But after Taksin reconstituted much of the former kingdom, the old Ayutthaya elite turned against him. Led by the powerful Bunnag family, trader-aristocrats of Persian origin, they possibly saw Taksin's ethnic Chinese allies as a threat to their own commercial interests. Taksin was also said to have become dangerously delusional in his power and sacrality, alienating his top officials. In the same kind of treachery which characterized the old court, in 1782 the old nobility supported the two foremost generals in overthrowing and executing Taksin. General Chakri, from a prominent Ayutthaya court family and Bhumibol's great-great-great grandfather, became the first king of the eponymous dynasty.

Buddhist principles of kingship were used to explain the regicide. Taksin was painted as a paranoid tyrant who ignored the ten kingly virtues while claiming magic powers and divinity, like Hindu kings. He was said to have brutalized those in the sangha who refused to accept his lead, dividing the sangha and the kingdom.

Like Ayutthaya's Uthong, General Chakri took for himself the title of Ramathibodi, which was later turned into the modern dynasty style, Rama I. He moved

Chakri

the court to the eastern bank of the Chaophraya, building palaces and temples using designs and recovered statuary that were intended to re-create the grandeur of Ayutthaya, as in the impressive Wat Chetuphon (Wat Po), named after the monastery where the Buddha had lived. To assert his sovereignty, he installed in his new palace the *Phra Kaew* palladium, or Emerald Buddha, captured from Vientiane in 1779. The Janusian representation of the Buddha and the Hindu god Indra was made the centerpiece of worship for the entire kingdom. He named his capital for it: Krung Thep Rattanakosin, or the "divine city of angels, the jewel abode of the god Indra." Enshrined in a glittering, gilt-trimmed Grand Palace chapel, today the Emerald Buddha remains the kingdom's paramount icon, the symbol of Chakri rule.

Legitimacy was not automatic. The king reconstructed the court and bureaucracy on the Ayutthaya model, modifying the legal codes and social-economic class structure, known as *sakdina*. Then he purged the sangha of Taksin's supporters and presented the move as a purification of the corrupted priesthood by a king of superior sacrality. He convened sangha scholars to rebuild the priesthood's integrity while reorienting its loyalty to himself.

To exorcise some of the Hindu-Khmer influence from the palace, Pali, the language of Buddhism, replaced Khmer and Sanskrit as the language of court and law. Old Hindu manifestations of gods were restated as Buddhist icons or symbols of the state. Rama I also ordered recensions of the Tripitaka, the most important of Buddhist texts; the Ramayana, the epical Hindu cosmology; and the Trai Phum Phra Ruang. In the Ramayana, the almighty Prince Rama was now referred to as Phra Chakri, or Lord Chakri. The Trai Phum's dhammasat, the code of dhamma, was inserted at the head of the new kingdom's legal code. Still, society needed an at least ambiguously divine king to assure it of the realm's stability and its farmland's fertility. Royal titles and language and Brahman rituals continued to assert the king's deity. The coronation and royal cremations portrayed him dwelling atop Mount Meru, the abode of the gods.

Rama I still faced political challenges from many, including the offspring of both Taksin and his own brother General Surasi. To maintain control he redistributed assets, state offices, and economic concessions, and took into his harem members of rival families like the Bunnags and apparently Taksin's daughter. In a determined effort to establish dynastic paramountcy, Rama I fathered 42 children. When he died, at age 72 in 1809, the throne passed without event to Prince Itsarasunthon, the elder of his two sons by Queen Amarindra. To protect against infighting, the king had established a succession panel headed by the sangha supreme patriarch, whom he had appointed himself, and filled by loyal princes and favored monks. Tentatively, claim to the throne was refined into one family line.

Itsarasunthon, King Rama II, reigned over a relatively quiet realm from 1809 to 1824. For safety the king awarded high positions to relatives of his mother and his first queen, Suriyendra (his first cousin), as well as many of his own 73 children. He generously supported the monkhood and ritual ceremonies, to consecrate his dhammaraja status. When he died after a lengthy illness, his first son and top administrator, Prince Chetsadabodin, became the dynasty's third king.

Chetsadabodin would decades later be characterized as an Ayutthaya-style blemish on the Chakri bloodline. Although he was trusted by his father and skillful in the power game, because he had been born to a non-royal concubine he was denied the celestial title of *chaofa,* lord of the skies. The position of official heir fell to the fully royal-blooded Prince Mongkut, born in 1804 to Rama II and Queen Suriyendra. The tension between the two over the succession was evident before Rama II died. Perhaps in response to a threat on his life, 20-year-old Mongkut entered the monkhood a few months before his father expired, ceding the throne to Chetsadabodin. Afterward Mongkut's younger brother Prince Chudhamani complained that his side of the family had been robbed of its blood-born rights.[3]

To demonstrate his legitimacy, Rama III performed all the standard rituals of kingship. He also deified his predecessors with posthumous titles that suggested they were incarnations of the Buddha: Rama I was called Phra Phuttayotfa, Lord Buddha Atop the Heavens, and Rama II became Phra Phuttaloetla, Lord Buddha Atop the Earth. The king also had Buddha statues cast and named after the two kings, to be placed beside the Emerald Buddha.[4] For 27 years, Rama III ruled the country firmly in the face of the British imperial challenge, in which London's trade demands were backed with threats of invasion. As the king's principal backers, the Bunnag family took control of the kingdom's finances, military, and internal administration, making them the real power behind the throne. Although he raised his sons as his successors, Chetsadabodin couldn't extinguish the question of his blood legitimacy. From the monkhood, his rival Mongkut educated himself not only in Buddhist theology but also in European rationalist culture and languages. He built a powerful network of supporters, including other royals, ambitious businessmen, and foreign missionaries.

The monkhood constituted a powerful foundation of support for Mongkut. His royal rank allowed him to rise to a sangha leadership position and he started his own reform sect, an ostensibly more austere, less ritualistic and pure Buddhism. The new movement took the potent name Thammayut, or the Order Adhering to the Dhamma. Its leaders sarcastically branded the Mahanikay, the larger popular orthodoxy, as the Order of Long-Standing Habit. This was an implicit challenge to the king's own claim of sangha leadership. With the purest of royal blood, Mongkut rivaled the king for the mantle of the top practitioner of the dhamma.

This had the desired effect. In 1850, when the king entered a lengthy illness, he dithered about the succession. The country faced imminent challenges from Western gunboats, and the economy was weak. The English sought a puppet leader, or a casus belli, to advance their own trade and colonization interests. The Bunnags focused on what would best augment their own wealth and power. Fears of civil war rose as Rama III's sons squared off with Mongkut and his brother Chudhamani. Reportedly, the king doubted the ability of his sons to rule but also viewed Chudhamani as irresponsible and Mongkut as a religious radical. When the king finally died, in April 1851, chief minister Dit Bunnag handed the crown to Mongkut. To neutralize the late king's family, Mongkut immediately took two of Rama III's granddaughters as royal consorts, of whom Thepsirin became the primary queen. He also took into his large harem offspring of Rama II and of other well-connected families. These moves sealed Mongkut's legitimacy, but at a steep price. While Mongkut had both pure Chakri blood and unsurpassed religious virtue, the Bunnags controlled the military and the kingdom's finances. Mongkut was completely beholden to a non-royal family.

As for Rama III's record, the modern palace treats the reign as a non-Chakri interregnum. He is never called a usurper, but palace figures claim he never wore his crown, or took a formal queen, or designated his children chaofa, supposedly out of respect for genuine Chakri lineage.[5] Ignoring his efforts to perpetuate his own line, today Rama III is portrayed as simply a virtuous throne-warmer for Mongkut's eventual accession.

Popularized internationally by Yul Brynner in the musical *The King and I*, Mongkut, as Rama IV, was a curious, complex sovereign who mastered the symbols of the monarchic tradition and modernity. King Bhumibol, it is said, likens himself most to his great-grandfather. Indeed, certain traits and conundrums connect the two.

The official view of the Fourth Reign is of a man of great spiritual virtue and learning who purified Siamese Buddhism and upheld Sukhothai dhammaraja ideals, and a brilliant progressive who introduced Western science and education and whose skillful diplomacy fended off the colonialist threat. Another view that emerges from historical accounts is of a mercurial and undisciplined conservative given to a fearsome irascibility, whose inability to modernize the sacral kingship in more corporeal ways left it dangerously weakened.

Outwardly, Mongkut recognized that modernizing the monarchy, at least on the surface, was a means of fending off the European threat of forcible colonization. He opened his door to foreign diplomats and broke traditional taboos by shaking their hands. He recruited Western tutors to educate his children, like the famous Anna Leonowens, whose book became *The King and I*. He also purposively accentuated the idea of the Sukhothai dhammaraja tradition as the direct forerunner of the Bangkok dynasty. During his reign the famous Ramkhamhaeng inscription was unearthed (or, some later scholars insist, fabricated). He also consciously copied the ostensible Ramkhamhaeng practice of accepting petitions from common people, reportedly personally doing so from a palace door once a week. To appease the Europeans, who viewed the country's Hindu and animist traditions as superstitious and backward, he stressed publicly the monarchy's Buddhist activities, while camouflaging devaraja rituals.

Yet he also kept up the old trappings of bloodborn sacrality. Starting with his lavish coronation, Mongkut skillfully deployed Hindu and Buddhist religious symbols and rituals to make himself appear as both divinity and dhammaraja. He installed a new Bangkok city pillar that carried the city's horoscope, its fortune, and people made offerings to it. He created a new icon, Phra Siam Dhevathirat, as the protective deity of the kingdom.

In a distinctly un-dhammaraja-like conceit, he built a major temple and named it after himself. He broke tradition to personally award ranks and decorations to senior monks, and he commissioned Buddhist images that wore the faces of previous kings, similar to the Khmer practice of portraying kings as divinities. He also made the king's birthday and coronation anniversary special celebrations, following European practice—but in Siam they became holy days. It all added up to the king's own equation of himself with a higher presence, an assertion which rankled even some of his court.[6]

The Europeans were more irritated that Mongkut let their trade demands fester, and they responded with direct challenges to the throne's inviolateness. English newspapers in Bangkok and Singapore attacked him for his assumption of deity, for amoral antics in his huge harem, and for the royal monopolies and corruption. It was all proof, they said, of Siam's need of colonization.

How to deal with this new type of challenge, of nonbelievers, of modernism? Putting a foreigner to death for lèse-majesté would provoke armed reprisals.

Bowing to the challenge required demystifying the throne, at the risk of losing the awe of the people. Ignoring the threat gambled the king being seen as weak and virtueless.

Unlike the Japanese and the Chinese, the throne responded pragmatically and engaged the colonial powers in trade. It was a move that saved the monarchy and set Mongkut's reputation. But it was not all Mongkut's doing. The British emissary Sir John Bowring, who in 1855 made the first trade accord between Siam and the West, portrayed Mongkut as zanily taken with diplomatic ceremony and said he found the real power and brains in the minister Chuang Bunnag (also known as Chao Phraya Srisuriyawongs), son of Dit Bunnag. Other foreigners called Chuang the real king.

Still, Mongkut's compromises worked. Freed-up trade brought more wealth, permitting the construction of roads and canals and the purchase of modern ships. By exchanging letters and gifts with his European counterparts like Queen Victoria, Mongkut even garnered recognition of sorts as a fellow monarch. He also made an unparalleled contribution to the Chakri bloodline, fathering 82 children by 35 mothers. Rama III's granddaughter Queen Thepsirin bore him the next king, Chulalongkorn, Bhumibol's paternal grandfather. A favorite concubine, Piam, bore three daughters whom Chulalongkorn later took as queens, one of them Bhumibol's grandmother.

Even these accomplishments could not hide the court's internal problems. By the mid-1860s, the monarchy was at its frailest point during the dynasty. Mongkut was aware that his prerogatives and riches rested in the hands of his nobles, specifically Chuang Bunnag. The tale of Mongkut's death revealed how much he had become captive to his own sense of deity. In the 1830s he had studied astronomy with missionaries, and at the beginning of his reign he awed the court by predicting an eclipse, which in Hindu tradition represents the evil god Rahu swallowing the sun. This trick revealed the new king's ability to foresee dangers that not even court Brahmans could anticipate. In August 1868 he again forecast an eclipse. Making a party of the occasion, he invited many foreign guests to accompany the court to Petchburi to observe. As the eclipse took place, the Europeans watched, the Siamese cowered, and the king took a ritual bath of purification. Rahu did not swallow the sun, and again Rama IV demonstrated his mastery of the Siamese cosmos.

Within a few days, though, many of those who had attended came down with malaria, including Mongkut and his eldest celestial son, Chulalongkorn. By September, eight had died. And on October 1, 1868, his own birthday, Mongkut also succumbed, but not without reiterating his dhammaraja sacrality. On his deathbed, he assumed the position of the Buddha, and before expiring he uttered the phrases spoken by the Buddha himself when he died—likewise, on his birthday.[7]

Chulalongkorn survived the malaria that killed his father. Yet his succession was not automatic. Only 15, he was too young to serve as full king. An elder cousin had a lesser, but legitimate, claim to the throne. And Chuang Bunnag's power made him a potential usurper.

With the colonial powers looking for signs of instability, Chuang opted to remain the power behind the throne, and he named Chulalongkorn king, Rama V. As regent, Chuang expanded his family's hold on the most important ministries and commercial concessions. Chulalongkorn faced a life as a puppet king, like the similarly-aged Meiji emperor who inherited the Japanese throne only 10 months earlier. And his grandson Bhumibol might have become as politically insignificant as the current emperor in Tokyo. Instead, over four decades Rama V became the dynasty's strongest ruler. Overcoming the Bunnags and finessing the colonialists, he restored the absolute powers of the Chakri throne. Ironically, his success ensured that he was the last king to enjoy them.

The Bunnag family had severely disadvantaged the royal household. In 1871 the king even had to borrow 8 million baht from Chuang for palace and government needs.[8] But over time, as the Bunnags' older allies in government passed away, Chuang himself dying in 1883, Chulalongkorn replaced them with young Western-educated princes from among Mongkut's 82 children, loyal directly to him. With them Chulalongkorn formed two advisory councils, tellingly named, on the English model, the privy council and the council of state.

Advised by European counsels, he gave his government a modern bureaucratic shape. Professional schools were established for the civil service, the *kharajakan,* or servants of the king, and for the army and navy. A central budget set appropriations for each ministry and division, and a separate privy purse funded the palace. State income grew as trade was progressively freed up, graft was reduced, and the Bunnags' influence slashed.

Chulalongkorn reapportioned concessions and assets like land to his generation of Chakris, ensuring that economic power remained in the king's family. But he also delineated between state and private wealth, by turning over vast tracts of real estate to his relatives to help make them self-supporting. Renting property to city residents and land to farmers soon became the greater royal family's chief source of income.

The king meanwhile brought his image closer to earth. He appeared more in public, and allowed others to touch him. He ended the rule that subjects must prostrate themselves before him, though it didn't really stop them. Casting himself as democratic, Chulalongkorn called his adviser group a legislative council, and characterized himself as a "prime minister almost exactly like the British prime minister."[9] Yet his reforms further concentrated monarchic power. He filled top bureaucratic and military posts only with family members. Young princes by-passed the academies and training to be made generals and ministers.

In the Buddhist priesthood, Chulalongkorn elevated King Mongkut's Tham-mayut order to a superior position over the much larger Mahanikay order, and he installed his cousin Prince Wachirayan Worarot as the Thammayut head. In 1899, Wachirayan was made supreme patriarch, the head of the ecclesiastical commis-sion governing both sects.

At the time the sangha was still officially self-governing. Wachirayan made palace control systematic in the Sangha Reform Act of 1902, which asserted the royal government's responsibility for the priesthood, with sole right to confer clerical rank. This rendered the king the de facto head of the church. A hierarchy of monasteries was formalized, with royal temples (*wat luang*) at the top. The king took personal control of the appointment of ecclesiastical officers in Bangkok and in royal temples.[10] The new monastic structure and its operatives were developed methodically to the village level, making the monkhood an important instrument of Chakri promotion and control.

Chulalongkorn also further propounded and deepened Chakri mythology. The stone Ramkhamhaeng inscription describing a liberal Sukhothai state under a just and absolute dhammaraja was promoted by Chulalongkorn's cultural chief, Prince Damrong Rajanupap, to justify the Chakris as heirs to the Sukhothai tra-dition. Meanwhile, through ritual and symbols, Chulalongkorn maintained the throne's ambiguous devaraja-dhammaraja image. The emphasis, as with his father, was more on conspicuously demonstrating his observance of the dhammaraja's thotsaphit rachatham through rituals and the building of monuments and temples.

By the turn of the century, Chulalongkorn ruled supreme. There were no challengers, to himself or to his officially designated successor. In two official tours to Europe, in 1897 and 1907, which were well hosted by the European royal families, he confirmed the Siamese monarchy's equal status among the world's royals. He became the first Thai king to understand the monarchy as an institution of govern-ment, in the way that the Europeans saw it.

Yet time was ticking for the absolute throne. Providing modern educations to a new generation of Chakris and then to non-royal civil service officials opened the door to new political ideas. Already in 1885, 11 Western-educated members of the elite, including three half brothers of Chulalongkorn, petitioned him to create a Westminster-like parliamentary democracy. They argued that the absolute monarchy, dependent as it was on one person to manage the country, left Siam vulnerable.

Chulalongkorn defused the challenge by encouraging these reformers to further study European government for eventual application to Siam. This gave credibility to the idea of constitutionalism, and reminders of it kept cropping up in other troubled monarchies in Japan, China, and Europe. Before he died in 1910, Chulalongkorn confided his fear: "When the descendants of the bureaucracy have acquired more knowledge, we shall face the same situation as experienced in previous reigns, that is, the monarchy and royalty will become increasingly helpless."[11]

Even so, he prepared for Chakri perpetuity, siring 77 children by 36 of his 92 consorts. His official queens, by which he had 18 children, including Bhumibol's father, were all his half sisters. They seemed to guarantee that the pure Chakri blood was generously sustained into the next generation. The assumption, however, nearly proved fatal to the dynasty.

The system of primogeniture, by which Chulalongkorn selected his heir, is notoriously fickle. While sometimes it begets unexpected greatness, like the passage from vacillating Mongkut to sagacious Chulalongkorn, just as often the reverse occurs. It was a testament to Rama V's restoration of the absolute throne's powers that it took two poor kings in succession to bring down the absolute monarchy.

Born in 1881, Chulalongkorn's heir, Prince Vajiravudh, was the first Thai sovereign to be educated abroad. He studied in England at Oxford and then Sandhurst military academy, and by the time he was crowned in 1910, he was thoroughly exposed to the affairs of state. His inheritance was generous: a well-staffed, loyal government; Chakri blood, with all the accumulated merit of a great king; and absolute power. As his nephew wrote later, "No monarch of Siam had ever succeeded to such a noble or well-secured heritage."[12]

Captivated by the industrialization and the nationalist fervor of Japan, England, and Germany, Vajiravudh moved in a new direction. He endeavored to imbue Siam with the same unified, disciplined patriotic drive and sense of national duty that those countries enjoyed. Yet his formula was to direct his people's loyalty not toward the geopolitical or cultural state but on the body of the king himself. He fashioned a new cosmology in a mantra that was to become the seminal code of 20th-century Thailand: *chart, sasana, phra mahakasat,* or nation, religion, and king ("lord great warrior"). Every Thai was called on to love and serve this "trinitarian mystery," as historian David Wyatt has called it. Without any one of the three, the people were told, the Kingdom of Siam could not exist.

The pivotal component was the monarch. Making it easy to understand in traditional terms, Vajiravudh established the style for Chakri kings Rama I, Rama II, and so on, evoking not only the Ramayana's warrior hero but also Sukhothai's Ramkhamhaeng and Ayutthaya's Ramathibodi. He created two new holidays, one to celebrate the Chakri Dynasty's founding and the other for his father Chulalongkorn's birthday.

To advance his vision beyond the small literate population, the king promoted mass education. He also popularized his concept of the state in the media and the arts. And to serve as the platform for his new nationalism, Rama VI launched a nationwide paramilitary group, the Sua Pa, or the Wild Tiger Corps, directly answerable to the throne. At his coronation, he declared that the aim of the Sua Pa was "to instill in the minds of the people of our own race love and loyalty towards the high authority that controls and maintains with justice and equity the political independence of the nation; devotion to Fatherland, Nation and our Holy Religion; and not the least of all, the preservation of national unity, and the cultivation of mutual friendship."[13] The ceremonial army reached 4,000 members in its first year, quickly becoming a new elite rivaling the civil service.

Vajiravudh also modernized the army and the navy with new equipment; he created a Siamese bank (foreign banks had dominated the country until then) and the Siam Cement Company, which more than 90 years later remains Thailand's leading industrial conglomerate, mainly owned by the crown. He also raised Siam's international profile by sending several thousand men to help the Allies in World War I.

Vajiravudh's nationalism was timely and utilitarian, but several things got in the way. First was the immensity of the royal family his father and grandfather had begotten. King Mongkut had some 500 grandchildren, with 28 families descending from his sons alone. Aside from Chulalongkorn's 77 children, another prince of the same generation had 73, and several had 40 to 50.

These people were a gigantic load on state coffers. Chulalongkorn lightened the burden somewhat by preventing his huge surplus of daughters from marrying, at least officially. But in the Sixth Reign many royals were shockingly profligate, traveling the world in lavish style, and moving money offshore in case of a revolution like China's or Russia's. Vajiravudh responded by placing limitations on the royal titling system, and introducing family surnames in the Western style to make it clear who was who. He also declared a national policy of monogamy. Still, it didn't shrink the immediate burden much.

Another problem was the king's own introversion and alleged homosexuality. Vajiravudh spent his time not with the high princes who guaranteed his throne but with his own coterie of often ambitious young men, mostly commoners. He avoided the day-to-day duties of government while pursuing personal pleasures in literature and drama, and in military pomp and pageantry. This was doubly significant. His behavior revolted much of the court, including the princes his father had most trusted. And because Vajiravudh took no blue-blooded queen or consort, he could foster no natural line of succession.

Moreover, his establishment of the Sua Pa alienated the army, and in early 1912 several dozen young military officers plotted to overthrow the new king. They proved disorganized and their goals were unclear: some wanted to do away with the monarchy altogether, while others wanted to install another king with a constitution. The cabal was exposed before they ever moved. But it was an important development, because for the first time significant resistance to the throne came from outside the court and the aristocracy.

In addition, Vajiravudh's interest in the modern-style state somewhat shifted the identity of the king away from a sacral bodhisattva toward a kaiser-like figure.[14] This step toward desacralization of the monarchy endangered the all-important construct of the dhammaraja king. Saving the throne was the powerful sangha supreme patriarch, Prince Wachirayan. Through the kingdom's temples, Wachirayan could propagandize the nation-religion-king mantra. This kept the modernizing state, Buddhism, and monarchy together in a sacral context.

By 1920, mismanagement and the global economic downturn took the budget into deficit. The main problem remained the king's spending on the military, his corrupt courtiers, and the Sua Pa. The princes couldn't change him or remove him, so some took to publicly maligning the throne in newspapers. Royal prestige began to deteriorate, not only within the court but among the people of Bangkok.

Yet the court remained so bound to uphold royal inviolateness that it was only in 1925 that the princes ventured a stronger challenge. With the country's finances on the verge of complete collapse, an emergency cabinet meeting was held in early May. The senior princes decided to demand large cuts in expenditure, especially in the royal household. Their decision represented a bold challenge to the absolute king, so much so that one concurring very senior prince dared not sign it. In response to their audacity, the king defiantly replied that it was his sole, absolute prerogative to decide state policy. Although the consequences were immense, no one dared fight back.

Another problem had unfolded along with the fiscal malaise. Around 1920, Vajiravudh woke up to his primary duty to sustain the Chakri line. He launched into a series of attempts to produce an heir, changing one princess or noble daughter for another, all in vain. Given Chulalongkorn's abundant progeny, it should not have been an obstacle to the maintenance of the dynasty. Chulalongkorn left behind him seven celestial sons, including Vajiravudh: five by first queen Saowabha, one by second queen Sawang, and one by third queen Sukumala.

But it wasn't enough, due, some believe, to the family's intense inbreeding. First, none of Vajiravudh's four celestial brothers (the sons of Saowabha) had produced his own pure royal-blooded heir. They produced very few children at all. Two had sons who were unqualified to succeed in normal circumstances, one by a foreign wife and the other by a maid.

Moreover, Saowabha's sons were all given to chronic illness, and between 1920 and 1925, three of them died. That left in early 1925 only three celestial princes, one by each former queen: Vajiravudh's full brother Prince Prajadhipok, Queen Sawang's surviving son Prince Mahidol, and Prince Paripatra, Queen Sukumala's son. Again, it should have been enough, but for the details. Prajadhipok was the natural choice as heir, but he too was childless after five years of marriage. In late 1925 Mahidol had a newborn son, but by a commoner. Only the last-ranked Paripatra had a fully blue-blooded son. But Vajiravudh hated the prince.

In one of his lasting legacies, Vajiravudh attempted to resolve the succession problem systematically. His 1924 Palace Law of Succession established primogeniture as the principle, with first in line being the eldest son of the previous king (rather than the late king's brother, for instance). Second would be the next-oldest son, and so on. Vajiravudh still believed he might conceive a son, but if he didn't, the law established Queen Saowabha's line first in succession, followed by Sawang's, and then Sukumala's. It made Prajadhipok, younger than both Mahidol and Paripatra, the heir. Above all, the law prioritized the king's own discretion in choosing the heir. It also expressly ruled against women ascending the throne.

The kingdom was saved, just barely, by Vajiravudh's demise later that year. In early 1925, one of his consorts became pregnant. As the delivery date grew near, Vajiravudh fell ill. On November 24, the consort gave birth to a daughter. "It's just as well," the bedridden king supposedly said. Two days later, he died.

Despite his modernization efforts, Vajiravudh had nearly wiped out his father's immense legacy. Prince Damrong wrote in 1926: "The authority of the sovereign had fallen much in respect and confidence, the treasury was on the verge of bankruptcy, and the government was corrupted."[15] But his motto "nation-religion-king" created a new consciousness of the Siamese nation, providing the people with a modern identity as members of a corporeal state. Membership was defined foremost by allegiance to the king; the king was the captain and the nation the ship. It was a radical new basis for monarchic rule, bordering on desacralization into a hereditary martial autocracy. In firm, percipient hands, this new concept might have worked. Instead, the throne passed to a conscientious but weak king dominated by old-school princes who clung to a mythologized vision of past thrones.

Born in 1893, Chulalongkorn's youngest celestial son, Prajadhipok, attended Eton and then Woolwich Royal Military Academy, returning to Siam in 1914 to oversee the king's artillery. In 1917 he ordained for three months under the supreme patriarch, Prince Wachirayan, who urged him to stay in the monkhood so that he might succeed him as supreme patriarch. This showed Wachirayan's belief in the essential pure virtue carried by royal blood, as well as the need for continued palace control of the monkhood. Prajadhipok declined, and in 1918 he married his first cousin, Princess Rambhai Bharni. After his three elder brothers died in the early 1920s, he became the key prince and first heir. Yet he too was childless.

To his great credit, the new Rama VII attacked the job with a sense of urgency. Three days after Vajiravudh's death, he constituted a new Supreme Council of State, a super-cabinet comprising the top-ranked and most experienced members of the royal family: Princes Bhanurangsi, Naris, and Damrong, all sons of King Mongkut; and Princes Paripatra and Kitiyakara, the eldest sons of Chulalongkorn. Within five months, they replaced most of the late king's ministers and chief bureaucrats with their own people, most of royal or noble blood. They slashed palace expenditures, laid off many bureaucrats, and reduced the king's own annual stipend by half. Within a year the government's position turned around.

In certain areas the new reign was fairly progressive. The princes traveled across the country promoting modern agricultural methods to combat poverty. Making himself accessible to the growing urban bourgeoisie, the king attended scholarly lectures and civic association meetings. He personally awarded diplomas at university graduation ceremonies with the hope of binding students to the throne.

Likewise, the king presided over military school commencement, presenting the new officers their swords as bonds of loyalty. About 40 percent of the civil service in number, the military was a key to his survival, so he left its budget untouched. This move kept the soldiers happy, internally, but war minister Prince Boworadej warned that mounting indiscipline and corruption in the military could endanger the throne.[16]

Yearning to recover the power and prestige of the Fifth Reign, the king reinstated the many rites that Vajiravudh had let lapse, traditional sources of royal prestige like the royal tonsure and plowing ceremonies, and the kathin merit-making ceremony to Wat Arun, with its opulent royal barge procession. Rather than erecting grand new temples like his predecessors, Prajadhipok turned austerity into a virtue by repairing existing ones. Other traditional symbols of monarchic power were highlighted. When a baby "white" elephant was discovered in Chiangmai in 1927, it was, as in ancient times, heralded as a great omen for the reign. As a symbol of prosperity and the exclusive property of the king, this white elephant, the first discovered in decades, was received in Bangkok with three days of religious rites and celebrations.

As Prajadhipok hoped, royal prestige again climbed, with the help of some enforcement. Monarchist newspapers again generously praised the king. Critical papers were threatened and strident republican papers were closed down. Despite the turnaround, Prajadhipok was acutely aware of the dangers confronting the throne. He knew many Bangkokians resented royal privilege and monopoly on high positions, and he knew of the Thai students in Europe who openly discussed alternatives like parliamentary democracy, national socialism, and communism. In a letter the king wrote in July 1926 to Francis Sayre, the American adviser to the Sixth and Seventh reigns, he acutely laid out the conundrum of the modern monarchy.

> As you well know, the king has absolute power in everything. This principle is very good and very suitable for the country, as long as we have a good king. If the king is really an elected king, it is probable that he would be a fairly good king.[17]
>
> But . . . the kings of Siam are really hereditary, with a very limited possibility of choice. Such being the case, it is not at all certain that we shall always have a good king. The absolute power may become a positive danger to the country.
>
> Besides this . . . in olden days the actions of the king were hardly ever questioned. . . . The king was really respected and his words were really

laws. . . . In the reign which has just ended, things got much worse. . . .
Every official is more or less suspected of embezzlement or nepotism.
Fortunately the princes were still respected as being on the whole honest
folks. What was very regrettable was that the court was heartily detested
and in the later years was on the verge of being ridiculed. The birth of
free press aggravated matters still more.

The position of the king has become one of great difficulty. The
movements of opinion in this country give a sure sign that the days of autocratic rulership are numbered. The position of the king must be made
more secure if this dynasty is going to last. Some sort of guarantee must
be found against an unwise king.[18]

But Rama VII balked at real reforms. He insisted that a European-style parliament was unsuitable for Asians, and that the Siamese were not ready for representative government. He told Sayre that the Supreme Council of State was ideal
because its high-minded princes were unlikely to succumb to corruption and
influence peddling. Prajadhipok did propose creating the position of prime minister to supervise the cabinet's work. But the supreme council was vehemently
opposed. Prince Damrong argued that it would dangerously suggest to the people
that the king no longer ruled the country.

The king did create a practice legislature called the Committee of the Privy
Council. This powerless body was assigned to debate public policy to show how
democracy works. The members were all appointed by the king, and they were
mostly of royal descent. Again the high princes objected. Prince Dhani Nivas, the
education minister, argued that the whole thing was unnecessary because democracy was not applicable the world round. Others said the Privy Council would put
the monarchy in a bad light because it would propose things to the throne, rather
than only respond to royal requests. Prajadhipok finally gave up after a test case
revealed that the faux legislature was unable to decide even on the design for a
national flag.

The king meanwhile remained committed to the primacy of royal blood. He
stayed within royal circles in appointing supreme councilors, ministers, and advisers. He told younger princes that it was their duty to study abroad, in order to
prepare for government service. To strengthen the family's weakened bloodline, at
the end of 1927 Prajadhipok promoted a group of young, middle-ranked princes to
just below the celestial level. They included the two-year-old Ananda, son of Prince

Mahidol, and the second son Mahidol would soon have, Bhumibol. Mahidol, now first heir because the king remained childless, was called home from Boston.

At the end of 1930, America's financial crash circled the globe and caught Siam up with it. The principal source of state income, taxes on exports and imports, collapsed. Over 18 months the king and his Supreme Council of State battled almost openly over what to do. The king proposed implementing general income and property taxes. The princes flatly rejected the measure, because it would hit hardest their own fortunes. Demonstrating their power over the king, the princes instead forced reductions in civil service salaries and rolls, and then the military budget. The cuts predictably angered Bangkok's middle class. Rebellion was in the air, fueled by the fast-spreading story of an ancient prediction, supposedly made in Rama I's court, that the Chakri Dynasty would last only 150 years—to 1932. If the princes needed any reminder of their vulnerability, it came when republicans overthrew King Alfonso in Spain in 1931.

The king was in great distress. After 14 years of marriage, he remained without an heir. His brother Mahidol returned in 1929, only to die months later, leaving two half-commoner sons. The celestial royal bloodline, seemingly so full after Chulalongkorn's great harem, had almost dried up. On top of that, the obstinate princes and the insurmountable forces of global economics left him lost. At the end of 1931, Prajadhipok admitted to a dinner party of fellow royals that he could not master the new complex economy. "I'm only a soldier. How can I understand such things as the gold standard?" he moaned.[19]

On another occasion the king, who had restored the fertility rituals of the royal plowing ceremony, complained that people unfairly held him personally responsible even for bad weather. And in front of a group of army officers he said: "The financial war is a very hard one indeed. . . . I have never experienced such a hardship; therefore if I have made a mistake I really deserve to be excused by the officials and people of Siam." It was a stunning confession that Prajadhipok lacked the dhammic virtuosity and kingly omnipotence so painstakingly constructed through history and culture. The inviolate dhammaraja himself conceded that the king wore no clothes.[20]

In desperation, in October 1931, Prajadhipok assigned a small committee to draw up a draft for a democratic government and constitutional monarchy. The group comprised foreign minister Prince Devawongs Varodaya, his bright assistant Phraya Srivisarn Vacha, and American adviser Raymond Stevens. None of them believed it was the right time, but they understood that some shift to constitutionalism was inevitable, eventually. They designed a government run by a prime minister who names his own cabinet and answers first to a legislative assembly, half royally appointed and half indirectly elected. The king retained the right to choose the prime minister and to veto laws and policies. The supreme council of princes would continue to advise the king but would not oversee the cabinet. Prajadhipok saw this as a way of ensuring that the cabinet worked in harmony with the executive. It also shifted royal power back to the king from the princes.

In an environment of near panic, in early March 1932, Prajadhipok handed the draft constitution to the princes. He wanted to promulgate it on April 6, the dynasty's 150th anniversary. The supreme council flatly rejected the draft and any other ideas for political reform. The princes again overruled the king's economic reforms and further insulated themselves from new taxes, while passing the burden to the middle class. As newspapers strongly attacked the injustice, Prajadhipok belatedly wrote to Prince Dhani expressing envy of foreign fascists' ability to inculcate support for their governments.[21]

Siam's absolute monarchy fell to a coup on June 24, 1932. The revolt was carried out by frustrated members of the new bourgeois elite, well-educated civil servants, and army officers. There was no mass uprising, no involvement of the peasantry. The coup took place while the palace community enjoyed its annual hot-season sojourn at the seaside resort of Hua Hin, where a few years earlier Prajadhipok had built a splendid beachside palace that he named Klai Kangwon, or Far from Worry. The princes were seized without violence, and the revolution was all over in less than 24 hours. The king was playing golf on the Hua Hin course with Queen Rambhai and visiting British arms dealers that morning. Receiving the news on the eighth hole, he turned to the queen and said, "So, as I told you."

3   1932: Revolution and Exile   ❧

ALTHOUGH BHUMIBOL WAS ONLY FOUR AT THE TIME, the story of the revolution, and how it was later rewritten by the royalists, became an essential component in his restoration of the powerful throne after 1946. The battle to control the story was as toughly fought as the royalist battle to overturn the revolution was.

The June 24, 1932, revolt was essentially a coup by non-royal army and navy officers and their allies in the civilian bureaucracy. Calling themselves the People's Party, they seized the top princes and palaces and presented Prajadhipok with a fait accompli. They had begun as a clique of students in France in the twilight years of the Sixth Reign. The key plotters included leftist intellectual Pridi Bhanomyong and young army major Phibun Songkhram. An ideologically mixed bunch, beyond stripping the throne of its powers and creating a constitutional government they lacked a uniform idea of the kind of state they sought. They left the result up to the reaction of the royal establishment. The coup was launched with a menacing public declaration written by Pridi that calculatedly stripped away the king's inviolate cloak. It was designed to convince the royals that, if they did not accede, the alternative was a republic.[1]

All the people,

When this king succeeded his elder brother, people at first had hoped that he would govern protectively. But . . . the king maintains his power above the law as before. He appoints court relatives and toadies without merit or knowledge to important positions, without listening to the voice of the people. He allows officials to use the power of their office dishonestly. . . . He elevates those of royal blood to have special rights more than the people. He governs without principle. The country's affairs are left to the mercy of fate, as can be seen from the depression of the economy and the hardships. . . . The government of the king has treated the people as slaves. . . . It can be seen that from the taxes that are squeezed from the people, the king carries off many millions for personal use. . . . The People's Party has no wish to snatch the throne. Hence it invites this king to retain the position. But he must be under the law of the constitution for governing the country, and cannot do anything independently without the approval of the assembly of the people's representatives. . . . If the king replies with a refusal or does not reply within the time set . . . it will be regarded as treason to the nation, and it will be necessary for the country to have a republican form of government.

The ultimatum shocked not only the palace but even some People's Party figures who couldn't really imagine Siam without a monarchy. Indeed, the language of a private letter the coup leaders delivered to Prajadhipok in Hua Hin was a great contrast to Pridi's ultimatum. It exalted the king's position in traditionally formal terms, and respectfully sought his blessing for the revolt. It began with a phrase of ultimate submission in the elaborate court language, *rajasap:* "May the power of the dust and the dust under the soles of your royal feet protect my head and the top of my head."[2] The phrase refers to the belief that the head is the most sacral part of the body, the feet the most vulgar. The writer is thus prostrating himself to the extreme, placing his head below the dust under the dust of the king's feet. Such language was pro forma in letters to the king, with every word designed to project an air of supplication to a deity. Even the members of the People's Party couldn't bring themselves to dispense with this self-abasing language. Their letter formally ended: "Whether the matter will be proper or not, in whatever respect, ultimately will be up to royal kind consideration."

Accompanied by a provisional constitution, the letter was an ultimatum nonetheless. The night he received it, the king discussed with the court whether to muster a counterrevolt, or even to flee the country. With the top princes under arrest, he had little choice but to concede. But he made a show of independence and monarchic status when he was commanded to return to Bangkok by a naval vessel. Prajadhipok refused, and instead took his own royal train. On June 26 the king met the coup leaders in his Bangkok throne hall to discuss the constitution and a blanket amnesty for the plotters. They were conciliatory, some even prostrating themselves. These gestures allowed Prajadhipok to further reassert his stature. He demanded that the revolutionists' tanks be removed from around the building and insisted that he be approached with traditional respect.

The British parliamentary structure was the general model for the new government. But because of the roughshod language of the first coup announcement and because the wording and government structure in the draft constitution evoked Russian Bolshevism—particularly the establishment of a ruling "Committee of the People" dominated by the People's Party—Prajadhipok took advantage to show his offense and umbrage. He refused to immediately sign the charter, implying that the People's Party had communist leanings. Moreover, he declared that in fact he himself had long been considering a constitution. It was a skilled assertion of superior royal virtue. He now had the revolutionists backpedaling, almost begging for his endorsement. Some of them became angry with Pridi, the author of both documents and the most leftist among the People's Party leaders.

The next day the two sides met again. Employing the humbling rajasap, the People's Party leadership apologized for the coup and their disrespect to the throne. Only then did the king sign their pardon and the constitution. He emphatically added to the document the words *chua khraw,* provisional, forcing the coup leaders to agree to draft a more substantial constitution in consultation with the palace. Still Siam's unifying symbol, the king had already recaptured a measure of his power.

Even so, Prajadhipok was forced to forswear a countercoup and to accept new limitations on his ancient powers and prestige. British constitutional scholar Vernon Bogdanor calls constitutional monarchy a contradiction in terms, because, by definition, monarchy is an absolutist system of government.[3] Under a constitution, the throne remains hereditary but has little authority. As mostly a rubber stamp for parliament and the cabinet, the constitutional sovereign reigns but doesn't rule. "The crucial function of the monarchy in a democracy is to sustain the legitimacy of the state," Bogdanor writes.[4]

Ultimately, the constitutional king's influence rests on how he exploits the prestige of his person and the powers of his office. How the constitution establishes the basis of royal existence and allocates royal prerogatives is then crucial. Even when equality is the bedrock of the constitution, it must somehow defend the king's inviolateness and endorse the blood mythology that underpins royal succession. This is most often simply declared, and justified by tradition, for continuity in the culture and the state itself. Like language and religion, monarchy is presumed a part of the community's identity and natural order. And so throne-specific incongruities are accepted.

Beyond that, the constitution usually reestablishes the king's traditional position as the source of justice, the leader of the military, and the head of the church, even if he lacks full power over those institutions. The sovereign will usually receive the right to sign off on or veto bills and appointments, and to assume more responsibility in grave crises, such as hung parliaments and war. The scope of such powers is set in part by the word of the constitution, and also founded in tradition and precedent, in the flexibility of the government and society, and in the sovereign's skill in deploying his prerogatives. This skill is pivotal, for each royal intervention carries the potential for enhancing the king's stature and the people's trust in him. But each occasion also brings the risk of demeaning royal prestige, and so reducing his future influence.

In England an arrangement evolved in which the government exercises most of the king's prerogatives on his behalf, on the grounds that the king is first consulted and that the government accepts full responsibility for any outcome, whatever the king's input. This allows him to appear as a sovereign with real powers and to get his views across, while not dipping his hands into the messy details of government. It is a no-fault clause, protecting the king from the negative consequences of exercising his prerogatives. He can remain infallible. Even then, the king must ensure that the government does nothing to severely damage the state or the throne itself. So behind the scenes, the throne remains in constant discussion with the government, and forewarns against dubious or risky policies, appointments, and plans.

Walter Bagehot, the 19th-century expert on the British constitution, summed up the arrangement by saying that the art of the modern sovereign is to quietly steer government and society without actually calling on his powers for overt use. In a distillation now used almost globally, he wrote: "The sovereign has, under a constitutional monarchy such as ours, three rights—the right to be consulted, the right to encourage, the right to warn. And a king of great sense and sagacity would want no others. He would find that his having no others would enable him to use these with singular effect."[5]

King Prajadhipok wrote "provisional" on the constitution of June 27, 1932, because while the draft had the crucial effect of preserving the throne—reciprocally ensuring the new government's legitimacy—it fell short of the British allocation of royal power and prestige. The document began by downgrading the king's status, declaring that "the supreme power in the country belongs to the people." Those empowered to exercise power on behalf of the people included equally the monarch, the People's Assembly, the People's Committee, and courts of law.

Selection of the government did not involve the king. The representative People's Assembly and the administrative People's Committee would be determined at first by the People's Party, and over the long term by election. The committee alone would appoint and oversee the prime minister and his cabinet. The king could order nothing without the countersign of at least one committee member, and he would have no power in the assembly. In England, the elected lower house of parliament was offset by the House of Lords, filled by aristocrats chosen by the monarch, whom they then steadfastly protected.

Prajadhipok would also have had no real veto power under the proposed constitution. He could send an act back to the assembly for reconsideration, but this move could be rebuffed with a simple majority vote. It was unlikely his veto would ever hold. Perhaps most significantly, the 1932 provisional constitution denied the king's infallible status and his sacral family hold on the monarchy. Although he could not be prosecuted in an ordinary court of law, the assembly could impeach and try him. The assembly also reserved the right to sign off on succession, even as the 1924 Law of Succession remained in place.

The new government didn't cut the royals out completely. Only the most senior princes were purged, and only one was exiled, the former military chief and potential heir to the throne Prince Paripatra. Many pro-palace officials remained in government, and while most members of the 15-strong People's Committee were revolution leaders, four were high-born bureaucrats of the old regime. Two of those joined the People's Party, but two others remained solidly in the royal camp, and both took top jobs. Made prime minister was senior court judge Phraya Manopakorn Nithithada, a member of Prajadhipok's privy council whose wife served Queen Rambhai. Phraya Srivisarn Vacha, a hard-line royalist but one of the drafters of Prajadhipok's proposed constitution in 1931, was named foreign affairs minister.

Prajadhipok meanwhile fought back. Knowing that foreign powers were watching critically, on June 30, 1932, two days after the People's Assembly first met, he told the new ministers that his health was bad and his eyesight failing, and that he was mulling abdication. With Paripatra in exile, he suggested a successor, the first son of the late Prince Mahidol, six-year-old Ananda. The message was clear: Prajadhipok saw little reason to hold on to his position, and if the government leaders pushed him too far, he would exit, taking their legitimacy with him. Ananda would be seen as a puppet.[6]

For several months the government tried to assuage Prajadhipok. They kept him informed of important issues and policies. When the government dismantled the king's private secretariat, slashed the palace budget, and retired many senior royal household officials, the king was consulted and seemed to agree. He approved a new tax system that hit large landowners heaviest, specifically the old sakdina nobility and royals. On the other hand, the government ignored the fine points of royal prestige. The palace was miffed when the assembly gave 6,000 convicts amnesty, for this traditional display of compassion had always been the king's right. The high princes meanwhile agitated behind the scene, painting Pridi as a communist and lobbying the British and the Americans for support. The permanent constitution became a flashpoint. In an interview published in the American media in September 1932, one top prince again threatened the king's abdication if the charter did not satisfy the palace. The result might be war involving foreign powers, he warned.[7]

With the People's Party wary of foreign intervention, the king's threats to go into exile or abdicate seemed to have an impact. Finalized that December, the permanent constitution gave the palace much of what it wanted. The preamble fully honored the king, invoking both devaraja and dhammaraja images in the language of Ayutthaya:

> King Prajadhipok, the great power of the world . . . a great in the sun's dynasty who is god's beloved; a pure descendant of the kings who are warriors; the great man of the royal family; the king of the world . . . strict in monarchical morality code with incomparable power of merit . . . full of merit from the former life, and incarnation of god . . . clever in war strategy and with quick and errorless decision . . . the great protector, the observer of the Buddhist precepts and respecter of the three gems.[8]

In the first chapter, the king is elevated to high status, but not quite as high as before 1932. "Sovereign power emanates from the Siamese people," it says, then adding, "The king, who is head of state, exercises it in conformity with the provisions of this constitution." The king is assigned his multiple traditional identities.

He "professes the Buddhist faith and is the upholder of religion," and he is named head of the Thai armed forces. He is declared "sacred and inviolable," while members of the royal family, from the rank of serene highness and up, were made above politics. Confirming the Chakri and particularly the Chulalongkorn lineage, succession is left to the 1924 law.

The constitution refined the king's power along British lines. The king "exercises legislative power by and with the advice and consent of the People's Assembly"; he "exercises executive power through the council of ministers" and "judicial power through the courts." These bodies became conceptually the agents of his power. The king's practical powers included the appointment of ministers and other top officials, convening, proroguing, and dissolving the national assembly, and approving bills passed by the assembly. As in England, most of these powers required the countersign of the president of the assembly. This essentially assigned to the government primary responsibility for the king's actions. The king also retained prerogatives of emergency decree, declaring war, and concluding treaties.

Still, the king lacked a say in the composition of the government. The People's Committee was renamed the State Council, which kept Phraya Manopakorn as premier. The assembly would be much the same as in the provisional charter. It would nominate the prime minister and other ministers, and the king would approve the appointments. But he had no independent choice in the composition of either the executive or the legislative branch.[9] Furthermore, his veto could still be overruled by a simple majority.

The royalists weren't happy about this. But on December 7 the charter was introduced with great ceremony that seemed to signal the restoration of royal authority. For the first time since his own coronation, Prajadhipok wore his crown and full regalia. The People's Party leaders presented him with flowers, incense, and candles, just as they would a venerated monk, and in the humblest rajasap they begged the king's pardon for the nasty language in the original coup announcement. In fact, they conceded, "The kings in the House of Chakri and many members of the royal family have in fact brought progress to Siam in their own time."

Pleased, Prajadhipok thanked them for "seeking pardon from me and the House of Chakri." He said: "One thing which makes me feel more gratified is that in your request for the pardon, you mention that the kings and a number of the princes of the House of Chakri had made contributions in their own way to bring progress to Siam. This is true. . . . This action of yours should be a great honor to you because you have shown that you have dhamma in your heart. . . . The confession of your error, I believe, will help you gain much public confidence."[10]

He said nothing about democracy or constitutionalism; his speech was all a reassertion of royal infallibility and superiority. Three days later, on December 10, 1932, Siam's first permanent constitution was promulgated. In the preamble, the revolutionists generously credited the king: "His Majesty had it proclaimed that his civil servants, his members of the fighting forces, and his people had asked him to grant a constitution so that the Kingdom of Siam may have the same form of government as that of a civilized country. . . . In accordance with the royal command, the Constitution of the Kingdom of Siam was given to His Majesty's people."

Decades later, in the reign of King Bhumibol, this statement would be held up as proof that democratic constitutional government came to Siam not by revolution but from King Prajadhipok himself. The achievement of the People's Party would be blotted out.

Even though the new 20-man state council included nine officials from the old regime, the royalists kept fighting back. While the princes secretly mulled a military revolt, Prajadhipok urged Prime Minister Manopakorn to break the People's Party politically. When in January 1933 the government moved to create a formal political party system, the king advised Manopakorn to reject all new party applications and to dissolve the People's Party.[11]

That wasn't possible, yet. But a month later, the king found a wedge to drive between the factions of the People's Party. Faced with a stubborn recession, Pridi had drafted a master economic plan that proposed giving the government control of much of the country's means of production, land, and capital. Working with Manopakorn and Srivisarn, the king publicly branded Pridi a communist. In a lengthy written critique he sardonically asked whether Pridi copied Stalin or Stalin copied Pridi.[12] Manopakorn published the critique as a pamphlet, which was then heavily reported in the press.

Raising the stakes, Prajadhipok again threatened abdication, citing Pridi's plan. Then he pressed Manopakorn to purge the revolutionists from the government by royal decree.[13] Manopakorn essentially did so by banning government officials from political party membership. Many in the People's Party, and almost all of Pridi's faction, were bureaucrats.

Having made a very public gambit, the king himself was now out on a dangerous limb: failure could mean the loss of all his remnant prestige. Amid extreme political tension, the Mahidol family was sent off to Lausanne, Switzerland, for safekeeping. The palace believed that if Prajadhipok did abdicate, or was forcibly removed, the People's Party would be hard put to gain international legitimacy while the heir lived abroad.

The People's Party countered with a no-confidence motion against the premier. Sensing that Manopakorn might lose the vote, the king prorogued the assembly on April 1, 1933, and Manopakorn commenced to rule by decree.[14] Royalists were promoted throughout the bureaucracy, with Prajadhipok signing off at each step. A tough anticommunist law was promulgated, and under its threat Pridi was forced into exile.

Striking back, on June 20, the People's Party ousted Manopakorn in a coup led by Phibun Songkhram, a key party figure in the army. In Hua Hin, the king was requested by letter to reopen the assembly and appoint a new state council. Avoiding a challenge to the king personally, the letter deferentially confirmed the throne's position as laid out in the constitution. Royal prestige remained intact as Manopakorn was blamed for all. Prajadhipok complied with the request, and two days later the assembly elected army general and 1932 revolt leader Phahon Phonphayuhasena as prime minister. Phahon invited Pridi to return and join the state council on the condition that he renounce extremist views.

The struggle continued over the next several months. Rumors of new coups filled the air, labor groups demonstrated as proxies for both sides, and Mahanikay monks agitated against the royalist Thammayut monks who controlled the sangha. Meanwhile, the king desperately sought international support. He implored the country's British financial adviser James Baxter to persuade other foreign advisers to resign, to put pressure on the government.[15] The king reiterated to Baxter that his strongest weapon was "the threat to abdicate—effectively used several times already.... The revolutionaries have only to get hold of [the king] to effectively stop any kind of movement on the part of the royalists.... With the king at large and free to lead a revolt they have to be more cautious." Assembly members responded with an unprecedented motion to impeach the king, and a labor leader lodged a defamation suit against Prajadhipok for his attack on Pridi. Although these measures were blocked by the government, both were daring public insults to the king's inviolate status.

Pridi's return brought things to a head. On October 12, the pre-1932 army chief Prince Boworadej led an insurrection of royalist military officers on behalf of the throne. Phibun Songkhram directed the counterattack, and the country plunged into civil war, with airplanes bombing Bangkok and fighting in the streets of many towns. Both sides sought the king's endorsement; physical possession of the monarch was seen as a key to victory. Again conveniently in Hua Hin, Prajadhipok maintained the appearance of neutrality. Seeing Boworadej blunted early on, he retreated with his court to the border of British-controlled Malaya. *Phibun*

After two weeks of fierce fighting, Phibun claimed victory. A number of rebel leaders were killed, and Boworadej fled abroad. The rebellion ended the People's Party's willingness to work with the palace. A few weeks after the failed rebellion, Prajadhipok announced plans to go abroad, ostensibly to have his eyes treated. On January 12, 1934, he embarked for England with much of the court, leaving Prince Naris, the 70-year-old son of King Mongkut, as regent.

From London, Prajadhipok laid out an ultimatum. In exchange for his return, the king wanted greater constitutional powers, including the right to select half of the members of the assembly, control over the royal budget, and a veto power that could be overridden only by a 75-percent majority in the assembly. Against the government's plan to execute captured participants in the Boworadej rebellion, the king also insisted on his traditional right to decide capital cases, and in this instance he wanted the prisoners freed. Without these concessions, Prajadhipok said, he would abdicate and meanwhile sell his substantial royal possessions, including palaces, shrines, and the Emerald Buddha, according to one report.[16]

No longer afraid of losing royal sanction, the government in Bangkok rejected nearly every point. Consequently, in early March 1935, the king stepped down. "Nothing remains but animosity," he wrote. He would stay in exile in Europe for the rest of his life. *[king stepped down]*

As he resigned his crown, Prajadhipok made an elegant last claim to superior virtue. It didn't save him, but his argument later became a cornerstone of royal prestige in the reign of his nephew Bhumibol. "I feel the government and its party employ methods of administration incompatible with individual freedoms and the principles of justice," the king wrote. "I am willing to surrender the powers I formerly exercised to the people as a whole, but I am not willing to turn them over to any individual or any group to use in an autocratic manner without heeding the voice of the people."

Interestingly, Prajadhipok's letter implied a significant shift in what constituted royal virtue. Instead of the thotsaphit rachatham, the ten dhammic kingly traits, he asserted virtuous leadership by the modern concepts of democracy and freedom. Prajadhipok personally may have deservedly claimed a greater sense of both, but because of the palace's reactionary fight, his defense rang hollow. In response the government published correspondence with the court that contradicted the abdication statement. It was yet another insult, showing just how much the monarchy had lost its cloak of inviolateness.

In the snowy mountains of Switzerland, the ceding of the Chakri throne to Ananda came as no surprise.[17] The young prince's mother, Sangwal, had agreed months earlier that her son would accept the crown. Yet when the time finally came, Prajadhipok declined to officially nominate his heir. In a strange lapse of effort to protect the Chakri bloodline, he wrote to Prime Minister Phahon that he would leave it to the government to "elect" a king.

The cabinet didn't know how to respond, because few people outside the palace grasped royal practices or had seen the 1924 succession law. Only the palace secretary still in Bangkok, Yen Israsena, fully understood rankings and titles, and besides him, ironically only Pridi understood palatine law.[18] The question was complicated by another young prince who lived with the exiled court in England, twelve-year-old Prince Varananda. Varananda was born to the late Prince Chutadhuj, who ranked higher as a celestial son of King Chulalongkorn than Ananda's father, Prince Mahidol. Both boys' mothers were commoners. But Varananda's mother was a household retainer whose match with Chutadhuj wasn't official. Sangwal's marriage to Mahidol had royal sanction. After five days of meetings, finally, on March 7 the cabinet concluded in favor of Ananda. After fighting Prajadhipok for nearly three years, the revolutionists were content to have a child on the throne.[19]

Ananda's mother, however, proved an equally formidable challenge. Sangwal was determined to control her children, insulating them in Switzerland for as long as she saw fit. Her obstinacy left both the government and the court unhappy. Because of her ethnic Chinese commoner roots, Sangwal's control over two principal heirs to the Chakri lineage unsettled many courtiers. Her American-style modern approach to mothering was immensely different from what the boys would have experienced in Bangkok. Some in the court wanted her pushed aside like the non-royal mothers of the king's sons in earlier reigns. Having the children reared exclusively by blue-blooded courtiers would ensure that Ananda and Bhumibol would grow up thoroughly committed to the Chakri institution.

But, crucially, Sangwal had the backing of the seniormost royal of all, her feisty mother-in-law, dowager queen Sawang Vadhana. For Sawang, who had been demoted in the politics of succession from Chulalongkorn's first to second queen, the two boys and their sister Galyani represented her own dynastic posterity. And she trusted her daughter-in-law to raise them.

The family was comfortable in Lausanne. When they arrived in 1933, the three children were boarded at the school Champ Soleil, while their mother stayed with a Swiss family to learn French. After several months they took an apartment near the center of town, with a Thai maid and a Swiss woman as live-in help, and several women of the court living nearby.

Pictures from the time show two slight, cheery, and curious boys, constantly together, appearing neither wildly uncontrolled nor cowed by excessive discipline. However, Ananda's health was a problem. In letters to Sawang, Sangwal complained that he suffered a constant flow of mostly minor ailments.[20] Bhumibol, in comparison, was rarely ill. His mother also struggled with Ananda's disinclination to study. "Ananda doesn't concentrate at all on his schoolwork, and wants to play all the time," she wrote in September 1933, while diligent Bhumibol "understands the importance of studies" and was good at memorizing vocabulary. Ananda's health improved in 1934, and the family traveled in the countryside around Lausanne. In April they met King Prajadhipok and Queen Rambhai in Paris. During the summer, they escaped from the heat at a mountain resort.

Siam's politics descended on the family with winter that year. In November, European newsmen showed up chasing the story that Ananda would soon ascend the throne. Sangwal declared her determination to protect Ananda from the court and the public, if indeed he became king. Awaiting the arrival of the government minister in February 1935 to discuss the imminent abdication, she wrote to Sawang: "I will tell him, it is not up to me to decide if it is accepted or not. It is up to [Prajadhipok]. But I have the right to say that Ananda is physically still not strong at all, and not suited for hot weather, and should remain here."

At the first official audience with palace officials after Ananda's accession, Sangwal was kept from the room, to her great indignation. But with Sawang's support, her demand to remain in Lausanne was accepted. She also refused to have Ananda and Bhumibol take a traditional Siamese education at home, and instead entered them into the Ecole Nouvelle de la Suisse Romande, known for its progressive, Eurocentric program. There they studied French, then English and Latin, and later German, leaving little time for Thai at home.

Another troubling issue was religion. As king, Ananda was protector of the Buddhist faith and an incipient bodhisattva full of superior merit. He needed a Buddhist education. Yet the Mahidols' life was surrounded by Christianity, and, the whispers said, Sangwal herself had become Christian.

There was a seed of truth to that. Sangwal, like many Siamese who had been educated in Christian schools, saw no great contradiction between Buddhist and

Christian principles. At home she kept an altar for the family's Buddhist statues, and she taught her children to pay respects to the statues, lighting incense and saying basic prayers. On their birthdays and other occasions, she had them make merit with gifts to the poor. But there was no Buddhist temple or monk in Lausanne, and Sangwal at times attended Christian services.

The pressure on her over these issues intensified, her letters revealed. In May 1935, she wrote to Sawang that, if people criticized her for being a commoner, they were criticizing her children, including the king. Half the king's blood came from her, she argued. "If they say I am not suited to be the mother of a king . . . let them find another king whose mother is a royal." In essence, less than two months after Ananda became king, she was threatening his abdication—not to the government, but to the royal family.

She did agree, tentatively, to return to Siam at the end of the year for a coronation. Without the performance of Brahman and Hindu rites, the new king was not consecrated, and the throne would remain unpropitiously vacant, the land unsettled. The Siamese people needed to see their king.

That August, Ananda's Swiss doctor said he was still too frail to travel abroad, and again Sangwal was accused in Bangkok of controlling Ananda for her own pretensions to power. She told Sawang that her family could happily live without all this. "They cannot change the fact that I am his mother," she wrote. She continued to threaten Ananda's abdication through 1936, directly to the throne's regents. Her son would be nobody's puppet, she declared.[21]

Feeling things deteriorating, Sawang told both the government and the court to step back, and she then sent her daughter Princess Valai Alongkorn, and Prince Rangsit, a son of Chulalongkorn whom Sawang had raised as her own, to calm the Mahidols. They became the family's close advisers.

The government meanwhile provided the Mahidols a princely stipend of 100,000 baht a year. With that, in August 1935 the family moved to a palatial home in Pully, just outside Lausanne. It had three stories with 13 rooms and a large garden. The house was renamed Villa Vadhana, after Sawang, and became the Mahidols' home for the next 16 years. The family added a bevy of new retainers and bought a stately limousine befitting their status.

As Sangwal gained respect, life settled down for her family. Official visits to the fidgety little sovereign were restricted to Saturdays. Otherwise, there was little formality. Servants did not overly prostrate themselves to the children, who ran around in play like all their classmates. They visited area sights, took weekend picnics, and went to the mountains for relaxation and sports in both summer and

European influence

winter. The children grew more European by the day, speaking French among themselves while using Thai with their mother and the staff.

Ensconced outside London, however, Prajadhipok's court plotted with a core of die-hard monarchists for a comeback, claiming they were fighting for democracy.[22] In Bangkok, the government stabilized the country politically and economically, bringing together left-leaning leaders like Pridi and many former members of the absolutist regime who embraced constitutionalism. The cabinet and the bureaucracy were led by capable People's Party men working alongside progressive princes and aristocrats from the ancien régime. They included Sixth and Seventh reign courtiers Chao Phraya Sridharmadibes and Prince Wan Waithayakorn, with the latter in charge of foreign affairs.

The royalists were increasingly marginalized. Even before the abdication, the government had begun to attack the throne's traditional sources of power and popularity. Some palace ceremonies lapsed, and others were transformed into state rituals. The government assumed control of the sangha and built new temples, with the resulting virtue and merit no longer accruing to the throne.[23] People made offerings to shrines that had representations of the king, Buddha, and now the constitution too, which was sometimes placed higher than the other icons. December 10, the day the first full constitution was promulgated in 1932, was made a national holiday, and it was celebrated more lavishly than the king's birthday. To King Vajiravudh's mantra of nation-religion-king was added the constitution.

After the abdication, the government installed three politically weak men on the Regency Council to oversee the monarchy: the elderly Prince Anuwat Chaturon, known as Prince Oscar, a grandson of King Mongkut; 31-year-old Prince Aditya, a grandson of King Chulalongkorn; and the aristocrat Chao Phraya Yommaraj, a powerful minister in the Sixth Reign who had been pushed out in the Seventh. Yommaraj and Aditya both owed their status to the People's Party.

Through them, the government transferred traditional royal operations to the bureaucracy. The privy purse was moved to the Finance Ministry, its assets divided into crown, state, and personal royal property. Fearing confiscation, many royals who had left their property with the privy purse and the palace-controlled Siam Commercial Bank scurried to pull them out.

In his abdication statement, Prajadhipok had laid claim to any private property he held prior to becoming king in 1925. The government rejected the claim and accused him of having removed state assets to Europe. Prajadhipok had taken a lot with him, including cash and gems accumulated by earlier reigns, like the famous jewelry set with massive diamonds and emeralds once owned by Napoleon III's empress Eugénie, which Chulalongkorn had bought in 1897. When Prajadhipok rejected demands to return it all, the government confiscated much of his family's assets left behind in Bangkok.

This had a tragic outcome. Heavily pressured by both the government and the royalists, in August 1935 chief regent Anuwat committed suicide. The job fell to the highly pliable Prince Aditya, further weakening the royalists' position.

Propelled by his defeat of Boworadej, army chief Phibun Songkhram became the power behind Phahon. Trained at France's Fontainebleau Academy in the 1920s, Phibun had his own ambitions. He was an admirer of the militaristic nationalism that had taken root in Germany, Italy, and Japan, and he coveted the adoration of those countries' fascist leaders. The royalists now saw Phibun as a greater threat than Pridi. Even before Prajadhipok's abdication, in February 1935 Phibun was slightly injured in an assassination attempt at a football match. Six months later another unsuccessful attack, on both Phibun and Pridi, clearly had royalist backing.

Failing to kill him, the royalists were more successful in embarrassing Phibun during 1937, when they exposed the People's Party government's dividing of confiscated royal real estate among its members. The scandal forced the resignation of the regents, prime minister Phahon, and his cabinet. Phibun's threat of an army coup stifled the public uproar, and he restored the government leadership to office. But even as the royal property was returned, the revolutionists had lost much credibility and the royalists regained some.

With plots and counterplots rumored by the day, the environment turned more deadly. In November 1937 a royalist scheme to kill both Pridi and Phibun was uncovered. During 1938, there would be three allegedly royalist-backed attempts on Phibun's life.[24] Phibun grew in power, but not altogether in popularity, even within the original revolutionary clique. His enemies spread stories that Phibun had Napoleonic designs to sit on the throne himself.

During this period the government persisted in pressing for Ananda's return from Switzerland, at least momentarily, for his official coronation. Even Phibun was sensitive to the need for the appearance of royal endorsement, for in the minds of many Thais, the monarchy still represented the state. In Lausanne, Sangwal stubbornly resisted, threatening to have her son abdicate each time the pressure increased. Her main reason was that chronically frail Ananda wasn't fit for the journey. Trips planned for the November–January cool and dry season in each year following his accession were each time canceled on a doctor's recommendation.

In fact, Sangwal was reticent to expose her son to the harsh and confining pressures of kingship. She was determined that he have a normal childhood and complete his education in Europe. And given the continuing threats of violence, she also reasonably feared for her sons' safety in Bangkok. Even though Phibun and others believed the royalists were conspiring to deny them political legitimacy, the royalist cause also suffered from Ananda's continuing absence. The longer the king was gone, the less important the throne became. Key royal rituals like the plowing ceremony and the kathin merit-making ceremony to Wat Arun, an essential demonstration of the king's patronage of the sangha, were discontinued.

Finally, in 1938, Sangwal relented and headed back to Siam with her two celestial boys. Embarking on October 17, Ananda and Bhumibol spent nearly a month on shipboard, taking instruction in the Thai language and in royal etiquette. Their reception overwhelmed everybody. As the Mahidols' vessel headed up the Chaophraya River from the Gulf of Thailand on November 15, hundreds of thousands of bowing and cheering Siamese jammed streets and riverbanks to greet them. When they disembarked at the Grand Palace, they were greeted by top officials of the government and the court, led by Ananda's grandmother, dowager queen Sawang, all prostrating themselves at his holy feet. The only leader missing was apparently Phibun, who feared another assassination attempt.[25]

The visit was filled with rituals and appearances for Ananda, with Prince Bhumibol constantly at his side. They attended royal temples, gave early morning alms to barefoot monks, presided over inner-palace Brahman rites, and reviewed Phibun's troops. At every step, Ananda was treated as a holy, righteous dhammaraja. Sangwal also made sure the boys had ample time to play. They took drives around the city and to the seaside. On Bhumibol's birthday, December 5, there was a grand garden party for the royal circle, with a monkey show as the featured entertainment. For a few weeks, it appeared as if the royals and the government had resolved their differences. Ananda was recognized as Siam's sovereign king, and Sangwal gained stature within the court. Her son bestowed upon her the full royal title of "her royal highness the mother of the king," in English shortened to "princess mother."

But the originally planned highlight, Ananda's coronation, never took place. It was said that he hadn't learned formal Thai or Pali well enough to recite crucial oaths and prayers over a week of rites. To temporarily consecrate Ananda's crown, a ceremony paying respects to the Chakri ancestors in the palace was substituted for the coronation. Apparently that was good enough for the Siamese people. As the Mahidols embarked for Europe on January 13, 1939, the capital's cheering crowds made it clear that the sacral prestige of kingship had survived.

Meanwhile, the war between Phibun and the royalists was boiling over. A week ahead of the Mahidols' arrival, Phibun had survived another assassination attempt. His patience gave out and he forced Phahon to resign, taking the premiership for himself. Shortly after the Mahidols departed, Phibun swept the capital and arrested 50 royals, nobles, and soldiers in the clique of his People's Party rival Colonel Song Suradej for plotting his overthrow. Some were executed immediately, and the rest were held for trial on treason charges, accused of plotting against the government of King Ananda and for the restoration of Prajadhipok. The arrestees included several high princes, foremost among them Prince Rangsit, Queen Sawang's adopted son who had personally chaperoned Ananda and his family throughout their visit. Rangsit was ignominiously thrown into a common jail, stripped of his title, and sentenced to death. He was saved, apparently, by Sangwal's threat of Ananda's abdication.[26] At the end of 1939, Rangsit's sentence was commuted and he was imprisoned on a remote island, along with 21 others. Eighteen more, mostly junior officers, were put to death.[27]

Whatever the truth behind the cabal, its quashing came to represent the final victory of the 1932 revolutionists and the constitutionalists over the monarchists. To mark it, Phibun commissioned a huge monument to the constitution, later called Democracy Monument, in the middle of the city's main thoroughfare, Rajadamnoen ("royal progress") Avenue. He slashed the remaining vestiges of royal power. Senior royals were restricted in their travels and activities. Prajadhipok's Bangkok home and possessions were seized. Government offices were banned from displaying his portrait, and Phibun's, not Ananda's, replaced it.

When Sawang's daughter Princess Valai Alongkorn died in 1939, the government refused to pay for her cremation ceremony. When Prajadhipok died in England in 1941 from heart failure, return of the body for a royal cremation wasn't even pursued. The Siamese embassy in London insultingly called the death *thiwongkhot*, a term denoting much lower status than *sawanakhot*, the sacralizing royal expression used to describe a king's death. There was no cremation pyre representing Mount Meru, the Hindu abode of the gods, and the ambassador sent only a wreath, on behalf of King Ananda but not the government.

After a year, Phibun also no longer feared Sangwal's threats. He made it clear that he was ready to install the puppet regent Prince Aditya on the throne to do his bidding. Meanwhile, he began to assume traditional royal powers and symbols for himself. He adapted Vajiravudh's nationalist triune to a tetrad of nation, religion, constitution, and king. Taking Vajiravudh as his personal model, Phibun declared him the greatest Siamese king and erected a statue of him. In 1939 he made June 24, the date of the 1932 revolution, National Day, celebrating it massively to emphasize the victory over the Chakris.

That same day he launched his program of *ratthaniyom,* or state conventions, employed like an absolute king's decree. The first changed the country's name to the more modern-sounding Thailand, signifying the break with the old dynasty. Another convention ordered the people to show respect to the official icons of Thailand, the national anthem and the flag, but not the monarchy.

Phibun eliminated other features of royalism as well. He ended the system of peerage titles granted to prominent people, titles like *luang, phraya,* and *chao phraya,* severing a once important palace link to influential commoners and senior bureaucrats. He also ordered the Thai language simplified by removing esoteric letters most often used in fancy royal names and terms, and by eliminating complicated linguistic class distinctions.[28] In addition, the new premier issued a mandate changing the way people referred to King Chulalongkorn. On the anniversary of his death in 1943, Thais were instructed to no longer call him Phra Phutta Chao Luang, which translates as the Lord Buddha King. Phibun said it made Rama V greater than the Buddha. He wanted him desacralized.[29]

Phibun assumed the royal role of directing the sangha, with the purpose of undermining the royalist Thammayut sect. In 1937 the monarchist supreme patriarch, the Chakri prince Phra Chinaworasiriwat, died. A Mahanikay monk, Phra Phuttajan (Phae Thissathewo), was named as his replacement by Phibun himself. Phuttajan was from the northeast, home to a long tradition of anti-palace monks.

In 1941, Phuttajan overhauled the Sangha Act of 1902, which had given the palace official control of the clergy. The new structure followed that of the constitutional government. In it, the supreme patriarch (the *sangharaja,* the sangha king) remained on top of the hierarchy, but he was powerless, like the postrevolution Chakri king. Power devolved to a fixed-term *sanghanayok,* a title evoking that of the laic prime minister. He administered through a sangha cabinet and a deliberative body, a parliament of monks. Control over the titling and promotion of monks was transferred from the palace to bureaucrats in the Ministry of Education. The king could choose the supreme patriarch, but the government would select the sangha prime minister and his cabinet.

Conscious of the sacred foundations of the king's power, Phibun began to engage in acts that implied his own superior practice of dhamma. In September 1940 he launched the construction of a new temple, Wat Phra Sri Mahathat. Traditionally, temples were used to commemorate kings, monks, and great spiritual beings. Wat Phra Sri Mahathat commemorated instead the 1932 revolution. Phibun donated an auspicious Buddha statue to the new wat and, in an encroachment of the throne's prerogatives, had it declared a royal temple, though it held no relics or connection to royalty. Its biggest association was with the military. Wat Phra Sri Mahathat was located in the military-dominated suburb of Bangkhen, far from the palaces. The former premier and army general Phahon was the first to ordain as a monk there.

Phibun intended the temple to become headquarters of the sangha after unification of the two rival schools. He named the senior Thammayut monk Somdej Uan as the first sanghanayok, and installed him as abbot of the new temple. Uan laid out a 10-year plan to unify the sangha on a democratic basis, which would weaken the Thammayut.

Phibun saw himself as a nationalist, building a tough and proud country like the autarchic leaders of Italy and Japan. He provided the royalists good reason to believe that he had his own dynastic pretensions. While he compared himself to King Vajiravudh, his cultural propagandist Luang Vichit Vadakan likened him to King Ramkhamhaeng, the exemplary Sukhothai king. Phibun was stealing the Chakris' proprietary symbolism. Going even further, he had the regent Prince Aditya grant him the highest royal decorations, and he sought to possess Vajiravudh's scepter.

Phibun might have succeeded. But he alienated the liberal democrats of the People's Party, including his longtime ally Pridi. After Phibun allowed the Japanese to occupy the country in 1941, he sacked Pridi from the cabinet and installed him in a presumably powerless position on the regent council. Still very popular, Pridi used the position to mask his leadership of the anti-Japanese and anti-Phibun underground, the Free Thai Movement.

Eventually Phibun's support in the army and parliament frayed. In mid-1944, he made what was said to be a veiled attempt to end the Chakri Dynasty and launch his own. He proposed relocating the government by building a new capital at Petchabun, far to the north of Bangkok and its royal palaces. He also wanted to move the sangha administration to a new national Buddhist center at Saraburi, some 100 kilometers outside the capital.[30]

Pridi organized the assembly to defeat the proposals in July, and Phibun was compelled to resign. He was replaced by a liberal politician, Khuang Aphaiwong, one of the 1932 revolutionists. Regent Aditya also resigned, ironically leaving Pridi, once the bête noire of King Prajadhipok, as the principal agent for the throne. To demonstrate to the royals that he had toned down his anti-monarchism, Pridi freed all those who had been imprisoned in the 1939 plot, including Prince Rangsit, in King Ananda's name on the concurrent birthday of Ananda and Chulalongkorn, September 20, 1944.

When World War II ended, Phibun and his henchmen were arrested and members of the Free Thai Movement took power. Pridi dutifully called upon King Ananda to return and assume the throne upon reaching his majority in September 1945. Accepting, Ananda, the princess mother, and Prince Bhumibol returned on December 5, Bhumibol's 18th birthday, to formally begin the Eighth Reign. Pridi resigned the regency and was bestowed the new title of Senior Statesman by the king. To nearly everyone it seemed a new beginning. Ananda would sit on the throne, receiving full regal respect and honor, and a new constitution would be written.

Sangwal planned to stay in Thailand only several weeks and then return to Switzerland for her two sons to complete their university studies. The main duty while in Bangkok would be for Ananda to put his name on a new constitution. Turbulent politics and social obligations prolonged their stay to six months. Finally, with a new constitution in place and the throne's future apparently secure, the Mahidols set June 13 as the date of their departure for Lausanne. But events soon took a dramatically different turn.

4   *Restoration to Regicide*   ‿

UNTIL THE FAMILY'S ARRIVAL IN BANGKOK IN DECEMBER 1945, life had been comfortable and carefree for Prince Bhumibol. Being a Mahidol put him at the center of the Chakri hierarchy, and it went unquestioned that he would always sit alongside Ananda in some capacity. But Bhumibol grew up free of the pressure that his brother endured as a king-to-be. It made a huge difference.

In Lausanne, Sangwal managed to insulate her three children from the court for an almost typical European life. The boys studied Latin and German and woodworking at school, collected pictures of fighting tanks and ships, raised pet cats, tended a vegetable garden, bicycled and picnicked, and hiked and skied in the Alps.[1]

Sangwal taught the boys of the greatness of their grandfather King Chulalongkorn and King Mongkut before him. She checked any sign of haughtiness, insisting on them being disciplined and humble like their father. She instilled her commoner's ideas of Buddhist sacrifice and service, Bhumibol later recalled. "When we received something—money—we had to put a percentage in the box for the poor. If we did something wrong . . . we paid the fine not to mother, but to the box for the poor people."[2]

Most of the pressure on Ananda came from Sangwal herself. She tried to prepare him for kingship, but he was frustratingly inattentive, she complained in letters to Sawang. Pushed hard, he became introspective and moody. Bhumibol meanwhile was merry, energetic, and curious. His mother's letters make it clear that he was her favorite, noting that he readily completed his schoolwork and chores before running off to play. Still, the difference between the two boys was only a few degrees. They were their own constant companions and best friends, and Bhumibol looked up to Ananda.

After their return to Switzerland from Siam in 1939, when Phibun arrested the boys' favorite uncle Prince Rangsit and executed other royalists, there seemed little likelihood that the Mahidols would ever go back. They remained in neutral Switzerland during World War II, in the company of many other refugee royals. Sangwal hired a tutor from the Ecole Nouvelle, Cleon Seraidaris, to watch over the boys. A trained scientist, he fostered their interest in model making, radio electronics, and music, becoming a father figure and constant companion.

As teenagers, Ananda and Bhumibol passionately followed the drama of the war and its heroes, and they became avid fans of American popular music and French and American films. Although neither studied music seriously, both learned several instruments well enough to play popular tunes together with classmates and other expatriate Thais. They also loved fast cars, traveling to watch their raconteur uncle Prince Birabongs, one of Europe's leading drivers, race in Bern.

With most attention focused on Ananda, Bhumibol worked in solitude on numerous hobbies like photography. From the late 1930s he was the family photographer, and a camera hung from his neck whenever and wherever they traveled. At home, he would concentrate quietly until he could produce something—a drawing or a wooden model of a battleship, or a simple song on the clarinet—to impress the adults around Villa Vadhana.

In 1944, Ananda boarded outside the home as he entered Lausanne University to study law. With a sense of freedom, he made a few friends in the café society where students passionately discussed the arts, literature, and politics. He discovered a soulmate in the one Swiss woman in his first-year law class. Alone at home, Bhumibol fancied himself becoming a professional musician, or like Birabongs a race car driver. When he entered Lausanne University in 1945, though, he leaned toward engineering, apparently inspired by Rangsit, a German-trained irrigation engineer.

At the war's end, Ananda and Bhumibol had become like many other well-heeled European youths: in love with jazz music, abstract painting, fast cars, summers hiking in the mountains or driving to Paris, winters skiing in the Alps. Speaking between themselves in French (they spoke Thai with a slight foreign accent), they had little interest in the culture and politics of their homeland, much less the antiquated life of the Chakri court. A Swiss upbringing left both far better prepared for life in Europe as bon vivants than in Thailand as Lords of Life.

So the call to return to Siam in late 1945 must have been greatly unsettling, especially for Ananda, who was expected to give up Europe altogether for the dhammaraja kingship. The brothers' lives would be turned upside down and thrust into the simmering hostility between the 1932 revolutionists and the old princes.

The greeting the Mahidols received upon arriving on December 5, 1945, was encouraging. At Don Muang airport, north of Bangkok, they were welcomed by a kneeling Regent Pridi, behind him the new prime minister, M.R. Seni Pramoj, and the highest military officers, many of them participants in the 1932 revolution. The 20-kilometer rail trip into the city was lined with cheering and bowing Thais, and when they reached Chitrlada Palace station, there was a second official greeting led by Rangsit; behind him were other princes, top government officials, foreign diplomats, and again Pridi, who presented the royal seal to Ananda, formally restoring to him the throne's authority.

Then Ananda, Bhumibol, and the princess mother rode in an open car to the Grand Palace, where they would reside. Tens of thousands of Thais flanked the long broad avenues offering blessings and cheering. It demonstrated how deeply the monarchy remained embedded in the culture, even though the country had survived virtually kingless for 13 years. Beyond the political experience of sovereign and subjects, the parade had a religious facet. Thais believe that one can absorb spiritual greatness merely by witnessing it. This sense filled the air as the king passed: the people beheld and experienced his unmatched virtue, heightening their own spiritual state. Many held up their personal Buddha statues and icons to witness and absorb the king likewise, sanctifying the icons.

Even so, the enthusiastic reception was not automatically convertible to power. The throne had been stripped of so much that there was little else besides popularity for Ananda to inherit. The court was weakened from lack of practice and lapses in the decorum that affirmed the throne's prestige. Many details of rituals had been forgotten as ancient courtiers passed away. People didn't stand up in theaters for the royal anthem, and thieves boldly stole palace assets, even vehicles and religious icons. Bangkok's educated and elite had a low sense of reverence about things royal.

Perhaps more crucially, the institutions that had underpinned the absolute throne's power were now disconnected. The bureaucracy was filled with people who had never served the monarchy. They, not the palace, were responsible for justice, the economy, culture, and the sangha. The majority Mahanikay sect had taken control of the priesthood from the palace-backed Thammayut. Palace financial resources were in government and private hands, so that even the basic distribution of largesse and patronage, crucial to deepening loyalty to the crown, was severely constrained.

Working in the Mahidols' favor was that, in the wake of the war, the country needed a unifying leader. The postwar government couldn't offer that. Phibun's regime had been replaced by the factionalized Free Thai Movement, which included progressive royals who embraced constitutionalism but not the decline of royal privilege, and liberal democrats and socialists who accepted the throne only as a symbol. The leader of the first group was Seni Pramoj, who, based in Washington, had overseen the U.S. wing of the Free Thai during the war. The leader of the second group was Pridi.

Pridi was by far the more popular and powerful figure. But Seni's group constituted a potent challenge. They were abetted by a small group of high-born royals driven equally by their commitment to the Chakri legacy and their hatred of Phibun and Pridi. These true believers—with Princes Dhani, Rangsit, and Bhanuband Yugala, and Seventh Reign official Srivisarn Vacha foremost among them—would set the stage for the Bhumibol restoration with the initial reinstatement of royal prestige in the 1940s and 1950s.

Immediately upon the king's arrival, the princes launched into a program of royal culture revival. The first aim was to establish Ananda as a Buddhist king in the Sukhothai dhammaraja tradition. Rangsit and Dhani vigorously stressed to the king and his brother that ritual meant everything to their positions. In a lecture on Siamese kingship in March 1946, with Sangwal, Ananda, and Bhumibol listening in the front row, Dhani quoted the anthropologist Bronislaw Malinowski: "A society which makes its tradition sacred has gained by it inestimable advantage of power and permanence. Such beliefs and practices, therefore, which put a halo of sanctity round tradition, will have a 'survival value' for the type of civilization in which they have been evolved. . . . They were bought at an extravagant price, and are to be maintained at any cost."[3]

Ananda and Bhumibol, the latter constantly present as apprentice and sometimes stand-in king, found their schedule in Bangkok filled up with ritual appearances. As soon as the family reached the royal palace on December 5, 1945, the two were taken to make offerings to the Emerald Buddha, the royal palladium that General Chakri had brought from Vientiane two centuries before, and then to Phra Siam Dhevathirat, the patron spirit of the kingdom created by King Mongkut. Next they paid obeisance to the remains of previous kings in a hall reserved only for the highest royals.

The following day, in the presence of Brahman priests, senior monks, and princes, Ananda donned the crown and ascended the throne in a sort of mini-coronation, surrounded by the holy symbols of state and sovereignty: a discus, a bow, sword and trident, royal fan, scepter, yak-tail and white-elephant-tail whisks, each full of Hindu and Buddhist symbolism. The ceremony set out the kingdom's spiritual hierarchy: bowing to the dhammaraja were the land's foremost civil and religious leaders.

Then came secular rituals that projected Ananda as the head of government and the military. On December 7 he received the prime minister, his cabinet, and the commanders of the armed forces, who, kneeling before him, presented him with the decorations and uniform of a field marshal, declaring him supreme commander of the Thai armed forces. For the next two days, Ananda and Bhumi-bol made merit, offering alms to their dynastic predecessors and hosting a cere-monial meal for leading monks, personally offering the monks rice and fruits as the humble patrons of the sangha.

December 10 was Constitution Day, celebrating the document that repre-sented the throne's loss of power. The palace approached the occasion with deliber-ate ambiguity. In a nationally broadcast speech, probably written by a senior prince, Ananda called for unity, diligence, and patriotism, but he stopped short of exalting the constitution itself. The last of the priority ceremonies was less weighty but equally important. This was a palace tea party held on December 12 for the titled royal community, giving them a chance to bond with the symbol of their privileged status.

Afterward began the workaday program to establish a rapport with the people. Audiences were given to top politicians and civil servants, and Ananda and Bhumi-bol visited numerous royal temples. Military units put on mock war displays for them, after which they were seen in newspapers inspecting naval vessels and sitting in the cockpit of an air force fighter.

As head of state, in January 1946, Ananda presided over the conclusion of a peace treaty with Britain, and with the British queen's dignitary Lord Louis Mount-batten he reviewed British troops that had occupied Thailand after the war. And because postwar parliamentary politics were extremely fractious, over six months the king officially convened the parliament twice, appointed the prime minister three times, and promulgated a new constitution. The May 9 promulgation cere-mony showed the king in his golden regalia and jewel-studded crown atop his

throne, handing the document down to government leaders: the democratic constitution was bestowed munificently by the sacral hand of the good king.

Twice, Ananda, with Bhumibol alongside, was presented to the people as the
Solomonic source of justice in courtroom trials. On one occasion, a hearing on
May 24 in Chachoengsao, a woman with an infant child had confessed to theft,
pleading poverty and hunger. It was her first offense, and the court had earlier
sentenced her to six months in jail. Reviewing the case in an open courtroom, the
public gaping from open windows, Ananda noted the woman's remorse, and
pointing out that she had an infant son that needed care, he suspended her
sentence. Then he offered a small sum of his own money to feed the child. For the
people it was an uncanny sign of the wisdom, compassion, and generosity of the
Buddha, bound up in the DNA of a 20-year-old Chakri.

Ananda presented degrees to graduating university students two times, a practice begun by Prajadhipok to connect the monarchy to the future government elite.
Several times Ananda and Bhumibol traveled into nearby provinces to show the
throne's concern for peasant farmers. These trips invariably took them to the local
temples, where they performed popular rituals of contrition by releasing captive
fish and birds to their freedom.

Two noteworthy efforts were made to address groups that had been marginalized by Phibun. First was a meeting with leaders of the country's Muslim minority. Second was an outreach to the ethnic Chinese community, branded by both
Rama VI and Phibun as unpatriotic and greedy, a threat to national security. In the
widespread postwar privation, the business-minded Chinese had been an easy
target. Just before the Mahidols returned, the Sampaeng district, Bangkok's China-
town, was wracked by riots. On June 3, Ananda and Bhumibol made a half-day
visitation to Sampaeng. As they peered into shops and waved to the residents, the
Sino-Thais prostrated themselves, presented offerings, and held out religious icons
to witness the royal aura. News reports said some collected the dust from where
Ananda and Bhumibol had walked. All of these activities were glorified in newspaper and radio reports that, couched in the long unused and unfamiliar courtly
rajasap language, reminded everyone of the Mahidols' special sacrality.

Ananda and Bhumibol also began learning to preside over the court. They
took classes in language, history, the classic principles of Buddhist kingship, the
thotsaphit rachatham, and the ancient cosmologies like the Trai Phum. Sangwal
invited the aristocrats to family meals, and there were also fairly frequent gatherings outside the Grand Palace, especially at the Srapathum Palace of the brothers'
grandmother Sawang. Taking up his role as the hub of court society, Ananda

presided over a charity ball and the wedding of Prince Rangsit's son Piyarangsit to Princess Vibhavadi Rajani. Social functions like this placed a high value on associating with the king. But there was yet another purpose, to find a queen for Ananda. There was a dire need to strengthen the Chakri bloodline's depth and sustainability, so King Ananda needed to get married and have sons quickly.

Outside the palace, the Mahidol brothers attended sports matches and went on holidays to Ayutthaya and Hua Hin. Inside the Bangkok palace, they had recent American movies to watch and a collection of musical instruments to play. The Free Thai gave Ananda a U.S. Army jeep, which he and Bhumibol would spin around the many throne halls and chapels inside the Grand Palace's high whitewashed ramparts. Some evenings, too, they drove around the city incognito.

Less burdened by official duties, Bhumibol snapped photographs, composed songs, and built models. These activities likewise fed into the development of royal prestige. At one charity ball, the orchestra played a Bhumibol-composed foxtrot, auctioned off his photographs for 3,000 baht each, and auctioned an airplane and a ship model he had made for a huge 30,000 baht.[4] It was probably the first time Ananda or Bhumibol realized that their position could be used to draw money from the wealthy for charitable, or other, purposes.

The most important day of their visit, it would turn out, was December 23, 1945. Pridi took them on a day-long trip to a Free Thai camp. The king was thrilled as the soldiers performed a mock battle, reported Alexander Macdonald, an American who had worked with the Free Thai. "His eyes shone as the carbines, machine guns, light mortars, and grenades boomed and crackled in the woods. There was a chair for him, but he stood, absorbed in the show." Afterward, the brothers got to shoot as well, firing off hundreds of rounds between them. "Wincing with anticipation of each charge, he gradually gained confidence as he fired several rounds from a Colt automatic and a sub-machine gun," Macdonald recalled of Ananda. "He spent nearly an hour at it before he was ready for lunch."[5]

At the end of the day, the Free Thai presented the king and the prince each with their own working weapons, including a Colt .45 pistol for Ananda. From then on shooting became a favorite pastime in the palace. Targets were set up inside a garden, at which Ananda and Bhumibol would fire from the second-story balcony of their Barompimarn residence hall in the palace compound. Some days they expended several hundred rounds, and each assembled a miniature arsenal in his bedroom. Bhumibol, for instance, had a carbine, a Sten gun, and two automatic pistols.[6]

It is unclear what Ananda and Bhumibol thought of their kingdom. Having grown up mostly in the rationalist, egalitarian environment of Switzerland, were they impressed or repelled by the fawning of their subjects? Or did they begin to believe the royal mythology, of their own purer blood and greater sacrality? There is some evidence that Ananda didn't like what he was being pushed into. Both Mountbatten and Macdonald recalled him as almost neurotically shy and sensitive, extremely dependent on his mother for decisions, dreading public appearances and holding in his emotions. He clearly missed the relative freedom of Lausanne.

Yet he also apparently began to imagine that he might contribute something to Thailand's development. With briefings by top officials and aides several times a week, both young men became familiar with the country's problems and political developments. They read the local and foreign newspapers, which were filled with the machinations of postwar politics and even discussions of the monarchy's role. Ananda, however, reportedly showed signs of straying from the confines of the throne. Inspired, said some, by the writings of George Bernard Shaw, he mentioned to several people his idea of turning over the crown to Bhumibol and running for election, with the goal of eventually becoming prime minister. Seni Pramoj's brother Kukrit later said Ananda had queried him on how to conduct a campaign for political office.[7]

Ananda was better off remaining above politics. The postwar competition for power had turned into a snakepit. After the Free Thai Movement and its allies took power, their ranks split between pro-Pridi and anti-Pridi factions. Behind the latter lined up the monarchists, still plotting revenge for 1932.

Having spent the war running Free Thai activities under the guise of regent, Pridi had many supporters and acolytes in the bureaucracy, in education, and in banking (he had earlier been finance minister). He had also improved his standing with some royals, by having shown full respect for Ananda as king and having provided strong care for the royals who remained in Bangkok during the war, including dowager queen Sawang. Pridi also gained an important ally in the London-based Free Thai leader Prince Subhasvasti, known as Tan Chin. The brother of Queen Rambhai and formerly the head of King Prajadhipok's body-guard, Subhasvasti came to trust Pridi once Pridi agreed to release Prince Rangsit and other royalists from prison after Phibun fell from power in 1944. Pridi declared Ananda's birthday a national holiday and restored Rangsit's title and decorations. At the end of the war, Pridi also reinstated the honors Phibun had stripped from Prajadhipok.

But neither Pridi nor Subhasvasti got along with Seni, the Thai ambassador in

Washington during the war and the leader of the U.S. wing of the resistance. A descendant of Rama II, he was one of a conservative clique of blue-blooded Thais who studied in England in the 1920s, including his brother Kukrit, Prince Prem Purachatra, Prince Chumbhotpong Paripatra, Prince Chula Chakrabongs, Pin Malakul, and Manich Jumsai. All were dedicated royalists who would have enjoyed bright careers in the court and government if the 1932 revolution hadn't taken place. They all detested Pridi. Seni's war record was marred by his petty disruption of cooperation between the different sides of the Free Thai. Why he did so was never explained, but clearly Seni saw Pridi and Subhasvasti as rivals for postwar leadership.

After the war ended, Khuang Aphaiwong resigned as prime minister. To avoid reigniting the 1932 fight, Pridi stepped aside for Seni to take the premiership, on September 17, 1945. But Seni had virtually no domestic support base, because Pridi's men still dominated the assembly and the cabinet.

So within a few weeks, Seni dissolved the parliament and set elections for January 6. Ostensibly, this was to give the returning Ananda the chance to oversee the formation of "his majesty's government," new and democratically elected, and to sign in the new prime minister and open the parliament. But Seni aimed to bring the royalists back into politics as his backers. Just before the dissolution, he proposed changing a constitutional clause that banned members of the royal family from partaking in politics. This required royal approval, and, according to a later newspaper report, he sent a letter of request to the royal secretary Chaleo Pathumros. But Chaleo, a longtime Pridi man, wrote back on November 1—after the dissolution—that Regent Pridi had polled the royal family and they agreed to continue with the ban.

The election formally laid out the lines of postwar struggle. There were several political parties allied with noncandidate Pridi, representing his broad public support and strong networks in government and business. Khuang Aphaiwong set up the Democrat Party to vie with Pridi's clique. His backers included some members of parliament, Free Thai men, and anti-Pridi royalists. Seni and Kukrit formed the Progress Party, which included revenge-minded men jailed by Phibun in 1933 and 1939. Seni aside, they equated the Free Thai with the People's Party and wanted Pridi and all the revolutionists imprisoned. Prince Subhasvasti observed in 1947 that "the extremists amongst them still hope against hope for a restoration of the absolute monarchy as a means of restoring their own lost privileges."[8]

In the polls, Pridi's bloc won a majority in parliament, and Khuang's Democrats came in second. The Pramoj brothers' party garnered only a handful of seats.

Pridi then declined a nomination as prime minister; his royally granted title of senior statesman gave him the power to advise both the cabinet and the palace, without the vulnerability of a political job. But when Pridi suggested one of his backers, the parliament instead turned to Khuang. At the end of January, in a landmark ceremony of the revived monarchy, King Ananda signed Khuang's appointment as prime minister.

To shore up his position, Khuang named several royalists to important jobs, and in doing so he gave a figurative slap in the face to Pridi. The most aggressive appointment was of the palace diehard Srivisarn Vacha as finance minister. In 1933, under the Manopakorn government, Srivisarn was responsible for Pridi's being exiled as a communist. The two were mortal enemies, and Srivisarn now became the government spearhead of the monarchist agenda.

The main task was to craft a new constitution. The drafting panel was split fairly evenly between Pridi's men and royalists appointed by Khuang: Seni and Kukrit, Srivisarn (a drafter of Rama VII's ill-fated 1931 constitution), the moderate Prince Wan Waithayakorn, and Phraya Manavarajsevi, a legal official in the Seventh Reign and a parliamentarian after. Pridi was committee chairman. Among them all there was no dispute that the basis of the government would be constitutional monarchy. In discussing how much power to give the throne, they reviewed constitutions from other monarchies, including Britain and Japan. The palace and the king himself were also polled for their views.

What emerged then was noteworthy for how little was changed. The 1946 constitution begins identically to the 1932 charter, unambiguously establishing the king as the sacred and inviolable head of state, exercising the sovereign power that emanates from the people. The king's power is exercised through the parliament, ministers, and state courts. Beyond that, royal power remained quite limited. The same demands that Prajadhipok made in 1934 before abdicating were considered and mostly rejected by the panel. The king was still denied viable veto power: he could be overridden by a simple majority.

The palace remained dependent on the government for its finances and staffing. And a palace proposal to establish a permanent body of advisers to the king, independent of the government, was rejected. The committee apparently felt this resembled too much the powerful pre-1932 Supreme Council of State, and would manipulate the monarch and compete with the elected government. So Ananda was left with no formal advisory body.

The major setback for the throne's advocates was the organization of parliament. The primary house of representatives was now converted from partly appointed and partly elected to fully elected by the people. A second house was created, a senate with limited powers in lawmaking and state affairs. But instead of being appointed by the throne, like the British House of Lords, the senators would be elected by the lower house for six-year terms. The palace would have no hand in it. This favored Pridi. Since his followers dominated the lower house, he stood to control the senate as well, thereby dominating the entire parliament for years to come.

Some changes favored the throne. One was originally a Prajadhipok demand, a ban on active bureaucrats and soldiers also serving as members of parliament or the cabinet. Prajadhipok had sought this provision in 1933 to undermine the People's Party. Now Pridi himself supported it, probably to stifle the many Phibun supporters who remained in the civil service. At the same time, the ban on senior royals participating in electoral politics was repealed. This was the change Seni had pushed in vain the previous October. Now only the immediate royal family and the regent, just five people, were precluded from politics.

But it wasn't an absolute gain for the royal clique. Allowing royals to take political office was potentially injurious to royal prestige. It could fog the distinction between the pure and selfless virtue of the Chakris and the impure, venal nature of politicians. It would smear the line between royal inviolateness and democratic equality, eroding the justifications for royal privilege. The shield of royal inviolateness would be partially dropped when a prince in parliament simply took sides. If he misbehaved in office the royal family could be exposed to criticism.

But with the royally titled Pramoj brothers on the drafting committee, such concerns were pushed aside. Indeed, most remarkable about the 1946 constitution is that it was agreed to by all sides. The palace, hardly unaware of the ramifications of each and every clause in the charter, readily embraced it. Finally, on May 9, 1946, King Ananda signed it into effect.

The stormy action in parliament meanwhile gave a taste of the politics to come. As soon as the assembly opened in January it bogged down in infighting. Pridi's men constantly checked the government, and Seni's group tried to smear Pridi. At one point, Seni openly accused Pridi of swindling $500,000 that Seni claimed he had sent to Pridi for the resistance during the war. An investigation showed that Pridi was never sent more than $49,000, none of it unaccounted. Seni could only apologize for his faulty memory.[9]

Khuang resigned in March after being defeated on a minor bill. Pridi was drawn into accepting the premiership, and the monarchists stepped up their campaign against him, spreading stories that Pridi was a republican, a communist, and corrupt. When in April the government decided to drop war-crimes charges against Phibun for his collaboration with Japan during the war, the royalists were incensed, for they wanted Phibun hanged.

While they made little ground in parliament, the royalists did slash Pridi's influence in the court. It wasn't easy. As regent, Pridi had served the royal family attentively and developed a close rapport with Ananda and Bhumibol. A number of his people served in the palace, including royal secretary Chaleo and a key royal aide-de-camp, Lieutenant Vacharachai Chaiyasithiwet. The leading figure in the court, Prince Rangsit, helped by Seni and Kukrit, strove to reduce Pridi's influence, in part by poisoning the Mahidol family against him. It seemed to work; several months into 1946, the relationship between Pridi and Sangwal had become "hopelessly bad," according to one diplomat.[10]

Crucially, Rangsit persuaded Ananda and his mother to replace Chaleo and Vacharachai in May 1946. Rangsit may have had concrete reasons to oust at least Chaleo. It appears that in late 1944 Chaleo had raided the business and staff of the palace-owned Siam Commercial Bank, over which he held some supervisory authority during the war, in order to launch the new Bangkok Bank together with a number of other Pridi allies. By the time the war ended, Bangkok Bank, with Chaleo on its board, had become very powerful while Siam Commercial Bank had weakened. Enjoying much business from the government, Bangkok Bank appeared to be a vehicle for the Pridi bloc.[11]

None of this jockeying for power interfered with the progress of royal duties or the plan for the Mahidols to return to Lausanne. Sangwal was adamant that both boys complete university studies there before fully assuming royal duties.

Fifteen days after King Ananda promulgated the new constitution, members of parliament selected the senate, predictably packing it with Pridi men. On June 1, Ananda opened parliament, with Bhumibol at his side. Pridi formally stepped down as premier, and six days later Ananda signed his reappointment. Having put his stamp formally on the formation of a government, the constitution, and the leadership, the king was free to return to Switzerland, and he set a departure date of June 13.

On the evening of June 7, Ananda met Pridi to discuss naming the regency council for his absence. Acting on the advice of his mother, Ananda proposed Prince Rangsit and Prince Dhani. Preferring someone he could get along with, if not control, Pridi first proposed former queen Rambhai, who was also supported by some other royals, including Prince Subhasvasti.[12] As for the other regents, various accounts have Pridi proposing Prince Dhani; Prince Alongkot, another pliable royal; constitution drafter Manavarajsevi; and Duen Bunnag (Chao Phraya Pichaiyati), Rama VII's agriculture minister but also a longtime Pridi ally.

At any rate, Ananda and Pridi disagreed, with the deepest point of contention certainly being Rangsit. Whether it was a serious argument, and whether it was resolved, remains an open question. Years later, the official palace line became that Pridi disrespectfully rejected the king's desires and left in anger. What happened two days later made this point crucial to national politics for the next decade.

For Ananda never had a chance to make the appointments. On June 9, shortly after nine in the morning, around the time that Ananda and Bhumibol normally prepared to take breakfast, a single gunshot shattered the stillness of the palace residence. Servants, Bhumibol, and Sangwal rushed to Ananda's room, where they found him lying on his back on his bed, his blue silk Chinese pajamas neatly secured under a coverlet, his head straight on the pillow as if asleep. He was already dead from a single gunshot to the forehead, fired at close quarters. A U.S. military-issue Colt .45 pistol lay on the bed next to him, a few inches from his lifeless hand.

As the palace plunged into shock, suddenly, life changed prodigiously for Bhumibol. Within hours, the bright, often smiling and joking prince, more interested in European cars and American jazz than anything Thailand had to offer, would be named king of a country in which he had spent less than 5 of his 18 years. He would almost never be seen smiling in public again.

Whether he considered it or not, Bhumibol had little choice: the family line that threaded from Rama I through the great Rama V, King Chulalongkorn, his queen Sawang, and their son Prince Mahidol, had to remain intact. Prince Rangsit, Princess Mother Sangwal, and the other senior princes prevailed upon Bhumibol to accept. Following emergency parliamentary approval, in a hastily organized accession ceremony with Buddhist and Brahman priests, Rangsit handed the crown to Bhumibol, who crowned himself the Chakri king Rama IX. Years later Bhumibol dryly explained: "It was the only way I could be sure of giving my brother a proper funeral. In any case the people asked me to succeed, and there was a vacuum which had to be filled."[13]

Who killed King Ananda? To this day, despite the tragic effect it had on the lives of so many, the answer remains a mystery. More than any other person concerned, Bhumibol prefers to leave it so. The death opened political fault lines and triggered years of Ayutthayan intrigue. And as it placed the palace at the center of politics,

Ananda's death perversely raised the monarchy's profile and, eventually, vastly increased its power.

Two of the possible explanations considered at the time were simple and understandable. Ananda killed himself, either accidentally while playing with the gun, or deliberately; or Bhumibol, in play, accidentally shot him. Both were feasible, because Ananda and Bhumibol kept loaded guns immediately handy by their beds.

The nefarious third theory was that Ananda had been assassinated for political reasons. Given the tension between the factions and individuals competing for power, this was plausible. But few could imagine it, since Ananda was still an innocent and impotent force in Thai politics. The popular hypotheses were, first, that Pridi had the king shot, and second, that others, Phibun's clique or possibly the younger royalists, had Ananda killed to embarrass and frame Pridi. That the effect of the king's murder on political developments was unpredictable makes both theories difficult, but not impossible, to fathom. There was no clear utility in it.

A fourth theory, proposed in a biography of King Bhumibol published in 1999, *The Revolutionary King,* was that the notorious wartime Japanese commander Tsuji Masanobu killed Ananda in an effort to retain Japanese influence in postwar Thailand via Phibun. The theory would be easily dismissible save that author William Stevenson had unprecedented private interviews with Bhumibol. Even so, Tsuji specialists reject the theory, arguing that he wasn't even in Thailand at the time.[14]

In the event, the first government statement on June 9 concluded that Ananda had accidentally killed himself while handling his gun. Made by Pridi with the agreement of Rangsit, the princess mother, other top princes, and government officials, the statement respectfully maintained royal prestige and infallibility by explaining that the fatal error occurred because Ananda was suffering intestinal troubles and a loss of vitality for the previous week. This was partly true. Mild stomach problems had forced Ananda to miss two appearances, and he had deputized Bhumibol to go in his place.

Few were convinced. There were rumors about family trouble, leading to a deliberate suicide. One of these accounts said Ananda had quarreled with his mother over "some dirty story about her getting mixed up with his private secretary."[15] Another had him despondent over being forced onto the throne, and over a thwarted relationship with a Swiss woman at his university.

But the strongest rumor was that the king had been murdered, by Pridi or his men. Within a short time Pridi was forced from government, and a year later he,

Chaleo, and Vacharachai were named by a new royalist government as the master-minds. Pridi and Vacharachai fled into exile, and the case was pursued by royalists through 1954, when a court finally sentenced Chaleo and two others to death for regicide. They were executed in 1955.

There is no irrefutable proof that they did not murder Ananda. Yet the evidence for the case has been shown to be so weak, and the political machinations behind the trial so deliberate, as to render the court's conclusion highly questionable. In a modern Western court, none of the accused would have been convicted, possibly not even tried. On the contrary, there is much evidence to show that the conservative princes and the Pramoj brothers created and sustained the fiction for decades afterward that Pridi had plotted Ananda's death.

Most foreign missions concluded that either Ananda killed himself or Bhumibol did it accidentally. The best-known independent work on the case, the 1964 book *The Devil's Discus,* by Rayne Kruger, methodically exposed the failings of the trial and concluded that the lovelorn Ananda, infatuated with his Swiss classmate, had killed himself. Prince Subhasvasti, who encouraged Kruger to write the book, stuck to the story that, enfeebled by illness, Ananda accidentally shot himself.[16] In the 1990s, the palace itself seemed to concede the falsehood of the Pridi murder plot by recording Ananda's death in official publications as simply mysterious, as if it was something supernatural.

The theory that Bhumibol killed his brother has never been examined closely. An investigation would have questioned the infallibility of the king, bringing the entire institution into disrepute, possibly destroying it. The royal family's behavior after the accident gives no indication. If the Mahidols themselves knew it was suicide or fratricide, one might expect them to have intervened in the hearings or convictions. Both King Bhumibol and the princess mother gave testimony and could have defended the accused without pointing to an answer. Likewise, the king could have granted amnesty to those sentenced to death, had he known they were innocent.[17] On the other hand, possibly neither mother nor brother is certain of what happened. If unconvinced by the suicide explanation, they may have been persuaded by the murder arguments.[18] One of the most important influences on the family after the war, Prince Dhani, testified in the case that he suspected murder.

Even had he known the truth, though, the king's intervention in such a politicized case would have been difficult. He was politically weak in the early 1950s, when both the royalists and Phibun's clique were determined to destroy Pridi. Nonetheless, one cannot say with certainty that Bhumibol did not try to intervene.

Contrarily, the royal family's apparent inaction could protect a secret. An intervention on behalf of the innocent would have left the case still open, forcing the question, who did kill Ananda? To prevent attention from shifting to Bhumibol, his mother, and Ananda himself, other suspects would have to be dredged up, and there were none. A new investigation would be very uncomfortable for the palace and the government.

Whichever way one turns, there is not enough evidence to confidently reach a conclusion. Does Bhumibol's refusal to be seen or portrayed smiling in public since Ananda's death hint at the truth, as some believe? Not really, for even his dour mien is purposely ambiguous. There is no reason for King Bhumibol to not take the truth, if he knows it, with him to his cremation pyre.

5 Revenge of the Monarchists, 1946–49 ⌘

THE TRUTH OF ANANDA'S DEATH, ultimately, was not what was important: it was the simple absence of any convincing explanation that fired politics for the next six years. The palace princes, and Khuang and Seni's parties, which merged as the Democrats, together leaped on the Ananda mystery to expand their own power. While Bhumibol remained on the sidelines, they would successfully leverage Ananda's death for a new, very royalist constitution, electoral dominance, and replenishing the palace's emptied coffers.

Their first step was to discredit Pridi. Many Thais were unwilling to believe that the young dhammaraja Ananda could have killed himself, accidentally or deliberately. The princes were happy to encourage that view. A day after the death, the Democrats, the Pramoj brothers in particular, authored an alternative explanation that Pridi was behind it, and with little subtlety they hired a dozen men specifically to spread the story through the Bangkok community.[1] Seni's wife told the U.S. chargé d'affaires that Pridi had the king assassinated, and other senior royals told the British ambassador the same.[2] The diplomats dismissed the story, but after Ananda's own nanny said she believed he had been murdered, the plausibility of Pridi's guilt grew. Just a few days after the death, in the middle of a crowded movie theater a Democratic member of parliament yelled out, "Pridi killed the king."[3]

If Ananda had been murdered by Pridi's men in an effort to destroy the royal institution, the plot decidedly backfired. With the Mahidols still living in Lausanne, over the next few years an elected government might have grown confident in its ability to run the country without a king physically present, and the throne would have remained a one-dimensional cultural symbol. Instead, the tragedy put the royal family and the monarchy in the newspapers and on the radio every day, making even people in the more detached corners of Thailand understand that the throne mattered. The palace had more opportunity to demonstrate the unparalleled virtue of Chakri blood. In Ananda's death, the monarchy became much more alive and essential.

This began with Ananda's body. Few people who were summoned to the scene understood the issues of handling the royal cadaver. Ananda's blood-spattered corpse had already been cleaned by the princess mother when government officials arrived and began poking around it. But they stopped when Prince Rangsit sternly insisted that only certain high palace priests could touch the inviolate corpse. Later the same day, Rangsit told the assembled leaders that deliberate suicide could in no way be reported to the public. A dhammaraja could never purposefully kill himself. Even the word suicide could not be used; the king was too holy for that. It left Pridi little choice but to report in a roundabout way Ananda's death as self-inflicted, but accidental.[4]

With some compromise to modernity—doctors from Chulalongkorn Hospital were allowed to embalm the corpse—the palace Brahmans took the body through a ritual bathing with scented water blessed by Buddhist monks. It was wrapped in gold-trimmed robes, trussed like a mummy in white bandaging, and inserted crouching upright into a jeweled silver and gold urn. Bhumibol placed a crown on his brother's head, after which the urn was sealed shut, to be carried on a palanquin and set high into the Dusit Throne Hall, under the broad, golden royal umbrella.

For the next hundred days, Ananda's body lay in state. That arguably had more effect in scoring the monarchy's presence into the collective Thai mind than the entire first six months of the Mahidols' visit. Royal funerals heavily emphasize the sacred nature of the monarchy. There had not been an opportunity to demonstrate this in a large ritual involving the public since the early 1930s.

For hours on end each day, a group of monks would chant prayers in the funeral hall. Setting the standard for proper obeisance, late every afternoon the princess mother and King Bhumibol themselves would sit in meditation for an hour or two. They made offerings to the monks, making merit in the name of the late king. Meanwhile, organized groups of officials and royal family members would enter the chapel to likewise bow and then kneel in prayer. After the first week, prominent institutions and families would sponsor a particular day of mourning, attending with all family or staff members, and making their own offerings to the monks.

Then on Sundays members of the general public were given the unprecedented opportunity to prostrate themselves before the jeweled urn encasing the late king's corpse. As they filed through the imposing gold and crimson throne hall, they would witness the diligent daily attendance of the new king and his mother, and the large number of top monks chanting prayers on Ananda's behalf. It all projected the unmatched sacrality of pure-blooded Chakris.

It is customary in Thailand to issue special commemorative volumes to the public at the funerals of prominent figures. The family might print a biography of the deceased accompanied by his writings, or works that were of special importance to him such as Buddhist sermons, old stories, historical tracts, or even popular literature. On the fiftieth day after Ananda's death, King Bhumibol issued such a volume for his brother, which was revealing of how the modern monarchy wanted to be seen. It was a special impression of the Trai Phum Phra Ruang, the cosmology that identified Sukhothai's kings with the Buddha. Probably the decision of one of the senior princes, the act reminded people of the Buddha-Sukhothai-Chakri lineage of virtue.

Shortly after, Bhumibol performed another important rite. Ananda had never been formally crowned king, and technically this left him consigned to a celestial prince's seven-tier umbrella, rather than the nine-tier golden parasol of a fully invested Lord of the Realm. In a creative adaptation of ritual, on August 11 Bhumibol presided over a posthumous coronation, presenting Ananda's remains with the formal regalia of the king. Ananda would thereafter be regarded as a full Chakri king.

As the daily rites for Ananda continued, around the capital the politics of his death began to overheat. An investigation was launched, ensuring that the cremation would be delayed for some time. Rumors spread that Bhumibol himself was in danger, further stoking the Ananda assassination theory. The princes had to officially deny that attempts had been made on his life.

Whether it was due to a sense of danger, or simply the imminent opening of the university term in Lausanne, Bhumibol and his mother didn't remain in Thailand for the entire 100 viewing days. They departed for Switzerland on August 19. The story of their leaving marked the beginning of Ninth Reign mythology. The day before was a Sunday, normally the public's day to pay respects to the late king. It was also the last opportunity for Bhumibol and Sangwal to do the same, so the palace intended to keep the public out. Bhumibol, however, generously insisted that the people be permitted to enter as usual, even while he and his mother were inside.

On the morning of the 19th, as Bhumibol and his mother were being seen off by the government leadership, a woman ran up to the royal limousine and thrust something at the king. It was not a bomb as feared, Bhumibol later recalled for the Thai media. It was tasty homemade toffee, proof, he suggested, that the Thai people could in no way think to harm the Mahidols. Who but evil politicians could want to hurt the dhammaraja king?

The Mahidols left behind a formidable team of princes determined to keep up the momentum of the nascent restoration. They saw themselves as custodians of the pivotal traditions of Siamese culture and polity, and true defenders of the nation they still insisted on calling Siam. Their patrons were the dowager queens Sawang Vadhana and Rambhai Bharni, and their leader was Sawang's adopted son Prince Rangsit, who was named regent for the underage Bhumibol. Rangsit was born in 1885 to King Chulalongkorn and a concubine from the influential Sanitwongs family, descended from Rama II. After his mother died, he was raised by Queen Sawang. Schooled in Europe as an engineer and married to a German woman, he served the Sixth and Seventh reigns in part as an irrigation official. In the 1930s he helped Sawang take care of the Mahidols while allegedly scheming to overthrow Phibun.

The second royalist leader was Prince Dhani Nivas, a grandson of King Mongkut born the same year as Rangsit. A scholarly recorder of royal history and ceremony, Prince Dhani oversaw King Prajadhipok's coronation and became his education minister. After the revolution he kept his head down even as he remained a hub of the palace network. Dhani's voluminous research and writings deftly combined critical historiography with a highly favorable appraisal of previous kings. It made him best qualified to direct the tutoring of Ananda and Bhumibol in the 1940s. While he disliked Phibun, he recognized Pridi as bright and assisted his Free Thai operation on occasion. But he also apparently saw Pridi as ideologically threatening.

Other crucial palace defenders included Prince Alongkot Suksawat, an army leader for Rama VII; Prince Chumbhotpong Paripatra (known as Chumbhot), son of the exiled Prince Paripatra and so a potential successor to the throne; Prince Bhanuband Yugala, a grandson of Rama V; the relatively liberal diplomat Prince Wan Waithayakorn, a longtime friend of the Mahidols; Srivisarn Vacha, a Seventh

Reign civil servant; and English-educated lawyer brothers and parliamentarians Phraya Manavarajsevi and Chao Phraya Sridharmadibes.

They fronted a reenergized network of noble families all carrying bits of Chakri blood—the Diskuls, Devakuls, and Kridakorns, all celestial descendants of King Mongkut, the Kitiyakaras, from a noncelestial son of Chulalongkorn, and the Pramojs and Malakuls, descended from Rama II. Their members and networks spread well through the palace, the bureaucracy, and business. Most accepted constitutionalism but also yearned for a more powerful monarchy and the restoration of blue-blood entitlements. Faithful to the historical construct of the Sukhothai patriarchal monarchy, they held that the 1930s under Phibun and Pridi were proof of the failure of the kingless state.

Prince Dhani supplied the intellectual defense of this position. Advising Prajadhipok, Dhani had argued that constitutional democracy was unsuited to Asian culture. Explaining his view 24 years later, Dhani said the traditional Siamese method of selecting kings was already "democratic" because, in Dhani's interpretation, succession had never been automatically governed by primogeniture and blood heirs.[5] It was really determined by a council of leading statesmen, who were the representatives of the people. This was like the election of the virtuous Roman Catholic "king," the pope, by the Vatican's college of cardinals. Dhani argued that strict primogeniture was an imported Western concept that created succession problems, as in Ayutthaya. Archetypal Sukhothai had resolved these in the superior, traditional way, Dhani maintained. Since no one knew as much about Siamese history as he did, no one could contest his argument.

In March 1946 Dhani gave a lecture on kingship in Siam attended by the Mahidols.[6] This seminal work, reproduced in his own funeral volume in 1974 and cited in many later government publications, stressed that the good kings of Siam had always ruled in accordance with the dhammasat, the laws of dhamma. Making frequent reference to Brahman and Hindu and Khmer tradition, to the Trai Phum Phra Ruang, and to the Ramkhamhaeng inscription, Dhani laid out the standard for Ananda and Bhumibol:

> The old Thai had their own traditions of kingship. The monarch was of course the people's leader in battle; but he was also in peace-time their father whose advice was sought and expected in all matters and whose judgment was accepted by all. He was moreover accessible to his people, for we are told by an old inscription that in front of the royal palace of Sukhothai there used to be a gong hung up for people to go and beat

upon whenever they wanted personal help and redress. The customs survived with slight modifications all through the centuries down to the change of regime in 1932.

What formalized this patriarchal kingship was the "Constitution of the Dhammasat," as Dhani called it: "The Dhammasat describes its ideal of a monarch as a king of righteousness, elected by the people; . . . the ideal monarch abides steadfast in the ten kingly virtues, constantly upholding the five common precepts and on holy days the set of eight precepts."

Having shown that the kings of Siam had always ruled by a "constitution," the revolution of 1932 was thus unnecessary, Dhani suggested. The modern constitution-limited monarchy was "a pure foreign conception." But it was admittedly a logical reaction to "new problems," which had arisen through contact with the West and were "no longer within the radius of the Constitution of the Dhammasat." Dhani conceded that modernization posed difficult technical challenges to the old system, and he twisted logic to squeeze past this jam. "In absence of proper sanction of the dhammasat," to meet challenges like public hygiene and education, the king went ahead and "exercised full legislative power"; that is, he himself authored modern laws and policies that were appropriate. This was the main value of constitutional democracy, Dhani rationalized.

Conscious of the challenge of modern science, Dhani avoided the mystical issue of royal blood and dynasty. Royal sagaciousness was a given. All the successful modifications of government by Ramas IV, V, and VI, Dhani said, "came from the sovereign's own initiative." When natural laws failed, royal wisdom found the way. To stifle argument, he added that, at any rate: "As has been said by scholars of legal history, the function of the king was not to legislate but to protect the people and preserve the sacred law."

Royal sacrality and deification were likewise problematic in the modern context, and Dhani told his two young celestial students that this was simply a false relic of the Khmer:

> The average Siamese, then as now, has never taken up seriously the idea
> of his king being connected with Hindu divinities, who after all had no
> place in his Buddhist faith. . . . The Siamese king has never in theory
> or practice been a high priest at any time whatever. What duty he was
> required to perform in this connection was either that of a worshipper or
> an "Upholder of the Faith." The Buddhist priest, really a monk, seeks

release from worldly ties, and the king cannot really afford to do that, unless he is prepared to be accused of neglecting his duties.

Dhani's views on the throne's relationship with the sangha were detailed much later to an international Buddhist convocation, where he said: "The position of the king of Siam vis-à-vis the Buddhist church, or in fact any church in the kingdom, is one not of defender but protector. We Siamese are ingrained with the Master's tolerance to such an extent that the idea of defense never occurred to us."[7] Citing Rama I's cleansing the corrupted sangha, Dhani implied that the king's natural-born purity qualified him best to protect Buddhist doctrine and practice:

> Among the first problems he tackled was the monastic practice of the clergy and the consequent moral degradation of the laity, especially those armed with official privileges. His was the duty of protection of the church, not necessarily from external encroachments, but from the monks' own failings.
>
> The constructive protection of the church given by the monarchy lies principally in the civil aspect, wherein the state supports the church in the performance of its duties and in education. Thus Siam has been enabled to keep her monasteries in a healthier condition than in neighboring countries which have been till recently governed by non-Buddhistic administration which took a more or less noncommittal attitude on the problems of Buddhist churches.

Dhani's king is thus a spiritual leader of greater virtue than monks and amoral government. He summarized elsewhere that the king brought stability and development to the modern era: "Our national prosperity and independence in the first 150 years of the Bangkok era was the result of the wisdom and statecraft of our kings. And I cannot see how we can maintain such a state of affairs without good kings."[8]

This mythology underpinned the princes' determination to turn Ananda's death in 1946 to advantage, to destroy the remnants of the 1932 revolutionists. Within just a few days, Pridi was bogged down by rumor implicating him. He banned media reportage on the king's death, to protect royal dignity, and organized an official committee to investigate and rule conclusively on the case. The committee included senior police officials, judges, and Princes Chumbhot, Bhanuband, and Dhani. The secretary was the young judge Sanya Dhammasakdi.

Pridi failed to calm the air, and the royalist bloc, united now as the Democrat Party, made Ananda's death a key issue in the August general election that the new constitution required. Running for office alongside Khuang and the Pramoj brothers under the Democratic banner were palace allies Prince Upalisarn Jumbala, Srivisarn Vacha, Sridharmadibes, Boriraks Vejjakarn, and Srisena Sombatsiri. Except Upalisarn, all would eventually become King Bhumibol's privy councilors.

After the votes were counted, the pro-Pridi parties still held the balance of power. But when parliament opened, Seni and Khuang tied up the government over the king's death case until, days after Bhumibol's departure, Pridi resigned. He went abroad for several weeks to cool off, and Admiral Thamrong Navasavat, one of the revolutionists of 1932, assumed the premiership.

At the end of October, the investigating committee announced its conclusion, that the king couldn't have accidentally killed himself. The committee declined to decide between deliberate suicide and murder, but it didn't matter. The conclusion encouraged a belief that Pridi had engineered a cover-up to hide foul play and protect himself. Stoking the anti-Pridi fire as well were Phibun's old army allies, who resented losing position and benefits to the Free Thai after the war. With Phibun's backing, in March 1947 they formed a new party and began to agitate against the government. Surprisingly, the monarchists joined with them.

The general postwar environment did the rest. During 1947, the economy deteriorated as rice shortages fueled high inflation. Corruption scandals buffeted Thamrong's cabinet and were exploited by the opposition. The divisions became so tense that by May fears of civil war spread. Encouraged by the royalists, people began to imagine that Rama VIII's death had cast a foreboding shadow across the land. Finally, on November 8, the military ejected Thamrong in a coup. Pridi narrowly avoided being murdered and escaped abroad with the aid of British and U.S. diplomats.

The coup surprised nobody. Phibun allies General Phin Choonhavan and General Kat Katsongkhram had sounded out not only the military leadership but also Khuang, Seni, and the palace. Through Kat's son-in-law Prince Chakrabhand Phensiri and others, the coup makers were assured that the palace would go along. Although Phibun was plotting his own comeback, the princes decided Pridi was the more important foe.

The coup showed just how far the palace had advanced politically since Ananda's death. Phibun's generals now saw the throne as crucial to their own legitimacy. With the United States and England likely to object to the coup—Phibun was still viewed as a war criminal, for one thing—the generals attached themselves to the palace's virtue in their justification for seizing power. While noting the people's suffering, government corruption, and uncontrolled Chinese immigration, they emphasized that the coup was primarily a defense of royal prestige. They said the Pridi-Thamrong government had not respected the holy trinity of nation, religion, and king. General Kat explained that government corruption had demeaned the sacredness of the constitution signed by King Ananda, and that proof was in the appearance of vultures at the royal cremation ground, Sanam Luang. Vultures appeared in Ayutthaya before it fell to the Burmese, Kat reminded people, so the military had to intervene to rescue the kingdom.[9]

Moreover, the generals claimed to have conclusive evidence implicating Pridi in Ananda's death, adding that he had also plotted to kill King Bhumibol to eliminate the monarchy altogether and replace it with a communist state. They arrested two royal pages, Chit and Butr, and former royal secretary Chaleo Pathumros as Pridi's conspirators. Also named was former royal aide-de-camp Vacharachai, who like Pridi escaped abroad.

Palace support for the coup was evident in how quickly the regent, Prince Rangsit, approved it. He gave his official acceptance in the king's name in less than 24 hours, and immediately promulgated the new constitution the plotters had drafted. Some later accounts claimed that Rangsit had done so only at gunpoint.[10] But the content of the new constitution, and Rangsit's quick action on one particular clause, supports the view that the royalists had actually helped draft it, to the palace's benefit.

The preamble made the overthrow of the government sound like a pact between the generals and the throne. It read: "To meet this present grave situation, the majority of the Siamese people and members of the Siamese military forces have united in petitioning his majesty the king for the repeal of the present constitution and for the promulgation of a new constitution."[11]

The first substantive change was the introduction of a permanent Supreme State Council to advise the king and handle his personal affairs. The palace had been denied this in both previous constitutions. The council's five members would be appointed by the king and act as a regency council in his absence. A second key change was the creation of a senate selected by the king, its 100 members equal in size to the lower house of representatives. So while the king's veto power was not changed from 1946—parliament could still override with a simple majority—a united, palace-allied senate could sustain a royal veto.

Other changes increased palace control over its own operations and strengthened the king's emergency powers, such as declaring war or martial law. One change could have proved momentous if ever called into use. The new constitution stated that policies of one government could not be altered by a succeeding government without royal approval. This established the king as the source of stability and constancy, essentially giving him the power to decide which policies were of long-term good for the country.

Immediately after signing the document, Rangsit took action to name the council of state: himself as the head, Dhani, Prince Alongkot, Manavarajsevi, and General Adul Decharat. The urgency was apparently to circumvent Phibun's ambition to become the council head. The appointment of Adul, a politically vague but venerable People's Party man, may have mollified Phibun. But by choice or palace demand Adul never attended council meetings.

The generals dispatched Prince Chakrabhand to Lausanne to present the new charter to King Bhumibol. If Bhumibol had any qualms about the coup, they were not aired in his letter of endorsement, written on November 25: "Those who were involved in this operation do not desire power for their own good, but aim only to strengthen the new government which will administer for the prosperity of the nation and for the elimination of all the ills suffered [by the people] presently."[12]

The military men assumed that they would be the real power in the government, and the throne would remain a benign symbol of the nation. They were mistaken. Very deftly the palace and its allies seized the upper hand and moved to extend their power.

The first demand, apparently made by Dhani, was that Khuang be made prime minister and that new elections quickly follow.[13] With the United States and Britain withholding recognition of the new regime until it proved its democratic nature, the generals had to go along. Then, Rangsit flatly rejected the coup leaders' full slate of senate nominees, mostly soldiers and bureaucrats. Insisting that the choice was solely the king's, Rangsit proceeded to fill the senate with princes, nobles, and palace-friendly businessmen. Only eight of the 100 came from the coup group.

The royalists methodically expanded their power in other ways. Although the military removed the ban on civil servants taking part in politics, Khuang accepted only a couple from the coup group into his cabinet. The cabinet then gave Rangsit more autonomy for palace operations, including control over the royal household, the privy purse, and the royal guards, all denied since 1932. A later report noted that he then retired nearly 60 royal household officials, clearing out anyone, like the many Pridi appointees, who might not be loyal.[14]

With an eye on further expanding the throne's powers, the royalists persuaded

Phibun, Phin, Kat, and the others in the military clique to agree to draw up a new, more extensive constitution following the elections. The generals had little choice but to support the government to gain the crucial recognition of the United States and England, or risk intervention by them.

As expected, in the polls of January 29, 1948, the Democrats won a majority and returned Khuang as prime minister, who packed his cabinet with palace allies. The generals, and the still substantial remnant of Pridi backers, now recognized the royalist power grab for what it was. They likened the new state council to the prerevolution super-cabinet of princes, and Rangsit, Thawiwong Thawalyasak, head of the royal household, and Nikornthewan Devakul, the king's personal private secretary, were accused of plotting to turn back the clock to 1932. Incensed, the generals made veiled threats to expose Bhumibol as Ananda's killer and replace him with Prince Chumbhot, who was considered more pliable.

The Democrats stood their ground until, finally, on the Chakri Dynasty anniversary on April 6, groups of generals met simultaneously with Khuang, demanding his resignation, and Rangsit, demanding that he name Phibun prime minister. Two days later Khuang stepped aside, and Phibun was again the leader. It was a great, but not absolute, setback to the royalists. Khuang embarrassed Phibun by spelling out in a letter to King Bhumibol that he had resigned at gunpoint, and naming the generals involved.[15] Desperate for approval, Phibun responded by declaring his conversion to a "constitutional monarchist" since his last stint as premier.[16] "I did not force the crown to appoint me [as prime minister]. The crown graciously selects me," he announced.[17] For proof, he left Khuang's royalist cabinet mostly unchanged, and gave justice minister Seni Pramoj the go-ahead to draw up a new, permanent constitution.

A year earlier that might not have saved Phibun from American and British opposition. But suddenly Southeast Asia was swept up by the geopolitics of the Cold War. By 1948, with Mao Zedong's forces gaining strength in China and the Viet Minh rising in Vietnam, the United States was eyeing Thailand as a bulwark against communism. With its first arms deals with the Thai military arranged in early 1948, Washington conveniently forgot about Phibun's wartime alliance with Japan. It was the first sign of how the United States' global fight against communism would help set the course of politics in Thailand, and the monarchy's revival, over the next 40 years.

All of this—Khuang's letter and Phibun's declarations, and the foreign role in politics—must have bewildered King Bhumibol. He had personally endorsed the November 1947 coup. Now he found that his prerogative of signing into office the democratically chosen prime minister and cabinet had been wiped away in an instant by the ambitions of the army, and that his exhortation for moderation and selflessness fell on deaf ears. Whatever the constitution said, the generals did as they pleased. And yet, oddly, Phibun, the throne's longtime enemy, still asked for the king's blessing.

For the rest of 1948 there was a tenuous balance between the military under Phibun and the palace-Democrat alliance. The military grew stronger as the United States started to funnel arms and money its way as part of anticommunist efforts. The generals behind Phibun, Kat, Phin, Phao Sriyanond, and Sarit Thanarat, tapped the flow to build their own huge fortunes and formidable political and business machines. The Democrats and the palace threw themselves into casting a new constitution. What they came up with by the end of 1948 was a stunning rebuttal to everything represented by 1932. It almost restored the absolute throne.

Prince Rangsit himself launched the drafting committee on July 12, and head drafter Seni set the tone with an impassioned call for all to uphold the principle of constitutional monarchy. Declaring the royal system more stable than a republican one, he said, according to one newspaper report, "I do not favor an absolute monarchy. But as a democrat, I want a king. I give the king my unlimited loyalty and hope that the monarchy will live forever and ever."

Such hubris aside, the drafting was long and thorough. Debate referred in detail to the structure of the most enduring limited monarchies and the faults that had destroyed the French and Russian thrones and weakened the Japanese emperor. The drafters tapped the writings of people like Walter Bagehot, the 19th-century expert on the British constitution. And they rejected the most extreme proposals, such as one for the king to appoint his own prime minister, and another to make the royal veto absolute, with no possibility of overrule.

That said, the final document was democratic only by the terms laid out in Prince Dhani's interpretation of Siamese kingship. The throne was elevated to a consecrated position above politics, and then given immense powers to direct the government. The Supreme Council of State was revamped into a nine-man privy council, selected solely by the king, for his own advice and consultation. As earlier, a 100-member senate would be wholly selected by the king. Now, however, it was not the prime minister who countersigned but the president of the privy council, making the senate entirely a palace affair. Automatically, too, the head of the senate would become president of the parliament. The elected lower house would be slightly larger than the senate. Against that, however, the king's veto was strengthened with the stipulation that overruling it required a two-thirds vote of the entire parliament.

The king was given the power to dismiss any or all cabinet members by decree, as well as military and civil officials at the three top layers of the bureaucracy. It also put the military directly under the king's supreme command, bypassing the executive. In lawmaking, the king was empowered to issue his own decrees in general, and emergency decrees with the force of full government acts, in issues dealing with taxes, duties, and currency that might require urgent secret consideration. This power appears to have been arranged for such acts as a currency devaluation, harking back to Rama VII's predicament over the economy in 1931–32. However, as these matters required specialized knowledge and information, such powers were normally reserved for prime ministers and presidents.

In addition, the throne gained a new power of plebiscite, by which the king could bypass the government and parliament to amend the constitution by polling the general population, with approval requiring only a simple majority of voters (compared with the two-thirds required in the parliament). So the king could go straight to his subjects to alter the country's basic law against the elected government's wishes.

As for succession, the 1924 Palace Law was again invoked. But now the charter added that the 1924 law could be neither repealed nor amended. And at succession the privy council, not parliament, would name the heir. The king might be elected, as Prince Dhani said, but certainly not by anyone outside the palace.

This was a momentous document. Such a range and depth of royal power was highly uncommon among constitutional monarchies. In its whole it implied that parliament was an innately troublesome and dangerous thing. The 1949 constitution attempted to codify in modern terms the absolute power of the past. It presumed that, by his pure blood, a Chakri king was necessarily wise and good and, guided by the "Constitution of the Dhammasat," was fully and uniquely deserving of power.

When it was released, the final draft created an uproar among the generals, Pridi supporters, and many in the public at large. It was attacked as contrary to the spirit of the 1932 revolution, and Prince Dhani and Prince Upalisarn were accused of planning to form a royalist political party. In response, Dhani claimed that there was no need for such a plan, because in fact "all the political parties now support the throne," while other royalists branded the critics as republicans and communists.[18] A writer to the *Bangkok Post* insisted that the new charter followed the thinking of Rama VII, a king who had protected democracy.[19]

In fact, it was a palace fait accompli. At the outset, the government had cleverly established rules requiring the parliament to accept all or none of the final draft; changes would not be permitted at that stage. On January 27, 1949, the constitution passed in the house by a vote of 125 to 30. Phibun and his generals were now staring at their demise. The holding of elections to form a new government after promulgation meant Phibun would have to resign. The Democrats were certain to be restored to power, and the senate stuffed with the throne's men. Bhumibol would then be invited back to sit on the throne, and 1932 would become a distant memory.

The palace held its ground in the midst of new coup rumors and threats from Phibun. In early March 1949 the new charter was sent to Bhumibol, who studied it closely, together with a drafting committee member. He wasn't likely to have suggested changes, for it was all quite abstract and complex for a 21-year-old student. After the palace made public the king's cabled approval, on March 23 the Supreme State Council signed and promulgated the charter. The council then metamorphosed into the privy council. Rangsit remained regent, and Dhani was made privy council president. They must have found it difficult to contain their triumphant elation.

There remained a lot of work to do for the palace. The case of Ananda's death still overhung Bangkok, and Pridi was still influential. Just as the constitution fight peaked, at the end of February 1949, he snuck back into Thailand and, with support from the navy, attempted a coup. It failed, but it was clear that there was still considerable resentment of both the generals and the royalists.

On the Ananda case, the palace and the generals worked together. In September 1948 the three men arrested for murdering the king went on trial. Palace officials provided dubious evidence pointing to Pridi, along with motives, mainly his argument with Ananda over the regents. Against such a weak story, lawyers for the defense made a convincing case clearing all three. Police chief Phao Sriyanond countered them, brutally: in early 1949 his men murdered two of the defense lawyers and several defense witnesses, masking it as an anticommunist operation. The case continued into 1950, and scores of royal witnesses, including the very top princes, incriminated Pridi with hearsay and circumstantial evidence. From exile in China, Pridi could do nothing in his own defense.

Meanwhile, the palace reclaimed its influence in other areas of the state, including crucially the sangha. Ploddingly replacing Phibun-selected Mahanikay administrators with monks from the Thammayut sect, the royalists eventually reversed Phibun's reforms and returned ecclesiastical power to the throne. Prince

Dhani most likely guided the process, which began as soon as Phibun was forced from power in 1944. Conveniently the Mahanikay sangharaja installed by Phibun died that year. The vacancy was filled by the royal-blooded Prince Vachirayana-wong, abbot of Wat Bovornives, the Thammayut headquarters.[20] When the position of sanghanayok, or ecclesiastical prime minister, became vacant in 1946, another Thammayut monk, Phuttakosajan of Wat Thepsirin, was invested.

In 1947 Phuttakosajan called outright for the repeal of Phibun's 1941 sangha reform and reinstatement of the Sangha Act of 1902. Two years later, inspired by the new royalist constitution, Vachirayanawong ordered Thammayut monasteries to "secede" from the sangha administration, preventing the planned merger of the two schools.[21] In 1951, Vachirayanawong skipped over several more senior Mahanikay officials to name the Thammayut monk Juan Uttayi to replace Phuttakosajan, who had died.[22] The move put the Thammayut in a position to dominate the Mahanikay sect, which was 20 times larger, and restore King Chulalongkorn's 1902 act.

Such successes for the royalists meant little to the farm-bound, poorly educated majority of King Bhumibol's 19 million subjects. If the throne was to mean more to them than the generals and politicians did, they had to witness and feel its presence and superior dhamma sacrality. So while the king was physically absent, the high princes created a sense of his omnipresence for his subjects.

This took the form, in the first place, of frequent press and radio bulletins detailing Bhumibol's activities in Europe, including his schoolwork, travels, and meetings with high officials. His comments on state affairs were reported as commands; for instance, during the review of the constitution draft, royal secretary Nikornthewan Devakul announced that the king had a great interest in all constitutional matters and instructed that he be informed of any further developments.[23] It told the public that the king was, even from a distance, managing his kingdom.

This promotion also involved the assiduous revival of royal ritual and ceremony, which, Dhani and Rangsit both understood, was essential to the peasantry's understanding the monarchy's importance in limiting the suffering in their own lives. Royal ritual gave people faith. So the senior princes revived the rituals that had disappeared after 1932, performing them in the king's name with extensive publicity.

Typical was Chakri Day, the April 6 annual paean to the dynasty. In 1948 Prince Rangsit invigorated the celebrations with more royal and public involvement. The day began with the regent leading a large group of royals in prayers and offerings rites in the palace chapel reliquary of previous Chakri kings. Afterward, the whole group, dressed up in traditional Thai silk finery, moved down the road to pay obeisance to the statue of Rama I on the riverside, as the public watched.

That was tradition. Modernity was expressed in parallel. Chakri Day was also the occasion of the annual Red Cross Fair, for which the royal family was sponsor and patron. This made the fair a royal festival and, for high society, the social event of the year. It suggested that the Red Cross was itself a palace operation, its relief and medical programs an expression of Chakri virtue.

With generous publicity, Prince Rangsit revived a number of ancient rituals of the inner palace. In the king's place he carried out the thrice-yearly changing of the robes of the Phra Kaew, the Emerald Buddha, a ceremony that identifies the king with the country's holiest icon. In early November 1948, Rangsit undertook the royal kathin ceremony to key royal temples, in the king's name presenting robes to top monks to mark the end of the Buddhist lent. Even without being physically present, Bhumibol was making merit and supporting the sangha, demonstrating his own pure practice.

In May 1949, Rangsit similarly revived Brahman-Hindu fertility rites associated with the royal plowing ceremony. Since the 1930s, the actual plowing of the land with holy oxen and celestial virgins, the *chot phranangkhan,* had been performed sporadically by civil officials. But the less visible palace chapel rites of fertility, the *phuetmongkol,* the blessing of the grains, had not been practiced. In 1949 Rangsit renewed the phuetmongkol, leading the offering of alms and prayers to the gods. It emphasized the magic link between the crown and the fruitfulness of the kingdom's farms.[24]

Other revived rituals included the October celebration of Chulalongkorn Day, and the king's birthday, now December 5. At the latter, in the king's name the princes presented alms to monks in the morning. Later in the day there was a party in the palace, while the public enjoyed a holiday. The press meanwhile reported the king's own activities of merit-making in Lausanne, emphasizing his pardon of several thousand prisoners for the occasion. This exhibited the king's mercifulness while indebting the prisoners and their families to him, even though it was the government that had drawn up the pardons list. On that day in 1948, the *Bangkok Post* lamented his absence, saying: "Enlightened leadership is needed in the kingdom today probably more than it ever has been."

History was being rewritten by ceremony. The royal birthday was followed by Constitution Day, December 10, which was made into a three-day holiday. Tellingly, activities focused not on the charter or the 1932 revolution but on King Prajadhipok as the one who had personally bestowed a democratic constitution to the people. Likewise, National Day on June 24, celebrating the 1932 revolution, became an homage to King Prajadhipok, not the People's Party. A new holiday was made of the day of Bhumibol's accession. Rangsit led palace religious rites in Bhumibol's name, while Phibun himself had to preside over government celebrations, at which all present publicly pledged their loyalty to a giant picture of the king.

There were many other small ways in which the verisimilitude of Bhumibol's presence was established. For instance, the throne resumed its sponsorship of funerals of minor royals and respected commoners. Rangsit presided in the king's name over university and military academy commencements. In May 1949 he presented swords to 176 newly commissioned officers of the Chulachomklao Military Academy, a reminder of their service to the crown. A few weeks later, he presented degrees at Chulalongkorn University.

Also effective were the celebrations held on the return to Thailand from exile of senior royals, alive or dead. In June 1948, Prajadhipok's widow Queen Rambhai returned carrying her late husband's ashes, and he was glorified as a great reformer. Only slightly less fanfare greeted the May 1948 return of Prince Boworadej, exiled since the failed 1933 counterrevolt, and later the return of the remains of the late princes Naris and Paripatra. Royal treatment was also accorded the remains of the commoner Phraya Manopakorn, the postrevolution royalist premier.

One other example shows just how complete was the princes' strategy to restore the throne to the center of Thailand's culture. In August 1948 a huge fervor was whipped up following the discovery of a white elephant. White elephants were traditional symbols of power and prestige, automatically becoming the possession of the king. Those reigns in history blessed with white elephants were said to be the greater reigns of Siamese history. Conversely, the unhappy Sixth Reign and the ill-fated Eighth both lacked the giant talisman. Thus it was a momentous occasion when a rural villager captured a white elephant and gave it to the palace of Bhumibol. The villager was given a reward and the royal honorific luang, and the palace held religious rites to receive the animal in Bangkok and induct it into the royal household. It too was given a sacral royal title.

Most important for the king's prestige, though, would be to have a direct impact on the lives of his subjects through relief programs and largesse. The king had to be seen as the most willing to sacrifice his assets, the most generous and unattached to his wealth, to truly claim the status of dhammaraja.

In this he faced tough rivals. Politicians and generals, with their hands on state budgets and access to funds from private business, were already building their own personal stature, their barami, through "selfless" philanthropy. The throne was at a disadvantage. After 1932, the government had seized much of the assets of the royal family and household, mostly real estate and shares in companies. The total was substantial: the royal family had owned an estimated one-third of all the land in central Bangkok before the war, including the buildings housing the government.[25] Much of this was transferred to the state by Phibun, leaving the palace with little independent income by the end of World War II.

In the late 1940s, a key goal of the princes was to recover pre-1932 assets and restore the royal family's private income. The money would both support palace operations and family needs and fund the effort to establish the king as the people's most important benefactor. Regaining political muscle in 1947–48 was a big step toward this goal. The Khuang government substantially increased the throne's allocation in the state budget, meanwhile quietly returning to the Mahidols many former palace assets (though the government-occupied buildings and palaces mainly in the old city center remained the state's).

In 1947 the palace assets and finances—the Bureau of the Royal Household, the privy purse, the Crown Property Bureau, and some private royal family assets— were put into the hands of M.R. Thawiwong Thawalyasak. Born in 1901, the Cambridge-educated Thawiwong had been a page to Rama VI, and thereafter he remained deeply involved in royal society.

Thawiwong rebuilt the royal fortune skillfully and aggressively. He persuaded the government to recognize the palace's ownership of property that had fallen unofficially into private hands after 1932. Tens of thousands of people lived in homes and shophouses in the old city, which was originally crown real estate. Thawiwong made these residents resume paying rent to the Crown Property Bureau (CPB), acknowledging its ownership, and from late 1948 the bureau sought to increase this income by leasing out more real estate, raising rents, and evicting nonpayers, even the parliament itself. The legislators had long occupied the huge Ananta Samakhom throne hall, for which the palace had little use. Nevertheless, Thawiwong's bureau threatened to evict the parliament unless it paid rent to the crown. This was unreconstructed royalism, the assertion of the king's traditional claim to ownership of all property. The legislators, unsurprisingly, refused.

Meanwhile Thawiwong restructured the holdings of the broader royal family. He claimed for the Mahidols official ownership of royal palaces and estates that had lapsed into the hands of cousins, uncles, and aunts. He didn't want these properties to be passed on irretrievably to descendants outside the Chakri core. His measures generated some tension within the greater royal family, but Thawiwong apparently

traded annuities from the royal purse for the properties. In the postwar environment, cash was more needed than land anyway.

Thawiwong also made capital investments in the palace and Mahidol family
name, with private-sector partners like banks and insurance firms that hoped to
benefit from royal prestige as well as funding. Siam Commercial Bank became the
foundation for the expansion of crown investments. Together with the CPB and
Princess Galyani privately, for instance, the bank supported the development of the
new Princess Hotel on crown land by businesswoman Chanut Piyaoui. This investment would later develop into the prominent Dusit Thani hotel group, a joint
venture of Chanut and the CPB.

Within a few short years, Thawiwong piled up a hefty war chest of discretionary funds. This allowed the palace to pay its staff better—shoring up loyalty—and to
provide steady income for the senior royals who emerged from the war relatively
impoverished, including former queen Rambhai. The money also underwrote
Rangsit's revival of palace rituals and social activities.

Most important, the money enabled building the king's reputation as a source
of charity. Even though he wasn't really there, in June 1948 the king donated
100,000 baht (U.S.$5,000) to purchase radio receivers for distribution around the
country, so that rural communities could listen to the national news (which included reports on the king). The money was said to come from the king's personal
funds.[26] On his birthday in 1948, the king made a "personal" donation of 3,000 baht
to the United Nations Appeal for Children in Bangkok. By July 1949, the king could
muster 300,000 baht for a tuberculosis inoculation campaign by the Saowabha
Institute, the local branch of the Pasteur Institute, named after King Chulalongkorn's first queen. As time passed, such donations became larger and more frequent, and all were highly publicized. Since Rangsit and Thawiwong handled them,
it wasn't clear if Bhumibol was even aware of these transactions. But it didn't
matter; the people understood the gifts came from him personally.

None of this went unnoticed by the king's competitors, especially Phibun, who well
understood the power of such symbolism. With his hand on the government
budget, he could, for the moment, outspend the king and call it his own munificence. But in the other areas where the royals were making advances, such as
influence over the sangha, and religious ritual performance, he was losing ground.

It wasn't for not trying. Because he was the prime minister, government
publications and radio extolled him, holding a position neither above nor beneath
the king. He assumed the mantle of the country's leading anticommunist, to give

him a modern importance the throne did not yet have. But he wasn't completely successful. In 1948, Phibun named himself head of a revived National Council for Culture, which would conceivably give him the opportunity to depreciate royalism. Taking note, the royals forced him to name Prince Bhanuband, Prince Prem Purachatra, and M.L. Pin Malakul to the council's board. Their presence ensured that royalism still defined national culture.

6 Romance in Lausanne ∽ Bhumibol Prepares to Reign

THE AXLE AROUND WHICH THIS WHOLE COSMIC WHEEL SPUN, meanwhile, was ensconced in Lausanne, Switzerland, maybe pondering his schizophrenic life. One persona was a European university student caught up in the postwar reconstruction zeitgeist. The other, less familiar identity was the sacral dhammaraja king of Thailand, turgid, conservative, confined by an entourage of elderly men who emphasized only the old.

His brother Ananda had balked at this. But after the tragedy of June 9, 1946, Bhumibol displayed nothing but a firm sense of duty—or guilt, as some believe—to wear the crown. It wasn't only temporizing for a future way out. Bhumibol's loss of his public smile for much of the next five decades made clear that his acceptance was complete and permanent. Bhumibol was better suited to kingship than Ananda anyway. He was more disciplined at work and more obedient to his elders, foremost among them his mother Sangwal. In Switzerland he stuck to a circle of expatriate Thais, never straying too far into European life and the profusion of new ideas that filled the air. He liked Europe, but the prospect of life in the Bangkok palace didn't overwhelm him with anxiety. He was not particularly ambitious, so the confines of kingship seemed to fit.

Life with his mother in Villa Vadhana during 1946–50 was filled with an air of transience. The king took more tutoring in Thai culture and things royal. He dropped his formal university studies for a customized course covering political science, government, and law.[1]

His life was already that of a king. He was awakened every morning by crouching pages instead of his mother, delivering his croissant-and-coffee breakfast in bed. All but his mother addressed him in the equivalent of "your royal majesty," and they were wary of even touching him.

He received regular communications from the Bangkok regent on the decisions being made in his name, and he was helped in this official king's business by a private secretary. A stream of visitors ensured that the king and his mother were attentive to Bangkok's muddy politics, many asking them to intervene. These included Pridi in early 1947, followed by Prince Subhasvasti, who endeavored to bring the royalists and Pridi together. Subhasvasti wrote the king a 120-page memorandum on postrevolution politics that outlined how Seni Pramoj and the Democrats were framing Pridi for Ananda's death in order to take power. He also gently offered a plausible explanation of how Ananda could have accidentally shot himself.[2] Subhasvasti later wrote to Pridi, "From my audience with his majesty and the princess mother this time, I dare tell you positively that they did not believe that you were the assassin."[3]

After the November 1947 coup, too, the generals pressed the Mahidols to return for Ananda's cremation and Bhumibol's official coronation. But Sangwal resisted. The new constitution was yet incomplete, and Lausanne, home to many royals in exile, offered a constant reminder of the postwar perils for monarchies. The most famous resident was King Leopold III of Belgium, whose son Prince Baudoin, though three years younger, became one of Bhumibol's closer contacts among European royalty.

Leopold's fate illustrated the difficulty of a king negotiating the twists of democracy. He was resented by many Belgians for allegedly capitulating to the Nazis, and also for having married a commoner soon after the death of his much-loved royal-blooded queen. For five years after the war, the Belgian government couldn't decide whether to reinstate the monarchy or, if it did, whether to keep Leopold or pass the crown to Baudoin. The questions were first put to parliament, and then to the people in a general plebiscite. The monarchy risked a massive embarrassment by putting itself up for a popular referendum.

The Mahidols, moreover, had reasons to fear the nationalist and communist movements that had turned violent in many Asian countries, ejecting colonial powers and old elites alike. In China, Mao's communists were close to victory, and they were believed to support ethnic Chinese communist undergrounds throughout

Southeast Asia, such as the insurgency in Malaya. On Thailand's western border, the Burmese coalition led by Aung San—unfairly branded a communist in the West— ousted the colonial British in January 1948 and then refused to restore the Burmese monarchy. To the east, turmoil in Laos and Cambodia threatened their monarchies, while in Vietnam, Ho Chi Minh's nationalists were fighting France's reinstatement of Emperor Bao Dai. A report about Bao Dai ran in the *Bangkok Post* in July 1949 with the headline "As Indochina Goes, So Goes Thailand."

Switzerland gave Bhumibol protection from all this. His personalized studies left him much free time to travel, play his music, and socialize. He frequently drove himself to Paris to go shopping and pass nights in smoky jazz clubs. He helped his car-racing uncle Prince Birabongs in the pits at the Grand Prix des Nations in Geneva, and in August 1948, during a motor tour of northern Europe, he watched Birabongs take first at Zandvoort. Bhumibol put even more time into his photography and music, fancying a second career as a jazzman. *Life* magazine described him as having "probably the most intricately gadgeted orchestra in Europe," with every manner of musical instrument and recording and amplification equipment spilling from his music room.[4] With a band of mostly expatriate Thais, including his sister Galyani's new husband, Colonel Aram Ratanakul, a royal aide, he held jam sessions that ran through the night.

The palace proudly announced his compositional achievements. In September 1948 the press splashed the news that a foxtrot penned by the king, "Heart and Love," would soon arrive in Bangkok carried by Prince Chakraphan, who wrote the lyrics. An earlier composition, "Rainfall," was popularized via band concerts and national radio. Both pieces were sweet, slightly bluesy ballads of a prewar type. It was reported that an American film studio wanted the rights to "Rainfall."[5]

But it was *Time* magazine that fingered the principal reason for the Mahidols' continuing stay in Europe. As *Time* suggested, other things were being plotted for Rama IX. "In Lausanne, Bhumibol's studies consisted of a passionate interest in photography, music and racy automobiles. He also sometimes read a law book. . . . Many mammas of the Siamese nobility got the idea that . . . Lausanne would be good for the daughters. Quite a 'court' developed around Bhumibol."[6] In fact, the pool of heirs to the dynasty was ominously scant, and finding a match for the king was the first priority for the palace and the Mahidols. Soon after the return to Lausanne, Rangsit prepared a list of eligible women.

Bhumibol seemed dutifully willing. His first known interest was a daughter of Prince Dhani, M.R. Supicha Sonakul, whom he met in 1946 and then again in early

1948, when she and her father dropped by Lausanne on their way to England. Thai newspapers reported a royal courtship in process, but apparently Dhani wanted Supicha to finish university first and blocked the relationship.

In the meantime, Bhumibol met the daughters of the Thai ambassador to Paris, Prince Nakkhat Kitiyakara. Nakkhat was familiar to the Mahidols, having been minister in the London embassy before Paris. His family was also well known for its push to insinuate itself into the core Chakri bloodline. Nakkhat's father was Prince Kitiyakara, the noncelestial son of Rama V by a favorite concubine. While most of his generation of princes disappointed when it came to sustaining the Chakri line, Kitiyakara stood out: he had 25 children by five wives. It made his family important to the dynasty by its sheer numbers. These offspring married strategically into other families that were influential in the palace, such as the Sarasins and the Sanitwongs. Large in number and very wealthy, the Sanitwongs, descended from the Second Reign, were likewise bent on reclaiming a central role in the dynasty.

By lineage Prince Nakkhat, born in 1898, was the best of his generation. His mother was Prince Kitiyakara's primary wife, herself of sparkling royal lineage, born to Rama V's half brother Prince Devawongs (founder of the Devakul family). That made Nakkhat and Bhumibol cousins. Nakkhat tightened that relationship by marrying strategically to M.L. Bua Sanitwongs, who carried the blood of both Rama II and Rama V and was a senior aide to Queen Rambhai. With deliberateness, their children married equally well. Their first son, M.R. Kalayanakiti, born in 1929, married a Sanitwongs; second son M.R. Adulyakit married M.C. Bhandhusawali Yugala, daughter of Prince Bhanuband, the seniormost prince of the postwar era.

Prince Nakkhat had even loftier goals for his daughters, M.R. Sirikit, who was born in 1932, and M.R. Busba, born two years later. He brought the girls to Europe to be schooled in the comportment of modern, Europeanized Thai ladies, and also to get close to the new king. It wasn't difficult, given Bhumibol's frequent visits to Paris. Pretty and precocious, the 15-year-old Sirikit caught his eye in 1947.

Even so, a distance came between them when Nakkhat was transferred to London in mid-1948. Bhumibol was planning to return to Thailand in early 1949 for the cremation and coronation, occasions that would provide an opportunity to meet more girls. But a near tragic accident intervened, providing Nakkhat the opportunity to set the hook. At 10 p.m. on October 4, 1948, Bhumibol crashed his sporty Fiat Topolino into the rear of a truck 10 kilometers outside Lausanne. He was driving about the town with Galyani's husband, Aram, presumably speeding. The Thais blamed the truck driver; the perfect dhammaraja king could not have erred. (The following year, Galyani and Aram were divorced, possibly as a result of the accident.)

The Thai press reported the crash as a near catastrophe for the kingdom, which was true, given the diminished Chakri line. But the king's injuries could have been worse. His back was hurt, and he incurred cuts on his face that cost him most of the sight in one eye. The Kitiyakaras made the most of it. Sirikit and Busba rushed from London to assist Sangwal in caring for the hospitalized Bhumibol. Sirikit stayed on, enrolling at a local academy in Lausanne. It was later said that when the king came to after the crash, he asked for his mother and Sirikit.

Attempts to restore his eyesight delayed the homecoming, for which the now very royalist government budgeted some two million dollars, inclusive of a new Daimler for the king. It was further stalled to let his romance with Sirikit blossom. Courting and negotiations went fast. On July 19, 1949, the couple were secretly engaged in Lausanne's Windsor Hotel. Three weeks later, the formal announcement was made at Sirikit's 17th birthday party in London, where Bhumibol played solo piano and joined with the dance band on the saxophone. He presented Sirikit, Western-style, with the ring his father had given Sangwal for their own engagement 30 years before.

In her own inimitably charming, and maybe fact-bending style, Sirikit later recalled her romance for the BBC, starting with the first meeting in Paris.

> It was hate at first sight . . . because he said he would arrive at four o'clock in the afternoon. He arrived at seven o'clock, kept me standing there, practicing curtsey, and curtsey. [But the next time] it was love. . . . I didn't know that he loved me, because at that time I was only 15 years old, and planned to be a concert pianist. He was gravely ill in the hospital. . . . He produced my picture out of his pocket, I didn't know he had one, and he said "send for her, I love her." I thought of being with the man I love only. Not of the duty, and the burden of [becoming] queen.[7]

The engagement filled Thailand with immense excitement. The king's return was now slated for early 1950. In quick succession there would be Ananda's cremation, Bhumibol's wedding, and the coronation. With the royalist constitution in place, it would be an opulent, two-month celebration of the monarchy and its victory over the 1932 revolutionists.

The new monarchism, though, wasn't proceeding as smoothly as hoped. After the 1949 constitution was promulgated, Phibun and his generals looked to reclaim the upper hand in elections. Helped by police chief Phao's campaign of murdering and intimidating opposing candidates, and by paying off independent members of parliament, Phibun's group gained a solid majority in the lower house. But because Democrats and royalists still dominated the senate, Phibun couldn't consolidate control. Rangsit again rejected his request for a privy council seat.

The armed forces, though, had a source of power extraneous to the constitution, the parliament, and the throne: the United States. Washington had concluded that Thailand would play an important role as a frontline ally in the Cold War. In 1948, U.S. intelligence units began arming and training a separate army under General Phao, which became known as the Border Patrol Police (BPP). The relationship was cemented in 1949 as the communists captured power in China. The generals demonstrated their anticommunist credentials by echoing U.S. propaganda and killing alleged leftists. At midyear a CIA team arrived in Bangkok to train the BPP for covert support of the Kuomintang in its continuing war against the Chinese communists on the Burma-China border. Later in the year the United States began to arm and train the Thai army and to provide the kingdom general economic aid.

The supposed communist threat and American support essentially legitimized the generals' claim to political power for the next four decades. Yet this wasn't all a loss for the palace. The Americans saw the king as a useful figurehead in the fight against communism. And so, even before his coronation, Bhumibol was being shaped into a potent icon of the Cold War, and the United States became his throne's guarantor.

This was all beyond most Thais, bound to their farms and living according to the seasons and traditional calendars. The jousting for power since 1932 had done little to improve their lives. The dhammaraja king's repatriation held more promise for them. In a radio address on December 31, 1949, Bhumibol reassured them that he would very soon return despite his studies and eye injury. These were small burdens to bear for the sake of his subjects. He called on them to uphold unity and work for progress.

But at 22, Bhumibol was far from reassured himself as he sat on the ship heading to Bangkok in early 1950. Although he was with Sirikit, his main sources of strength were now all absent: his brother had died, his sister had settled in Switzerland with her daughter, and his mother had fallen ill and was unable to make the trip. While in transit he received a letter from Francis Sayre, the former government adviser and Mahidol family friend, who wrote:

> Do not let yourself become discouraged. The Thai people . . . yearn to
> have back in their midst their king and leader. They will be loyal and true
> to you. . . . [Economic] problems which menace so many countries do
> not beset Siam. The country's greatest dangers lie in other directions than
> these. To meet such problems . . . you will follow the pathway which your
> father always followed, the pathway of selfless service for his country and
> its people. Your ideals like his must be kept untarnished and shining;
> your constant compass if you would avoid shipwreck must be utter good-
> ness and integrity of character. Nothing else will so surely win your peo-
> ple's hearts and strengthen your reign.

To which the king replied: "I shall try not to get discouraged, although sometimes, I nearly got discouraged even in Switzerland. . . . But I know I must hold on [to] what I think is the right thing to do, and I can assure you I shall try my best." To ensure the best, on a stopover in Sri Lanka he visited two old temples, one founded by one of his own ancestors, where he planted a tree, lit incense, and prayed, presumably, for safe passage in his life ahead.[8]

Bhumibol's ten-week stay in Thailand was an immense triumph. He was received with all the fanfare and glory of a beloved, long-absent king. To astrologers, the heavens proved the great event: three days before Bhumibol arrived, hail fell on Bangkok for the first time since 1933. Every facet of his visit was designed to accentuate the monarchy's greatness. Before his arrival, the government spent weeks searching for a white elephant to present him. The day of his arrival was declared a holiday, and arrangements were made for a squadron of jets from a nearby American aircraft carrier to fly over Bangkok in his honor.[9]

On arrival he was presented with the Golden Sword of the Realm, the symbol of his sovereignty. Each branch of the armed services awarded him its top rank, and the national mint struck new coins with his image. As he came ashore, airplanes dropped bunches of flowers and lucky puffed rice over the city. Following the government's greeting, he went to the Grand Palace to light candles and pray to the

Emerald Buddha and Phra Siam Dhevathirat. Then he proceeded to the chapels of the Grand Palace to pay respects to his ancestors, and to the golden urn holding his brother Ananda.

The next morning he and Sirikit made merit to 64 monks at the dilapidated Chitrlada residential estate where they would stay. There was no interest in returning to the bloodstained memories of the Grand Palace's Barompimarn residence. Following a parade, the king led princes and monks in a propitious circumambulation procession at the Amarind Throne Hall, ended by a ceremonial cleansing of the king's feet and shoes. He also presided over separate Mahayana rites with Chinese and Annamese monks.

Sunday, March 26, was a rest day. In the late afternoon, a casually dressed Bhumibol drove his own car to the Grand Palace area accompanied only by his aide-de-camp, Luang Suranarong. They were quickly recognized by the many people gathered near the Sanam Luang royal cremation ground for a concert. The commotion forced the king to speed back to Chitrlada. The next day began with a formal procession to Sanam Luang to raise the nine-tiered royal umbrella over his brother's pyre. While there, a man broke free from the crowd and rushed toward the king's car. He was a poor Ayutthaya farmer who wanted to petition the king over some 40 acres of land that had been cheated from him. It was a reminder to Bhumibol of the things people expected from him as a perceived omnipotent king.

Later in the day a series of royal proclamations by the king reshaped the palace hierarchy. Prince Rangsit, stepping down as regent, was appointed privy council chairman, with Dhani as his deputy. Princess Galyani, who had been forced to give up her title five years earlier for marrying a commoner, had her rank as a princess restored, now that she had divorced. Other high-level royal honors were granted to Sirikit and her father, Prince Nakkhat. In subsequent weeks Dhani and Nakkhat were elevated to senior prince level, and Nakkhat was made an army general. The rolls of the bluest-blooded Chakris were now reinforced around the Queen Sawang-Mahidol core, enhancing dynastic survivability.

For the solemn spectacle of Ananda's day-long cremation rites on March 30, the extended Chakri royal family, the top military brass and government officials, and a legion of soldiers, monks, and Brahman priests, all led on foot by the king and the supreme patriarch, escorted a crimson and golden chariot bearing Ananda's urn-encased body through the streets around the Grand Palace. Up to a half million Thais watched from the side as they paced their way, precisely timed by palace astrologers, to Sanam Luang.

Every act and detail of the cremation was designed to amplify both dhammaraja and devaraja identities of the king. The pyre was an elaborate multiple-storied representation of Mount Meru, the Hindu abode of the gods. The lineage between the modern king back through Ayutthaya to Sukhothai was restated in various incantations by officials and monks. In a funeral volume commemorating his brother, Bhumibol published a biography of King Naresuan, the greatest warrior-king of Ayutthaya, implying a consanguinity between the two.

The entire group returned in the afternoon for a ceremonial igniting of the pyre. In stifling heat, Bhumibol led the hundreds of family members and officials, one by one, in placing lit candles under the urn. Then, late at night, Bhumibol returned with a small group of immediate family members and priests for the actual cremation of Ananda's body, which had been removed from the urn and placed in a sandalwood coffin. The next day they collected the ashes for placement in a royal temple and in the palace hall reserved for royal relics.

A steady routine of rites and socializing filled the run-up to the royal wedding and the coronation. There were two more royal cremations at Sanam Luang, for the late Prince Paripatra (who died in exile in 1944) and Prince Naris. April 6 was Chakri Day, with ritual paeans to all the previous kings. Beautiful Sirikit stole all the attention as the royal couple opened the three-day Red Cross Fair. A week later it was the same when the couple joined various rituals for Songkran, the kingdom's traditional New Year.

The royal wedding was, by comparison, private and subdued. After paying the official civil marriage fee of 10 baht, on the morning of April 28, Bhumibol and Sirikit went to Sawang's Srapathum Palace, where the former queen bound the couple with lustral water originally sanctified by Rama I. In the afternoon a similar public ceremony took place in the Grand Palace, with members of parliament and Phibun as witnesses. At the end, the king personally bestowed the jeweled decorations of the Order of Maha Chakri on Sirikit, raising her title and blood status to that of queen. Paid for by the government, the Maha Chakri piece had 750 diamonds set in gold. Tradition had it that the newlyweds were to spend the next three nights in the Grand Palace. But with Bhumibol still bothered by the memory of Ananda's death, they stayed only one night. Afterward, he and Sirikit embarked for the Klai Kangwon palace in Hua Hin for four days.

The coronation on May 4–5 involved mostly inner-palace Hindu-based rituals evoking the devaraja cult: a ritual bath of the king in waters collected from auspicious sites, followed by the anointment of the king by Prince Rangsit representing the royal family, and an anointment by the sangharaja. The king then donned the royal robes and climbed atop an elevated octagonal throne, the faces of which represented the eight cardinal points of the compass, the expanse of his realm. He received homage at each side, a Brahman priest pouring holy water from 18 spiritually significant stupas. Then the president of the senate, representing the people, pledged the kingdom's loyalty.

Bhumibol then moved to another throne, shielded by a nine-tiered umbrella. The Brahmans presented him with the official royal regalia: his conical golden crown, the royal sword and cane, the whisk made from a white elephant's tail hairs, a fan, golden slippers, and two rings of kingship. Kneeling, the priests recited Sanskrit incantations summoning the Hindu gods to descend and take up residence in his person. Bhumibol poured some holy water from a small ewer and, finally imbued with the correct spirit and tools to take the ultimate step, he crowned himself. Making a pledge to rule with justice, he scattered silver and gold flowers on the floor, symbolically spreading goodness over his kingdom.

Other holy acts, like formal horoscope readings and two hours of lying on the royal bed in the ceremonial residence of the king, sealed his deity. After two days, Bhumibol finally emerged in front of his subjects, accompanied by trumpet fanfares and a cannon salute. The now fully crowned Rama IX declared that he was deeply attached to the Siamese people and would reign with righteousness, for their benefit and happiness.

Other rituals filled out the visit. Bhumibol handed out degrees at seven military academy and university graduations. He awarded new ranks and decorations to the highest military and police officers, naming many as honorary royal guards. He led the observation of major Buddhist holidays, and he pardoned, for the coronation, 2,000 prisoners.

There were also charity duties that portrayed the Mahidols specifically as the source of modern health care. Bhumibol unveiled a statue of his father at Siriraj Hospital as the father of modern doctoring, and donated several hundred thousand baht for a medical school, which would be named Mahidol University. Another 88,000 baht was given to the Royal Thai Air Force's new hospital, which was named for the king. He also made a "personal" donation of three kilograms of a new antituberculosis vaccine to the Public Health Ministry. The drugs came from the Swiss, but the king accrued the merit. Meanwhile, Sirikit became patron of the Red Cross and the Foundation for the Blind.

Promotion of the king was comprehensive. His songs were performed by government orchestras and university groups. His compositional brilliance was confirmed with the news that five Bhumibol songs would be used in an upcoming Broadway review called *Peep Show,* by the famous producer Michael Todd. The king declared that the royalties would go to charity. *Peep Show,* a sexy song and dance burlesque, opened in early June 1950. Todd had originally sought out the king's music to help publicize the show.[10] In the end, however, all of Bhumibol's songs had been dropped except for "Blue Night," which was performed to a backdrop of a Thai temple and Thai-style dancing. A favorable reviewer termed it a "haunting beguine." Less excited, the *New York Times* said "Blue Night" was "okay," "a competent blues song composed out of office hours by the King of Thailand."[11] To the Thais, this was a great Chakri accomplishment all the same.

The trip was not completely cloudless. There was an air of instability due to constantly fractious parliamentary politics, and the situation of King Leopold in Belgium again reminded Bhumibol of the pitfalls of democracy. In March 1950, Leopold finally, but only barely, won support for his reinstatement in a plebiscite. After another three difficult months getting parliament to ratify the reinstatement, the *Bangkok Post* opined that the long battle had weakened Europe's once strongest monarchy.[12] It was food for thought for Bhumibol. Engaging public opinion to settle issues of royal power was a minefield.

Also constantly overhanging the Thai capital was the Ananda case. Hearings continued throughout the king's stay, and each new revelation and rumor was avidly covered in the press. Khuang, Kukrit, Phibun, Phao, and the supreme patriarch testified, each stoking the case against Pridi. In early May the police official appointed by justice minister Seni Pramoj to run the investigation—Seni's own brother-in-law Pinit Chongkadi—produced a man who claimed to have been hired by Pridi to kill Ananda. Much later it would come out that the witness was Pinit's friend.

The king himself was interviewed by the court in Chitrlada Palace over two days. As in earlier testimonies, just after the event and later in Lausanne, Bhumibol punctiliously avoided suggesting any particular conclusion. Yet he provided just enough facts to damn Pridi: that Pridi had argued with the king, had abused some privileges like using the king's car, and that Chaleo had left the palace under a cloud. There was nothing in Pridi's defense.

Also hanging over the visit was the growing communist threat, real and fancied.[13] As the communists consolidated their power in Beijing, leftists carried out political assassinations in Singapore, Malaysia, Indonesia, and Vietnam. The

United States told Bangkok it could be the next "domino." Pridi, now branded a Chinese agent, was reported to be building a base in the northeast. This ominous picture brought the palace, the Democrats, and the generals somewhat closer, and the palace actually ceded some of its hard-won powers to the military. Just before the coronation, Bhumibol signed two protocols of the government's formal anti-communist policy. The first allowed the government to mobilize troops in case of a communist uprising, and the second to declare martial law, both without the throne's approval. The king's sharing of his prerogatives made him a co-combatant in the war against communism. In Washington the Truman administration immediately approved an extended aid program for Thailand, with the first tranche totaling $10 million for the military.

King Bhumibol's last ritual duty before departing was the opening of parliament on June 1. It was a special session, expressly held for the purpose of demonstrating the bond and hierarchy between the throne and the legislature. Dressed in an army field marshal's uniform, the king warned of an unpredictable and worrisome "ideological conflict" in the world and in neighboring countries. But he said that things were looking much better in his own kingdom and that there was reason for optimism. The performance was not altogether inspirational, but it showed him as an alert and comforting all-seeing king.

It isn't clear why he had to leave. It was probably hoped that the royalists would force Phibun and the remnant 1932 revolutionists permanently into the political abyss before Bhumibol settled permanently on the throne. The royal astrologers chose June 6 for his departure, and before the date Rangsit was reappointed as regent.

Bhumibol took advantage of his last 18 months abroad like any young, well-off, and recently married man. Shortly after they returned to Lausanne, Sirikit became pregnant, tentatively satisfying their paramount duty to secure the dynasty's future. Meanwhile, the couple whirled about Europe attending parties, concerts, and other shows. They saw the latest movies, and their attendance at *Gone With the Wind* in early 1951 was touted by MGM as an endorsement.

The king dropped his university studies as he took on an increased load of palace paperwork, guided by Rangsit and the privy councilors. For New Year 1951, a taped radio message gave what was becoming his standard call for unity and peace. It also took note of the growing political tensions across Asia: "History has told us that nations are annihilated when their people lack unity, when they divide into factions which try to take advantage of each other. I enjoin upon the Thai people to recall with gratitude how our ancestors worked with unanimity and were ready to bear sacrifice for the good of the nation."

On April 5, 1951, auspiciously the eve of Chakri Day, the royal couple's first child was born, a girl who was given the name Ubolrat. For a country that had been waiting 40 years for a true heir born of a king, a girl was a slight disappointment. But this king clearly promised more than his three predecessors.

In Bangkok, the battle between the royalists and Phibun's generals continued. Both sides worked to boost their financial strength. Palace money manager Thawiwong launched new real estate developments, one of which eventually became the Siam Intercontinental Hotel on family land next to Srapathum Palace. The Crown Property Bureau formed the Muang Thai Insurance Company with the Lamsams, a wealthy ethnic Chinese banking family. The CPB also evicted the parliament from the Ananta Samakhom throne hall.

At the same time, the ambitious and venal rival generals Phin, Phao, and Sarit each gained wealth and influence on the back of the intensifying U.S.-Thai military relationship. In June 1950 the government agreed to send 4,000 Thai troops and 40,000 tons of rice to the just-erupted Korean War. In return a formal U.S. military advisory group arrived, pouring more money, arms, and training into the Thai armed forces, particularly Phao's BPP. It marked the beginning of an overt U.S. military presence that would grow steadily over 25 years.

The two sides squabbled over the official royal stipend and over the royal couple's refusal to return home to give birth. Just after Bhumibol departed, the palace faction in parliament proposed to reinstate two old traditions, the swearing of an oath of allegiance to the king by all government officials, and the award of such aristocratic peerage titles as luang and phraya to favored supporters of the throne.

Phibun, who had halted both traditions when he was prime minister in the 1940s, blocked their reinstatement. But then his own proposals were rebuffed. In December 1950 Phibun proposed to Rangsit that he have a weekly audience with the king, and also asked to sit in on privy council meetings. Arguably, Phibun's proposals were reasonable: in Britain there is a regular meeting between the sovereign and the prime minister, as well as direct links between the government and the privy council. But Rangsit flatly rejected both, denying Phibun increased influence in the palace.

In fact, Phibun was no longer completely antipathetic toward the crown. He adhered to royal protocol, dutifully leading demonstrations of respect for the king on royal occasions. He declared the king's birthday a three-day holiday in December 1950, and a few days later on Constitution Day seemed to accept the ceremonial assignment of credit for democracy to King Prajadhipok. It could have been that Phibun was seeking an entente with the palace because, as 1951 opened, holding Phao, Phin, and Sarit in check was increasingly difficult. Indeed, when rebel navy officers kidnapped Phibun in an attempted coup in June 1951, the generals deemed Phibun expendable, bombing the vessel on which he was being held. The premier barely escaped by jumping into the water and swimming to shore.

Phibun also may have seen an opening in early 1951, when one of the main barriers to better relations, Prince Rangsit, died, on March 6. Rangsit's death was a major blow to the Mahidols. He was the last surviving of King Chulalongkorn's many sons, the most strong-minded and clever of the royal restorationists, and almost a father to Ananda and Bhumibol. His replacement as regent and royalist spearhead was Prince Dhani, who was formidable though not as politically driven.

Yet Dhani proved nearly as tough as Rangsit. Around midyear, the generals made a play for greater powers to deal with rising security threats. Phao traveled to Switzerland twice to lobby the king for constitutional amendments to expand the executive's emergency powers. He returned from his first trip believing he had the king's agreement. But Bhumibol stalled, probably at Dhani's advice, hoping the issue would be dropped. On Phao's second visit, in October, the palace's refusal was direct, and it left the generals fuming. Increasingly, they were losing patience with the royals.

Further adding to the unsettled climate in Bangkok were the unending twists and turns of the king's death case. When the first judgment came out on September 27, 1951, the court acquitted royal secretary Chaleo and the page Butr but found the page Chit guilty. By implication the verdict absolved Pridi, although the conviction of Chit alone was inexplicable. With both the government and the royalists angry and embarrassed, the government called for a new trial.

This made it hardly an ideal time for Bhumibol to return to Bangkok for good, which was planned for early December. Around the world there were harbingers of what he could face with such turbulence at home. In July 1951, King Abdullah of Jordan was assassinated. In Spain, the dictator Francisco Franco tried to make a puppet of exiled King Alfonso's son Don Juan, to shore up his own legitimacy. In Japan, an unprecedented anti-monarchy demonstration by 3,000 leftist students had Emperor Hirohito momentarily imprisoned in a university building.

These warnings would have been better heeded. On November 29, 1951, just as King Bhumibol's vessel entered Thai waters, Generals Phin, Phao, and Sarit undertook a coup against their own government and stripped the throne of the powers it had gained in the 1949 constitution.

7 The Cold War, 1952–57 ∾

THE COUP OF NOVEMBER 1951 was no less of a blow to the monarchists than the overthrow of the absolute monarchy in 1932, executed firmly and underpinned by ugly personal threats to the king and the princes. It came at the very moment the palace was preparing to celebrate the culmination of a pertinacious six-year fight to restore the primacy of royal blood.

A crescendo of anticipation had grown at each stage of the king's journey. From his grand send-off by the city of Lausanne, and another at quayside in Genoa, daily radio and newspaper reports mapped his progress. Personal messages from the king en route were broadcast, to stir excitement in Bangkok. The arrival was planned like a second coronation, with cannon salutes at riverside to be followed by religious rites at the various Grand Palace shrines. Then in quick succession would be Bhumibol's birthday on December 5, celebrating his second 12-year cycle, and Constitution Day celebrating the throne's "gift" of democracy.

Three days before the king's arrival, several generals arrived at Prince Dhani's doorstep demanding that he dissolve parliament, dismiss the cabinet, abrogate the constitution, and declare a new government with them in charge. When Dhani argued that it would be better to consult the king first, the generals carried out their own demands, nullifying the 1949 charter and stripping the throne of its powers. They blocked communications with the king's vessel so that Bhumibol wouldn't turn around and go back to Europe.[1] Adding insult to injury, Phibun assumed the job of regent in Dhani's place.

For the public, the generals put on a great display of fealty when the king, Queen Sirikit, and their infant daughter Ubolrat finally disembarked on December 2, greeted at riverside by Prince Chumbhot and Phibun. Meanwhile they banned political parties and sacked royalists who had dominated the parliament and government for four years. The junta restored the 1932 charter and Phibun named a single national assembly of 123 members, 103 of them from the police or military.

On December 4, Phibun became prime minister, General Phin Choonhavan deputy premier, and Generals Sarit Thanarat and Phao Sriyanond ministers without portfolio controlling, respectively, the army and the police. The king had no voice in the matter. The generals held that he was abroad at the time of the coup and royal approval was in the hands of the regent—Phibun.[2] As justification for the coup, the new leadership claimed that, because parliament was corrupt and ineffective, the country was vulnerable to communism, which, Phibun explained, threatened the holy Thai trinity of nation, religion, and monarchy.

The Cold War made it expedient for the United States and England to recognize the new government. They rationalized that the head of state, King Bhumibol, had not changed. It meant, however, that Phibun had to preserve the monarchy, if he had considered otherwise. Keeping up appearances, on December 6, Phin presented the king with the symbolic sword of leadership of the Thai military.

It was an ominous beginning for the 24-year-old king's rule. Severely shaken, the palace maintained appearances of normality. Bhumibol and Sirikit stiffly went through the arrival ceremonies, and the Bureau of the Royal Household declared four days of celebrations for the king's birthday. Dhani and Prince Bhanuband meanwhile geared for a fight: on their advice, Bhumibol launched his reign with a direct challenge to the generals. On December 6 he received the 1932 constitution to sign as a temporary charter, to be modified later. The king demanded changes up front that would give the throne representation in the junta cabinet and a central role in the amendment process. As in 1947, the palace sought to lock in influence early to control the outcome. But after visits to the palace on December 6–7 by Phibun and other generals, Bhumibol gave in and signed the charter, unchanged. What transpired exactly isn't clear, but it appears Bhumibol was threatened with removal if he didn't cooperate. Summoning the example of King Prajadhipok in 1932, he declared the document provisional, to be amended.[3]

He then registered his indignation publicly by reneging on a commitment to

open the Constitution Fair in Dusit Park, and canceling the palace's annual Constitution Day garden party. On December 10, Bhumibol instead performed rites
emphasizing the story that Prajadhipok gave constitutionalism to the country.

Then Bhumibol began the routine that would govern his life for decades:
meeting dignitaries, presiding over official functions, and socializing. He gave an
audience to the deputy director of UNESCO. He and Sirikit attended a grand party
for Queen Rambhai's birthday. On December 26, he accepted the gown of a Thai
barrister at the Ministry of Justice. On the final day of the year, the king and queen
joined Bangkok's high society at the Royal Turf Club, where they presented the
Derby Cup. That evening he made his annual New Year broadcast, asking for
people to practice true morality in order to combat evil, and to think of the country
rather than themselves. The next day he followed religious rites in the palace with a
garden party for officials and families of the royal household.

Behind this confident mien, the palace was desperate. Prince Dhani told
diplomats that if the constitution didn't satisfy the palace, Bhumibol would return
to Switzerland, or even, he hinted, abdicate.[4] But Dhani's threats were ignored. On
January 3 the constitution committee, led by Phin, began forwarding draft amendments to the palace. There was almost nothing for the throne.

The monarchist community reacted by taking the fight public, through newspapers. The domestic and international media reported that the military was
tightly controlling the movements of the Mahidol family. It was untrue, but Phao
was forced into denying it. The Democrats declared a boycott of the elections
scheduled for March. The palace sought ways to embarrass the generals and claim
the moral high ground. When the generals tried to buy off the king by allocating 5
million baht for a new palace for Bhumibol and Sirikit at Tha Vasukri, the king
branded it an unnecessary luxury. According to newspaper reports, he told the
government it should budget only for essential things, adding that the new palace
would require evicting scores of families who had no place else to go. The king's
riposte, the royalist *Bangkok Post* said, was "a timely lesson in frugality."[5]

The generals didn't budge. Phin's committee submitted more unfriendly
amendment drafts and rejected palace changes. Taking a new tack, on January 17
Bhumibol proposed that there should be an entirely new constitution, since it
would be the first truly promulgated by himself. That was rebuffed as well. Instead, on January 24 the military-controlled assembly unanimously accepted the
revised 1932 charter in its first reading. A month later, the final document passed
unchallenged.

In decorous language the document sustained the inviolate character of the throne. It enshrined the holy foundations of Thailand, amended to four as Phibun had done in the 1930s: nation, religion, monarchy, and the constitution. It left the king full discretionary power over the royal household staff and a nine-man privy council. Beyond that, there was little difference from the charter that had led to Prajadhipok's abdication. The king's powers would be controlled by the recommendations and countersignatures of political leaders. The unicameral assembly had two categories of members, elected and appointed by the prime minister. A simple majority could override the king's veto.

Bhumibol acted unfazed by pursuing his normal duties. At the end of January he donated 10,000 baht to the army hospital. In early February he presided over graduation at a royal secondary school. Later that month he took his family to Hua Hin for vacation, returning with Sirikit to Bangkok momentarily to open the annual fair at the royal Wat Benjamabophit. That evening the couple attended a benefit ball for the Foundation for the Blind, which made the queen its patron. One of Bhumibol's new compositions was performed, and a photo portrait he made of Sirikit and their daughter was auctioned. That night the main news was that Queen Sirikit was again pregnant.

Risking everything like Prajadhipok in the 1930s, the princes now openly threatened the king's return to Lausanne and abdication. Phibun and the generals calmly retorted that they could name their own king, mentioning Prince Chumbhot. The showdown took place when the government asked for a date on which the king would promulgate the constitution. Bhumibol didn't answer, and, as he returned to Hua Hin, the cabinet scheduled the morning of March 8. When by March 7 it became clear that he wouldn't return, the ceremony was canceled. The state radio announced only that the king felt promulgation should not be rushed.

That afternoon Phao led a group of officers to Hua Hin to confront Bhumibol. Several hours later, they returned to Bangkok, ushering the king along with them. At 11 the next morning in the Ananta Samakhom throne hall, to the braying of conch-shell horns, Bhumibol promulgated virtually the same constitution his uncle Prajadhipok had signed thirty years earlier. Premier Phibun stood by to countersign.

It was an extraordinary event. Bhumibol had just made his first determined attempt at political intervention, the deployment of the powerful royal prestige he had been told so often was in his crown and his blood. He failed resoundingly. Precisely how the venomous Phao intimidated the king remains secret. The general belief is that, if he didn't threaten the king's life, he threatened to expose Bhumibol as Ananda's killer and to force him off the throne.

In the event, Bhumibol went through the paces regally, ever unsmiling, making a brief speech and quickly departing for Hua Hin. The shock of it all showed when he did not return again for the March 12 seasonal changing of the robes of the Emerald Buddha. The important ritual was done instead by another prince.

In the late-March general election, the military had limited success. Yet it hardly mattered, for the appointed assemblymen were all their men. The next official ceremony was the opening of parliament. When the palace again stalled, Phibun opened the body without the king and formed a new government. Finally conceding defeat, on March 25, Bhumibol formally accepted Phibun's nomination as prime minister.

It was a wise choice. There were many contemporary signs of the fate of monarchies that crossed their armed forces. On July 28, 1952, the profligate King Farouk of Egypt was overthrown by his army and exiled in Italy. His six-month-old son was named puppet king. The next year the army gave up pretenses and declared a republic. In Jordan in August 1952, the new king, Talal, was ousted and replaced with the 17-year-old Hussein. And the corrupt shah of Iran was forced temporarily into exile during a near-successful revolt to oust him. King Sihanouk of Cambodia also floundered in mid-1952. He dissolved the government and assumed the premiership himself, and a few years later he was forced to abdicate. And in Vietnam, the embattled French puppet emperor Bao Dai was near to giving way to a republic.

The Thai generals continued to gain strength courtesy of their Cold War alliance with the United States. Nascent insurgencies wreathed the country, in Burma, Malaysia, Cambodia, Vietnam, and Laos. In January 1952, the Viet Minh exploded large bombs in Saigon as part of their nationalist campaign against the French, and May Day 1952 brought bloody communist riots in Tokyo. As small leftist cliques appeared in Bangkok, Washington named Thailand the forward bulkhead against communism, the generals its agents. The CIA stepped up training of the police and army in combat and social control.

CIA support made Phao and his Border Patrol Police especially powerful. Phao spoke the American anticommunist language, and he was Phibun's likely successor. Phao took advantage of the situation to monopolize a number of key trading and finance businesses, including the export of opium from Burma, and skimmed huge sums from U.S. aid. The Thai police and army institutionalized their extraordinary power following passage of the repressive Un-Thai Activities Act (also called the anticommunist act) in November 1952. This legislation, which would justify much brutality and corruption for the next four decades, was muscled through the national assembly in an audacious three readings in one day. Praised by the Americans, it equated "un-Thai activities" with communism and sedition, and defined them as any activity that could be construed as undermining nation, religion, and king. Any political opponent could be branded a communist and jailed for ten years, if Phao didn't first have them murdered.

Regrouping, the palace shrank from the overt fight and reverted to reinforcing the traditional bases of royal prestige: the king as national patriarch, the sacral near-bodhisattva, the selfless source of welfare and the embodiment of national culture and tradition. Over time the tactic would work brilliantly: by not being seen to seek political power, the throne would prove itself an able rival to the generals.

Bhumibol was hardly capable of plotting the strategy himself. The real work was done by a very experienced team of princes and nobles through their extensive networks. The principals were Bhumibol's privy councilors, personal staff, and a handful of senior princes, all with links to the Seventh Reign, and several to King Chulalongkorn. Since Prince Rangsit had died, the privy council was chaired by Dhani, the canny traditionalist. Alongside him were palace veterans Sridharma-dibes, Manavarajsevi, Srivisarn Vacha, and Prince Alongkot. After the royal marriage, Sirikit's father, Prince Nakkhat, also joined the privy council, as well as Prince Vivatchai Chaiyant. Alongkot and Nakkhat died in 1952 and 1953, respectively, and were replaced by M.L. Dej Sanitwongs and Luang Suranarong.

This was a formidable team. Vivatchai was one of the country's leading diplomats and financial experts. A Cambridge graduate and a nephew of Rama V, during World War II he ran the Bank of Thailand, the central bank. At the war's end he led the tough treaty negotiations with the British. He had intimate knowledge of postwar politics and an impressive set of global contacts, leading Thailand to join the World Bank and taking a position as adviser to the UN secretary general.

Dej too was a diplomat and a finance specialist. Related to Sirikit's mother, M.L. Bua Sanitwongs, he counted as a representative of the queen's side of the palace. But he was also close to Bhumibol, sometimes joining the king's band. Luang Suranarong, a royal aide-de-camp since the 1930s, was a trusted Mahidol family retainer and a link to the military.

Other important royal team members were M.C. Nikornthewan Devakul, secretary of the privy council and later also the king's personal private secretary; Thawiwong Thawalyasak, master of palace finances and by the 1960s the controller of all palace operations; and Prince Bhanuband, an influential businessman and publisher of a popular royalist newspaper. Outside the palace, the royalist network included foreign minister Prince Wan Waithayakorn, the palace's éminence grise in the bureaucracy; Prince Chakraphan in the Ministry of Agriculture; Prince Ajava-dis Diskul, heading Bangkok Electric Works; M.R. Suksom Kasemsant as manag-ing director of Thai Airways, the national carrier; and many other royals in high bureaucratic jobs.

The Chakri network was equally strong in the business community. Thawi-wong and his agents held influential board and shareholder positions in several banks. Wan, Dhani, and Srivisarn were all at times governors of the Bangkok Rotary Club, the leading society for Thai and foreign businessmen. They also controlled the Siam Society, which through its sponsorship of cultural and histori-cal research and popular events promoted the royalist line. Palace officials main-tained positions in several conservative religious societies. Thawiwong headed the Old England Students Association, a significant networking point for the Thai aristocracy and foreign capital.

Such networks helped to protect Bhumibol. But further promoting him wasn't easy. After the constitutional defeat, the princes tried to send the king on a national tour, to let the people witness the dhammaraja. Phibun rejected the idea on grounds it would be dangerous, and instead cut the palace's official budget while embarking on his own rural tour. So the palace went back to the basics, ritual and social activity. The hectic first six months in Bangkok showed how this alone could have a substantial impact.

Even before the constitution debacle, Bhumibol undertook numerous rituals that asserted his position at the top of the kingdom's hierarchy. The king's role as a source of justice was established in ritual court appearances. In one of two cases he judged, a man who had stolen a small rice-flour mill pleaded guilty and received a jail sentence of three months. The percipient and merciful king proposed a sus-pended sentence, noting that the man was genuinely contrite. In the second, several naval officers had sued a member of royalty for damages in a car accident. Under the king's guidance, the royal conceded fault, while the navy men showed they were not simply greedy by donating the proceeds to the naval hospital.[6]

Through ritual the king sustained his identity as head of state. When Bhumi-bol received the new Phibun cabinet, its members had to acknowledge his superi-ority by prostrating themselves. The same happened in the many familiarization audiences he held with government officials and bodies. At the end of March he attended the Royal Thai Air Force annual day, where he was honored in front of thousands with a fly-by. The next day he visited the Interior Ministry. During the ceremony, the power failed, and subsequently several top officials submitted their resignations for embarrassing the king. He generously refused them.

In April and May the palace openly celebrated Chakri Day, the royal wedding anniversary, and coronation day. For the latter Bhumibol presided over the induction of privy councilors and conferred royal decorations and titles upon several princes and princesses, identifying those who were most important to the throne. Two days afterward he undertook the royal ceremony for crop fertility, phuet-mongkol, inside the palace. The grains of rice he consecrated were then used in the public plowing spectacle.

Such work and promotion increased when the royal family moved back from Hua Hin to Bangkok in mid-June. On the way the king visited the country's oldest Buddhist shrine, the Phra Pathom Chedi, giving Thais in the countryside a rare opportunity to witness the young and handsome dhammaraja with his beautiful wife as they devoutly lit incense and prayed. When they arrived in Bangkok hours later, thousands saw the king, queen, and Princess Ubolrat received with great respect by Phibun and his cabinet. Bhumibol then launched into a steady schedule of meetings with government officials, diplomats, and rural civil servants attending seminars in Bangkok. He again undertook the tedious job of handing out each diploma at university graduations. On June 24, National Day and the 20th anniversary of the coup that ended the absolute monarchy, the king opened the new session of parliament, asserting his leadership whatever the meaning of the date.

As the year passed Bhumibol held regular meetings with ministers and senior civil servants to be informed of their work. He received a steady flow of foreign diplomats, military officials, and capitalists, including U.S. vice president Richard Nixon, German industrialist Alfred Krupp, Belgian and British royals, and frequently the embattled King Sihanouk. It might have been expected that Sihanouk and Bhumibol, both French-speakers of similar age and predicament, would become soul mates. Ultimately Bhumibol found the Cambodian prince a nuisance, in part because in 1954 Sihanouk apparently borrowed a gold-plated saxophone of the king's and didn't return it.[7]

His work exposed Bhumibol to the complex issues and interests of domestic and global politics. It gave him the opportunity to practice expressing his views in a delicate royal way. To selected guests, he began to make calculated, discreet aspersions of the government, referring condescendingly to Phibun and the generals as "ces gens là."

The palace kept Bhumibol on a steady schedule of religious rituals. At the beginning of 1952 he began regular meetings with the supreme patriarch Prince Vachirayanawong and other senior monks, displaying his personal relationship with the most sacral men of the sangha. It connected Bhumibol to Wat Bovornives, the Chakri family temple, where Vachirayanawong was abbot, reinforcing the idea that the young king already had a high level of sacrality. In June he anointed candles for issue to temples around the kingdom for phansa, and on July 7 he inaugurated phansa at three royal temples. At the end of October he closed the period with the kathin, offering robes to monks, in one of the country's most important popular holy rituals.

The other activity that the princes made sure Bhumibol undertook was charity. From their first weeks in Thailand, the king and queen, and later Princess Galyani and the princess mother, made regular donations for scholarships, temples, and poor hospitals and schools. Typical donations in 1953, out of many, were 36,000 baht ($1,800) for a group of schools in northern Thailand, and two large refrigerators to a Bangkok hospital in honor of the late Prince Nakkhat. When communities were hit by disasters like fire or flood, the Mahidols contributed for relief and rebuilding.

The most substantial donations went to health care, to establish the royal family as the source of well-being in the kingdom. In late 1952, they gave three iron lungs and 1.5 million baht to Siriraj Hospital, where Sangwal had once trained. The money was to start a new nursing school under royal patronage. Health care was smart turf to claim in the campaign for prestige, for it was apolitical and touched everyone. However much the faceless government spent itself, the Mahidols were seen as personally doing more. Most of their donations were in the name of Prince Mahidol, who was declared the father of modern Thai medicine.

This was the pattern of work that would govern the rest of Bhumibol's life. At the beginning there were up to 150 such official duties every year, each making a particular visual statement about the king's prestige and sovereignty. Phibun and the generals couldn't hijack the ceremonies; contrarily, they had to show their own fealty at many.

Bhumibol and Sirikit would have become popular without trying. The king was intelligent and good-looking, with a worldly panache. Sirikit was a perfect fit: precocious and vivacious, with natural social skills, her smile, poise, and fashion sense made her an instant model for Thai women. Together they brought the romance of monarchy to a new generation of Thais who had never really lived under a king and queen, mostly didn't know what happened in 1932, and disdained the corrupt generals and politicians. To them the king was fresh and attractive, and provided a real sense of Thai culture. Feeling akin to the Europeans with their glamorous, fashionable royal families, urban middle-class Thais sought to see the royals in person and to attend royal ceremonies. They again stood to attention when the royal anthem was played in movie theaters.

Behind this was canny promotion from the palace. Newspapers and magazines were fed official photographs of the Mahidols at formal balls and informal garden parties, passing popular Thai holidays with their children, celebrating their birthdays. They published the king's own candid snapshots of his family at work and play, while his home movies appeared in theater newsreels. In late 1952, a 90-minute feature using Bhumibol's own footage, depicting a contemporary middle-class family like those in American television shows, was shown around the country. It provided a distraction from wearisome politics. In 1954, Kukrit Pramoj launched a newspaper called *Siam Rath*, which was targeted toward better-educated Thais. Woven throughout its reportage, essays, and literature was an intellectual argument for the monarchy and consistent criticism of the king's rivals, Phibun in particular.[8]

Music occupied much of Bhumibol's free time in the early 1950s, and his musical interests earned special promotion. He composed tunes for concerts and charity benefits, and the simple melodies were given heavy airplay, even on local U.S. government broadcasts, as part of its Cold War propaganda. Knowing the king was a radio buff, in 1952 the government presented him with a powerful transmitter. He launched his own station, Radio Aw Saw (the initials for Amphorn Palace), broadcasting programs on palace culture and history and popular music. As his own announcer and disc jockey, Bhumibol did a weekly show of his favorite music.

Not long after, he formed the Aw Saw Band to perform on Friday night broadcasts. They played popular Thai and Western tunes, along with the king's own pieces. The band became Bhumibol's most enduring pastime and his bandmates became his closest chums, the earliest members being mostly royals and palace officials. The band gave occasional public performances, which allowed the king to be seen by his subjects in nonceremonial venues. It was hugely popular, even if to many Thais the Western music was odd. On stage Bhumibol was treated with great deference; he was still king.

All these facets of a young, handsome, talented, and dedicated leader came together on July 28, 1952, when Sirikit gave birth to a *chaofa chai*, a boy lord of the skies, named Vajiralongkorn. It was a dynastic landmark, the first birth of a celestial prince since King Chulalongkorn's reign. Military bands outside the palace struck up the royal anthem, cannons thundered salutes, and thousands who waited throughout the day cheered. Over the next weeks the newspapers and magazines ran pictures of the Chakri heir, all shot by the doting father himself.

As long as the palace appeared to stay away from politics, the junta was supportive. It made both the king's and the queen's birthdays national holidays and invited the king to preside over military ceremonies, including officers' academy graduations and senior officer promotions. In late 1952 the government conceded the throne direct control of the palace guards. And in an important act that bound the military rank-and-file with the throne, Bhumibol was invited on several occasions to present colors to military and police units.

In fact, the generals didn't want to appear opposed to a popular monarch who was integral to the war against communists, and promoted by the United States as such. The CIA and the U.S. Information Service put out handbills and booklets in Thai declaring how communism opposed nation, religion, and king. They exaggerated the threat by manufacturing fake communist tracts in Thai that attacked the monarchy. Over time the United States expanded the effort into pictures, books, and movies. In 1956 USIS had eight mobile teams putting on film and music shows contrasting the beloved king and queen with the evil specter of communism. While communism did not become much less abstract, the monarchy became more real.

The palace reciprocated by offering controlled friendship to Phao, Phin, and Sarit. None of them were particularly savory, but the palace wanted to exploit their rivalry and protect itself should any one take power. The generals were invited to join in palace ceremonies and sometimes to dine with the royal family. In 1953 they were given royal decorations, allowing them the appearance of royal favor. Some links were carved through business. Thawiwong put palace money into a few joint investments with the generals, who held monopoly control over many industries, legal and illegal.

The palace made a special effort to befriend Phao. In 1953 the king presided at major police ceremonies, granting Phao and other police generals special ranks and decorations and conferring the promotions of senior officers. Bhumibol also presided over the investiture of Phao's personal brigade of *aswin,* or knights, actually the thugs who ran Phao's drugs and protection rackets. The key to this relationship became the BPP. As the CIA client for anticommunist operations, the BPP was better trained and armed than the regular army. Its training center was next to the king's Hua Hin palace. As he used the BPP airfield, and they served as his local escort, a special relationship blossomed. The king frequently visited the camp, joining the BPP soldiers in sports and shooting. When in 1954 the BPP began building a rural Volunteer Defense Corps of 120,000 men across the country, the king became their patron, presenting flags to corps units.

This special relationship was encouraged by both Phao and the CIA. Eventually, noted a study, the BPP "came to view themselves as holding special responsibility for protection of the Thai nation and the king."[9] This suited the palace because the relationship transcended Phao, and could function in Phao's absence, or if he ever challenged the throne. Phao evidently relished the king's attention, telling diplomats that the palace favored him while disliking Phibun.[10] In 1955 he did the throne perhaps the most important favor ever: he wrapped up the Ananda death case. It wasn't pleasant, but it was final.

The case had festered in the courts, always overhanging politics and the palace. Despite the almost nonexistent evidence, repeated investigations and trials remained focused on Pridi and Vacharachai, both still in exile, and the three men arrested in 1947, former royal secretary Chaleo and royal pages Chit and Butr. Lower courts would not convict the three. It fell to Phao to keep pushing, until in October 1954 the Supreme Court found Chit, Butr, and Chaleo guilty and sentenced them to death. Only the king had the power to block their execution, but for four months the palace remained silent. While Phibun was out of the country, on February 17, 1955, Phao quietly had the three executed by firing squad.

Four decades later, King Bhumibol would suggest that the execution had caught him by surprise while he was still considering commuting the sentences.[11] But his four months of silence doesn't support this claim. Another sign that it was expected was Princess Mother Sangwal's beginning a private course in soul-clearing *vipassana* meditation two days before the execution. For one month she confined herself to Srapathum Palace, emerging only to meet her meditation teacher Phra Thepsiddhimuni at Wat Mahathat. Sangwal's sudden desire to meditate was later explained as a result of her suffering from insomnia, but the timing suggests that she sought to clear her conscience.

Phao's dirty work ended the case. Had Bhumibol intervened, people might always have asked, if they didn't do it, then who did kill Ananda? Now Bhumibol would have to answer the question only to himself.

In spite of their cordiality with the generals, the palace princes had no appetite for cooperation with Phibun; he was the archenemy now that Pridi was gone. In the 1950s, Phibun remained a popular figure, handsome and charismatic. His efforts at nation building had touched many, and he was skillful in distributing largesse. To survive above the generals' internecine rivalry, he needed the people to look to him as leader. But he kept colliding with King Bhumibol. Phibun was perhaps the only one to recognize the potency of traditional royal symbolism, having appropriated it for himself in the late 1930s. Now he had to vie with the palace on its own turf, and the princes wouldn't share the limelight. In 1952, for instance, they again rejected Phibun's request to join the privy council.

It turned into a competition of merit accumulation, where desire for popularity had to be masked in a show of non-desire. With Bhumibol confined to the capital, Phibun promoted himself as the country's beneficent patriarch. He traveled the country, at each stop donating money to temples and health centers and handing out Buddha statues. Concurrently serving as the minister of culture, he promoted the idea that Sukhothai had no real royal king, but instead simply a father and his children. This effectively dismissed the blood basis of kingship, qualifying Phibun for the position.

The competition spilled over into economic development policy. Reviving a key fight of the 1930s, Phibun moved to dismantle the huge landholdings of the old aristocracy, including possibly the royal family. By most accounts it was necessary. Under King Chulalongkorn, the royals and the aristocracy expanded their holdings of farmland, especially fertile central plains land served by state-built irrigation. Many branches of the royal family—the Sanitwongs family especially—depended heavily on renting out rice and orchard land to peasants. The princes' refusal to tax this income was a spark of the 1932 revolution.

Two decades later, still less than half of farm families owned their land. With 80 percent of the population dependent on farms, Phibun proposed legislation in 1952 to limit the maximum land any person could hold at 50 rai (20 acres) for farmland, and 10 rai for industrial property. Large landholders were to be given seven years to dispose of their surplus. Longtime squatters would also be helped to obtain title to their land. The proposal provoked a two-year battle with the biggest landowners, including the throne. The palace insisted that redistribution was unnecessary because of the plentiful land around the country. But such land was mostly state-owned forest and not legally available to farmers. The palace also argued that the law would leave small landholders vulnerable to abuse by powerful people.

Finally, in 1954, the law passed parliament. When it was sent to Bhumibol he declined to sign it, avoiding a test of his weak veto power. When parliament submitted the bill to him a second time, again he took no action. For a third time, in December 1954 the parliament sent the legislation to the throne. The king's prestige was directly on the line: if he refused again to sign, parliament could vote again and make it law anyway. So Bhumibol finally signed. The seven years they would have to comply, the princes knew, was a long time in Thai politics.[12]

The palace fought back. The princes asked foreign governments to support the king's proposed rural tours, as part of the campaign against communism. Bhumibol himself lobbied the British ambassador, who afterward recommended that London pressure the government to allow the king to travel, to "exploit the fundamental loyalty of the people towards the monarchy" as "a most potent antidote to communist subversion."[13]

Nothing came of it. But the palace found other openings. In 1953 the Viet Minh, fighting the French, moved deep into Laos, and Thai troops went on alert along the Lao frontier. Not allowed to visit the soldiers, Bhumibol instead made an unscheduled national radio broadcast in which he told the people on the frontiers not to worry, and that he would visit them soon. It was meant as a reminder that he was their supreme leader.

In spite of his best efforts, Phibun was losing this contest. He took the blame for the junta's intense infighting and corruption. Lacking support in the military and the palace, he sought to remake himself as a proponent of constitutionalism and democracy, in the process rendering the king extraneous to politics. In early 1955, Phibun spent two months traveling to 17 nations of the anticommunist bloc. He met the pope in Rome, lauded General Franco in Spain, and lunched with Queen Elizabeth. The highlight was three weeks in the United States, where Washington briefed him on the American democratic system and the dynamics of the Cold War.

After returning home, Phibun launched weekly press conferences and encouraged criticism of the government. He revoked the ban on political parties and announced elections would come soon, while declaring that military coups constituted an attack on the system of monarchy. Extending an olive branch to the throne, he gave in to the king's countryside tour.

Phibun would regret it. Two one-day test trips in late September 1955 to central plains provinces revealed a peasantry hugely excited about seeing their king. Finally, on November 11, Bhumibol's first grand excursion into his realm began, a 20-day tour of the northeast, known as Isan. Thailand's largest region by area and population, Isan was also its most impoverished, due to extremely poor soil and weather conditions. Illiteracy and malnourishment were widespread, and as a language Thai ranked third after Lao and Khmer. Central Thais regarded the region as a rebellious and uncultured colony.

The tour was a modernized version of the ancient kings' grand processions. A huge entourage of army and police generals and government officials accompanied the king. Alternating car and rail transport, each day the procession moved to a new provincial seat, holding ceremonies in government offices and military camps, and making occasional side trips to ancient monuments and important temples. Film records show people lining the roads as the king's train or motorcade passed their scrubby rice fields, or crowding thickly into city centers and temple court-yards to prostrate themselves to the sacral Buddhist sovereign. Massive crowds saw off his train in Bangkok and at each station along the way.

Most of the trip, however, was given to rituals of state. At each stop the king was feted by local civil servants. He sat at length while offerings were made and the governor delivered a tedious statistical report on the state of the province. These meetings were held openly, and the people could see in the seating arrangements and behavior of officials that the king commanded all, even the most holy monks and fearsome generals. After the presentation the king would receive gifts and walk among the people, slowing for their prostrations, touching their holy icons, and handing out coins. Sometimes he would sheepishly pat the tops of their heads, the holy blessing of a Buddha-to-be. It was enough to convince all that here was a good and omnipotent power above the oppressive and corrupt police, bureaucrats, and merchants.

Petty issues that erupted during the trip served the king's virtue. In one minor fracas, the department of highways was attacked for the poorly maintained and dust-covered Isan roads. Critics said the department should have watered down the road in advance, and that it had left nails on the road that caused several tire punctures in the royal motorcade. The department responded that the king himself had commented that the roads were better than those in Bangkok, and second, he had told the department specifically not to water down the dust because the water should be reserved for needy farmers. The nails came from careless workers who had built the arches of welcome for the king.[14]

The trip's huge success startled Phibun, and he disallowed similar tours planned for the south and north. But meanwhile the two sides launched into a grinding battle over whose religious sacrality was greater. In this, the king had the upper hand.

Phibun well understood the religious power of the dhammaraja image. In the late 1930s, he seized control of the national Buddhist administration, installing allied Mahanikay monks in positions of authority. After Phibun was ousted in 1944, the palace moved quickly to restore royalist control by placing Thammayut monks in the two top ecclesiastical positions, the sangharaja and the sanghanayok. The palace's uncompromising stance showed when the sanghanayok position became vacant again in 1951. Rather than rotating to a Mahanikay monk, the job went to another Thammayut leader, Juan Uttayi.

Three years later, Juan's expiring term was renewed, uncompromisingly maintaining the royalist monopoly. This was in part the work of M.L. Pin Malakul, the Education Ministry official who oversaw the religious affairs department. Since he served as a page to Rama VI, Pin had been a consistent supporter of the monarchy's interest in the bureaucracy, and he had close relatives working in the palace. The move plunged the sangha into open turmoil. With Phibun's apparent support, incensed Mahanikay monks openly accused the palace of destroying democracy. Under intense pressure, Juan's renewal was rescinded and a Mahanikay monk, Plot Kittisophana, was made sangha premier. For Phibun, however, it was not much of a victory.

Aside from controlling the sangha, the princes understood that projecting the king's superior virtue was the key to spiritual hegemony. The foundation for this was ultimately ritual acts. By its nature the throne essentially owned the highest rituals, which depicted Bhumibol as a figure of matchless virtue. These ceremonies could also be tuned to have a political impact. In 1952, for instance, the throne resumed full observance of the royal kathin ceremony at royal (and so the most prestigious) temples—something Phibun couldn't do because he wasn't royal. Bhumibol, his family, and the princes presented new kathin robes to monks at the first-class royal temples, and did so yearly ever after. But they conspicuously omitted two such temples: Wat Mahathat, the center of the Mahanikay, and the Phibun-built Wat Phra Sri Mahathat.

Fighting back, Phibun offered himself as Buddhism's promoter by launching a national program of temple refurbishment, using state funds. Temple renewals went from a few hundred a year in 1950 to more than a thousand, peaking at 1,239 in 1956.[15] Attached to the work was the name of Phibun, not the king, who remained hampered by limited financial resources and controls over his travel.

Another tack was Phibun's efforts to rebuild relations with Burma, the country's ancient rival and likewise a mainly Theravada Buddhist culture. The starting point was to be religious exchanges, managed directly by Phibun and Burmese leader U Nu. The palace took umbrage because it felt the king should lead in making peace with the country that had destroyed Ayutthaya.

In December 1955, Burma invited Phibun and the king to attend its commemoration of the 2,500th anniversary of Buddhism, planned for 1956. (Due to different calendar interpretations, this was a year earlier than the Thais planned to mark the occasion.) Phibun accepted, but the king declined the invitation. Prince Dhani, probably the one behind the king's decision, gave the excuse that King Bhumibol could not accept the Burmese requirement that he remove his shoes to enter a Burmese temple. Phibun went alone then, and months later U Nu returned the gesture by visiting Thailand, during which he planted a tree at Wat Phra Sri Mahathat and donated a large sum of money to repair temples in Ayutthaya. All this helped Phibun's image.

With unlimited government funds and state diplomacy in his hands, Phibun was making a discomfiting challenge to the king's proprietary turf. Bhumibol was dhammaraja, but to truly win the battle of virtue, he had to demonstrate his superior munificence by spreading around more money. The anthropologist Christine Gray laid out the problem in terms of traditional cosmology: "Bhumibol's pure blood and magical touch gave him a clear lead in the race for virtue. Objects given 'by the hands of the king' were still considered to be sacred, . . . [and] all the king needed was the cash to buy them. . . . King Bhumibol may have been born with barami but he could not become a fully realized dhammaraja if he was poor."[16]

It was the palace money master Thawiwong's job to surmount this problem. In the early 1950s his rebuilding of royal finances had funded an appreciable level of royal donations to needy causes. In addition, the royal family began to extract funds from the Thai elite at royal balls and charity events. To bolster this the palace awarded royal honors and decorations to those who contributed larger sums. In the early 1950s, 26 of the country's most prominent Chinese businessmen received not only medals from the king in return for their donations but also legitimization as loyal Thais, along with useful business connections.[17]

As funds were turned around and redonated to worthy causes in the king's name, the palace became a charity collection center for natural disasters and calamities. During the early 1950s polio epidemic, the king launched a relief fund in his name and quickly raised 540,000 baht.

But such efforts were still not enough. The king needed to be able to donate unimaginably large sums, sustainably, so that his generosity would reign unmatched. The princes evolved a brilliant mechanism to increase the resources available to the king without requiring him to be rich. This was a circle of ever multiplying merit, through which all Thais were encouraged to contribute to the king to participate in his virtue. This arguably emerged as the single most important factor in the Bhumibol restoration, as it rendered him the undisputed master of social welfare and the absolute paragon of selfless sacrifice.

Merit can be made and counted in numerous ways. The elegant scene of Thai villagers presenting alms, food, and other necessities to queues of orange-robed monks in the dim predawn light is the most visible manifestation of the practice. Popular Thai belief holds that the merit received is relative to both the size of the donation or sacrifice and also to the virtue of the recipient of the largesse. The wealthy layman who builds a new worship hall or donates a Buddha sculpture to the temple gains far more merit than the poor farmer who offers only rice. (Few would question how the donor had come by his wealth, presuming only that it arises from his karma.) Likewise, offerings to monks rather than, say, to an impoverished layman, have special weight because of the monks' closeness to the dhamma. As recipients, the monks add to their store of merit, because they have humbled themselves to create the opportunity for others to sacrifice. The ritual becomes a mutual exchange, enhancing the stored virtue of both giver and recipient.

So it was with Bhumibol in the mid-1950s. As he gave more and more to charity, forfeiting substantial assets for his subjects, they increasingly understood that he was, like a real dhammaraja, full of wealth and full of merit. People believed that donating to the king, and participating in his charity, would accrue superior merit to themselves. They would share some of the sacrality of the kingdom's most sacral person. At a higher level, a multiplier effect kicked in. The king turned around and donated all of the receipts in his own name, more money than anyone else could, so he appeared ever more virtuous. There was a magical snowball effect, drawing in ever more donors. Eventually even the peasantry sought to participate in his karma with small donations.

Unlike the Catholic Church's selling of indulgences, the princes behind Bhumibol didn't coarsely attach dhammic redemption to the exchange of cash. But they knowingly encouraged the idea, and quickly the magic circle of merit took root. By the second half of the 1950s, the royal family was able to donate several million baht a year to public needs. The king appeared to have the financial power of a truly world-commanding and selfless sovereign, even as other greedy men really controlled the economy.

What finally sealed the king's projection of unmatched virtue was his ritual ordination as a novice monk in October 1956. Short-term ordination is a rite of passage for young Thai men, traditionally undertaken during phansa, coinciding with the

July–October rainy season. For modern Thais this had evolved to a two-week stint. Ordaining was extremely important for the king as a would-be dhammaraja, to both his kingdom and his mother.[18]

A traditional novitiate combines solemn study and introspection, work for the temple, and early morning processions to receive alms. Widely published newspaper photographs show Bhumibol at the time as a shaved-bald, saffron-swathed novice proffering his bowl to people receiving the opportunity to make the merit of a lifetime, with the king himself. In his dark sunglasses and monk's robes, the sinewy Bhumibol resembled a Buddhist beat poet from California. In fact only a small part of Bhumibol's temple stay involved meditation, study, and accepting public alms. The two weeks were consumed by rites, ceremonies, and audiences heavily attended by the royal, political, and ecclesiastical elite. Like the Isan trip, each one was designed to accent the king's virtue and sovereignty.[19]

The ordination period was planned in minute detail by a committee under Prince Dhani. The biggest job of preparation was to renovate Wat Bovornives, where the king would reside. The cost was underwritten as meritorious donations by the privy purse, the Ministry of Culture, and Princess Mother Sangwal. The formal launch was the king's grand audience with top officials of the government and palace on October 18. He announced his "journey," after which the officials all followed him in a symbolic circumambulation of his "kingdom," represented by carrying candles around the palace chapel housing the country's patron Phra Siam Dhevathirat.

On the morning of October 22, Bhumibol swore in Sirikit as regent, giving her status a significant boost beyond simply being the mother of the king's children. The king was then formally shaved, not by the Brahman priests who normally cut the royal hair, but by Sangwal. The act asserted her own lofty royal rank. The ordination took place at the astrologically auspicious time of 4:23 p.m. at Wat Sriratanasudaram, the chapel of the Emerald Buddha. Bhumibol prayed in the middle of 30 abbots and monks of the top royal temples, after which he received saffron robes and the Pali novice name Bhumibala Bhikku.[20] The queen and Sangwal then offered him various implements for his novitiate.

He moved to Wat Bovornives in a procession led by Kukrit Pramoj. For the next two weeks the temple was constantly full of Thais, mostly organized groups of women who waited to witness the monk-king stepping outside his meditation room, the same one used by the Fifth Reign's supreme patriarch, Prince Vachirayan. The first few days were dominated by prayer and study. After eating (no predawn alms collecting was practiced), the king attended lectures, and in the evening he washed his own robes, about which much was made in the press. Each day he was accompanied by Phra Yanasangworn, a 43-year-old senior Bovornives monk.[21] It was the beginning of what would be a lifelong sharing of virtue and fate. Yanasangworn would become the king's personal spiritual adviser, promoting the monarchy as he himself rose in the sangha to finally become supreme patriarch in 1989.

After the first two days, the king's schedule was overtaken by ritual visits to other royal temples, where he paid respects to the prominent abbots, and by ceremonial opportunities for others, principally the Thai elite, to make merit with him. From the very first day they queued for the opportunity to offer alms to the king, led by Queen Sirikit and prominent princesses. Bhumibol traveled to several royal palaces for the same purpose, including his own. In a famous photograph, five-year-old Prince Vajiralongkorn crouches in front of his father to make an offering, proving the purest blood and spiritual link between the two leading heirs to the Chakri tradition.

In the second week, Bhumibol joined the induction of other novices and made a trip to the royal temple at Nakhon Pathom for more ritual. In another ceremony, Queen Sirikit carried out the royal kathin at Wat Bovornives by presenting robes to Bhumibol. In between the king made two or three short, semi-orchestrated trips out into the streets to receive alms, uncommonly performed in the hot midday sun. This produced the photographs that would be used to represent the entire two weeks.

The ordination period ended with a rush of opportunities for high officials to make merit with the king. The Burmese ambassador offered alms from his prime minister; the Indian community in Thailand sent its gifts. Finally Phibun and his wife prostrated themselves in front of the monk-king to make an offering. On the final day, Bhumibol planted commemorative trees in the temple compound, and then he formally exited the monkhood. There was another audience with the government and royal elite, to recover his crown from Sirikit and report on his "journey." He was greeted with hugs from his proud mother and sister, posing with them for one of the few photos ever that shows him smiling and laughing. He had hardly been away from the normal royal rigmarole, but he was treated like it had been two weeks of sheer isolation and denial.

In spite of his surging personal popularity, in the mid-1950s Bhumibol politically remained in the shadows. "When I'd open my mouth and suggest something, they'd say: 'Your Majesty, you don't know anything.' So I shut my mouth," he recalled much later.[22] Instead, he went about his routine of meetings and cere-monies and passed time with his hobbies and his family, which had grown with the addition of a second daughter, Sirindhorn, born in April 1955. Even so, by early 1956 Bhumibol was already winning the battle of virtue against Phibun. Youth and forced exclusion from the corrupt world of politics proved an advantage. As the people began to see Bhumibol as embodying their own ideals, the princes sought to test his political muscle.

In the first move, in his annual radio speech for Army Day on January 25, 1956, Bhumibol told soldiers to not shirk their appointed duties to play politics and abuse their power. Soldiers were for the whole country and did not belong to any one group of people, he warned. As modest as this may have seemed, it was understood as a challenge to the junta. Defending the government, senior member of parliament and jurist Yut Saenguthai suggested on the radio that the king had exceeded his appropriate role under the democratic constitution. The king should comment on economic, political, or social concerns only indirectly, through a government minister, Yut said.

Technically, Yut wasn't wrong. But royalists reacted with forced outrage. The palace-linked newspaper *Sayam Nikorn* attacked Yut by citing not the Thai consti-tution but Bagehot's prescription of the English sovereign's prerogatives "as giver of happiness to the people": "conferring with anyone, giving advice to anyone, and warning anyone if he sees that somebody is doing wrong, especially a bad government. . . . Thus it is not necessary for the king to speak through anyone."[23]

Kukrit wrote in *Siam Rath* that he couldn't even repeat what Yut had said because it risked offending the king, adding that, as head of the armed forces, the king needn't consult anyone before speaking.[24] Shifting the line of attack to the government itself, Kukrit asked, "Where is the democracy that permits a prime minister to be an active military man? Where is the democracy when regular civil servants dare to criticize the king using the government radio as their tool?" A few days later, a royalist member of parliament filed a formal charge of lèse-majesté against Yut. At the time, conviction under the rarely enforced law could mean up to seven years in prison and a fine of 5,000 baht. (Not long before, peasants who had merely obstructed a vehicle delivering a petition to the king had been jailed for 43 days.) But police chief Phao personally ruled that Yut was innocent.

For the king, moving into the realm of an active player of politics wasn't free of danger, as Yut's criticism suggested. Bhumibol risked getting caught up in differ-ences between the government and the people. But the princes pushing him no longer worried about this. They saw the opportunity to hurt Phibun and the generals. Phibun must have understood this, for he avoided talking about the case. Instead he continued to advertise his new democratic spirit in advance of elections in early 1957. He seemed to believe that the palace wouldn't interfere with popularly elected officials.

But actually, the royals' thinking in this regard had gone through a significant transformation. They had now concluded that Western-style popular democracy was unimportant for Thailand. In 1954, privy councilor Srivisarn Vacha had divulged this view in a speech on kingship in Siam to the American Association of Bangkok. Srivisarn began by saying that a modern state comprises a unified community of people with a common purpose, a fixed territory, and full sovereignty. Focusing on the first, he noted that to express itself, the community chooses and empowers people to represent them in the legislature. However, he said, "these representatives of the people are elected individually by certain groups of people and they do not, in fact, represent the whole people."

Nor, he added, could one suppose that the executive or judicial functions of government represented the general population's aspirations and needs. "None of them can be said to incorporate all the functions of the state and so none of them can properly be regarded as representing the state as a whole." Thus, he concluded, even an elective democracy still needed a unifying institution, "so that law and order can be proclaimed within the territories and contact and intercourse with foreign countries can be made abroad. In a republic you have the president, in a monarchy the king. . . . The forms of government may be different, but both the president and king fulfill the same functions and are regarded, at least in the eye of the law, as being in the highest degree the best type of the very people they represent." The difference between presidential and royal systems was minor, Srivisarn said, because, "up to this day," Thai kings have always been "elected by the people." Because of its history a king was simply more appropriate to Thailand.[25]

This was Prince Dhani's earlier argument. But Dhani had never dismissed democratically elected lawmakers as representing only narrow minority interests. Srivisarn had moved a step further, equating the hereditary king with an elected president, and implying that the prime minister was no more than a parochial member of parliament.

Srivisarn had to justify the Chakri hold on the "elected" kingship, and for that he reverted to ideas of bloodline and tradition. There may have been bad kings in the past, he said, "but of the present Chakri dynasty . . . it can truly be said that their reigns have been beneficial to the people." He cited King Mongkut as a democratic modernizer who allowed his ministers to decide succession, a scientist in his people's service who nevertheless spoke Bodhisattva-like words of wisdom on his deathbed: "a savant, a philosopher, a man with common sense, a patriot who is both fair-minded and just." Chulalongkorn was a forward-looking administrator who reorganized government and fostered public education.

Srivisarn then laid down the new royalist thinking about government. "Since June 1932 we have adopted the form of constitutional monarchy and the rights and duties of the king are governed by the constitution. But the tradition of kingship still lives. Our kings still abide by the ten kingly virtues and the four principles of justice, for they are, in fact, the guiding principles of good government. . . . The criterion of a good government is the result of its administration and not in the form in which it functions." In case that wasn't clear, he repeated a verse of Alexander Pope, the English poet: "For forms of government let fools contest / Whatever's best administered is best." Srivisarn's argument reflected the princes' deep belief that, constitutionalism aside, only the blue-blooded Chakris could ever truly serve the needs of the Thais. To them, this was real democracy.

In 1957 the palace efforts to promote Bhumibol bore fruit. The year began with political change in the air, in the form of the general election on February 26. The campaign released a barrage of attacks on the government, and Phibun and Phao specifically, from the monarchist community, progressive liberals, and one of the generals themselves, Sarit Thanarat. Sarit, it was widely rumored, now had palace backing.[26] The palace itself tested the waters when Bhumibol suggested in his New Year's Day speech that the government eliminate appointed members of the national assembly. These constituted Phibun's political base.[27]

Phibun still reaped a huge victory in the polls. But Sarit declared to students that it was the most corrupt election he had ever seen, unleashing large protests against Phibun. Sarit was suddenly popular with both the people and the palace.

Things worsened for the government. Severe drought struck the northeast, and the government did little for the refugees who flooded the capital. Phibun's denouement came, though, out of a particular skirmish involving Thailand's own celebration of Buddhism's 2,500th anniversary. When the occasion arrived, the palace aggressively undertook to undermine the prime minister.

Phibun and Phao took the lead in planning the event. Phibun accelerated his temple restoration program, and he revived his plans from 1944 to build a Buddhist city, Phuttamonthon, relocated now 50 kilometers west of Bangkok. The activities were to include an opulent procession of the royal barges, and the king's inauguration of the Phuttamonthon project. The apex would be the visit of Burma's premier, U Nu, to Ayutthaya to join in casting 2,500 Buddha images and oversee the ordination of 2,500 novice monks. The palace wasn't left out, but the plans gave only passing recognition of the king as a religious leader.[28] The event was made out as a "state" ceremony rather than a "royal" ceremony.

The princes saw this as a heist of royal sacerdotal and peacemaking roles. "It was felt that the prerogative for righting an ancient conflict was that of the king and not a commoner like Phibun—not only as modern head of state but as descendant of the monarchs of Ayutthaya," wrote Thak Chaloemtiarana. Contrarily, Phibun saw it as a way of demonstrating that he was the real head of state.[29]

At first Bhumibol seemed a willing participant, breaking ground as planned for the Phuttamonthon project. For the occasion the palace distributed 20,000 copies of a commemorative volume of the king's ordination. But then, on the big day in May, King Bhumibol closeted himself in Hua Hin, claiming a cold. The royal barge procession, the Phuttamonthon rites, and the ceremony at Ayutthaya went off without the Mahidol family's presence. Prince Dhani attended the Ayutthaya event, giving face to the Burmese, but the palace snub was well recognized nonetheless. Newspapers pointed to the unseasonably dark skies and high winds in Ayutthaya that day as a heavenly sign that Phibun had grievously offended the dhammaraja.

Afterward the princes went to great lengths to portray the occasion as Phibun's near usurpation of the throne. British diplomats reported that the king told them Phibun was "drunk with power" and desired to be "a second king" or to even replace him on the throne.[30] On the defensive, Phibun declared the government's full respect for the monarchy, and he denied any split between the palace and him.[31] For many, it simply confirmed the point.

To shore up his position, in June Phibun proposed increasing the number of unelected members in the parliament. King Bhumibol openly expressed opposition, and the palace questioned the move's constitutionality. A decade earlier the throne had tried to control the appointment of these members as its own power base.[32]

Sarit, meanwhile, made his own moves. A political party he sponsored challenged the government in parliament, culminating in a mid-August no-confidence motion, in which Sarit's party accused the government of encouraging criticism of the throne, committing lèse-majesté. This forced Phibun closer to the strongman Phao, who made things worse. A newspaper Phao controlled directly attacked the royal circle. Referring to the Buddhist anniversary, headlines in the paper read, "The royalty snub religion" and "The royalty would all die."[33] The text accused the palace of trying to overthrow the government and of insulting Buddhism. Privately, Phao was also said to accuse the king of giving 700,000 baht to the Democrat Party.[34]

The royalists countered by spreading rumors that Phao was plotting the king's arrest. With Phao's reputation irretrievably sunk, Sarit demanded that Phibun sack him or be overthrown in a coup.

Phibun's lifelong struggle against the throne collapsed. On September 16 he went to beg the king's support for his government.[35] The court's self-satisfaction must have been viscous as Bhumibol told this man, twice his age and with many times his experience, to resign to avoid a coup. The palace still preferred a constitutional transfer of power.

Phibun refused, and that evening Sarit seized power. The speed in which he and his aide, General Thanom Kittikachorn, obtained royal sanction exposes the palace's complicity. The two rushed to the palace, and just two hours after the coup was declared the king decreed martial law and named Sarit as Bangkok's military custodian, "Defender of the Capital." It empowered Sarit to control the country and to countersign royal decrees. Phibun and Phao took this as notice to leave Thailand.

The next day Sarit declared he had acted in defense of the nation, monarchy, and religion. The palace responded generously. "His Majesty the King has graciously observed that the Revolutionary Party's objective of protecting the people, safeguarding national welfare and interest and promoting the prosperity of the country is a noble one. Having set yourself a noble objective, you are expected to proceed with your work with loyalty and uprightness, placing the interest of the nation above all. . . . You will have His Majesty's full blessing if all this is carried out," the king said in a statement.[36]

If foreign embassies had any reservations over the palace's sentiment or Sarit's ideology, they were quickly reassured. Dhani and other privy councilors fanned out on the embassy circuit delivering the message that Sarit was a loyal royalist and anticommunist, and that the palace supported the coup wholeheartedly.[37]

8   *Field Marshal Sarit* ∽ *The Palace Finds Its Strongman*

SARIT'S COUP HAD A GIDDYING EFFECT ON THE PALACE. After 25 years of struggle, the men behind the 1932 revolution, Phibun and Pridi, were both exiled and never to return. Their era was left behind like a Cromwellian interregnum. In its place was a revitalized royal institution ready to use its muscle. Everyone now sought the king's support. A desperate Phibun pleaded for the throne's protection. Sarit found the king's endorsement necessary for the takeover. In the aftermath, even the U.S. embassy rushed to the palace to obtain assurances that the new regime would remain on America's side in the Cold War.

The Sarit coup was a landmark of the Ninth Reign in two other ways. There was no more dreaming of absolute monarchy. The royals stopped fighting military government and embraced it. In the decades to come, Bhumibol found his greatest comfort in alliance with military autocrats, most of whom took power by royally endorsed coup. Equally significant, the palace lost interest in Western-style constitutional democracy. Constitution and parliament had been all-important to the royalists before 1957, but now the princes concluded that both were immaterial and even obstructive to royal power. The crown supported Sarit when he abrogated both institutions.

Field Marshal Sarit Thanarat was a cinematic picture of the Third World generalissimo: a smiling, generous man of the people, a heavy drinker, an opium trafficker, a vain womanizer, and a ruthless dictator who summarily executed criminals and political rivals to scare others. None of that was important to the princes. What they appreciated was that, never having studied abroad, Sarit subscribed to the idea of a grateful and obedient peasantry under the traditional monarch and his loyal government. One of his fondest memories was said to be his 1927 officer's school graduation, where King Prajadhipok presented swords to the graduates.

Like Phibun, Sarit saw himself as a fatherlike leader.[1] But where Phibun had tried to be equal with, or even superior to, the king, Sarit put the king above himself and promoted traditional hierarchy while attaching himself to royal prestige. Sarit understood the tradeoff: honor the king, and he could have the power he wanted. He wove this hierarchy throughout his speech, popularizing phrases like "the government of the king" and "the army of the king."[2]

His social values also evoked the imagined traditions of the absolute monarchy. They stressed discipline, harmony, and unity as the binding agents of the Thai cosmos, summed up as "Thai-ness," *khwam ben thai*. Another code word was *khwam riaproy*, which refers to order, neatness, and presentability, both public and personal. For both Sarit and the palace, there was no room for unsightly pedicabs on the streets, unruly union protests, socialists scorning aristocracy, or noisy liberal political activists. The princes evidently saw no need to intercede against Sarit's violent enforcement of these ideals.

Even so, neither the royals nor Sarit had any strategy for the post-Phibun era. To assuage critics of the coup, Sarit installed an interim prime minister and scheduled elections for a permanent one. The throne's ambitions showed in the short list for the temporary premier. Most of the candidates were pro-palace aristocrats, including the serving privy councilors Sridharmadibes and Srivisarn Vacha. Unsure of the princes' ambitions, Sarit chose the most neutral, Pote Sarasin, a former ambassador to the United States, who accepted only following assurances that the throne had approved the coup.

The elections of December 15, 1957, demonstrated that Sarit retained real power as supreme commander. Parliament was filled with his supporters and a slightly smaller contingent of Democrats. His army allies General Thanom Kittikachorn and General Praphas Charusathien became prime minister and deputy prime minister, respectively. Quickly they purged Phibun and Phao partisans and slashed the budgets and arms of the BPP and the regular police, the heart of Phao's power.

The new government in place, Sarit went to the United States for treatment for liver cirrhosis. Before he left, in a well-publicized flourish, King Bhumibol sent him a huge bouquet of flowers and offered prayers for his recovery. Never before had he made such a public display for a politician. Weeks later, Bhumibol fused the alliance by signing the promotion of more than 50 Sarit-favored generals. The king personally conferred upon Thanom the rank of full general. Bhumibol was building his own ties to the officers corps.

Over his nearly eight months abroad, Sarit signed up as a pro-American cold warrior. Unlike Phibun, however, he wasn't swayed by Western-style democracy. He concluded that Thailand really needed traditional command leadership. King Bhumibol was coming around to that idea as well. Ineffective government, continuing turmoil in parliament, and a rise in public disorder were inimical to the idea of an orderly, obedient Thai nation. In October 1958 a healthier Sarit slipped back into the country and undertook another coup. Bhumibol and his advisers apparently raised no objection.[3]

The October 20 coup overthrew not the political leadership but the system itself. Sarit abolished the legislature and declared martial law, giving himself autocratic powers. Ruling through a military-dominated Revolutionary Council, he staunched critics by arresting more than 100 prominent intellectuals, journalists, and politicians. For justification, Sarit turned to traditional cosmology. He cited a growing moral disorder that stemmed from transplanted Western ideologies, those Phibun and Pridi represented. Parliamentary democracy had not worked, because the people lacked discipline and respect. This turbulence and the rise of communism posed a direct threat to nation, religion, and king. Something more "Thai" was needed. "In this revolution, certain institutions must be changed," he stressed. "However, one institution which the Revolutionary Council will never allow to be changed is the institution of the monarchy representing the nation as a whole."[4]

Thanat Khoman, Sarit's royalist ambassador in Washington, said the near anarchy of the national assembly proved that the Western democratic system was alien and unnecessary. In fact, Thai people already had an ingeniously structured society: "The fundamental cause of our political instability in the past lies in the sudden transplantation of alien institutions onto our soil without proper regard to the circumstances which prevail in our homeland, the nature and characteristics of our own people, in a word the genius of our race. . . . If we look at our national history, we can see very well that this country works better and prospers under an authority, not a tyrannical authority, but a unifying authority around which all elements of the nation can rally."[5]

The condemnation of foreign ideology as the root of the country's problems recalled the Chakri dismissal of Ayutthaya as poisoned by Khmer and Hindu culture. With Prince Dhani and privy councilor Srivisarn having argued that the monarchy is all the constitution and representation the people require, the palace only needed Sarit and Thanat to rationalize eliminating parliament altogether. Sarit replaced them with the abbreviated provisional constitution of February 1959, which gave sweeping powers to the premier and his council.

This was hardly the progressive government in which Bhumibol had been schooled for sixteen years in Lausanne. But whatever he thought, he was still directed by the privy councilors and the princes, who never objected when the promised full charter was never drawn up and a representative parliament never elected. The former charter drafter Kukrit Pramoj wrote that Thais shouldn't be too concerned, because Sarit had the nation's best interests at heart.

The palace's needs were not Sarit's priority when he took power. The priority was the Cold War, which was foisted on his government by the events in surrounding countries. China had taken control of Tibet, and during 1958 it shelled Quemoy Island, which was occupied by exiled Kuomintang soldiers. In Laos, the nationalist-communist Pathet Lao, led by the "Red Prince" Souphanouvong, gained strength with backing from Hanoi. The long Lao-Thai border, and the presence of more than 10 million poor ethnic Lao in the Thai northeast, led Sarit to invite U.S. intervention.

By the end of 1960 there were 250 U.S. marines in the Thai northeast on standby, and in early 1962 the United States and Thailand crafted a bilateral defense pact. The agreement between Thanat Khoman and U.S. secretary of state Dean Rusk rendered Thailand officially a frontline state against the communist threat, and marked the beginning of what some call an American neo-occupation of Thailand to prosecute the Indochina wars. Launching a flood of U.S. money, arms, and advisers, the first of 10,000 American soldiers pledged by President John F. Kennedy arrived within a month, backed by fighter jets and an aircraft carrier task force. The conflict in Laos cooled momentarily, but the U.S. military presence in Thailand inexorably grew.

The Cold War became fundamental to the power of the monarchy and its military partners. King Bhumibol began to make his own warnings about the red menace. The pact with the United States, Sarit said, emphasized the looming threat to "precious traditions and institutions of the Thai nation, ranging from our Buddhist religion to our king and our freedom." Hundreds of government opponents, from students to liberal politicians to activist monks, were jailed as un-Thai communists and enemies of the monarchy.

The economy also expanded under an economic plan designed by the United States and the World Bank that encouraged competition and private investment. In the hands of technocrats, more effort went into building infrastructure and educational and health-care services. Bhumibol endorsed the plan in his 1961 New Year's address, which exemplified the stiff, baffling manner of speaking that was becoming his style: "The government is trying to promote national development in a most competent way. . . . This plan will be implemented this year. I believe that it will be useful for the nation. However, the important thing depends upon the carrying out of programs under the plan with togetherness from all sides. Only then would the nation profit. I hope that you will cooperate with the government on these matters in the future."[6]

Having seen the princes undermine Phibun, at first Sarit was reluctant to cede the palace much ground. He did accommodate apparently benign needs, for instance after the 1957 coup quietly allowing the king to resume his countryside tours, which had been halted after the successful 1955 trip to the northeast. In March 1958, the royal couple spent two weeks in the north, again with a fast mix of stops at provincial seats, notable temples, government offices, famous landmarks, and some villages in between. Peasants lined the roads waving flags as their motorcade sped by. This was repeated a year later in southern Thailand, deep in the territory of Thai Muslims, many of whom felt greater allegiance to Malaysia's sultans. The third trip completed the traditional king's ritual establishing possession of his kingdom.

Over time, Sarit gave more leeway. After two years he allowed the palace to reclaim control over national ceremonies and holidays. Since 1932, many important holidays had been separated from the palace, essentially secularized, like National Day on June 24, the date of the 1932 revolution. In 1960, Sarit had National Day moved to December 5, Bhumibol's birthday. Kukrit Pramoj wrote in *Siam Rath* that this was most appropriate, as the founding date of the country could be debated. The royalists were expunging the 1932 revolution from collective memory.

The annual royal fertility rites were expanded, to bring the king into the plowing ceremony. And in November 1959, the government underwrote the revival of the splendid royal kathin procession, parading the king's fleet of ornate red and gold barges on the Chaophraya River.

The king's role as titular head of the armed forces was also increased. The soldiers had always had to swear allegiance to the throne. But now the oath was sacralized in an annual ritual of drinking holy water in front of the king or his portrait. Top government officials, members of the court, and recipients of high royal honors (the so-called Rama knighthood) and their families also undertook the ritual. In 1959 Bhumibol presented flags carrying his personal relics to each military regiment, a mark of bonding for the king and his soldiers. He had done the same for the army, the police, and the Volunteer Defense Corps in the early 1950s. But its repeat with Sarit and his own generals, accompanied by much publicity, forged a deeper connection between the throne and the military, as did the king's unveiling on Army Day in 1959 of a statue of King Naresuan, the Ayutthaya warrior and the symbol of the army. Afterward, until at least 1970, Bhumibol unveiled or paid homage to a Naresuan statue at a different army camp each Army Day.[7]

Sarit increased the palace's control over royal guards as well. For the king's birthday in 1959, the army's 21st regiment was transferred to palace duties, and Queen Sirikit became its honorary commanding colonel. On the occasion Sarit took royal praise to new, holy heights:

> It is clear to all both within the country and abroad that your majesty has followed the guidelines on thotsaphit rachatham in national affairs and has been the most exalted leader of the nation. . . . You are a king of great ability and interested in the work of the government although these in-volve new methods and plans. . . . You have advised and cautioned myself and others to carry out our duties faithfully for the development of the nation and happiness of the people. All your ideas have been useful and have provided constant encouragement for this government. . . . You have a personality worthy of worship. Your visits to the countryside have swayed the hearts of your people towards unity within the nation. . . . Foreigners also praise your impeccable personality. . . . It has become internationally well-known that Thailand is lucky to have a king worthy of worship.[8]

Sarit also increased the palace budget by nearly 28 million baht in 1958, with the amount rising steadily each year after, bolstering the royal family's own sub-stantial financial base.[9] He also financed the refurbishment of the Chitrlada resi-dential palace. More substantially, in January 1959 Sarit repealed Phibun's 1954 land reform, securing the landholdings of the powerful old aristocrats from breakup. Five years earlier, the law's cancellation would have met significant protest. Now no one dared.

Taking advantage of the opening, the palace expanded royal rituals and duties. Until 1957 the king's official activities, from government functions to ceremonies and audiences with business and social groups, never numbered more than 155 in a year. In 1958, the number shot up to 191. By 1962 it hit 377.[10] The number of traditional ceremonies surged by half, but the biggest increases came in meetings with private business and industry, and with foreign dignitaries and agencies. King Bhumibol was widening his network of contacts and information sources, and deepening his constituency.

American diplomat U. Alexis Johnson described the king as greatly interested in what he could learn from visitors.[11] Johnson's own palace meetings usually began at 11 a.m.—the king already had a habit of waking up late each morning—and continued for three or four hours, often without lunch, until Bhumibol was reminded of his next commitment. Usually accompanied by his aide Luang Suranarong, the king listened closely, asked many questions, and wasn't afraid to criticize, including the United States. He complained frequently that the Thai peasantry wasn't benefiting from American and Thai development programs. He also expressed fears, Johnson noted, that Pridi and his followers remained dangerous to the country. "He was extremely open, direct, and friendly, with wide-ranging interests," which included politics, farming, health, religion, water skiing, and movies, Johnson said. Nevertheless, "He spoke softly but sat straight, never forgetting he was king."

After the regional tours, Bhumibol seldom ventured back into the countryside. Still a publicly shy, Westernized urbanite with a family to raise, he didn't yet appreciate what he might accomplish. Instead, he embarked on an extensive series of state visits during 1960–63. Because he hadn't been out of the country since 1951, these trips gave the king's reputation and personal confidence an immense boost. The visits abroad were initiated by Sarit and the United States to bring Thailand more deeply into the anticommunist bloc, while obscuring the Sarit regime's dictatorial face. Furthermore, by visiting the world's mainstream monarchies, the Mahidols would gain recognition as equals in that rarefied fraternity.

The anticommunist theme was emphasized in the first trip, to South Vietnam for three days in December 1959. It was an archetypal state visit: reviewing military units, stopping at an important national monument, receiving an honorary university degree, visiting an important religious edifice and an ancient cultural site, along with other institutions like an industrial plant or scientific institute, and exchanging state banquets and gifts with the hosts.

The trip went like clockwork, and Bhumibol and Sirikit showed a flair for diplomacy. Two months later they spent eight days in Indonesia, their host the flamboyant nationalist President Sukarno. They traveled through Java and Bali, with the focus, as with most of their visits to fellow Asian countries, on displays of traditional culture. Queen Sirikit, despite her love of French fashion, would don elegant, traditionally patterned Thai silk outfits, Bhumibol meanwhile sticking to a Western suit or military uniform. In early March their visit to Burma confirmed the political nature of the king's snub of Phibun a few years earlier, when he had declined to attend Rangoon's celebration of Buddhism's 25th centenary ostensibly because Bhumibol would be forced to remove his shoes to enter a temple. Now the king gladly doffed his shoes.

These three trips were a warm-up for a seven-month tour of the West, including state visits to 15 countries mixed with generous family vacation time. The trip began on June 14, 1960, with an entire month in the United States. The Americans went all out with a mix of soft entertainment and gushing political recognition that put Bhumibol in a light comparable to that of the West's most powerful leaders.

The first stop was Honolulu, where sightseeing included a visit to the Pearl Harbor war memorial. At a formal dinner with the state's governor, the king sat in on clarinet with the dixieland jazz band. The following week was spent in California, where the Mahidols stayed at the residence of Henry Kearns, a close associate of Richard Nixon and the head of the U.S. Export-Import Bank. California was mostly entertainment: a family trip to Disneyland and a meeting with Walt Disney, a tour of Paramount Studios and photos with Elvis Presley on the set of GI Blues, and visits with comedians Bob Hope and Lucille Ball.

Depositing their children at Kearns's ranch, the king and queen headed eastward. By the time of their arrival in Washington, D.C., on June 27, the visit had become a national media event. Bhumibol waved at crowds from a convertible limousine in a parade down Pennsylvania Avenue. That evening President Dwight D. Eisenhower presented him with the Legion of Merit, as commander-in-chief of the Thai armed forces.

On June 29 the king addressed Congress, where he lauded American political principles and praised U.S. concern for small countries. "Your people have given, by their own sovereign will, full freedom and equity to a Southeast Asian nation," he said. "When a Far-Eastern country [South Korea] was being overwhelmed by a war fought for its oppression, the United States without hesitation went to war to save that country." He characterized this as a Buddhistic act of selflessness. In Thai culture, he noted, even if the recipient of assistance does not show it, he is grateful. For the donor, not insisting on praise or credit, "the giving of aid is a merit in itself."

He added, "In view of the present world tension and the feeling of uncertainty apparent everywhere, it is my sincere feeling that the time is ripe for an even closer cooperation."

Bhumibol and Sirikit next went to New York, where Governor Nelson Rockefeller hosted a huge party for members of New York's high society on July 4 at his estate. The entertainment was the master of jazz clarinet, Benny Goodman, who invited Bhumibol to play along on a couple songs. The next day tens of thousands of New Yorkers turned out for a tickertape parade honoring Bhumibol and Sirikit. That afternoon he joined Goodman in his apartment with Gene Krupa, Teddy Wilson, and other top jazz musicians for a jam session. For two hours they played swing standards like "The Sheik of Araby" and "Honeysuckle Rose." Goodman presented his guest with a new saxophone, and Bhumibol would ever after be called "the king of jazz."

The king also made a sentimental return to Boston, to meet the doctor and nurses who had helped with his own birth, and to be feted at Harvard Medical School where his father had studied. The rest of the trip included visits to Tennessee, Montana, and other stops before returning to California. The king was taken to see monuments, grand public works, and America's most advanced technologies and companies, like IBM.

The United States had rarely rolled out the red carpet so intensely for a foreign leader. It showed the importance Washington now placed on Thailand, and Bhumibol as a symbol of anticommunism. None of the attention was accidental, not even the Benny Goodman jam session. Goodman was a notorious taskmaster who had no patience for those not near to his standard of musicianship, and Bhumibol wasn't close. Arranging such a bevy of jazz stars to play with the king was the work of the White House. But it helped make the U.S. visit an unqualified success. The American press lathered praise on Bhumibol and Sirikit, who captured hearts with her charm and beauty. Back in Thailand, U.S. propaganda arms distributed newscasts of the trip, making sure the events of the visit were seen by as many Thais as possible.

The tour of 14 European capitals that followed was no less triumphant. Europeans generally had little interest in Thailand, but they had a tradition of monarchic diplomacy. So they too laid out the red carpets, and the media covered the visits with great enthusiasm. With their children left behind in Thailand, over a leisurely five-month stretch the Mahidols made mostly three-day state visits each to Great Britain, Germany, Portugal, Switzerland, Denmark, Norway, Sweden, Italy, the Vatican, Belgium, France, Luxembourg, the Netherlands, and finally Spain.

There was a ritual pattern for all visits: the couple was received by the corresponding head of state and reviewed troops; the king laid flowers at a national war monument or tomb; the two sides exchanged state banquets, gifts, and decorations; and then there were visits to significant institutions, cultural, scientific, or economic. Usually too they had lunches or dinners with the mayor of the host city. Certain places did a bit more. France put on a special fashion show for the queen and then a late night classical and modern dance concert in the Opera.

In between the trips the Mahidols returned to a hired estate in Switzerland, or did some private socializing and tourism. Escorted by their old friend Princess Alexandra, a cousin of Queen Elizabeth, they stayed in London for several days following their official duties, taking a double-decker bus tour, visiting Cambridge, and supping with Britain's royals. They returned to England twice more, for shopping, theater, and meals with the queen. At a final party at the Thai embassy on December 14, Bhumibol kept everyone up into the early morning playing saxophone with the band.

The trip was another roaring success. The European monarchies greeted the Mahidols as full members in the club of kings and queens. The royal couple appeared fully modern, the king wearing fine-cut London suits when he wasn't in official uniform, and the queen showing off a constant change of French haute couture. She was most stunning when she met Pope John XXIII in a shimmering Pierre Balmain gown and diamond-studded tiara. The press made as much of her style as it did of Bhumibol's jazz, and soon she was rewarded by being named to the list of the world's ten best-dressed women. The trip ended with a skiing holiday with Princess Alexandra in Gstaad over the New Year holiday. Finally, in mid-January 1961 the Mahidols returned home to a huge, enthusiastic public welcome. An estimated one million people lined the royal couple's route from the airport, while across the kingdom monks chanted, temple bells pealed, and fireworks were launched.

Over the next few years the king and queen made similar visits to Pakistan, Malaysia, Australia, and New Zealand (in 1962); Japan, Taiwan, and the Philippines (1963); Austria (1964); Iran and England a second time (1966); and the United States again and Canada (1967). All of these were key noncommunist allies.[12] Pointedly bypassed were close neighbors India, North Vietnam, Cambodia, Laos, and China, as well as the Soviet Union.

At home, Thais had the impression that the world essentially stopped for their sovereign. Enhancing this idea was Kukrit Pramoj, who accompanied the king and queen as a semiofficial palace publicist. He reported their European trip as a mystical journey, noting in *Siam Rath,* for instance, that as the king arrived in London, England's never-ending rain had magically halted. Media promotion of Bhumibol and Sirikit, and their now four children—a third daughter, Chulabhorn, was born in July 1957—became slicker, helped by members of the court who were deeply involved in newspapers, magazines, and movies. Prince Bhanuband and Thawiwong were leading filmmakers, and the Crown Property Bureau owned leading movie producer and theater owner United Cinema. This ensured that the principles of nation, religion, and king were woven throughout the popular entertainment of the period.

The United States was critical in this as well. By the early 1960s, the U.S. Information Service had virtually taken over public relations for the Thai government, heavily funding equipment and programming for television and radio broadcasts with an anticommunist, pro-monarchy theme. Recorded on film by American and Thai cameramen, the king's journeys abroad were shown on U.S.-funded Thai television and in movie theaters and open-air venues around Thailand. The U.S. Agency for International Development and USIS also printed hundreds of thousands of posters and calendars with the king and queen's pictures each year for distribution throughout the countryside. These became often the only wall decoration one could find in the homes of poor peasants. As *Time* magazine wrote in 1966, "American information officials in Bangkok concluded long ago that USIS funds could not be better employed than in spreading the likeness of His Majesty."

Some efforts sank to absurdity, as with the soap bars distributed around the countryside that, as they were used, wore away to reveal seven layers with different slogans exhorting the bather to love the king, follow Buddhism, and fight communism. "The government of His Majesty the King sends its good wishes to all the Thai people," read one of these messages.[13]

Soap was not enough to cement the throne's popularity, nevertheless. The palace needed to create around itself an exclusive corps of dedicated supporters from the non-royal elite. In the past this had been achieved through family marriage and business alliances, and by a system of peerage titles for favored commoners. The former had lost currency, however, and Phibun had eliminated the peerage titles.

In the 1960s, the palace fostered a new extended royal community by offering select upper-class families, friends, big donors to royal charities, and volunteers close proximity to the king and queen. This perquisite could consist of invitations to palace parties, or the royals attending a function outside the palace. It also included taking wives and daughters into the court, as ladies-in-waiting to the queen and the princesses. The creation of a school inside Chitrlada Palace also allowed children of the select elite and foreigners to mix with the Mahidol children. The palace expanded its royal sponsorship of funerals and weddings, which in the 1960s grew nearly tenfold, totaling some 200 weddings between 1964 and 1971.[14] Many if not most involved commoners who had earned, and could now advertise, royal favor. A further way the royal community was delineated was a government decision in 1962 to allow only royals and select palace friends to take five-syllable names, while others were limited to a maximum of four syllables.[15]

To replace the lost peerage titles, the palace restored a hierarchy of royal decorations. Aside from a senior class of honors extended to those who were particularly dedicated to the court and the royal family, there was a second class for wider distribution. Recipients and their wives would earn medallions, brightly colored sashes and gold pins, and the women getting the highest decorations would also garner the titles *khunying* or *thanpuying,* essentially "lady," indicating their connection to the court. By awarding these decorations systematically to the top bureaucrats, generals, and leading capitalists and charity donors, the palace deepened its constituency base among the wealthy and powerful.

To reinforce the ties between the throne and this new elite, palace activities actually grew more stiff and ceremonious, after a century of slow relaxation in royal formalities. Crucial was the revival of rajasap, the court language rich with ornate terminology for everything related to the king, including his movements, his implements, and even the parts of his body.[16] Rooted in Pali and Sanskrit, the intensely sacerdotal court dialect had always been an identifier of royal proximity. But after the 1932 revolution it became an anachronistic affectation of the feudal past, remembered only by the old princes and courtiers.

Key to the sacerdotal effect of rajasap is the ubiquitous prefix *phra*. It carries a nonspecific sense of not just royal and grand but sacral. "Phra" is the everyday term for a monk or a priest, as well as a generic noble title. As a prefix it could be translated as "excellent" but also "holy one"; combined with "chao," or lord, it becomes a term both for king and for god. *Phra Yesu,* for instance, is the Lord Jesus. "Phra" is applied to the special terms for every part of the king's body, his implements, and his activities, imbuing all with sacrality. It is also key in the king's formal titles, such as *phra maha kasatriya,* which translates as "excellent/holy great warrior-king." Another formal title for the king is *phra chao yu hua,* "the holy lord above my head," or even "the god above my head."

The sense of hierarchy is particularly strong. In a royal audience, the royals speak in everyday language, while the commoner must address them in the tongue-twisting court dialect. The mechanics of class become clear in pronouns. In addressing the king, one refers to the self as *kha phra phutta chao,* which translates as "the servant of your excellent and enlightened holy being" but also "the servant of the Lord Buddha." The way to address the king is *phra bat somdej phra chao yu hua,* literally "the excellent feet of the supreme Lord (Buddha) above (my) head." Coupled with prostration, this implies a deep sense of inferiority, but also high honor for being able to place the highest possible part of one's body, the head, in proximity to the holy king's most inferior part, his feet.

As one gets deeper into rajasap, the positioning becomes more exaggerated and more physical. The beginning and ending of a formal address to the king is often *khoh decha fa la ong thuli phrabat bok klao bok kramom:* "May the power of the dust on the soles and the dust under the soles of your royal feet protect my head and the top of my head." What this expresses is not only the placement of one's head below the king's feet, but putting the very top of one's head below *the dust which is under the dust* on the bottoms of the king's feet. This expression was used, most ironically, to begin the first letter to King Prajadhipok by the 1932 revolutionists. And it was announced in British-accented Thai, to everyone's amazement, by the head of the honor guard receiving King Bhumibol on his state visit to Great Britain in 1961.

Such language is only slightly compromised in a meeting between the king and a monk. The monk need not express such humility as a commoner does, yet he still must acknowledge the king's greatness. The average monk addresses his king and his supreme patriarch with the same term: *phra chao,* lord holy one. In rajasap, wrote political scientist Sombat Chantornvong, "Even a foreign monarch or the Lord Buddha, himself royal by birth, does not receive as much reverence and exaltation as the Thai king."[17]

The court language's decline had been reinforced by Phibun's efforts to eliminate royal culture. At the end of World War II, few educated Thais knew even the simplest rajasap, and the popular media used the most informal term for the king, *nai luang,* or "sir king." Sublimely, in the 1960s rajasap was resuscitated and became an anchor of the royalist revival. Books about royal ceremonies, comportment, and language became a small growth industry, many of them issued by the royalist-dominated Ministry of Education. On television and radio, royal activities were reported now in correct basic rajasap. Not being able to master a few key terms became the sign of an uneducated peasant.

With this linguistic hierarchy came a revival of physical positioning. Mandatory prostration to the royal family, officially ended in the Fifth Reign, continued out of habit until Phibun came to power. In evidence presented in the Ananda death case, Pridi and royal secretary Chaleo were both accused of disrespect for not bowing to the king. By the 1960s, prostration returned as fashionably correct deportment. If Bhumibol's own children and servants kowtowed to him in public, and if top politicians did the same, then so should everyone else. The effect of this royal culture revival was ultimately political. Sombat wrote: "A linguistic system which demands the utmost humility on the part of a subject and presupposes the budding Buddhahood on the part of the ruler works out best in a traditionally Buddhist society under an absolute monarch." And Thai society was drifting back in that direction.

The rajasap revival was closely tied to the palace men's retaking control of the state apparatus over education and religion, both within the Ministry of Education. Through the 1950s and 1960s, the palace's point man was Pin Malakul, who had been a page under Rama VI and served in top positions in the ministry before becoming minister himself. Pin's family traced its lineage to Rama II, and its members remained committed servants of the modern palace. A close relative was the palace's chief of rituals and ceremonies during the 1950s. As education minister, Pin doggedly pursued the royal agenda. He could focus history and culture lessons on Chakri kings and their link to Sukhothai, while deleting the record of the 1932 revolution. Religion reverted back to a royal-centered activity, reinforcing the idea of the king's dhammaraja and devaraja godliness.

Pin also helped regain full palace control over the sangha, a process that involved one of the most crude and cynical displays of royal power during the period. In spite of gains the Thammayut sect had made just after the war, during the 1950s the rival Mahanikay school, backed by Phibun, retained a number of top sangha administrative positions. These monks blocked the palace's plan to abrogate Phibun's democratizing Sangha Act of 1941 and restore King Chulalongkorn's 1902 code, which allowed the throne direct control over the monkhood.

Leading the Mahanikay resistance was Phra Phimontham, the abbot of Wat Mahathat, the foremost Mahanikay temple, located near the Grand Palace. Phimontham's abilities as a wat manager and leader, his monastic discipline, and his religious scholarship were undeniable. By his high rank, he was one of the monks who oversaw the king's ordination in 1956. In the 1950s he was a certain candidate for the sanghanayok, or sangha premiership, and after that possibly supreme patriarch. Very politically minded, and with a power base rooted among activist monks in northeastern temples, Phimontham had long fought Thammayut elitism as well as government oppression of peasants. When the government said communists should not be allowed in temples, Phimontham countered that a good monk will accept anyone, communist or not. Phimontham's obstinacy and political views rendered him, to the palace and government, a serious threat. Beginning in the Sarit period, they took strong steps to repress him.

In 1958 the Thammayut supreme patriarch died. The presumed heir was the sangha prime minister Plot Kittisophana, a Mahanikay monk whom palace officials had found fairly cooperative. But they worried that Plot's vacated sanghanayok place would fall to Phimontham. Working in the palace's favor was the fact that Plot himself deeply disliked Phimontham. After the supreme patriarch died, the palace, represented by Pin and Prince Dhani, cut a deal in which Plot would be promoted in exchange for freezing Phimontham's rise.[18] Plot also agreed to abrogate the 1941 Sangha Act and reinstate the royalist act of 1902.

Days after his installation on May 5, 1960, Plot obliged. He named the Thammayut monk Juan Uttayi sangha premier. A few weeks later, after the new sangha cabinet declared a policy of weeding out communist monks, Phimontham was arrested and charged by police, falsely, with homosexual behavior, improper dress, and communist leanings, and was ordered to disrobe. When he refused, in October Sarit and Pin had him dislodged as Wat Mahathat abbot. Two weeks after that he was stripped of all of his clerical titles and reduced to a common monk. The scandal rocked the sangha and the public. Phimontham was released from jail after several weeks for lack of evidence. But he returned to Wat Mahathat as a rank-and-file monk.

Plot meanwhile created a new sangha act that, based on the 1902 charter, recentralized administration under Thammayut control. The sangha premier and cabinet were eliminated, and replaced with the *mahatherasamakhom,* or sangha council, made up of the most senior titled monks, which in numbers the Thammayut dominated. This new act had several important effects. Although doctrinal differences between the schools had become less significant, putting Thammayut on top ensured that the sangha remained closely allied with the palace, whoever controlled the religious affairs department of the Education Ministry. The monks would advance the palace agenda.

This achieved, on June 20, 1962, Phimontham was declared a threat to national security for supporting communists and rearrested, under Sarit's order. He was forcibly disrobed in a police station with Sarit and two top Thammayut sangha council members watching, and imprisoned for four years. In prison he wore white robes as a symbol of his rejection of civil and royal authority over the sangha.

Phimontham's neutralization completed the palace's capture of national culture. In schools and temples, history, worship, and tradition could now be manipulated to ensure unquestioning support for Chakri culture and power, and for the triune of nation, religion, and king. By the mid-1960s the memory of 1932 and the Phibun-Pridi interregnum was almost completely snuffed out, or twisted into something evil.

As the Phimontham case showed, Sarit was the royal enforcer. Beginning in 1960, he applied lèse-majesté laws toughly to eliminate troublemakers and demonstrate the throne's sacrality.[19] He often combined the charge with allegations of communist sympathies. In one instance, a writer who named his dog after the king was thrown in jail. Characterized by the historian Thak Chaloemtiarana as "despotic paternalism," Sarit's harshness and corruption never seemed to bother the throne. Bhumibol made well-publicized demonstrations of confidence in the field marshal. He presented Sarit with gifts, visited his farm, and proclaimed how much the country owed him. Sarit was allowed to share in the throne's prestige by performing royal ceremonies on the king's behalf, undertaking a royal kathin in Khon Kaen, for example.

As Thak said, this alliance was a pragmatic secularization of power and leadership. In his sphere, the king was allowed all the sources of legitimization he needed. In return, Sarit as prime minister enjoyed the cosmological sanction of the throne, managing the country "on behalf of" the throne, and in doing so deriving his own public legitimacy. This was a momentous shift. As a foundation of its power, the palace traded the constitution for partnership with the loyal military. Royal interests would no longer be defended by princes or aristocrats but by common-born army generals. If anything symbolized the closeness of the relationship, it was when the die-hard royalist Srivisarn Vacha resigned from the privy council in 1962 to become Sarit's primary adviser on everything from national security to managing the national assembly to cultural development. Until his death in 1968, Srivisarn also led the National Security Council, connecting the palace to the center of state policy.

Cooperation with Sarit and other generals carried substantial risk of embarrassing the king and eroding his virtue. But it never appeared to blemish Bhumibol. When Sarit died from liver failure in December 1963, the event was at first shaped ritually to reflect the moral goodness of the palace-military-bureaucracy hierarchy. The king made a televised display of touching Sarit's forehead, a Buddha-like blessing of honor, shortly before he died. A photograph of the gesture was distributed like a religious icon that proved Sarit's proximity to the virtue of the dhammaraja.

King Bhumibol declared an unprecedented 21 days of mourning in the palace, and Sarit's body lay in state under royal sponsorship for 100 days, encased in a gold urn under a royal five-tier umbrella. Bhumibol and the queen presided at Sarit's cremation on March 17, 1964. Srivisarn later noted that no prime minister ever had such intimate relations with the Thai monarch as Sarit Thanarat.[20]

But within weeks of his death came revelations that Sarit had amassed a fortune of $140 million and 8,000 acres of land by robbing government assets and foreign aid. With the money he had kept more than 100 women as concubines, and they began fighting over the spoils. Embarrassed, the succeeding government of General Thanom Kittikachorn had to launch an investigation just two days before the cremation.

Yet the scandal failed to tarnish Bhumibol even slightly. By having survived seven prime ministers and five successful coups over 17 years, Bhumibol's monarchy was now virtually stainless, unaffected by the failings of even those enjoying his favor. The dhammaraja kingship had irrevocably reestablished itself as the nation's pillar of continuity and stability, independent of its secular surroundings. The throne's popularity was founded in the people, who expected the sovereign to protect their interests and lead the country to prosperity. Everything else, everyone else, was dispensable.

9   *Bhumibol in the 1960s* ॡ
A Dhammaraja's Brilliance Unfolds

WITH SARIT'S DEATH, THE MONARCHY FINALLY, as the princes had long
desired, moved to the center of Thai national culture, unstained by all the political
ugliness around. Like beauty, longevity was related to karma and merit, and although he was still young, 17 years on the throne rendered King Bhumibol automatically a figure of virtue. Sarit's successors, Generals Thanom and Praphas, had
no choice but to bow to him for their own legitimacy.

Even so, Bhumibol wasn't ready to take charge of his position. During the early
1960s the aging princes continued to direct official business. Meanwhile the king
pursued a wide range of personal hobbies and disciplines that inevitably crystal-
lized into radiant new facets of his dhammaraja personality: the warm father,
excelling sportsman, fine arts genius, king of jazz, development economist, and
meditation master. Not only would each of these facets be advertised and mythologized incessantly for the rest of his life to remind his subjects of Bhumibol's
unsurpassed brilliance. They would also prove useful in raising more funds for
palace operations—funds that, in the creative hands of the palace managers, continued to multiply, quietly attesting to the crown's unmatchable wealth.

A sports and fitness buff since his youth, Bhumibol regularly rowed and
worked out with weights in the 1950s and 1960s. Seemingly always seeking a
challenge, he was also an enthusiastic competitor in badminton and tennis, playing

with the palace and military staff and others in the royal circle, and favorite daughter Ubolrat when she reached her teens. Understandably, he always had difficulty knowing just how good he was, because he could never be certain if his opponents were as submissive on the court as they were off it. Those who dared to beat him honestly became his more enduring chums, like the swaggering Prince Bhisadej Rajani, not only a sporting buddy but also later the manager of the king's development projects. Perhaps reflecting this conundrum, Bhumibol's greatest sporting passion was small-boat sailing. It offered exercise and self-trial, as well as the means of achieving a slight but important distance from the constantly present palace staff, who noted for history the time and duration of his every act.

This was not the grand yachting of Europe's royals. Bhumibol took to the humble OK dinghy, an uncomplicated four-meter, one-man boat that provides a good test in a stiff wind. Alone on the sea off Klai Kangwon palace in Hua Hin— albeit with a flotilla of navy cruisers ever on guard in the distance—Bhumibol could fiddle with the controls, turn whichever way he desired, push himself and the boat to the limit, suffering at most an occasional dunking for his own mistakes. For someone who was rarely seen smiling, he was said to appear happiest when he was drifting along the breeze with abandon, enjoying a smoke and a nip of whiskey from a hip flask. After a time he also sailed Enterprise class boats, agile two-man racers that provide a more challenging workout. The king's favorite partners again were Ubolrat and Bhisadej, with whom he could share helm duties without proto-col problems.

Bhumibol's enthusiasm launched a sailing fervor among the aristocrats who likewise flocked to Hua Hin in the hot months. A fleet of boats was acquired at Klai Kangwon and the Mahidols put on day-long regattas, complete with a raucous awards banquet. The regulars of the dinghy community became the king's pals, some of them comfortable enough to defeat him in races. Even at that humble level, sailing was still an elite sport in undeveloped Thailand, difficult to construct as a royal virtue. But three ways were found to extract prestige from it. The first was hobbyist Bhumibol's building of his own boat. He and Bhisadej obtained plans from England, and the king set up a workshop in Chitrlada Palace. In 1964 he completed his first boat, an Enterprise. The following year he built an OK dinghy, and in 1966–67 he built two 3.5-meter Moths, another popular dinghy.

In the world of small boats, these weren't remarkable accomplishments. Thou-sands of hobbyists around the world had constructed their own OKs, Enterprises, and Moths. Nevertheless, the palace and government made it out to be little short of a miracle that, on testing in the Chitrlada pond, the first Enterprise actually floated. Bhumibol was portrayed as the king of persistence and accomplishment, building an oceangoing vessel with his bare hands, and a master of tools and technology, whose innovations improved the boats' performance.

Likewise, when Bhumibol undertook a solo marathon sail, it became a display of exemplary tenacity. On April 19, 1966, he piloted his OK dinghy across the Gulf of Thailand, covering the 60 nautical miles from Hua Hin to Sattahip in 14 hours. The feat was portrayed as a solemn, lonely, and difficult sail, but that wasn't quite true. The winds were very light and the seas calm. He was alone in the boat, but sailing alongside were Bhisadej and the car-racing champion Prince Bira. A flotilla of navy and private vessels followed them. Success was presupposed; a huge boulder at Sattahip had been inscribed earlier to mark the occasion. Like building the boat, it was an accomplishment, to be sure, but not a singular one. Later it was said that the Hua Hin-Sattahip route could not be made an annual race because it was too grueling.

The third way sailing was etched onto Bhumibol's shining image was his victory in the Southeast Asia Peninsula Games of December 1967. How it came about is revealing. Air Chief Marshal Davee Chullasap, a Hua Hin sailor and member of the Thai Olympic Committee, explained that "[we] wanted the king to be like the Norwegian king who marveled in sports, winning a gold medal at the Olympics."[1] With only Burma, Thailand, Malaysia, and Singapore participating, the event was hardly the Olympics. There were few competitors. Bhumibol and Ubolrat led the Thai team. Halfway through the six-race series, Ubolrat held first, and her father second. At the end of the fifth race, the teenage princess remained marginally ahead. The king could take the gold only if he won the final race and his daughter finished third or worse. It was an interesting situation for royal prestige. A victory would underline the dhammaraja's perfection. If Ubolrat won, gracious sportsmanship and fatherhood could be highlighted. But if some other competitor came first, the king's prestige could suffer.

The final result was remarkably perfect. The king won the last race and Ubolrat took second. With equal points, father and daughter shared the gold. Was Bhumibol good enough for the Olympics? No one knows, for that was the end of his formal racing career. What mattered was, the day he and Ubolrat received their gold medals from Queen Sirikit, December 16, 1967, became the annual national sports day. For the Thais, Bhumibol certainly was as good as Norway's king.

King Bhumibol's efforts in the fine arts also refracted into exaggerated brilliance. In his oldest hobby, photography, he mostly took snapshots of family and friends and gathered crowds during his travels. But a small output from experimenting with shooting and darkroom techniques made its way into the mass media and books about the king, garnering widespread acclaim. Artistically speaking, these photos were undistinguished. But in a country where very few people had a camera before the 1960s, the work was held as legendary.

For a more determined effort at art, Bhumibol took up oil painting, perhaps because canvas and brushes provided a freer operating environment. Starting in the late 1950s, he studied with the kingdom's leading painters and some famous foreign artists passing through. He turned his palace into a bohemian salon, putting on dinners for his favorite painters, after which they would sketch and paint, smoke and drink beer and whiskey late into the night. Sometimes they would hold painting contests, inviting a lady-in-waiting to pose. It was typical of Bhumibol, adding a dose of competition to strip away the formality and obsequiousness.

Bhumibol put a lot of time into painting, completing some 100 medium-sized works, mostly oils, between 1959 and 1967, after which he retired his easel. Mostly still kept by the palace and shown in exhibitions, his earliest works were realistic and impressionistic portraits and landscapes. He painted many portraits of Sirikit, some of them good likenesses, and some nudes never seen publicly. Although he showed skill in color and composition, the works are fairly flat and textureless, and understandably for his experience they are short on emotional content.

In the 1960s he experimented with the exaggerated shapes and colors of expressionism, under the guidance of Piriya Krairerks, member of a family of Chakri courtiers and a student of Oskar Kokoschka. Some paintings from this period are psychological portraits with disturbing colors and shapes, evoking darkness and chaos. Others draw on the feverish intensity and blue moodiness of jazz. There is clear inspiration from Kokoschka and Edvard Munch, as well as Indonesia's Raden Basoeki Abdullah, a favorite of the king.

Although these paintings lack maturity, anyone who looks at them is prodded to imagine some dark torment or a beboplike fiendishness in the painter's soul. Sirikit is still pretty, but darkly so. Faces and bodies appear out of infernos. Nudes are ambiguously dangerous, surrounded in fiery reds and yellows. Others writhe in seductive dark green. One of the most memorable is *Forest Fire,* swirling with black-green and red waves of heat. Does the darkness of this later work reflect a deeply held pain or rage, as some Thais speculate? Angst hardly seems descriptive of Bhumibol, who from his youth was methodical and pragmatic. Even so, these paintings are a dark picture of the world. "Every artist has a feeling of being crammed in, and every artist wants to explode," the king reportedly once said.[2] He later told a visitor that he liked to paint when he was depressed or unhappy, and that he painted better when he was a little drunk.[3]

Bhumibol's greatest release from being "crammed in," however, was music. He spent so much time on it that the queen told an American reporter in 1960 that Bhumibol didn't need a harem. "For him, the orchestra is one big concubine."

Inspired by big-band leaders like Les Brown and Count Basie, Bhumibol took up composing songs when he was still in Switzerland. By 1960, there were some 60 official compositions by the king, including marches written for the armed forces, dixieland rags, and piano blues. All were simple, sweet, and sometimes forlorn melodies set to basic chords, often with lyrics written by Prince Chakraphan, Seni Pramoj, and some palace ladies. Because Bhumibol lacked arrangement skills, others like Seni scored them for bands and orchestras. Promoted by the palace, they became a staple of official bands and popular combos.

Even more ambitiously, one story has it, Bhumibol attempted to get famous European classical musicians to score some of his music.[4] For his visit to Austria in 1964, the government hired an Austrian professor to arrange the works for a performance in Vienna's concert hall. During the visit, Bhumibol became the first Asian to be named an honorary member of the Vienna Academy of Music.

Bhumibol found greater pleasure in playing music. The Aw Saw Band, formed in the early 1950s from obliging royals, military musicians, and the small community of nightclub professionals, played a couple nights a week, broadcasting live on the king's radio station on Fridays, with its signature tune the king's own "Friday Night Rag." The group also held Sunday jam sessions with invited musicians, and these sometimes also turned into radio concerts. Photos from the time show a jazzy-cool Bhumibol, in dark glasses with a saxophone hanging from his neck, clearly enjoying himself.

His larger ensemble, the Laicram band, had vocalists, often ladies of the palace, and matching uniforms. The group did radio concerts and performed in public, especially at universities in front of the assembled faculty and students. No driving big band in the Count Basie style, Laicram played syrupy Thai popular songs and Broadway musical tunes more than jazz. Even Bhumibol's own bluesy compositions came out sounding peculiarly Thai. And by some descriptions, a Laicram concert came across like a stiff royal ritual, with everything designed as an appreciation of the king and his family.[5] Professors, dignitaries, and honored visitors would sit formally across the stage rather than in the audience. At center stage would be the king and queen, sometimes with their children, and behind them sat the band. The programs could last four hours, each piece receiving a lengthy introduction by the king, with his thoughts on other subjects intertwined. To make a request, at the designated time students would creep forward, prostrate themselves in front of the sacral jazz king, begging beneath the dust of the dust of his feet to offer a song idea. A smoke-filled room of free-flowing improvisation and soulful blues this wasn't. Yet it served to bring the king and his younger subjects together over something they could share, music.

As the king found more talented musicians, his Aw Saw palace jam sessions became more frequent, sometimes happening four times a week. These gigs did feature jazz riffing and improvisation. The musicians would perform on air, have dinner, and then play privately well into the night, according to legend, often breaking only at dawn. With royal procedure minimized, and stoked by beer and whiskey and the king's favorite Lucky Strikes, the band went through a playlist of dixieland, blues, and swing standards. Like the expressionistic painting, playing around a simple dixieland melody required less discipline and technical ability, allowing the king to leap straight into his feelings and blow them out. Bhumibol, whose favorite musicians were Johnny Hodges and Benny Carter, flitted from clarinet to one sax and then another and back again.

As the "king of jazz," Bhumibol was invited to play whenever he went abroad. He played at embassy parties and receptions. And musicians visiting Thailand were inevitably summoned to the palace to jam with him. Already by the mid-1950s, in fact, Bhumibol's jazz obsession was such that it was considered a path to palace access. At the end of 1956 the U.S. government, which sponsored global tours of American musicians, had Benny Goodman and his combo stop in Thailand for the Constitution Fair week. Besides adding the king's compositions to his concert lineup, Goodman and his group played at the palace with the king while the queen danced along. Diplomats, said a report from Bangkok, commented that "there could be no better way of cementing friendly relations with King Bhumibol Adulyadej than for Benny to stay indefinitely."[6] This extended to popularizing the king's own compositions. In 1958 the U.S. government brought Jack Teagarden's jazz band to Bangkok. A year later Teagarden recorded Bhumibol's dixieland rag "When" on a live album.[7] In the 1960s bandleader Les Brown, likewise on a U.S. government tour, arranged the king's "HM Blues" (for both "His Majesty" and "Hungry Man") for the king.

The king tried in vain to make his children as enthusiastic about jazz as he was. He provided them instruments and teachers, and put them on stage in Laicram performances. Photographs show the young crown prince struggling with a big saxophone, and Chulabhorn singing meekly in front of thousands of students. But none caught the bug. Nor was the country infected by his enthusiasm for swing and dixieland. Like people everywhere else in the 1960s, Thais preferred Elvis Presley and the Beatles. Bhumibol scorned the Beatles, telling an interviewer in 1967: "They are through. You know, they were really a part of the British drive for exports."[8]

With music so important in Bhumibol's life, was the king as good as his official reputation had it?

His compositional talents were very limited. His simple melodies are pleasant and almost memorable, and he could clearly shape a song to an identifiable style—foxtrot or waltz or ragtime blues. But his inability to arrange them, or offer harmonies and counterpoint, or insert rhythmic shifts, left them without depth. With a little arranging they were playable, as Jack Teagarden demonstrated with "When." But none were particularly memorable, except that, even to this day, they are played so constantly in Thailand on television and radio, in shopping malls, movie theaters, and concerts, that residents can't help but hum and whistle them—without even knowing the composer.

As an instrumentalist, assessing his skill is difficult because recordings of his palace sessions and concerts are nearly impossible to access. For a king so well promoted, surprisingly, there aren't any publicly available recordings of his musicianship. But from the comments of some of those who have heard him play, and from one rarely seen filmed performance, the faults of very limited formal study are manifest.[9] Although able on clarinet and saxophones, and secondarily trumpet, guitar, piano, and organ, Bhumibol never had much training, or the experience of playing in a band as an equal under a demanding leader and being forced to repeat exercises and scored parts day in and day out to perfection.

As a king beyond criticism, Bhumibol developed as a soloist, and one imagines that he played along with recordings a lot. Swing and dixieland jazz, like the Aw Saw standards "When You're Smiling" and "C Jam Blues," suit this perfectly. They required everyone to play a basic melody in unison, and then turn to lengthy solo breaks, ending up in one cacophonous climax with everyone playing around the melody. Such a structure was not complex, progressive, or technically demanding. Indeed, according to some who played with him, Bhumibol took little interest in the more challenging and abstract jazz of the period, like the music of Charlie Parker, John Coltrane, or Miles Davis.

This was all evident in a performance of three songs by the Aw Saw Friday group filmed in 1964.[10] Two of the six band members are professionals, the others well-trained amateurs. The first song, "Autumn Leaves," quickly makes it clear that Bhumibol, playing baritone and alto saxes, is the least skilled in the group. His tone is clear and he hits no sour notes, but his solos are rambling and dull, without beginning or end. There is no crispness or stylistic phrasing, no change of pace, almost as if he never heard himself play. It is hard to find the influence of Hodges or Carter. It is the same for the next two songs, "Them There Eyes" and "Isle of Capri," both performed with Thai vocalists who themselves lack any feel for the genre. Bhumibol switches to clarinet and remains noticeably the poorer of the instrumentalists. The other sax-and-clarinet man in the band, even as he plays with demurring restraint, is clearly far better.

The point of such criticism is not to be uncharitable, but only to indicate the vast gap between reality and King Bhumibol's intensely palace-promoted image as a jazz legend. Moreover, whatever his skill, there is no denying Bhumibol's immense pleasure in jazz, undiminished even today. He is an avid collector of recordings, and through the 1990s the Aw Saw group remained a jam session on call, subject to preferred hours from evening deep into the early morning. It has always been his greatest escape from his job, his minders and supplicants, and the weight of the Thai cosmos.

Two other early hobbies bear mentioning. First was Bhumibol's interest in radio, which began in Switzerland. In Bangkok, in addition to his palace commercial station, Bhumibol was provided the most current short-wave and long-wave equipment to listen to police and military broadcasts and international transmissions. By the 1960s he had lined his personal offices with numerous such radios. Like photography, it became a tool of work: a way to eavesdrop on the rest of the world and hopefully understand what really went on, what people really thought.

The second of these hobbies was range shooting. He practiced with pistols and rifles regularly at the Hua Hin BPP camp, learning to handle various modern combat weapons. In the late 1960s shooting became a pastime he was able to pass on, with more success than jazz, to Prince Vajiralongkorn. Despite his single useful eye, the king's small-arms skill was apparently appreciable, though maybe not as great as a U.S. army officer recalled: he said that in the early 1970s, at the Lopburi army base shooting range, Bhumibol calmly shot a 93 out of a possible 100, at 200 meters distance. If true, he might have been on the national shooting team.[11]

Bhumibol didn't spend this period only indulging his hobbies. He was always deeply earnest about serving the people as Thailand's king, and from the late 1950s he took interest in the relief and rural development projects being carried out in his name. As they expanded, these projects would be shaped into the most prominent facet of Bhumibol's reputation as a great king.

Even as it expanded quickly, the monarchy's spending on charity and disaster relief in the 1950s was fairly small compared with the government's. In the country-side the king and queen distributed food, medicine, and other health-related items, like mosquito nets to protect against malaria and blankets against the cold. When people lost homes in village fires, they donated household necessities and support for rebuilding. But the strong palace media promotion in the 1960s, and the mechanism of the magic circle of merit, helped expand these works. The more money the people saw the king turn over for social needs, the more they were willing to give him, in exchange for a share of his great merit.

The impact of royal charity became sizable. During a cholera outbreak in 1958–59, King Bhumibol collected 884,000 baht (U.S.$44,200) for victims over a few days. In October 1962, after a huge storm wrecked great swaths of southern Thailand, he raised 10.8 million baht. As the sums grew, the palace created formal bodies to manage the collection and distribution of charity funds. The surplus from the 1962 collection became seed money for an ongoing disaster relief opera-tion, the Rajaprachanugroh Foundation. Bhumibol also created a scholarship fund in the name of his brother, the Ananda Mahidol Foundation, to finance study abroad for the brightest of Thai students.

Driven by the public's desire to partake in the king's sacral generosity, the collections and disbursements of these operations grew exponentially for years. The Rajaprachanugroh Foundation built assets eventually estimated in the hun-dreds of millions of baht. As the Ananda scholarship became known as the king-dom's most prestigious academic award, money flowed in from individuals and companies entrusting their own scholarships to the Ananda foundation to admin-ister. Awardees got to meet the king, creating a bond of loyalty between the throne and the kingdom's best minds.

But Bhumibol wanted to get his own hands dirty in the development of his kingdom. His efforts in fighting poverty and championing development, what were eventually called the Royal Projects, came to form the core of his reputation and the way he most sought to identify his reign. Official accounts have the king leaping headfirst into combating rural poverty, and especially fostering water resources development, as soon as he occupied the throne in 1951. The mythology even goes so far as to say Bhumibol was born with a hydrological bent, predestined to develop sustainable water supplies for all his people, not unlike the Hindu devaraja as source of life and fertility to the land.[12]

In fact, the king did little that early. Probably the first effort he was associated with was fish farming. At the beginning of the 1950s, the UN's Food and Agriculture

Organization was promoting freshwater aquaculture around the world, focused on the easy-to-raise tilapia genus. By the time Bhumibol returned from Switzerland, hundreds of Thai farmers were raising tilapia.[13] In May 1953 the Food and Agriculture Organization and government fisheries officials presented the king with 2,800 fingerlings to raise in a Hua Hin palace pool. A few months later, in honor of the first anniversary of Prince Vajiralongkorn's birth, some 65,000 tilapia were distributed to farmers in Hua Hin and elsewhere by fisheries officials. This led, years later, to the king being credited with introducing tilapia to the country.

Bhumibol also took an interest in artificial rainmaking during the 1950s, coaxed by friend and Agriculture Ministry official M.R. Theparit Devakul, a member of a venerable inner-court family. As the ministry allocated only a very small budget for rainmaking research, Theparit evidently got additional funds from the king.[14] Little came of it until the early 1960s, when the United States offered more substantial funds for experimentation. The U.S. government was dubious of the potential benefits; cloud seeding was a new and expensive science, with very mixed results. But because of the king's enthusiasm, an American official later suggested, the government decided to fund it anyway: the program involved the king in development efforts, which was important in fighting communism.[15]

By the beginning of the 1960s, the king himself understood the links between poverty and domestic insecurity. He latched on to two popular concepts of the time: the Green Revolution's increase of food production with improved plant hybrids; and the presumed link between dairy product consumption and the healthy development of children. With Theparit, he set up an experimental rice farm inside the walls of Chitrlada Palace. It was redundant to government rice research ongoing for decades, but the palace paddy served to teach the king about the primary occupation of half of his subjects.

Bhumibol's second project had its conception in a visit by Danish officials in 1960 and the king's own visit to Denmark later that year. The Danes were pursuing a large joint venture with the Agriculture Ministry to develop milk production, which eventually became the semi-monopoly Thai-Danish Dairy Farm. To get the support of the king—whom they knew had grown up drinking milk, unlike most Thais—they set up a mini-dairy in the palace with five cows and a bull. This became the Chitrlada Milk Project, providing milk to the children in the Chitrlada School.

For a third early project at Chitrlada, Bhumibol planted some 1,250 seedlings of the towering forest dipterocarp *ton yang*. Although the forestry department was already propagating the species, his project made the king out as a pioneer of conservation, which was an important Buddhist virtue.

Bhumibol's interest in water problems came somewhat later. The $100-million Yanhee multipurpose dam project in Tak province, built in the late 1950s, was renamed the Bhumibol dam and reservoir. Aside from christening Yanhee, however, Bhumibol had little to do with it. Afterward, all large hydropower projects were named to honor, and by implication to credit, the royal family.[16] The king's first real work in water problems grew out of visits to the villages around Hua Hin. There he was exposed to the constant struggle Thai farmers had with geography and the elements. Much of the country, especially the northeast and the upper south, which included Hua Hin, was dry as desert for half of the year. In areas of the northeast, in some years no rain fell. And outside the fertile central plains, soils were often parched and unable to hold moisture.

Such a place was the isolated scrubland of Hup Kapong, about 20 kilometers from Klai Kangwon palace. The soil was very bad and water supplies were uneven. Local peasants struggled to farm rice, vegetables, and various palm tree fruits. Land tenancy was high and productivity was low, and to eat, the residents relied on collecting forest products.

In 1963 the king got BPP soldiers to bulldoze roads into Hup Kapong and build a small reservoir. This was no revolutionary idea; with UN support the Phibun and Sarit governments had built hundreds of small reservoirs and catchments around the country. But those efforts reached only a few among thousands of villages generally ignored by Bangkok. Without the king's attention Hup Kapong probably would have remained unchanged for another decade or two. Instead, with more regular water, farming supplies from the king, and intensified attention from officials, the lives of the residents began to change. It also changed Bhumibol. Hup Kapong showed that with a little effort he could have a positive impact on his people's lives.

Another early effort was the interest the king and his mother, Princess Mother Sangwal, took in the country's upland minorities, known as the hill tribes. There were some 200,000 people belonging to the Akha, Hmong, Karen, Shan, and other ethnic groups scattered in the mountains of the northern and western border areas. Scorned by most Thais and bound by tradition and poverty, they were deprived of the government's educational, health, and other social services. Many farmed opium poppies to sell to lowland Thai traders. In the 1950s, the BPP created a string of posts in hill-tribe villages to monitor border security, and in a handful of places it also built rudimentary schools. The BPP hoped to foster some integration, but more important to forestall communists who, it was believed, aimed to exploit Thailand's minorities. This program received a boost in the early 1960s when the

United States pinpointed the hill tribes as a source of intelligence and manpower for the Cold War.

Around the same time, the royal family began taking regular trips to the northern capital Chiangmai, where the Thai army built a new palace, Phuping, on Doi Suthep. Taking an interest in the hill tribes in the area, in 1963 the king and queen sponsored the construction of several small schoolhouses using public donations. In 1964, Sangwal, who still spent most of the year in Lausanne but had begun to pass the winters in crisp Chiangmai, began focused efforts to help the area's hill-tribe population. Supported by the BPP, she sponsored new schools and health clinics in upland villages, coaxing money from the government and public donations. Eventually, as an extension of the king's munificence, she became a patron of both the BPP and the hill tribes.

What the royal family spent on development and relief was still small compared with what the government spent, and also with U.S. social welfare spending in Thailand. Yet because of the publicity given the king's work, people in distress directed their hopes toward the king and Rajaprachanugroh, as they had in the time of the absolute monarchy. When the government itself funded palace efforts, the throne garnered the credit. The result was to create an intimate bond between the king and his people that the government and politicians found difficult to replicate.

One area of Bhumibol's personal development in the late 1950s and early 1960s related more directly to his image as a sacral dhammaraja. This was his deeper exploration of his own spirituality. In the Sukhothai tradition, royal power rests on the dhammaraja's perceived deeper grasp of the truths and mysteries of the universe, and of the conscious and subconscious. This indication of at least incipient enlightenment underlies the sovereign's omniscience.

Bhumibol's inner development was guided by the monk who had chaperoned him through his 1956 novitiate, Phra Yanasangworn. Because of this association, in 1961, at a relatively young age, Yanasangworn became abbot at Wat Bovornives, the Chakri family temple. The two met often, and through Socratic-style teaching Yanasangworn coaxed Bhumibol through the meanings of dhamma and pure practice, life and morality. This likely inspired the king's own habit of discussing deep issues in an elliptical way that, as with a high monk, tries to elicit from listeners the realization of truth without spelling it out. The technique itself was evidence of having grasped the essence of dhamma.

Later Yanasangworn instructed the king in vipassana insight meditation, a path to enlightenment that didn't require renouncing the world and going into seclusion.[17] This was apt for the busy king. Bhumibol could progress while still performing his regal duties. He was said to advance very quickly—naturally, for a dhammaraja. None of this was overtly publicized, but Thais in elite circles learned that the two men had deeply penetrated dhamma, and they too flocked to see the Bovornives abbot and take up vipassana. Setting trends in religious practice was another sign of an enlightened figure.

More visibly, Bhumibol associated himself with the most sacral Buddhist icons, monks, and places of Thailand. He visited non-royal temples with special holy characteristics and contacted obscure older monks who stood out for their teachings or their alleged special or magic powers. People were impressed that Bhumibol was aware of these men, who often were known only in the immediate area of their temples, or only by the sangha cognoscenti. It demonstrated his omniscience while seeming to confirm the monks' abilities, a two-way amplification of virtue.

Yanasangworn took Bhumibol beyond mainstream Thai Theravada practices to the mysteries of *samadhi* concentration meditation. Samadhi is a path to personal psychic conquest, said to sometimes bring practitioners supernatural experiences. Only the most advanced monks could understand and achieve samadhi. Unqualified to teach the king himself, in the 1960s Yanasangworn invited to Bangkok three of the most famous disciples of Acharn (teacher) Man, a storied ascetic monk from the northeast who was renowned for profound knowledge and technique in both vipassana and samadhi.[18] After his death in 1949, a devotional movement elevated him to an *arhat,* a Buddhist saint.

Bhumibol built special residences inside the palace walls for the three disciples to live, and he studied and meditated with them frequently, especially with a favorite, Acharn Fan. The royal family made a pilgrimage to the monastery in Sakhon Nakhon where Acharn Man died, and the king undertook joint ritual acts with Man's students, like making amulets with the royal cipher on them. These observances reinforced Bhumibol's reputation as a pioneer in spiritual knowledge and practice. As they learned of his patronage of the Acharn Man tradition, others from the court and then the social and political elite likewise made pilgrimages and pursued study with students of Acharn Man.[19]

The king went even further, it is said. Having exhausted the knowledge and experiences of Thai Buddhism, Yanasangworn reportedly invited for him a Tibetan lama teacher of more esoteric tantric meditation. Such experiences were completely unattainable to nearly all Thais, and so displayed the king's spiritual reach as that of a true bodhisattva-to-be. Bhumibol, insiders understood and gossiped, was indeed the kingdom's most spiritually advanced figure.

Because Bhumibol's spiritual achievements couldn't be declared outright, the palace stepped up the ritual activities that served as indicators. This began soon after Sarit took power in 1957. The most obvious change was the revival of the grand royal barge procession for the king's annual kathin to Wat Arun in both 1959 and 1961. Because the spectacle had been absent for 25 years, few Thais had ever seen the colorful display of dozens of long, narrow rivercraft trimmed in gold and decorated with mythical beasts, each rowed by oarsmen chanting paeans to the dhammaraja. The barges projected the king's wealth, refinement, and power.

Turning Bhumibol's birthday into a national holiday during the same period allowed the organization of mass gatherings to honor him in a religious way, with merit-making and candle lighting. This was further exaggerated with the 1963 observation of the king's 36th birthday, his auspicious third 12-year cycle. The Brahman rites performed on this occasion had rarely if ever been seen, and indeed were never performed again in such a manner. The day began with the king giving alms to monks and prayers to the dynasty, followed by an elaborate public bathing of purification attended by Brahman priests and high princes. Afterward, Bhumibol was dressed in royal regalia, plus a jeweled cowboylike hat and his cool dark glasses, and was carried on a hand-borne open palanquin through the Bangkok streets.

Another way of projecting the idea of the king's advanced sacrality was his production of holy icons identified with himself. Thai Buddhists elevate their own sense of grace by collecting icons, medallions, and statues. Especially popular are pocket-sized amulets, usually an impression of the Buddha or a famous monk, and identified with a specific trait, like luck, protection, or fertility. They are often worn on gold necklaces or carried around in purses. Such icons are sought avidly by collectors, feeding a speculative trade that can elevate the cost of a valued piece to thousands of dollars. Recognizing this, monks and temples produce amulets and statues as a means of raising funds; the more famous the monk, the more saleable the piece.

As he visited temples around the country, Bhumibol regularly joined local monks in casting new statues and medallions, which then became highly sought after. In 1965, he began making his own icons.[20] The first was a bronze Sukhothai-style seated Buddha figure, 32 centimeters tall. It copied a statue minted to honor his reign at Wat Thewasangkaram in Kanchanaburi, the original home temple of Phra Yanasangworn. Two changes were made. One was to add in gold the official cipher of the Ninth Reign, which is crowned with the radiating white beams of light, *rassami,* commonly seen over the Buddha's head representing wisdom and purity. The second was to inscribe it in both Pali and modern Thai to read, "The Thai people can preserve Thai-ness by consciously striving for unity."[21] This became a principal icon of the reign, to be used, a government publication said, "for personal worship by the Thai people."[22]

In 1966 Bhumibol minted a slightly smaller bronze statue, again a seated Sukhothai-style form, in the position known as Buddha subduing Mara, the representation of evil. It was named Buddha Navarajabophit, or "The Buddha of the Holy Ninth Reign." This suggested Bhumibol as a Buddha-king who repels danger. Although these were stylistic copies of traditional images, the statues were said to incorporate Bhumibol's own personal artistic and spiritual ideas. The ability to adapt and refine religious icons, like scripture, signaled sacral virtuosity.

Attached to each of these statues was an amulet the size of a silver dollar featuring a seated Buddha image that the king had also created in 1965. As a government publication describes it, the king "used a special mixture of auspicious and consecrated materials to make the amulets," including flowers from garlands the king had placed next to the Emerald Buddha; the king's own hair, trimmed by Brahman priests; petals from garlands that had hung on the king's umbrella and sword on the Coronation Day anniversary; dried paint from the king's paintings; and pitch and paint from the king's handmade sailboat. The materials were blended and cast into the small votive tablets by the hundreds, which were then handed out to palace favorites and top government and military officials. Recipients were instructed to adhere a piece of gold leaf to the backs of the amulets, as well as the larger statues, an act of self-abnegating anonymity in merit-making. Only those crudely desiring recognition put gold leaf on the front of an image. This was to become a key message of the king: to work earnestly without desire for recognition.

The king's amulets rose quickly in appeal and value. They garnered names that reflected the image of the king: the venerable monklike title Luang Pho Chitrlada (the Old Holy Father of Chitrlada Palace), and Phra Kamlang Phaendin, the lord who gives strength to the kingdom.

Family life, and family image, filled out the roster of activities for Bhumibol in the years up to the mid-1960s. At ever more official audiences, charity balls, and social events, he and Sirikit together struck a handsome sight, although she grabbed most of the attention. Vivacious and fashionable, the queen was a constant feature in the Thai media, appearing on nearly every women's magazine cover at least once a year.

On one side she was portrayed as a model wife and mother, able to cook and clean for her man and her children while looking beautiful in a simple dress, like her modified traditional silk sarong and blouse. At the same time, she was the focus of high society, brightening parties in expensive jewelry and lavish French dresses by Pierre Balmain and Madame Carven. On state visits she won the world over, alternating between stylish modern suits, with gloves, hats, and pearl chokers, and luxurious evening gowns and furs. She became known as Asia's Jackie Kennedy, and in 1965 she topped the list of the world's best-dressed women. The impression the royal couple made was far from frivolous. Thai Buddhist culture peculiarly relates fame and beauty to merit, so, elegant and celebrated worldwide, Bhumibol and Sirikit clearly had a great stock of karma.

Bhumibol was also an interested and even doting father to his four children. Palace photographs show the king on the floor with Ubolrat and Vajiralongkorn playing with toy cars, stringing a kite for them, holding and embracing them. Still, Thais leave the job of child raising almost completely to mothers, aunts, maids, and other women. If Bhumibol hoped to give his children some of the normalcy and discipline of his own upbringing, it was a losing battle. With all the indulging caretakers, they could hardly avoid being spoiled. Prince Vajiralongkorn later recalled that at 12 he couldn't tie his own shoes, for they were always tied for him.

What the public saw in palace-issued photographs and movies, however, was a dhammaraja king who, besides all his other incredible talents, was a caring, sensitive patriarch of his handsome family. The Mahidols were a metaphor for the nation.

There was one real problem in this picture, theoretically at least. When she was born in 1957, Princess Chulabhorn proved to be the last of the king and queen's children. At 25, Sirikit inexplicably stopped having babies. Four children was a respectable-sized family, but in this case there was only one son, one qualified heir to the Chakri throne. It left the dynasty at a huge risk. In the six decades since Chulalongkorn had produced his 32nd son, almost all the possible lines of succession had hit dead ends. Prince Varananda Dhavaj, born to celestial Prince Chutadhuj but passed over for the throne in 1925 and again in 1935, had married an English woman, disqualifying their two children from succession. Varananda divorced and later married the king's sister, Princess Galyani, a good dynastic strategy, but the couple never had any children. Galyani herself had only a daughter by her own first husband, a commoner.

Chulalongkorn's son Prince Paripatra left one son, Prince Chumbhotpong or Chumbhot, by his first, royal-blooded wife. Chumbhot however, had only one daughter by his royal wife before he died, in 1959. Paripatra's second wife, a commoner, also gave him a son, Prince Sukhumbhinanda, who could have been promoted into the line of succession if necessary. Sukhumbhinanda's wife, though, was also a commoner, leaving their sons, M.R. Sukhumbhand, born in 1953, and M.R. Vararos, born in 1959, as distant options for succession.

The shortage of royal heirs meant that, if Vajiralongkorn died young, the dynasty risked a massive succession crisis involving the numerous ambitious families descended from the Fourth Reign. So it was odd that Bhumibol and Sirikit would stop having children in 1957 with only one son. Possibly Sirikit simply decided that she was tired. Yet it would have been a decision the whole court objected to, though maybe not the king. Her relatives also would have pressured her as the one responsible for the Kitiyakara family's dynastic position.

Another plausible explanation is that physical problems prevented Sirikit from having children again. If so, there were no public revelations. Perhaps, too, the practical-minded Bhumibol himself decided that four children was enough. But again, there was the unshirkable mission of securing the dynasty. The issue is never discussed, at least in public, but it is crucial. The problem of the king's having only one son would become obvious to all by the early 1970s.

The point raises another question, which is whether Bhumibol ever had other women. His ancestors kept enormous harems, and Thai culture accepted, especially among the elite, men having second and third wives or concubines. A number of men in the king's circle made little effort to hide their mistresses. Sirikit's father and grandfather, as well as Prince Bhanuband, were all famous for their many women. It would have been inevitable between jazz numbers and sailing races that talk among the king and his chums turned to women. On the other hand, Bhumibol's uncle King Prajadhipok was monogamous to a fault, leaving no heirs, and Bhumibol's father was too. In addition, the Swiss environment Bhumibol grew up in frowned on extramarital relations.

Thai tradition accepted that powerful men should have their sexual needs freely gratified. Women offered up themselves or their daughters to enhance their own status. Sometimes a powerful man's wife would herself select the mistresses, so that she could retain control over her household. Without a doubt, it wasn't long after Bhumibol returned to Thailand before women were offered to him, attractive and educated women, by their families and by themselves. The Thai royal circle repeats numerous such stories. But how the young king responded is one of the palace's most tightly held secrets. Did he indulge in one of the great fantasies of kingship?

Some say that he had at least one discreet affair over a lengthy time with an unidentified woman from the court circle in the 1960s. Others say there were several affairs, though again no names are available. In addition there are two rumors that spread in the 1970s and featured in later Communist Party of Thailand (CPT) propaganda. The first had it that Queen Sirikit gave her own younger sister, Busba, to the king. Two years younger than Sirikit, Busba was a palace fixture, and in 1957 she remained unmarried. If the rumor was true, it wouldn't have been surprising. Many kings, including Chulalongkorn, made queens of several sisters. Bhumibol might have done it both for pleasure and to strengthen Sirikit's dynastic mission. If Busba bore the king a son, it would have ensured the Kitiyakara family's position in Chakri posterity.

Around the very end of 1957—five months after Sirikit had her last child—Busba became pregnant with no publicly recognized suitor. Four months into her pregnancy she suddenly married M.L. Thavisan Laddawal, a palace adviser who later became the king's personal private secretary. Their marriage and Busba's giving birth to a daughter in September 1958 made the rumor of Bhumibol's involvement moot—neither mother nor child had any impact on the royal succession. He never displayed any paternal attitude toward the girl. Busba and Thavisan had no more children and divorced a few years later.

The second story repeated in CPT propaganda was of the king's affair with the exceedingly beautiful Thai woman who captured the Miss Universe title in 1965, Apasara Hongsakul. She was said to have been presented to Bhumibol by her father, Air Chief Marshal Harin Hongsakul, or by Queen Sirikit. But the official record doesn't reveal any more. Apasara married Sirikit's cousin M.R. Kiartiguna Kitiyakara in 1968, and a year later she gave birth to a boy, M.L. Rungkhun. Ever since, Rungkhun has had no obvious connections to the palace. He apparently was sent to study abroad, and not long after returning to Thailand as a teen he disappeared into a monastery. Those who entertain the idea of a Bhumibol-Apasara relationship note the tradition of rival heirs to the throne, like Mongkut in 1824, donning a monk's robes for safety.

Ultimately there is no proof that the king ever took a lover outside his marriage to Sirikit. Nothing has ever blemished the public picture of a happily married, monogamous royal couple.

Although they were not particularly extravagant, the activities of King Bhumibol and the Mahidol family did cost money. Thanks to the palace administrative and financial manager Thawiwong Thawalyasak, however, there was no shortfall in the

1960s. The palace became sophisticated and even innovative at bringing in money. Collecting funds for palace charities became an important part of royal activities. With the expansion of royal culture, class-conscious aristocrats and businessmen gave regularly to the throne, like a tithe. Business associations also made frequent large donations. When the king and queen returned from Europe in January 1961, the Thai Bankers Association handed them 100,000 baht, for example, and foreign banks donated another 50,000.

To encourage them, the palace awarded the biggest donors from commerce and industry the king's royal symbol, the *karut*, or garuda, in Hindu mythology a half-man half-eagle figure that carries the god Vishnu. Between 1954 and 1961 only eight companies received the garuda, with most of them already having palace ties. From 1963 to 1973, 22 more, mostly unconnected to royalty, received the royal garuda mark to post above their doors and place on their letterhead. Recipients included the biggest Sino-Thai businesses, like Bangkok Bank, which could now suggest they had the dhammaraja's endorsement and trust.

Palace receipts rose as more wealthy business families enjoyed royally sponsored marriages and earned royal decorations. Reported donations doubled from 1963 to 1965, when the king took in nearly eight million baht. This was still small compared with the big pools of money that Sino-Thai tycoons, top generals, and some politicians had access to. Thawiwong took the palace to their level by the mid-1960s by recovering prewar royal properties into Mahidol hands, and by positioning the family and the Crown Property Bureau in finance and industry just as the economy took off on the huge influx of American money and military forces.

A crucial gain was made when Sarit restored to the palace official ownership of the scores of properties occupied by the bureaucracy and claimed as government possessions after 1932. The ministries lining the grand boulevard of Rajadamnoen Road in the old city now paid rent, albeit a nominal amount, to the throne. The expanding economy allowed Thawiwong to raise rents on crown-owned real estate. It also generated greater dividends from the throne's business assets, particularly Siam Cement, the leading construction materials group, the now-large Siam Commercial Bank, and holdings in insurance, trading, and agribusiness. Palace real estate was made available for joint-venture developments, including several top-flight hotels like the Siam Intercontinental, the Erawan, and the Dusit Thani.

With both connections and cash, the CPB became the choice partner for domestic and foreign investors entering the Thai market. The bureau formed joint ventures with Firestone Tires, banks and insurance companies, and the leading Thai textiles manufacturer (and perhaps the largest single employer), Sukree

Bodiratanagura. By the late 1960s, the CPB had 500 staff members to oversee its investment and property portfolio, as much as the smaller banks.

Thawiwong's work acknowledged the shift in economic power from princes and aristocrats to a much more powerful community of mostly Sino-Thai capitalists like Sukree. By sharing the palace's protective cloak and capital in exchange for a share of profits, he created new allies. He also made allies of the large community of small traders: typically the CPB, owning thousands of shophouses in the old city occupied by Chinese merchants, kept its rents well below market prices, sometimes so low that the tenants relet the properties to others at market rates. It may have robbed the palace of potential profits, but it rendered the beneficiaries dependent on the throne for theirs.

The palace also effectively subsidized the two elite recreation clubs in central Bangkok, the Royal Bangkok Sports Club and the Royal Turf Club. Both operated as exclusive sports, golf, and horse racing clubs for the rich, the titled, and the powerful (the Turf Club more for the military), and both were on royal property leased for a pittance. At both as well, untaxed backroom betting operations on horse races dwarfed the official tote, while enriching club management and membership, invariably the aristocratic and military elite. Similarly run by the military, the city's two heavily gambling oriented Thai kick-boxing stadiums were also on extremely cheap crown land.

By putting most of the business through faceless institutions like the CPB, Siam Commercial Bank, and Siam Cement, Thawiwong ensured that few people took notice of this growing business group. He was wary of the dhammaraja being seen as a grasping capitalist. Instead, the king appeared wholly disinterested, involved only in distributing the proceeds for his subjects' benefit. The Mahidol family did reveal capitalist ambitions underpinned by economic nationalism when it ambitiously tried to start an airline, Air Siam, in 1965. The decade-long struggle to make it work would provide the family a tough lesson about modern business.

The amulets made by Bhumibol demonstrated how popular culture, religion, and the king's hobbies could be used to build his stature. Another innovative program combined with subtle brilliance ritual, sangha politics, capitalism, and development to spread the king's aura into the countryside, all the while raising money for the palace. This was the extension of the royal kathin ritual into the kingdom's hinterlands. The annual kathin was traditionally a community rite of presenting robes and other necessities to the monks of their local temple at the end of phansa, the Buddhist Lent. It confirmed the intimate ties between villagers and their local temple.

The royal kathin was traditionally performed by the royal family at only the 18 first-rank royal temples, nearly all in Bangkok. The king did the three most important temples and deputized other royal family members to perform the ceremony in his name at the others. The king could also make a *kathin ton,* a private kathin to non-royal temples. In the early 1960s Bhumibol undertook several such kathins to the temples of prominent conservative monks outside Bangkok, for instance, in October 1963 at Yanasangworn's first temple residence, Wat Thewasangkaram. In October 1966 he performed a private kathin at Bangkok's Wat Sutthiworaram, a favorite of privy councilor Sridharmadibes and attended mainly by ethnic Chinese.

The kathin season lasts only several days, however, and the Mahidol family couldn't cover very many temples. Some royals would carry out the kathin at second- and third-class royal temples. But there were scores of them, most very distant from the capital, where few of Bangkok's elite wanted to travel. They disdained the local people and feared for their own personal safety in far-flung areas like the northeast. Moreover, undertaking a kathin required money. Addressing the issue brought together Thawiwong, the education minister Pin Malakul, and his religious affairs chief Pin Muthukan, a conservative former military officer. They came up with a scheme to farm out the royal kathin to these lesser royal temples to wealthy non-royal Thais willing to spend their own money to advance royal prestige in exchange for palace connections and a share of royal merit.[23]

Selected carefully by bureaucrats in the religious affairs department and the palace, these proxies would deliver the king's kathin offerings, robes, and other gifts at remote temples. The ceremony pulled the temples and villages into the throne's orbit, demonstrating the palace's attentiveness in contrast to the government's lack of care. There was also a momentary injection of cash into the village by a visiting Bangkok entourage, whose members were compelled to improve village clinics or schools and donate cash to the temple, all in the king's name. Under the dynamics of the magic circle of merit, the king's kathin surrogates would accrue substantial merit for performing the ceremony on his behalf. At least some people found it could be worked into their own capitalist strategies. Bangkok Bank made it a core of its expansion in Isan. The bank cleverly offered to sponsor the ritual at selected northeastern towns where it was opening branches. Through the kathin, the bank could attract the temple's deposits—usually the largest in any community—and also impress potential customers that it was part of the king's circle. With the royal kathin as a key element in its strategy, over a decade Bangkok Bank would come to dominate the northeastern market.

The surrogate royal kathin wasn't supposed to be commercialized. But the religious affairs officials accepted that, without cost to the palace, more communities were being pulled into the king's cosmos. In the often rebellious northeast, especially, it helped orient the people's allegiance toward the king. A leading development economist of the time, Sunthorn Hongladarom, later told an interviewer that "*kathin prarachathan* [the royal kathin] was part of economic planning, part of developing the countryside."[24]

By the mid-1960s, King Bhumibol's prestige was greater than that of any king since Chulalongkorn. Without challenging the official constitutional, democratic basis of the country—and anyway in the mid-1960s there was still no constitution or elected parliament—the king was set out as an alternative leader, one with virtue and true insight, a Sukhothai-style dhammaraja. As an incipient bodhisattva, a handsome modern family man, an internationally recognized statesman, an artist and musician, a generous protector of his poorest subjects, a partner of industrialists and traders, and a pioneer of development, he became bigger than government, and the public became his real legitimizing force.

David Wyatt has described the 1960s as the period of bourgeoisation of Thai monarchy.[25] Charmed by royal culture and disgruntled by the dominance of corrupt generals and businessmen, Thais learned to look to the throne for respite, inspiration, and actual leadership. More and more Thais sought out Bhumibol and Sirikit with petitions for help, for money, and to heal their illnesses. Increasingly, the king substituted for the government in social welfare, both in the imagination of the people and somewhat in reality. This further propelled the king's charities, the circulation of merit, and the kathin sponsorships, a phenomenon that Christine Gray has called a new "civic religion": " 'Sacrifice to the nation' through private support of schools and hospitals was portrayed as a form of religious purification. The king and the royal charities were hailed as exemplars of this religion: inspired by the king's selfless behavior, ordinary citizens, rich and poor, would donate money to the royal charities."[26]

The new royalism was reinforced by snubbing and intimidating nonbelievers. The palace shunned anyone not expressing unqualified monarchism. It chose its associations, for instance rural temples and monks, for their potential to further advance dhammaraja culture. Mahanikay temples allied with the anti-palace monk Phimontham were bypassed for their rivals, especially in the surrogate royal kathins.

Beginning with Sarit, too, a generation of liberal political and social scientists were forced from academia or simply hushed for questioning royalism. It made educators docile loyal subjects and killed any debate over the throne's political and social role. This stifling of dissident views was enforced by the increased use of lèse-majesté allegations and formal charges. Showing how sacral all things royal had become, lèse-majesté was even alleged, though never formally charged, when the Paris newspaper *France Soir* discussed Queen Sirikit's personal measurements in a piece on her new Pierre Balmain swimsuit.

What isn't clear is the effect that all this promotion of the monarchy had on the king himself. Somewhere along the line Bhumibol became a true believer in the Chakri dhammaraja mythology and in himself as embodying it. This elemental transformation would have him take as his model his great-grandfather King Mongkut, who, in the official history, had combined the best of traditional dhammaraja attributes with modernist insight, all accrued from his years in study as a monk.

Likewise, Bhumibol in the 1960s began to display confidence in his superior insight into his kingdom, his people, and the world. He understood the power and use of his position, his accumulated prestige, and Buddhist symbolism. He had learned to look at visitors intently, piercingly, radiating a concentration that stilled Thais and foreigners alike and reinforced royal protocol. He queried visitors sharply, demonstrating that he knew the subject at hand and that no pertinent information should be kept from him. He learned to speak in Thai without referring to himself, never using the first person and rarely the second or third, leveling all of his statements with a measure of ambiguity as well as evoking the semi-deity of his position. (In English he spoke more directly.) It was a technique he learned from European royals, said one foreign official, making him both engaging and imposing.

His consciousness of this powerful ambiguity was clear in an interview he gave to America's *Look* magazine in 1967. The king answered questions about his archaic royal rituals by combining a modern, rationalist explanation with hints that mystical forces were also at work. At one point he explained what was done with the water used in his seasonal ritual bathing of the Emerald Buddha.[27]

> It becomes holy water. . . . I decided that the people outside, the ordinary people, would believe the water would bring them goodness, and they would look upon the ceremony as more than an honor. For if you believe the water will do you good, it will do you good.
>
> The first time, a taximan told his friend that I had given him the holy water. His friend would not believe a king had done that! But I had sprin-

kled him, and he was happy. The honor—it is nothing. It is just the happiness that is important, and that man had the feeling that he was pure and good. . . .

You saw the ceremony. Who was there? Men, women, children, tourists, and taximen. Everyone was free to come and go. When your president came to Thailand, there were many FBI men and security men around us, and you couldn't walk. . . . Anyone can petition me. . . . [A]nyone can see me if he has a good interest in his heart.

And, showing that he understood likewise how to define all this in more palatable modern terms for the unknowing West, Bhumibol added: "I am really an elected king. If the people do not want me, they can throw me out, eh? Then I will be out of a job."

10　*Going to War*　∾

AS IF TO REWARD THEMSELVES FOR ALL THEIR WORK, in mid-1966 the royal family took an 11-week holiday to England. They settled into the maharajah of Jaipur's suburban London mansion for a leisurely schedule of stage shows, museums, and sightseeing. Bhumibol studied the modern paintings at the British Museum and bought art supplies. Twice the family went to the Frensham Pond Sailing Club, a center of OK dinghy sailing, where the king and Princess Ubolrat sailed, and he exchanged notes on small-boat construction. Strolling in the gardens near their residence, the king took photos of Sirikit amid the flowers.

Toward the end of July they retrieved Prince Vajiralongkorn from King's Mead Preparatory School. Bhumibol took him to the Imperial War Museum and various science museums. On July 28 the London Thai community was invited to the residence to celebrate the prince's 14th birthday. He started the day by presenting alms to monks, and then later shared a birthday cake and opened gifts. On a tour of the continent, they motored to their old home in Lausanne and around Bavaria, attended the Salzburg festival, and visited with the Belgian royal family. There were official duties on the trip as well. On August 1, Bhumibol inaugurated a Thai temple in London, and a few days later he and the queen gave an informal audience to Thai students in England.

The British press generously celebrated the royals' youth, freshness, and modernity. Elegantly dressed in a Parisian skirt and jacket, Sirikit charmed the reporters as she fielded a slew of questions about fashion. On the controversial miniskirts sweeping the Western fashion scene, she gave her conditional approval, saying they were lovely on teenagers but not suited for herself. Later during the trip, she was interviewed by American television's ABC network for a series on the beautiful women of the world. She demurely brushed off the interviewer's comparisons between herself and Jacqueline Kennedy. Photographs and reports of royal meetings with the press were splashed across the newspapers back home. These pictures showed a happy, handsome, and confident family, including one poignant shot of the king walking hand in hand with Sirikit and Princess Ubolrat.

During the same summer, *Time* magazine published a very positive report on Thailand, featuring Bhumibol on the cover.[1] In a land where "nearly every Thai household boasts a picture of the king," *Time* wrote, Bhumibol has "taken it upon himself to mold his emerging nation's character." The article went on to say: "Militant communism, poverty, misery, illiteracy, misrule and a foundering sense of nationhood are the grim order of the Asian day. With one important exception: the lush and smiling realm of Their Majesties King Bhumibol and Queen Sirikit, which spreads like a green meadow of stability, serenity and strength."

Without irony, *Time* then described all of the king's ceremonial and celebratory work on Chakri Day in April 1966: he received a new yellow Mercedes Benz limousine; he presented graduation swords to police; he unveiled a new statue of Rama VI; he handed diplomas to 868 graduates of two universities. That evening, the anniversary of Bhumibol's first musical composition was honored with 1,400 Thai musicians in an all-night concert of the king's works. The king himself stayed until 2 a.m., playing saxophone with his own band which, it was noted, now broadcast four times a week on Radio Aw Saw.

Time also briefly explained that Bhumibol often journeyed into the countryside. On one occasion he had walked more than 15 kilometers to visit a remote village, where the king and his beautiful queen gave food and medicine to the primitive hill people, who were the frequent targets of communist subversion. "Their tribal leaders value nothing more than the tiny silver medals distributed by the king," the magazine said. More space was given to Bhumibol's "equally strenuous hobbies." The king had built a boat and sailed it across the Gulf of Thailand, accompanied by "a motorboat using a new design of jet propulsion that Bhumibol himself had conceived," according to the report. His current project, *Time* said, was "a do-it-yourself helicopter." Such hyperbole—Bhumibol created neither a jet boat engine nor a helicopter—was by then common in Thailand, but it was perhaps embarrassing to have it repeated internationally.

The writer summed up by saying that all is happy in the kingdom, despite the large prostitution industry fueled by the U.S. presence, and the 250,000 poor opium-growing hill-tribe people. Importantly, the third white elephant of the Ninth Reign had been found just the previous week. As for politics, *Time* added, only outsiders are impatient for democracy and a constitution: "Members of the Constituent Assembly have been at work on a constitution for seven years, and may go on with the job indefinitely. No one is rushing them. The fact is, the easygoing Thais simply do not care very much one way or another. Nor does class and status trouble anyone very much, even though titled aristocracy . . . abounds."

The problem was that, for more than a few Thais, the stories from the royal family's England trip and *Time*'s upbeat coverage were sharply at odds with the real situation in Thailand. For many, including some from the royal circle, the media images showed the king playing at being monarch when they wanted him, faced with the menacing communist insurgency, to begin to rule and not simply reign. Under uncommonly direct criticism, a clearly offended Bhumibol took up the challenge. He curtailed his hobbies, stopped traveling, and began to assume a role as the country's paramount executive and commander in chief.

Ironically, when this transformation took place, the communist threat inside Thailand was smaller than in most other Asian nations. It was more the repressiveness of the Sarit and Thanom-Praphas regimes, combined with the lack of economic development in the countryside, that stoked the rise of the Communist Party of Thailand (CPT). Since the end of World War II, much of the country had remained untouched by progress. A large percentage of farmers rented or sharecropped their land. For the quickly growing population, moreover, farmland was increasingly scarce and the urban job market didn't offer good alternatives.

Unchanged, too, was the imperial way the government in Bangkok dealt with the poor. Distant provinces were administered like remote colonies, with the government's main interest being to extract something of value—food, timber, and taxes—and to quash rebellions. Traditionally, the most troublesome areas were Lao-dominated Isan, the heavily Muslim south, and the hill-tribe areas on the northern and western borders. The people in these regions often saw Bangkok's bureaucracy and military agents as oppressors, while the Bangkok elite regarded the local residents as rebellious non-Thais, and increasingly branded them communists.

There had been no Thai communist movement when Field Marshal Sarit seized power in 1957. A few months earlier, however, a respected young academic, Jit Phumisak, published his seminal Marxist history of Thai society, *Chom Na Sakdina Thai,* or "The Face of Thai Feudalism," which, like Pridi in the 1932 revolution, directly challenged royal culture and history.[2] Jit traced the modern political and economic power structure back to old royalist society, arguing that the Thai class system had been little different from European feudalism, and implying that the king had been simply the biggest landlord. For many dissidents, this explained the continuing great discrepancies between wealth and poverty in the kingdom.

Sarit's reaction was to jail or eliminate hundreds of the political opposition, journalists, and intellectuals, including Jit, who was imprisoned for eight years. It was perhaps as much this repression as Jit's ideology that gave birth to the CPT. In June 1961, a popular member of parliament, Khrong Chandawong, who had been a Free Thai operative during World War II and was an advocate for the northeastern poor and Isan autonomy, was arrested and summarily executed for allegedly being a communist. Afterward, Khrong's wife and daughter and a mixed bag of followers, socialists, farmers' rights advocates, and ethnic Lao nationalists fled into the Phuphan mountain range in Sakhon Nakhon, in the far northeast. From this redoubt they built contacts with the Pathet Lao and the Viet Minh, to become the core of the CPT.

The CPT slowly expanded in small pockets, encouraged by bombastic propaganda and a small amount of aid from Hanoi and Beijing. From mountain bases in the north and northeast, they recruited hill tribes and lowland farmers who felt oppressed by government officials and local traders. In their support, in late 1962 China launched the "Voice of the People of Thailand" radio broadcasts out of Yunnan province. In early 1964, CPT membership numbered probably in the high hundreds rather than thousands. Nevertheless, alarms rang out in Bangkok and Washington that January, when the communist Pathet Lao army attacked the Laotian border city of Thakhek, only 100 kilometers from the Phuphan hills.

The first real government clash with the CPT took place only 20 months later. In August 1965 in the same region, police stumbled into a small CPT meeting in a village. A scuffle followed in which a villager was shot dead and a policeman was injured. Eight months later, Jit Phumisak, recently released from prison, was arrested and summarily executed by government officials near Phuphan.

Many Thais saw this as evidence that the country faced a full-scale insurgency, like those taking place in neighboring Laos and Vietnam. Government officials said a communist takeover was possible, via either parliament or popular revolt.[3]

Political analysts declared Thailand the next domino. Yet, as one historian of the period put it, "Paradoxically, the counterinsurgency effort not only pre-dated the insurgency, but it outgrew the latter by many times over."[4]

Bangkok reacted by forming a counterinsurgency task force, the Communist Suppression Operations Command, or CSOC, run by Deputy Prime Minister Praphas along with U.S. advisers. Behind them was the massive force the United States had built up in Thailand, consuming the country like an occupation. In the early 1960s the Americans, together with Thai soldiers, were already conducting guerilla raids into Laos and launching air strikes on Laos and Vietnam from Thai bases. By 1965 there were roughly 14,000 U.S. military and intelligence personnel in Thailand. A year later the total topped 34,000, accompanied by 400 aircraft. The American force was there as much to prevent the rise of a domestic Thai insurgency as it was to support South Vietnam, and it legitimized the Thai military's political control of the country.

The United States did not ignore the poverty and exploitation that fed the nascent CPT. Washington threw huge resources at winning the people's hearts and minds through development, hoping to avoid the problems of Vietnam. U.S.-directed projects built roads, dug fish ponds, and established social services in rural villages. Within a few years U.S. annual spending in Thailand equaled the total economic product of the entire northeast, where the lion's share of it was deployed, all accompanied by anticommunist and pro-monarchy propaganda.

Arguably, the extensive U.S. presence and aid worsened the problems. Much of Washington's hundreds of millions of dollars dropped into the pockets of the traditional elite, the landowning aristocrats, Sino-Thai traders, and powerful bureaucrats and generals. Bangkok spent up to three times as much on arms as it did on education, and health services got much less. Strong economic growth came with high inflation near military bases, GIs on holiday carousing drunkenly throughout the kingdom, and a very visible explosion in the sex industry.

Meanwhile, security conditions in the countryside worsened. Following the incident in August 1965, clashes between the CPT or other rebellious groups and the government grew to more than 150 skirmishes during 1966, mostly in the south and the northeast, killing 47 police and government officials and 97 insurgents.[5] In 1967 the troubles spread into the north, the number of incidents doubled, and the casualties rose similarly. The alarmists of the Thai government, as well as some of the Americans advising them, insisted that a substantial communist insurgency was already under way, and that it needed to be crushed before it opened the door

to invasion by Vietnam. It was highly exaggerated, but the alarmists' view nevertheless fed a growing hysteria over the communist threat.

In this atmosphere of panic, accompanied by a corrupt and ineffective military
leadership, Bhumibol himself came under criticism. At first a small group of
conservative intellectuals dared to suggest that the king wasn't doing anything
useful, that he was little different from the dilettantes of European royalty. Sulak
Sivaraks, a one-time protégé of Prince Dhani, almost openly taunted Bhumibol to
quit playing as king and use his power to lead the country. Criticism like this
paralleled international media reports that characterized the king as nice but
largely ineffectual, and Thailand itself as uncommitted to its own defense in the
Cold War. What could be imputed from the 1966 *Time* cover story was said more
directly by a number of journalists, Thai and foreign, the next year: that Thailand's
military-controlled government was deeply corrupt, that the U.S. presence had a
deleterious effect on Thai society, and that poor government and lack of democratic institutions was exacerbating poverty and feeding the insurgency.

Amid all this, the respected leftist American writer Louis Lomax wrote in a
book on Thailand that the king was barely material.[6] Facing the imminent eruption
of "another peoples' war," Bhumibol was no more than a "Linus blanket," he said,
referring to the insecure blanket-snuggling character in the cartoon strip *Peanuts*.
At best the king limits the "excessive excesses" of the government, Lomax wrote,
but meanwhile, "the military have destroyed his divinity and the intellectuals have
destroyed his authenticity." Referring to rising dissent, Lomax declared, "The king
can no longer unify Thailand."

Beneath his fixed, never-smiling mien, King Bhumibol must have felt the insult
painfully. He had already suffered much indignity for the position he inherited two
decades before. People saw him as committed not to his subjects' well-being but to
his jazz, sailing, and relic ceremonies. His indignation spilled out when he told
Look magazine, a rival of *Time*, in 1967:

> Americans, and writers especially, seem to prefer stereotypes. Now, you
> are in the exotic Far East. Is that what you call it? With the rajas, the lion
> hunting, the elephants. But the people who see only the jewels on the
> temple roof, they do not realize the jewel is in the heart, not on the roof
> of the temple. Now they call me the "jazz-loving" king. I must put up
> with it. The truth is, I do not have a saxophone of pure gold, and I never
> had one. It would probably be too heavy anyway. And the "fast-driving,

speed-loving" king. I must live with it. I'm not angry about these stereo-
types, but I don't believe that they are constructive or in the best interests
of Thailand and the United States.[7]

Answering criticism that he was out of touch, Bhumibol fell back to the idea
that a dhammaraja had a sort of natural omniscience. Because he was king, he said,
people told him things they didn't tell others: "I believe I am in touch with my
people and the government. In government, we have two kinds of reports, official
and unofficial. Many departments write unofficial reports about each other, and I
see them."

But the criticisms hit a nerve, and Bhumibol understood Lomax's point. The
rebuilding of the monarchy on the old princes' model had failed to bring many
concrete benefits to his people. Its ritual and symbolic promises of a better world
hadn't fundamentally improved village life. To the contrary, continuing under-
development and bureaucratic and capitalist abuse of peasants were driving the
CPT's expansion. One reason Bhumibol's work had remained mostly ritual and
symbolic was that the old advisers from the Chakri ancien régime didn't imagine
him doing anything else but building his image and bolstering national unity.
Aside from his hobbylike farm projects, Bhumibol hadn't himself shown much
initiative. But he was nearly 40, an age when many Thai men born into privilege
aspire to transcend their lives of ease and really accomplish something. Bhumibol
now conducted the routine of kingship by rote. His children were taken care of; the
prince was at an English boarding school and Princess Ubolrat was soon to attend
university. And he had exhausted his potential in sports and arts.

Moreover, his two decades on the throne had given Bhumibol more intimate
knowledge about Thai problems and politics than most Thai leaders acquired. He
had a fairly solid understanding of national security issues, thanks in part to his
longtime adviser Srivisarn Vacha heading the National Security Council. He regularly met privately with the leaders of noncommunist nations and was briefed by
diplomats, intelligence specialists, military leaders, capitalists, and development
experts. In addition to receiving daily reports on Thailand from his own government, and a constant flow of letters from his subjects, he monitored Thai and
international radio transmissions and news reports in his personal work space in
the palace—his "intelligence center" lined with radios, teletypes, televisions, and
map-filled cabinets.

When the criticism surfaced, then, it had a galvanic effect. Determined to gain
respect as a real leader, Bhumibol curtailed his hobbies, at least in the public eye—

the regattas at Hua Hin, the jazz jams on the radio, and painting parties in the palace—and thrust himself into the war against communism. At first, this just meant intensifying the usual activities. Bhumibol and Sirikit's official appearances and audiences increased from 341 in 1965 to 553 in 1969.[8] Ever more royal medals, honors, and titles were dispensed to donors to the king's charity operations. But now, as a rule, they were given to almost all senior military officers and top bureaucrats.

There was a distinct change in the atmosphere of these rituals, however. There was more of a focus on the idea of national unity against a looming, though often unnamed, threat to nation, religion, and king. Bhumibol increasingly alluded to the insurgent threat and to problems in neighboring states and spoke of the relationship of poverty to Thailand's situation. To strengthen national unity around the person of the king, Bhumibol began a program of distributing his own Buddha Navarajabophit statues, with his own amulets attached, for display in each of the 73 provinces and to key military units, as representations of his omniscient presence across his realm. The anthropologist Frank Reynolds compared them to Angkor ruler Jayavarman VII's spreading his own image throughout the kingdom.[9] The very first was presented in Nongkhai, the province directly opposite the Laotian capital of Vientiane, which was often blamed for the troubles in Isan. It appeared to be a combination sacral and secular message to the ethnic Lao and communists on both sides of the border that this was Bhumibol's dominion.

Another anthropologist, Charles Keyes, described one provincial presentation ceremony as well scripted to portray Bhumibol as both head of state and paramount religious leader.[10] To Keyes, it "conjured up images of the durbars held in India in the last century at which representatives of the diverse peoples of a particular district were brought together to demonstrate their fealty to the British raj. . . . The arrangement of the grounds for the ceremony thus made evident the constituent elements of the Thai state: the monarch, the Buddhist sangha, the officials, and the populace." An adjunct program was the religious affairs department's effort to designate a royal temple representing the Chakri dhammaraja's presence in each province, even if the temple had no historical link to the monarchy.

In his new posture, Bhumibol also revealed a distinct militaristic streak, as if he was taking seriously his ceremonial position as head of the Thai armed forces. He began to openly and stridently advocate tough U.S. and Thai military action against the region's communists. In February 1966, Bhumibol had already pleaded with visiting U.S. vice president Hubert Humphrey for more help to defend against a communist invasion as they discussed the parallels between Vietnam and Thailand.

He requested specific equipment for fighting communist infiltration, and also complained of delays in the delivery of aid from Washington.[11]

That summer, on his holiday in England, Bhumibol declared several times that China and Vietnam seriously threatened Thailand. He told reporters that one of his purposes in Britain was to buy aircraft for his military, and he visited several aircraft factories in England and Germany and attended the large Farnborough military aircraft show.[12] Aircraft purchasing for the Royal Thai Air Force wasn't really among his responsibilities, but he was getting involved. Later the same year he lobbied the United States to escalate its war against Hanoi, even criticizing Washington for pausing in its air strikes on North Vietnam.[13] He pressed Thanom to allocate more soldiers to CPT suppression operations in the northeast, and to demand even more American support since Thailand had agreed to Washington's request for a large Thai combat troop deployment to Vietnam.[14]

Bhumibol's view of the Cold War was simplistic, though not out of line with conservative thinking at the time. Despite his awareness of internal causes, he took the position that the roots of the communist threat were essentially external. In his 1967 *Look* interview, he revealed his view of the imperiled Thai cosmos.

> The Chinese have always been a threat to Southeast Asia, because they are an expansive people. . . . In Thailand, there are many of them, and it is hard to absorb them. . . . In the northeast villages, the communists are either Thai Chinese or North Vietnamese. . . . Generally, the people do not believe them, but in the remote areas, if the people do not cooperate, the communists kill them. . . . Now of course, some government officials upcountry do not do their jobs properly, so the peasants have a reason to become bitter and rebel. But their bitterness is not against Thailand, it is against the officials.
>
> Thai people are not communists. For example, if you consider our religion and consider all of its rules, it is democratic. Thus, the monks all have their rights, and they operate in a manner similar to that of a parliament. Each has the right to say what he thinks. We in Thailand have, then, a basis for democracy and good living.
>
> Communism is impractical. Life is not each to his needs. The one who works today should get the money and the goods, not the one who doesn't work. Communism can be worse than the Nazis or fascists. In practice, it is more terrible than dictatorship.

Dictatorship, of course, was exactly what Thailand's generals were being accused of, increasingly by antiwar activists in the United States. Bhumibol told *Look* that the American student protestors were ignorant, victims of communist manipulation. Thailand had to be wary of such communist trickery and prepare for "a very special kind of war," he argued. "While millions of Chinese are starving, China has the luxury of the bomb. Now, many people in India want the bomb. We in Thailand have been too modest, but perhaps in the future, the Thai people won't be so modest. If the Thai people want the bomb, then they shall have it."

As the king's statements became more hawkish, he spent more time with the armed forces, strengthening his bonds with the rank and file, and showing his wartime leadership, like a traditional kasatriya. The Mahidols had long paid personal attention to Thai soldiers and police officers injured in the line of duty, visiting them in the hospital and providing funds to their families and sponsoring funerals.

Now the king made an extra effort to visit camps and field positions, wearing combat fatigues, often with a pistol on one hip and a walkie-talkie on the other. The press generously published photographs showing Bhumibol shooting carbines, M-16s, and larger machine guns from forward bases. Queen Sirikit was frequently at his side, likewise clothed in army greens and posing with a carbine. The elite group of soldiers headed for Vietnam became her "Queen's Rangers."

Prince Vajiralongkorn joined the family militarization as well. Before being sent off to England to study in January 1966, he was, at 13, named a sublieutenant in all three armed services. Whenever he returned to Thailand on holiday he put on a field uniform and accompanied his father to BPP and army camps. At 15 he participated in military basic training and learned to shoot sidearms. Not long after, he graduated to large-caliber machine guns and grenade launchers. The palace released photographs of father and son shooting together, and the prince learned how to dismantle, clean, and reassemble various weapons.

Showing he recognized the social roots of the insurgency, Bhumibol also ratcheted up his development initiatives. His keystone project was the Hup Kapong area near Hua Hin. Despite the construction of roads and small reservoirs, farming wasn't taking off. The reason, Bhumibol observed, was that the people themselves weren't determined enough to overcome poverty. He had expected them to achieve bucolic farming lives once they were provided with the means, but they didn't work together, he noted. Instead, as soon as roads and other facilities were built, some sold their property to land speculators. It was a cycle that deeply vexed the king all his life: when offered fast cash for their land, peasants took the money and moved to the city or to other state-owned lands, only to end up poor again.

As a way of combating the cycle, in 1967 the king introduced to Hup Kapong the idea of a village farming cooperative modeled on an Israeli kibbutz. If it worked, he wanted the program copied around the countryside, as in Israel, converting poor land into miracle farms while boosting unity and national security. First he communalized the land at Hup Kapong. Using royal and government funds, land was purchased and merged with other land already owned in the community, and then marked out for group farm plots. Ultimately, 120 families shared some 4,000 acres as joint owners, so no one could sell it off. Palace, government, and military officials under the king's direction improved the soil, constructed irrigation facilities, introduced cash crops that mixed well with rice cultivation, and taught the people new farming methods. They helped set up community credit, buying, and marketing cooperatives, and they installed power and water infrastructure. Merit-seeking Thai businessmen and the Israeli government donated supplies and equipment. With all the inputs, it could hardly fail.

Bhumibol's other early project, the Danish milk business, was similarly converted into the Nongpho cooperative. The palace offered cows from its original herd to farmers in the hills northeast of Bangkok. Again with royal funds and donated equipment and materials, central milk collection, processing, and distribution facilities were built, and credit, purchasing, and land sharing cooperatives were organized. The palace managed and subsidized the distribution of the milk products to schools.

The palace also intensified the BPP's hill-tribe development efforts, with the king represented by Princess Mother Sangwal during her yearly stay in Thailand. She still offered health support to the hill-tribe hamlets, but increasingly her visits had a more military accent and focused on unity under the dhammaraja. Suited in green BPP jungle fatigues, Sangwal would descend from the sky into a hill-tribe village in a BPP helicopter, flanked by heavily armed soldiers. She was presented as a magical princess, the personal representative of a great, distant sovereign who protected the people—as opposed to the government or the communists, who did little for them. Doctors accompanying her would treat the villagers, and the team would hand out blankets, medicines, and money. She would expound on Buddhist principles and hand out Buddhist tracts and magical amulets, and then fly away.

It was a potent presentation for the shamanist hill tribes. Sangwal was named their personal patron, like a benevolent holy spirit, and called Mae Fah Luang, the "royal mother from the sky," a reference both to her magical helicopter descents and to the monarch's traditional image as chaofa, lord of the skies. Where once they were simply numbered, the BPP-run hill-tribe schools were now named for members of the royal family. Sangwal recruited more city doctors to make upland helicopter visits, and in 1969 she formalized the operation as the Princess Mother's Medical Volunteers foundation. She also used public donations in 1967 to endow a support fund of one million baht for the BPP soldiers and their families.

Several examples during this period show just how involved Bhumibol had become in the nitty-gritty of national security and state economic policies, two coming in his 25-day trip to North America in June 1967. Aside from a three-day state visit to Canada, the entire time was spent in the United States. This time there was no Hollywood, jazz, or tickertape parades. Instead, it was all about the U.S.-Thai security relationship.

Earlier in the year the United States had requested Thailand to supply 20,000 ground troops to South Vietnam, as a part of the Americans' own 200,000-strong escalation. Bangkok wasn't opposed, but there were several issues to resolve, including the depth of the U.S. commitment to Thailand. Bhumibol went to the United States to negotiate these issues himself. The trip was not without formal ceremony, including the king's dedication of a Thai pavilion at the East-West Center in Honolulu, and his presiding at a charity ball for children in Los Angeles. But the main focus was impressing Thailand's needs on the Americans, including influential figures like President Lyndon B. Johnson, New York governor (and possible future presidential candidate) Nelson A. Rockefeller, and James Linen, publisher of *Time* magazine.

In New York, Linen hosted a dinner for the king at the Metropolitan Museum of Art. Bhumibol then took *Time*'s corporate jet to Williamstown, Massachusetts, to receive an honorary degree at Linen's alma mater, Williams College. The occasion was nonpolitical, but the king suggested in his acceptance speech that other things were on his mind: "There is at this moment a maze of ideals, of interests. The present society is crisscrossed by propaganda and counter-propaganda, so in any issue our minds should be keen enough and clear enough to perceive . . . where the truth lies." Back in New York, the Rockefellers hosted a dinner for the king and queen with a group of top policy- and opinion-makers. In an interview with reporters, the king stressed the global communist threat and repeated that American opponents of the Vietnam War were victims of brainwashing.[15]

He finally met Johnson at the White House on June 27, and spent much of the next day with defense secretary Robert McNamara and then Johnson again. Beforehand he had already asked the United States to firm up its guarantee of Thailand's security and to quit fueling Thai government corruption and mismanagement. The record of their meetings remains secret, but they apparently focused on how Thailand should address the insurgency and respond to the U.S. request for Thai troops in Vietnam. Related documents show the king negotiating the terms for allocating Thai soldiers to the American war, demanding that they be volunteers and receive more training, better weapons, and increased pay. Bhumibol also said that Thai soldiers who were not going to Vietnam were also underpaid and badly trained, and they too required further help from the United States.[16]

In addition he apparently asked the Americans for a strong restatement of their security pledge to Thailand. The question arose from the perceived weakening of the U.S. commitment to South Vietnam, and also because Bangkok feared that sending Thai troops to Vietnam would incite North Vietnamese bombing raids on Thailand. Yet the Americans remained ambiguous. Johnson wouldn't commit to an escalation, and the king learned that the U.S. presence in all of Indochina was greatly subject to American domestic politics. Johnson told him that the only way Thailand could defend itself was to get its troops real fighting experience in Vietnam, and warned that Thailand needed to prepare as many men as possible in case war erupted on its own soil.[17]

During the trip, the king also met with Henry Kearns, the businessman who had hosted the royal family in Los Angeles in 1960. Kearns was planning several substantial investments in Thailand, particularly a pulp and paper plant, but was hampered by bureaucratic issues. The subsequent joint venture between the Crown Property Bureau and the paper plant indicates that Bhumibol personally intervened after his return to make it happen.

Another example of the king's involvement even at a lower management level of Thai national security is shown by an episode involving the BPP, which by the mid-1960s was an important actor in the Thai counterinsurgency. Although it was organized under the national police department (a division of the Interior Ministry), the BPP was almost completely autonomous. It operated about 23 U.S.-supplied aircraft to move its men around the mountainous terrain of the country's northern borders. In an indication of the force's favored status, the United States armed BPP squadrons with new M-16s in 1966, while the regular army was stuck with older weapons.

The regular police were meanwhile being funded by another U.S. government arm, the State Department's secretive Office of Public Safety. This office appears to have encouraged the police to create their own aviation division directly under the national police chief. The office offered the police 100 new aircraft and fuel, but only if the police chief established a unified police aviation division, merging the BPP air operations into his own. Doing so, however, would effectively strip the BPP of its aircraft and force it to use mules in the hills, as it had done in the 1950s.[18]

The police chief agreed, and the Americans began to ship in aircraft, including a first delivery of 22 helicopters. But the administrative change did not take place. To protect the BPP, King Bhumibol refused to sign the royal decree merging the two aviation operations. Moreover, with apparent support from the palace, the BPP grabbed the best of the new equipment and, a few years later, assumed control of all police aviation operations. The king had protected his protectors.

11   *Reborn Democrat?*   ℘

BHUMIBOL'S INCREASINGLY STRIDENT PUBLIC STATEMENTS, his posing with the troops, and his trip to the United States to discuss security arrangements served to quench the criticism that he was just a figurehead who spent his time on jazz and sailboats.[1] As he had requested, Washington increased the money and equipment it was sending for Thai soldiers. In return, the first of 10,000 Thai troops arrived in Saigon in September 1967. Although Washington still conducted the relationship mainly through Thanom and Praphas, Bhumibol began to establish his authority in Thai politics.

The king also returned from Washington, apparently, a reborn believer in democracy and good government. The trip made him acutely aware of the ground-swell of opinion in America against the Vietnam War, and its corrosive effect on the U.S. commitment to Thailand. The American press portrayed Thailand, after two decades and a billion dollars of U.S. aid, as led by corrupt, inept, and dictatorial generals who presided over an uninhibited narcotics trade, a booming sex industry, and unremitting poverty. In Congress, the prominent antiwar senator William Fulbright branded Thailand as undemocratic and not worth supporting. The message from President Johnson, too, was that Thailand had to clean up its image, first by getting Thanom to restore the constitution and democratic elections.[2]

Bhumibol couldn't reject the criticisms. A new constitution had never materialized after 1958. Meanwhile, corruption was ravaging the nation, helping the CPT grow. "If all corrupt persons were executed, there might not be many people left," he told college students in 1967, adding, "I am at my wit's end to know how to remedy it."[3]

Upon returning from Washington the king pressed Thanom to reinstate the constitution and hold elections. His own birthday was set for promulgation, to reiterate the idea that Thai democracy flowed from the throne. Thanom moved slowly, however, in part worried that deputy premier Praphas would seize power for himself. Finally, on June 20, 1968, Bhumibol promulgated the new Thai charter.

Although it was democratic on the surface, in its details the constitution essentially legitimized Thanom's military-dominated government. Nearly as brief as Sarit's 1958 "interim" charter, the 1968 version created a bicameral parliament, with a 219-member elected lower house and an upper house of 164 senators appointed by the king. Bhumibol approved Thanom's mostly military senate nominees, so that, with only a small representation in the lower house, Thanom would easily control parliament. Furthermore, lower house members were forbidden to serve in the cabinet; the senate leader was automatically president of parliament; and the senate had the power to delay any legislation for one year, in essence its own veto, in addition to the king's.

The new charter also validated all legislation made by previous governments, rendering unchallengeable the dictatorial laws that Praphas used to repress dissenters, such as the sweeping Anticommunist Act. Like Sarit, Thanom reserved for himself strong emergency powers. In the February 1969 elections, with Washington's and possibly the throne's financial help, Thanom's supporters won a majority in the lower house, giving him a lockhold on the government.[4] The new regime was unchanged, but the constitution and the elections were enough to assuage Washington.

But in a perhaps unintended effect, Bhumibol emerged appearing committed to liberal democracy, free elections, and the rule of law. This emboldened many Thais to criticize the government, while in parliament the opposition assailed the regime for corruption and for overly close relations with the United States, and demanded improved civil liberties. The annual budget was stalled for months by advocates of cutting military spending. Thanom and Praphas reacted by arresting some critics and shutting down publications. Yet they had to be cautious, not only because of bad publicity in the United States. The pro-democracy voices claimed that the king was on their side.

This reaction caught King Bhumibol between his pro-democracy stance and his support for a tough response to the insurgents and dissidents. He understood the importance of improved governance. But the growth of the insurgency, and events in neighboring countries, encouraged a military solution. By 1967 the CPT had spread to the northern mountains, particularly the provinces of Chiangrai and Nan on the Laotian border, both heavily populated by Hmong hill tribes. In 1968 the rebels gained a foothold in the mountainous Khao Khor area where the north and northeast come together. More insurgents cropped up in the middle south, and a separate struggle arose on the western border, where the forest-dwelling Karen people had conflicts with lowland Thais.

These were mostly local insurgencies, but CPT networking made them a loose confederation. The number of incidents between insurgents and the police and soldiers grew to 372 in 1968. In Chiangrai that April, an 18-man army garrison was wiped out by a CPT hill-tribe force, with the attackers taking no losses.[5] A few months later insurgents attacked a U.S. airbase in the northeastern province of Udon Thani, killing and injuring several guards and damaging two aircraft. Even so, in 1968 the CPT network numbered fewer than 4,000 armed men, with no lowland or urban base and limited links to external communist parties. They lacked the weaponry and personnel to challenge the government, and showed no signs of attempting to do so.

But after early 1968, when Hanoi shocked Saigon with its Tet offensive, the Communist Suppression Operations Command gave up on wooing the peasantry with reforms and aid and, rejecting the lessons of Vietnam, made "search and destroy" its mode of operation, using shakedowns, torture, and summary executions in rural areas suspected of supporting the CPT. The army and the BPP began to terrorize rural Thais by pushing CPT suspects from hovering helicopters and, in the south, plunging prisoners into red-painted drums of boiling oil. The BPP turned harsher toward the hill tribes as well, now pushing brusquely through hamlets suspected of CPT sympathies rather than taking time to develop a relationship. The government began to forcibly relocate hill-tribe villages to the lowlands, causing new problems over land and resources with lowlanders.

Also in 1968, badly stung by the Vietnam War, President Johnson declared that he wouldn't run for reelection. Both Hubert Humphrey and Richard Nixon, consequently, campaigned on pulling American troops out of Vietnam. Nixon won the election, and shortly after taking office in January 1969 he announced the "Vietnamization" of South Vietnam's defense, followed two months later by his plans to reduce the 50,000 U.S. troops in Thailand. Meanwhile the U.S. Senate banned those troops from fighting in Thailand or Laos, as Senator Fulbright again attacked Thailand as a corrupt and undemocratic U.S. dependency.

This sent the Thai elite into collective shock. It appeared that the United States was giving up on Thailand as well as Vietnam. American cutbacks would cause a recession. More worrisome was that, with more than 10,000 Thai soldiers in Vietnam, Bangkok feared an escalation of direct hostilities between the two countries. Without the U.S. security umbrella, war between Thailand and North Vietnam seemed possible.

Thanom responded by sharply escalating the counterinsurgency campaign. In Khao Khor, Chiangmai, Chiangrai, and other areas his forces aimed their heaviest equipment, bombers, artillery, and attack helicopters at CPT redoubts. They incinerated vast forests and suspect villages with missiles and napalm bombs, just like the Americans did in Vietnam.

Also like in Vietnam, the campaign was not very effective. Knowing their terrain better than the government troops did, CPT fighters avoided capture and injury. More government soldiers were injured in clashes than insurgents were. Moreover, the attacks appeared to turn even more rural Thais against the government, as was the case following the February 1968 razing of the Chiangrai village of Meo Maw. The CPT had entered the village one night to attack a small group of visiting police. Afterward, the villagers insisted that they had not aided the insurgents, offering as proof of their loyalty the fact that only a few years earlier King Bhumibol had granted honors to the grandfather of the village chief, and just a year before Princess Mother Sangwal had dedicated the village school. Nevertheless, airforce planes bombed the village and ground soldiers torched the school and granaries.[6]

In an escalation of its own, in 1969 the CPT formally announced the establishment of the People's Liberation Army of Thailand. While this was alarming to Thais in Bangkok, in fact the poorly equipped insurgents showed no potential for moving out from their rural mountain and jungle hideouts. Their threat as a communist movement was little more than theoretical. As Jeffrey Race, an expert on Asian insurgencies, said at the time, the only people who considered the CPT truly communist were the heads of the CPT and the heads of the Thai government. Otherwise, they were just hill tribes fighting abuse.[7]

Moreover, the CPT's followers remained firmly loyal to King Bhumibol. As one reporter wrote in 1972, "Insurgency inroads in Thailand have been somewhat frustrated by the reverence the peasant has for his king, and by the pacific, nonpolitical nature of Thai Buddhism."[8] For that reason, the writer noted, the CPT had a firm policy of not criticizing King Bhumibol or the sangha.

This affection challenged Bhumibol's ability to balance his role as compassionate unifier with his concern about neighboring communist movements and his support for the government's tougher counterinsurgency campaign. Pulled in different ways, he and Queen Sirikit continued with their official ritual duties and charity work. Every ceremonial paean to the Chakri tradition was punctually performed. The king held the extravagant royal barge ceremony for the royal kathin again in 1967. When a white elephant was discovered in the south in 1968, it was adopted into the palace with great fanfare. On Sirikit's third-cycle birthday that August, in commemoration she issued a volume of historical writings that extolled each Chakri king. The royal couple displayed their support for the armed forces, visiting, always in army fatigues, injured soldiers in hospitals and the troops at the front, where the king tested weapons and gave tactical instructions.

At the same time, using his own royal development projects as examples, Bhumibol challenged the government's approach to the insurgency. With his sailing buddy Prince Bhisadej Rajani as his manager, he had expanded his royal projects, paying more attention to the needs of the hill tribes, who were still mostly untouched by government assistance. The king's operations introduced cooperatives to hill-tribe villages, starting first with community rice and seed banks. They launched small crop substitution projects to wean hill tribes from growing opium poppies.[9]

The king also, together with international agencies, pressed the government to accord full Thai citizenship, and so rights to state services, to the hill tribes. Over four years, to 1973, some 200,000 members of hill tribes were said to have received citizenship, although it turned out not to be full citizenship.[10] Going a step further, Bhumibol pointedly criticized the state's approach to development and the excesses of the counterinsurgency campaign. In several talks he advised that the military should be more restrained and the government more truthful, rather than spreading self-congratulatory propaganda.[11] After visiting northern Hmong villages that had suffered a military assault in late 1968, he suggested that the government's attacks were wrong. He insisted that few hill-tribe people had joined the communists, saying: "There are very few who are really reds. If we make mistakes, the whole tribe will turn red and cause incessant trouble for us later."

During 1969, Bhumibol's criticisms became stronger. He told one student audience about a village in Prachuab Khirikan, south of his Hua Hin palace, where people had settled in a reserve forest.

These people lived and earned their living in peace, having their own self-rule without any record of crimes. They would have been considered democratic but for the lack of district officers and officials, and in fact, they were more democratic without than with a district officer. . . . But apparently they are taken as offenders verging on communist terrorists. We have no wish whatsoever to have communist terrorists in Thailand, but we ourselves have created them by accusing villagers who were governing themselves in an orderly and democratic fashion of being trespassers of the reserve forest and driving them out.[12]

He told a group of businessmen that foreign interlopers had sparked the insurgency, but that it fed off bad local conditions: "If justice is not dispensed throughout the land, disorder will prevail. Many are driven into becoming insurgents by force of circumstances. . . . Troops we can fight, for we are a nation of warriors; but insurgency which is of our own making is much more difficult to defeat. . . . It is up to officials in rural areas to perform their duty with caution, justice, consciousness and greater sacrifice. Otherwise we have to concede victory to the insurgents."[13]

The king criticized businessmen themselves for feeding corruption and abusing the peasantry. He said middlemen kept farmers poor by paying too little for their crops. He also blamed land speculators. Whenever the government built roads into isolated areas, he explained, land dealers would flock in to pay uneducated farmers small but attractive amounts for their property. Inevitably, Bhumibol said, the money would be spent quickly and the now landless families would have to rent the same land, move to the city for low-paid work, or illegally carve out a new plot of barely fertile land from the forest, "to cultivate with little or no prospect of making good."

More daringly, Bhumibol encouraged students to pressure the government to act more justly, in the old Siamese tradition of petitioning the king for justice. "So I say to the generals," he told students at Prasarnmit College in 1969, "that they must learn to listen to the people."[14] He advised the students of Chulalongkorn University to think for themselves, rather than be dictated to by soulless bureaucrats, "so that our country may attain true democracy according to the dictates of the minds and hearts of the people."[15] For students and other activists, such words put the king on their side, opposed to the military-dominated government of Thanom and Praphas.

The students were wrong, though, for Bhumibol was headed in an entirely different direction. After two decades of study and observation, his views of modern government, economic development, Buddhism, and morality were beginning to crystallize into his own unique ruling philosophy, one with clear roots in the principles of the absolute Chakri dhammaraja monarchy. As only the most virtuous men can do, Bhumibol was embarking on his own interpretation of the dhamma for the modern world.

At the center of his view was the modern maxim promoted by King Vajiravudh: every citizen's paramount duty is to the unity of the nation under the king. The simple components of this were diligence, selflessness, and duty to the family, implying both one's immediate family and the national family, of which the king and queen were father and mother. Like Vajiravudh, Bhumibol emphasized national unity as almost a religious commandment. To achieve unity, everyone had his or her own job to do: "A nation is made up of various institutions in the same way as all the organs which make up a live body. Life in our body can endure because the organs, large or small, function normally. Likewise, a nation can endure because its various institutions are firm and fully discharging their respective duties."[16]

In talks he singled out specific sources of the nation's lack of unity. A primary problem, he noted—as, ironically, did the CPT—was selfish capitalism, which lacked morality and was by nature divisive. Capitalism didn't reward most the hardest workers or those who performed their duty. It benefited more those who took advantage of others, and this eroded unity. Bhumibol said traders and land speculators who took advantage of peasants "may be on the side of the terrorists."[17] And when he criticized a faulty government program that gave heavy equipment to peasant farmers who really needed more fundamental assistance, he added: "Not everyone can have tractors, except capitalists who have no regard for common villagers anyhow."[18]

For the Marxists of the CPT this was political economy, but for Bhumibol it was a matter of dhamma. To Bhumibol, national unity arose only from selfless motivation, or, in the words of the dhamma, pure intentions. He lectured that rural development should be carried out with "a high degree of ability, wisdom and intelligence coupled with honesty without any thought for financial gains. Anyone who wants to make money had better resign and go into business."[19] And he added: "Only clever and discerning people will be able to distinguish between those who really want to bring about development and those who want to do it for the devious benefits of their own party."[20]

Not only capitalist businessmen possessed this destructive selfish mentality, the king said; it also infected scholars, politicians, and bureaucrats, people who often worked, consciously or not, counter to national unity. He admonished students and bureaucrats to work hard without thinking of personal gain. And he applauded the work of doctors in the countryside as "a most progressive activity": "The subjection to physical exhaustion, the running of risks and encountering of obstacles and difficulties in the way of living all make up a round of activities benefiting good doctors, good men and good patriots."[21] He held himself and his family as examples. He told students to study in order to serve the country, like his daughter Ubolrat, who intended to study nuclear physics at the prestigious Massachusetts Institute of Technology to benefit the kingdom.

Bhumibol didn't fault only capitalism. He also said the modern bureaucratic and legal systems equally sabotaged national development and unity. From his speeches in the late 1960s and early 1970s, it was clear that he blamed officious and misguided bureaucrats, and the inflexible laws they exercised, for much of the insurgency's growth. Although this was a widespread view, the lesson Bhumibol drew from it was not. He concluded that modern government just wasn't as good as traditional rule by a Chakri dhammaraja. As the princes of the old regime had taught him, the modern Thai system of government had been imported from the West, and wasn't appropriate to Thais. While laws, like capitalism, might stem from laudable concepts, he suggested, in practice they were a tool for abuse and exploitation that weakened the kingdom. "We have reformed our administrative systems on the basis of principles of foreign countries, without any regard for the way of life of the people. . . . Law and reality may differ, and there are no small number of loopholes," he told the Chulalongkorn University law faculty in March 1969.[22]

He frequently illustrated his point with the example of the Prachuab Khirikan community, which was democratic in spirit but abused by legalistic officials. "Treating them as simple villagers, we oppressively demand that they must know the law. But such a law . . . is no true law. . . . It is not a matter of blaming people for not knowing the law. . . . If we are to govern and help achieve law and order in this country, we cannot afford to observe the law to the letter. . . . Think in terms of your own personal responsibilities and not your official ones which are colored by bureaucratic strait-jackets of chain of command superiors, subordinates and the rest."[23] In another speech he said: "The law is silent on human beings who are in the forest [already]. . . . Once a reserve forest is opened up, the newcomers come in driving off the previous occupants, sometimes rather brutally, giving rise possibly to terrorism. . . . The weight of real humanitarian consideration together with the precepts of human kindness and of acting really for the common good should be brought to bear and to resist the application of the law in support of the oppressors of the people."[24]

As for the bureaucracy, he cited numerous examples of its sluggishness, wastefulness, and lack of a rational approach to rural problems. In a speech to the Bangkok Rotary Club in 1969, he pointed out that government agencies were perennially hampered by bureaucratic procedure and bound by cumbersome rules of planning and execution, so they never really helped the people. His own royal projects, by comparison, were efficient, didn't cost a lot, helped reduce poverty, stopped deforestation and the narcotics trade, protected people's livelihoods, and made them good citizens. The projects did all this by avoiding frequent meetings, delays, red tape, and the loss of resources to corrupt people. In other words, his projects were superior because he didn't work like the government.[25]

This became a key theme of Bhumibol's reign. He would repeatedly contrast the failures of the bureaucracy and law, and the selfishness of capitalism, with the success of his own initiatives, which arose from pure dhammic practice. But King Bhumibol also understood that dhamma-based unity and selflessness were not enough to build a strong and unified nation. Thais, he saw, were too docile in their acceptance of fate, or karma. This was the downside of non-desire, and it was a dangerous vulnerability of Thai society.

To address this, Bhumibol had to modify the moral code that guided Thais, to advance a profoundly modern shift in dhammic interpretation. He introduced as a moral concept the idea of hard work, beyond duty. This was a radical addition to the catalogue of generally fatalistic Theravada Buddhist virtues, for it tied successful unity to diligence and perseverance, not just karma and good intentions. This was a radical idea, because hard work suggested having goals and making concentrated efforts to achieve them—that is, desire for success and achievement, which was at odds with key principles of Theravada Buddhism.

Under Bhumibol's interpretation hard work had merit in itself. Combined with pure intentions, it brought one closer to happiness, to nirvana, not so much as an individual but as a part of the Thai nation. It even had a karmic value of protecting one from evil and suffering, from communist terrorists and bureaucratic persecution.

The message of hard work began appearing in Bhumibol's speeches in the late 1960s, directed at both educated urbanites, whom he considered generally selfish, and peasants, whom he thought lazy. Sounding more Swiss Calvinist than Siamese dhammaraja, he told them that they would advance if they worked hard, and that they could protect themselves if they were more self-reliant. In a speech he gave in June 1969, for instance, he told development experts that providing modern tractors to help poor farmers clear some forest would only make them lazy and dependent. Already they didn't even bother to weed their crops, he said. Spades and pickaxes were hardly obsolete, and if they did their own work they would be more successful.[26]

Bhumibol also adapted the dhammic virtue of pure intentions. Pure intentions, even together with hard work, were not sufficient to uphold unity and protect the state. Pure intentions still allowed for a fatalistic acceptance of error and failure, a perfidious attitude that weakened not only the poor but the entire country, he told a group of bureaucrats in 1969.

> Errors or breaches of rules and regulations, if motivated by good intentions, are fair enough, but they become more serious if, as sometimes alleged, they are committed through ignorance, for executors of [development projects] are supposed to be proficient and expert and cannot be that ignorant. . . . Mistakes and errors, if committed with honest intentions, can be passed over. But if they are not, it may mean treason. . . . He who causes failure must be a traitor. This may sound too harsh and too strong, but it is within reason, because . . . any chance opening provided for terrorists or infiltrators to make headway is an offense committed against the nation.[27]

What was needed was not well-meaning ignorance but thinking, reason, and knowledge, he told students: "When there is a task to attend to, please pause to consider first . . . means to find out what the task involves and what you are told to do, and then use your own thought or reasoning. There must be a reason for everything, and what you are told to do must be backed by reasons. . . . When in doubt, ask questions so as to perfect one's knowledge. Silence [may] result in some act detrimental to oneself, to the community and to the nation."[28]

Bhumibol's thinking remained rooted in a traditional karmic causality: one receives good by doing good; selflessness and sacrifice bring benefits, while greed and exploitation yield bad consequences. His innovations were on what specifically constituted good, or meritorious behavior or correct practice of dhamma. Advancing his interpretation of dhamma was a sign of his confidence as the kingdom's conscience and wise guru. He detected faults in the national spiritual code and was fulfilling the dhammaraja's role of remedying them.

That his audience didn't always get the message was understandable. His addresses often came across like a Buddhist monk's rambling didactic sermons, employing a dialectic method to reveal the truths he understood. His opinions were couched in ambiguity, hedged by "on the other hand" and flecked with unclear code words for duty and honesty. He always cautioned people to stick to one's specific job and uphold unity and khwam riaproy, social order. And he rarely recommended a clear course of action, leaving his talks to be read in several ways, like the words of an elliptical mountaintop guru.

Apparently much to his chagrin, though, Bhumibol's criticisms struck liberal Thai politicians, students, and workers as a direct attack on the government. After being repressed for more than a decade, they thought he was blessing a people-power movement.

Thailand was ripe for this kind of reaction. Deep changes had taken place in the country since the late 1950s. Bangkok's population had doubled, to four million; its professional white-collar class had multiplied almost tenfold, to more than 200,000; and the number of university students had grown from 20,000 to more than 100,000, most of them in the capital. People in this literate urban middle class had their own expectations. They worried about communists, but with CPT activities consigned to the far countryside they were more concerned about jobs, government corruption, and the ill effects of the U.S. military presence.

Added to this was the rise of urban labor. The country's non-agricultural work force had grown by 50 percent over a decade, mostly in Bangkok-area industries. These workers were poorly paid, lived in slums with few social services, and enjoyed little protection from exploitive employers. Though still few, labor strikes were growing at the end of the 1960s. This made fertile ground for anti-government agitation, particularly by university students and workers arriving from the poor countryside and Thai students returning from Europe and the United States, where they were exposed to vocal antiwar, pro-democracy activism. Increasingly, their sentiments fed into parliament, where Prime Minister Thanom now ran into strong opposition to his arms spending from MPs demanding money for social services.

For many Thais with these new attitudes, King Bhumibol's support for restoring the constitution and parliamentary elections, and his criticisms of the government, sanctioned bolder dissent. A whole generation of students had grown up indoctrinated in Chakri mythology, understanding that the monarchy alone had given the country democracy and constitutionalism and was committed to the people's rights and aspirations. Bhumibol's criticisms showed them that their aspirations were aligned with royal virtue, increasing their righteousness. This perspective received a further boost when Seni and Kukrit Pramoj both attacked the government in 1970. Kukrit wrote in *Siam Rath:* "What is happening to our country? The people are becoming steadily poorer and suffering increasing hardships, . . . crime and banditry are widespread and political bandits seem to be springing up everywhere. . . . I am loyal to our king, but when I consider the conditions in the present day, I cannot help but feel that our country will not be able to avoid having a leftist policy." Given Kukrit's status as a palace mouthpiece and a liberal intellectual, the left could only believe that these were the king's own sentiments.[29]

This placed the king in a compromising position, for he continued to support the military-dominated government. The military and the government were the throne's primary protectors, and he personally liked Thanom, although he didn't care much for Praphas. With emboldened students, labor, and politicians growing more noisy by the day, Bhumibol seemed to realize in 1970 what had been unleashed. Changing his language and message, he exhorted students to curb their passions, not to imitate their counterparts abroad, and remain patient. Their duty was to study now and change society later, when they were employed. Meanwhile, they should let authorities do their jobs.

At Thammasat University in March 1970, he reproached students for holding a protest at the Justice Ministry. The ministry's affairs were not their concern, he said.[30] "Whenever a defect develops in an organization, those who can best correct it belong to that organization. For example, if the courts are going astray, it is up to the members of the judiciary to alleviate the problem." A year later he scolded students for protests at their own universities. At Chulalongkorn University, students and faculty were fighting a deal made by Praphas, who was university chairman, to sell some university land cheaply to his cronies. At an address by the king, students boldly asked him to look into the matter. He replied that they should fight against corruption, but in this case they shouldn't protest but instead broach the issue with the prime minister.[31] Two months later, at Kasetsart University, students audaciously petitioned the king for the reinstatement of an expelled student leader. He told them to be more reasonable and discreet in their initiatives.

But it was too late. The government became more vulnerable when President Nixon suddenly normalized U.S.-China relations in mid-1971. It threw open all questions of who were Thailand's friends and who were its enemies, and whether the United States was still a dependable ally. Fierce political debate erupted in Bangkok, student and worker protests grew, and parliament fell into disarray, with many parliamentarians sensing the possibility of finally replacing Thanom and Praphas.

Seeing their control slipping away, on November 17, 1971, the two leaders overthrew their own government. As in 1958, parliament and the cabinet were dissolved, martial law was declared, and control was placed in the hands of a National Executive Council. Thanom consolidated power in his hands as prime minister, supreme commander, and foreign minister. Praphas was deputy prime minister, interior minister, chief of police, deputy supreme commander, army commander, and head of CSOC, as well as chairman or vice chairman of any number of state enterprises and private companies. The two quickly pledged their loyalty to king, nation, and religion, and explained the coup as necessary to counter grave external and internal threats.

The palace was silent, reluctant to make a concrete show of support. But Thanom was known to be a personal favorite of the king, and when he appeared on TV opening a purported letter of approval from the king presented on a gold tray, a royal endorsement was understood.[32] The king also made no push for the reinstatement of the constitution. The palace, in fact, had every reason to support Thanom, given the rising turbulence. Thanom promised the restoration of order, and that was most important.

Thanom's subsequent actions only inflamed the public, however. Soon afterward, he tried to claim control of the judiciary, still a stronghold of integrity and independence in the government. Student protests against Thanom had public support. The king, who a few years earlier had chosen the respected supreme court judge Sanya Dhammasakdi to be a privy councilor, probably registered his concerns behind the scenes. Thanom was forced to back down. With that victory, wrote political scientists Chai-anan Samudvanija and David Morell, "The students had become the most powerful extra-bureaucratic force in the country . . . all without having attracted the notice of military leaders and politicians."[33] The government handed them one inflammatory issue after another, guaranteeing that their public support base grew.

Over the next year, the economy plunged further into recession, accompanied by high inflation. Because of government cutbacks, graduating students no longer found jobs easily. The rice crop shrank; in 1973, for the first time in memory, Bangkokians had to queue to buy rice. Suddenly worker protests skyrocketed, with 34 strikes in 1972 growing to hundreds in 1973, involving almost 180,000 workers. The war with the CPT intensified as well, yet it didn't go well. The government launched its largest offensive so far in March 1972, arraying 10,000 men for an assault on several hundred CPT soldiers in the lower and upper north. It was a disaster. A few hundred government troops were killed, while the CPT had minimal losses. A second offensive the following October also flopped. Unlike earlier failures, these were well reported in the media. Some commentators compared them to the failed American effort in Vietnam, specifically blaming General Narong Kittikachorn, the particularly repugnant son of Thanom and the son-in-law of Praphas.

Narong came to symbolize all that was going wrong with the government. Deeply unpopular, he was closer in his brutality and ambition to Praphas than to his father. But both depended on him to control an increasingly factionalized and unruly army. Fed by a generous state budget and substantial U.S. support, the army had grown top-heavy, with a surplus of senior officers, and divided into factions dedicated to advancing their own interests in promotions, money, and political ambition. Narong controlled the most powerful and corrupt group, designed to propel him to the job of army chief and, after that, he hoped, prime minister. His venality outraged the public. In 1972, for instance, he took charge of a new government anticorruption agency, which he manipulated to expand his own businesses and extort and terrorize competitors. Thanom and Praphas let him do as he wanted, for they benefited as well.

This left other ambitious army cliques looking for opportunities to dislodge Narong, and Thanom and Praphas as well. One rival was the army deputy commander, General Krit Sivara. A more professional and thinking soldier than most, Krit kept his ambitions and business interests well hidden. He was trusted enough that Praphas delegated to him the army leadership duties. This became a key in the ruling trio's downfall.

In August 1972 activist students from several universities created a new federation, the National Student Center of Thailand (NSCT), to coordinate political activities on a national basis. Led by Chulalongkorn University student Thirayut Boonmee, the organization quickly demonstrated an ability to turn out tens of thousands of protesters on the streets within a few hours. The NSCT's first act was to attack not the government but the Japanese. Japanese businesses dominated Thai industry, and Japan exported a large quantity of goods to Thailand, but it imported little in return. The NSCT launched a ten-day boycott of Japanese products, giving a hefty boost to the group's credibility nationwide.

Throughout 1972, King Bhumibol had remained ambivalent about this rising student and labor juggernaut, and his ambiguous stance encouraged the activists. Most Thais joining the protests were moderate, concerned with social justice, opposed to the U.S. presence, and angry about corruption. A large majority still swore allegiance to the pillars of nation, religion, and king. But Bhumibol wasn't firmly on their side. Because there were a handful of hard-line leftists in their ranks circulating Marxist and Maoist materials, the king and others worried that they represented a CPT front. In a speech at Thammasat—the university started by Pridi Bhanomyong—he made little reference to the Thanom government's misrule, while focusing on the alleged leftist underpinnings of student activists. He also betrayed a deep-seated disdain for intellectuals.[34]

> At present there seems to be a new theory that all things that have been formerly established must be abolished and destroyed by violent means so that something new may be initiated. It is an expression of intellect and creativeness on the part of the highly educated. This new theory originated abroad and has gained considerable influence. . . . You should make special research into this theory, to find out whether the destruction of old established things for the sake of bringing about the new would lead to entirely good results. . . . Moreover, there seems to be no guarantee that the new things thus brought about will be good for certain. . . . After due consideration, it is my view that real creativeness may be expressed only by peaceful means . . . allowing all sectors and all men to participate in the correction of things.

The king and government clearly took the student-labor protest movement seriously. Probably at the king's suggestion, in December 1972 Thanom attempted to head off the rising pressure by restoring the constitution and the legislative assembly. But as in 1968, the new charter simply reinforced his power. It established a wholly appointed 299-member National Legislative Assembly, which was then filled by 200 men from the armed forces and police, with the rest, less than one-third, civilians. As before, the executive retained strong control over the government.

In reaction, the opposition intensified. Amid the crumbling economy and constant street protests, rumors were spread that Thanom, Praphas, and Narong intended to declare a republic and hold power permanently. Two years before, Thanom and Praphas had already breached the law by refusing to retire from their military positions at the statutory age. Narong supposedly boasted that he would become Thailand's first president. This was branded an offense to the king, provoking Kukrit Pramoj to call for the government to resign. Now people openly branded Thanom, Praphas, and Narong "the three tyrants."

Bhumibol stayed on the sidelines. He repeated to students that they should study rather than demonstrate, and leave government to the officials. But he also obliquely criticized the government. In one speech he even drew on the language of Marxism in declaring peasant landlessness the country's most pressing problem.

> At present, changes are taking place rather ominously; people are becoming slaves on the land under the oppressive yoke of capitalists. . . . Ours is a system in which each has his own land and shelter, but all that is now being turned into the reviled system of feudalism of medieval Europe, with a hierarchy of oppressive rule down to the lowest stratum. . . . People used to work on their land or land which could be theirs but for the capitalists' offer to buy it, which was accepted out of the illusion that the money thus received could bring them to happiness. But in reality . . . with the money gone, they had to hire themselves out and cheaply, too, and finally became the capitalists' slaves.[35]

An accident sparked the denouement. On April 29, 1973, an army helicopter crashed in the Thungyai wildlife preserve. It was full of Narong Kittikachorn's army cronies on an illegal hunting trip, shooting animals from the air. When nine students from Ramkhamhaeng University were expelled for producing a political satire of the incident, the NSCT mobilized tens of thousands of students and nonstudents to protest. The government shut the universities, a tactical mistake, for it only put more students on the street. Students, labor leaders, and opposition politicians attacked the government on every front, seizing up the city.

The demonstrations and government responses became, in part, competing claims of loyalty to nation, religion, and king. The government insisted that the students were driven by leftist, "un-Thai" sentiments, implying that they were communist, godless, and opposed to the throne. The students paraded holding high pictures of the king and queen, at times turning toward the palace to sing the royal anthem. Still Bhumibol did not commit himself, but the students presumed his support after he told the police to refrain from violence during the June protests and had tents and food laid out on Chitrlada Palace grounds for the protesters.

Worried about a coup from within the army, in September Praphas named Krit the commander in chief. But he then put Narong in control of all strategic army units in Bangkok, assuming this would prevent Krit from attempting a takeover of the government. On October 6, Praphas had 13 students, including NSCT head Thirayut, arrested for sedition after they distributed leaflets demanding a new constitution. Rumors spread that they had been killed, and students and others poured into the streets en masse, protesting day after day at parliament, at Thammasat University, and at Sanam Luang next to the Grand Palace. Another focal point of protests was the Democracy Monument in the middle of Rajadamnoen Road, the monument that Phibun had erected following his vanquishing of the royalists in 1939. Now it had become a potent symbol for constitutionalism under a monarchy, and against dictatorship. The depth of the protesters' support was illustrated by Thanom's brother, retired police major general Sa-nga Kittikachorn. He announced at the time, "If the demanding of the constitution is to be interpreted as treason, then there are probably 38 million traitors in Thailand at present."[36]

The monarchy became a focal point of the battle. Students demanded to know, if the king's position as head of state was guaranteed only by the constitution, then where was the constitution? Without it, they said, the Three Tyrants were guilty of republicanism and lèse-majesté. Against claims like this, the junta had difficulty arguing that the students were a threat to the throne. But it also put the king on the spot: he hadn't openly expressed a desire for a constitution himself.

With tacit support from General Krit, on October 13 some 400,000 demonstrators gathered at the Democracy Monument and at parliament, just a short walk from Chitrlada Palace, where the king lived and worked. As the protesters sang and chanted peacefully, they hoisted portraits of the king and queen in the air. What then took place is murky in later accounts, especially, and very deliberately, what the role of the king was. To defuse the confrontation, probably at the king's request, the authorities released the 13 arrested students from a distant suburban Bangkok facility that morning. Late in the afternoon, Bhumibol summoned Thanom and Praphas and ostensibly obtained their agreement to draft a new, democratic constitution. After they left, the king invited into the palace a group of student delegates, though not including any of the 13 arrested leaders, who hadn't yet returned to downtown Bangkok. After over an hour, the students emerged to report that the generals had conceded to a new constitution.

In fact, Thanom and Praphas had agreed to draw up the new charter only over 12 months.[37] This wasn't completely convincing. After having stalled for years on the same promise, there was no guarantee of their follow-through. Some observers believe that King Bhumibol let Thanom promise the charter simply to get the students off the streets.

Later reports by his top aide and liaison with the students at the time, police general Vasit Dejkunchorn, suggest that Bhumibol was unsympathetic to the students' demands. Vasit recounted that the king told them the government had been generous, giving more than they asked, and that they were young and should just try to benefit from the experience of their elders.[38] Other reports suggested that Bhumibol was much more patronizing in explaining why the students shouldn't protest: "Even the wisest of monkeys uses its feet to scratch its head. Men are wiser than monkeys, for we use hands to scratch our heads and we use our feet to walk with. Therefore, when we have some problems, we should use our head to try to find the solution and should not use our feet for that purpose."[39]

Even so, the students were apparently overawed and empowered by their personal audience with the king. They emerged from Chitrlada claiming victory, and told fellow protesters to go home. However, not all of the student leaders understood the results of the royal meeting, or agreed that it was a real victory. The twelve months was too long, and the Three Tyrants still held power, some felt. As they tried to obtain clarification and reach a common stance, 50,000 protesters remained outside Chitrlada Palace through the night. Seeking a more concrete statement from the king, two student representatives entered to meet with Vasit and another top royal aide, M.R. Tongnoi Tongyai, who said the king wouldn't see the students again. Vasit went out and repeated the king's agreement with Thanom and Praphas. After he did so, he recounted later, the protesters cheered, sang the royal anthem, and began to disperse.

As they decamped just at sunrise, fighting broke out—due to accidental pushing, or police heavy-handedness, or, some believe, deliberate provocation. Whoever was responsible, the result was that police beat several students, a riot erupted, and the police and army reinforcements began shooting. This brought thousands more protesters out into the streets, and Narong directed foot soldiers and tanks to fire on the crowds. Narong himself shot into the crowds from above in a helicopter. At least 70 people were killed, although the exact number was never determined.

It fell to the patiently waiting Krit, not the king, to end things. Under pressure from the cabinet, Thanom and Praphas resigned their political jobs. But they refused to give up their respective positions of commander and deputy commander in chief of the armed forces. When they ordered in more troops to confront the demonstrators, Krit blocked the command and, now working with the king, forced them to resign all positions and leave the country. As Praphas and Narong fled to Taiwan, and Thanom to the United States, Bhumibol appeared on television to announce that it was all over, directing the protesters to go home. He named Sanya Dhammasakdi, his privy councilor and also the rector of Thammasat, to be prime minister. The next day Krit led the heads of the armed forces in declaring their loyalty to the king.

October 14, 1973, has ever since taken on legendary proportions, in Thai consciousness and in Bhumibol's own record. To the students of that and succeeding generations, it was an unprecedented people's uprising against tyranny. "It was the first time in modern Thai history that the masses had rallied to take up arms against the ruling elite, to demand a change in leadership," said the historian Joseph Wright.[40] People power was the very thing that the 1932 revolt lacked, and the 1973 protest and massacre offered more than 70 martyrs as symbols.

In official histories, however, it was the king who had single-handedly restored constitutionalism and democracy. Rather than credit the popular uprising, later books and articles overwhelmingly emphasized King Bhumibol's intervention against the dictators, saving the country from disaster.

However it was characterized, the October 1973 uprising marked a new zenith in the restoration of the throne's power and grandeur. For the first time in his reign, Bhumibol publicly inserted himself into a very tense confrontation. He did this much on his own. At 46, with 27 years on the throne, Bhumibol no longer had savvy old princes to advise him; he had more experience than most anyone inside the palace or out. The issues he had to wrestle with weren't complicated and, with his extensive network of loyal informants, he had months to assess his options. The 1971 coup made plain to everyone the problems of the military's unchecked political power, which the king had accepted. In 1972 and early 1973, the full scope of government sordidness was laid bare for all to see. The students' loyalty to the throne, their earnest desire for greater democracy, and the public's support for them were also evident. Even the military was fed up with the Three Tyrants.

Equally evident, at the beginning of October, was the strong possibility of a violent clash. Yet the king's first settlement supported the government and gave the students little of what they had asked for. Thanom and Praphas remained in power, and a new constitution was promised only for a year later. This suggests that Bhumibol did not view Thanom and Praphas as the paramount problem, and his attempt to placate the students without truly giving ground helped lead to the violence. Only after the army killed scores of demonstrators did he move decisively

against the Three Tyrants. As one analysis of the period said: "His open intervention in October 1973 to end the uprising . . . should be understood as a necessary
move to reestablish calm and stability, not as support for major socio-political
reform in Thai society—as the reformers chose to interpret it."[41]

Emerging as the hero of democracy, then, was a considerable act of alchemy
that rested in the people's—and the students'—faith in Bhumibol's dhammaraja
virtues. This required emphasizing his altogether remarkable move to meet with
the students, which elevated them to the status of the generals; his letting them take
cover inside the palace when the shooting began; and his then agreeing with Krit to
expel the tyrants. With those elements highlighted, he emerged as the savior of
the day.

But by claiming to represent the peoples' aspirations in this episode, Bhumibol
validated the student movement and the political power of the masses. That clearly
left him disconcerted. Meeting a group of student leaders in the aftermath of
October 14, he lectured, back in his Buddhist monk mode, that they should control
themselves: "For instance, when we are angry, we generate much energy which may
however be dispersed and not used to the full for failure of control by the intellect
or moral fiber. Anger thus saps your full physical power, because, in anger, our
mind is not clear but befogged."[42]

12   Royal Vigilantism and Massacre, 1974–76 ᐬ

THE UPRISING OF OCTOBER 1973 MARKED THE BEGINNING of the most turbulent three years in modern Thai history, which culminated in a barbaric massacre at Thammasat University on October 6, 1976. The three years also marked an important turning point for the throne. King Bhumibol began the period as a classic unifying monarch and a leader committed to democratic government. By 1976, he had cast his lot with the fanatical right, abandoning moderates and the left. Breaking a primary precept of dhammaraja rule, he split his kingdom.

October 1973 put Bhumibol at the acme of his reign. "After twenty-seven years," wrote Chai-anan Samudvanija and David Morell, "King Bhumibol had become the most powerful figure in his nation's political system."[1] The journalist T. D. Allmann gushed more hyperbolically: "There is little doubt here that the king, if he so wished, could restore to himself the absolute power which Thai kings, the traditional Siamese 'lords of life,' enjoyed until 1932. . . . Instead, the king's actions since October have been deliberately self-effacing." Allmann added an increasingly popular exaggeration: "There is hardly a village in Thailand where the king has not opened a school or clinic, and very few Thais have not seen the king, at least once, performing his duties with a seriousness that seems at times almost incongruous in this normally easy-going country."[2]

In fact, there remained thousands of villages without schools or clinics, and most Thais had never seen the king. But such details were easily overlooked in the widespread yearning for a true dhammaraja. Everyone saw in Bhumibol what he or she desired. Conservative Thais saw him leading the fight against disorder, socialism, and anything that challenged the status quo. To the students, Bhumibol supported democratic change and an open society. "He is to us what the constitution is to the Americans: our last recourse against tyranny," said one.[3] To some foreigners, he demonstrated the enduring value of sovereign monarchy.

Only a handful of liberal politicians and academics quietly understood the ascendant power of the throne itself as contrary to representative democracy. A young lawyer and politician, Chuan Leekpai, said at the time: "The voters themselves are the most important component of the society. They must understand the mechanisms and procedures and be able to make judgments on those persons who presume to represent them. . . . What is needed is to let the people have an opportunity and enough time to gain political experience on their own. It is a pity, however, that in the past 42 years the people have never had such a chance."[4]

October 1973 had brought all these people together around the goal of expelling the Three Tyrants. After they were gone, there really wasn't anything binding them together. Although the king took the lead to oversee the crafting of a new constitution and restructuring the government, the unity behind him lasted only a few months.

Sanya Dhammasakdi, the privy councilor Bhumibol named as prime minister, was an honest jurist and a pious Buddhist who had been close to the palace ever since he took the king's deposition in the Ananda death investigation. He was no commanding leader. But as the king's adviser and proxy, he channeled the palace's momentary enthusiasm for constitutional government and the rule of law. Sanya named men he and the king personally trusted to the cabinet and the constitution drafting committee, which included respected justice minister Prakob Hutasing, Kukrit Pramoj, and a number of academics. They produced their first draft by January 8, 1974.

Vetting the draft democratically posed a problem, however. The old parliament hand-picked by Thanom remained in place. Leaving the charter's approval to them would undermine its legitimacy. So it was decided that Bhumibol would choose 2,347 Thais "from all walks of life," including farmers, laborers, businessmen, professionals, students, and civil servants, to elect from among themselves a 299-man convention to scrutinize the draft. With this solution, the king's prestige as a democrat was further heightened.

The king announced the 2,347 names on December 10, 1973, Constitution Day. A week later they met inside the Royal Turf Club, where the king consecrated their duty as a royal mission. On December 19, they were each told to nominate 100 people from among themselves to the final convention. Because few delegates even knew 100 names to select, they chose bureaucrats and famous Thais like Kukrit and Puey Ungphakorn, the incorruptible former central bank governor and new Thammasat University rector. As a result, the constitutional convention took on a distinctly conservative face: most of the 299 were from Bangkok, half were from government, and 12 percent were businessmen and bankers.

The draft charter they received resembled the constitution of 1946. It didn't increase the king's powers, and it shifted power away from the executive to a bicameral parliament in which the elected lower house would choose the upper house itself. Ministers, including the prime minister, had to be national assembly members. The drafting committee also required a referendum for approval of the constitution before the king received it. Since the king could hardly reject such an overt act of popular will, it placed, on this one issue, people power on an equal level with royal power.

Publicly the palace appeared content with the draft. Yet it was blocked by a large conservative faction in the constitutional convention organized by Kasem Chatikavanich, the head of the Electricity Generating Authority of Thailand (EGAT) and an intimate of the king. Over the next nine months Kasem-led conservatives tore up the draft and wrote their own. On the face of it, the conservatives' draft indulged the democracy movement. The preamble declared that this constitution had been demanded by the people on October 13–14, 1973, and then said that the king had examined the draft and found it acceptable. The constitution came, then, from both the people and the palace, as opposed to previous charters' assertions that the king was the sole source.

The constitution also laid out a progressive set of the rights and responsibilities of the Thai people. Men and women were equal. Workers had the right to organize. Meanwhile all Thais were bound to uphold the nation, religion, and king as well as the democratic form of government. The constitution and the monarchy were given equal status. State officials and privy councilors had to swear allegiance to both, and amnesty was to be denied anyone who overthrew either the king or the constitution. In previous coups the king had granted amnesty when the constitution was abrogated.

Beyond those points, the charter watered down many of the original's democratic aspirations, restored power to the executive, and increased royal power like the 1949 constitution. Emergency powers were moved from the executive to the king. The king's prerogative to appoint and remove officials was expanded to cover all top ranks in the military and bureaucracy. The conservative draft also gave the king the power to appoint the senate with the countersign of his chief privy councilor. The senate would have strong checks over the larger lower house, and overriding the king's veto required a two-thirds majority of both houses, meaning the palace could block any legislation with the full senate's backing and a handful of MPs. Moreover, the senate had the ability to kill any legislation by sitting on house bills for six months without voting.

The final draft included a ban on sitting bureaucrats (including soldiers) serving in parliament. This was a wish of the king, who felt civil servants needed to focus on their jobs and remain, like him, above politics. Likewise, the constitution allowed the prime minister to choose half of his cabinet from outside the parliament, again reflecting the bias against politicians.

Finally, the new constitution would not be subject to national referendum; it needed passage only by the constitutional convention. Indeed, by the time the final draft was promulgated in October 1974, it was the convention's creation, and not at all what Prime Minister Sanya had envisioned. At one point he even resigned, only to be pushed by King Bhumibol to stay on. The palace, on the contrary, found the final product democratic enough, with one exception: early in 1975 the palace had it amended to stipulate that the prime minister countersign the king's senate appointments, rather that the privy council president. The original approach made the king too overt a political actor.

The king likely embraced the right's hijacking of the constitution because of the unnerving turbulence that marked Sanya's tenure during 1974. October 1973 released stresses that had festered for two decades. Chaos descended on Bangkok as everyone with complaints about social justice, corruption, abuse of power, and economic exploitation took to the streets, incited by an explosion of new media voices—177 new newspaper licenses were issued in 1974. As Thailand succumbed to the global recession, in December 1973 alone there were 249 labor strikes.

Farmers and workers had good reason to complain. Real wages had declined over the previous decade, and the minimum wage was mostly unenforced. When inflation jumped to 5 percent a month in late 1973, the financial situation became untenable for many. The royal family's investments became involved. During 1974 workers went on strike at the luxury Dusit Thani Hotel, partly owned by the Crown Property Bureau. With the strike drawing negative attention to the king's business interests, the hotel was forced to make concessions. Throughout 1974 groups of farmers poured into Bangkok to complain about crop prices, rising rents, land seizures by lenders, and tenancy. Students helped mobilize them, at one point busing to Bangkok thousands of farmers who had been cheated out of their land. Also supported by students, in September 1974 about 7,000 farmers in eight provinces threatened to declare their lands "liberated zones."

Pursuing their own issues with great effect, the students exposed the CIA's manipulations of the government and U.S. involvement in official corruption. They revealed the Thai military's fabrication of insurgent atrocities while carrying out its own, such as the grisly murder of southern activists by putting them into drums of boiling oil. In a notorious case, the student leader Thirayut Boonmee showed that the total destruction of an Isan village, Ban Na Sai, had not been the handiwork of the CPT, as the army claimed, but of the CSOC. The students showed that the counterinsurgency program was out of control, doing more damage than the CPT.

In the sangha, too, pro-democracy monks also held protests. In late 1974 a group of reformist monks launched a hunger strike to force the supreme patriarch to reopen the case of Phimontham, the palace-hated senior monk whom Sarit had forced to disrobe. Under their pressure Phimontham was formally cleared, though he wasn't granted the senior rank he merited. Kukrit Pramoj declared that Bhumibol had refused Phimontham the rank "because his stars are not consistent with those of the king."[5]

As leftist as they may have sometimes appeared, the protesters did not threaten the state. They liked Sanya for his real efforts to address rural poverty and injustice. He set up a committee to mediate disputes between farmers and landowners and money-lenders. He controlled paddy rents and established a land redistribution program that would allow people to occupy degraded reserve forests, though without receiving ownership rights. The king himself considered these the primary social issues. Sanya's tenure was nevertheless too short and his legitimacy too tenuous for him to make much headway on other pressing social problems. He survived in office mainly through the protection of the king and the popular army chief Krit Sivara, who quashed talk of rebellion among army hard-liners by declaring that the overthrow of Sanya would constitute a coup against the throne.

Protests subsided in advance of the elections in January 1975. But none of the 22 separate parties winning parliamentary seats came close to a majority. The fragmented parliament was dominated by businessmen and professionals, many linked to military and bureaucratic cliques. The Democrats, led by Seni Pramoj, had the most seats, and to the apparent dismay of the king and the far right they formed a center-liberal coalition and made Seni prime minister.

Seni was never given a chance to lead, however. Within a few weeks the conservatives brought down his government, replacing it with an uneasy alliance between three right-wing parties and the liberal Social Action Party created by Kukrit Pramoj, who became prime minister. The new coalition's far-right underpinnings were more reassuring to the palace, and the king trusted that Kukrit's commitment to royal traditions was greater than his belief in parliamentary politics.

Kukrit's oratorical talent, earthy sense of humor, and ingrained distrust of the army made him widely popular with the people, including academics and students. He launched a progressive social agenda seemingly matching the king's. Prior to the election Kukrit had declared himself in favor of better distribution of wealth via improved taxation, administration, and education.[6] He said land reform was crucial to solving rural problems. And as for the insurgency, he said, "past governments haven't been doing anything to lessen it." Improving rural livelihoods and income "would bring many people in from the jungle. Most of them are not ideological."

After taking office Kukrit established a respectable minimum wage, improved funding for rural development, land reform, and public housing, and moved to decentralize government. He created the position of Bangkok governor to give the city its own administration. In the king's name he made an earnest attempt at land reform, asking the land-rich to donate property, or sell it cheaply to the government, to then be made available to landless farmers. According to one account, the first donor was program head Chitti Tingsabadh, one of Sanya's colleagues in the Justice Ministry who quietly gave more than 10,000 acres to the king, who then donated it in his own name to the program as an example.

Apparently less to the palace's pleasure, Kukrit set a one-year deadline for the departure of the 25,000 U.S. personnel and 350 aircraft that remained in Thailand, and made friendly overtures to Vietnam and China. He declared his intention to abolish the Anticommunist Act, which served the police and military as a tool of repression.

Kukrit's policies were popular, but between the military, the parliamentary opposition, and Kukrit's own far-right coalition partners, they were stifled or sabotaged. Farmer support programs stalled in the bureaucracy, and there was no enforcement of the minimum wage. Kukrit faced constant threats of an army coup, and his coalition partners cooperated with the army to protect the Anticommunist Act and abort Kukrit's foreign policy initiatives. The land-reform program flopped completely. Despite the king's involvement, no one else, not even from among Bhumibol's own circle of the wealthy and powerful, donated land.

To some, Kukrit's tenure demonstrated that parliamentary government could work if given a chance. To others its ineffectiveness proved the opposite. When King Bhumibol gave a quiet nod to Kukrit's removal at the beginning of 1976, it appeared he had given in to the latter view, after barely a year of trying out elected government.

In fact, well before Kukrit's short term in office the king had thrown his lot in with the Thai conservative forces. Throughout Sanya's tenure, publicly Bhumibol appeared committed to the spirit of the 1973 uprising. On October 14, 1974, he attended a memorial service at Sanam Luang for those who had been killed a year earlier. Afterward, a piece of CPB land on Rajadamnoen Road, near the Democracy Monument, was set aside for a monument to the 1973 martyrs. But even at that time the king was building strong bonds with the most hard-line factions in the armed forces, politics, and business, who were organizing to oppose what they perceived as the leftward drift of the country, threatening nation, religion, and the monarchy.

Thai conservatives were convinced that protesting students, workers, and farmers were a fifth column for the CPT and North Vietnam. They had taken notice of the student-led Red Guard tearing apart China in the Cultural Revolution, and the American students who helped force Richard Nixon from office and the United States to abandon South Vietnam. Western conservatives told them Thailand was Hanoi's next target, saying—as the U.S. ambassador to Bangkok did in 1974—that protesting Thai students were a dangerous "neo-Marxist" movement.

There was little evidence for this conclusion. To be sure, the CPT insurgency had grown by 1974–75 to an estimated 8,000 armed combatants, controlling territory involving over 100,000 people.[7] Their rhetoric on the radio often talked of revolutionary war. But they were far from a unified force, and they appealed to peasants by focusing on social injustices while avoiding attacking the monarchy and Buddhism. Their expansion was arguably fueled more by the government's alienation of the peasantry. "The communist threat has been demonstrably exaggerated," said one writer in late 1974. "After more than 20 years of effort, the communists are still confined to border areas."[8]

Moreover, Marxist ideology failed to attract a significant following among urban Thais. There was some creeping radicalism among the student, farmer, and labor activists. Leftist literature like the martyred Jit Phumisak's *The Face of Thai Feudalism* was revived, and socialism was a hot topic of discussion. Some students declared sympathy with Indochina's so-called national liberation movements. Yet leftist ideological activities involved very few students. Throughout 1974 most student leaders continued to regard King Bhumibol as a beacon of justice and democracy. The small minority who were critical of the monarchy kept their views to themselves.

This was despite the king's repeated criticisms of the students. He lectured those attending Chulalongkorn University to study diligently and quietly, that the noisy activists' ideas were wrong: "Nowadays, free thinking is understood by some . . . to mean to think differently from others. Such understanding is not quite right. Thinking must primarily aim at thinking things out so as to have a clear idea as to what they are. . . . To pursue a way of thinking only for the sake of being different from others can also be done, but it is doubtful whether any benefit will result." He had a similar message for protesting farmers: "They believe that if they come to Bangkok, their problems would be solved. But demonstrations are expensive. I agree that sometimes it is necessary so that the government will wake up and see the problem. But demonstrations should not be carried out too often since the demonstrators themselves will waste both their time and money."[9]

The students failed to notice how Bhumibol had grown much closer to the military hard-liners. Most of his original advisers and mentors had died by the early 1970s or were very old and feeble. They were replaced unofficially with generals whose discipline and loyalty the king and queen valued. That the generals weren't blue-blooded princes didn't matter. Queen Sirikit surrounded herself with the wives of officers, when not the officers themselves. Crown Prince Vajiralongkorn was pointed toward a military career. After grade school in England and a prep school in Sydney, Australia, in 1972 he entered Duntroon Royal Military Academy, Australia's prestigious officer's school. Whenever back in Thailand, the prince spent most of his time with military minders.

The close palace-military relationship ignored, and possibly exacerbated, the rampant corruption and indiscipline in the military brass. Extremely top-heavy, Thailand's military had 600 generals and admirals, and 24 four-star generals in the army alone. Many spent their time enriching themselves and pursuing political power, further entrenching the military's deep factionalism. Meanwhile, poor training and indiscipline meant the soldiers themselves had very limited combat ability and no strategic vision.[10]

If the king understood this, he made no efforts to change it. His occasional comment about corruption singled out civilian bureaucrats and politicians. Although the generals he became closest to were relatively clean, he made no signs of distinguishing between the honest, professional officers and the corrupt and

destructive ones. Army chief Krit Sivara wasn't in the inner palace circle, despite his
moderating role in October 1973 and his support for Kukrit.

Bhumibol's closest advisers, his new inner court, were key generals in the
Internal Security Operations Command, or ISOC, which replaced CSOC in the
name of reform after the overthrow of Thanom and Praphas. Many hoped the king
would push ISOC to make more social-based efforts to lure the peasants from the
CPT. Instead, counterinsurgency operations became harsher. In November 1973,
ISOC launched a bombing campaign on hill-tribe villages in the far north, and
continued with the same tactics in the months afterward. Less overtly, ISOC and
other conservative leaders formed several operations designed to subvert the left in
the city and countryside through propaganda and violence, in the name of preserving nation-religion-monarchy. Bhumibol knew of and sanctioned all of these.

The first was a mass rural patriotic organization, the Village Scouts.[11] During
the 1960s peasants were instructed to simply trust the king and queen and their
agents for protection from evil and injustice. The main sources of trouble, they
were told, were communists and capitalists. A typical propaganda poster placed in
villages had two panels. The one labeled communist showed a Chinese man (both
communists and capitalists were typically characterized as ethnic Chinese) lording
over miserable, destitute peasants. The other, labeled peace, showed the king grace-
fully greeting a crowd of smiling, healthy Thais. The poster resembled popular
temple murals depicting the Buddhist heaven and hell.

As the insurgency grew, the palace needed a more resilient link with rural
Thais, one not mediated by unthinking bureaucrats and soldiers. Inspired by the
Wild Tiger Corps of King Vajiravudh, in August 1971 a BPP officer, Somkhuan
Harikul, founded the Village Scouts as a community team for resisting the CPT.
Ideally, one person from each family joined the local scout unit. They became a new
village elite after undergoing a rigorous three-day initiation by the BPP, described
by the anthropologist Katherine Bowie as ideological indoctrination and bonding
through high-pressure psychological techniques. All their activities were designed
around traditional royalist definitions of Thailand and Thai-ness, joining virtues
of loyalty, unity, non-desire, orderliness, and discipline to Vajiravudh's nation-
religion-king mantra. They stressed familial bonds, with Bhumibol and Sirikit the
nation's patriarch and matriarch.

Village Scout directors from the BPP stressed and exaggerated the imminent
danger of the communists to the kingdom. The scouts were told that North
Vietnam, allegedly an ancient enemy, was using the CPT for a planned takeover of
Thailand. South Vietnam, Laos, and Cambodia were already lost because those

countries had no indivisible trinity binding the people. As the local scout units promoted this thinking through their village, they effectively extended the BPP's intelligence network. Their sole uniform was the "king's kerchief," blessed personally by King Bhumibol just as a monk blessed holy medallions. The kerchiefs were awarded in a religious-like ritual, also sometimes personally by the king.

King Bhumibol himself wrote a code of behavior that said a lot about his own view of a well-functioning Thai cosmos.[12] The Village Scouts did not get involved in politics or show off their power, he instructed. They were not to organize under the official government system. Their affairs were conducted "of the people, by the people and for the people," and they were leaders in local self-development. They worked as a group, not individuals, to promote unity and readiness. The Village Scouts also set the pace in building discipline and thrift, did not spend money excessively for scout activities, and did not use political funds, the king wrote. Alcohol was not permitted in scout training activities, and scout leaders would promote Thai-produced goods and food. Finally, the scouts were instructed to be leaders in restoring and protecting the "good traditions and culture" of each village. It was about everyone performing his assigned task, working in unity without desire, complaint, or criticism, and staying away from the government system, that is, from corrupt politics and inefficient bureaucracy. Bowie observed that "the movement . . . encouraged an orderliness and a passivity compatible with an authoritarian government."[13]

The royal family was involved with the scouts from the very beginning. As BPP patron, Princess Mother Sangwal presided over one of the first initiation ceremonies in November 1971. She presented Somkhuan with a book on counterinsurgency, an act revealing the Mahidols' growing sense of being under siege.[14] The following March 19, the king and queen graced an induction ceremony, awarding initiates their kerchiefs. Later the king invited the movement's BPP founders to the palace and offered his official patronage with 100,000 baht.

The movement tied into the king's magic circle of merit. The BPP's budget wasn't large enough to finance it fully, and cash-poor villagers couldn't fund the induction rites. The king ordered that the movement not be a burden on the government. But his endorsement allowed the scouts to attract donations from the fretful middle and upper classes, who could fight communism and share royal merit at the same time. Charity kept the Village Scouts out of the government's control and under the monarchy directly, binding an elite of hyperloyal rural peasants. "We do not want scouts to be the private army of anyone," the king said in a 1973 speech.[15] Instead they became his own.

By 1974, Village Scout membership had risen to tens of thousands, almost all in rural, CPT-confronted Thailand. That year ISOC and its allies in the Interior Ministry took control of the movement, turning it into a national organization that spanned the entire countryside and cities. Behind this expansion was the BPP leader and ISOC associate General Suraphon Chulabrahm, a longtime confidant of the king and his mother.

Membership grew exponentially as the scouts filled up with minor business-men, street-stall operators, low-ranking civil servants, and the wives of govern-ment officials, military and police officers, and even palace staff. Hundreds of thousands of Thais went through the three-day initiation, which was filled with invective against the CPT, the Vietnamese, and student protesters. These forces were said to be on the verge of destroying the nation-religion-king triune, like the Burmese who had destroyed Ayutthaya. In ceremony after ceremony, the king, the queen, and their children now handed out more Village Scout scarves and flags than they did university degrees. Like holy royal amulets, the kerchiefs gave each scout a sense of proximity to the throne.

After the ISOC takeover, the Village Scouts metamorphosed into a fascist-style mass political movement. Now, Bowie wrote, "The urbanized Village Scout move-ment was not focused on winning the hearts and minds of villages in the border areas, but . . . on changing the course of national politics."[16]

Much less visible than the Village Scouts was the formation of two organizations that would undertake vigilante actions in the name of nation-religion-king. These were the Krating Daeng, or Red Gaur, and Navapol. Named after a very large and testy native Thai forest ox, the Red Gaur consisted mostly of former soldiers and mercenaries, ex-convicts, and technical school punks organized in early 1974 by ISOC officer Sudsai Hasdin. Told that students and other activists were monarchy-threatening communists, they became the right wing's street enforcers, disrupting demonstrations and menacing the leaders of the left. Their first show of force was when King Bhumibol commemorated those who were killed in the October 1973 uprising in a ceremony on October 14, 1974, at Sanam Luang. Before the ceremony began, a group of toughs led by Sudsai marched menacingly through nearby Thammasat University. During the rites, they surrounded Bhumibol and his fam-ily, declaring that the king was in danger of being shot by students hiding inside the school. The king made no effort to distance himself from them.[17]

Navapol was far more secretive and sinister. It was an ISOC operation orga-nized in 1974 by the former military intelligence chief General Wallop Rojanavisut,

CIA associate Wattana Kiewimon, BPP chief General Suraphon, ISOC head Sai-yudh Kerdphol, and former northern region army chief General Samran Bhaetya-kul. The name Navapol meant "nine strengths" or "power of the Ninth," suggesting the Chakri Ninth Reign. Citing the king's own worries, General Wallop said Nava-pol had been created to "build a Thai wall against the communists," who endan-gered Buddhism and the monarchy.[18] He claimed that activist students received support from Pridi Bhanomyong, the KGB, the International Socialist Party, and the CPT.

At its highest level, Navapol was a sort of Masonic elite of men intellectually committed to the traditional construction of Thai culture and values. They came from the top echelons of the bureaucracy, the armed services, business, the sangha, and the palace. They were proud of their dedication and of not being part of the corrupt business-political establishment. One key nonmilitary figure was the su-preme court judge Tanin Kraivixien, an ardent monarchist and anticommunist, and a friend of the king. At a lower level, Navapol built its membership from local businessmen and officials in the towns. They held anticommunist rallies to recruit members and money from others in the bourgeois strata. Some were selected to take part in secret units of saboteurs, provocateurs, and hit squads designed to terrorize the left.

A key link between the two levels was the notorious monk Kittivudho Bhikku. Kittivudho had risen through the sangha ranks during the 1960s in part on aggres-sive campaigning against the reformer monk Phimontham. In 1967 he opened Jittiphawan College, a very unusual ordination and training center in Chonburi province that operated outside the official sangha organization. At Jittiphawan young monks were trained in social activism of a kind that promoted a state founded on a "natural" Thai system of paternalistic social welfare, rather than a "modern" or "Western" government-directed system. This ideal state's social hier-archy was based on relative merit, gained through birth and pure dhamma prac-tice. That made the hierarchy immutable, and trying to change it was an act of destroying the state.

Such ideas dovetailed with Bhumibol's own thinking, and he together with Queen Sirikit inaugurated Jittiphawan in 1967. They returned frequently even after Kittivudho began to focus on communism, students, and liberals as the enemies of his "natural" state. When Navapol adopted Kittivudho and flew him around the country to make rabble-rousing anticommunist, anti-student speeches, he turned Jittiphawan into a training facility for Navapol's secret operations. These included assassinations.

By the end of 1974, the sinister direction of these organizations was becoming apparent. As conservative media began to brand protesters communist and accuse them of lèse-majesté, a famous student activist, several farmer and labor protesters, and an American journalist who wrote about them were all murdered. None of the murders were ever seriously investigated. In December, a faction of army and ISOC hard-liners brought the exiled former premier Thanom back into the country, momentarily. Only after several days were Sanya and General Krit able to force him to leave again.

Even before the January 1975 elections, the network connecting the ISOC, the palace, and the extreme right ensured that the Kukrit government would never succeed. While Kukrit pursued improved relations with Beijing and Hanoi, the conservatives grew fearful at the U.S. withdrawal from Indochina, which led to the fall of Cambodia to the Khmer Rouge and Saigon to the North Vietnamese in April. Despite Kukrit's warning that it only made things worse, ISOC's counterinsurgency campaign grew more brutal. A rising air of panic was stoked by well-circulated but bogus U.S. intelligence reports detailing Hanoi's strategy to take control of all of mainland Southeast Asia.[19]

The vigilante groups stepped up their activities. When Kukrit proposed the introduction of regular democratic elections in local districts and villages, Navapol organized 500 village leaders from upcountry to protest in parliament.[20] Just before the first-ever visit to Bangkok of a Hanoi government delegation as part of Kukrit's détente program, the defense minister and ISOC figure Pramarn Adireksan declared that the Vietnamese were plotting against Thailand.[21] Navapol agents then incited riots in the northeastern provincial capital of Sakhon Nakhon, home to Thailand's largest concentration of immigrant Vietnamese. In another operation, later widely understood to be Navapol's, over nine months in 1975 more than 20 prominent farmer activists were methodically assassinated.

The Red Gaurs meanwhile wreaked havoc on city streets. They provoked fights at student and labor demonstrations, beating up activists and wrecking the offices of leftist newspapers. In May 1975, the staff of the partly palace owned Dusit Thani Hotel again went on strike. Called in by management, the Red Gaurs menaced protesting workers into dispersing and were then hired as the hotel guard force. The workers were all sacked and the hotel shut down, reopening a month later with all new staff. In fear for their lives, the strike organizers went underground and eventually joined the CPT.

In July 1975, just as Kukrit embarked on a trip to Beijing to establish formal relations with China, the Red Gaur stepped up its attacks, provoking violence at several small labor strikes and invading the operations of leftist political parties while the police stood aside. When Kukrit returned, he accused the police of abetting mob rule. In reaction, on August 19 hundreds of policemen, many associated with the Red Gaur, marched to Kukrit's house and ransacked it. The next day the Red Gaur, Village Scouts, and Navapol joined the anti-Kukrit protests using police vehicles and radio equipment. Neither Kukrit nor army chief Krit could intervene without fear of provoking a bigger backlash, or a military coup.

Even as he remained silent, by his appearances and associations King Bhumibol revealed his lack of support for Kukrit and his commitment to the right. The royal family took part more frequently in military and Village Scout activities and attended ceremonies at Kittivudho's college and Red Gaur training camps. The king's swing to the hard right was symbolized by his first-ever appointment of a soldier deeply involved in national security issues to the privy council, in March 1975. This was General Samran Bhaetyakul, the just-retired assistant army commander. Samran's father had served King Vajiravudh, and Bhumibol had known him since the 1960s, when Samran oversaw the first Thai soldiers going to fight in Vietnam. He also wrote important papers on the need to address the insurgency problem among the hill tribes with a social-political approach, backed by tough military tactics.

Samran's commands toward the end of the 1960s involved combating insurgents on the western border and then in the far north, both areas the royal family frequently visited under military escort. His tactics paired earnest social development efforts with fierce search-and-destroy campaigns, bombing, and shelling. During 1973–74, Samran was deputy president of parliament and continued working with ISOC, importantly helping to direct Navapol. As an adviser, he met Bhumibol's need for an honest and professional soldier who could brief the king straightforwardly on national security. Their views coincided: both understood the social and economic roots of the insurgency but also saw the country under dire threat and had no qualms about taking tough action on a large scale. As one of his fellow ISOC officers wrote about Samran, "if it came to a need for violent, clearcut means, he was resolute and thorough."[22]

Ultimately the right's campaign of violence and murder against the student-labor-farmer movement became a self-fulfilling prophecy, for it forced the left to radicalize and join the CPT. In the countryside the harsher counterinsurgency campaign drove more innocent people to the CPT as well. As the king let lapse many of his development initiatives, in some areas peasants started to identify the throne directly with government oppression. Those raiding and bombing the villages were understood as the very people whose patrons and leaders were the king, queen, and princess mother.

In the cities, students made the connection between the vigilante groups, security organizations, and the palace. They came to see October 1973 as a manifestation of the monarchy's commitment not to democracy but to its own power and status. One leading activist later recalled that in October 1973 his circle had believed unquestioningly that the king was on their side. By early 1976, that had changed completely.

> What we learned was that the king was not above politics; that he was just another political player. We discussed the king's differences and alliances with the military; and that he could be corrupt. We saw the king as his own player in changing alliances. The more we learned, we understood the issue of the monarchy being overthrown in 1932 and then trying to restore itself into power for its own interests. In looking at it this way, we of course were influenced by Marxism and Maoism. We discussed feudalism and the sakdina system. We saw the king as a remnant of all this. . . .
> We saw the king as an obstruction to either democracy or socialism, a force of absolute conservatism. We knew we could not talk about this in public. . . . No one would follow us [and] we hardly ever discussed what to do about it.[23]

For some, the king's position became clear when in 1975 the piece of land the palace had made available for a monument to those killed in the October 1973 tragedy suddenly became unavailable. After the first stone for the monument had been laid by the supreme patriarch and Prime Minister Kukrit, the Crown Property Bureau declared that the land was tied up in contracts with others. In fact, the king, who reviewed all important CPB transactions, had changed his mind. The monument would be stalled for another 25 years.[24]

For the palace, the final straw was the abolishment of the monarchy in Laos by the Pathet Lao on December 2, 1975, three days before Bhumibol's 48th birthday. He and most of the extended royal family were horrified, for the Thais saw the Laotian monarchy as a sister throne sharing the same traditions, history, and even bloodline. Vientiane's fall was the final catalyst that sent Thailand back to military rule.

As 1976 began, right-wing vigilantes increased their assaults on the left, driving frightened student, labor, and farm activists to join up with the CPT. With support from the scheming defense minister Pramarn Adireksan and army factions still loyal to the exiled leaders Thanom and Praphas, Kittivudho led a rally of 15,000 Navapol activists to demand that Kukrit turn power over to a military government. Kukrit held on with the tenuous support of General Krit, who himself singled out Navapol as a greater danger to society than a Vietnamese invasion. But Kukrit's government reeled under other forces. With one million Thais already unemployed, the government was hit by a strike of 200,000 public enterprise workers over the high cost of living. When Kukrit caved in to their demands, signing the government's first-ever labor agreement with a state enterprise union, he was called weak and even leftist.

Then even Krit broke away when Kukrit gave the United States a deadline of March 20, 1976, to demobilize its 7,000 men inside Thailand and begin returning control of some important bases to the Thais. Fighting back, the United States together with the Thai right produced "evidence" that the Vietnamese were planning to invade, and the military undertook threatening mobilizations. Finally, on January 11, the armed forces leadership demanded Kukrit's resignation and the dissolution of the national assembly, vowing to seize power otherwise. The next day Kukrit obliged, and the king, without any sign of disagreement, gave his blessing to the dissolution. Elections were set for April 14.

The public was by no means behind this move. Many Thais were fed up with the turmoil and the extreme right, and there was a good chance that a liberal coalition would result from the elections, combining Kukrit's Social Action Party, Seni's Democrats, and the leftist Socialist Party. In the campaign, these parties emphasized ending the U.S. troop presence, greater economic justice, more help for the poor, stronger controls on ISOC, and removing corrupt military-controlled business monopolies.

The right countered with fear-mongering, saying the liberal parties were communist fronts for the CPT and the Vietnamese, who intended to conquer Thailand and destroy Buddhism and the monarchy as in Laos. A daily army radio program run by Queen Sirikit's cousin Lieutenant Colonel Utharn Sanitwongs made liberal use of the king and queen's names while broadcasting false reports and virulent invective against the left, even accusing Kukrit and Seni of being in league with the communists. Because the army radio had the strongest signal in the nation, it was what most Thais listened to.

The palace's biases were now openly discussed, as the royal family championed the Village Scouts and the Red Gaur while warning against unnamed dangers facing the nation. Queen Sirikit publicly condemned activists on the left and expressed her preference for the police and military over politicians. A newspaper-man wrote that the queen had called the 1973 student demonstrators trouble-makers and had described wealthy people as human while others were nonhuman. After he then said that the monarchy was not staying above politics, he was jailed for three years for lèse-majesté.[25]

The king's partisanship was nearly as open as the queen's, as Kukrit's ouster implied. Bhumibol had received proposals for a military coup, at least one of them from Admiral Sa-ngad Chaloryu, the military supreme commander. A later report suggested that he had told Sa-ngad that it just was not the appropriate time, while proposing that, if and when a coup took place, the new government be led by Tanin Kraivixien, the jurist and senior Navapol member.[26] Tanin by that time had become famous for his regular radio program, which mixed rabid anticommunist invective with unconstrained monarchism. He had also recently published a lengthy paper that advocated a strong king and minimized the importance of the rule of law and the democratic process.[27]

King Bhumibol also inserted himself elsewhere. As interim prime minister during the election campaign, Kukrit pushed the United States to meet his March deadline for the departure of all troops. Stalling, U.S. ambassador Charles White-house went to Chiangmai to discuss the issue with the king. Shortly after, an embarrassed and angry Kukrit retracted his timetable and set a new June deadline, after the election and so unlikely to hold. Bhumibol had overruled Kukrit, and the humiliation would contribute to his loss in the polls.

Another episode showed the king's turn against Kukrit and the law and for the armed services. After his house was trashed by policemen in August 1975, Kukrit had their leader arrested. In April 1976, just before the man's trial opened, he was allowed to ordain as a monk, protecting himself from the law. Normally this was against the rules of the sangha. But in this case the protection came from the king's personal spiritual mentor, Wat Bovornives abbot Phra Yanasangworn. Yanasang-worn ruled that the evidence in the case—before it was even heard in court—was not strong enough. It was tantamount to the king himself intervening.

The twelve-week election campaign turned into a deadly drive to frighten liberals away from the polls. Navapol launched its own anti-left party, and Sa-ngad stirred up fears by announcing that communist saboteurs had entered Bangkok.[28] Pra-marn, who had direct links to both the Red Gaur and the Village Scouts, launched his Chart Thai Party's campaign with the slogan "Right Kill Left."

On February 15 the Red Gaur attempted to bomb the headquarters of the leftist New Force Party, but the bomb exploded prematurely and killed the bomber. At the end of February, the moderate Socialist Party chief, university professor Boonsanong Punyodyana, was assassinated in central Bangkok. A few weeks later, Red Gaurs threw bombs at a student protest, killing four. By election day more than 30 people had been murdered nationwide, nearly all of them progressives or leftists. Under threat for their lives, many others abandoned the election.

Even so, the public rejected vigilantism and red-baiting and gave Seni Pramoj's Democrats the largest share of MPs, 114 of a total 279. Kukrit's Social Action took 45 seats, but Kukrit himself, running in an area of Bangkok heavily dominated by military troops, lost to Samak Sunthornvej, a favorite of Queen Sirikit and the head of a renegade hard-right faction of the Democrats.

To become prime minister again, Seni compromised by forming a coalition with Pramarn's Chart Thai and another conservative army-business clique party. Seni's policy objectives were not too different from Kukrit's, but he toned down the rhetoric and sought a compromise on the American military presence. He balanced rival military factions by naming Krit defense minister and Pramarn's men as Krit's deputies. In a huge shock, though, just days after the appointment Krit died of a heart attack. As rumors circulated that Krit had been poisoned, Seni was suddenly in trouble again, for without the moderate general there were no longer any restraints on army extremists.

In the meantime, Village Scout growth accelerated. The group added more than a million new members in 1976, ten times the inductees of 1975, mainly from the cities. Almost 10 percent of the nation's adults would become members, their inductions ever more stridently martial, anticommunist, and emphasizing nation-religion-king. During the first half of 1976, the king and queen presided over at least 19 scout gatherings, often together with daughters Sirindhorn and Chulabhorn. Sometimes tens of thousands of scouts massed together to see the king and hear his short addresses that set out the scouts as a special brotherhood built around the virtues of cooperation, discipline, and hard work, the king's new dhammic values.[29] Bhumibol stressed the scouts' role in maintaining *khwam mankong*, or stability and security.[30]

Although Bhumibol never directly enunciated who the threat to security was, from his context everyone understood him to mean the students, farmers, and workers, and other alleged communists—those who weren't Village Scouts. In May the king addressed a massive gathering of scouts at Jittiphawan College.[31] After a ceremony to enshrine Buddha relics in a new building dedicated to the late supreme patriarch, the king told the scouts their purpose was to help the country survive. He said that unity "will allow Thailand to survive on like it has for centuries. No one can topple us if we don't topple ourselves." And in July he told a group of scouts in Singburi: "The collective will-power of each individual becomes a united strength acting as an impenetrable shield against the enemies who dare not come to shatter the united whole."[32]

There was no possibility that the palace was ignorant of the martial and vigilante activities of the Village Scouts, Red Gaur, and Navapol. These were widely reported and discussed in the Thai newspapers and international media. The violence of the 1976 election campaign was well known to be the work of the Red Gaur and Navapol. Moreover, there was no ignoring Kittivudho's extremist declarations. In the middle of the year he infamously told a magazine interviewer that to kill a communist was not a sin. In fact, he said, in terms of merit, killing communists was a Buddhist duty. The magazine reported:

> He said such a killing is not killing persons "because whoever destroys the nation, the religion, or the monarchy, such bestial types are not complete persons. Thus, we must intend not to kill people but to kill the devil; this is the duty of all Thai." He continued . . . to say that while any killing is demeritorious, the demerit is very little and the merit very great for such an act which serves to preserve the nation, the religion, and the monarchy. "It is just like . . . when we kill a fish to make a stew to place in the alms bowl for a monk. There is certainly demerit in killing the fish, but we place it in the alms bowl of a monk and gain much greater merit."[33]

Kittivudho's statement caused such public outrage that there were strong demands that he be censured or even defrocked. The pro-palace sangha council retorted that there was no evidence against him. He repeated his statements, declaring that killing 50,000 Thai communists would bring sufficient merit for the 42 million other Thais. Such talk was echoed by other monks with palace links, like Phra Phawonawornkhun in Samut Sakorn, who suggested that, to save the monarchy, 30,000 students should be killed.[34]

Bhumibol and Sirikit made no attempt to distance themselves. They continued to hold private meetings with Kittivudho, and attended Red Gaur functions and a training camp where, with great publicity, the king test-fired Red Gaur weapons. Indeed, some Village Scout units trained for vigilante operations at the BPP's

Camp Naresuan next to the Hua Hin palace, where the king and his son liked to practice shooting.

Such tacit encouragement turned glaring and aggressive in the second half of 1976. With anticommunist hysteria infecting large numbers of Thais, Seni's government began to buckle. Radio and television, all state-owned and mostly military-controlled, intensified their anti-left propaganda and attacked Seni, while under Pramarn and Samak the Interior Ministry began to arrest leftist activists. The communist threat was still hugely exaggerated. The CPT remained limited to attacking remote police, BPP, and army outposts. The communists didn't gain any ground, and they still declined to criticize the monarchy. The best insurgency experts discounted their threat to the state, and a respected journalist wrote that the CPT's success or failure ultimately depended on the Bangkok government.

> Crime and violence is rampant throughout the country, corruption pervades the entire Thai administration, and though the government talks of bridging the income gap between Bangkok and the countryside and introducing much-needed social and economic reforms, there is considerable skepticism here about how effectively such measures will be implemented. As one Western diplomat put it: "The Thai Government and press are forever explaining away their national problems by pointing at the communists and Thailand's neighbors, but the real enemy is alive and well and living in Bangkok, driving around in air-conditioned Mercedes."[35]

Ignoring such comments, the palace turned its back on Seni's reform efforts. When he reintroduced Kukrit's 1975 bill to extend democratic elections down to local levels in June, parliament voted the bill through by 149–19. But the king declined to sign the bill or send it back, an undeclared veto. Likewise, Seni got no support in his attempts to achieve an agreement with the Americans over the U.S. troop presence, with the Supreme Command imperviously rejecting the government.

In August the palace, the military, and far-right politicians became even more audacious. Knowing it could cause an explosion in the streets, they moved to bring the former leaders Thanom and Praphas back to Thailand. Protected by a military escort, Praphas returned on August 17, claiming that he needed medical treatment. Some 20,000 students demonstrated at Thammasat for four days, until a clash with Red Gaur and Navapol toughs left four dead. Praphas then met the king and shortly afterward returned abroad. It appeared that Bhumibol had originally okayed the return, and then decided it wasn't the right time.

As Praphas left, Thanom's wife returned to negotiate with the government for her husband's repatriation. Fearing more turmoil, the cabinet stalled. But then deputy interior minister and queen's confidant Samak went to Singapore and told Thanom he had the throne's support to come home. On September 19, Thanom returned, disembarking from his airplane unexpectedly in the saffron robes of a Buddhist monk. He went straight from the airport to Wat Bovornives, where sangha rules were broken to ordain him in a private ceremony. Ordinations normally must be open to the public, but that would have allowed someone to challenge the rite.

The significance of this taking place at Wat Bovornives is paramount. Bovornives had been the Chakris' personal temple ever since King Mongkut was abbot there. Celestial princes from Chulalongkorn to Bhumibol were ordained at Bovornives. The royal Thammayut school had its headquarters there. The abbot, Yanasangworn, was the king's personal spiritual adviser. The umbilical cords of Bhumibol's four children were ritually buried there.[36] Everything important that happened at Wat Bovornives was a palace matter. Thanom's acceptance there could not have happened without King Bhumibol's explicit instruction.

For Thanom's arrival, Wat Bovornives was ringed day and night by a cordon of the Red Gaur. As Seni's government scurried to ask Thanom to leave before trouble broke out, Samak declared to the cabinet that the king and queen had endorsed his return.[37] Expectedly, massive protests broke out, and it wasn't only students. Among many private groups, the head of the Thailand Lawyers Association called for a police investigation into Thanom's culpability in the October 1973 killings. On September 22, outraged Democrats and the opposition in the House of Representatives joined hands to vote a resolution that Thanom be again expelled.

At the time of Thanom's return, Bhumibol and Sirikit were in the south, keeping their distance from the quickly unfolding events. When it appeared that Thanom would be exiled again, they hurriedly returned to Bangkok and, three hours after arriving, made a highly public visit to Thanom at the temple, the king wearing his official army uniform. Just behind him at the temple were the leaders of Navapol. It was a stunningly brazen rejection of the cabinet, parliament, and much of the public. The king's politics, for so long ambiguous, were now on the table and highly incendiary. A stunned Seni sent in his resignation, which was refused by parliament. He tried again to assemble a workable government, proposing to expel Chart Thai from the coalition and to bring in Kukrit's Social Action Party.

Again the king intervened, by rejecting the exclusion of Chart Thai.[38] All Seni could then do was to drop Samak and another rightist minister from the cabinet, which he did on October 5. In reaction, Chart Thai and Samak mobilized the Village Scouts in a large demonstration, where they demanded the expulsion of three Democratic cabinet ministers whom they branded communists. As Seni strained to stabilize the government, on the ground mobilizations by both the left and the right grew more tense. On September 25 in Nakhon Pathom, west of Bangkok, two activists putting up anti-Thanom posters were beaten to death and hung from a wall. It would soon come out that police killed them.

On September 30, 10,000 students together with labor groups demonstrated at Sanam Luang. It went off peacefully, as did their next major protest on October 3. Students then declared a united front with labor and other groups, to boycott classes and hold strikes until Thanom departed. The palace responded by having Crown Prince Vajiralongkorn abandon his military training in Australia to fly back to Bangkok. Arriving in his military uniform, he went straight to Wat Bovornives and paid respects to Thanom.

For two more days both the left and the right held demonstrations at various locations, with few clashes. On October 4, inside the walled campus of Thammasat University, students performed a dramatization of the hanging at Nakhon Pathom. Deliberately or unfortunately, the student at the end of the garrote bore a resemblance to the prince. It was the spark that would set everything off.

The next day, as Seni struggled to install his cabinet, the ultra-rightist newspaper *Dao Siam* published a photograph of the mock hanging on its front page, declaring in outrage that the students had hanged the prince in effigy. (Some would later claim that the photograph was altered to better resemble the prince.) On army-controlled radio stations, announcers including the queen's cousin Utharn accused the students of lèse-majesté, and called for Village Scouts and Navapol to rally and attack them for offending the throne.[39] They claimed that the students planned to assault the palace and Wat Bovornives. "Kill them," the radio announcers chanted, "kill the communists."

With Village Scouts, Red Gaurs, and Navapol cells already mobilized in Bangkok to protest Seni's new cabinet, there was a charged force ready to respond. After dusk fell on October 5, some 4,000 rightists massed at Thammasat University: Village Scouts, the Red Gaur, local police, and BPP commandos from Camp Naresuan in Hua Hin flown in by helicopter.

Just before dawn on October 6, 1976, a day now ingrained in most Thais' memories as simply "6 Oct.," they began shooting into the campus, using M-16s, carbines, pistols, grenade launchers, and even large-gauge recoilless rifles. Prevented from leaving the campus, or even sending the wounded to the hospital, the students begged for a cease-fire. The actors in the mock hanging had already turned themselves in to Seni at the prime minister's offices. When one student came out to surrender, he was shot and killed. After a free-fire order was issued by the Bangkok police chief, the campus was stormed like an enemy army's redoubt, with the king's preferred BPP troops in front.[40]

With the exits from the university blocked, the result was horrifying carnage. Students diving into the Chaophraya River were shot at by navy vessels. Others who surrendered, lying down on the ground, were picked up and beaten, many to death. Some were hung from trees and beaten; some were set afire. Female students were raped, alive and dead, by police and Red Gaurs.

The savagery continued for several hours, and was only finally halted at noon by a rainstorm. But it was not clearly over. Tens of thousands of Village Scouts had now arrived in Bangkok. They gathered at the statue of King Chulalongkorn near parliament and at the Royal Turf Club, chanting "Kill the communists, kill the three leftist ministers, defend nation-religion-monarchy." They were poised to attack whatever they were pointed at, until early evening, when the BPP head and Prince Vajiralongkorn thanked them and said they could return home. A military junta had seized power and, with royal endorsement, the government was now in the hands of a group of generals calling themselves the National Administrative Reform Council. A few days later, palace favorite Tanin Kraivixien was named prime minister.

To this day the details of how and why October 6 happened remain deliberately obscured by the participants. Officially only 46 died in the conflagration, with 167 wounded and 3,000 arrested. Many survivors claim that the death toll was well over 100. The new government first justified the attack as protecting the monarchy and the country from a Vietnamese-backed revolt starting from inside Thammasat University. They showed pictures of a body from the university on television, claiming it was a Vietnamese guerrilla. The military also claimed that shots had first been fired at them from inside. Both stories were lies.

Later explanations painted the carnage as the result of fast-evolving political rivalries involving three separate political-military factions. The attack on the university was not intentional or planned, but the result of chaos as the rival groups stirred things up as a pretext for seizing power. The palace unfortunately simply got swept up in it all. There is some truth in this second argument, but ultimately, like the first, it amounts to calculated mystification of an event that did involve planning and deliberation. The buildup of right-wing groups nationwide for the previous year anticipated just such a battle. In Hua Hin, BPP troops had trained together with Village Scouts in mock attacks on students. Village Scouts in Nakhon Pathom, where the two activists had been hanged, had actually undertaken a mock beating and hanging of students not long before.[41]

The willingness of the Bangkok police commander to give orders to shoot also gave away the planning, as the rector of Thammasat, Puey Ungphakorn, wrote afterward. "It is completely inexplicable that a police commander would accept responsibility for the killing in Thammasat if he had not received the assurance that the events would lead to a military coup."[42] It was the pattern of several previous coups, including October 1973: initiating violence, leaving the police to show they could not establish order, then allowing the military to step in. In October 1976, the very heavy-handedness at Thammasat gave the military an excuse to take control. Yet afterward there was no investigation or charges. Puey called it "a carefully planned drama leading to a long-prepared conclusion."

The orchestrators were many, but the palace's hand was everywhere, going along if not directing, all year stirring up the frenzy. The king and queen consistently interfered with the government's attempt to establish its authority and enforce the law. Most brazenly, with Red Gaur and Navapol at his side, Bhumibol introduced the catalyst to the violence, Thanom's return. That made it impossible for Seni to calm the city. When the students protested against Thanom, there was no attempt to muzzle the incitement to violence by people like Utharn.

The final use of the lèse-majesté claim in the students' mock hanging as a pretext for the violence was likewise telling. It turned the crime back a century and a half, to when critics of the throne were summarily put to death. Some people claim to have seen Prince Vajiralongkorn on the scene at Thammasat on October 5 and 6, in the company of police and Village Scouts. Afterward newspapers gave him prominent photo space, authoritatively dressed in his army fatigues and a pistol on his hip, surrounded by Village Scouts, Red Gaurs, and police and army officers. Four days later, the prince presided over a flag and awards-giving ceremony of Village Scouts in Lopburi and Singburi, the source of many of the soldiers and vigilantes in Bangkok that day. It was a conspicuous endorsement.

As if to confirm it all, the generals who seized power declared, as in each and every previous coup: "The takeover of power . . . is aimed at safeguarding the institution of the monarchy. The king and the royal family are being protected. . . . They all are safe."[43] It presumed that, for the Thai people, this was purpose enough.

13 *What Went Wrong* ❧
Cosmic Panic, Business Failure, Midcareer Crisis

OCTOBER 6, 1976, CONSTITUTED the throne's most explicit and assertive intervention in politics since the Boworadej revolt of 1933. King Bhumibol openly supported, if not instigated, an attack by his soldiers on his own people, setting his subjects against one another. Up to 10,000 students and leftists fled into the arms of the CPT in the jungle afterward, doubling the size of the insurgency and bringing the kingdom close to civil war. The constitution was again abrogated and the government replaced with a military junta. The new government and the king were unapologetic, to their own people and to the international community, which castigated Bangkok for the brutality. Bhumibol's lack of hesitation to support a new far-right government led by Tanin Kraivixien was startling to those who had learned to see him as a dhammaraja king of compassion.

On one level, King Bhumibol's embrace of the violent right, as both its leader and its tool, was understandable. The cardinal duty of any sovereign king is to defend and sustain the monarchy. As communist regimes took power in neighboring states and the Thai insurgency grew, the Mahidol family became obligated to ally itself with the forces that would protect the throne above all other. But this doesn't explain Bhumibol and Sirikit going so far as to aggravate a hysteria that turned one half of Thai society against the other half and left no room in the middle. It cast a shadow over the monarchical institution itself—the dhammaraja was no longer the nation's unifier.

The reasons for this momentous change were much deeper than the surrounding communist threat, and didn't take place suddenly. There had been a generational change in Thailand, not noticed or understood in the palace. As in 1932, the palace misread the rise of native Thai reformism as a radical revolutionary movement with foreign roots. It was confident and chaotic, antithetical to the quiet and orderly traditional cosmos the palace sought. The throne's response, the political scientist Benedict Anderson explained, was "not simply cynical conservative maneuvers against the left, but . . . genuine cultural-ideological panic."[1] Another academic, Roger Kershaw, called it "profound culture shock."[2]

Why the unflappable, broad-minded Bhumibol succumbed to panic, however, is more complex. To understand his response, one must contrast his formal training with a number of less-known experiences in the early 1970s, experiences that affected his worldview as deeply as the rise of the insurgency.

For the first two decades of his reign, two notions were drummed into Bhumibol's head. The first was that Thailand could not survive without a pure-of-practice dhammaraja, following the ten cardinal points of kingship. The second was that the ideal king had to be a full Chakri, a man who carried the blood and spiritual inheritance of previous dhammarajas. With this birthright, he was told, he would naturally rule justly and wisely and the people would follow.

In the mid-1960s Bhumibol began to truly assimilate these notions. He was constantly reminded that, like his great-grandfather King Mongkut, he was blessed with a singular appreciation of both Western rationalism and Thai spiritualism, of global modernity and Thai tradition. He could discuss important spiritual and secular issues as an equal with heads of state and religious leaders. He understood, both as a sociologist and a Buddhist guru, the causes of his people's suffering. Amid corrupt politicians and generals and greedy businessmen, he was selfless. And he had, thanks to his advanced religious study and meditation, a level of perspicacity that bordered on divine insight.

This spiritual backbone gave the king confidence to discern the nature of governance in the modern state. Nearing three decades of dealing with greedy and corrupt men, he concluded that politics was an inherently dirty and futile process that neither attracted men of virtue nor produced capable leaders. Competitive Western democratic government of the type adopted in 1932 generated confrontation and disunity, and stymied the people's progress and development. The alternative was Thai tradition, good government under a sagacious sovereign who selected the most virtuous men to lead. A system like this, Bhumibol had been taught by Prince Dhani, was truly democratic.

The king saw in his own palace operations proof of this. In the hands of honest men he selected, the royal charities and relief operations took in huge sums of money from the people and then disbursed it to much greater effect than the government. Avoiding the selfish haggling typical of the parliament and bureaucracy, the throne could deliver aid quickly where it was needed the most, and the results could be seen very fast.

The king also concluded that Western-style law hindered more than helped his people. He had seen the constitution and civil law used to exploit and punish honest Thais while protecting the powerful and corrupt. It did not deliver fairness or justice. As he said in a 1973 speech on land rights problems, "the fault rests with the law-enforcing side rather than with the one upon which the law is to be enforced."[3] He spoke instead for a traditional, "natural" law:

> In forests designated and delineated by the authorities as reserved or re-
> stricted, there were people there already at the time of the delineation. It
> seems rather odd for us to enforce the reserved forest law on the people
> in the forest which became reserved only subsequently by the mere draw-
> ing of lines on pieces of paper. . . . With the delineation done, these peo-
> ple became violators of the law. From the viewpoint of law, it is a
> violation, because the law was duly enacted. But according to natural law,
> the violator of the law is the one who drew the lines, because the people
> who had been in the forests previously possessed human rights, meaning
> that the authorities had encroached upon individuals and not individuals
> transgressing the law of the land.

Bhumibol's conclusion was that a hierarchy under the king and the men he chose to govern would best serve the aspirations of the people, creating order, justice, and happiness.

These conclusions extended to economics, the nature of which Bhumibol began to fathom in the early 1970s. His small development projects and large capital investments represented his challenge to the Western capitalist model. His huge frustrations in these initiatives ultimately contributed to the royal panic of 1976.

By the 1970s, persistent poverty and its connection to the insurgency led the king to distrust American-style market capitalism. He observed that in the free market, farmers benefited the least from their labors while the merchants, middlemen, and traders who did less work profited the most. Landless farmers especially suffered, paying a huge portion of their production to idle landowners. In the urban milieu, likewise, workers didn't always earn a living wage while factory owners took all the profit and lived grandly.

Thai peasants and workers weren't greedy, the king knew; mostly they wanted simply to make enough from their labors to be comfortable. This was the concept encapsulated in the iconic Ramkhamhaeng inscription that Bhumibol had studied in his youth: let them plant their fields, fish the waters, and trade in their produce under a benevolent monarch, and the kingdom would be content and peaceful. The problem with capitalism, as the king saw it, was that, like the contentious parliamentary system, it emphasized selfishness and desire that turned men against one another.

Bhumibol found contemporary reinforcement of his views in E. F. Schumacher's bible of the new sustainable development movement, *Small Is Beautiful*, published in 1973. Schumacher preached that development should not be defined by accelerating growth and consumption. Instead, it should stress self-reliance and self-sufficiency, and focus on making small, sustainable improvements in people's lives. He argued that encouraging capitalist and consumerist desires was destructive. If treated justly and gently, people would work hard in their lives and be happy with less material rewards, and nations would advance with greater certainty.

For Bhumibol this was not just economics but the basis of the paradisiacal Buddhist kingdom. Each person worked hard and performed his or her job—giving in to neither absolute non-desire nor excessive greed—and contributed to the better of the whole, all the while accepting what in their lives couldn't be changed. Revealingly, in 1975, Bhumibol translated Schumacher's chapter "Buddhist Economics" into Thai, but not the rest of the book, notably the chapter that stressed the importance of education.

To counter market capitalism, King Bhumibol drew on the generous resources of his charities and the Crown Property Bureau. At one end were his rural development projects, mostly built around cooperatives inspired by Israel and communist China. After his initial success at Hup Kapong in 1967, Bhumibol put cooperatives at the forefront of his thinking. In a cooperative, he explained in a later speech, "no one should be under the order of anyone else," but "every member must have strict discipline. . . . If everyone can set his own discipline, it will be a more solid and more durable rule; it will be better than to have others impose their will, their discipline on you."[4]

Another theme was appropriate or small technologies that could help farmers without much capital. For farmers who had nothing at all, he established a handful of breeding banks for water buffalo. For those with more resources, he promoted a hand-operated plowing tractor that he tested in his experimental Chitrlada paddy field, and then had it produced and sold cheaply by his own Siam Cement Group. (Bhumibol is often credited with inventing the tractor, but it was already popular in Japan at the time.) Further exploring this concept, in 1971 he erected two small rice mills (donated by foreign governments) inside Chitrlada and, four years later, built a plant to convert discarded rice husk into inexpensive fuel. The hope was that such plants could be copied cheaply around the country to help farmers extract more value from their rice. On a similar rationale, in 1969 the king built a milk-powder plant in Chitrlada to add value to the Nong Pho cooperative milk program he launched in 1962.

Cooperatives, new technologies and techniques, and non-market-based assistance came together in his program to wean hill tribes from dependence on opium production. The idea was to substitute for opium poppies new cash crops like red beans and coffee. The palace, the BPP, and the army together would operate a heavily subsidized processing and marketing program for the new products, ensuring that the hill tribes made more money from these products than from opium.

A third theme of his initiatives was the development of water resources. This would become a key facet of Bhumibol's popular and sacral profile. Although begun in the early 1960s with a dam project at Hup Kapong and cloud-seeding research, his water resource efforts started in full only at the end of the decade. The first successful experiment in cloud seeding took place in 1969, after which the king pushed for a fully funded program. In 1971, regular rainmaking efforts began, becoming popularized as the Royal Rain, reinforcing the king's devaraja image, as the source of the kingdom's fertility. In October 1972, Bhumibol proudly invited foreign diplomats to a show of rainmaking in Petchburi province.

Around the same time, he began developing water resources on the ground. Hup Kapong demonstrated that family storage tanks and small local reservoirs could go a long way. Bhumibol had Siam Cement fabricate cheap cement water jars for distribution across the countryside, often sponsored by royal charity donors. Getting personally involved in the Agriculture Ministry's royal irrigation department, he pushed to expand programs of building small reservoirs, water tanks, and water diversion projects. There was a lot of domestic and foreign expertise and impetus behind these programs, but each one was credited to the personal initiative of the king.

More ambitiously, he took on the perennial rainy season floods that beset numerous areas around the country. The government itself had made few efforts in this area. The king's first large-scale project was at Bachoh in the southernmost province of Narathiwat. With large swaths of the province's lowlands covered in phru, or peat swamp forests, there was a shortage of land for rice cultivation. In addition, the peat swamps frequently overflowed into cultivated land, destroying crops. This economic problem was seen as underpinning security problems: many people in Narathiwat's largely Muslim population supported the local CPT and advocated seceding from Thailand to become part of Malaysia.

The idea attributed to King Bhumibol was to cut lengthy canals to the Gulf of Thailand to drain the Bachoh forest. Not only could flooding be averted, but the drained land could be turned into paddy fields. The king closely followed the royal irrigation department's progress on the job, often giving directions. Not long after the canal was completed and the water drained, in January 1974 much of the south was inundated by floods. The Bachoh area was an exception. The happiest day of his life, Bhumibol years later told an interviewer, was when the irrigation department head rushed to him exclaiming, "Bachoh works!"[5]

Although later publicity suggests otherwise, the king's projects were not unmitigated successes. As they do anywhere, the cooperatives required constant effort to function smoothly, and they still had to deal with wily traders. The Royal Rain often fell in the wrong place, including once on coastal salt-drying flats. And Bachoh, after several years, proved unexpectedly counterproductive: acid leaching from the drained peat forest damaged nearby crops, and the drained land itself was unsuitable for farming. Moreover, natural compacting of the drained soil lowered its ability to absorb water, resulting over time in new flooding.[6]

In most of these projects, too, the external subsidies could be huge and never ending. The cooperatives required outside financial support just to exist, and the Royal Rain operations were very expensive. For crop substitution, red bean prices were set artificially high just to build production; the beans were exported to significant losses by the state and royal projects. To King Bhumibol, the social benefits far outweighed any cost accrued. His view was that it might run contrary to classic economic concepts, like the economic rate of return, but they didn't suit Thailand anyway.

And yet the king remained disappointed. The impact of his efforts on the overall economy was minimal. His programs didn't generate spontaneous imitation or inspire government implementation on a greater scale. In the 1970s, too, they were overwhelmed by the war on insurgency. As 1975 drew to a close, Bhumibol mostly suspended his attention to development projects and focused on fighting the leftists.

Even more frustrating were Bhumibol's experiences in large-scale capital investment. Palace investment boss Thawiwong Thawalyasak had made the throne an important player in the economy, and the palace reaped several million dollars annually from rents and dividends, all available for additional investment.

Thawiwong died in 1970, leaving the job to his understudy, Grand Chamberlain Phunperm Krairerks. But Bhumibol then took a greater hand in the throne's investments, with a strategy motivated not simply by cold profits but by the desire to contribute to Thailand's development. He aspired to demonstrate a more constructive business model for his domain. But by the mid-1970s, Bhumibol's good motives left him in several cases betrayed, cheated, hurt by unfair competition and unpredictable economic circumstances, and finally accused of being just the kind of capitalist he disdained. Some of this came to a climax precisely in 1976.

One case was a controversy over the development of palace land. The CPB owned the Bangkok plot of land on which sat Mu Ban Thepprathan, a slum of longtime squatters. Since the 1950s the crown had collected a nominal monthly rent from the residents, without rental contracts. One day in the early 1970s, a private developer arrived and ordered the occupants to vacate. The CPB had leased the land to be developed commercially. The very public fight against eviction generated comparisons between the CPB and officials who evicted poor farmers from degraded state forests. When student activists got involved and likened the palace to a landowning feudalist, the embarrassed palace halted the project. It undoubtedly added to Bhumibol's dislike of the student movement.

The labor movement likewise put the throne in a bad light. After 1972, labor strikes hit a number of palace-linked textile factories, banks, and hotels. In most cases, the palace was able to keep a distance and protect its image from accusations of exploiting workers. This proved impossible in the 1974 strike at the Dusit Thani Hotel, which refused to offer wages and benefits commensurate with the rest of the industry. The palace couldn't distance itself: the building was on CPB land, CPB members were on its board of directors, royal family members personally held shares, and the hotel was a center of royal society. When the strikers boldly pointed out the royal connection, the government had to step in to manage negotiations, just to keep the king's name out of it. Finally the hotel grudgingly changed its pay scale. It wasn't clear, however, where the king stood: on the side of management, or workers, or his own image.

The answer was clearer a year later when the Dusit staff again went on strike. The issue was the same, pay and benefits in a high-inflation environment. This time the management called in the Red Gaur to menace the workers and break the strike. The hotel closed until it could replace the entire staff. With that result, the students and workers began to talk more openly of the monarchy as an exploitive capitalist.

Two other important cases set the king's interests against the government, against economic trends, against corrupt competitors, and against his own partners. Both were particularly difficult because they involved very large sums of money and represented Bhumibol's personal attempt to hold a role in big-capital, nation-building investments.

The first began with influential California businessman Henry Kearns, at whose estate the Mahidol family had stayed when they were in Los Angeles in 1960. Early in the 1960s, Kearns turned this connection to advantage by launching several Thai investments with his American Capital Corporation, starting with an industrial estate and a Firestone tire plant.[7] In both, his principal local partner was the Crown Property Bureau. Kearns subsequently pursued the largest single investment ever in the country, a $30 million pulp and paper plant. At first it was stalled by vested Thai interests as well as questions of financial viability. Then King Bhumibol became interested, not so much in potential profits but in Kearns's pitch that the plant, Siam Kraft Paper, would benefit farmers, who would grow the raw materials for pulp. It would also substitute for imported kraft paper, and possibly even export a surplus. Siam Kraft was financed by the U.S. Export-Import Bank, but the palace took a controlling interest through the CPB, Siam Commercial Bank, and Siam Cement. When the plant began production in 1969, the king awarded Kearns a high royal decoration.

Yet the project was already in trouble, and it quickly broke into scandal. Kearns had brought in another company, Parsons & Whittemore, to share a 35-percent ownership and to manage plant construction and operation. By the time production started, Parsons had apparently more than recouped its own investment by paying itself handsome management fees and inflating the costs of equipment it bought. In so doing, Parsons wiped out Siam Kraft's total equity, so that at startup it couldn't service its loans. Kearns too was believed to have recovered his investment through consultant fees. That left the Thai shareholders, mainly the palace, holding all the risk.

The case must have taken much of Bhumibol's time. Parsons was sued for mismanagement and embezzlement, and newspapers portrayed the Americans as cheating Thailand and the king. Kearns eventually saved the day when he was named head of the U.S. Export-Import Bank, where he obtained for Siam Kraft an uncommonly long loan rescheduling. Under new management, Siam Kraft made a small profit in 1972, mainly because the government banned imported kraft paper, controversially allowing the company to set its prices high. Even then, it still struggled to service its debt. By that time Kearns had washed his hands and graduated to an even larger scandal, a corrupt deal between the Northrop Corporation, a handful of Thai air force generals, and the Thai construction group Italthai to develop a new Bangkok airport at the aptly named Cobra Swamp.

In 1975, Siam Kraft was hit triply hard, by economic recession, more mismanagement, and the arrival of an aggressive, better-run competitor. The foreign partners had bailed out, and the palace moved to sue Kearns after he sold his shares in both Siam Kraft and Firestone to Japan's Mitsui group. Wiped out a second time, the king had Siam Cement take over Siam Kraft. It was a particularly difficult move. Siam Cement monopolized Thailand's cement production, a virtual guarantee that it could remit millions of dollars a year in profits to the throne. But in 1975 the Kukrit government froze cement prices, and Siam Cement lost money. That meant it didn't have surplus funds to service Siam Kraft's millions of dollars of debt. Finally, in November, Siam Kraft announced it was bankrupt.

That wasn't the end. Over the next year, the palace and Siam Cement worked together with the Thai and U.S. governments to restructure the debt again and revive the company. Just as that deal was finalized, in early 1977 Thai customs authorities charged the company with having cheated on duty payments on imported raw materials years earlier. Although Siam Kraft blamed corrupt customs officials themselves, the court levied a whopping $3.3 million penalty, enough to send the company back to bankruptcy proceedings. Only tough intervention by Prime Minister Tanin and the U.S. embassy got the company a new cushion.

Concurrent with the Siam Kraft story was the saga of Air Siam, the royal family's airline. Air Siam was started in 1965 with the Mahidol family as core investors to compete with the state carrier Thai Airways, which was controlled by the Scandinavian Air System together with Thai air force generals. Leading the project was Princess Galyani's consort, Prince Varananda.

Air Siam almost never took off. It lacked adequate capital, Thai Airways controlled most international flight routes, and it was hard to find pilots and technicians. Finally in 1970 Air Siam launched a cargo service between Bangkok and Hong Kong with a leased plane. In 1971 the airline appeared headed toward success when it began flying twice weekly from Bangkok to Los Angeles, a prime route for the U.S. military in Thailand. But like Thai Airways, the company had to hire high-priced foreigners to manage and fly the planes. Then in 1972 the economy turned bad. The United States began to reduce its presence in Thailand, and the first OPEC oil shock sent fuel prices skyrocketing. Thai Airways barely survived, and Air Siam had to halt its trans-Pacific run. To stay alive, the company brought in new capital from the group of the much-hated Colonel Narong Kittikachorn. Air Siam survived, but it was presumed to involve something corrupt.

It isn't clear after this point how much interest the royal family retained, but in 1975, with Narong exiled, the Kukrit government was compelled to deploy public funds to bail out the airline. This brought open opposition from the staff of the likewise struggling Thai Airways, who complained about unfair government support for the competitor. So the government fashioned a deal by which it would inject funds into Thai Airways to take over Air Siam, absorbing all its losses and liabilities. The original shareholders were to be repaid, suggesting the royal family would not incur the loss. Thai Airways' management and the air force together angrily contested the deal and, remarkably, in August 1976, amid the growing tension between the right and left, Thai Airways' entire staff of 5,300 stopped work for a day in protest. In February 1977 Air Siam was shut down. How the losses were distributed was never clear.

Considering all of the other things going on at the time, these problems must have demanded far more of the king's attention than he had to spare. When the crown's investments began to fail, he was put into the position of either writing them off or protecting them. This put him in conflict with workers as employees, with the bureaucracy, with foreign partners and governments, with competing businesses, with the military's vested interests, and with the government itself. It was a deep antinomian conflict for the throne. Bhumibol wanted to foster development while the students branded him the "big feudalist" (sakdina yai). The sheer frustration had to be an essential ingredient in his descent into reactionary panic.

Yet the most important element lay in Bhumibol's family life and his primary obligation to the dynasty's survival. By the beginning of the 1970s it had struck home that, in raising only one son and three daughters, Bhumibol and Sirikit had not created an adequate Chakri blood pool for future generations. By the Palace Law of Succession of 1924—endorsed by each post-1932 constitution—only male descendants of King Chulalongkorn by his official queens were permitted to ascend the throne. Other than the Mahidols, the only remnant viable line was the Paripatra family. However, Prince Paripatra's grandson M.R. Sukhumbhand Paripatra, born of a prince father but a commoner mother, was not formally considered an alternative.[8]

That left the throne without a backup for Prince Vajiralongkorn. There were more than enough recent reminders of how quickly successors could disappear: the high rate of premature mortality for Chulalongkorn's sons and their scant offspring; Bhumibol's potentially fatal auto accident in 1948; and most of all the tragic death of King Ananda. The CPT posed another danger to the royal family.

Then there was the problem of the heir himself. With Vajiralongkorn, the palace wasn't certain of sustaining the prestige of the royal institution. By the beginning of the 1970s, he had become a disagreeable young man lacking any of the intellect, charm, curiosity, or diplomatic skills of his parents, much less any adherence to dhammic principles. He treated aides with little respect and women as objects, using his power to get them to sleep with him. One common tale was that his first sexual experience was arranged by his aide-de-camp while he attended secondary school in England.

It wasn't a complete surprise. None of Bhumibol's children were raised with the discipline of his own childhood. Vajiralongkorn grew up surrounded by fawning palace women, including Sirikit, who granted his every desire. The king tried in vain to pass on to the prince his own enthusiasm for hobbies, music, or sports. The only thing he and his father seemed to do well together was to go shooting. By his own later recollection, the prince's insulated upbringing kept him from having a normal life and meeting normal people.[9] At 13 the king sent him off to boarding school in England, where it was hoped he might learn some discipline and humility, and mix with his peers. It wasn't too successful. The prince later said he was intensely lonely and couldn't make friends. Rumors in Bangkok said he got in trouble for fighting and theft.

At 18 in 1970, he was already asocial and impervious to criticism. The logical choice was to send him to a foreign military academy, to instill in him discipline and leadership qualities, and maybe draw out some latent intellectuality. He was sent to the Australian highbrow preparatory academy King's School in Sydney to prepare for entering Australia's elite officer's academy, Duntroon.[10]

As for the problem of succession, the palace began to consider changing the 1924 law, to allow a female successor. This wasn't hugely radical; King Chulalongkorn had deputized one of his queens as his stand-in when he traveled to Europe, and Bhumibol had made Queen Sirikit and Princess Mother Sangwal regent at various times. Moreover, Thais understood from England and the Netherlands that a regnant queen wasn't terribly problematic. Yet the palace refused to allow the issue to be discussed publicly.

Allowing a female successor would make the king's popular first daughter Ubolrat second in line. Ubolrat was Bhumibol's favorite child, attractive, outgoing, and capable in school and sports, everything the prince wasn't. She wasn't as spoiled by palace life, although she was automatically awarded top grades in school, and in her teens she ran around Bangkok partying in discotheques. (She called herself Julie, after sultry American singer Julie London.) She could get along with people and didn't overly abuse her status.

In 1969, Ubolrat went to America to study at the Massachusetts Institute of Technology, supposedly pursuing the goal of becoming a nuclear physicist.[11] Her proud father held her up as an example to Thai students. In 1972, however, she broke his heart and upset plans for plugging the vulnerability in succession when the palace discovered she was dating an American classmate, Peter Jensen. Although several of the king's uncles had married foreigners, Bhumibol and Sirikit attempted to block the relationship, as they apparently had in an earlier involvement she had with a non-royal Thai student. Stubborn and resentful of the confines of royal life, Ubolrat declared her intention to marry Jensen. In July 1972 the king reacted by angrily stripping her of her title, meaning her children would not be royal. A month later the young couple married, and Bhumibol virtually disowned Ubolrat. She did not return to Thailand for the next eight years.

How much this related to father and daughter's once very close relationship and how much to Bhumibol's dynastic planning has never been clear. He pushed ahead with his plans anyway. In December 1972, at the end of Vajiralongkorn's first year at Duntroon, the king had the prince return home for his coming-of-age ceremony. This comprised nine days of Brahman-led rites inside the palace, symbolically acclaiming him as a future holy devaraja-dhammaraja. On December 28 the prince was invested and presented to the public as the heir to the Chakri throne.

After the Three Tyrants were overthrown the next year, the drafting of a new constitution conveniently allowed the king to change the succession rules. Indeed, if the final outcome of the 1974 constitution is any guide, King Bhumibol's primary interest was the quietly inserted clause that said, as usual, that succession would be according to the 1924 law but added that, in the absence of a prince (specifically, a son of the king) the national assembly may select a daughter of the king (and not, for instance, Queen Sirikit). The 1924 law specifically disallowed a regnant queen, and previous constitutions had declared the law immutable. So the new constitution added that the 1924 law could be amended in the same manner as an amendment to the constitution. This indicated that the king intended to have parliament change the old law.

By that time, the prince's bad reputation had spread more widely, and people cheered the change. To them it meant that the well-liked 19-year-old Princess Sirindhorn, Bhumibol's and Sirikit's third child, would succeed if the prince couldn't measure up. That may have also been in the king's mind, but the primary reason was one of safety and security for the dynasty. Sirindhorn was simply a fallback.

Bhumibol certainly understood that Vajiralongkorn was a problem. He complained to friends in the 1970s of his frustration in controlling the prince.[12] He was at a loss to understand how his son had turned out so unmanageable. Duntroon was both bad and good for the prince. The academy trains the future leaders of the Australian army, and its course and field work is rigorous. Some 40 percent of starters fail or drop out before the four years are ended. The prince worked hard, but from the beginning he couldn't keep up physically or academically, say former schoolmates. Describing the prince as "panda-like and slothful" when he arrived, one schoolmate said Vajiralongkorn wouldn't have made it past two years if he hadn't been passed for diplomatic reasons.[13] "It was clear he was not prepared," this fellow student recalled. "He needed sorting out, taking down a peg. The king was right to send him to Duntroon. But he was also very soft, pudgy and overweight. He had problems keeping up with hard workouts. It was clear he was never going to make it."

He entered in January 1972, avid but carrying a huge sense of privilege. It made for a very difficult four years. His academic performance was middling at best, and he didn't make many friends in his class. To his credit, the schoolmate said, Vajiralongkorn strained to make the grade, pitching in on all the jobs conscientiously. He was genuinely apologetic when his poor performance hurt his unit. By his last year, he held the most junior rank possible, corporal. He ostensibly completed the school, but he never received an official diploma, presumably because he couldn't truly pass the coursework.

Even so, the experience taught him military discipline and probably left him more advanced in soldiering skills than most of the Thai army. After leaving Duntroon in December 1975, he joined advanced counterinsurgency training at the Special Australia Air Service Regiment in Perth, covering special forces weapons, demolition, and unconventional warfare tactics. He remained there until being called back to Bangkok days before the October 6 massacre. In Bangkok, Vajiralongkorn already had a bad reputation, particularly for violence. Some people were quick to pick up his bills and offer him women, to curry favor and exploit his name. The military was said to be reluctant to accept him in any command position. For the time being, he was attached to military intelligence.

This gave King Bhumibol and Queen Sirikit further reason to fret about the dynasty's future. Their son was bad, they had lost one daughter, and the other two princesses showed little of the dynamism needed to be a leader. This burden was brought home during 1974–76 when the last but one of Bhumibol's mentors from the ancien régime, the men who had built the Ninth Reign and shaped Bhumibol, passed from the scene. The longtime privy councilors Prince Dhani Nivas and M.L. Dej Sanitwongs both died in 1974. Prince Wan Waithayakorn and Chao Phraya Sridharmadibes died in 1976. The only old-timer left was privy councilor Phraya Manavarajsevi, who, at 86, was essentially retired.

Each had been important to the king for different reasons, and they had spanned a political spectrum from unreformed absolutists to advocates of constitutional democracy and a limited king. After they passed away, the king was on his own. Within the palace he knew more than anyone else about the past and the present. He replaced the old princes with bureaucrats, mostly honest men but uniformly conservative and excessively deferential. There was no liberal-progressive among them to offset several almost paranoid rightist-monarchists. If anything, they encouraged the king's plunge into the right-wing maelstrom.

Outside the court, Bhumibol also lost perspective. Judging the Sanya and Kukrit governments as failures, he gave up on these liberal allies and, more important, on the idea of Western democracy. Sanya's tenure was the first time Bhumibol personally faced the complexities of government and responding to people's needs. He was overwhelmed far more than Sanya was by the fractious politics, stubborn bureaucracy, and all the noise in the streets. By the end of Kukrit's year in office, Bhumibol no longer supported any democratic reformism.

This view came through when he translated a mid-1975 article from the *Economist* titled "No Need for Apocalypse."[14] The *Economist* warned of a dangerous breakdown in British government and society due to the Labour government's socialist policies and the intransigence of mine workers. There weren't many similarities in Thailand's and Britain's situations at the time, but by his translation the king seemed to conclude that democratic elections only served to permit leftists to gain power and destroy the country.

One other important event that pushed Bhumibol and the palace at large into panic was an alarming reminder of his own mortality. In January 1975, just as the newly elected Seni government took office, the king fell deeply ill with a fever he had contracted in northern Thailand, later reported as scrub typhus. His temperature was above 40 degrees Celsius for ten days running, and the palace worried he would die.[15] He was back up and about in February, but he had a relapse in April, canceled numerous commitments, and only after a few more weeks' rest fully recovered.

It was the synchronicity of all these things—the insurgency, his health, his son and the succession, frustration with capitalism and rural development, abandonment by allies, and the communist takeover of neighboring states—which propelled King Bhumibol's and Queen Sirikit's panicky descent into an unapologetic, violent conservatism, leading ultimately to the Thammasat massacre. The fall of the Laotian monarchy in December 1975 was the final straw. From then on, Bhumibol rejected flatly the view of many experts and intelligence reports that the CPT had no ability to undermine the government, and that Vietnam had no intention of invading Thailand.

The final factor in Bhumibol's giving up on liberal governance and his plunge to the right was his assimilation of the mythology of the dhammaraja state and his own superior wisdom. After years of Buddhist study and meditation, he crossed the line to a sense of bodhisattva-like clarity about the world and himself. He concluded that civil law and the secular civil authority behind it are temporary, unprincipled, and indiscriminate, ultimately serving the wrong purpose or skewed intentions. Together with the modern market economy, he came to believe, they foment unjustness and distort the natural world. To rectify this required reviving the natural state founded on the dhammasat, a permanent guide for behavior based on personal morality and conscience, reinforced by the personal burden of karma. To define and shape the dhammasat, to govern through a dhamma-based hierarchy, required a powerful, wise, and just sovereign. It was tantamount to a sort of Buddhist theocracy.

For King Bhumibol, at first it had been enough to try to strengthen unity by emphasizing moral behavior and karmic causality. As social turbulence grew, though, making merit and being patriotic wasn't enough. Expanding the definition of virtuous behavior, he promoted discipline, industriousness, and sacrifice. He stressed that hard work with erroneous goals or outcomes was more important than well-intentioned passivity. Bhumibol made clear in speeches that this was about religious virtue, and not simply civic duty. He preached it to the sangha, and supported a program of "development monks" who traveled the country to proselytize hard work as meritorious behavior. These concepts were also the original basis of the king's association with Kittivudho, whose college trained monks in agriculture, engineering, and business as part of their dhammic commitment to nation-religion-king.

The king even projected the message in rituals. Instead of traditional offerings of new robes and other items for daily temple life for some royal kathins in the 1970s, the king pointedly sent carpentry tools, as if the monks should themselves construct temples, homes, and schools. This was a radical adaptation of the Buddhist ethic. Karma, the king was saying, was not destiny; it was the cumulative achievements emanating from hard work and sacrifice to the community and nation. Pure dhammic practice was founded not on non-desire but instead on striving to achieve certain goals through honest hard work. It was these values that brought salvation, personal and national.

Bhumibol's new interpretation of morality hardly went unnoticed. Some lay and monk critics argued that the sangha was supposed to live passively in pure thought and practice, that goal-oriented work compromised pure practice, and proselytizing like the development monks did was worldly activity that didn't build merit or karma. But King Bhumibol could ignore the critics. As the dhammaraja, he was the country's leading theologian, the most lofty interpreter of the dhamma. Endorsed by the top monks (whom he installed in office), he countered that people who spoke from any theory or dogma other than that of the Thai nation-religion-king had their heads in the clouds.[16]

In glaring contrast, too, Bhumibol, the head of state, was silent on the secular rules of the modern state. Aside from his momentary support for the constitution in 1974, he didn't speak of the need to obey the law or its principles, or even civil authority. Nor did any of his children, future leaders of the country, study modern law, government, or philosophy, the subjects Bhumibol himself had studied in his last years in Lausanne. His son studied soldiering, and his first daughter science. The throne's alternate, Princess Sirindhorn, wrote her thesis at Chulalongkorn University on the thotsaphit rachatham, the tenfold code of a Buddhist king's behavior.

At times King Bhumibol showed signs of really believing in the magical powers of his position. Throughout the 1970s crisis he unfailingly performed the religious rituals of the office, tweaking them to suit his views. He visited monks known for magic and supernatural powers and still followed a daily schedule advised by royal astrologers. Even as he reviewed all the geopolitical and economic principles behind his kingdom's fate, he sometimes explained the world in terms of cosmic and astrological forces. In a 1975 speech to the Bangkok-based UN agency ESCAP, he warned not of communism or capitalism but a mysteriously undulating universe: "The operations of the United Nations . . . must like all other operations be normally subject to periods of prosperity and deterioration following one another in cycles according to the changing times and circumstance of the universe."[17]

Although confident in his insight, Bhumibol certainly didn't ascribe to himself bodhisattva attributes. Doing so fell instead to those around him, especially Phra Yanasangworn, abbot of Wat Bovornives. The monk virtually apotheosized the king in a speech on the occasion of Bhumibol's 10,000th day on the throne, on September 20, 1977.[18] The title of the lecture itself evoked sacral revelation: "At the Conclusion of the Meditation Period Dedicated to His Majesty the King." Yanasangworn's deep contemplation had divulged important truths about Rama IX.

Officially, Yanasangworn and the king did not subscribe to divination or numerology. But there was something magical in this 10,000-days date, for it coincided with the birthdays of both King Rama V and King Rama VIII. This, said Yanasangworn, "becomes even more significant if we pause to consider how his majesty has drawn on the merits which have accrued to him from the past as well as from his present constant actions, and has patiently transferred them through various activities into benefits of increasing happiness and prosperity for his people. . . . We have always managed to overcome all threatening dangers owing to the constantly overriding virtue of his majesty. The virtuous state which his majesty has reached through accumulated merits is so massive that it stands out so clearly for everyone to see."

He detailed how Bhumibol had fulfilled each of the tenets of the thotsaphit rachatham. For *tapa*, diligence, King Bhumibol did a full day's work on each of the 10,000 days, and on some days even more. He "never tires of trying to overcome evil with goodness." As for *akkodha*, not displaying anger, he said: "Ask anyone if he or she has seen his majesty angry and everyone will answer in the negative. . . . [T]here are only kindness and compassion in his heart." For *avirodhana*, rectitude, the monk dangled the possibility that the king could make a mistake, by saying he was "very rarely wrong both in initiation and execution, because his majesty always considers well and hard before committing himself to any action or any course of action." On the other hand, he added: "Naturally, there may be some cases where mistakes become apparent or changing circumstances indicate a change of course. Then his majesty never hesitates to make the required change or correction which usually brings about the desired results in the end or may even improve on the envisaged objective."

Having run through the list, the high monk summed up: "He has indeed kept his words by maintaining to the full the . . . Ten Principles of a Perfect Ruler. . . . His majesty thus merits to be classified as the best among kings according to the criteria which our Lord Buddha indicated." The very best king, Yanasangworn quotes the Buddha as saying, is one who upholds dhamma, respects dhamma, depends on dhamma, who regards dhamma as supreme and uses dhamma to protect and relieve his people. The Buddha himself respected, regarded, and followed dhamma.

Yanasangworn then explained that King Bhumibol was perfectly invincible due to his achieving the Buddha's five righteous attributes of a king, and that the king furthermore adhered to the layman's five principles for achieving *vimutti*, release from suffering. Following that, the abbot outlined the stages of higher consciousness that are achieved by pure practice. The fifth stage is nirvana, full enlightenment. He didn't dare say Bhumibol had achieved that, but in declaring Bhumibol's mastery of the thotsaphit rachatham, the five righteous attributes of a king, and the five layman's principles, it was the unmistakable conclusion. In conclusion, Phra Yanasangworn asked the audience "to concentrate your mind in dedicating your merits and all blessings which you have attained to his majesty the king, the glorious defender of our faith, as well as her majesty the queen."

An essay that accompanied Phra Yanasangworn's revelations reiterated this brilliance in more contemporary, secular terms. It explained that, after the frail regimes of Rama VII and Rama VIII, Bhumibol had restored the monarchy, giving a modern meaning to the Thai throne. "With a perceptive as well as imaginative mind and an inborn sense of intense dedication . . . his sense of involvement, be it in small or insignificant duties, is always so total that he would never feel relieved until each duty is carried out to his complete satisfaction. . . . His total dedication . . . can never see an end."

Given his upbringing, thoroughly indoctrinated in Chakri mythology, Bhumibol's turn to the way of Buddhist dhammaraja kingship in the face of universal chaos was not surprising. Christine Gray wrote that, as unmodern as it seemed, the Thai Buddhist canon taught that "in times of great trouble, only a great world renouncer can restore order by analyzing the causal sources of suffering and prescribing appropriate, and radical social remedies."[19] Amid the political turmoil, it was what the Thai people appeared to want, wrote Benedict Anderson. For them the monarchy "was both a talisman and a moral alibi. The historical depth and solidity of the institution appeared as a kind of charm against disorder and disintegration. . . . Thus any assault, however indirect, on the legitimacy of the throne was necessarily sensed as a menace to that alibi."[20]

It explains why, at first, many people were comforted by Bhumibol's choice of Tanin Kraivixien to lead the government in the wake of October 6. Some Thai political scientists would come to call his approach to government "dhammocracy," like a modern Buddhist theocracy. This approach was summed up in an exegesis on democracy from a booklet that accompanied a 1978 royal kathin ceremony. "The people must have complete and perfect value in themselves before democracy will appear. . . . Buddhism is the oldest model of democratic ideology in the world. . . . Only by obeying the laws of the sangha . . . will men come truly to reside in the principles of democracy."[21]

Yet there was an important fault in all of this. Charles Keyes, in *Thailand: Buddhist Kingdom as Modern Nation-State,* wrote that the key to stable progress in this Buddhist kingdom was "tolerance for different value systems . . . as against an ideology based on a narrowly militant Buddhist or Buddhist-monarchical nationalism. If King Bhumibol or his successor were to support the promotion of the latter type of ideology, the consensus would undoubtedly collapse. So, too, would it collapse if the king or his successor were to give unqualified support to efforts by any military faction to extend its power through violent and coercive means."[22]

This, though, was the precise direction in which Bhumibol turned in 1976. He supported an extreme militant nationalism that attacked and alienated a large sector of society. By turning against students, farmers, and workers, Bhumibol divided his kingdom and exposed the Chakri monarchy to nearly as much danger as it had faced in the early 1930s. Confident in his wisdom, and desperate to protect the throne, he forgot the real sources of the kingdom's problems, and its real enemies. Nevertheless, the cataclysm of October 6 only hardened his resolve, and he eventually fell into the trap that was the second part of Keyes's warning: giving unqualified support to a military faction.

14   *Who's the Enemy?*   ∾

THE COUP OF OCTOBER 1976 GAVE KING BHUMIBOL the chance to create his own government and, for the first time, truly rule his kingdom. With his proxy Tanin Kraivixien as prime minister, his interventions became regular, planned, and purposeful, as the political scientist M.R. Sukhumbhand Paripatra wrote, "predominantly aimed at increasing the monarchy's political power . . . as a guarantee against disorder and communism."[1] The throne seemed to be, said Sukhumbhand, "attempting to transform itself into the most dominant institution in the body politic." That made the backlash against Tanin, when it came after barely a year, all the more stunning to the king. Bhumibol's politics were soundly rejected by a collaboration of moderate generals, businessmen, bureaucrats, and the general public.

The group that seized power on October 6, 1976, was made up of relatively moderate military officers associated with the late Krit Sivara. One view of the still-murky affair is that they headed off a takeover by extreme rightists connected to Thanom and Praphas, Pramarn Adireksan, and Samak Sunthornvej. The military men called themselves the National Administrative Reform Council, or NARC, with Admiral Sa-ngad Chaloryu, the military supreme commander, as chairman. The power behind Sa-ngad was General Kriengsak Chomanan, a Krit-like moderate in his soldiering and politics. To obtain palace approval for the coup they were obliged to install the king's choice as prime minister. Bhumibol's insistence on a civilian suggested both distrust of the NARC generals as well as concern over foreign perceptions of the new government.

As a supreme court judge, Tanin was the kind of bureaucrat the king most appreciated: honest and dedicated, never showing ambition or greed. A second-generation Sino-Thai the same age as King Bhumibol, he studied law in England, married a Danish woman, and was almost more monarchist than the king himself. Tanin was best known for his anticommunism. He wrote books like *The Use of Law to Fight Communism* and, with university psychology lecturer Dusit Siriwan, hosted a Navapol-sponsored television program called *Democracy Talks*. On it they constantly harangued communists, students, and progressive politicians as a monolithic threat to the kingdom. Tanin's 1975 book on the monarchy made him a leading new-generation exponent of Chakri royalism.[2] He explained the Chakri king as a patriarch who would deliver a good life to his subjects as long as they remained faithful, docile and orderly. As proof he cited mostly the great reforms of King Chulalongkorn.

He argued ultimately that Thais cannot survive without the monarchy because the Thai race is not defined by genetic or geopolitical traits, but by "Thai-ness," khwam ben thai, a concept that, Tanin wrote, cannot exist separate from the king. Without the monarchy, he implied, the land and its people would fall into some identity-less perdition of the type communists would bring. Earlier Ninth Reign ideologists Prince Dhani and Srivisarn Vacha had argued that the dhammaraja king is by nature supremely democratic. Tanin went a step further, citing Bhumibol's three decades on the throne as evidence that institutions like the parliament and voter-based representation, and even constitutional law, were unimportant. Participation of the masses in government was unnecessary, because the throne best advocated their welfare. That, Tanin said, was true democracy. Tanin approved the October 1973 uprising, but only because the students were acting in harmony with the king.

In the wake of bloody October 6, 1976, the king and Tanin rejected any thought of moderating their hard-line policies. Consequently, as many as 10,000 leftists fled into the countryside to join the CPT, making civil war a real possibility. The economy sank as investors pulled out, and Thailand's old ally Washington cut off aid, criticizing the government as undemocratic and abusing human rights. Tanin later explained unapologetically: "When you deal with politics, you've got to be wary of the middle ground because that is where the communists creep in, disguised as liberals."[3] That is what happened after 1973, he said.

The new government set out a new, abbreviated constitution that gave Tanin near absolute powers, ruling through an appointed national assembly of bureaucrats and soldiers. The charter made the prime minister's orders law, and he had the power of summary justice. It resembled Sarit's dictatorship of 1958, except that Tanin was the king's proxy. In an indication of the palace's intention to rule, the charter created a new royal prerogative, that the king could introduce legislation directly into the assembly.

Tanin largely ignored the NARC generals, rejecting their shortlist for the cabinet and naming his own men. His television partner Dusit became senior minister in charge of political policy. The reviled Samak Sunthornvej, a favorite of the queen, became interior minister, with power over the police. Aside from three NARC men in defense-related slots, the rest of the cabinet members were Tanin's friends and government technocrats. The royal imprimatur compelled the NARC to go along as Tanin moved brutally against the left. He put criminal cases under the jurisdiction of military tribunals, and the police were given sweeping powers to detain people. The government branded all those who backed the insurgency as traitors and communists, allowing them to be held without charge for six months. Several thousand people were then arrested, the government alleging they were communists plotting the overthrow of the government and the monarchy.

Lèse-majesté law was also toughened. Before October 1976, a lèse-majesté conviction carried up to seven years' imprisonment. This gave judges great leeway, and many people who were accused got off lightly, with suspended sentences or a few months in prison. Many judges understood that lèse-majesté had become a political tool used by the right, often without justification. Two weeks after taking power, though, Tanin had the penal code amended to assign a minimum of three years' imprisonment and a maximum of 15 years for lèse-majesté. There was a surge in arrests. In 1975, 10 people were arrested for lèse-majesté; in 1976, 21; and in 1977, under Tanin's tough regime, 42.[4] One man was accused of royal desecration for wiping a table with a royally-bestowed Village Scout scarf.

Like Sarit, Tanin ordered a few summary executions of hardcore criminals to send a message to miscreants. The difference in his law-and-order regime, appreciated by the palace, was that he was almost equally tough on corruption and the abuse of bureaucratic power as on communists. The new regime strictly censored the media and banned all protests. The police scoured homes, schools, and offices to confiscate "dangerous" books, going so far as to burn any book with a red cover. In schools, discussion of political thought, whether Marxism or democracy, was banned. Textbooks were rewritten and movies produced to expound on Thai values—defined as allegiance to the royalist state—as the very antithesis of communism. Tanin's book on Thai kingship was reprinted by the government and distributed throughout the country's schools.

In the countryside, counterinsurgency efforts escalated to near full-scale war. But reports showed more innocent villagers being killed than CPT regulars. In the south the use of napalm destroyed entire villages and great swaths of coffee, rubber, and rice acreage, the basis of the local economy. The CPT's strength was hardly dented. Guerrilla attacks continued at a measured pace, and the government's death count jumped to some 550 troops in the first three months of 1977.[5]

Tanin's bellicosity extended to foreign relations. He tossed aside Kukrit's and Seni's overtures to China and Vietnam and again declared those countries mortal enemies. To its neighbors, it was now Thailand that appeared to be preparing for war. It was a dangerous swing to the far right, and was reported as such by academics, foreign embassies, and journalists. Within several weeks Tanin had alienated much of Thai society, making it clear that he answered to none but the throne.

Bhumibol himself was unyielding, declaring the October coup "a manifestation of what the people clearly wanted."[6] In his December birthday address, he said: "At a time when our country is being continually threatened with aggression by the enemy, our very freedom and existence as Thais may be destroyed if Thai people fail to realize their patriotism and their solidarity in resisting the enemy. . . . Accordingly, the Thai military has the most important role in defense of our country at all times, ready always to carry out its duty to protect the country."[7] Just a few weeks later in a well-publicized audience he welcomed back Praphas Charusathien from exile.

In its toughness, the monarchy risked losing "ownership" of the virtue of democracy, after wresting it away over decades from the 1932 revolutionists and convincing Thais that democracy was King Prajadhipok's idea. The new government of Jimmy Carter in Washington strongly reprimanded Thailand for abandoning democracy, and the CPT was calling the government a palace dictatorship.

The Tanin-palace regime countered with a concerted effort to define itself as democratic. Despite abrogating the constitution, Tanin told critics he believed in "a form of democratic socialism as practiced in England and Denmark." Like the high princes before 1932, he said his government would hold elections and respect civil rights, but that the people first needed more education, which would take 12 years. He called this long-term plan to restore democracy the Chulalongkorn Plan. Meanwhile he launched a campaign to reiterate the monarchy's fostering of democracy ever since King Ramkhamhaeng. The government repeated like a mantra a defining phrase from the shrunken constitution: that democracy is a form of government "with the monarch as head of state." King Bhumibol's own speeches shifted to explain democracy as a system of order and discipline, suggesting then that the 1973–76 period could not have been democratic.

To seal these assertions in cement, literally, Tanin planned to royalize the students' favorite rallying spot, the Phibun-built Democracy Monument in the middle of Rajadamnoen Road, a black-painted podium atop which rested a volume representing the constitution.[8] By the early 1970s, historical revisionism and student activism had converted the monument's identity from its original association with the overthrow of absolute monarchy to democracy as bestowed by King Prajadhipok. This gave it its potency in rallies against the Thanom-Praphas dictatorship. After they were banished, the monument was painted a shimmering gold, making it an emblem of the liberal Western variety of democracy.

Following October 6, the palace recognized that it had to either appropriate Democracy Monument's symbolic power or destroy it. Tanin immediately assigned a huge budget for erecting a large statue of Prajadhipok atop the monument in the place of the constitution. It proved to be an engineering problem, so instead the government decided to raise the Rama VII statue in front of parliament. It would be inscribed with the one sentence from his abdication statement that immortalized him as the father of the parliament and constitutionalism: "I am willing to surrender the powers I formerly exercised to the people as a whole, but I am not willing to turn them over to any individual or any group to use in an autocratic manner without heeding the voice of the people."[9]

As for Democracy Monument, the Tanin government decided to destroy it altogether. Conveniently, a historic preservation committee decided it wasn't worth conserving because it was not associated with anything royal.

Meanwhile King Bhumibol, Queen Sirikit, and their children went to work more intensely than ever, seeking to rally the people behind them personally, both to protect Tanin and to protect themselves if he didn't survive. To stress that the kingdom's very existence was at stake, the royal family bustled across the country making contact with as many Thais as possible. They presented themselves before military units, civil servant groups, and especially Village Scout gatherings. Numbering over three million, the scouts were now the primary locus of support for the throne. The royal family also visited many temples and monks, including again Kittivudho's Jittiphawan College, and consecrated a number of new royal temples, the first since the 1960s, mostly in Isan where the insurgency was worst. They increased their visits to soldiers on the front lines and attended to the wounded in hospitals, wearing fatigues and sometimes sidearms. Prince Vajiralongkorn, just out of guerrilla warfare training, made well-publicized visits to forward army positions.

This concentrated effort included strengthening the Mahidols' own ranks. While the country was still reeling from the shock of October 6 and the Tanin government's repressiveness, at the beginning of December 1976 newspapers carried the picture of a relatively unknown girl, M.R. Somsawali Kitiyakara, calling her Prince Vajiralongkorn's fiancée. The future queen had been decided. The engagement took place in a hurry. The prince had just spent most of six years in Australia, and had even fallen in love with the daughter of a Thai diplomat there, M.L. Laksasubha Kridakara. But she wasn't acceptable to Queen Sirikit, who insisted on Somsawali, her own niece, the daughter of her brother Prince Adulyakit Kitiyakara.

Somsawali represented not only the dynastic ambitions of the Kitiyakaras but also those of the Sanitwongs family of Sirikit's mother, and a third prominent royal line at risk of marginalization, the heirs of King Chulalongkorn's son Prince Yugala. Somsawali's mother was M.R. Bhandhusawali Yugala, whose own mother was a Sanitwongs. For the three families' dynastic aspirations, Somsawali was genealogically near perfect. But genetically she was a potential disaster. In a dynasty deeply defined by endogamous marriage and mating, the king and the queen were closely related direct descendants of King Chulalongkorn. So Somsawali had much the same blood as the prince.

On top of that, the prince didn't like her. He preferred beautiful, clever, and forthright women. At 19, Somsawali was plain, dull, timid, and not well educated or hugely intelligent. Totally inexperienced with men, she had none of the spark that the prince liked in women. Still, he obliged his mother. On January 3, 1977, the couple married in a traditional royal ceremony, blessed by all the elders of the court, the Brahman and Buddhist priests, and the king and queen. Somsawali was given a title that established her as the future queen of Thailand. Almost immediately, the couple began touring the country, to show the people that the royal family was united and that the dynasty had a future.

The royal family's campaign was one of open and aggressive partisanship. This effectively made them out as combatants, putting royal prestige and even their bodies directly in the line of fire. After years of steering their criticisms around the throne to avoid alienating people, the insurgents responded accordingly. After

October 6, the CPT began attacking the throne directly, calling it the "great feudalist" and blaming the institution directly for the Thammasat massacre and Tanin's repression. On February 13, 1977, the CPT knowingly fired near the army convoy of the crown prince in the mountains near Lomsak, Petchabun. By some accounts the shots were meant only as a warning, and the prince was never seriously endangered. Nevertheless, the incident was inflated in Bangkok to portray the savage un-Thai behavior of the communists, as well as to demonstrate Vajiralongkorn's frontline bravery.

Three days later, in the south, the queen's aide M.C. Vibhavadi Rangsit was killed when her BPP helicopter was shot down. Vibhavadi was the sister of Bhumibol's chum Prince Bhisadej, and she was married to the son of Prince Rangsit; their marriage in 1946 was the only one ever blessed by King Ananda. She was particularly close to the royal couple and very popular. But her flight in the south was hardly innocent. The war there was full-scale, with the army and the BPP conducting bombing attacks from the air. Her helicopter went deep into the war zone near the Thai-Malay border to retrieve two wounded soldiers, and the insurgents didn't know she was on it.

Bangkok reacted to her death with outrage. The government and palace characterized her as a royal and so having the status of a beneficent neutral, never to be harmed. Accused of savage terrorism, the CPT replied by calling the royal family aggressors. In radio broadcasts they said Vibhavadi was helping a murderous regime repress the people: "Amidst the dead bodies, the odor of blood, and the crying of the people who were victims of the reactionary piratic clique, Princess Vibhavadi boarded a BPP helicopter to encourage those murderers. . . . What about the people in the area who are now facing difficulties and hardships, those whose relatives were killed or wounded by the police and volunteers, whose houses and farmland were destroyed, and whose children, wives and sisters were raped and killed? Princess Vibhavadi never paid any attention to these people."[10]

With her death, the royal family could no longer feel immune. Making use of the newly recruited intellectuals who better understood Thai history and royal symbolism, the CPT attacked royal wealth, in history and the present. They assailed the king's predecessors Rama IV and Rama V for living off the people's backs "in luxurious palaces and having large harems of . . . 60 to 70 children. They reproduced like rabbits." The CPT struck at the palace's indulgent ceremonies and identified its investments and properties, saying: "They promulgated a law saying this institution is sacred and inviolable. However, ... the more powerful the monarch becomes, the poorer the people become, and the more the monarch's income from land rental, his shares in commercial companies, and his bank savings increase."

The insurgents reserved their strongest attacks for the queen and the crown prince. Sirikit was compared to China's imperious dowager empress who destroyed the kingdom while holding the real emperor prisoner, while the prince was uncontrollably violent, as October 6 demonstrated, they said. This had an appreciable impact, for among educated urban Thais, the reputations of the queen and the prince had been sinking steadily. Many people blamed Sirikit for the palace's support for rightist vigilantism, and for choosing Tanin to be prime minister.

But eventually the CPT went too far for most Thais. In a broadcast on April 1, 1977, the former student leader Thirayut Boonmee called the monarchy "obsolete and deteriorating," and said, "I think that if our people were to destroy it, there would be no adverse effects." This was a strategic mistake. Most Thais still saw the monarchy as essential to their culture and nationhood. The broadcast proved to them that the CPT intended to overthrow the monarchy and so destroy the kingdom.

With this evidence, Bhumibol boldly and unrepentantly took his campaign to the universities, where there remained huge enmity and distrust toward the throne. Instead of healing wounds, he lectured that students had no business meddling in politics. They should study hard and quietly and leave national policy to leaders and bureaucrats.

On June 17 he delivered his message to Thammasat University's graduation ceremony. Extremely resentful students underwent body searches before the king arrived, surrounded by bodyguards. Bhumibol made no direct reference to the massacre that had taken place there eight months earlier, but indirectly he condescendingly suggested that the students themselves were to blame:

> An idea exists among certain groups of people that it is necessary to destroy and uproot existing things before progress or prosperity can be accomplished. This idea must be scrutinized to find out whether it is correct and worth thinking about or implementing. Existing things constitute foundations and models, whose strength and weaknesses should be studied to eliminate the weaknesses and achieve more developed advancement. How can progress be made if the foundation for it is destroyed?
>
> For example, a person must treat his headache so that he can once again think about more progress. If he crushes his brain by pounding on

his head to cure his headache, what will be left to think with? Smart and intelligent graduates should fully study the progress which has already been made and solve the current weaknesses in order to bring about new progress.[11]

But Bhumibol was ignoring the fact that Prime Minister Tanin's unpopularity had deepened to the point that, by April 1977, he survived only by dint of the king's backing. Tanin and Interior Minister Samak evoked possibly more fear among the public than the CPT. Among businessmen, Tanin's intractability frightened investors as much as the insurgency did, and many shifted their assets out of the country. In the military, competing factions varyingly resented Tanin's hard line, his snubbing the NARC, and his anticorruption thrust. Nor did Tanin find support among the peasants. While he increased budgets for the military and for promoting the monarchy, he slashed spending for rural development. For important projects he revived the use of unpaid corvée labor, which the CPT cited as evidence of the regime's feudalism.

The resentment surfaced in late March when an army general mustered a group of officers to overthrow Tanin. The plot collapsed from inadequate support, but only after the coup leader killed another officer. Tanin took the extraordinary step of ordering the leader executed, while four accomplices were given life sentences. To reiterate their unwavering support for Tanin, the royal family attended the funeral of the officer who was killed, and the king awarded him royal decorations posthumously.

But public sentiment against the king's government grew daily. The families of the 3,000 activists who were arrested and the many more who fled into the jungle after October 6 objected to Tanin and Samak's branding them communist terrorists. NARC moderates got Tanin to release most, but halfway through 1977 several hundred still faced charges of conspiracy against the government and the monarchy. Attention focused on the Thammasat 18, core student activists who were charged with sedition and lèse-majesté. Tanin was widely believed to want them executed.

Their trial opened in September. Rather than beg for mercy, the defendants declared that they didn't recognize the authority of Tanin or the military courts, saying Tanin's regime had violated the law by overthrowing a democratically elected government. They rejected the specific charges of organizing and participating in illegal protests and strikes, because laws banning such activities were made only after October 6. Their arguments were a powerful direct act of defiance to Tanin and his patron King Bhumibol, and to traditional Thai hierarchy in general. Unlike peasants, the students knew the law, the same law Tanin relied on for his own power. They accused Tanin of never investigating the October 6 massacre or arresting anyone for it. The coup-makers themselves were given full amnesty, but no one else, they pointed out. The obvious real question being posed was, was the king, represented by Tanin, truly fair and just? Did he accept the law? Was he really democratic?

As the trial got under way, competition for power among the political and military elite heated up. In August a clique of ambitious young military officers called the Young Turks lobbied deputy NARC leader General Kriengsak to lead a coup. As Kriengsak demurred, the government was embarrassed by an incident that illustrated just how messy things could get when the throne got mixed up in politics. In late September, while the king and queen were appearing in Yala in the deep south, small bombs exploded in a market close to them. As they sped off in their limousine unharmed, two drunken policemen on a motorcycle crashed into the royal motorcade.

The incident revealed the deep split in the political establishment. Immediately rivals attacked Interior Minister Samak for not providing adequate protection to the royal family. When Samak countered that someone had planted the bombs specifically to embarrass him in front of the king, he was accused of lèse-majesté, the very tactic he used on others. Although demonstrations were banned, Red Gaur and Navapol brigades now hit the streets to protest against Samak, as one general declared that a protest "could be permitted if it was an act of allegiance to the king."

The palace was now being tested directly on its commitment to a deeply disliked government. Kukrit Pramoj ridiculed Tanin as "a sort of blue-eyed boy talking about ideologies, self-sacrifice and rural development by sheer voluntary service." Peasants had no choice but to join the insurgents, Kukrit said, because Tanin's government was "completely neglectful of all the vital problems, the life and death of the farmers." In the south, he added accurately, "anybody who looks suspicious would be declared an insurgent, would be arrested and disappear completely."[12] Kukrit, who had also been delicately pressing the palace to withdraw from politics (while suggesting that an out-of-control Queen Sirikit was the real problem), was offering King Bhumibol room to distance himself. But the king held his ground. He still didn't see Tanin's visceral anticommunism as bad for the country.

Finally Kriengsak moved. Just after he was promoted to supreme commander in early October, he and the Young Turks demanded that Tanin fire Samak. Tanin replied that his government had been royally appointed and would stand or fall as one. But the royal imprimatur no longer worked. On October 20, it took only several truckloads of soldiers to eject the government. Coups by this time were accepted among large parts of the Thai elite as a natural political change, especially if they were not violent. The king had given his blessing to several such takeovers during his three decades on the throne. But inside the palace, this time was different. Kriengsak's coup had not received the royal go-ahead, which meant that it showed great disrespect for the king's political primacy. With his prestige momentarily punctured, Bhumibol struggled to maintain royal composure by asserting his claim to moral superiority. With no sense of irony, palace agents spread the word that the king was unhappy with the coup because he stood only for smooth, democratic, and constitutional changes of government. They said he felt Kriengsak's coup made Thailand appear like a "banana monarchy."[13]

Kriengsak's coup looked like other coups. The NARC became the National Policy Council, which then named him prime minister. A new interim constitution was written, creating a 360-member National Legislative Assembly, with more than two-thirds of its seats occupied by members of the military or the police.

But there was a difference. Kriengsak's first acts promoted national reconciliation, a role the king should have assumed himself. The new prime minister promised freedom of the press, the end of martial law, and normalization of relations with Indochina, China, and the Soviet Union. Calling Tanin's 12-year Chulalongkorn Plan to restore democracy too slow, he pledged a new constitution and elections by 1979. He named to the national assembly moderate politicians like the Pramoj brothers, and his cabinet was filled with technocrats. Only three ministers came from the National Policy Council, including the deputy interior minister, Lieutenant General Prem Tinsulanonda, who would soon prove very important to the Ninth Reign story.

Kriengsak made significant attempts to address the deep shortcomings outlined in a World Bank report from 1978 that said nine million Thais still lived in absolute poverty, and that real incomes among rural Thais and the urban lower class had declined for years. It was a damning indictment of the monarchist view that King Bhumibol's presence had steadily improved Thai life. Kriengsak also declared a compromise toward the insurgency, promising security and justice to any students who returned from the jungle. It wasn't exactly amnesty, and it got few takers at first. But it was a move in the right direction.

These initiatives gained widespread approval. Yet the king still snubbed Kriengsak, as if to deny him legitimacy.[14] With a flourish, Bhumibol named Tanin to the privy council as compensation for his ignominious downfall. The king limited his public associations with Kriengsak and declined to wear his military uniform on appropriate occasions. Bhumibol also stalled the proposed amnesty for the Bangkok 18 for another year, purportedly out of resentment. And the palace reportedly even considered appointing the vile Samak to head the CPB, until strong objections from various corners forced it to scotch the idea.

Kriengsak's three years in power achieved only tentative progress toward what he promised. Heightened tensions on the Cambodian border, first with the Khmer Rouge and then the Vietnamese who forced them from power, made it difficult to relax military control in rural areas. Hundreds of thousands of refugees spilled into Thailand from Cambodia. The economy was battered by OPEC's early-1979 oil price hike. On top of this, Kriengsak presided uneasily over a coalition of competing military factions, all vying to succeed him by evolution or by coup.

Yet internally things were calmer than they had been for a decade. Kriengsak neutralized the most extreme groups behind the turmoil of 1976. He took control of the BPP and delinked it from the Village Scouts, whose activities were slashed back. Navapol disappeared and the Red Gaurs were sent off to fight on the border, where many died. Toward the insurgency, Kriengsak downgraded the combat footing to launch a new hearts-and-minds strategy. The government finally gave amnesty to the Bangkok 18 in September 1978, which gave credence to his earlier offer to CPT defectors. By coincidence, the CPT had begun to fracture—mainly, the more democracy-focused newcomers fell out with the older Marxist ideologues, and the pro-China group split with the pro-Vietnam. As the movement stalled, Kriengsak squeezed commitments from Hanoi, Beijing, and Vientiane to reduce support for the insurgents. Soon some senior CPT members threw in the towel and returned to Bangkok, and the forgiving reception they received pulled some 400 insurgents in their wake in 1978. It was the beginning of the CPT's end.

No anti-monarchist, Kriengsak kept the throne enshrined and defended royal virtue. In the 1978 constitution, royal power was reduced only slightly. The charter declared that democracy had been granted by King Prajadhipok, and defined Thai government as "a democratic form of government with the king as head of state." Although he no longer appointed the senate, the king had substantial veto power, which only a two-thirds vote of both houses could override.

Kriengsak involved the king in important diplomatic moves as well. Bhumibol gave audiences to the Vietnamese foreign minister in January 1978 and the Laotian premier in early 1979. Deng Xiaoping too had an audience in his 1978 visit, and he attended the crown prince's ordination. These steps reinforced the king's image as head of state and peacemaker. The monarchy was still portrayed at the top of the national hierarchy. Every night on the television and radio, the news broadcast led off with a 5–10 minute report on the royal family's activities, first the king, then the queen, the prince, and the princesses. Then, without a break, it segued directly into what the military leadership did that day as well, and following that the government.

Behind the scenes, intellectuals at ISOC and the National Security Council tried to determine why the nation-religion-king and "democracy with the king as head of state" ideology had failed to unite Thais. An important conclusion was that neither concept had given the peasantry any status or told them how they would benefit. The concept of the state had been wholly focused on the royals and their idealized view of culture. The solution was to redefine the Thai nation to reflect a more balanced mix of royal and rural importance. Now self-sufficient village life, together with the monarchy and Buddhism, was stressed as defining Thai culture. The strength of this culture was in the diligence of simple peasants working in the community's interest. This wasn't so different from Village Scout themes, but there was much less emphasis on danger, fear, and elitism. Reacting to the specifics of peasant and urban-dweller discontent, the national security thinkers paid more attention to the social, economic, and political hopes of the people themselves.[15] They aimed to codify and expound on these ideas through the National Identity Board, created in 1980 to officially answer the questions "What is Thai?" and "What is Thai democracy?"

Kriengsak had no objection to using the traditional monarchy to organize the people. But he preferred to keep the palace a neutral object of politics, a figure of national ritual, so when it came to important political issues, the king was left out. Kriengsak, supported by an unspoken consensus of the non-palace elite, under-stood that the country's problems had become too complex to address with tradi-tion and royalism. Nor did Kriengsak want the palace too able to rally the people on its own. Aside from restricting the activities of the Village Scouts, he blocked the project to build a monument to Rama VII at parliament, claiming budget constraints.

This was an immense setback to Bhumibol, whose political influence had taken decades to construct. With his characteristic persistence, he almost defiantly returned to his earliest lessons on the throne, that ritual and public-spirited ac-tivities were the real source of his prestige. As he stepped up his ritual appearances, he also moved to rebuild the palace's circle of allies through the award of royal honors. These were especially meted out to top bureaucrats and military men, whose wives then received the coveted aristocratic titles of thanpuying and khunying. For others, royal honors were tied more clearly than ever to the size of contributions to royal charities, which grew as the palace played on the fear of the insurgency and the problems of poverty. Bhumibol's continuing ability to draw donations in exchange for a little of his dhammic aura was demonstrated in an appearance at a temple in Bangkok's heavily Sino-Thai Yaowaraj district, where 120 people received his amulets for donations of 20,000 baht (U.S.$1,000) each.[16]

The king resumed with great vigor projects like village cooperatives and water storage. His highland opium-substitution projects were expanded, and he kept up his experimentation in crops and small-is-beautiful technologies in Chitrlada Palace. Drawing on his experiences with capitalism and cooperatives, he joined CPB capital with money and technology from the legendary secretive Israeli trading magnate Shoul Eisenberg, in an attempt to implement the farm cooperative concept on a more corporate basis, like the Israeli kibbutzes that melded farming with food processing. The idea was that the Eisenberg Group would introduce Israel's innovative drip-irrigation systems and agriculture management skills in core demonstration farms. It would also set up and run processing plants for the crops produced by the demonstration farms and by independent Thai farmers using the new farm technology. The farmers would share in the profits of the final factory output, increasing their earnings while avoiding the profiteering middlemen the king so detested. (Ironically, Eisenberg would one day be called "the world's greatest middleman" for his commercial empire.)

Eisenberg wasn't elsewhere involved in manufacturing or farming, so presumably he had his eye on other deals in Thailand, possibly arms related.[17] By late 1977 the Eisenberg-CPB project had several companies in the lower north: one to make tomato paste, another for dehydrated vegetables, a third for frozen vegetables, and a fourth, the Thai Farming Corporation, running its own farm on 3,600 acres. Many other farmers joined the project, producing corn, beans, coffee, tomatoes, and other crops. With an airfield and well-equipped military patrols, the farms doubled as a buttress against the CPT in the area.

Many things went wrong, however. There were fights over land rights between farmers and the company; farmers refused to shoulder the costs for equipment problems; and outsiders offered the farmers higher prices than the Eisenberg plants. Rather than gaining their confidence, the palace succeeded in alienating the local people. They gave up quickly: by 1979, most of the Eisenberg-related operations were shut down or transferred to the government.

That Bhumibol still refused to concede any errors was clear in several interviews he and Queen Sirikit gave to Western journalists during this period. He brushed off criticisms, saying people didn't understand that he was nonpartisan. (He knew that international press reports would be taken more seriously by educated Thais, those who most questioned monarchic government.) The most important of these interviews was for a BBC television documentary in 1980, a two-hour feature on Bhumibol called *Soul of a Nation*. The interviewer David Lomax portrayed Bhumibol as a savvy but humble modern leader guided by Buddhist insight, a king intimately in tune with the problems of his country and above the pettiness of politicians. Spliced with footage of the king and queen at work, in the countryside and in royal ceremonies, the documentary built from the premise that Bhumibol was protecting his kingdom from the imminent threat of communism.

Lomax interviewed Bhumibol late at night in the king's makeshift office in his recently built palace in the Phuphan mountains in Isan. The king sits on the hard floor in his socks and a short-sleeved shirt, not facing his guests or the camera—they are interrupting his never-ending work, represented by maps sprawled across the floor and a table and the constant clabber from several radios against the walls. The scene suggests a bare-bones war operations center, where this simple, hardworking king struggles far into the night to solve the people's problems. The film calls this operation his "intelligence network," giving an impression of Bhumibol's royal omniscience, a one-man CIA and MI5 who knows all that happens in his realm.

As Lomax questions him, the king's unsmiling face and pained voice suggest that the filmmakers not only could never comprehend what he does, but that the interruption is stalling his progress. Bhumibol almost contemptuously replies to a question from Lomax about the CPT threat by correcting him: "We are not fighting against people, we are fighting against hunger. If we make this and they have a better life, the people you call the communist insurgents will have a better life also. So everybody is happy." He explains that what he does is part of a lengthy tradition, which the Thai people recognize.[18] "My great-grandfather was the philosopher king. . . . People in this country . . . have respect especially for King Mongkut. [As in the movie *The King and I*] he is a wonderful fellow, intelligent, strong. . . . He did have a very strong character [and] a very strong sense of duty for the country."

This tradition was carried on by Mongkut's son King Chulalongkorn, who began at 15, Bhumibol said, working on the foundation laid by Mongkut. "He had to fight also to keep the country free from encroachment from other countries," Bhumibol said. Bhumibol himself adhered to his ancestors' examples. Coming from a Chakri king, his work was necessarily good for the people. "I do things which I think are useful, and that's all. I do not know what can be defined as king. . . . I am called a king, but my duties . . . are not the duties of a king. It is something that is quite different, difficult to define. I have no plan. Just like . . . today, we are going [to do] something. . . . We don't know what the something is, but we are going to do something that is good." The primary goal is the people's security, he explained. But beyond that are spiritual goals, toward which the king also provides direction.

> The Thai people have to fight for their freedom. . . . So the main thing is to be a good general and then after that, when the country is more set-tled, is to have law and order, law and administration. At the same time we must have enough food, . . . enough facilities to have good homes, to have shelter. These are essential things.
>
> Then we must have social order, more things of the heart. We must be good people, so that there would not be disorder. . . . So we must have religion. The king is the leader of religion also.

Bhumibol explains his rural development activities, citing as his main contribution more than 400 irrigation projects. He refers only to his own work, as if the government doesn't exist. The people in the countryside follow his advice because he (and not the government) recognizes their needs and problems. "They are very happy when somebody comes and knows about their village," he says of his countryside visits. "They are on intimate terms with us, it's like a big family," he says. "They like us, and we like them."

Bhumibol characterized his work like that of a reclusive guru. "I am not lonely. I have work to do," he said. "The way of doing work is to have some concentration and some peace. . . . It is a way of preparing oneself to be able to do whatever circumstances will have me do. I gather information by listening, I gather information by looking at the maps, or reading, or thinking, and then when the time comes I have the material in my head."

Spirituality is important to his work: "Meditation . . . is very important because, first you must have concentration, you must concentrate your mind. So that you have a peace that is, perhaps, not lasting, but a peace in which you can see many things. To have a peace, a real peace, and then with this peace you will be able to see, very clearly."

Buddhist thought is rather complex and has many grades. There is the grade of Buddhism [in which] the highest level is to attain absolute purity, which you call selfish motive. That is true, it is selfish, purely selfish. But to attain this purity you must do everything that is not selfish, which for you perhaps is a paradox. One must sacrifice, one must discard everything that one thinks that is one's goal. Charity is one way to discard. . . .

Usually the one who practices politics in any doctrine wants to get on the top. If you think of Buddhism, one does not want to be on the top, because there is no top, there's no bottom. It is just pure purity. . . . There is the original purity, which has been spoiled by, or covered by, what we call sin. The original thing that is light, is beautiful.

It was an extremely rare moment, for Bhumibol to enunciate his Buddhist principles. To get his message across to his own people, he had mostly employed his own silent acts and rituals. But then, the BBC interviewer wanted to know, how did the king reconcile these principles with his role as head of the armed forces, directing men to kill?

Most important in life, he replied, are correct intentions and performance of duty. "When a soldier holds a gun, this gun should be intended to shoot, and shoot what, shoot an enemy. That is a living being. But if he holds that gun, with the intention of guarding, preserving his country, with this intention he is not sinful. And even if . . . he must shoot, he has to shoot, and why? Because he has the intention of guarding his country, of preserving his country and, by the way also, the religion. But if the enemy comes, and the country is gone, is destroyed, there's no religion, and there's no good."

He gave Lomax no ground when pressed on specific controversial events. There was no reason to dwell on the past, especially the death of his brother Ananda:

The investigation provided the fact that he died with a bullet wound in his forehead. It was proved that it was not an accident and not a suicide. One doesn't know. . . . But what happened is very mysterious, because immediately much of the evidence was just shifted. And because it was political, so everyone was political, even the police were political, [it was] not very clear.

I only know [that] when I arrived he was dead. Many people wanted to advance not theories but facts to clear up the affair. They were suppressed. And they were suppressed by influential people in this country and in international politics.

When Lomax asked about politics and October 6, 1976, the king bristled, not because it was sensitive, but because the interviewer still didn't understand that he, a Buddhist king of pure intentions, couldn't be political.

It seems to be a very bad thing to defuse a crisis because one touches politics. But if we try to speak and to put some reason into the heads of people, I don't think that is so bad. And even the words "defusing the situation"; I don't think that is very bad. If you don't defuse a bomb it will blow up. And if it blows up, it will be a good fireworks for the one who looks from afar. . . .

The royal family is in the limelight, so that if we think something, we do something, [others will focus on it]. It doesn't mean that we are playing politics. . . . It is not October 6 only. Any action, even if I am going out to look on the site of a small dam, or asking the people if they have had enough to eat this morning . . . I am accused of playing politics.

It is quite normal that people will use the king. He is here to be used. . . . But the way of using depends on us also. That we are doing things that are good for the country, or the people. And we don't have any secrets.

We keep in the middle, neutral . . . in peaceful coexistence with everybody. . . . We could be crushed by both sides, but we are impartial. One day it would be very handy to have somebody impartial. Because if you have in the country only groups of political parties, which have only their own interests at heart, what about those who don't have the power, just ordinary people who cannot make their view known? They must have somebody impartial. And if one wants to destroy somebody who is impartial, one destroys oneself.

Queen Sirikit spoke more readily to Lomax of her husband's brilliance, as well as her own: "Kings and queens of Thailand have always been in close contact with the people. Really. And they usually regard the king as father of the nation. That is why we do not have much private life, because we are considered father and mother of the nation. We are all the time with the people. . . . We are an underdeveloped country. So the task of mere visiting the people as a conventional duty of the head of state is nonsense. If we cannot participate in helping to alleviate the misery of the people, then we consider it a failure."

Their Buddhist beliefs sustain and guide them, Sirikit explained. "I believe what the Buddha taught us, that never dwell in the past, never look at the future, doing your best now, and then you can be sure that the result will be good."

> It is extraordinary when your mind is at peace, tranquil, then you don't feel the tiredness is so much. . . . Just like the monk, the one I have here [holding a picture]: he died of cancer of the throat. I asked whether he felt the pain or not. He told me that if your mind is tranquil, then you don't feel any pain, at all. You feel only that you have done the best of your life, for the others. He said, that is the only way to achieve happiness.
>
> To give, not to take, only to give; to love, so that is the reason my husband and I can work, year after year, day after day. We have been ill. But we know that when it is time to die nobody can escape. So it's better that we contribute as much as we can to society, and reserve some small limited time for us.

How they achieved this, Sirikit noted, was in part through meditation. In this her husband had achieved a very high level, because, she said, "he could control his breathing and he could really concentrate. But I cannot concentrate and meditate yet, I'm learning."

Soul of a Nation brilliantly allowed the king and queen to explain themselves in a rational way. It gave just enough hint of the magical dhammaraja guided by Buddhist principles to persuade the average Thai viewer, while not appearing ridiculous to foreigners and Thai intellectuals. It was only about the dhamma-adhering king helping his nation, with no mention of the government's efforts, or the role of modern democratic institutions, or international aid, or the Thai people themselves. The film concluded: "The king strengthens the nation by reminding it of the nature of its soul."

In a later interview, after Kriengsak was gone, Bhumibol distilled his role in a convenient quip: "They say that a kingdom is like a pyramid: the king is on top and the people below. But in this country, it's upside down. That's why I sometimes have this pain around here [pointing to his neck]."[19]

15 *In the King's Image* ↜
The Perfect General Prem

KRIENGSAK'S COUP OF 1977 was by no means something King Bhumibol took as a lesson that he had pushed too far in politics. After Tanin, the only lesson was that a civilian proxy wasn't enough, that the king needed his own soldier to lead, someone both powerful and selfless who would make the king's needs his priority while controlling the military. One of Kriengsak's ministers, General Prem Tinsula-nonda, fit the bill perfectly. It only took finding an opportunity to push Prem into the premiership.

As he promised, Kriengsak restored the constitution in 1978. It reconstituted the bicameral parliament, with a 225-member senate appointed by the prime minister—no longer by the king—and an elected 310-member lower house. Serving bureaucrats and military men could be made senators, and neither the prime minister nor the members of the cabinet had to be a member of parliament. This permitted Kriengsak to keep a cabinet of technocrats, most of them people Bhumibol appreciated.

It also allowed Kriengsak to become prime minister without his own political party. Before the April 1979 elections, he packed the senate with nearly 200 supporters from the military and police, enough to hold on to power, but weakly so. He could barely manage the several competing military factions, and he had no firm support in either the house or the palace. The governing coalition parties were only tentatively supportive, while in the opposition, the Social Action Party's Kukrit Pramoj, looking to become premier himself, made fierce assaults on Kriengsak. Any crisis would weaken him. But it took Bhumibol to give Kriengsak the final, decisive push, replacing him with Prem as the dynasty's new strongman.

Born in southern Thailand in 1920, Prem was a career soldier with a creditable field record. A stern but well-liked commander, he stayed clear of controversy while serving in the national assembly and the senate under successive governments. In charge of the northeastern military region in the mid-1970s, he took on the insurgency by combining social development with tough military tactics. He was a senior officer in ISOC, and one of his oldest friends, Sudsai Hasdin, was the leader of the Red Gaur. Sudsai and Prem had attended high school, military school, and special training in the United States together. Prem was extremely soft-spoken and respectful of hierarchy. He was so discreet that no one could ever expose his homosexuality, and so firm and disciplined that almost no one tried to. He was oblique and hid his alliances, yet he vainly encouraged the sycophancy of officers below him and didn't always promote professional soldiers like himself.

Mostly, Prem was absolutely loyal to the Chakri hierarchy and honored King Bhumibol unhesitatingly. Their special affinity surfaced in August 1978, when Kriengsak was preparing to name the politically moderate general Serm Na Nakhon to the concurrent posts of supreme commander and army commander in chief. Then Kukrit Pramoj wrote in the newspaper *Thai Rath*, "I think the person who should be given the post of army chief is General Prem Tinsulanonda." Many observers took it as a message from the throne, and six days later Kriengsak named Prem the army chief. Serm got the less powerful post of supreme commander.[1]

The promotion meant that Prem bypassed a number of more senior officers. It allowed him to fill key military positions with his own supporters for the next several years, also giving him substantial leverage in the military-saturated senate. Around the same time, Kriengsak's leadership was weakened by the plummeting economy, soaring oil prices, and the security emergency that arose with the Vietnamese invasion of Cambodia. As Kriengsak's parliamentary base crumbled, Prem and the palace smelled opportunity. In early January 1980, Prem abruptly canceled plans to escort the queen and the crown prince to the United States.[2] Instead, he began criticizing the government on issues like the rise of oil prices. Not coincidentally, on January 24, Sudsai Hasdin used the occasion of a Red Gaur anticommunist protest to attack Kriengsak as well. Kukrit saw this as his chance to recover the premiership, and in early February he launched a no-confidence motion against Kriengsak. But then the Young Turks, the military faction that had helped Kriengsak to power, called for Prem to become prime minister, even though he was officially a noncandidate.

With tension in the air that reminded some of 1976, the palace wanted a smooth, certain transition: another coup would draw criticism from Thailand's allies. But if Kriengsak dissolved the government and set new elections, it risked putting a nonmilitary politician into power, and not necessarily Kukrit. On February 28, Kriengsak and Prem flew to Chiangmai to see the king. The next day Kriengsak resigned without dissolving parliament, and a frustrated Kukrit was pressed by Bhumibol to organize the legislature to endorse Prem as prime minister. The change appeared to be democratic, but in fact it was a royal coup. When Prem ritually declared that his coalition was the "government of the king" as he was sworn in on March 3, the statement held a much deeper truth than ever before. He would stay on "reluctantly" for eight years, closely protected by the king's hand.

With Prem, the king finally had a powerful leader who would honor him as monarch and govern with the virtues the king espoused. Sarit was loyal but corrupt and lascivious; Thanom and the crude Praphas were ineffective and propped up by the United States; Sanya and Kukrit were weak, too concerned with democratic forms and popular support; Tanin was inflexible and couldn't control the military; and Kriengsak was too independent.

Prem, however, was firm, disciplined, and showed no appetite for wealth and no pleasure in power. He understood that Bhumibol was uninterested in day-to-day administration but wanted someone to act when he issued instructions or voiced opinions. The two shared a belief in a natural Thai hierarchy and the value of social and public order, established and enforced first by example and then, when necessary, by force, not law. During the 1980s Prem fostered a new era of adulation for the throne, a real second revival, with the weight of the military and the private sector behind him. Over his eight years in power, he would take the Mahidol family through a nerve-wracking institutional climacteric into golden senior citizenship. During the 1980s King Bhumibol intervened with unabashed regularity on Prem's behalf. Prem, likewise, was hardly shy about tapping into palace support. "Whenever he was bruised," said one 40-year observer of Thai politics, "he would go to the palace and get his injection, get a pick-up."[3] As Prem emerged from Chitrlada, his foes would quickly fall back into line.

More than that, the Bhumibol-Prem partnership attempted to institutionalize the idea of a king's government, and formalize it constitutionally as a palace-army hierarchy. Ideally, the king's man would sustain the system by promoting similarly loyal professionals into the leadership ranks of the armed forces, and these virtuous generals would become the new princes. Instead, Prem's rise fueled more corrupt competition for the palace's favor, and military factionalism and indiscipline only increased. It ironically made Prem-era politics highly unstable, at times violently so. Yet the palace took that as vindication. After several episodes of internecine military fighting, privy council secretary Tongnoi Tongyai declared that it showed that only the king could lead the country. "Do you think even the most popular person who becomes president of a nation would be able to lead the country through difficulties once a crisis erupts? People have no faith in him. But in the meantime the royal establishment and our king can."[4]

At first, Prem's rise wasn't an issue for most Thais, for whom the Vietnamese and CPT threats still justified military leadership. With the king's support, Prem quickly parlayed this receptiveness into more institutionalized military control. The first step was to lay out the philosophical framework, which took the shape of Order 66/2523, a landmark decree issued by Prem just seven weeks into his government. Together with a follow-up in 1982 (Order 65/2525), this was, at face value, a comprehensive refooting of counterinsurgency policy. Its stated aim was to beat the CPT by addressing the real problems of distressed peasants. Meanwhile, a forgiving hand would be offered CPT defectors, codifying Kriengsak's earlier policy. Indeed, the CPT was already imploding, and so Prem appeared immediately successful.

But more important, in these orders the military declared outright its paramount role in government and society. The orders legalized and legitimized the military's any effort to construct a "truly democratic" political system. The armed forces would undertake a "political offensive" to create social justice and root out corruption and exploitation. It was their "sacred duty" to confront both the civilian bureaucratic forces and monopoly capitalism that made the people resent the state. This was the real silent coup of 1980. The two edicts declared support for the constitution and a parliamentary democracy with the king as head of state. But within that framework, the constitution and parliament were to be stifled while Bhumibol and Prem administered through the army. The armed forces gained legal powers that set them above both parliament and the constitution, and just below the throne.

Prem was not all that clear what to do with this new power. Beyond the palace-military hierarchy, he had no particular plan. He spent much of his first four years just protecting his job, for which he depended heavily on the king. The first instance came only a few months after Prem's takeover in 1980, when tradition and law were thrown by the wayside to increase his power. When he became premier,

Prem held on to his other jobs, as minister of defense and army commander. Holding a top civil service post while taking political jobs was highly unusual. After the Thanom-Praphas dictatorship it was specifically proscribed in the reforms of 1974–75. But Bhumibol, who had to approve the arrangement, made no objection. There were grumbles among the public, but it was accepted that Prem would retire from the army job when he turned 60 that October.

In late August, however, senior officers led by Arthit Kamlang-ek, a rising general and favorite of Queen Sirikit, petitioned the king to postpone Prem's retirement for another year. Seeing himself as Prem's heir, Arthit wanted to head off the advance of a more senior rival, the deputy army commander, General Sant Chitpatima. The extension proposal was criticized as subverting the regularization of bureaucratic processes, and even members of Prem's government disapproved. Critics recalled that a similar continuance given to Praphas had helped cause the 1973 revolt. Nevertheless, on September 1, Prem emerged from meeting with King Bhumibol and announced that the king supported the extension. When cabinet ministers demanded proof, they were summoned to meet the king. Whatever he said wasn't reported, but the ministers emerged endorsing Prem's extension.

Some younger politicians were not silenced. The Democratic member of parliament Chuan Leekpai called the extension antidemocratic, and some Young Turks objected as well, though mainly because they opposed Arthit. As significantly, the student movement emerged from dormancy to hold small protests. But the students stopped when they were threatened by the Red Gaur leader Sudsai, who declared, "I want people to know that I am a dangerous man."[5]

In his December 1980 birthday speech, King Bhumibol summed up his support for Prem with a message to pro-democracy critics: "Some intelligent people develop theories usually borrowed from abroad. I use the word 'borrowed' because they are not ours. Scholars borrow technology and try to put it to a successful end in Thailand, so they would be lauded as adept by imparting technology and theories which are not Thai."[6] So it was that the Prem-palace alliance was cemented into place.

Administratively, Prem focused on the insurgency. Order 66/2523 accelerated the collapse of the CPT, and cadres came in from the jungle by the thousands. By 1981 the movement was a spent force, though pockets of resistance remained in the deep south and around Khao Khor in the lower north. In January 1981 it was announced that King Bhumibol planned a river development project at Khao Khor. General Pichit Kullavanich, an aide to Prem, launched a massive five-month air and land campaign to clear the area of insurgents. Given the CPT's collapse, it was a costly effort of questionable utility, as critics noted. There were 1,300 lives lost on the government side alone and a range of mountains was left completely denuded.

In Bangkok, meanwhile, after barely a year Prem was struggling politically. With the country in recession, the political parties that made up his coalition in parliament grew unruly over not benefiting in return for their support. The government was further damaged by several corruption scandals. Moreover, the public reacted badly when, in early 1981, it emerged that Prem would request yet another extension as army commander. Hoping to take advantage, several ministers resigned and Kukrit, still gunning for the premiership, pulled his party out of the government.

Prem was unwilling to step down, and he formed a new coalition with rightist-military parties. He named Sudsai and one of his cohorts, General Prachuab Suntharangkul, to the cabinet, provoking widespread fears of a return of the extreme right of 1976–77. King Bhumibol duly approved the new cabinet roster. The consequence of this was known soon enough. On the night of March 31, 1981, a large cross-section of the military attempted what became known as the April Fools' Day coup. It became the defining moment of the Prem-Bhumibol relationship.

The April Fools' coup was led by the Young Turks, the cocky military clique whose members had graduated in 1960 from Chulachomklao Military Academy, also known as CMA Class 7. Their confidence and cohesiveness stemmed in part from the fact that many had combat experience in Laos and Vietnam, making them more militarily professional than other army cliques, particularly their rivals in Class 5. Their support for Prem in 1980 grew from his own image as a professional soldier, as well as the close personal relationship between Prem and the Young Turk leaders Manoon Roopkachorn and Chamlong Srimuang. After Prem took power in 1980, Chamlong became secretary general of his office. On the other hand, the Young Turks did not particularly enjoy the royal court's patronage.

Many details about the April Fools' coup have been obscured by the palace and the participants, mainly to protect the reputations of Prem and Queen Sirikit. It wasn't at first a coup against Prem, but against Prem's having to depend on unsavory military officers to survive the rebellion in parliament. The Young Turks and allied officers were unhappy as well over the promotion of more political and corrupt officers, including certain palace favorites like General Arthit. According to various accounts, Manoon and General Sant Chitpatima approached Prem on March 31, asking him to abrogate parliament and the constitution and take control in the manner of Sarit in 1958. It appears that Prem at first agreed. As the coup leaders mustered their forces to control Bangkok, however, the queen intervened and summoned Prem to Chitrlada. According to some accounts, her main interest was to protect Arthit. Sirikit reportedly held lengthy phone discussions with the coup leaders, demanding that they come to the palace for talks. When they refused, she supposedly persuaded Prem and the king to withdraw their support for the coup.

The coup leaders went ahead and declared a takeover early on April 1. Prem meanwhile evacuated the entire royal family by helicopter to the 2nd Military Region, 300 kilometers away in Nakhon Ratchasima, where Arthit was commander. From the second floor of Prem's private mansion there, Sirikit, Arthit, and Prem launched a battle of propaganda, the crux of which was who truly enjoyed royal favor and honored the king. On the afternoon of April 1, Prem broadcast that the royal family was with him and that the coup group "harbored ill will against the country and the throne." He branded them shameful and insulting for rejecting a decree to meet the king in audience.[7] Then Sirikit, not Bhumibol, called for unity and criticized the plotters for trying to overthrow "the government of his majesty led by Prime Minister Prem."[8] Her statement was rebroadcast constantly over the next 36 hours. As further evidence of the throne's position, on April 2, Princess Sirindhorn's birthday, her picture ran on the front pages of the newspapers with a caption noting that she was at the 2nd Military Region headquarters with Prem.

With the king himself still silent, the coup leaders retorted by accusing Prem of abducting the royal family. They declared that Prem had sheltered himself "in the graciousness of the institution of the monarchy, thus involving his majesty the king in politics. It will be noted in Thai history that a Thai officer has taken part in sabotaging the institution of the monarchy."[9] They also said that, far from refusing a royal audience, they had been denied one by Prem. "The revolutionary council would like to send an emissary to the king and queen. We hope General Prem will not attempt to monopolize loyalty to the king. . . . We must explain the truth to the king and to the people."[10]

But Prem had the upper hand. "Almost all the army is in my hands, and the king is with us," he declared.[11] In fact it took two days of tense lobbying before most of the regional commanders sided with Prem, finally forcing Manoon and his men to surrender to Arthit on the morning of April 3. Prem's leadership was rescued with barely a shot fired.

King Bhumibol's ambiguous position in the April Fools' Day coup left his reputation mostly intact. Afterward his sticking by Prem was explained as support for orderly, democratic change of government. But it was clear there was much more involved. A royal amnesty was rapidly granted to nearly all the coup participants, as if it had been a misunderstanding among the king's children. Yet whenever the royal family appeared in public during the following weeks, security was extraordinarily high. Over the next year both Prem and Arthit narrowly avoided assassination several times, and the culprits were presumed to be from the army.

Conceivably this might have convinced King Bhumibol that the military's politicization and factionalization endangered the throne, and that the problems were being fed by the palace's personal patronage of specific officers. But the king gave no sign of afterthought. Prem did forgo extending his army commander post another year. It no longer mattered, because the king's endorsement during the coup and the purge of the Young Turks guaranteed Prem at least another year in office. Arthit was promoted to the second most powerful army post immediately, and then in 1982 he was named army commander. It made him Prem's undeclared political successor.

For the next seven turbulent years the king's umbrella sheltered Prem from challenges in both the military and the parliament. The two met constantly, and the king made regular reminders to the public of his support. One occasion was striking in its use of traditional Buddhist symbolism. In July 1982, Bhumibol fell very ill of a mycoplasmic infection and pneumonia, and the palace feared he might die. He later said he went "through the twilight zone." After three weeks in bed, he emerged for a stroll around the Chitrlada gardens. He walked alone, with the crown prince, Sirindhorn, and then Prem following behind. The very positioning ranked Prem like a senior prince of Chakri blood. Bhumibol asked a lady-in-waiting to pick a lotus from a palace pond. She passed the lotus to Prem, who knelt and proffered it to the king. He accepted the flower, gazed at it, and then gently presented it back to Prem.

The scene was reproduced on television and in newspapers, and the symbolism was readily apparent. The lotus represents purity and enlightenment, and is commonly presented to monks as recognition of their spiritual transcendence. For the palace lady to give the flower to Prem recognizes that he is the most virtuously qualified to offer it to the dhammaraja. Holding the flower, the king further imbued it with his own grace. He then presented it to Prem, confirming Prem's own great virtue.

The king recovered, and Prem's hold on power strengthened, despite continued economic woes across the country. The military leadership enjoyed special access in the court as Sirikit surrounded herself with police and military generals, their wives serving as ladies-in-waiting. The most frequent guests at palace parties were military officers, and the generals would take their turns dancing with Sirikit and singing while the king played his saxophone. Politicians and businessmen were rarely invited.

Meanwhile, the government continued to brand its critics as enemies of the state and communists. When at the end of 1982 students held small protests over economic issues, both the Red Gaur and the Village Scouts were mobilized to face them down. Village Scouts were implicated in the murder of a student in Prachuab Khirikan who led a protest against bus-fare rises.

The government sought to permanently institutionalize military power under the king. The 1978 constitution had a transitional phase that kept the military-dominated senate strong and permitted serving military officers to hold political posts. The transition period was to expire in April 1983, after which the senate's powers would be reduced and civil servants and military men would be banned from political office. At the same time, political parties would be forced to consolidate, the goal being to end the forever fractious four- and five-party coalition governments that, for lack of cohesion, never achieved much. In fact, their fractiousness had benefited Prem, who played them off against one another. With tacit palace support, in January 1983 Prem moved to make the interim structure permanent through a constitutional amendment. When he ran into unexpectedly strong resistance from parliament, and even from some progressive generals, his aide General Pichit hinted that there could be another coup if the army didn't get its way.[12]

Indicating his backing, King Bhumibol declared a special session of parliament for the amendment. The military-dominated senate ensured that it passed the first and second readings, which required only a simple majority in both houses. The third reading, slated for March 16, needed a two-thirds vote. By then strong public opposition had surfaced, and the amendments narrowly met defeat.

Prem had a fallback plan, though, which required a precision in timing that made the king's support explicit. The transitional government phase was to end on April 21. At Prem's request the king dissolved parliament on March 19, setting new elections for April 18. This meant a new government would be formed under the old rules, with a potential lifespan of four years. Military dominance could be sustained.

The ruse became an issue during the election. The Democratic and Social Action parties called it a choice between democracy and military dictatorship. The implied issue was the king's support for Prem. When the votes were counted, the winner of the largest number of seats in parliament, thanks to the rural vote, was the Chart Thai Party of Pramarn Adireksan and Chatichai Choonhavan, two venal, ambitious figures directly linked to the right-wing vigilantism of 1976. When Pramarn challenged for the premiership, Prem, who hadn't stood for election himself, took advantage of the widespread fear of Pramarn to pressure the other major parties to support him instead, forcing Chart Thai into the opposition.

Prem then showed the politicians who backed him what he really thought of them. Rather than draw on their ranks, he named over a dozen outsiders as ministers, men loyal to Prem alone. He then reasserted the legitimacy of the palace-army alliance: "The armed forces will play an important role in the defense of the country, national independence and the democratic system under the monarchy."[13]

In approving each of Prem's moves, Bhumibol made his support clear. He verbalized it on the eve of his birthday in December 1983 with a chatty 45-minute monologue that made numerous slights against elected officials and civil servants, but none against Prem and the military leadership. He blamed public officials and politicians for badly handling the floods that had inundated greater Bangkok for weeks on end two months before. Like the sorcerer's apprentice in Walt Disney's *Fantasia,* he said, instead of draining the water out to the sea, officials stupidly moved it from one point to another, creating new problems.[14] The king made it clear he felt they were generally incompetent—as opposed to the military.

In return, Prem made constant efforts to protect and promote the monarchy. He spent a great deal of his time hiding the Mahidols' blemishes, which became increasingly difficult to keep from the public. As soon as he took office in 1980, Prem reactivated the construction of the large monument to King Prajadhipok at the parliament, which had been initiated by Tanin Kraivixien in 1976 to assert the throne's ownership of the virtue of democracy. To make the point, the statue was inaugurated with great fanfare on Constitution Day in 1980. There was even a proposal to rename the day after Rama VII. That didn't happen, but it didn't matter. Around the same time the government delisted the student-favored Democracy Monument from national heritage protection, with the expectation that it would be demolished.

It was all about expunging June 24, the date of the 1932 revolution, from official history and collective memory. After nearly fifty years, few people were left who remembered the truth. It fell to Prem to take care of two of them, the revolutionary leader Pridi Bhanomyong and the monk Phimontham. When Prem took power, Pridi was in Paris, 80 years old, and longing to come home after more than three decades in exile. His family and friends appealed to Bhumibol to permit his return, challenging the king's sense of compassion and forgiveness. But the palace feared that Pridi remained a political threat, still a hero among a generation of students from the 1970s, many of them now teachers and bureaucrats.

Prem finessed the challenge for the king. Privately the government circulated the news that Pridi could return, and that the palace didn't hold him responsible for Ananda's death.[15] But official permission never came, as if there was a bureaucratic snafu for which no one was blamed. Pridi died in Paris on May 2, 1983, and what happened afterward bared the palace's vindictiveness. His body was repatriated, but the government refused him a state funeral, and the palace declined to sponsor his cremation, which it had done for every other Thai leader except Phibun.

The powerful anti-palace monk Phimontham proved more problematic. After being defrocked and jailed on false charges by Sarit in the 1960s, Phimontham had regained some status in the 1970s. At the end of 1980 the abbot of Wat Mahathat died, and the monks voted to restore the position to Phimontham. But the palace- and government-guided ecclesiastical council, the Mahatherasamakhom, stalled, naming no one to lead one of the country's most important temples. After nine months, public criticism and threats of monks' protests forced the council to relent, and Phimontham was made abbot.

That wasn't the end, however. As in the royal family, where it designates a high prince, the highest sangha rank is *somdej*. It is granted for achievement and age, and only six somdej positions exist, with all of them serving on the Mahatherasamakhom; the supreme patriarch is chosen from among them. Just below is the *rong* (deputy) somdej, held by only 12 monks at any time. The king awards all of these positions under recommendation of the sangha council and the religious affairs department, and he personally confers the ranks on his birthday, December 5.

Phimontham attained the rank of rong somdej in the 1950s. Sarit stripped him of the title, and it was restored only in 1975. He was already fully qualified for full somdej rank at the time, but the palace refused it. When one of the six somdej monks died in July 1983, a popular movement arose in favor of giving the position to Phimontham. He was more qualified than any others; indeed, he had become rong somdej before two other monks who had already gone on to become supreme patriarch. The Isan sangha council unanimously voted to support him.

Prem and the palace responded by reviving accusations that Phimontham was a threat to national security, the monarchy, and the priesthood. They particularly worried that he could contest for the supreme patriarch's job, for which another somdej monk much junior to him was already in preparation: this was Phra Yanasangworn, the king's personal spiritual adviser.

As with Pridi's return, the issue was handled in the secret networks that ran between the palace, the sangha council, and the government, and accidents were contrived to block the appointment. At first the sangha council simply stalled. Then, with the king's birthday rapidly approaching, on November 20 the head of the northeastern region on the Mahatherasamakhom formally nominated Phimontham. Eight days later the supreme patriarch asked the religious affairs department to put the proposal on the council agenda. But it never came up, it was explained afterward, because the supreme patriarch's letter was misplaced. This was implausible, since it was tantamount to misplacing an order of the king himself, and it did involve Bhumibol's own affairs. Still, no new somdej appointment was made on December 5.

In mid-1984 another somdej monk died, leaving two vacancies. Again that December the king's birthday passed with no action. Because naming the top monks was a prerogative crucial to the construction of the king's own sacrality, it was now clear that Bhumibol himself opposed Phimontham.[16] The monk was 83, and the palace simply hoped he would, like Pridi, soon die. As 1985 passed with no movement in the sangha council, the 17 monks of the Isan regional council threatened to return their royal-bestowed ranks and regalia. The action verged on secession from the sangha. Facing a great embarrassment, finally that December the king elevated Phimontham to somdej. The other position was filled by a conservative monk. In fact, by then Phimontham was too old to cause any trouble. He died a few years later and Yanasangworn was unopposed as supreme patriarch.

As he cleaned out the remaining witnesses to the ugly past, Prem spared no effort to promote the king and royal culture. It began with his own exemplary obsequiousness. He consulted the king at least once a week, in the court fashion of a century earlier, prostrating himself and speaking in a humble whisper only when spoken to. While his predecessors had worn military uniforms and Western suits, Prem made a fashion of a Thai silk, Nehru-collared button-down jacket called the royal suit, *chut prarachathan*. The style dated back to the Fifth Reign, although some Thais ascribed its design to King Bhumibol. After Prem's model, bureaucrats, politicians, and businessmen sought to also consult the king and queen and adopted the chut prarachathan as their work dress. High-society Thais and ambitious climbers competed ever more to be seen donating funds and participating in royal events. They sought to take part in a full-fledged court society fostered by Prem, centered in part in the Dusit Thani Hotel. The Dusit became the site of regular royal charity balls, its restaurants preferred by Sirikit, Prem, and their circle of royally decorated ladies. It became the place for businessmen, politicians, generals, and their wives to be seen and do business.

Prem accommodated the royal family in almost every area possible. He obliged their increasing requests—especially from Queen Sirikit—for promotions of palace favorites in the military and civil service, as well as recommendations for government contracts. Meanwhile, using the state budget he built several more palaces for the royal family, including a massive mountaintop chalet in Chiangrai for the king's mother, Sangwal, who only in the late 1980s abandoned Switzerland for a permanent home in Thailand. Prem enlisted state enterprises like the national carrier Thai Airways, the Tourism Authority of Thailand, and the national power monopoly EGAT to deploy their own funds to advertise and celebrate the throne. With their help, every holiday, even the strictly religious ones, became a royal promotion with the Mahidol family's activities featured heavily on television and radio. The king's and queen's birthdays were promoted as, respectively, Father's Day and Mother's Day.

The monarchy was made the focus of the Bangkok Bicentennial in 1982, while the original communities and peoples of greater Bangkok garnered little attention. The highlight was a reenactment of the royal barge ceremony. Originally performed only for the royal kathin ritual at Wat Arun, now it was re-created simply to celebrate the monarchy and advertise for tourists. The Bangkok Bicentennial celebration came with its own miracle indicating the magical Chakri brilliance. The king's aide Tongnoi Tongyai pointed out that on the day of the anniversary, April 5, at 11 a.m. the sun broke through the clouds and around it appeared a halo. It was just as a wise monk had predicted, Tongnoi said—and the same thing had occurred on that very day 200 years before.[17]

The foreign press caught the royal bug as well. *Asiaweek* magazine wrote that the Chakri Dynasty had produced a succession of monarchs of truly outstanding character, calling the current king a "guiding hand that sees the country through each constitutional crisis."[18] The magazine cited 1973 and 1981—neither one a constitutional crisis—while at the same time ignoring October 1976. *National Geographic* ran a long feature that ignored the many military coups and said the king and Buddhism stabilized the country.[19] In an interview, Bhumibol told the magazine that Thailand's development was about "looking at the good things of the past. Traditions perpetuated and transformed. That is the lesson: we take old traditions and reconstruct them to be used in the present time and in the future."

Ironically, perhaps, as the king stressed the past, the same issue of *National Geographic* carried a cover story about the silicon chip's revolutionary effect on people's lives.

Death and sickness were equally valued occasions to promote the throne. For King Bhumibol's 1982 illness, the government and the military marshaled large public displays of fealty, led by the Village Scouts. The religious affairs department organized nationwide mass merit-making ceremonies and group meditations for the king, some led by the supreme patriarch.[20] The good wishes sent by world leaders were publicized as evidence that Bhumibol was a universally respected dhammaraja.

When Rambhai Bharni, dowager queen to Rama VII, died in May 1984, Prem stretched the normal 100 days of official mourning to eleven months. This compelled visits to the throne hall holding Rambhai's body by every organization and social group possible from around the country. Rambhai's opulent cremation in April 1985 cost the government several million dollars in the middle of a recession and was well-promoted by the tourism board. The gilded pyre, a representation of the holy Mount Meru, was 29 meters high. The three-kilometer procession from the palace to the pyre featured elaborate red and gold chariots carrying the body in its jeweled funerary urn, and a thousand soldiers, drummers, and trumpeters dressed in early Chakri costume. Seen on live television broadcasts, the Mahidol family led hundreds of the Chakri clan in the procession while 300 cannon rounds concussed the air.

Prem's most important contribution was the huge expansion of the royal development projects. It was through these that Bhumibol most defined himself, and during the 1980s, with Prem's help, they became the way Thai people most defined their king. In 1980 the king's projects numbered a few hundred, mostly underwritten by his main charity, the Chai Pattana Foundation. The projects were already important to his image. Well-circulated photographic and television images showed the king trekking across unpaved paths in remote rural areas, a Canon camera around his neck and map and notebook in hand while quizzing villagers and officials on seasonal water flow, rainfall, and farm practices. His aides would explain wondrously how the king could look at a map and immediately understand the landscape and the water resource potential.[21] It was like Rama IV predicting a solar eclipse, the Chakri genius.

Yet Bhumibol remained disappointed that the government hadn't applied his successes on a nationwide scale. In a 1981 seminar on agriculture in northern

Thailand, he criticized the bureaucrats and development specialists for ignoring the kind of simple and inexpensive solutions to farmers' problems that he himself had adopted. The bureaucrats' methods were "useless," their data unclear and imprecise, in part because they never listened to the peasants, who, he said, were more clever than everyone assumed.[22]

Using his own projects as a reference, he lectured the audience on how unresponsive and wasteful the bureaucracy was. Typically, as he described it, a small village water project would take the palace a few days and a few thousand baht to deal with. With the government, it would take more than a year and the cost would rise tenfold. This frustrated the king hugely. Every day he received letters from villagers pleading poverty, exploitation, and lack of roads and water. To help them all, Bhumibol's operations needed far more manpower and money than the magic circle of merit charity structure could supply.

Prem gave him both, by committing the full force of the government and its budget, and especially the military, to royal projects. Whatever the king wanted to do was declared a priority over each agency's normal work. A new unit chaired by Prem himself, the Coordinating Committee for Royal Projects, was formed to ensure they progressed expeditiously. In 1981 the CCRP created the Royal Projects Development Board inside the state planning bureau, the National Economic and Social Development Board. This made Bhumibol essentially the bureaucracy's new chief of development, with the entire resources of the government to undertake operations that he alone would enjoy credit for.

The royal projects board was run by an economist and National Security Council veteran, Sumet Tantivejakul, a close adviser of the king. Since the 1960s Sumet had worked at the planning bureau's division that dealt with preparing for natural disasters and war. He also spent time in Vietnam studying the potent links between rural discontent and insurgency, and returned committed to economic and social development. Sumet called the RPDB "an integrated service for His Majesty the King and Royal Family."[23] He later explained how it worked, using the example of the agency's intervening when bureaucrats blocked a palace effort to give peasants tilling rights on denuded state forest land. The officials couldn't see through their soulless rules and regulations to virtuous policies, Sumet noted.

Once the RPDB was in place, spending on royal projects increased tenfold, the money mostly earmarked from normal ministry budgets. Most of the projects were the same as earlier: crop research, large and small water resources projects, training for doctors and medics, more medical extension services, and the like. Prem funded the creation of six royal development centers around the country, each occupying thousands of acres, usually at the king's regional palaces. Each had its own staff to experiment in crops and animal husbandry, work that was little different from the research done in the ministries and universities, although often more location- and result-focused.

The king had lots of new ideas, like producing biogas, fruit juice, and mushroom canning; turning water hyacinth into fertilizer and compressed fuel; herb gardens and rattan farming. For his small water diversion and storage projects the king worked closely with EGAT, which controlled hydropower-cum-irrigation dams around the country, and the royal irrigation department at the Ministry of Agriculture. The top people in both were now frequently seen at King Bhumibol's side.

The army became Bhumibol's personal task force for royal projects. The armed forces built a million-dollar development center on 5,300 acres at the royal palace in Phuphan, and it spent another $1 million for a small palace and development center near Khao Khor, the mountain area cleared in the bloody anti-CPT campaign of 1981. Khao Khor became one model for the king's ideas. Responsibility for restarting economic life in the area was turned over to General Pichit, who had overseen the Khao Khor battle. The army developed water resources, introduced crops, and subsidized farmers, all as royal projects. It succeeded with the introduction of cash crops like asparagus and passion fruit for canneries and fresh markets in Bangkok. After that the military's budget for royal projects was increased, and Pichit was moved to the Thai-Cambodian border to replicate his success.

As news of the royal projects spread, the palace received a constant stream of petitions from rural Thais begging for help. The king's staff followed up each case, and either the palace made a direct intervention, in the case of people with particular health problems or a hamlet needing a small bridge to connect it to the world, or an inquiry was sent on to the appropriate ministry with the implication that the problem should be solved there. Details about these petition cases remain a closely held secret of the palace, with the secrecy enhancing the very mystery of the king's wisdom and ability to improve the lives of his subjects. The cases divulged a greater truth, though: the more the king's works were advertised by Prem at the expense of the government's, the more the people looked beyond the government to their king for escape from misery.

As the number of royal projects grew exponentially, the risk increased that some might go wrong and embarrass the king, so a new classification system was created to insulate the throne. In the highest classification were projects initiated and pursued directly by the king and queen. Then there were three other classifications that essentially left the responsibility to others involved, the government, and citizens' groups. This allowed the throne to take credit for all successes, while others would shoulder any failures.

Two particular projects embodied the king's holistic view of culture, economics, and development. The idea of his model "royal development temples" was that, as the center of traditional communities, Buddhist temples rather than insensitive state bureaucrats were in the best position to organize a village. Monks would promote the virtues of non-desire, cooperation, sharing, and hard work to overcome rural poverty. Their guide would be self-sufficiency, not the production of surplus cash crops for sale in large markets. The king believed that peasants would be happy if they had just a bit more than enough from year to year.

The archetype was Wat Thudong Kasathan Thavorn Nimit, in Nakhon Nayok, about 100 kilometers east of Bangkok. Established as a royal project in 1985, the temple occupied 140 acres, with only a small part reserved for religious activities. The rest was turned into a reservoir and farm that, with palace guidance, raised various crops for experimentation, seed production, and food, all to support the village. Monks would manage distribution of the temple's surpluses.

The second model project of Bhumibol's was a new community fashioned out of a thousand-acre temple in Chonburi, southeast of Bangkok. The land was originally donated to the king's spiritual mentor Yanasangworn in 1976. A temple was built and named after him, Wat Yanasangwararam Voramahaviharn. More land was then acquired and the monk offered it to the king as a royal monastery. When Bhumibol visited in 1982, he decided to convert it into a model cooperative and center of dhamma-based development.

It was literally built from the ground up. Only a few people lived on the denuded, hardscrabble ground. To turn it into a harmonized farming community, tens of millions of baht were spent on developing water resources and improving the land with thousands of truckloads of soil, compost, and fertilizers. Slowly, food crops and fruit and pulp trees took root, and surrounding denuded forest was allowed to recover naturally. A community with a hospital and school grew up, supervised by the monks. The development was funded mostly by donations, especially from the kingdom's richest businessmen, civil servants, and military figures, all prodded by Prem. Numerous huge buildings were constructed, turning the community into a monument to the Chakri Dynasty and the Ninth Reign. Today there are many buildings and statues dedicated to King Prajadhipok, Bhumibol, Sirikit, and Bhumibol's parents Prince Mahidol and Sangwal.

Prem didn't merely promote the palace; he also protected it. He controlled critics through selective application of the lèse-majesté law. According to the constitution, only the king, queen, crown prince, and regent were inviolate under the law. But under Tanin and then Prem, the law was applied to protect the institution of the throne, the Chakri Dynasty, and all of Thai kingship. Making disparaging remarks against, for instance, Rama II, could draw charges of lèse-majesté.[24]

To the media, Prem made it clear that royal matters, even those broached publicly by members of the royal family themselves, were not for public discussion. Any newspaper that published, knowingly or not, anything that might have a negative connotation for the palace would be warned by a phone call from the police or the national security office. While in the United States in late 1981, for example, Queen Sirikit gave interviews to the American media in which she directly criticized Prince Vajiralongkorn. The palace made no complaint about American reports of the interviews. But when local papers reported Sirikit's comments, they were strongly rebuked, even threatened with closure. For those who were caught publishing underground material critical of the throne, the punishment was tougher. The people behind several 1981 tracts criticizing Sirikit were tracked down and imprisoned, one for eight years.

Prem's efforts didn't stop at Thailand's borders. Not long after he became premier, the government banned an issue of *Newsweek* for cover pictures that unmindfully positioned Prem higher than the king. In January 1982, the *Asian Wall Street Journal* was banned completely for an opinion piece titled "Can Thailand's Monarchy Survive This Century?"[25] The author, a former UN official in Thailand, suggested that the throne wasn't as popular as it appeared, and that its political interventions were self-endangering.

Even with Prem's generous promotion, King Bhumibol and Queen Sirikit impressively never let up on their own rigorous schedule of royal duties. In the 1980s the king went out to the countryside for four to six months of the year, usually with either Sirikit or Princess Sirindhorn, who acted now as his personal secretary. Sirikit ran her own large government-backed program helping village women to develop handicraft skills for extra income.

Bhumibol and his family performed the old rituals without fail. With 20 universities in the country by this time, the annual royal dispensing of every degree now verged on crippling Bhumibol's arm and shoulder. He insisted on doing it alone it until an old doctor friend, Prawase Wasi, publicly criticized the practice as dangerous. Bhumibol relinquished part of the task to his children, though he continued at Thammasat and Chulalongkorn universities and at the military academy. His reluctance to stop was portrayed as a sign of his great virtue.

Traditional symbolism wasn't forgotten either. In January 1984, Bhumibol returned to the courtroom, for the opening of a new court in Chiangmai, to sit in judgment and remind the people that he was the source of justice. In 1983 the 13th white elephant of the reign was discovered, an unparalleled number in history, and was received in a great celebration.

Supporting this picture of tireless dedication were testimonies from the king's associates. In 1982, Bhumibol's aide Vasit Dejkunchorn told an audience that every night the king and queen took piles of documents into their chambers, and these would "often require the whole night to read and decide upon."[26] This explained why they only emerged from their bedchamber at noon each day. Immediately though, Vasit said, they would launch into a tight schedule of meetings and ceremonies. They also squeezed in exercise. The queen did calisthenics and the king, at 55, jogged two kilometers in under 12 minutes five days a week. The only days he didn't jog were Friday and Sunday, the days he reserved for jazz. Vasit explained: "Music is the king's only recreation. And he plays with rare zeal. I was mesmerized, and later shocked, watching the king play a nonstop jam session beginning at nine in the evening and ending at dawn. He never once left his seat. Later . . . I began to understand. Music, like anything else he performs, is treated by the king with the greatest concentration. It is this concentration, the result of a long, rigid self-discipline, that has made the king immune from emotion and sentiments that would otherwise interfere with his calm and correct decision-making."

What was remarkable about all this promotion was that it fell back on the most traditional interpretations of the monarchy while mostly ignoring the conclusions of a National Security Council task force that had tried to find out what went wrong with royal democracy that led to October 6, 1976. As recounted by Michael Connors, an elite team of academics and security specialists assembled in the late 1970s to analyze what had caused the nation to split so sharply. This group concluded that the "nation-religion-king" and "democracy with the king as head of state" construction had failed to keep the nation united because such mantras did not connect to the lives of the people, especially the rural peasantry. Left out of official national culture, the people were more susceptible to CPT propaganda.[27] The academics concluded in part that the government needed to expand the sense of participation in the state by widening the realm of public political and social discourse. The peasants were to be made to feel they were a key facet in national culture.

But in the hands of Prem and a younger generation of palace advocates, royal promotion in practice reverted to tradition. Certain areas, like economic policy and administrative issues, were open to a more bounteous public discourse, but it was still limited to the educated elite, and still only inside the strict parameters of the traditionally defined nation-religion-king formulation. Since the king had legitimized Prem, criticizing his leadership was out of bounds.

The security group's conclusions on national culture and ideology were to be disseminated by the well-funded National Identity Board. But, despite its progressive approach to the job, what the board promoted was a decidedly old-fashioned ideology. In its approach, national culture was still something that came from the leaders and was broadcast to the people. It remained focused on preserving the nation as defined by nation-religion-king. The National Identity Board published books like *The Chakri Monarchs and the Thai People,* in 1984, which focused on Bhumibol as "the Farmer King" and "the Developer King," connecting him to both Ramkhamhaeng and a modern economist-leader. The board also sponsored academic conferences, like one discussing the modern importance of the Trai Phum Phra Ruang, the Sukhothai Buddhist cosmology. The uniformly conservative attendees at these gatherings, wrote one historian, "emphasized the continued relevance of the text's ethical teachings to contemporary life, government, and 'national security.'"[28]

In all this the people were still recipients, and at times participants, in officially established culture. Their connection to the state was mainly through their discipline and work in building society—the king's modern dhammic values. As for democracy, it remained defined and bounded by the needs of national security—as interpreted by men from the national security apparatus who still insisted throughout the 1980s that Vietnamese or Chinese communists threatened to conquer the kingdom. They continued to downplay modern democratic institutions like the constitution, parliament, and the rule of law as Western imports. Instead, the National Identity Board stressed the Ramkhamhaeng inscription as a constitution-like liberal democratic pact between the leadership—the king—and the people. "The people are not the government; taking the opinion of the people as an instrument to define policy is just the same as letting the people be the government, which is likely to lead to a political crisis," explained one board publication.[29]

In parallel, the king's foreign relations adjutant and privy council secretary Tongnoi Tongyai emerged in the early 1980s as the palace's modern theoretician. Tongnoi made a lengthy argument for the king's power based on a mixture of science and sentiment in a series of chatty articles in the *Bangkok Post* in 1983, using the pen name "Concensus."[30]

Consensus, he said, was considered by scholars "the psychological basis of an

Asian nation," which was true especially in Thailand, "the only country left in the world literally living in Buddhism." Consensus was thus a spiritual virtue. Historically, Tongnoi said, Thai kings ruled by consensus. People united behind their ruler, who protected them from threats like Western imperialism and represented their interests generally. In modern Thailand, Tongnoi wrote, politicians by nature were too venal and power-mad to defend the public interest. The press too was unreliable, just "another branch of entertainment." Only the king had the historical knowledge and experience, the omniscience and the selflessness to embody the national consensus.

The Thai people understand this, according to Tongnoi. When the king falls ill, everyone flies about in a panic; when the government falls, no one cares, because government is only entertainment. This clearly reflected Bhumibol's own thinking. In an interview in 1982 the king revealed a belief that he might be better prepared to choose the prime minister. "In the constitution it is written that the king appoints the prime minister. This is a system in which, perhaps, the experience of a king can be of use. . . . The president of parliament will come and have a consultation, but the king may have more power because the people have faith in their king."[31]

From his consensus theme, Tongnoi made a metaphysical leap. He declared that a constitution is really unnecessary, because consensus embodied in the king is the equivalent of democracy. He said that Great Britain, a renowned democracy, has never had a real constitution. Moreover, he argued, since 1932 Thai constitutions have been tools for self-serving, power-seeking elites, including the Thai military. Citing the two very different former Thai prime ministers on the privy council, Sanya Dhammasakdi and Tanin Kraivixien, Tongnoi defined democracy as "a method of government in which the rights of an individual citizen should be as fully protected as possible." Only the king can do this, he said. Still, Tongnoi conceded the idea of the constitution, acknowledging that Thais are habituated to it. In that case, it needs to have only three short articles:

1: Thailand is an independent nation, one and indivisible.
2: Thailand is a monarchy, with monarchy from the Chakri Dynasty.
3: Thailand should be democratic in so far as possible.

Tongnoi appeared to contradict the king when it came to soldiers in politics. He attacked them as inveterate power seekers whose attempts to monopolize government had exacerbated poverty, lack of development, and rampant corruption. But then, in an about-face, he declared a cultural, "consensus" basis for military power. Thais value soldiers as their "alter egos." They want soldiers to maintain stability. As for the frequent coups, Tongnoi said, referring to Bhumibol's own maxim, people must look to the soldiers' intentions, which he called democratic. Since 1973, the people and the soldiers have moved "at the same pace and in the same direction."

Such efforts to promote and enforce the throne's prestige during the Prem years nevertheless failed to stifle a number of critics who dared to question some of the directions those in power were taking. These included politicians whose own ambitions were impeded by the palace-Prem alliance, progressive academics, and former student activists, many of whom turned up working in the print media in the 1980s, which the government and military did not control as they did television and radio. A small industry of magazines arose that analyzed the power and money politics of Prem's government, very obliquely criticizing the Prem-king relationship.

Much of what these magazines and Thai intellectuals suggested about the throne and democracy was spelled out in the column that got the *Asian Wall Street Journal* banned at the end of 1981.[32] The author, Michael Schmicker, began by asking provocatively whether the monarchy would survive another 20 years in the face of challenges from various quarters. Aside from the CPT, he wrote, "a second, more serious threat comes from idealistic student activists and their liberal mentors within the Thai university system. They are unwisely being forced to choose between their conscience and their king by misguided monarchists unable to distinguish a sincere cry for social change from an attack on the throne. . . . The royal family is clearly committed—critics say overcommitted—to the preservation of the status quo."

Schmicker also pointed out a third threat: army factionalism, as exposed in the April Fools' coup, which had ended badly for all. "The coup collapsed, along with the monarchy's credibility as an impartial mediator between contending military cliques within the armed forces. The royal family is now dangerously identified with one faction and must accept the sizable risks that come with choosing sides." A final challenge was the unpopular crown prince: "Since his investiture nine years ago, 29-year-old Crown Prince Vajiralongkorn has struggled to meet the public's expectations of a future King. He appears to lack the intelligence, charisma and 'common touch' necessary to secure the affection of the Thai people for the Chakri dynasty and reportedly enjoys lukewarm support within the Thai military. His image as a Don Juan also has damaged his reputation and allowed critics to poke fun at the monarchy."

As might be expected, the government was outraged by the article and branded it a foreigner's distorted view. But in 1982, Sulak Sivaraks, an iconoclastic intellectual popular with students and foreign scholars, wrote in *Lorkrab Sangkhom Thai* ("Unmasking Thai Society") that the monarchy was going in the wrong direction and King Bhumibol misunderstood Thailand. Prem's government ignored the criticism until 1984, when it had Sulak arrested for lèse-majesté. Amnesty International and other international human rights groups, as well as a large number of Thai and foreign academics, strongly condemned the arrest. With the king being pulled into a difficult public relations fight, the palace intervened quietly to have Sulak let off.[33]

Another challenge was an unsigned critique of the king's interventionism that circulated among academics in 1983 in the form of a 69-page treatise, written in English, on the Chakri political tradition.[34] It was widely understood as the work of M.R. Sukhumbhand Paripatra, grandson of the Seventh Reign's Prince Paripatra and, in theory, in line to succeed to the throne.

After covering innocuously the political difficulties of the first eight kings, in his final pages Sukhumbhand, who taught political science at Chulalongkorn University, directly raised the dangers implicit in the Ninth Reign's open political partisanship. Recalling that rivalry between the palace and the bureaucracy, rigid conservatism, and resistance to institutional reform had led to the fall of the absolute monarchy in 1932, he warned: "The monarchy, once a beacon of hope for many in the days of military authoritarianism, is in danger of being perceived as factional, retrogressive and reactionary. . . . The paradox is that by seeking power to guard against disorderly change, the palace may in the end help to precipitate this very change itself. . . . The monarchy is attempting to act as both a symbol of national unity and a power seeker, without realizing that the two roles may be inherently and fatally contradictory. . . . Gone is the pragmatism and flexibility which had been the hallmark of the Chakris."

Because the essay was unsigned and had been distributed mostly to other intellectuals, journalists, and diplomats, and not reported on in public, the palace could still act as if nothing had happened. But Sukhumbhand's warnings proved prescient, the very next year.

16 Family Headaches ∽

JUST AS THE KING'S AIDE TONGNOI was setting out the rationale for the palace-Prem government, this structure's principal pillars were crumbling as palace critic Sukhumbhand had warned. Between 1984 and 1986, a series of intra-army clashes, coup attempts, financial scandals, and other crises battered Prem and the king. Outwardly it was a culmination of military corruption and factionalism. But the nucleus of the problem was the king's family, beginning with the queen.

Sirikit had spent her first two decades in the palace celebrating her fairy-tale queenship. As her beauty faded in the 1970s, she built a large court founded on competition for her patronage, which was manifest in her involvement with the rightist politics of 1976. She was a political force of her own, and *Parade* magazine in the United States labeled her a beautiful, ambitious "dragon lady."[1]

Outwardly Sirikit was a dynamic mirror image of the king. Her principal vehicle for aiding the underprivileged, the Support Foundation, brought health care to poor village women and children and helped them develop sources of extra income, like traditional handicraft production. Through charity balls and other sources she regularly raised tens of millions of dollars a year, which sustained her personal staff of 50 and many more in the Support Foundation bureaucracy. She made frequent, ritualized visits to the countryside. With a heavy army escort, Sirikit would emerge in front of peasants, adorned in modern fashions and a generous array of large diamonds, rubies, emeralds, and pearls. In the 1980s she often wore harem pants and a turbanlike hat that must have appeared to villagers as bizarrely foreign. Tongnoi explained: "She fears she will disappoint her subjects if she is not dressed well. . . . The people have their own idea that the queen is an angel with blessings."[2]

In the villages, she would meet with a preselected handful of diseased and crippled women and their infant children. She would give them medicine and tell them to take care of themselves, speaking slowly and simply like a mother giving instructions to a four-year-old—the way she talked to everyone outside the palace. Afterward her entourage dispersed more goods and health treatment and paid Support Foundation enrollees for their products, to be taken by the truckload back to distant markets.

This confident display concealed the fact that Sirikit was entering a period of personal crisis over her diminishing beauty, her busy husband's inattention, her controversial son, and criticism of her political meddling—all of which she sought to surmount through greater acclaim. In the late 1970s and early 1980s the government helped to arrange a series of international awards and degrees for her, with U.S. assistance.[3]

She desperately fought the aging process, dieting and exercising furiously and undergoing regular aesthetic surgery. "I jog and do yoga and when it rains I run up and down three stories, nine times. . . . I could afford to put on a little weight. But my husband says he hates me to be fat," she said.[4] She also took various diet and energy pills, and then sleeping pills to counter their effects, hardly a sustainable regimen. Answering rumors that she was unwell in 1983, Tongnoi explained that, because of her intense dedication to royal duties, she suffered from insomnia, going to sleep only at three or four in the morning and waking just two hours later.[5]

Her public image worsened with her support of ambitious generals like Arthit and widespread stories that charity receipts paid for the holidays, clothing, and jewelry of Sirikit and her courtiers. Critics said her social projects benefited the throne's image more than the people, that she distributed gifts but didn't have much permanent impact on the people's lives. "The queen is into social welfare, not social concern," said one academic years later.[6] Sirikit also generated ugly rumors for surrounding herself with young army officers, mostly the elite majors and colonels of a special queen's guard, recipients of the royal Ramathibodi decoration for bravery.[7] She was especially smitten by one, the handsome Colonel Narongdej, indiscreetly making him her companion in travel and at parties. "He was the son the queen never had, everything the crown prince wasn't," recalled one military officer.[8] People presumed they had a more intimate relationship, and the court was scandalized.

Her image plunged further with the spread of a damning underground account of her early 1980 trip to the United States with Prince Vajiralongkorn.[9] The CPT was presumed to have issued the report, in which the author characterized the trip as "67 days, 100 million baht" ($5 million), and had enough inside information and accurate details to be wholly believable. The book alleged that the primary reason for the trip was plastic surgery, with a second reason being to collect more money for her personal needs in the name of her charities, and a third to stash palace wealth abroad in case the monarchy was forced to flee the country. It described the queen's four large fund-raisers in different American cities, reaping hundreds of thousands of dollars. Then it detailed her subsequent purchases of two homes in exclusive southern California neighborhoods for her children, luxury cars for her son's consorts, and a $200,000 ring for herself. The authors cited meetings with specific New York banks as evidence that the royals were putting assets offshore. Such allegations appealed to the country's elite and educated, who were predisposed to believing bad things about Sirikit.

More troubling was Crown Prince Vajiralongkorn. By the early 1980s, he had become the very thing every modern monarchy fears, an heir whose intractable behavior endangered the throne's future. The problems were well known by the late 1970s. After returning from military training in Australia, he surrounded himself with people who would do his bidding, including disreputable businessmen who provided him with women and paid his bills, and military toughs who would take care of people who crossed him. With a pistol always on his hip, he gained the nickname Sia O—*sia* being the popular appellation for a Sino-Thai gangster, and *O* for *orasathirat,* part of his title as crown prince.

With little humility and self-restraint, Vajiralongkorn found it impossible to fit into his father's mold. His attitude only worsened when Sirikit forced him to marry her niece Somsawali. People were encouraged when she became pregnant in 1978, giving birth that December to the king's first grandchild, a girl named Bhajarakitiyabha. But while his wife was pregnant, the prince moved out of their downtown palace home to a new residence in the suburbs. Ostensibly this was to better facilitate his attending the Army's General Staff school, but he never moved back. It was in this period, stories have it, that Kampol Vacharapol, the godfatherlike owner of the country's biggest newspaper, *Thai Rath,* introduced him to the nightclub girl and aspiring actress who became his steady companion, Sucharinee Vivatcharavong.[10]

Sucharinee too became pregnant. The palace and high society were stunned when in August 1979 she gave birth to a boy, whom Vajiralongkorn reportedly took to Wat Bovornives to be blessed and named by abbot Yanasangworn.[11] The name selected, Chudhavajra, came in part from the prince's own name. The boy automatically received the princely but noncelestial title of Mom Chao. Even so, Chudhavajra was the sole male of the next generation of Chakris, making him the prince's heir. For Queen Sirikit this was a disaster: the boy threatened her own family's dynastic hopes, unless Somsawali gave birth to a celestial prince.

Vajiralongkorn performed his ritual and military duties sparingly. In 1978 he ordained as a novice in Wat Bovornives, an important step on the path toward dhammaraja kingship. But the problem of Sucharinee and numerous tales of his misbehavior involving money, including extorting businessmen, were said to have forced the king to step in. Bhumibol had Prem arrange for the prince to go to the United States in early 1980 for more military training. There, Vajiralongkorn attended special operations school at bases in North Carolina and Georgia. He was very troublesome, often refusing to take orders, according to a U.S. official familiar with the trip.[12] His marital problems followed behind him. Before reporting to the bases, he accompanied the queen to Washington and New York. Flying in to meet him was Sucharinee, and in hot pursuit, Somsawali. To assuage them, according to varying accounts, each was given a new luxury car. Later, Somsawali crashed hers near Fort Bragg, North Carolina, an accident that years later would take on greater significance.

Nevertheless, the U.S. visit proved successful in a way. Before the trip the prince had ostensibly qualified to fly helicopters in Thailand, but in fact he was passed without managing basic flight skills. In America he received more rigorous training and became very enthusiastic about flying. On returning to Thailand he moved from helicopter gunships to airplanes, and his ambition turned to jets. Militarily, it was rare for someone his age, 30, and not a career air force pilot, to take jet training. But Prem indulged him and in October 1982 he began training on the F5E fighter in Arizona. By most accounts he performed decently, advancing over one year to the level of flight commander. He returned to Thailand and flew in a live-fire demonstration in Lopburi, after which Prem gave him his own flight unit with three F5Es. For the government it was a hugely expensive pastime. Over the subsequent six years he put in 1,000 hours in the F5E, often using the jet as his personal transport, accompanied by the two others. For fear of being assassinated, he rarely scheduled his flights in advance, and three jets were kept on standby, the prince choosing his own only at the last moment.

The basic problem didn't go away, though. In June 1981, Sucharinee gave birth to a second son, named Vajaresra. The prince was rarely seen anymore with Somsawali, who became depressed and began eating her way to obesity, ensuring Vajiralongkorn's antipathy. Sirikit responded with a strong public admonition of her son, threatening to deny him the throne. While in the United States in late 1981 to receive another international award and to see her new granddaughter, Ubolrat's first child, she told a Texas press conference that her son's family life "is not so smooth." "My son the crown prince is a little bit of a Don Juan. He is a good student, a good boy, but women find him interesting and he finds women even more interesting." Then she added, unprompted: "If the people of Thailand do not approve of the behavior of my son, then he would either have to change his behavior or resign from the royal family." Two weeks later she repeated the message in Washington, saying: "In his job as a career military man, he's doing quite well, but for the crown prince of Thailand, not so well, because I think that he does not give enough time to his people. We [the royal family] do not have Saturdays or weekends, you see. And [the crown prince] demands his weekends. Well, he is quite handsome, and he loves beautiful women so he needs his weekends. . . . [The Thai people] know what they want, what kind of leader they want. And if they don't like such-and-such character, well, they won't choose him or her."

Sirikit's public threat was highly risky, for it opened up highly taboo royal subjects for public discussion. Even as Thai newspapers were warned not to publish or discuss Sirikit's comments, a foreign journalist in Bangkok wrote that the queen's going public "might have broader repercussions for the institution of monarchy. . . . [H]er public expression of dissatisfaction with her son is at odds with the discretion and self-censorship the Thai press has shown towards the royal family. . . . Some observers are concerned that debate over the succession, albeit within a narrow circle, could introduce a new element of instability into Thai society."[13]

Around the same time, in October 1981, the respected monk Panyanantha Bhikku gave a sensational sermon that included a barely disguised parable of a prince who placed carnal pleasures ahead of his duties.[14] This prince had a beautiful wife, but he spent his nights in a suburban palace he built for an actress on land seized from local people. A local monk warned the prince that he was like a tree he had torn down, that "people will uproot you from the throne." Tapes and booklets sold openly around the kingdom brought Panyanantha's sermon to tens of thousands of Thais. The parable rang very true with the public, knowing through the mainstream media that the prince had a new palace in suburban Nonthaburi and avoided Somsawali. Even people in distant villages came to understand that he had an actress girlfriend.

The bad publicity had no impact on Vajiralongkorn. He still played around, often with women proffered by powerful men, including generals in Sirikit's circle. And he remained beguiled by Sucharinee. In February 1983, she had a third son, named Chakrivajra after the prince and the dynasty. Apparently without the family's permission, Vajiralongkorn permitted her to call herself Mom Sucharinee Mahidol Na Ayutthaya, and their sons to use the family name Mahidol.

The king and the queen remained opposed to Sucharinee, and at one point Bhumibol reportedly reduced the prince's palace stipend to prevent him from supporting her. The prince only became more tempestuous. There were frequent stories of his staff beating and even killing people who angered him. Many Thais had heard tales like the one that he had pulled a gun on Princess Sirindhorn in the palace, or even shot one of her bodyguards, and that he took a monastery's land for business, booting out poor squatters. He became feared more out of legend than reality, and a rivalry with Sirindhorn began to play out through public sentiment. Her picture was found with the king's and queen's in most people's homes and offices, while the prince's pictures were seen almost nowhere, not even in the stores that sold royal photographs and posters.

Princess Sirindhorn was yet another kind of problem. Without trying, she was cast into a contest of virtue with her brother beginning in her teens. King Bhumibol, on his birthday in 1977, elevated the 22-year-old Sirindhorn to a full celestial ranking, inserting into her title the words *Maha (Great) Chakri*. This was a procedural follow-up to the 1974 changes in succession rules, ensuring that there was an alternate in case tragedy struck the prince. Nevertheless, most Thais took her promotion as the king's response to his son's reputation, and that she had an equal chance to succeed. Unofficially, it was acceptable to call her "crown princess" in English.

But Sirindhorn wasn't the perfect alternative. She was neither brainy, disciplined, and energetic, as Bhumibol would have preferred, nor a sleek and beautiful princess like Sirikit. Simple, youthful, and happily plump and indulgent in her eating, she took no interest in clothes, makeup, and jewelry. Her academic talents were mediocre, though the palace machine made sure she registered top marks nationally in examinations, as Ubolrat had done before her. Sirindhorn seems to have been genuinely embarrassed by the pretense. The public grew to love her for her dowdy dress and ready smiles; her popular name was Phra Thep, Princess Angel. At Chulalongkorn University in the 1970s, she studied Thai culture, history, and languages. Her own interest inspired a revival of Thai classical music. She then entered Silpakorn, the national arts university, where she studied archeology and the ancient Pali and Sanskrit languages. Her master's thesis topic was an analysis of the principles of barami underlying the thotsaphit rachatham.

The imposed competition with her brother was exacerbated by her closeness to the king, in contrast with Vajiralongkorn's better relationship with Sirikit. She was seen frequently at Bhumibol's side as he tended to his development projects. In 1981 she was delegated to be the first member of the royal family to visit China, a landmark in the long-estranged relations between the two countries. It was one of about a dozen official visits she made in the diplomatic shoes of the king during the Prem period, more than her brother. She also was far more visible than the prince in religious affairs and ceremonies. Prem added to the fire, in 1985 declaring Sirindhorn's birthday, April 2, as National Heritage Preservation Day, and in 1987 naming her "the Supreme Patroness of Thai Cultural Heritage." More important, she was made head of the history department at Chulachomklao Military Academy, which trains the future military and police leadership. This was a direct encroachment on the prince's turf of military affairs, and her students became her personal allies and protectors.

Still, people in palace circles say Sirindhorn left her father dismayed at her lack of drive and assertiveness. Nearing 30 in 1985, she still projected the image of an unmindful schoolgirl, and most of her activities were soft ones, like supporting traditional Thai orchestras and palace arts. But Sirindhorn strove to downplay the idea of a competition with her brother. To allay the prince's worries, she was said to have forsworn marriage by the early 1980s and chose an image of celibacy. The issue might have been moot anyway; knowledgeable Thais and diplomats say the princess prefers female companionship.

The two other Mahidol princesses generated headaches for their parents as well. After being banished in 1972 for marrying the American Peter Jensen, first daughter Ubolrat wanted back into the family and her title restored. With her husband, she returned to Thailand for the first time in August 1980, three months pregnant. The public still liked the attractive princess and saw it as the penitent return of a prodigal daughter. When she first alighted from her car at the palace, she prostrated herself deeply at the king's feet. With a fatherly but unsmiling hug, Bhumibol appeared to forgive her. The press called her Princess Ubolrat, though her only official title was the non-royal thanpuying, and asked her to remain in Thailand. But with no change in her status, the couple rushed back to their home in southern California after only four days.

In 1981 she gave birth to a daughter, Ploypailin. By 1982, when she returned for her sister Chulabhorn's wedding, there was a virtual popular draft movement to have her title restored. She wanted it, the queen wanted it, and the people wanted it. But Bhumibol was stubbornly silent, denying her any role in palace or family affairs. Nevertheless, she and her husband visited Thailand more often. They had two more children, a boy named Poomi after his grandfather, and then a girl, named Sirikitya after her grandmother.

The youngest Mahidol princess, Chulabhorn, disappointed for other reasons. Frail, frequently ill, and melancholic, she grew up more in her mother's mold, given to expensive fashions and jewelry, and was the haughtiest and most over-indulged of her family. Yet even the queen found her wanting, for her lack of energy and wit and for her lithe but flawed looks. Like her siblings, she took top honors in her classes and exams. She majored in organic chemistry at Kasetsart University, and then took a graduate science degree at Mahidol University, where, it was said, her research work and papers were handled by a team of palace-supported scientists. In 1985 she became an occasional professor in chemistry at the school and was the official royal family patron of the sciences.

The main issue was getting her married, but by her early 20s there weren't any appropriate or willing suitors. In 1981 she became attracted to Virayuth, the son of air force chief and Prem crony Prayad Didyasarin. It did not matter that he wasn't royal, nor, apparently, that he was said to already have children by another woman. His father and Prem prevailed on Virayuth to give them up, and in January 1982 he married Chulabhorn. She kept her title, and the two daughters she soon had were given third-level titles, filling out the thin Chakri family ranks.

Chulabhorn may have learned her royal bearing at the queen's feet, but she learned none of Sirikit's grace and common touch. She was highly demanding of her aides and very uncomfortable around peasants, and reluctant to visit the countryside. Instead she indulged in an expensive lifestyle and frequently traveled abroad. There were many whispers that she used funds from her own foundations to pay for the trips and buy expensive gems.

Prem did much to cover up the royal family's smaller embarrassments and prevent their most scandalous behavior from getting into the media. Recognizing that the prince was not going to give up Sucharinee, Prem brought together key officials from the palace and the bureaucracy to help spruce up his image. To cover the prince's shortfall in funds, palace finance manager Phunperm Krairerks, the military, and the head of Siam Cement supplied him with money, apparently unbeknownst to the king. They also found productive financial investments for the prince as regular sources of income. He was said to be a beneficiary in luxury hotels built by Prem cohort M.R. Tridhosyuth Devakul in Phuket, and also in the capital's hottest disco in the mid-1980s, the Nasa Spacedrome. In 1984 Prem's government arranged several well-publicized walkabouts in the Bangkok slums for the prince to show he cared for the poor. More than 20 free rural hospitals, known as Somdej Phra Yuparaj ("Royal Heir") facilities, were built and operated in his name by the government, though it was declared that the money came from the prince himself.

But beyond protecting the prince's image, and that of his family, Prem didn't achieve much in his first four years as leader. Left unimproved—and arguably further deteriorated—were the essential problems of governance. His military base was more factionalized than ever, its competing cliques each led by generals seeking to succeed Prem. They justified their political power by exaggerating the now almost nonexistent communist threat to the country. Corruption grew rife in the military and civilian bureaucracy, and among politicians, especially those who supported Prem, as he rewarded their support with special deals and contracts. At lower levels, crime, violent and otherwise, was widespread, with the country's regional crime lords working closely with the military, the police, and the bureaucracy.

There was a certain order about all of this, for it fit into the national hierarchy of the king on top, the next layer the military, then bureaucrats, businessmen and peasants. Prem substituted this structure for strengthening parliament and the institutions of law. The same structure, though, bogged Prem down as well in his second four years at the helm of the country. Constantly battered by challenges from the army and frustrated politicians, and from a public desirous of a more democratic and responsive system, at each major test, Prem fell back under the king's protective umbrella. But some problems were so entwined with the royal family that they further undermined Prem's authority.

In 1984 the economy fell into recession on the back of a regional downturn and large financial scandals. Several banks went bust and a number of large businesses began to collapse, creating a sense of panic. Amid all this, in August Prem fell seriously ill, and it wasn't clear whether he would recuperate. While Prem was laid up, General Arthit, now concurrently the army chief and supreme commander, poised himself to grab power, and meanwhile pushed his allies in the parliament to revive the constitutional amendments that would protect the military's paramount role, the same amendments that had been rejected a year earlier. Arthit needed them to guarantee his own power in the future, as he was scheduled to retire in 1985.[15]

But then his original patron, Queen Sirikit, intervened on Prem's behalf. Twice in nine days she made well-publicized visits to the prime minister at his bedside at home. One photograph, with Sirikit resting on her knees while Prem made an obeisance to her, was very deliberately placed in the press on September 2, three days after being taken but on the eve of the parliamentary debate on the constitutional changes. Sirikit's intervention forced Arthit to back off from the amendments, and talk of a coup disappeared. A week later Prem assuaged his challenger by elevating Arthit's favorites, none of them very professional soldiers, in the annual military promotions list. It only served to exacerbate the factionalism permeating the military officers' corps, as was immediately evident. Just hours after Prem left for the United States on September 15 for treatment of a pulmonary embolism, an incredible affair erupted. Police and military officials associated with Class 5 of Chulachomklao Military Academy suddenly arrested two of the leaders of Class 7, the Young Turks, Manoon Roopkachorn and Bunsak Pocharoen. Several former CPT members and liberal political activists were also arrested. They were accused of having plotted to assassinate Sirikit, Prem, and Arthit back in October 1982, at the King's Cup soccer final. That the case came to light two years later during Prem's absence made it dubious. Neither Prem nor cabinet security officials appeared aware of the arrest plan. And while the Young Turks were controversial, they had been mostly quiet since the 1981 coup flop. The arrest of CPT members conveniently cast a communist and anti-monarchist shadow over the group.

Even more bizarrely, the very next day, Manoon and Bunsak were released following the personal intervention of Crown Prince Vajiralongkorn, Generals Arthit and Pichit, and the police chief Narong Mahanond and his wife Bharani, who was a close lady-in-waiting to Queen Sirikit. The charges were dropped as suddenly as they surfaced, and no one could be sure there was ever such a plot. By the time Prem returned at the end of September, the whole case had disappeared.

But the army infighting hadn't. Prem returned to confront a rapidly crumbling economy, and on November 2 he was forced to devalue the baht by 15 percent. It wrecked the balance sheets of thousands of businesses and severely hurt many investors. Just as important was the collapse of the flourishing chit fund industry, which had attracted the savings of many thousands from the middle and upper classes. Chit funds were pyramid schemes that had blossomed over several years without intervention from the government, in part because many had strong government connections. One especially, the Mae (Mother) Chamoy Fund, was estimated at $300 million and involved large numbers of investors from the military and, it soon became apparent, the royal household, including probably Sirikit, Vajiralongkorn, Ubolrat, and Chulabhorn. With such prominent and politically significant people likely to lose massively in the Mae Chamoy collapse, Arthit stepped in again. He threatened a coup if the government did not rescind the devaluation and bail out the banks and chit funds.

This time, King Bhumibol himself rescued Prem, without saying anything. Prem went to stay at the Phuphan Palace for nine days, and each day the media ran pictures of Prem with the king, queen, and crown prince. Making the message clear, when Prem returned to Bangkok he was escorted by Prince Vajiralongkorn and Chulabhorn's consort Captain Virayuth. When Arthit then flew to the Phuphan Palace, Prem turned around and went back. What was said in their discussions with the king was not made public, but the episode ended with Prem still in power and Arthit unpunished for his series of mutinous acts. The devaluation stood and the Mae Chamoy Fund was shut down, but only after more backhall dealings managed by Prem. Fund manager Chamoy was arrested and held in secret by the air force until, it is believed, the losses of palace and military personnel and other high officials were recovered. Only afterward was she tried and sent to prison. Her hearing was held in camera and the records were sealed, presumably to protect the palace. Meanwhile thousands, possibly tens of thousands, of people who didn't have special protectors lost their savings.

To critics of the palace and Prem, the army infighting represented the corruption of the political elite that could be corrected only by increased democracy, rule of law, and transparency in government. Bhumibol responded with an opaque message that he would handle the military and it needn't concern anyone else. While he warned obliquely of "the enemies hidden within themselves" in a speech to the military at the beginning of December, he suggested that this was only a minor problem when he spoke to the whole country the following day in his annual birthday address: "Our country has long preceded other civilized nations in the sense that we can co-exist to conduct our respective duties. It can even be regarded that some of the people here are at odds, but then they have gathered here for they believe that they are Thais who have their duties to do for the good of our society." He added a condemnation of "textbooks" that suggested otherwise.[16]

Bhumibol and Prem were so confident of their regime in 1985 that Arthit was given an extension of his dual posts through September 1986. The king resumed regular sailing in Hua Hin and got his jazz band together more often. He explained that "it makes me happy and relaxes me. It washes away the cares and worries of the day."[17]

Then the army erupted again. In September 1985, while Prem was on a state visit to Indonesia, Arthit was in Europe, and the royal family was out of town, the Young Turks attempted another takeover. This time they took pains to claim loyalty to the throne, with their tanks and trucks sporting large framed photographs of the king, the queen, and the crown prince. The coup collapsed when several infantry divisions that were expected to join didn't show up. Prem rushed back from Jakarta and, after 10 hours of negotiations, it was all over. It was explained as another impetuous transgression by the Young Turks alone. But there was far more behind it than that, and far more players at the planning stage. Co-conspirators were never exposed, but fingers pointed in many directions: Arthit; Pichit, whose future had been hurt by Arthit's promotion; and Class 5. Some suspect that the Young Turks were the victims of a setup. Prem put 40 plotters on trial for rebellion, but in court it became clear that no one wanted the truth to surface. One key witness, tiring of lawyers' questions, abruptly threatened to reveal the real story if he was forced to continue.[18]

Preoccupied with such turmoil, apparently King Bhumibol hadn't noticed that Queen Sirikit had begun to unravel in the meantime. Besides her own lifestyle and the burden of her large court, she was distressed by Prince Vajiralongkorn's abandonment of her niece Somsawali. The prince made clear his rejection of Somsawali in an interview with local reporters in mid-1984. In the course of explaining that, as future king, he was dedicated to his role as a disciplined professional soldier and a committed servant of his father and the country, he pointedly made no mention of his wife.[19] Somsawali's family and supporters were outraged, at both the prince and the queen.

Added to that were the Prem-Arthit fight and the chit fund collapse, which had much of Bangkok gossiping about Sirikit's involvement. There was also a hushed-up scandal over a California gold-mine investment by Ubolrat and her husband, which apparently involved others in the royal family and was supported by a highly unusual $1.9 million loan from Siam Commercial Bank.[20] Then in May 1985 came the news that Sirikit's favorite Colonel Narongdej had died while in the United States. Supposedly he had a heart attack, but the queen pursued rumors that he was murdered. Her mourning became an embarrassment. For his funeral, which all top officials in the military and government had to attend, she issued a commemorative volume bearing photographs of the two together. Afterward a glorifying tele-

vision documentary was made on Narongdej, and it also conveyed their special
relationship.

The following month Sucharinee gave birth to another son. She was now
impossible to ignore as the mother to four royal sons in an otherwise male-heirless
dynasty. And she wanted to have another, for, it was said, a fortune-telling monk
had told her that if she bore the prince five sons she would become queen. This
story was taken seriously throughout the palace community.

These events and the mysterious September 1985 coup finally pushed Sirikit
over the edge. At the end of the year she had a massive breakdown, entering the
hospital for what was called a "diagnostic curettage." She disappeared from public
view for six months, reportedly isolated by Bhumibol personally from her courtiers and held to a healthy diet. Gossip spread that she was terminally ill, or might
even have died. She finally emerged in July 1986 for the consecration of the new
Bangkok city pillar. Somber and unsteady, she disappeared for another three
weeks, even skipping her birthday celebration. Instead, Princess Chulabhorn went
on television to praise her as a woman of supernatural dedication.[21] "Since her
majesty underwent an operation in 1985, she has been getting much better. Now she
constantly exercises and even though I am 25 years her junior, I can hardly keep
up. . . . If the people are going to get angry because of her disappearance from the
public view, it is us [her children] who should be blamed since we always insist that
she rests instead of making appearances. . . . Normally everybody has holidays, but
her majesty never had one." The queen wakes up at 10 or 11 a.m. each day, Chulabhorn added, and works more than 12 hours a day. "If she can't go to sleep, she will
continue working until the next morning. . . . [R]ight after waking up, she never has
time for anything else but work. . . . I have never heard her say that she is tired."

The princess used the occasion to address some of the long-festering stories
and the popular picture of a dysfunctional royal family. Denying rumors that the
queen controlled the palace, she insisted: "We all work for his majesty because of
our loyalty towards him. Nobody in our family wants popularity for themselves.
Everybody is sharing the work and we work as a team. . . . But again, there are
people who say that our family is divided into two sides, which is not true at all." As
if to prove the point, when on August 18 Sirikit felt well enough to receive well-
wishers—the very first being Prem—the occasion was made out to be a religious
awakening. She blamed her illness on fatigue and bad fortune and, asserting her
own superior sacrality, said that those who had prayed for her would achieve great
merit. "Had I followed the Lord Buddha's teaching of the middle path," she commented, "I would not have fallen ill and wasted so much time like this."[22]

Such statements revealed the cosmic importance the palace attached to such events as the queen's illness. By this time, however, the Thai public had become much less interested in royal affairs, and far more skeptical. The fact was, by the 1980s, broader education and economic advances had produced an ample Thai middle class with values and practices very different from Bhumibol and Prem's worldview. The urban population was nearly half of the country. Commerce and manufacturing had become larger than agriculture, driven heavily by exports to global markets. There were millions of struggling urban factory workers, their lives shaped more by forces like foreign capital, competition, and consumerism than by the traditional monarchy-topped ruling pyramid.

In the same period the students who had experienced the military dictatorships of the 1960s and 1970s had matured, becoming white-collar workers, private business owners, professors, teachers, journalists, politicians, and popular singers and writers. They were behind a growing number of activist independent agencies and nongovernmental organizations pushing into fields like poverty relief, education, and environmental protection, areas the government and the palace considered their own turf.

Moreover, after half a decade, many Thais had come to dislike Prem's aloofness and secretiveness. People openly called him undemocratic, for his refusal to answer questions about governance or take responsibility for scandals and failures, speaking only to the king. They expected more protection from the law rather than from the traditional paternal and feudal social arrangements his government fostered, and rejected the military's claim to special powers based on an allegedly extant communist threat. One sign of sentiment was the surprise election in 1985 of Chamlong Srimuang, a former Young Turk, as governor of Bangkok. The onetime Prem aide had turned against military politicking and become a strict Buddhist, living piously, abstaining from sex, not eating meat, and sleeping only on a thin mat. He had also joined the dissident Buddhist sect Santi Asoke, which held that the mainstream sangha was corrupt. His election was a sign of urban Thais' rejection of dishonest and unresponsive government under Prem, which had left the capital city a dirty, polluted, traffic-clogged mess. Chamlong promised voters honesty and responsiveness, implying the failure of the Bhumibol-Prem-army-bureaucracy pyramid.

In 1986, this change in the public's attitude became manifest when Prem was almost brought down in a bold parliamentary challenge. He responded with skillful patronage and by establishing his own political faction. He had his national security adviser Siddhi Savetsila take over the Social Action Party after Kukrit

Pramoj retired, and another ally, General Tienchai Sirisamphan, formed a second pro-Prem party, Rassadorn. Paradoxically, these moves served to further legitimize the parliamentary politics Prem and the king disdained, and also made the throne indirectly a partisan player in the legislature, opening itself up for challenge and criticism.

Within two months parliament again turned on Prem to defeat his new political base, forcing him in early May to ask the king to dissolve the assembly and hold new elections. But before the voting could take place, military factionalism reared its head anew. Arthit correctly read Prem's party building as a sign that he wasn't going to give up the premiership. When Arthit implicitly threatened a coup, the palace made it clear that opposing Prem was to oppose the throne. First, the crown prince made a public visit to Prem's home, not the other way around, as royal protocol should have it. A few weeks later the king conferred on General Prem the superfluous ranks of air chief marshal and admiral, multiple titles normally reserved only for the royal family. At the same time, from the safety of his Nakhon Ratchasima redoubt Prem released the king's signed order sacking Arthit as army commander.

It was the end of Arthit politically, but that didn't guarantee Prem's survival. Much of the campaigning for votes by progressive candidates attacked Prem's refusal to stand for election to parliament, as well as the military under him for being thoroughly corrupt and politicized. Prem's unbudging response was to set himself in the king's mold by claiming he was neutral and above politics—even as his personal aides now ran political parties. But Bhumibol and Prem were clearly worried. In yet another intervention, it was let out that the king wanted Prem in office at least through his 60th birthday celebrations in 1987, and then for the 1988 commemoration of Bhumibol's becoming Thailand's longest-reigning monarch ever.

The July 27 vote proved inconclusive. Receiving the most seats, 100 of 347, were the Democrats, the party with the cleanest reputation and the one making the strongest attacks on the Prem-royal-military alliance. This gave the Democrats the right to assemble a government under their own leader, Bhichai Rattakul. Much to his party's anger, however, Bhichai yielded to Prem. Who persuaded him and how was cause for great speculation.

Prem's ruling coalition included the Democrats, Chart Thai, and his own Social Action Party and Rassadorn. He then shortchanged the Democrats by placing his own men in the cabinet. The Interior Ministry was given to the former Red Gaur leader Prachuab Suntharangkul, who, as soon as a few students turned out to protest, put the police on high alert, just like in the 1970s. The most lucrative portfolio, transportation and communications, went to the new Chart Thai Party star Banharn Silpa-archa, an extremely venal business tycoon with a political machine in the central plains. Prem and the palace had again finessed the political system without force, but with a dubious standard of virtue. In hindsight, many realized that the election was a palace-military fait accompli. One Thai expert concluded to a foreign reporter, "The premiership is not decided by members of parliament, but by the military, the palace and other interest groups."[23]

As Prem circumvented yet another challenge, he also helped Vajiralongkorn spruce up his image even while he gave the shove to Somsawali. The prince seemed to have made a deal with the king: if he behaved properly and if Sucharinee rose above her low-class origins, she might be accepted into the palace. The prince made a number of visits to the poor, performed religious rites in upcountry temples, and gave out university degrees more frequently. He resumed the distribution of the king's personal Buddha statues to provincial seats, the program begun in the 1960s to register the king's rule over his kingdom. He stood by his father to receive the credentials of diplomats newly assigned to Bangkok and undertook state visits abroad, in February 1987 going to China as the king's stand-in. Often on these appearances, several steps behind the prince was Sucharinee, acting dutifully royal.

In mid-1986 Vajiralongkorn gave a lengthy interview to *Dichan,* the leading fashion and lifestyle magazine for the urban upper and middle classes.[24] The magazine was owned by Piya Malakul, whose family had long served Bhumibol and who himself had become the throne's unofficial public relations expert. In 32 pages of text and photographs showing him in his Nonthaburi palace, the article characterized the prince as a true working royal, dedicated to his father and his country, with little time for fun. The core of the interview combined an acknowledgment of his four children by Sucharinee with a character assassination of Somsawali. Although not naming her, the prince clearly painted his wife as wholly unsuited for marriage to a future king, lacking the ability to share and contribute to his life and duties, and so to the monarchic institution. He made the marriage out as a mistake, suggesting that it had been rushed and that, as a teenager, she wasn't even physically ready for a relationship with a man. He didn't elaborate.

He also discussed his own image. While denying stories of his misbehavior, he explained that every famous person suffered the problems of gossip and of others abusing their name for ill purposes. This was his suffering in his service to the king, and he dealt with it with Buddhist detachment. "Maybe in the previous life we did not make merit enough. Or maybe at some time we did things that attracted reproach. I have accepted this. . . . If the heavens think that one is not appropriate, or in the stars there is no benefit for the nation in one's duties, well then let us stop and end it. If you think like this, you are at ease. You don't think about being something. If the heavens give you a duty to the land, so be it. If they don't want you to work, okay."

Most readers couldn't help but be sympathetic, but the interview left the Somsawali faction in the court livid. The interview was a calculated step toward elevating Sucharinee into Somsawali's place, with the apparent backing of the king and queen. In fact, promoting Sucharinee was now even more likely, for when Vajiralongkorn gave the interview, she was three months pregnant.

For a moment at the end of 1986, Bhumibol, his palace, and Prem could relax in the comfort that they had overcome substantial political and family hurdles. They set their eyes on the king's auspicious fifth 12-year cycle, his 60th birthday on December 5, 1987, to be the centerpiece of a 20-month commemoration of the Ninth Reign and the Bhumibol-Prem palace-led state.

The celebratory spirit already filled the air when the king gave his annual rambling, grandfatherly birthday chat in December 1986. The audience of Prem and his cabinet, top civil service officials, the military brass, and others listened only half attentively until Bhumibol remarked, "The water of the Chaophraya River must flow on, and the water that flows on will be replaced." Ever unsmiling, he continued, "In our lifetime, we just perform our duties. When we retire, somebody else will replace us. . . . One cannot stick to a single task forever. One day we will grow old and die." Suddenly the old Siamese cosmos shuddered: Bhumibol was suggesting that someday, maybe soon, he might abdicate. It was unsettling, at least, because most Thais in the 1980s had never known any other king. They had been taught from birth that the dhammaraja monarch kept the kingdom on an even keel. Most knew also of the ancient prediction that the Chakri Dynasty would have only nine kings. Given the prospect of Vajiralongkorn becoming Rama X, this implied imminent chaos.

The king's hint was intentional, and the palace allowed that he might even abdicate sometime after the July 1988 longest-reign celebration. Over the next several months the palace spokespersons Tongnoi Tongyai and M.R. Butrie Viravaidhya spread the word that an abdication would mean no drastic change. Tongnoi said the king couldn't abdicate by the absolute definition of the word. Instead he might become a monk while keeping his hand in national affairs.[25] "The king will never abdicate, if by abdication you mean leaving his responsibilities [to the people] behind and retiring. . . . Once his majesty sees the crown prince reaching a more mature age and ready to take over all the royal functions, he may enter a monastery. . . . It does not mean he will simply remain a monk. The important thing is that he will continue to be there, behind the throne, and help his son solve any problems."

Tongnoi's words also confirmed that the crown would go to Prince Vajiralong-korn, who had stepped up his official duties and made more regal statements to generate confidence in him as a future dhammaraja. In June 1987 Vajiralongkorn received a delegation of Bangkok's foreign press.[26] His disciplined answers gave away little. He simply reiterated that he was a common man who served at the feet of the king, whom he extolled as having incredibly kept the country united for 40 years. His father's success came from strict adherence to the ten principles of dhammaraja kingship, he said.

The next month there was another interview in *Dichan*, 20 pages with photos of Vajiralongkorn alternately in his flight suit and jogging kit: the image of a working soldier-prince.[27] Sounding ever more like the king, he talked of the hard-ships of the poor southern villages he had recently toured, which were ignored by officialdom, he said. He had also straightened out the Somdej Phra Yuparaj hos-pitals, which had been mismanaged by the government, staining his own name. Highlighting the magical relationship between the people and the throne, he noted that however poor or ill they were, old or young, villagers had greeted him with handmade flower garlands and other gifts: they recognized Chakri virtue. The whole trip, he added, whetted his interest in the kingdom. "I'd like to go meet the people more. Really I would like to walk the whole of Thailand," he said wistfully.

The interviewer daringly brought up his public image. The prince answered stoically: "Some people like me, some people don't like me. It's their right. . . . Wherever you go there is gossip. If you are busy with gossip you don't have to work. We can set up a government office or division for gossip, and no one else has to work. . . . But those who gossip, if they want to know the truth, if they want to ask me, and they have a pure heart, and come to ask about the truth, I would respect them." Direct discussion of Sucharinee and Somsawali remained off-limits, but *Dichan* did broach the issue of the king's hinted abdication. Vajiralongkorn's reply sternly maintained the royal inviolateness, showing himself as real kingly material. "I have never heard this talk and I don't want to know about it. Any matters about the king are very high matters, higher than me. I am a servant of the king and as such will do my very best to do what he tells me. . . . We have a king who follows the thotsaphit rachatham. We should feel lucky to be born in this country. We should be satisfied enough to be close to the feet of the king."

Prem promoted the king's 60th birthday with the full force of the government budget. Posters and billboards went up all over the country, and nearly every act and event over the preceding and following year was dedicated to the occasion. Government offices produced massive commemorative tomes and lengthy television documentaries that emphasized Bhumibol's brilliance, his adherence to the ten kingly virtues, and the unerring leadership of all Chakri kings. Universities held seminars and issued scholarly analyses lauding the reign and the dynasty.

The royal family also contributed works. Princess Galyani wrote and the army published a 400-page volume on the childhood of Ananda and Bhumibol, laden with suggestions of how bright both were at a young age.[28] Princess Sirindhorn wrote an essay exalting the king's development miracles: "Wherever his majesty passes will in the succeeding year show a great improvement—the peoples' health is better, the environment is better, the economic situation is better."[29]

The Tourism Authority and Thai Airways together launched a global tourism promotion, Visit Thailand Year, which largely featured the king's anniversary. They arranged with the palace to put on the royal kathin barge procession in October, demonstrating how the Buddhist kingship and its holy rituals had become a core feature of the country's tourism pitch. The military's privileged relationship with the throne was also featured. In March 1987 Bhumibol performed the rare ritual of granting colors to military regiments, the staffs capped with the king's own personal relics. The military reciprocated by clearing swaths of protected forest at the summit of Thailand's tallest mountain to build two gigantic chedi, traditionally monuments to revered holy men, one for Bhumibol and the other for Sirikit.

At the end of 1986, Prem had the king officially declared "supreme artist," a prelude to offering him in December 1987 the new title of *maharaja,* King Bhumibol the Great.[30] Supposedly the maharaja title was decided based on a poll of all 41 million Thais. It placed Bhumibol in the rarefied pantheon of Kings Ramkhamhaeng, Naresuan, and Chulalongkorn, who were all named "the great" posthumously. (In 1983 Tongnoi had written that Bhumibol "steadfastly refuses" the encomium, because it should be decided by history.)[31]

Underpinning all of this was the persistent ritual attestation of Bhumibol's achievement of bodhisattva status. Monks made offerings to the king and the dynasty, and his dedication to Buddhist principles was heavily advertised. The religious affairs department launched a recension of the holy Buddhist text the Tripitaka for the occasion of his birthday. Such a rare and voluminous event signified that the king had the genius to recognize and repair faults in the existing liturgy. In a lecture to the Bangkok foreign press corps, Kukrit declared the king's near-deity. He told the reporters of the king's brilliant royal projects, which in the government's hands would have failed miserably. He credited this to the king's simultaneous and seemingly contradictory divine and human status:

> The king is something very near and dear to the people, especially at present. He is regarded as one of the family. And at the same time they still believe . . . that the king is god. It's somehow rather difficult for the people to find a balance between this intimacy which they feel towards their king and this sense of divinity, which they also believe the king has.
>
> The king at the same time must find it difficult to balance between being a friend of the family and the fact that he is divine. The king, on ceremonial occasions and on official occasions, has to show a certain amount of the divine aspect. He cannot be totally human and at the same time he has got to be very human when he goes to the countryside visiting villagers in their homes and in their houses. The divinity of the king has somehow given the country a kind of stability.

Kukrit supported this claim by relating what he called a "real miracle," the development of the Huay Klai wasteland near Chiangmai. Only after the king brought water and cooperatives did the lives of the people there improve. "If you go there today, you will find a veritable Garden of Eden. . . . This is what happens in this reign," he said.[32]

The press chuckled at the divinity idea but readily reported that Thailand's unity and development all magically sprang from King Bhumibol. The *New York Times* wrote: "The power of the king is most felt in the royal development projects, which he has been initiating and monitoring since the early years of his reign. The lending of his name to any plan means that things will get done; no bureaucrat would dare slow down or obstruct it."[33]

Royal boosterism did not protect Prem, however. During 1987 he faced increasing defiance and attack, some from the nascent nongovernmental organizations confronting the government on social and environmental issues. One effort, the campaign to block EGAT's construction of the large Nam Choan hydropower dam, demonstrated just how bold and powerful these groups had become. The proposal brought together a surprisingly broad group of poor farmers, merchants from the nearby towns, scientists, and other intellectuals and environmentalists, all fighting the dam because it would flood a huge area of protected wilderness on the western border and displace a large number of peasants. They attacked Prem for deciding the project without consulting the people, and EGAT management—the head, Kasem Chatikavanich, was a favorite of the king—for a long history of environmental destruction and mistreatment of displaced people. Indirectly, the king himself was under assault, because EGAT's dam-building program was credited to his own promotion of water management. The battle went on throughout 1987 and finally, in an embarrassing defeat, Prem and EGAT gave up the dam in early 1988.

Another challenge to the king-Prem hierarchy came over the recension of the Tripitaka. The monks assigned the solemn task saw the reason behind it, the king's anniversary, as spurious, as evidenced by the impossible two-year deadline to purify the immense text. They stalled until the deadline was given up.

The biggest fight during 1987 was over renewed efforts to institutionalize the royal-military government. In late February, King Bhumibol, lecturing a group of Thai reporters visiting his Chiangmai royal project center, emphasized that his own innovative ideas were most appropriate to solve rural poverty. He then added that the political system also had to be fitted to the Thai character.[34] This remark was open to many interpretations, but a week afterward Prem suggested to his ministers that the king supported the formalization of the military's dominant political role. Taking the ball was new army boss General Chavalit Yongchaiyut, one of the architects of Order 66/2523, on the military's socio-political role, from 1980. He had been involved in implementing it in the countryside—basically having the military run certain provinces—and he had helped Prem defeat the attempted coups. With Arthit gone, he also saw himself as Prem's replacement.

Repeating that it was the king's wish, Chavalit declared the army the kingdom's primary force for development and poverty alleviation, under the king's guidance.[35] "We have massive lands, water resources, disciplined labor and machinery. The know-how we can get from other agencies," Chavalit told a seminar.[36] To this end, soldiers underwent development training to tackle a long list of official royal projects. The biggest effort was Chavalit's famous *Isan Khiew,* or Green Isan, a massive program to ostensibly turn the dry impoverished northeast into a verdant land of plenty. More than $500 million was allocated through several agencies under the military's direction, and legions of soldiers went to work building reservoirs and water tanks and expanding water diversion projects. In the name of increasing forest cover, they also planted commercial eucalyptus farms for pulp.

Rather than attracting support, the army was strongly attacked for appropriating a governmental role in the king's name, exploiting the monarchy. The military was criticized for consuming more than a quarter of the national budget, far more than was spent on health and education. Critics called the army just another self-serving political party, using the government budget to build its power. They pointed to the lavish lifestyles of scores of millionaire generals as evidence of rife corruption, and some critics asked wryly whether the green in Green Isan was vegetation or just army uniforms. The military men defended themselves by arguing, like the palace had for years, that politicians and businessmen were corrupt and selfish.[37] But they no longer had the moral high ground. In April the parliamentary opposition lodged a no-confidence motion against Prem. By their numbers, it should easily have gone ahead. Instead, Prem's arm-twisting and outright buying off of a large number of votes prevented it.

Even so, the public saw on television MPs in parliament jeering the king's prime minister. They also heard uncommon attacks on Prem, such as Kukrit accusing him of behaving like royalty himself. "The fact that a certain government leader visits villagers and keeps on talking about his loyalty to the king is simply a tactic to boost his own popularity for future political benefit, in case there is an election of the prime minister. . . . The villagers would certainly vote for him because they too are loyal to the king. . . . [I feel] disgraced as a Thai in having to allow only one person to stay above politics and criticism—a person that has become like a king in an absolute monarchy but who behaves as if he was more important than the real king."[38]

Sukhumbhand Paripatra published a strong attack along the same lines, saying Prem had accomplished little in seven years and disdained democratic practices. "The substance of his accomplishments consists of balancing one military group against another to maintain his own position. His style of leadership is one of maintaining a royalty-like aloofness from all major political problems and ensuring that criticisms against him are contained at their sources." Sukhumbhand then suggested that Prem had not prepared the country for the king's abdication. "It is not surprising that everyone regards rumors about [Bhumibol's] abdication with great apprehension. . . . In the context where a crisis of confidence in the country's major political institutions is already developing, an early abdication would deal a damaging blow to the Thai political system. Because the king has been so dominant a figure, the crown prince, whatever his personal attributes, cannot immediately hope to fill the gap left by his father. The resulting vacuum will be dangerous indeed."[39]

That fall pressure intensified as a Prem-Chavalit effort to amend the constitution for the military played out against several corruption scandals and new outrages involving the prince, all as the king's anniversary celebrations reached their acme.

The prince had kept his worst instincts in check for the better part of a year. But in late 1987 he seemed to run out of self-control in his rush to gain official recognition for Sucharinee. At the beginning of January she had given birth to her fifth child, a girl christened Busyanampetch.[40] Afterward she accompanied the prince in appearances around the country, all broadcast on the royal news. Newspapers ran her photograph while avoiding Princess Somsawali. In November, *Thai Rath* reported that Sucharinee had earned two undergraduate degrees with top marks at Bangkok's Prasarnmit University, and newspapers and the televised royal news showed the prince himself presenting her certificate. Quietly, the public jeered, stoked by negative stories spread by Somsawali's camp. With abdication in the air, it appeared that Sucharinee was being prepared to be queen. But she had no official status yet, which led to a serious diplomatic incident with Japan.

In the final week of September 1987, Vajiralongkorn made an eight-day state visit to Japan. Beforehand, he had insisted that Tokyo receive him and Sucharinee together in an official capacity. The Japanese refused on the grounds of royal and diplomatic protocol: only his official wife could formally accompany him in meetings with the prime minister and the Japanese royal family. The prince was furious as he departed for Japan alone. He grudgingly followed the official schedule, but then he threw a tantrum and left three days early. After *Thai Rath* reported that the Japanese insulted him and the Thai monarchy in several incidents, a group of Village Scouts showed up at the Japanese embassy in Bangkok threatening violence if there was no apology.

Authorities in both Tokyo and Bangkok were shocked, with Prem himself scheduled to visit Japan within ten days. The accusations that the Japanese had humiliated the prince were fabricated, but the truth couldn't really be told. With his main responsibility to protect palace prestige, Prem had no choice but to make a formal protest, leaving only the palace to stop the case from snowballing into a diplomatic disaster. Presumably pressured by the king, the prince finally intervened to call an end to criticism of Japan for the sake of good relations on October 6. When Prem arrived in Tokyo days later, Prime Minister Yasuhiro Nakasone offered his regrets and gratitude for the prince's defusing the situation.

As he dealt with all that, Prem was battered as well by political problems of his own making. With little real official rationale other than the possible coming

succession and alleged continuing communist threats, in October Prem chaired an
ISOC meeting on changing the constitution to give more power to the executive
and the armed forces, declaring, in the language of Order 66/2523, that this "democratic" political reform was crucial for national survival. At the same time Prem's
personal virtue suffered in three consecutive corruption exposés. The first was
when credible graft charges were lodged against cabinet minister Chirayut Isarangkul, the son of a privy councilor and a palace and Prem favorite. Chirayut was
forced to resign but then went to work leading the Crown Property Bureau. In the
second case, communications minister Banharn was accused of massive corruption and vote-buying. Behind the accusations was sentiment that Prem, who relied
on Banharn's political support, was freely letting him pillage state assets and
contracts. The third scandal was over the army's corrupt arms deals, in particular
one involving Chavalit and his wife and the just-concluded purchase of American-
made Stingray tanks. The tanks had even been rejected by the Pentagon for their
high cost and low quality, and yet, despite the opposition of some senior Thai
civilian and military officials, Prem allowed the deal through.[41]

The scandals were serious enough to threaten bringing down the government
altogether, killing the constitutional amendment effort and spoiling the king's
fifth-cycle fete. Army officials responded by saying that the political instability
proved that democracy wasn't working, and Chavalit murmured that people were
asking him to lead a coup on Prem's behalf.

The political debate quieted in the first days of December, however, just before
Bhumibol's 60th birthday. As Japanese-sponsored fireworks filled the skies, Prem
formally presented the title of maharaja to the king. People celebrated and made
merit for their sovereign around the kingdom; Prince Vajiralongkorn's first son,
Chudhavajra, the possible future king, ordained as a novice in Wat Bovornives.

Just as the celebration began, unsigned leaflets attacking the royal family were
distributed openly at street intersections, placed in parliament letterboxes, and
photocopied and faxed around the country. Some criticized the king and queen
directly for the perpetuation of their power. Mostly they attacked the crown prince
for his general misbehavior, for the Japan trip, and for his mistreatment of Princess
Somsawali, declaring him unsuitable for the throne. "He is a disgrace and totally
lacking in morals," said one; "if we should choose to emulate him, chaos would
engulf the country."[42] They also attacked Sucharinee for her sham degrees, one
leaflet saying her graduation was rushed in hopes that the king would bestow her
full royal status on his birthday.

The leaflets went officially unremarked until December 8, when suddenly they were labeled part of a revolutionary communist conspiracy, the manifestation of "a group of enemies of the nation belonging to a movement bent on undermining the monarchy," the military and the police declared.[43] Actually, apparently several unrelated groups had produced the leaflets, one source believed to be the camp of Somsawali. The police hunted down some of the culprits, arresting a printer, some students, and a monk. They were quickly tried and imprisoned for lèse-majesté.

Bhumibol closed the tumultuous year with a gathering of the entire royal clan, scores of titled descendants of the Chakri kings, to commemorate the anniversary and the monarchy. In his address, he emphasized that the monarchy was democratic and that he represented the people's consensus. "Kingship is an institution [created] by the people, to be depended upon by the people and to act for the good of the people."[44]

Writing in a foreign magazine, Sukhumbhand drew on that comment to again mention the public's concern over his possible abdication.[45] He wrote that the December leaflets had left people anxious, not just about the prince, but about the overextension of the king's power and the power of the military. He gingerly laid out the problem:

> Given the monarchy's role in Thailand's political and economic development, as well as its place in the hearts and minds of the populace, any uncertainty regarding the future of the monarch inevitably causes a great deal of apprehension. Doubts continue to be expressed, mostly in private but now increasingly in the open, about the crown prince's capacity to evoke the kind of intense political loyalty from the people and the major domestic political groupings that his father is able to do. Doubts also persist as to whether the crown prince can match his father's subtle and mediatory role in politics. . . .
>
> Bhumibol has achieved a great deal for his country and for the institution he inherited without forewarning, but by doing so, he has set perhaps an impossibly high standard of attainment for his successors. Should the leadership provided by the monarchy become less effective for one reason or another in the future, there will be grave political consequences. The precarious balance among the major political groups and factions would certainly be destroyed. . . . This vacuum is one which only the military would be capable of filling, given its monopoly of coercive power, organizational cohesion and control of the media and grassroots politics. For many Thais this ultimately is the root of their apprehension.

Neither the king nor Prem showed any sign of accepting Sukhumbhand's analysis. Yet as his critique was published, palace officials began saying categorically that Bhumibol wouldn't abdicate. Apparently the king had changed his mind, presumably because of the prince's disquieting behavior. Also possibly influencing the decision were renewed challenges to Prem. After the king's birthday another skein of corruption cases erupted. Prem's customs and tax chiefs, supposedly honest technocrats, were caught smuggling luxury cars. Prem took their resignations, but there was widespread suspicion that he did so while protecting army smuggling rings. The prime minister wasn't cracking down on corruption; he was just reacting to bad press. Banharn became an embarrassment yet again by hijacking government contracts for his own benefit. When the overall economy began to show damage from one particular deal, even private industry attacked Prem.

Most embarrassing was a scandal that involved the prestige of the throne and Prem's own office. A large ring of top bureaucrats and monks was exposed for selling royal decorations and honors. The scandal had been long in coming. Awarding royal honors and decorations had been important in sustaining a palace-centered aristocracy and expanding royal culture among bureaucrats and businessmen. It also generated more donations to royal charities. Because of the increase in donors and decorations, the palace seconded management of this prerogative to the government and the sangha. Temples, charities, and certain government offices would report donations and suitable decoration candidates to the Ministry of Education, which would check the list and pass it to the prime minister's office. There other names could be added, and a final list would be passed to the palace and usually accepted without question.

As the awards carried not just social but economic value, by the early 1980s the process had become corrupted, with people buying their way directly on to the shortlist, bribing monks and officials and falsifying donation reports. The practice became public in December 1987 when a senior official in Prem's secretariat committed suicide. He was in charge of keeping the royal seals and the prime minister's specimen signatures, and had used his access to help people obtain decorations. Further investigation revealed at least two decorations rackets, involving officials in Prem's secretariat and a prominent monk from Wat Thepsirin, one of the foremost royal temples.[46] Police estimated that nearly half the requests for decorations that year were bogus, falsely reporting more than $55 million in donations.[47] The episode revealed just how debased royal decorations and the throne's magic circle of merit had become. It also revealed how unconcerned Prem, the king's virtuous premier, had been over corruption.

Prem's footing weakened further. After the Nam Choan protesters forced the government to give up the dam, a simmering border dispute with Laos erupted into open fighting and, despite superior firepower, Thailand got whipped. The blame fell mostly on Chavalit but also stained his patron Prem. Ahead of a possible defeat in parliament, Prem dissolved the body and scheduled national elections for July 24. It would at least allow him to preside over the longest-reign celebration on July 2.

Fully confident of palace and military support, Prem made clear his intention to be renewed as premier, again without standing for election. This time, however, the Bhumibol-Prem-military relationship became the main election issue. In the election campaign, Prem openly tied his renewed premiership to Bhumibol's coming longest-reign fete. Instead of running for office, he presumed that celebrating the monarchy—attaching himself to royal virtue—was enough. But in June, 99 well-known academics and professionals sent a petition to King Bhumibol accusing Prem of using the throne's name and the military's menacing support to hold on to power. In cautious language, the petitioners explained their concern with protecting royal prestige, and that they feared the military was corrupting the democratic process. But their real target was clearly the palace's permitting Prem to brandish the king's endorsement. The petitioners were boldly demanding that King Bhumibol stop hijacking democratic politics.[48]

Prem momentarily brushed them off as he led the celebration of Bhumibol's reign, which at just over 42 years surpassed any before in the Bangkok, Ayutthaya, or Sukhothai dynasties. After commemorating prior Chakri rulers in the Grand Palace, Prem traveled with the royal family to Ayutthaya to pay homage to its 33 kings.

When the elections were held, as usual the results failed to establish a dominant party. Prem positioned himself to knit together a new alliance and again assume power. But his refusal to stand for election and the general issue of democracy had become important to people, and the idea of having an elected prime minister caught fire among politicians and voters. As a thousand protesters demonstrated outside Prem's home, political party leaders and many others called openly for a prime minister chosen from among the elected legislators. As the nation waited to see whether Bhumibol would again intervene on his behalf, Prem decided to withdraw, saving the king a difficult choice between the people and the military leadership. Instead, replacing Prem was Chatichai Choonhavan, whose Chart Thai Party had captured the largest number of parliamentary seats. Cavalry officer, diplomat, and slippery business tycoon, and son of the notorious 1950s army chief Phin Choonhavan, Chatichai joined the rare ranks of elected prime ministers of the postwar period.

Why hadn't the people seen the virtue of the king's army-led government? In hindsight the answer was readily apparent. Prem had done little over eight years besides protecting his job and the monarchy. His government proved no less corrupt, abusive, and bureaucratic than a civilian one. Arguably, too, social problems had worsened. Bangkok was thriving, thanks mainly to increased foreign investment. But in the countryside poverty remained widespread. In 1988 more than 25 percent of Thai families lived below the official poverty line, little changed from a decade before. The rich had gotten richer, and the poor poorer: in 1988 the richest 20 percent of Thais captured 56 percent of income, while the poorest fifth got only 5 percent. In 1976, the split had been 49 percent versus 6 percent.[49]

Farmer landlessness was still a huge problem. In 1988 there were a half million farm households that controlled no land, roughly 10 percent of all farm families, and another half million whose landholdings were less than four acres, generally not self-sufficient. In addition, several million Thais lived illegally as settlers on degraded national forest land, lacking a legal right to till it. While money had poured into the military, health and education services hadn't kept up with population growth. At the primary and secondary school levels, dropout and matriculation rates were as bad as ever. More than one in five Thais never got beyond four years of education, learning just enough to respect the royal-bureaucratic hierarchy.[50]

Environmental degradation was beginning to look catastrophic. Millions of acres of supposedly protected forests were lost to loggers with political and military backing, while waterways and the air were becoming intolerably polluted. Violent crime was high and rising, and Thailand's narcotics traffickers brought in more than a billion dollars a year. And despite Prem's supposed personal cleanliness, his survival had taken precedent over stopping the corruption of those around him. His favored minister Banharn wasn't the only obvious example. In taking over the Social Action Party, Prem's top national security aide Siddhi Savetsila allied himself with two of the country's top crime godfathers, Kamnan Poh and Chat Taopoon, both party officials.

Perhaps most egregious was the uncurtailed factionalization and corruption of the military under Prem's watch. Rather than becoming more trim and professional, the military officers' corps grew fatter and more incapable of modern soldiering. Their involvement in politics, business, and crime was unabated, with the resulting disunity and indiscipline posing a constant threat to government stability.

Overall, a Thai society much changed since the 1950s was making demands that old-school politicians were not used to. That King Bhumibol didn't really comprehend it was understandable. His now mostly younger, less-experienced advisers deferred to him in all matters of analysis. None dared question or correct him, mostly serving to confirm his ideas, not inform them. His confidants told him the new people power was like the CPT, a threat to nation, religion, and king. It wasn't, but it sounded true enough for Bhumibol to continue endorsing the military's claim on political primacy.

17   Another Coup for the Throne   ❧

AS THE NEW PRIME MINISTER, Chatichai gave a fresh charge to the air. It wasn't only that he spun around on a motorcycle and wore the tag of playboy proudly as he shared lewd jokes with streetside vendors. Chatichai's rise proclaimed that Prem's style of government was outdated, that the Cold War was over and it was time to make friends with neighbors and leave behind the royalist national security state. While Bhumibol pointedly named Prem to the privy council, Chatichai replaced Prem's palace-approved technocrats with his own men. His advisers included men who had honed their politics in the anti-right movement of the 1970s, including his once CPT-associated son Kraisak and Prem critic Sukhumbhand. Chatichai's government even swapped out Prem's "royal suit" for Italian business suits and designer ties. It all said that the king and old royal culture was not their priority. The elected government was now the palace's competitor for prestige.

Chatichai inherited an economy that, thanks to the global currency realignment and a subsequent gush of investment from East Asia, would grow strongly for years. Constraints to economic growth like infrastructure and manpower were addressed with new approaches like increased competition and privatization, and quick action on grand projects that during Prem's years had bogged down in the bureaucracy.

For a while the boom enriched many more Thais and even increased general rural wealth, for many validating the move to a civilian premier. Like Prem, however, Chatichai presided over a fractious coalition, while in the wings awaited ambitious generals like Chavalit and the Class 5 leaders Suchinda Kraprayoon and Issarapong Noonpakdi, plotting their own political rise. To remain in power Chatichai had to keep everyone happy with pieces of the growing pie. Prem had done the same, but Chatichai took it to a new level, and his deeply corrupt government earned, deservingly, the epithet "the buffet cabinet." It validated everything the king had long said about venal politicians and opened the way for another coup.

Chatichai wasn't anti-monarchy. He accepted the ceremonial role of the king and, as a Geneva-based diplomat years before, he and his wife had regularly taken care of the royal family. But neither he nor his ministers thought it necessary to work closely with the king the way Prem had. As businessmen and politicians, too, they had never mixed with the court as the generals did.

While accommodating Bhumibol's royal projects and ceremonies, Chatichai tried to dismantle the machine that he and Prem had built. Their favorites in the cabinet and bureaucracy were shunted out. Chatichai kept Prem's foreign minister, the old cold warrior Siddhi Savetsila, on for two years, but finally forced him out as well. Siddhi then joined Prem on the privy council, making it clear where the king stood. Prem and palace allies at the state planning bureau, Thai Airways, and the central bank were also pushed out. The EGAT board of directors, which included two privy councilors, was sacked en masse at one point. Chatichai's government launched its own development initiatives without the palace or the military being involved. "Green Isan" was replaced with Chatichai's promise to make the northeast wealthy by "turning battlefields into marketplaces." Politicians and the civilian government were going to take credit for development.

Smaller things piqued the old establishment as well. Bowing to a younger generation of liberal MPs, the cabinet in early 1989 rejected a palace-military move to restore assets taken from Thanom Kittikachorn after October 1973. Later the cabinet also freed long-sequestered funds for the stalled monument to the October 1973 uprising. As the conservative establishment grumbled, new army strongman Suchinda made a loud, menacing objection.

There was also a collision of commercial interests. Businessmen like Chatichai's crony Prachai Leophairatana of the TPI Group were permitted to cut into the dominance of the crown's Siam Cement Group in the building materials and petrochemicals markets. Prachai, the country's first petrochemicals producer, resented that Siam Cement had earlier broken his monopoly. He convinced the Chatichai cabinet to license him to produce cement and aggressively went after

Siam Cement's customers. He also got special preferences over Siam Cement in new petrochemicals ventures. Other companies were likewise favored over Siam Cement in new steel and telecommunications developments. Sometimes Chatichai just disregarded palace interests. His government backed a mass transit plan known as the Hopewell project, whose elevated trains would run high in the air just past Chitrlada Palace and other important royal sites. This broke specific encroachment rules that protected the sanctity of the royal environment. The palace took umbrage and its supporters among the bureaucracy refused to cooperate with Hopewell.[1]

The Chatichai government also repudiated the idea of the army's predominant sociopolitical role. The prime minister moved to reduce the power of the appointed senate, which remained dominated by the armed forces, police, and conservative bureaucrats. While he couldn't reduce the number of senators overall, Chatichai wanted to have the parliamentary president come automatically from the house, rather than the senate as was the case. Since the president of parliament made the nomination of the prime minister to the king, a key role would be shifted away from the old establishment to elected politicians.

After eight years of Prem's hyperpromotion, Bhumibol's personal image was invulnerable to all this. But it felt like the beginning of the end of an era. In valedictory speeches the king and queen reminded listeners of all their past works and achievements, all that they had done for the people. The king received more honors, like the 1988 Ramon Magsaysay Award, Asia's most prestigious accolade. In 1990, Harvard University named a city square after him and in 1989, with the death of Prince Franz-Josef II of Liechtenstein, Bhumibol became the world's longest-reigning living monarch. In parallel, his own personal spiritual mentor, Somdej Phra Yanasangworn, rose to the zenith of the Buddhist clergy in 1989, when he was named supreme patriarch. This was the culmination of a path set when he first counseled the young Bhumibol in 1955.

The physical monumentalization of the Ninth Reign was under way as well. There was the ongoing expansion of Wat Yanasangwararam in Chonburi. In Bangkok the government built a huge new city park named for the king, with an exhibition hall of his projects. A major new road was christened Rama IX and the adjacent swamp, on a tract owned by the Crown Property Bureau, became Rama IX Lake. The king had the land developed as a cohesive community around a temple and school named for him. Yanasangworn's secretary became its abbot.

Another monument of sorts was the huge retreat built by the army for the king's mother, Sangwal, on Doi Tung mountain in Chiangrai. Doi Tung became a memorial to the royal family's care for the northern Thai hill tribes and the environment, and to Bhumibol's cooperative development ideals. Some 37,000 acres of surrounding mountain and valley land was appended to the estate, despite the land being already occupied by 27 hill-tribe villages, many there for generations. But none of the residents had title to their lands, and few had Thai citizenship. Instead they were blamed for destroying the area through slash-and-burn cultivation, illegal logging, and opium production. In fact many belonged to permanent settlements growing small crops of their own food and products to sell in area markets.

With government and palace funds, Doi Tung was turned into a large cooperative farm and community run by Sangwal's foundation, with tree plantations, fruit and nut orchards, and cash crops of vegetables and flowers. As employees the hill tribes enjoyed better schools, health care, and incomes, their products all marketed by the royal projects operations. Wearing shiny new traditional-styled outfits as they picked about the gardens, the hill tribes also became guides for tourists to Doi Tung, reverently explaining how the princess mother and her son had saved the area and its people from themselves. Over several years the project quadrupled in size to take in the entire mountain and surrounding valleys, like an old feudal estate. In Sangwal's honor in 1990, the army declared it would plant 90 million trees around the country, declaring her the protector of the environment of a country she had been absent from most of her adult life.

King Bhumibol adjusted his team to deal with the shift to an elected leader. He made Prem the de facto head of the privy council, in lieu of the infirm Sanya Dhammasakdi. Simultaneously, he awarded Prem the title of senior statesman, the same as Pridi had received after the war, allowing Prem to stay involved in politics. After a few years he also named Siddhi and Pichit Kullavanich, both cohorts of Prem, to the council. Together with Prem's former minister Chirayut Israngkul, manager of the Crown Property Bureau, and another new privy councilor, Seni Pramoj's son M.L. Usni, they became the core defenders of Bhumibol's royalism against Chatichai secularism.

This team was charged with readying the king's children for a transition. They renewed efforts to shape Crown Prince Vajiralongkorn into monarch material, giving him an expanded slate of duties and foreign missions to get exposure to other world leaders. He represented Thailand at Emperor Hirohito's funeral in Tokyo in February 1989, partly making up for the fracas over his visit 17 months earlier. Within Thailand, the prince represented the king at more sacral and civil ceremonies, and during 1988–89 he bestowed the king's personal Buddha statues to 31 provincial seats. His family problems seemed to subside. Sucharinee gained a grudging acceptance by involving herself in social development activities. Her children moved to the Chitrlada school, bringing them openly into the court atmosphere. Their royal status was underscored when the government built elementary schools named for each.

The prince seemed on track when he agreed to attend Britain's highly respected Royal College of Defence Studies during 1990. The course was intended to broaden the world vision of those destined for military and political leadership. They would study global politics, economics, and security issues, with briefings by many top international officials. The British made special efforts to keep him apace with his brighter classmates, but after a time he began to slip, not doing all the work. Things turned bad at midyear when he invited several classmates to Thailand on holiday. He was peeved when they continued to call him by his first name—in the style of the academy—rather than treat him as the crown prince. They, in turn, were said to be put off by his offerings of women as part of the entertainment.

During the second half of the school year, the students made study tours to various countries where they were hosted by the local military. One group went to Thailand and discovered that the prince remained unhappy over the earlier visit. In Bangkok their travel plans and accommodations had been downgraded without notice. At the end of the study tour, a military reception put on by the British embassy was boycotted by the Thai brass. The prince had ordered them to stay away.[2] Nevertheless, the prince returned at the end of 1990 a supposedly more mature and knowledgeable future leader. He was rewarded accordingly. On the queen's birthday in August 1991, the official Mother's Day, Somsawali's official title was reduced in stature by the king, from "royal consort" to "mother of the king's grandchild."

The prince's two younger sisters also went through something of an image refurbishment. Sirindhorn was the workhorse royal, also making diplomatic trips and handling minor appearances on her father's behalf, without overshadowing the prince. More plump and jovial than ever, she remained highly popular, even in neighboring Laos, which she visited in early 1990. For each of her frequent trips abroad, she published one or two books of notes and cute sketches, which were sold to raise funds for her charities and expand her popularity.

Princess Chulabhorn, on the other hand, still couldn't get things right. Her parents saw her as the royal family's scientist and wanted international recognition. In the late 1980s they even asked King Carl Gustaf of Sweden, in Thailand on a private holiday, to arrange for Chulabhorn to be awarded the Nobel Prize. They were apparently surprised and disappointed to be told that the Swedish king had no such power.

Much to her credit, in 1989 Chulabhorn boldly spoke out on the rapidly growing AIDS problem in Thailand, which Prem had refused to acknowledge. That led to her being named a goodwill ambassador for the World Health Organization's AIDS campaign. Her Chulabhorn Research Institute was designated host of an international scientific congress on the disease scheduled for Bangkok in late 1990. For a moment, she began to garner for herself and the Thai monarchy an international humanitarian image akin to that of Princess Diana, who had also joined the global campaign against AIDS. But Chulabhorn couldn't handle the job. First she balked at physically embracing an AIDS patient. Then WHO withdrew its support for the Bangkok conference, because Thailand refused to admit HIV-infected people into the country.[3] It led to Chulabhorn resigning her WHO position and again receding from public view.

If the throne's prestige wasn't increasing via the activities of the king's children, its finances were growing strongly. With the economy expanding at more than 10 percent annually, and the Thai stock market one of the world's best performers, palace assets and discretionary income grew exponentially. A soaring real estate market kept Siam Cement's building-materials factories running at full capacity year after year, and made real estate owned by the CPB and the royal family highly valuable.

Palace money manager Chirayut aggressively sought to develop as much as possible, directly and by leasing CPB real estate to developers in return for a share of rentals and equity returns. CPB property came to include everything from small restaurants to luxury condominiums, shopping complexes, hotels, and office towers. In one of the most ambitious plans, the royal family leased a 14-acre mid-city plot to an old Sino-Thai banking family, the Tejapaibuls, who planned a multibillion-dollar shopping, office, and hotel complex that would dwarf anything else in Asia, called the World Trade Center. After ignoring the Tejapaibuls' responsibility for the collapse of two banks just a few years earlier, the palace would reap the consequences several years later when they defaulted on the property.

New property leases increased CPB income by tens of millions of dollars per year, while generating a lot of business for the CPB-controlled Siam Commercial Bank, and related stockbroking and finance companies, which had preference for any CPB-related deals. In addition, between the Siam Cement Group companies, altogether some 35 subsidiaries and associates, and another two dozen CPB and privy purse companies ranging from farming to insurance to hotels and office machines, dividends accruing to the palace and the Mahidol family reached $30– 40 million a year by 1990, tax-free. By market value of their listed companies alone the Mahidols were worth more than $1 billion.

The palace used much of this income to expand its stake in the economy. Foreign investors lined up at Chirayut's door to propose partnerships. He chose to be a minority investment partner with companies like the Japanese electronics maker Minebea, Toshiba in television tubes, and Michelin for tires. Chirayut said the bureau did not want to be seen as competing with private capital, adding that in important projects like infrastructure, it could be "a good bridge between the public sector and the private sector."[4] Like many middle- and upper-class Thais, the Mahidols also personally invested in Thai stocks, according to people in the business. Even King Bhumibol traded shares, apparently more out of curiosity than pursuit of profit. One executive moaned privately on hearing the news that the king had bought 500 shares of his company. This meant unwanted pressure to demonstrate that it was doing good for society, he felt.

The economic boom brought more money into the royal charities as well. This proved advantageous when Chatichai's government stumbled, allowing the king to recapture the moral high ground and reinforce his argument that elected government was hopeless. The opportunity came with a series of natural disasters, the first only a few months after Chatichai took office. At the end of November 1988 violent storms caused massive floods and hundreds of deaths in the south. While the government and military undertook extensive relief efforts, more attention and credit went to the king's Rajaprachanugroh disaster relief group.

In early November 1989, the south was struck by another storm, Typhoon Gay, with a death toll of 450. Poorly informed, Chatichai brushed it off as a minor disaster. Before he could correct himself, King Bhumibol summoned him to the palace for what everyone understood as a rebuke. It showed that while the king watched over his people, the top politicians did not. Again, the palace's well-funded operations plunged into the relief effort and got most of the credit, despite the larger government rescue operations. Taking a page from her father's book, Princess Chulabhorn had her eponymous donor-funded foundation help restore villages and their livestock and fisheries operations, on the basis of cooperatives. The schools in a number of them were then named after her.[5]

The palace's work wasn't without problem. The disasters' severity, especially from flooding, stemmed in part from extensive logging of southern uplands. This gave impetus to environmental activist groups in their campaign to restrict log-ging. They assumed that because the poor were the most hurt by the disasters, then the king must agree with them on the need for stricter environmental protection. This set the king in a difficult position, which he recognized. He did agree on deforestation. But he strongly supported the building of large dams and reservoirs for development, and these were opposed by the same organizations that were against deforestation. They had led the defeat of the Nam Choan dam two years earlier. Bhumibol used his annual birthday speech in December 1989 to clarify his stance: in contrast with himself, he painted the environmental activists as essen-tially opposed to the people's good.[6]

In the talk he first asserted his superior understanding of the environment, ex-plaining the greenhouse effect and the global warming problem. He then pointed out that coal-fired power plants contributed to the greenhouse effect, while dams were clean and allowed Thailand independence from imported fuels. Referring without name to Nam Choan, he asked whether it was better to import coal for power plants or to cut a few trees in order to build a hydroelectric dam, which could also irrigate a lot of farmland. "The practical way is to keep and improve all the good things we have, like forests and water resources, and minimize all the bad things, like ignorance and pollution," he said.

The king was branding the environmentalists as impractical and uninformed, worse than loggers. He distorted some important facts: the environmentalists didn't advocate more coal plants; nor did Thailand import much coal, for it had its own deposits. But the facts didn't matter: he was attacking the environmentalists, and they took his comments hard. One of their leaders afterward said they had to muzzle themselves for months so they wouldn't be seen as contradicting the inviolate king and be charged with lèse-majesté.[7]

As Chatichai's cabinet continued to bicker and fumble, the supreme commander and army commander Chavalit and the deputy army commander Suchinda both tried to exploit the palace's discontent, each hoping to become another Prem. When in August 1989 Chatichai adviser Sukhumbhand countered their criticisms by saying that the military should clean up its own house and be depoliticized, Chavalit and Suchinda amassed some 1,000 officers in a menacing, drunken rally in a central Bangkok hotel. To ward off the threat of yet another army coup, Chatichai had Sukhumbhand resign and named Chavalit defense minister. Seeing it as a stepping-stone to the premiership, Chavalit retired from the military and took the job. Replacing him as supreme commander was General Sunthorn Kongsompong, a corrupt, pliable playboy.

The Machiavellian Suchinda then moved up to army commander, the real power in the military. Behind him was Chulachomklao Military Academy's Class 5, the most cohesive, ambitious, and corrupt class the school had ever produced. They plotted their rise together in the ranks by canny politicking, though always staying on Prem's side and in the queen's court. They operated as a highly unified political party and investment club, with their cooperative investments, stock trading, graft, and other operations making each member a millionaire in U.S. dollars by the late 1980s.

In his new job, Suchinda proved far more menacing to the government than Chavalit had. He brought his Class 5 mates along with him: four of the five top generals were from this group, setting them up to dominate the military for the next five years. In March 1990, Suchinda warned that he would not suffer any interference in military affairs from politicians. He also refused to swear off a coup. When some parliamentarians leveled accusations of military corruption, Suchinda replied threateningly that it wasn't their business. But then when Chavalit was criticized in parliament as corrupt and his wheeler-dealer wife called a "walking jewelry case," Suchinda cut short a visit to Singapore to take Chavalit and Chatichai into a hastily arranged meeting with Prem. The impression was that Prem, and Bhumibol by extension, were being asked to force Chatichai to resign and turn over power to a general, just like Prem's royally assisted coup in 1980. Chatichai refused to step down, and went to see the king himself. What transpired wasn't made public, but he emerged still holding the premiership. Chavalit resigned from the cabinet in a huff, and the next day soldiers in several cities held marches in his support. It took a few days before the fear of a coup waned.

No one was certain how to interpret the palace's position. While some people concluded that King Bhumibol had sided with the principles of democracy, there was other speculation that, although he was ready to trade Chatichai for another military-dominated government, he was wary of Chavalit's own strange political ideas.[8] A coup wasn't the problem; Chavalit was.

The game continued to focus on support from the king and his agent Prem. To secure his position, Chatichai named three Prem and palace associates to the cabinet in August 1990: economic adviser Virabongsa Ramangkura, Amaret Silaon, a former executive of Siam Cement, and police general Vasit Dejkunchorn, the king's personal aide of nearly two decades. Chavalit, snubbed by the palace, took the route of forming a political party, hoping the next elections would propel him to power. Suchinda, however, continued to agitate and menace the government. When Chatichai went abroad in November, Suchinda declared his control of capital security and banned demonstrations. Then the army demanded that Chatichai fire another government critic of the military. Fearing a coup, on his return Chatichai went directly to see King Bhumibol in the provinces. Right behind him was Suchinda. When they emerged with nothing specific to say, it again was read as the king's continuing support for elected government and against coups.

But when Bhumibol returned to Bangkok on December 2 for his birthday celebrations, that wasn't so apparent. Greeted at the airport by the regular phalanx of political leaders, military brass, and 400 Village Scouts, he said that the military and the government should unite for the common good and sort out conflicts through dialogue, taking into account the national interest and people's welfare. It was a neutral statement on the surface. But by not rebuking the generals for their coup threats, not telling them to return to the barracks, the king's word stood as a tentative endorsement of their gripes.

The next day Bhumibol and his family made their annual review of the palace guard, with the military leadership and Chatichai, in his capacity as defense minister, in the grandstand. The military-controlled TV cameras covering the event refused to show Chatichai, while highlighting the presence together of the royal family and the generals. Again the king seemed to give them his favor: "The military should . . . use its knowledge to its utmost in developing the country. . . . The military has done a good job in upholding the liberty and sovereignty of the country."

In sharp contrast were the direct criticisms Bhumibol made of the Chatichai government in his birthday address the next day. He responded to Chatichai's salutation praising the king for guiding the country with a rebuke. Bhumibol thanked the prime minister and then remonstrated, "Nobody can do everything alone. . . . The king at present does not carry the duty to run the country. He has someone else do it." His tone and phrasing implied disappointment with Chatichai as the king's servant.[9]

Bhumibol then suggested that modern, Western-style elected government was not as good as traditional Thai forms. Urgent problems required flexibility, not adherence to "theoretical principles," his referent for modern governmental procedure. His own charities and royal projects were superior, because they are not slowed by "western accounting methods." He criticized the government for not having built dikes and canals that would have prevented recent monsoon floods in the central provinces. The government's textbook solutions and principles exacerbated the damage, Bhumibol said.

The audience and the media understood that Chatichai's support in the palace had sharply deteriorated. All the players began to jockey for position. Chavalit recruited a Prem cohort, national security specialist Prasong Soonsiri, into his New Aspiration Party. Not yet a privy councilor, Siddhi Savetsila pulled his Social Action Party out of the governing coalition, as did the Democrats. To survive, Chatichai joined his Chart Thai with other parties, including the very small one led by the retired general Arthit, who became deputy prime minister. At the same time—baring the convolutions of Thai military factionalism—Chatichai rehabilitated the erstwhile 1980s coup maker Manoon Roopkachorn, promoting him to general and giving him a top Defense Ministry job.

The Class 5 clique was outraged, and Prem and the king were probably taken aback as well. For Suchinda this affront justified a coup, but a premise had to be engineered nonetheless. In January 1991, the Class 5 police general Boonchu Wongkanont, who had a long, ugly history as an effective hatchet man—on behalf of Prem and the palace, he took care of the Mae Chamoy chit fund scandal—suddenly revived the 1984 case of the alleged Young Turk-CPT plot to assassinate the queen, Prem, and Arthit. Despite the palace's intervention at that time to have the case dismissed, it was dredged up again, ostensibly on the throne's behalf. When Chatichai reacted by transferring Boonchu, Suchinda and his allies accused the prime minister of protecting people who had tried to kill the queen. On February 23, while Chatichai waited for a plane to go see the king in Chiangmai, he was seized by air force commandos and held while the military calmly established a new government. The next day Suchinda met with King Bhumibol, after which he announced that the king had blessed the coup, only instructing the generals to "not let the people down."

There was no way to tell whether King Bhumibol had truly approved yet another military takeover, and, as it had many times before, this ambiguity protected his image. But the fact was, by setting himself and Prem out as arbiters between the generals and Chatichai, the king had left the door open for a coup for many months. He and Prem made it clear that a military takeover was an acceptable alternative in modern Thai politics. And after a year of seeing Chatichai running to the king at every threat from Suchinda, the public was inured to the idea. Many blamed Chatichai himself when it finally happened. King Bhumibol's own view became unmistakable months later when he ridiculed Chatichai's cabinet as "comic."[10]

Nor did Bhumibol intervene, as his constitutional powers allowed, to trump the situation by dissolving the parliament. That would have maintained a semblance of constitutionalism by forcing elections. Protecting the constitution and the democratic process apparently wasn't high priority in the palace.

The new junta followed the script of earlier takeovers. This one named itself the National Peace-Keeping Committee, "peace" being the translation of khwam ria-proy, or social order. Supreme Commander Sunthorn was the NPKC chairman, but the Class 5 generals Suchinda, Kaset Rojananil, and Issarapong Noonpakdi held the real power. They dissolved parliament, abrogated the constitution, and formed their own national assembly of 292 military officers and sympathetic or obedient bureaucrats, businessmen, and academics. The head of the assembly was Ukrit Mongkolnavin, a lawyer and veteran of appointed legislatures from Thanom to Tanin to Prem, whom he had supported for five years as president of parliament. His wife was close to the queen and enjoyed the highest non-royal title, thanphuying. As the newspaper *Nation* branded the new assembly "a return to the sorry past," Ukrit was assigned by the NPKC to draft a new constitution.

The generals made well-practiced paeans to nation, religion, and king. They televised a supposed confession by one of the queen's assassination plot members, which much later was exposed as coerced and false. They accused Chatichai of taking the country toward a "parliamentary dictatorship," without saying what that was or why it was bad.[11] They put Chatichai and 24 other members of the former government under investigation for corruption. The NPKC also clamped down on potential critics, including allies of Chavalit, who was left out of the new power equation. They outlawed the state enterprise unions, threatened the press, and menaced the political opposition, students, academics, and social activists. Underscoring the point, state enterprise union leader Thanong Po-arn mysteriously disappeared, never to be found. And the activist Sulak Sivaraks, who made a speech attacking the junta, was accused by the generals of lèse-majesté, on the principle that the king had endorsed Suchinda. It was a twist on Sulak's own charge that the NPKC coup was an offense against the crown. Facing arrest, Sulak fled to Europe.

Suchinda was popular in the court, particularly among the women, for his suave good looks and manner. But he was no Prem, so to gain the king's confidence Suchinda named as prime minister a palace-favored civilian, Anand Panyarachun.

A disciplined, no-nonsense former diplomat and business leader with an unstained career, Anand had the respect of both the bureaucracy and mainstream industry. Although well acquainted with the palace, he had mostly steered clear of the court and high society. He also had avoided the military ever since right-wing militarists branded him a leftist in the 1970s. So while he disdained corrupt politicians like those filling Chatichai's government, he also had no love for the generals.

Anand put a good face on the junta and took government back toward the king's ideal. His cabinet mixed Prem-era technocrats with a handful of NPKC generals. They implemented a long roster of needed reforms, from banking regulation to taxes to rural administration, which the bureaucracy and politicians had stifled or just ignored. The generals lifted martial law after a few weeks, allowing print media to continue fairly uncensored and critical. More important to them anyway were radio and television, both of which were tightly controlled. As economic growth surged, many inside the palace and out could believe this was the ideal government for Thailand: the discipline and orderliness of the military and the selfless work of technocrats, watched over by a caring king.

But it wasn't permanent. Anand made his job contingent on the NPKC putting through a new constitution and holding fresh elections by April 1992. It was what he wanted, and also necessary to placate the large segment of the public that was unhappy about the coup, not to mention critical foreign governments. The NPKC men proved as corrupt as the politicians they ousted, interfering with many initiatives and projects to make sure they benefited financially. In the corruption investigation of Chatichai's government, half of those accused were cleared for lack of evidence, including Banharn Silpa-archa, the longtime Prem backer and arguably the most corrupt of all. Evidence was found only against ministers who resisted the NPKC, including Chatichai and his top aide. With Chatichai removed, Banharn became the leader of the Chart Thai Party, which he lined up behind the NPKC.[12]

The generals in the junta also turned a massive rural development program into a money grab for their cronies. Soon after coming to office, they announced a program to resolve all the problems of rural landlessness and encroachment on protected forests, issues that had occupied the king's attention for decades. In its first phase, the army-run program, Khor Jor Kor, was going to resettle more than 1.2 million people in the northeast to permanent homes with their own farmland. In the longer term, they planned to similarly relocate 10 million people around the country.[13] As with Chavalit's Green Isan, they declared they were doing the king's will. "The military's land distribution project is in line with his majesty the king's wish to help the poor in reserve forests by giving them a legal status and security in their lives. At the same time, the project will save forests from destruction," they said.[14]

Very quickly it proved to be something else: an eviction program to clear peasants from degraded forests and hand the land over for corporate plantations, mostly growing eucalyptus trees for pulp factories. People who had been promised years earlier that they could stay on the land, and even villages with decades of history, were forced to move. In most cases the army didn't have any new land or homes to provide them, and failed to deliver promised food and supplies. When an activist monk led villagers to resist peacefully, the army trucked in a mob of toughs to attack them, and the monk was arrested.

After six months most Thais realized the NPKC was just another group of old-style crooked generals. Yet King Bhumibol, who had taken ample opportunity in 1989–90 to criticize Chatichai's government over the peasants' welfare and various government programs, remained completely silent about the NPKC. The NPKC meanwhile made grand displays of support for the monarchy. At each royal anniversary they put on big shows and joined in private parties at the palace. When Princess Sirindhorn reached her third-cycle, 36th birthday in April, the Chulachomklao Military Academy had 117 cadets ordained into the monkhood by the supreme patriarch Yanasangworn in her honor.

The air force presented the crown prince with his own F-16A jet. (Not qualified to fly it himself, he used it to jet around the country with another pilot.) Then, at the start of 1992, the junta promoted the prince to four-star general, admiral, and air chief marshal, as well as making him commander of the directorate of the royal guards. It gave Vajiralongkorn more military stature, though he remained under the orders of the supreme commander.[15] In February 1992, Suchinda donated nearly four acres of army-owned land to the prince's suburban Nonthaburi palace.[16]

By mid-1991 there were signs that the generals intended to remain in power after the 1992 elections, and that Suchinda eyed the premiership for himself. In September, Sunthorn retired and Suchinda added to his army chief post the supreme commander job. Around him Class 5 men locked in all the key military commands. Air force chief Kaset assembled a new political party, Sammakitham (Unity in Dhamma), and formed an alliance with Chart Thai, which accepted into the party leadership another extremely corrupt air force general, Somboon Rahong. In November Kaset called outright for a military man to become prime minister, implying Suchinda or himself. Pressed by reporters, however, Suchinda pledged on camera that he would not use the NPKC springboard to take the premiership.

The drafting of a new constitution became the battleground between the junta and its opponents. The generals wanted something like the 1978 charter, establishing a privileged position for the military for an interim period—the arrangement that Prem had attempted to make permanent. Also as in 1978, the senate's powers and size would be expanded to allow it control over government work with the support of only one medium-sized party in the lower house. There was little doubt that Kaset's Sammakitham would be able to fill that role. The senate would be chosen by the NPKC, and the senate would take part in choosing the prime minister, who didn't have to stand for election. The senate head would be parliament president, responsible for nominating the prime minister. The cabinet would be open to serving government officials like themselves, so someone like Suchinda could remain army chief, not stand for election, and become prime minister even if the majority of the lower house opposed him.

What it meant was easily sustained control of the government by the NPKC and the Class 5 generals for years to come. There was widespread outrage when the draft was passed unanimously in its first reading by the military-dominated assembly. On November 19 at least 50,000 people protested at Sanam Luang, the largest public political protest since 1976. The draft was so one-sided that Prime Minister Anand, after the second reading passed, expressed his disappointment and encouraged the public to fight. As November ended, media attacks on the NPKC were bolder and students began to mobilize.

King Bhumibol, for most of the year, had remained in the background without comment. He regularly met Anand and Suchinda for consultation but kept to his annual roster of rituals and his family. As tensions over the draft constitution mounted, though, he made some purposively timed statements. On November 5, he addressed newly promoted military and police officers, in the traditional ceremony where they swore allegiance to him. The men at the front of the group were almost exclusively from Class 5. The king told them to reject criticism that, with the end of the Indochina wars, the armed forces should be cut back in size. "This is just a concept," the king said, ridiculing the idea; besides fighting the war and achieving peace, the armed forces had brought progress and contentment to the people. This, the king said, is their continuing duty, and they were following it without fault.

Bhumibol's clear endorsement of the generals fell on deaf ears outside the palace. As the final reading of the constitution neared on December 7, public opposition intensified and Bangkok grew jittery over the possibility of a clash in the streets. In response, King Bhumibol intervened more deliberately on the generals' behalf. In doing so he made the most explicit ever statement of his political beliefs, revealing that they had not changed since the Sarit coup of 1958. In his annual birthday-eve speech on December 4, he referred to democratic principles as simply highbrow ideals that could weaken society. He made clear that he thought little of constitutions. Viewed through Buddhist lenses, they were impermanent, always mutable, and not worth fighting over. He also contended that it was not the NPKC that was provoking a fight, but their opponents. He did this in a typically rambling, hour-long soliloquy, weaving from one thought to another in the vague manner of an elderly monk sermonizing on dhamma. Bhumibol had decades of practice in this technique, and he made his point with calculation and precision.[17]

He began by saying he would speak "in contravention with academic principle" on some issues, which he didn't name. His bottom line was what protects the "standard of living of the Thai people, how to give them peace and security, have safety and live under a fair and just government." The problem, he said, is that Thailand has adopted some inappropriate ideas from foreign countries. "Procedures or principles that we have imported for use are sometimes not suitable to the conditions of Thailand or the character of Thai people."

The kingdom needed to be unified for it to survive. In this case unity meant compromise, "accepting the acceptable," even if it isn't 100 percent perfect. Nothing is perfect, he said, and so "we must use what we have available" for unity and national survival. Indeed, countries that hold out for perfection in their principles, which don't compromise over them, can rupture. "It is evident in the past three years that several countries in the world established on the basis of idealist theories of government have collapsed." He then asked, "Is Thailand going to collapse too?"

King Bhumibol digressed to a story meant to illustrate that Thailand's home-grown way of doing things—if fact, the king's way—was superior. He called this "the poor man's way," in which sacrifice came before the payoff, and bureaucratic rules and principled ideals weren't allowed to block progress. His own royal projects were the example of this idea, which he called "our loss is our gain." Indeed, he said, doing things the way rich foreign countries do would be bad. "We have enough, enough to live. We don't want to be a very advanced country. If we become a very advanced country, then we can only go backwards. Countries such as this, that have advanced industry, are just going backwards. . . . However, if we have a 'poor-man' style of administrative system, that is, not too attached to dogmatic theory, but which has unity and mutual kindness, then we can survive forever."

The essential problem was constitutions, as was clear from the example of the United States, the king said. In New York City, he pointed out, the state welfare system pays people for not working, so people have no incentive to work. These are useless to society and to themselves. But this is the law: "It is their right, according to the American constitution, to receive welfare if they don't have a job," he said. "If we adhered to a law like that, it would waste our budget."

In contrast, his own royal projects proved the wisdom of avoiding "foreign-imported" principles. By being more agile, sometimes at a higher cost and with less official discipline, his operations help the people more effectively than the government by avoiding bureaucratic process and delay. This allows the people to reap benefits more quickly, within a year in the example he gave. "They will have income. So at the end of that year there is no need to give them welfare. . . . Real economic principles are like this," he said. Moreover, the people who donate to the royal projects, when they see the successes, readily donate more. It was a magically meritorious circle, in which a "loss" becomes a "gain."

So that there would be no misunderstanding, Bhumibol suddenly dropped the opacity and said he would address an unnamed current issue. He didn't mention the constitution. He first noted, in a long, twisting analogy, that anyone could be chosen to speak for the people, and it wasn't really important whether it was the community's eldest person or the one with the highest academic degree, or the prime minister or the president of parliament, or even the supreme commander. It didn't matter who represented the people, actually. Thailand simply has a system of the prime minister being the leader. "So we set up a system like this, having the prime minister be the one to speak. I am not sure if this can be considered democratic," Bhumibol added.[18]

Whoever it was would be fine; the people can decide on one national representative, on one system. "The current practice is acceptable," the king said. "If a change is desired for next year, that can be done; just make a resolution together and it can be changed. I will accept the resolution, and it can be changed. Whatever rules there are can be changed. It is not permanent; it can be changed. Just don't fight, don't fight to the point of spilling blood."

This was the king's main point. He found the current constitution fine, and any problems could be changed later. In fact, Bhumibol argued, other countries frequently change their rules, and don't always hold dogmatically to them. Again invoking the United States, he noted that, even with a principled system of quadrennial presidential elections, "it has happened that they have had a coup d'etat. . . . A president and a vice president who weren't elected were able to be president and vice president. It was a change that was not according to procedures." This was a remarkable interpretation of the Nixon Watergate resignation, but it served the king's point: even in the model democracy, leaders didn't bind themselves to highbrow principles and rules.

The king still avoided the word "constitution" (except in reference to the American welfare issue), as if it showed he was keeping his distance from politics, maintaining a dhammaraja's aloofness to mundane issues and biases. He summed up: "So change can take place. But it must happen without fighting, to the point of crushing heads and spilling blood. I speak like this because at present we have a headache over, 'will we change it or not change it?,' or, 'adopt it or don't adopt it?' Or 'adopt it and then change it?' or 'change it and then adopt it?' I don't know what is desired . . . if it works well, then stick with it; if it doesn't work well, it doesn't work smoothly, it can be changed. . . . and opening the way to change it is not difficult."

Change was easy, and, in fact, according to higher principles, "higher than textbook dogma," change was inevitable and nothing was permanent. Constitutions, in the king's view, were all but irrelevant, symbolic of the Buddhist truth of *anicca,* the impermanence of all things but the dhamma. Meanwhile, "If unity is not practiced today, there is no tomorrow."

Even couched in his mildly cryptic manner of speaking, everyone understood that the king was endorsing the NPKC constitution. The next day most newspapers had headlines akin to the *Bangkok Post*'s: "King calls for compromise on charter." In parliament, the weak opposition gave up and, three days later, the charter passed by 262–7. Even the pro-democracy activists in parliament voted for it. Such was the force of the king's words, backed by threats from the junta. It was an overwhelming defeat for the democracy movement.

While Bhumibol spoke from general principle, it was clear he had examined the draft constitution in some detail. The palace had certainly discussed clauses involving the king's own prerogatives, and the NPKC made minor adjustments in his powers at his request, for instance increasing the number of privy councilors to 19 from 16 (to have enough new blood to span the eventual succession).

Yet, as the democracy movement knew, he was wholly incorrect about one crucial aspect of the fight. He said the constitution would be readily changeable. But the way the draft was written, the military retained the ability to easily defeat any amendment they disagreed with. Change would not be possible for at least several years.

18   May 1992: October 1976 Redux   ❧

KING BHUMIBOL'S INTERVENTION ON BEHALF of the NPKC constitution meant Suchinda and the generals of Class 5 would be able to control government for years. With changing the constitution nearly impossible, their opponents in the democracy movement could do nothing but prepare for the elections. Already the big parties were in full gear as 1992 opened, spending heavily to buy members of parliament and the public's votes. The main question was whether Suchinda would take the premiership for himself or allow someone else to warm the seat first.

To dominate the March 22 polls, the NPKC-controlled Sammakitham and Chart Thai parties both shamelessly courted the most powerful and corrupt politicians in the country to join them. Sammakitham recruited as party leader the northern Thailand mafioso-politician Narong Wongwan, patron of a large bloc of MPs. Allied by their opposition to NPKC power, but not much else, were Chavalit's New Aspiration, the Democrats led by Chuan Leekpai, and Bangkok governor Chamlong Srimuang's Palang Dharma. The three campaigned on the need for greater democracy and less military control, stressing that the prime minister should come from among the elected MPs. That put the focus on noncandidate Suchinda, who still denied wanting the job.

Before the election results were known, the NPKC named the new senate. As expected, it was filled with military and police officers. Only 116 of 270 senators were civilians, mostly businessmen and bureaucrats with ties to the military. In a meeting with them at the Supreme Command a week after the election, Suchinda instructed them to vote with one voice—presumably the same as his own.[1]

In the lower house election, the generals' parties barely came out on top. That evening, NPKC chiefs Sunthorn and Kaset summoned the leaders of Sammaki-tham, Chart Thai, Social Action, and veteran rightist Samak Sunthornvej's small Prachakorn Thai to air force headquarters to form a government. The *Nation* wrote that the meeting before military leaders, as well as the location, were "un-becoming of important political leaders in a democratic system. It sent the generals a message that they could continue to interfere in the parliamentary system at will."[2]

The parties nominated Sammakitham's Narong for prime minister. Three days later, the U.S. embassy let on that Narong had earlier been denied a visa for suspicion of involvement in heroin trafficking. It fit Narong's reputation and his huge, unaccountable fortune. Now with a convenient excuse, on April 3 the NPKC generals and the party leaders substituted Suchinda as nominee. Many people believed Narong's nomination had been Suchinda's clever subterfuge. Still, even if it was long anticipated, Suchinda's nomination came as almost a second coup. As the four opposition parties attacked the government, students draped the Democracy Monument in black to symbolize the death of democracy. But there wasn't much else they could do. On April 7, General Sunthorn and Arthit Urairat, the new speaker of the lower house, submitted Suchinda's name to the king. Absolving himself, Arthit insisted that Sunthorn made the nomination alone as NPKC chairman. Ignoring the public outcry, King Bhumibol signed off on Suchinda's appointment.

The next day, the former Democratic MP Chalard Vorachart sat down in front of parliament and announced a fast to the death if Suchinda refused to step down. Chalard, who years before had undertaken a similar protest against Prem, ignited the opposition. Other activists immediately joined him in fasting, even as they endured harassment and threats by Red Gaur-type toughs.

The protesters' numbers grew daily, and when on April 16 parliament opened, the opposition could be seen on national television wearing black in protest. The next day the new cabinet roster said much about Suchinda's view of himself as a new Prem. While retaining the defense portfolio for himself and naming several Class 5 generals and allies in key positions, he chose technocrat veterans of the Prem and Anand governments for the main economic policy posts. The cabinet included 11 MPs from the Chatichai government whom the NPKC had accused of corruption. It also included political scientist Thinnapan Nakata, a political adviser to Prem for eight years who, sounding much like the king, insisted that neither elected politicians nor the bureaucracy worked effectively for the people. Just before joining Suchinda's cabinet he said he did not believe in fussing over the principles and methods of democracy. The focus should be the people's quality of life, not theory. "Democratic theorists must think of principles that are people-oriented. . . . [I am] for the majority of the people. The royal institution is also for the majority of the people."[3]

With more than 40 hunger strikers now together with Chalard, on April 20 the opposition political parties organized an anti-Suchinda protest of 50,000 people in front of parliament. Chuan and Chavalit demanded constitutional amendments that would require an elected prime minister, give greater power to the lower house, and shrink the senate. Although the government prohibited broadcast media from reporting the rally, the newspapers were full of the controversial events. Chalard finally collapsed on April 30 and was sent unconscious to a hospital. He lived, and the protesters began to run out of gas.

A presumed last big rally against Suchinda was organized for Sanam Luang on May 4, the day before the Coronation Day holiday. That evening about 60,000 Thais listened to opposition politicians and activists denounce the military and Suchinda, and demand the constitutional amendments. The demonstrators were peaceful and appeared resigned that the fight would be consigned to parliamentary politics as in the Prem years. Then everything changed, when Palang Dharma leader Chamlong read his melodramatic "last letter from Chamlong Srimuang." He declared that he too was going on a hunger strike, but unlike Chalard he would take only water and no glucose or other aids. "I have considered it thoroughly and decided to put my life on the line. . . . If I have to leave the world in a few days, I will not regret it. Goodbye." The crowd was deeply moved, and the government and the palace were shocked. Chamlong, a Class 7 graduate of Chulachomklao Military Academy who now lived a fairly ascetic life, was seen by some critics as bizarre and eccentric, while others considered him a potent demagogue. His declaration of a fast to the death seemed to confirm to the establishment that he had a very non-Thai way of thinking and acting.[4]

During Coronation Day rites the next day, as was customary, the king gave an audience to the top members of government and awarded royal decorations to 120 public figures. Leading the list were most of the members of the NPKC and their wives, which many in the pro-democracy camp called an insult. That evening, at a garden party at Government House, the atmosphere was edgy and defensive.

Suchinda told reporters menacingly, "It's not difficult to gather a mass of people. I can gather five million tomorrow. Do you want to see that?"[5]

The government tried to stifle Chamlong's challenge by censoring media reports. Television reported only on cabinet ministers and a senior monk criticizing Chamlong's behavior as destructive to nation, religion, and king. The king's media adviser Piya Malakul had his Jor Sor 100, the capital's popular talk-format radio station, run a barrage of denunciations of Chamlong and the protesters. Callers who criticized the government were cut off.

The next day in parliament, just as Suchinda began to deliver his formal policy statement with television cameras broadcasting live, the opposition walked out. Now people saw it was not just a fringe movement against Suchinda. That evening an estimated 80,000 people peacefully protested near parliament as Chamlong's wife and several others joined his fast. At this point the king was petitioned to intervene by a group of worried academics led by Dr. Prawase Wasi, a respected Buddhist ethicist whom Bhumibol had known since the late 1950s.[6] They told the king that the military had betrayed the people's trust by turning the 1991 coup into permanent political power, undermining democracy. They fretted that if Chamlong died, the result would be bloody chaos.[7] The king made no official response.

In fact, the military had already taken a key step toward that conclusion. On the day of the opposition walkout, May 6, new army commander Issarapong, Suchinda's brother-in-law, convened the police and military generals of the capital security committee to set in motion a tactical plan named *Pairee Pinat:* Destroy the Enemy. More than a thousand heavily armed jungle combat fighters and paratroopers were moved into central Bangkok and put on full alert.

The next day in parliament, the opposition criticized Suchinda's policy statement point by point. Then Suchinda mounted the podium and delivered, on live television, a furious five-minute denunciation attacking Chamlong as bent on destroying Buddhism, and Chavalit as a communist and republican. Suchinda declared it was his job to defend the nation, Buddhism, and the monarchy against such threats.

All of Bangkok froze at the premier's harsh language. The stock market immediately plunged and parliament was adjourned in pandemonium. Suchinda had drawn the line for a fight, and with a large force of well-armed troops at hand, he had already determined how it would go.

Pairee Pinat was a tactical approach for fighting a communist-backed insurgency and leftist urban terrorism.[8] It didn't involve police controls or modern riot equipment. The point was methodical suppression by methods including assassination of key figures, beating and shooting protesters, and mass arrests. It was devised by the United States and taught to allies like South Korea and Thailand in the 1970s. It clearly didn't work well in Vietnam, nor in South Korea against a pro-democracy uprising in Kwangju in 1980—likewise a year after a military coup—in which more than 200 Koreans were massacred.

When Pairee Pinat was initiated, the troops were issued live ammunition and were told that pro-democracy protesters threatened the country and the holy monarchy itself. Both the king and Prem knew about the operation: Suchinda and Issarapong communicated regularly with palace officials and Prem, who also had his own sources of information in the military. There is no sign that the palace institutionally or the king personally questioned this posture, even though the atmosphere on the streets evoked that of the days before the massacres of October 14, 1973, and October 6, 1976.

Suchinda's coarse parliamentary attack galvanized about 70,000 Thais to join a protest on May 7, ignoring Kaset's announcement of a strict ban on demonstrations. They remained entirely peaceful and cooperated with the small contingent of police standing by. The next day more than 200 university academics petitioned the king to dissolve parliament or push Suchinda to step down. Protest leaders found most palace channels closed to them, but Chamlong and Chavalit had direct lines to Prem, ensuring that the throne heard their point of view.

Suchinda maintained the theme that he was protecting the palace. He received a Buddhist group and told them he was fighting political and religious fanaticism. Army-controlled radio and television pressed the idea that Chamlong and Chavalit were communist, republican, anti-Buddhism, and, essentially, un-Thai, and refused to acknowledge the popular foundations of the anti-Suchinda movement.

The king finally responded, cautiously. While he declined to meet anyone from the demonstrators' side, he called in Suchinda and the military commanders. What was said wasn't clear, but afterward Suchinda announced on television that he wouldn't resign, but also would not order a crackdown on the demonstrators. At the same time, however, the military announced that Sanam Luang would have to be cleared for a Buddhist ceremony involving Princess Sirindhorn on Sunday, May 10, and the royal plowing ceremony, scheduled for May 14. This seemed to be the main result of his royal audience.[9]

Early that Friday evening, well over 100,000 protested at Sanam Luang. Still fasting, Chamlong arrived and told the demonstrators to march toward parliament. Before they had gone a kilometer down the broad Rajadamnoen Road, they were halted at Panfah Bridge by a barbed-wire barricade. Behind it were deep ranks of combat-clad troops with automatic weapons, blocking off approaches to parliament and Chitrlada Palace.[10] The next morning, a weakened Chamlong succumbed to what he said were the crowd's wishes for him to give up his fast. The government gave no ground, however, and instead threatened to forcibly clear the streets by Monday morning.

Bhumibol now intervened openly, pushing the political parties to compromise on amending the constitution. They agreed on amendments that included requiring the prime minister to be an elected MP, making the head of the lower house the president of parliament, and other procedural changes making the lower house more powerful. But because the government parties didn't commit precisely to when the changes would take place, some 25,000 protesters remained on the street the next day, Sunday. That afternoon the favorite princess Sirindhorn was scheduled to drive down Rajadamnoen for the five o'clock ceremony at Sanam Luang to launch Buddhism Promotion Week.

This became the focus of competing claims of allegiance to the throne. The government said the demonstrators, by not clearing out altogether, were interfering with the princess, and so offended the monarchy. Piya Malakul's Jor Sor 100 broadcast that the Chamlong-led demonstrators were blocking the path of the princess. To the contrary, under Chamlong's direction the demonstrators cleaned up the broad avenue and posted portraits of the princess and her parents at curbside hours before her arrival. The street was completely open and secure, like whenever the royal motorcade passed.

But the princess never came. Instead of traversing Rajadamnoen, under military guidance her motorcade took a long evasive detour to Sanam Luang. Demonstrators were confused: Did their princess not trust them? Or had the generals prevented her from coming? Slowly dismay turned to anger, and again the protest crowd began to swell, until late that Sunday night, finally, the government parties committed themselves to a fast amendment process. Just hours before the military moved on the demonstrators, they dispersed.

The king-brokered compromise was short-lived. By Monday evening government party heads Banharn and Kaset reversed themselves and declared there had been no agreement. They had refused, in effect, the king's demand. As they did, Suchinda threatened hard military retaliation if the demonstrators turned violent. Yet it was the week of the Buddhist holy celebration of Vishaka Puja, and the protest leaders had already decided to reduce their activities and soften their rhetoric. Thursday, May 14, was the annual observance of the royal plowing ceremony, and the democracy movement stayed quiet as King Bhumibol, Prince Vajiralongkorn, and Princess Sirindhorn attended the rites at Sanam Luang. When the royals traveled to the Temple of the Emerald Buddha in the Grand Palace that Saturday to perform rituals for Vishaka Puja, protesters again stayed away out of respect.

But with the government having reneged on amending the constitution, the protests resumed on Sunday, May 17, now guided by a new organization, the Confederation for Democracy. The confederation was led by a committee of nongovernmental organization directors, labor and student leaders, and political party heads, including Chamlong and Chavalit. They made the point that they were a broad-based movement and not simply a tool for Chamlong's and Chavalit's ambitions. When they resumed their demands for the amendments and Suchinda's resignation, Suchinda assigned a Class 5 police general with a brutal reputation to handle the protests, instead of the more moderate chief of police. The army deployed some 40,000 troops around the capital and established military check-points all around Chitrlada Palace. The palace gates were further blockaded by well-armed paratroopers. To some it appeared as if the military was cutting the palace's access to outside, rather than protecting it.

By eight in the evening on May 17, the crowd at Sanam Luang had reached about 150,000, a cross-section of Bangkok: poor workers, middle-class civil ser-vants and shop owners, and wealthy yuppies. They were much angrier than before. The Confederation for Democracy leadership had earlier decided to march to Government House, where the prime minister and his cabinet worked. Again they were halted at Panfah Bridge, where a brigade of disorganized traffic police waited behind razor wire. Behind them was a phalanx of combat troops with machine guns. Most people remained calm, but some in the crowd began throwing rocks and bottles, some of them clearly trying to provoke a violent confrontation. Over several hours they managed to tear down the razor wire and disable a fire truck that sprayed water on the crowd. Deliberately deployed without riot-control equip-ment, the police fled in disarray. This provided the military an excuse to step in, a modus operandi of both 1973 and 1976.

As the government declared a state of emergency, the military regrouped at another line farther down Rajadamnoen, with heavier equipment and armored vehicles. But the demonstrators didn't follow. Most remained at Panfah Bridge, where a small group of men burned a handful of cars and a vacated police station. They were organized provocateurs, both sides later agreed, though whose has never been established. Still no weapons were used, and injuries were minimal.

By two in the morning three-quarters of the protesters had gone home, and at

Chamlong's urging the rest sat down peacefully at the bridge, talking, singing, and dozing in the calm. Wholly unprovoked and without warning, at four o'clock the troops marched on the crowd and began shooting into it. As they scattered, a number lay dead and many more were injured. By the time the sun rose, the blood was being hosed off the street. On television, announcers reported that the protesters had tried to attack Chitrlada Palace. The military claimed the demonstrators had fired first. Both were lies. There was no shooting from demonstrators, and no guns or even knives were found. Nobody went near the palace, and no one had intended to. Nor was there any need to clear the street. Monday was a holiday, and no one was going to work on Rajadamnoen Road.

The palace spent that Monday morning collecting information. Prem talked to all the military men. The other privy councilors talked to their contacts. But prodemocracy groups said they were mostly brushed off.[11] It did not appear that the king was getting a full view of the situation, other than what Suchinda announced on television, that Chamlong's demonstrators had guns and threatened the throne. Early Monday afternoon, after Chamlong and several thousand people returned to sit in protest on Rajadamnoen, combat troops descended to arrest them. They mostly fired blanks in the air, but down side streets, away from cameras, more people were shot with live ammunition.

That evening the crowd swelled anew at Sanam Luang, its composition now younger and wilder. The protesters were prevented from marching down Rajadamnoen by new barricades, and as darkness fell, brigades of combat troops encircled the area. The military pointed machine guns at them through the razor wire, and there were sharpshooters on rooftops. They began firing when the protesters set alight several buses and began pushing them toward the barricades. Assassinlike, the rooftop marksmen cut down people at the front of the lines. The ground troops fired into the crowd, several times stopping for a break and then starting again. Scores of protesters were hit, with several dozen killed.

In the early morning hours, finally the military cleared the entire area, issuing arrest orders for leaders of the Confederation for Democracy. As news of the killing spread across Bangkok, people began to ask quietly, where is the king? Why hasn't he stopped this? Was he behind Suchinda, or was he prevented by the troops and armored cars around the palace from interceding? The questions came from average Thais on the street and from business leaders and members of parliament. Rumors spread that the king was being held prisoner by the military, or that he had fled the capital with Prem to Nakhon Ratchasima, as in 1981, to muster troops against Suchinda. All of the rumors presumed the king could not have supported

Suchinda. But meanwhile the army itself prepared for battle, apparently believing that Chavalit and Chamlong would call on their own loyal army troops to
fight back.

All through that Tuesday, May 19, there was no evidence where the royal family
stood. In a well-protected motorcade commanded by Kaset, Crown Prince Vajiralongkorn went to the airport and left for South Korea. Princess Sirindhorn had
left for Paris with Princess Galyani the previous week on an official trip. There were
pleas from all around to stop the violence and for the king to intervene. Phra
Yanasangworn led the sangha council in a public call for all sides to stop "killing each other," although no one from the government side had been killed.[12]
Sirindhorn made a taped statement from Paris calling for calm and unity. She said
she had tried to call her family but couldn't get through. This was normal; international telephone lines to Bangkok were usually poor, and at the time they were
swamped with calls. But people took it to mean she was prevented from speaking to
her father. After that, Suchinda came on television to deny that either he or the
royal family had fled Bangkok. He again denounced Chavalit and Chamlong as
bent on destroying Buddhism and the monarchy.

The next day, as more rumors spread of coming fighting between military
factions, there was still no indication of the king's position. Suchinda's forces had
blocked off all of the old city center and there was sporadic gunfire. Suchinda made
another short televised announcement, mainly to say that he had things under
control. With him were governing coalition party leaders Narong, Banharn, and
Samak. Samak, as in the 1970s, insisted that shooting the people had been acceptable because they were communists.[13]

That evening, several tens of thousands of demonstrators massed at Ramkhamhaeng University in eastern Bangkok, and the military began to move troops
in their direction. Just after ten o'clock, televisions flickered with a grainy picture,
the sound almost inaudible. It showed King Bhumibol on a chair with privy
councilors Prem and Sanya kneeling at his side, like temple guardians. On the floor
in front, their legs tucked behind them in near-prostration, were Chamlong and
Suchinda. The king spoke. "It may not be a surprise as to why I asked you to come
to this meeting. . . . But it may be a surprise as to why General Suchinda Kraprayoon
and Major General Chamlong Srimuang have been invited, when there may be
many other performers and actors involved. However, the two of you have been
invited because at the beginning there was a situation in which the two of you were
confronting each other, and at the end it has become a confrontation or a struggle

on a larger scale." Whatever the issue at stake, if the confrontation continued, he said, "It would only lead to the utter destruction of Thailand."[14]

To solve the problem, he said, some people had proposed dissolving parliament and holding new elections. But he claimed that the political parties almost unanimously rejected the idea, and so he couldn't do that. Another solution was to amend the constitution, which, he said, was exactly what he had already recommended in his December 4 speech. Although the constitution was already "reasonable," he said, this was still a good solution. He then said: "When I met with General Suchinda, General Suchinda concurred that the constitution should be first promulgated and it could be amended later; that was a possible alternative. And even lately General Suchinda has affirmed that it can be amended. It can be gradually amended so that it will eventually be improved in a 'democratic' way.... Therefore, I think that if possible, we should consider the alternative suggested in my address of the 4th December to solve the original problem, with a view to solving the present problem."

With the country headed toward collapse, he requested that Suchinda and Chamlong "sit down and face the facts together in a conciliatory manner, and not in a confrontational manner, to find a way to solve the problem, because our country does not belong to any one or two persons, but belongs to everyone.... What is the point of anyone feeling proud of being the winner, when standing on a pile of ruins and rubbles?" He ended with a Buddhist-like invocation to work together and rebuild the country: "You personally will feel much better, knowing that you have done the right thing. How you will achieve this will depend on your joint cooperative efforts. These are my observations."

Because the sound on television was so bad, for the public the main message was visual, simply that Bhumibol had Chamlong and Suchinda at his feet, with Prem and Sanya alongside as enforcers. "No man can argue on his knees," wrote Bagehot of a monarch's power. Not many noted the nucleus of the king's remarks. He squarely placed the blame for the eruption on Chamlong and the pro-democracy movement, because they had not acquiesced to his December recommendation to patiently seek the amendments—which, he implied, were of dubious necessity anyway. Suchinda, on the other hand, had generously accepted the king's position, and he had recently reaffirmed that he was prepared to accept amendments. The king appeared to be asking, so why were people in the streets fighting? Rather than recognize truly popular sentiment and acknowledge Suchinda's government's refusal to change the charter—and the impossibility of amending it against the military-controlled senate's will—Bhumibol had rendered it all as Chamlong's personal vendetta.

The next day, the world was in awe at Bhumibol's intervention. The violence and protests stopped, although troops remained on the streets. Chamlong was ordered, presumably by Prem in the king's name, to call off the protests, Suchinda to resign, and the political parties to amend the constitution. While Chamlong disappeared from view, the generals didn't. Suchinda, Kaset, and Issarapong defended their actions as legal and necessary acts of self-defense against protesters attacking with guns, grenades, and firebombs. There was no truth to it. Suchinda insisted on holding on to the premiership until parliament amended the constitution. He also demanded an amnesty to protect himself and his military cohorts. Although this outraged the democracy movement, the king went ahead and granted the amnesty. Finally, near noon on Sunday, June 24, after a private audience with Supreme Patriarch Yanasangworn at Wat Bovornives, Suchinda resigned the premiership, declaring that he had fulfilled the king's own wishes to bring about peace and reconciliation. The next day parliament opened with a longtime Prem and then NPKC legal adviser as acting premier. The lawmakers quickly passed the first and second readings of the desired constitutional amendments. The final reading was scheduled for two weeks hence.

Yet it was not all over. Suchinda remained as minister of defense, and Kaset, Issarapong, and the others kept their military positions. The parties that backed Suchinda still controlled parliament, with the support of the NPKC-appointed senate. Unrepentant, the generals defended themselves in several different forums, including one with incredulous foreign diplomats, declaring they had been protecting the king and country from seditious communist elements. When the pro-democracy groups called for rescinding the amnesty, they countered with coup threats.

A few days later the five government parties nominated Chart Thai's Air Chief Marshal Somboon Rahong as prime minister. But when house leader Arthit Urairat submitted the nomination, the palace silently stalled. While nothing was made clear, people understood that the king wanted the constitution amended first. Some perceived that he recognized that Somboon would cause more problems. After Somboon's nomination was unofficially rebuffed a second time at the beginning of June, Prem declared that the king wanted a premier acceptable to all people. There were strong rumors that the king wanted his own privy councilor, Chirayut Isarangkul. But the government coalition, still directed by Suchinda and Kaset, insisted on Somboon.

Everyone waited tensely for June 10, the date of the final reading of the constitution. After the amendments were passed, Arthit again went to the palace to submit Somboon's name. At his home with champagne on ice and surrounded by hundreds of supporters, Somboon waited for the phone call confirming his appointment. When it came, suddenly his face sank in disbelief. As he said into the telephone, yes, I understand, so did everyone else, and cheers erupted from reporters: the king had again named Anand Panyarachun interim prime minister.[15]

Over the next months Anand smoothed over tensions and stabilized the economy. He dissolved parliament and set national polls for September. They went off fairly well, with the field of parties polarized as devils—the NPKC-tied parties—and angels, the opposition. The latter came out in front to form a coalition government led by the Democrats, and Chuan Leekpai was made prime minister. It was seen as a new beginning for Thai politics.

Anand's other delicate responsibility was an accounting of the military's actions that May. General Pichit Kullavanich, a favorite of Prem and the king (and soon to be made privy councilor), undertook the confidential white-paper review over six weeks. The Pichit report was not released, but Anand revealed that it faulted the military for fundamentally misunderstanding the nature of the demonstrations. There was no broader analysis of why the Thai military produced such corrupt and ambitious cliques that assumed they had a right to hold power. Nervously, Anand transferred all the top generals involved in bloody May to powerless posts, effectively ending their careers. They took the transfers unrepentantly, still arguing that the demonstrators were a communist-like front bent on destroying the enduring pillars of nation, religion, and king.

Bhumibol's regal intervention, shown on television screens and newspaper pages around the world, quickly became a landmark act of great kingship. This was the same year as Queen Elizabeth's *annus horribilis*, when her family turmoil, acts of god, the uncontrollable London press, and, most of all, a downturn in public affection conspired to wreck the British monarchy's majesty. Rama IX's deft peacemaking provided new evidence for the monarchy's enduring value near the end of the 20th century.

Not only romanticists felt so. Pundits and scholars wrote paeans to Bhumibol as a Solomonic king who thinks beyond partisan politics and personal wealth to the people. Georgetown University's David Steinberg, an expert on Burma and a critic of its military junta, bemoaned the lack of a monarch in Rangoon to lessen the suffering of the Burmese.[16] For many Thais, it was yet another confirmation of their sovereign's greatness. Even Anand, never a man given to hyperbole or promo-tion, said: "The King is a sole personality who can tell all sides to stop fighting, to stop the confrontation. There is no place in the world where a civil war raged and then someone could come up and ask everyone to end the fight."[17]

There is little doubt that Bhumibol's intervention on May 20 cut short what could have been a much greater slaughter. Beyond acting as a symbol of unity, the modern constitutional king's most important role is to mediate in insoluble cir-cumstances and take up leadership when it is absent. Bhumibol did this with unquestionable skill, by reducing the entire episode to a personal feud between two ambitious men and then stopping it. He avoided alienating the demonstrators, his loyal subjects, and condemning the military, the men who protected him. He also skirted the real issues of the constitution.

But how things reached such a point is another question. Europe's modern sovereigns have overseen great efforts to develop other institutions and the rule of law to avoid such tragedies and to sidestep interventions that put at risk the throne's prestige. Bhumibol to the contrary had consistently undermined the development of other permanent institutions. He saw them as competitors to his prestige, and not as shields to protect it. This exacerbated the dysfunctional state of government that required his regular intercession. Bagehot spoke precisely to this issue in *The English Constitution*: "So long as parliament thinks it is the sovereign's business to find a government, it will be sure not to find a government itself." As long as the sovereign assumes such business, the deeper he is enmeshed in politics and the more at risk his own power becomes.

May 1992 was a manifestation of the faults in Bhumibol's ideal of a royal government, of his unrelenting prejudice against politicians, and his miscompre-hension of the social changes that had occurred during his long reign. Despite the popularity of politicians like Chamlong and Chatichai, the king remained com-mitted to his generals. They weren't even the best generals: the corrupt and merce-nary Arthit, Chavalit, and Suchinda all rose under Prem while professional, non-political soldiers fell by the wayside. Yet the king and queen preferred them to even clean politicians. When Bhumibol expressed his preference for soldiers in Decem-ber 1990, it provided Suchinda justification to seize power.

The king's defenders say that Bhumibol had no choice but to accept the NPKC takeover, while also insisting it was a popular coup. Neither is exactly true. There was a widespread swing of public sentiment against Chatichai—fomented by both the military and the king's own remarks—but it didn't represent a popular call for a military takeover. At the time Bhumibol made no point of standing for a constitution-based transition that might have denied Suchinda power. Moreover, he declined to exercise his prerogative to dissolve parliament and set elections. Such royal powers are not inconsequential simply because they are seldom used. They are specifically for political emergencies.[18]

After the coup, a few well-worded comments for constitutional and democratic principles would have left the junta on warning. Instead, following a year that exposed the generals' venality, in December 1991 Bhumibol generously endorsed Suchinda's leadership when he said there was no need to stick to theoretical principles or rule books. His intervention on the constitution, too, was premature: he did not wait until after the parliament voted. As the eruption five months later showed, the king's habitual interventions left parliament dependent on the sovereign to make its decisions. Responsibilities for controlling the military, changing the charter, and choosing a new prime minister were ceded to the king.

Bhumibol's skill in saving the day after the bloody convulsion of May 18–20 helped to hide his consistent bias against protesters and popular movements. But all the markers were there, from his silence on the Pairee Pinat preparations to the route change of the princess's motorcade, to the shrill propaganda in media controlled by palace agents like Piya Malakul. With practiced deftness, however, as in October 1973, the king reserved just enough distance from the generals to emerge still the people's king. When he appeared to blame Suchinda and Chamlong personally, the protesters could understand that he wasn't saying the people were wrong. Because the constitution was finally to be amended, they could believe that Bhumibol was on their side.

Even so, there is the problem that Bhumibol acted only three days after the first demonstrators were killed. Aware of this gap in time and credibility, the palace's defenders afterward insisted that Bhumibol didn't like Suchinda but, unable to control the general, had to wait until Suchinda's clique discredited themselves. It was almost an official argument, given how many people around the palace repeated it. One palace intimate explained: "When the king intervenes, he must succeed. He must know the territory he is charting. This explains the delay."[19] A senior prince called it the "silver bullet principle": the king has but one chance to intervene, and it has to hit the bull's-eye. He couldn't even risk declaring a dissolution of parliament, for fear Suchinda would ignore it. His prestige would have been exposed as lacking substance.[20]

Interestingly, the palace agents never claimed the king was out of touch or misinformed, which could have explained the three-day gap. That argument could have dented his omniscient image, and it also would not have been true. Early on he assigned Prem to take charge of the whole situation, and Prem communicated constantly with the generals and many others, and kept Bhumibol briefed. The other privy councilors worked their own networks of informants. There was no real sign that Bhumibol was held hostage inside Chitrlada. If one accepts the silver-bullet argument, it suggests a deep fault in his preference for the military, for clearly Suchinda and the NPKC generals were not more loyal, disciplined, or obedient than other Thais. And if Suchinda and his Class 5 cohorts were an exception, a rogue operation, how did they ever get so far?

Moreover, why then did the king pin most of the blame on Chamlong on May 20? Chamlong was rebuked for ignoring his December advice on the constitution, while Suchinda was praised for having agreed that amendments could be made. To assign guilt in this way, Bhumibol ignored the fact that the constitution and parliament were structured to defeat any amendment opposed by the generals. He also ignored Suchinda's broken promises to amend the charter.

In the same way, the king avoided the conclusion, widely accepted among respected Thais like Anand, foreign diplomats, and academics, that there was a massive institutional problem in the Thai military. This was clear in the generals' continuing defiance over the months after the May crisis. On the same day that Suchinda resigned, the army commanders held a meeting to declare their unity and defend the assault on the demonstrators. In July, Kaset threatened that a coup was still possible. Even after Anand sidelined the generals, the military openly assisted at least two parties in the election campaign, mobilizing the Red Gaur, Village Scouts, and ISOC to justify the May massacre to voters, insisting it was about a communist threat to nation, religion, and king.[21]

Indeed, Bhumibol himself defended the military in those months. At the end of October, he received in audience 256 newly promoted senior colonels and generals. He made no critical reference to May and instead took to task the military's critics. The *Far Eastern Economic Review* had repeated long-standing criticisms of the Thai military, that it remained incapable of convincingly defending its own borders, and yet maintained perhaps the most bloated officers corps in the world, with one general for every 300–350 troops, ten times the level of the West. Of the 600 generals in the army and supreme command headquarters, only half had identifiable jobs, the magazine noted.[22]

Bhumibol denied this, arguing that critics had counted retired generals—which they hadn't. The very number of newly promoted generals in front of him was clear evidence, but still he insisted: "It has been widely said today that we have too many generals. If so, then there would be no point in bestowing the rank of general on about 200 officers today. The criticism may hurt your feelings but as a matter of fact we have a lower number of generals than foreign countries, in the West or the East. . . . The number of generals in Thailand is not that high and our armed forces are not top-heavy as was said. In fact, [the number] is small."[23]

In December Bhumibol again placed the blame on Chamlong, Chavalit, and the protesters. He told the parable of a child who, confronted by a specific problem, ignored ready solutions to instead stir up an elephant, sending the elephant into a fury, setting off a violent chain reaction that finally resolved the original problem, only after much unnecessary chaos.[24] "The situation nowadays is like the story, confused. On any subject, one person says something, another comes to refute it, using irreconcilable arguments. And how can the country be governed, how can work be done, how can we have anything done, if everything is out of tune? . . . In the end, the obstinate, dogmatic one will win the argument; but that is not good, that is not right. . . . [O]ne must not stipulate too many conditions. Any action must be constructive and everyone will be happy."

The audience understood that the message was for the pro-democracy movement, those the king felt unnecessarily pestered the blameless military elephant until all turmoil broke loose.

Even after the dust of May 1992 settled, the king still rejected the conclusions of numerous Thai and foreign scholars, politicians, and businessmen, that the upheaval was the result of an undeveloped political system, one excessively reliant on the monarchy and military to govern and manage development. Bhumibol's stubborn hold on his own views was clear in an astonishing episode in early 1993. While Thailand was struggling with democratic processes and ambitious generals, neighboring Burma suffered the misrule of a paranoid and brutal military junta, known as the State Law and Order Restoration Council, or Slorc. They had crushed a popular revolt in 1988 and jailed members of the political opposition, including their leader Aung San Suu Kyi. Still under house arrest, in October 1991 Suu Kyi was awarded the Nobel Peace Prize in recognition of their struggle.

In February 1993 eight previous Nobel Peace laureates visited Thailand, as Burma's closest neighbor, to demonstrate their solidarity. Oscar Arias, the former president of Costa Rica, South Africa's Desmond Tutu, the Dalai Lama of Tibet, and five others were invited by Thai social activists, to the great consternation of the Thai military. After visiting the destitute Burmese refugee camps on the northern Thai border, the group was received by King Bhumibol. They were astounded to hear him lecture them on how Aung San Suu Kyi should give up her fight and return to England to raise her children, and let Slorc run the country. Military governments were good for developing countries, the king insisted, and there was no need to support the Burmese opposition. Suu Kyi was only a troublemaker.[25]

It wasn't the only time the king said such things. He lobbied American diplomats and foreign academics to accept Slorc as bringing stability to Burma. Like the Slorc generals, he argued from his palace chambers that because Suu Kyi was married to a foreigner and had been educated abroad, she didn't represent traditional Burmese values, so she ought to return to England and her family there. Outside Chitrlada Palace, however, a new generation of Thais was cheering for Suu Kyi, and the official policy of the newly elected government of Chuan Leekpai was to support her pro-democracy movement.

19 Sanctifying Royalty and Stonewalling Democracy in the 1990s ∾

THE INTERVENTION IN MAY 1992 DROVE King Bhumibol's popular renown as the nation's salvation to a new summit. He wasn't a salted memory of the past like Japan's emperor, or an extravagant playboy like the Muslim monarchs of Malaysia and the Middle East, or gaudy fodder for the gossip magazines like Europe's princes and princesses. Bhumibol was real, and good.

But for the institution of the Thai monarchy, it was a hollow peak. May 1992 marked a crucial turning point downward for the throne, when government and society in tandem veered sharply from the past and began to abandon the ideal of a dhammaraja-led state and culture. Many well-informed Thais understood the May cataclysm as the consequence of having allowed the king, and depended on the king, to be the arbiter of government, politics, and justice. Fundamental reforms were needed to reverse the deep corruption and mismanagement in government, to force the military back into their camps, and to push King Bhumibol back up onto his throne. Although they didn't blame the king for all that had gone wrong, they understood that political reforms couldn't take root as long as the palace continued to meddle. With Bhumibol at 65 in 1992, many were thinking also about the consequences of his power accruing to his dangerously capricious son.

In parallel was another profound transformation taking place in Thai culture. With the economic boom that began in 1987, and the technology advances sweeping across Asia, Thailand exploded with new wealth, businesses, consumer goods, and services. The country plunged headlong into a fast global culture with its new media, mobile phones, cable television from around the globe, and a massive surge in foreigners visiting Thailand. It all carried a sense of dynamic and democratic freedom from the heavy, hierarchical society of the past.

For the throne, democratic capitalism and globalist consumerism was a new type of intangible and popular adversary in the virtue stakes, unlike Phibun in the 1950s or communism in the 1970s. It was a far more daunting rival to Bhumibol's virtue-by-example, discipline-through-ritual dhammaraja ideal. It threatened to push Bhumibol aside, to propel him, his family, and the institution of the monarchy into a senescence as a greatly beloved, but never again powerful, cultural symbol.

With the clock ticking on his reign, King Bhumibol fought stubbornly against this turn, drawing deeply on the techniques and tricks for projecting royal virtue that had served him since becoming king in 1946. His 1991 birthday speech on the constitution became the model for more open political interventions to force his own agenda.

The September 1992 elections brought to power the anti-Suchinda coalition of parties led by Chuan Leekpai's Democrats and Chavalit Yongchaiyut's New Aspiration Party. The new prime minister was Chuan, a modest and incorruptible lawyer-politician and lifetime advocate of stronger democratic institutions and the rule of law. He was no republican, but all the same he was distrusted by the court.

Elected with a mandate to clean up and democratize government, Chuan inherited a society barely manageable after five years of 10 percent annual economic growth, and still moving at nearly that pace. The hallmarks of this economic boom were new cars, mobile phones, stock portfolios, heady real estate speculation, and holidays abroad. Even rural Thailand was swept by the freewheeling pursuit of wealth and consumer goods. Traditional values began to warp, with women demanding more say in society and MTV-inspired youths sporting dyed hair and pierced navels.

The people demanded more from government as well. In Bangkok, it was the quality of living: they wanted the endless traffic jams solved, the air cleaned, and the seasonal flooding stopped. In rural areas, peasants demanded solutions for age-old problems of land reform and farmer debt. They pushed for decentralized government, for elections of local officials and discretionary budgets for towns and villages.

The voters handed Chuan's government the task of doing all this, and also to amend or rewrite the constitution to make it more democratic. He struggled for nearly three years with an unruly coalition, demonstrating that some progress could be made without relying on the military or the monarchy. The biggest change was a more open political discourse. Community and social activist groups, the NGOs, had a greater input in many areas of public policy, especially the environment. They were assisted by a much freer mass media, as Chuan took steps to break the military-bureaucracy monopoly on television and radio. Increasingly frequent, aggressive news exposés began to reveal the breadth and depth of official and corporate corruption and poor governance, and the immunity of the Thai elite to the law. Such news replaced the official government and political party propaganda that had dominated coverage before. It also began to push aside news about the royal family. A new television station, ITV, didn't even broadcast the royal news in the evening when others did.

Chuan couldn't get everything done that he was mandated to. In 1995 his party fell victim to a corruption scandal. His government was replaced by a coalition led by Banharn Silpa-archa, with partner parties led by Samak Sunthornvej, Chavalit, and upstart billionaire Thaksin Shinawatra.

Forced to the sidelines, King Bhumibol and the palace recognized that they needed to keep the royal family in the spotlight to maintain their high standing in culture and politics. As ever, Bhumibol, Sirikit, and now often their children for them kept up the plodding regime of royal ritual and social ceremony. That clearly wasn't going to be enough, and the palace, and the king personally, turned to more aggressive methods of reminding people of his virtue. After only a short grace period, Bhumibol began fighting back aggressively when he saw his own views and ideas under attack. His targets were the usual politicians but now also environmental groups.

As with Chatichai, he branded Chuan's team as bumbling and selfish. After an acrimonious tussle over cabinet positions in a mid-1993 shuffle, with Chavalit at the center of the fray, in late September the king admonished Chuan's ministers for bickering. In December he revisited the issue, telling the assembled government leaders to "stop biting one another." "I think you all know what I'm talking about," he added sternly, as many looked at Chavalit. "Some of you are laughing. . . . People who know the value of unity are supposed to know what or what not to say."

But Bhumibol had much stronger words for the NGOs. He had become particularly angered by their impact on favorite projects of his. In 1992, for instance, several groups challenged a royal project managed by the king's chum

Prince Bhisadej Rajani. The project, at Ban Wat Chan near Chiangmai, was ostensibly to supply wood for royal handicraft projects. But the real goal was to cut and sell the timber from a protected primary pine forest. After the groups protested, supported by heavy media coverage, the palace had to cancel the project.[1]

Bhumibol was most bothered by the Thai environmental movement's opposition to several dams that he wanted built. Bhumibol had hung his poverty-fighter reputation on the harnessing of the nation's water resources. But as in other parts of the world, in Thailand in the 1990s large-scale dams were attacked for displacing massive numbers of people and destroying large swaths of the natural environment without real economic justification. Encouraged by their first victory over the Nam Choan dam in 1988, in the 1990s green organizations fought to stop or modify each successive one. Twice, during the Chatichai government and then during Chuan's first year, they blocked a hydropower dam the king and EGAT wanted built on the magnificent Haew Narok gorge inside Khao Yai, Thailand's most popular and pristine national park. The location was a key wild elephant habitat and included the country's most famous waterfall, and much of the public opposed it for those reasons.

Then the groups took on three more large water-control schemes. Pak Panang, a large estuary in southern Thailand, was already a royal project. After heavy rains flooded the estuary and damaged surrounding rice farms in 1989, the king ordered it to be widened and dredged so that water could exit better. A consequence, though, was greater saltwater incursion upstream in the dry season, which ruined the farms. Now the king wanted to build levees against this. The second and third projects were central plains dams. Pasak would submerge a massive area of prime farmland to regulate seasonal flooding, provide water for Bangkok, and feed dry-season irrigation. At nearly half a billion dollars, the cost was huge, and opponents insisted there were better ways to spend the money for similar results. Tha Dan was a tall dam that green activists disliked because it would damage scrub forest habitat on the edges of Khao Yai park. But the project, although pushed strongly by Bhumibol, wasn't moving ahead, mainly because it was low priority for the government.

The environmentalists considered the king somewhat mad about dams. And with projects like Pak Panang, they saw him piling one mistake on top of another. "The king represents the mentality of a conventional engineer: You can conquer nature and you should do so," said one.[2] Bhumibol in turn considered the activists impudent and, it was said, enjoyed making a pun on the acronym for nongovernmental organization, NGO, pronouncing it as the Thai word for stupid, *ngoh*.

In a televised talk to Thai diplomats in August 1993, the king insisted that dams were inherently good for the people.[3] He defended the twice-rejected Haew Narok project, saying people would accept it once they realized its value. The wild elephants could be moved to (unspecified) manmade sanctuaries, he added. Three months later in his birthday homily, Bhumibol drew on his accumulated virtue to launch a full-scale assault on the greens. He said the environmentalists had blocked the Pasak, Pak Panang, and Tha Dan projects for six years, against his support for the dams.[4] "Had they been constructed, there should have been no problem from drought and floods," he claimed.[5] Would he be making the same complaint again on his birthday in another six years? he asked rhetorically. By then, he warned, Bangkokians would have to cut back their water consumption by 90 percent.

Having pinned any flood-related suffering on environmental groups, the king then tied all three projects to his throne's inviolate prestige. He declared that Pak Panang should be completed by the Ninth Reign's 50-year jubilee in 1996 and the central plains projects by his sixth-cycle, 72nd birthday in 1999. He added with the knowing force of his crown: "We don't want to be confronted with protests. It is tiring and useless."[6]

The impact was powerful. The next day newspaper headlines screamed: "The King Orders Dams to Be Built." Immediately Pramote Maiklad, the royal hydrology adviser, released details of the three projects. The army volunteered to help build them. Chuan put them on the fast track and two weeks later the cabinet approved Pasak. (Tha Dan and Pak Panang needed more detailed planning.) Royal projects director Sumet Tantivejakul injected a sense of breathless emergency to it all. The country is direly ill, he said. Like an expert doctor, "His majesty sensed great danger if nothing is done. His majesty is very patient, but time is pressing. . . . The dams are like a cancer operation for a sick body."[7]

The environmental movement was bowled over. The king hadn't suggested dialogue or mutual understanding, or conceded any of their positions. They were painted like communists of two decades before, irrational, opposed to the people's welfare, and disrespectful. Now any argument they made could be construed as lèse-majesté. Six weeks later the king made what amounted to a victory trip to the Tha Dan site, where he told the people: "Don't sell your land. I am building reservoirs for you."[8]

Many months into 1994, the anti-dam voices cautiously resurfaced. They were less vociferous and mostly focused on technical arguments backed by scientific research. The king took note, because they were questioning his own veracity, and he replied on his birthday that December. He went through a list of selected points and simply declared each one wrong. Almost gloating, he added that he was happy to see the Pasak dam progressing as well.

This was an important demonstration that Bhumibol still could command politics from the outside. But Bhumibol still needed to convince people that his way was better than elected government. And he needed to convince a more difficult audience, urban Thais whom the king had ignored for decades as he helped rural peasants. So he turned his harsh criticisms to the government itself, addressing its handling of Bangkok traffic and seasonal flooding. Multiple government missteps bolstered his case.

By 1992 rapid growth had made the capital nearly unlivable. Traffic jams lasted from before dawn deep into the night, and many commuters spent at least two hours a day in buses and cars. Three separate mass transit plans were stalled, new highways wouldn't be completed for several years, and the exhaust of idling cars made Bangkok extremely polluted. The city's unregulated growth also exacerbated water problems, with shortages for consumers in dry years and more troublesome floods each monsoon season.

That year, after the May troubles, Bhumibol began to be seen on television giving advice on traffic management to the city government and police, telling them to make a road one way or stop U-turns, for instance. The king had always had meetings with officials, but rarely were they televised, and then only with an overlaid summary. Now frequent broadcasts showed bureaucrats submissively nodding at the king's remarks, which viewers could hear clearly and unedited. He would point at maps and talk about specific problems that the people themselves knew of, advising changes to the traffic configuration here and the traffic lights there.

The average TV viewer got no information on the utility of his ideas, and few even understood that there was already a whole bureaucracy working on traffic problems, backed by international expertise. It appeared like only the king was confronting the problem. This impression was amplified by news releases that portrayed the king in charge. One in October 1993 said the king gave the police chief a long list of things to do: build 23 traffic underpasses; increase shipping by river to reduce truck traffic in Bangkok; equip police with more motorcycles; upgrade police helicopters; and survey motorists, among others.[9] Another had Bhumibol instructing the Bangkok government to implement a city master plan done by the Massachusetts Institute of Technology. The queen, meanwhile, made her own suggestions on her birthday in 1993: reduce cars, get rid of large cars, and put more buses on the roads.

The king was giving voice to his own real frustrations. The traffic almost imprisoned him in the palace, because his motorcades would cause jams. And he rightly saw there was not enough coordination between various agencies on the problem. But by publicizing his own involvement, the king told Bangkokians steaming hour upon hour in their cars that he personally was leading the way out. They heard rumors that he made incognito forays out into traffic and surveyed the scene from helicopters, and that he ordered his children to stop their traffic-knotting motorcades and suffer like everyone else.

Bhumibol put substantial money behind his effort. Between 1992 and 1995 he gave at least three million dollars for traffic and flood-related work, for police motorcycles, road reconfiguration, and salary supplements for traffic cops. The palace explained the donations as the king's superior way around torpid bureaucracy. In a televised August 1993 address, he called for the government to quickly resolve traffic problems, whatever the price. The cost, he added, wouldn't be so high if traffic problems had been dealt with 20 years before—implying that he had foreseen it, even if no one else did.

He kept advising and criticizing through 1994, during which all the problems worsened. That December he warned that in five or six years the problems would overwhelm the country. "We must solve the problem by looking at the points of arrival and departure. We must shorten the distance between the two points so people will travel shorter distances and spend less time on the road," he said.

It sounded good, but it didn't mean much. Some of the king's advice was useful, but mostly it echoed what was already being done. Some ideas were fundamentally wrong, like several underpasses and his opposition to higher vehicle taxes. He never addressed key problems like unregulated building, the need for mass transit, or the huge growth in new cars: at one point Bangkok-area roads were getting over 15,000 new cars a month. But by going public with his ideas, he ensured that no one else got credit.

In early 1995 Bhumibol was preoccupied first with his mother's lengthy hospitalization and then his own. Dangerously close to a heart attack, he underwent an angioplasty to unblock a problem blood vessel. Rather than slowing his interventions, he seemed to gain a greater sense of urgency. As he recovered inside Siriraj Hospital, every few days he appeared on television studying maps with city planners. Because he usually met the officials in the evening, sometimes after midnight, people understood that the king was working day and night on the problem. Few Thais knew that he had always slept late in the morning and worked only in the afternoon and evening.

On television, he was audibly irritable and came near to scolding the officials. He didn't slow even when Sangwal died on July 18. For months, Bhumibol almost daily attended to his mother's body as it lay in state in a palace hall. But while others prayed, he could be seen studying traffic reports and sternly conferring with city officials. Sangwal died just as a new government came to power replacing Chuan's. With long, scandal-filled histories, the new leadership—Prime Minister Banharn, Samak, Chavalit, and telecommunications tycoon Thaksin Shinawatra—took office under a cloud of doubt, and, swearing them in, Bhumibol tersely warned them to perform. He afterward met with Banharn for 90 minutes, reportedly speaking mostly about traffic.

The government proved as bad as anyone expected. The two deputy prime ministers, Samak and Thaksin, fought openly for control of the capital and its traffic problems. After three weeks of their bickering, Bhumibol let loose, ridiculing the two ministers for achieving nothing on traffic. "Between these two sides there is only talk, talk, talk, and they argue, argue, argue." The stunning rebuke filled the headlines in every newspaper. For several days Thaksin, Samak, and Banharn leaped about frantically to display contrition. Banharn declared he would heed the king and coordinate the two ministers. Samak and Thaksin pledged to work together, even while denying they had not.[10] Four days later they met the king for several hours, poring over city maps and details of problem zones. "We had never thought about what the king had recommended," Thaksin said humbly.[11]

Bhumibol had again exposed politicians as incompetent and unconcerned for the people. His harshness was uncommon and unbecoming, but people understood it as the strain of his health problems, his mother's passing, and his own daily commute to the Grand Palace to attend to her body. Yet he made a very odd defense of himself, one that revealed the frustrations and contradictions he felt in his position, and in the monarchy itself. He claimed a constitutional right as a normal citizen to scold the leaders.[12] "My talking like this isn't very nice. Because it is close to talking politics. And they could feel angry that, why is the king talking politics? In truth, the king has the right. In truth, the king is also a Thai citizen, with rights and freedoms under the constitution. . . . In the constitution everyone has the right and freedom to speak. So I ask to use the right and freedom under the constitution to speak in this way. If they want to find legal fault with me, do it. I want to hear their charges."

For a moment, the king had brought the throne down to the level of commoners, dangerously divesting its special inviolateness. There was no need to claim a citizen's rights to intervene. But it had great effect. When he entered the hospital again in September to clear out scarring caused by the angioplasty, people said that Banharn had given him his second heart attack.

That did not end Bhumibol's gruff critiques. In early September, Bangkok was inundated by massive flooding. Still weak from surgery, he held a televised three-hour audience with city and irrigation officials. Jabbing his finger at a pile of maps, he demanded to know why people in Bangkok's suburbs were not protected from flooding. Again, he was right to a certain extent. The government could have done more to reduce the effect of the floods, like clearing canals and forcefully pumping water to get it moving. They should have built more canals a decade before, the king suggested.

Still, this too was more rhetoric than helpful advice. In late 1995 the Chaophraya River surged to an unprecedented high. Adverse tidal, river, and weather conditions made drain-off unusually slow. The cumulative effects of a decade of uncontrolled construction exacerbated the problem. But also, the suburbs were more flooded because the government had closed water gates to protect the inner city, with its government offices and palaces.

Some Thais had serious questions about the king's aggressive criticisms. They worried that he wasn't discrediting only the Banharn administration but the elected government system itself. "My concern is that people will look at this government and say that democracy doesn't work," said political scientist Kusuma Sanitwongs.[13] It wasn't clear that that wasn't the king's real point.

After the record floodwaters fell in late November, Bhumibol's hydrology aide Pramote announced that to stop future flooding it was absolutely necessary to build two more dams to the north, Kaeng Sua Ten and Kwae Noi. The king himself called for acceleration of the Pasak and Pak Panang projects, even though the latter's cost had grown to $600 million. The cabinet acquiesced without question. Thai environmentalists, strongly opposed to Kaeng Sua Ten because it would flood healthy virgin teak forest, couldn't argue any more than the ministers could. A year later, hours before he resigned as prime minister, Banharn obliged the palace and expedited cabinet approval of Kaeng Sua Ten, ignoring damning studies on the project's social, economic, and environmental impacts.

Bhumibol's intervention against amending the constitution was less open—Prem handled it in back channels—but no less effective. Chuan's election in 1992 left him mandated to pursue further changes to the charter to improve the democratic structure of government. With the senate still filled by NPKC-chosen men, amendments couldn't pass without the army's accord. They would also block any attempt to change the rules of amendment. In March 1994, Chuan approached Prem for support for his proposed amendments and received an effective slap in the face. Normally the military senators never showed up for senate meetings. But the day after Chuan met Prem, nearly every senator was there and, together with the lower-house opposition, solidly voted down Chuan's first amendment. Then in one swoop they submitted and voted through the first reading of an entirely "new" constitution of their own proposing. It was essentially the 1978 charter, which had enabled Prem and the military to hold power for so long.[14]

As Chuan persisted, veteran right-wingers made remarks that evoked 1976. Samak called Chuan's amendments tantamount to lèse-majesté, because they altered the structure of the government designed by Rama V.[15] Right-wing academic Poonsak Wannapong said the changes implied that the MPs could better represent the people than the king. Echoing the king's own sentiments, Poonsak said elected MPs were dirty and corrupt and that military coups were justified. "We must stop sticking too much to a written constitution, which no matter how good it is has proved a failure. We must give importance to our culture and history."[16] Meanwhile there were rallies by a militant Village Scout wing and a Red Gaur-like group, Apirak Chakri—Protectors of the Chakri. Their leader declared: "Thailand must not abandon constitutional monarchy. Our administrative system cannot be like that of the US, France, or communist countries. . . . The Chakri Dynasty is not a dinosaur."

The bluster continued throughout the year, and Chuan's every effort to get something through parliament was slapped down. In December he put some very watered-down amendments to a vote. Expecting Chuan to fail, Chavalit pulled his party out from the government in hopes of forcing its collapse. Chavalit saw himself then becoming prime minister, with military support. At this move Prem again stepped in, but now remarkably on the opposite side. Prem convinced the erstwhile leader Chatichai, now with his own new party, to join Chuan's government so it would survive in the majority, blocking Chavalit. Then the military senators also switched sides and voted for Chuan's amendments (which, in the broader context of the democratization effort, amounted to minor procedural issues). This spiteful intervention showed two things: that the palace, through Prem, still wielded a huge influence over the military, and was willing to use it frivolously; and that the palace distrusted Chavalit far more strongly than it did Chuan.

The Chuan government's tolerance for royal intervention had limits. Bhumibol's attempts to steer foreign policy on Burma and Cambodia in a different direction were rejected, and ended up embarrassing the throne together with the Thai military.

In the 1990s, Bhumibol remained bound to the thinking of the Cold War and even the absolutist monarchy. He believed China, Burma, and especially Vietnam had unremitting designs on Thailand. Vietnam's dominant role in Laos and Cambodia, both of which Bhumibol considered sister countries, directly threatened the kingdom, the king felt. He expressed this regularly to foreign diplomats and academics, as well as to Thai military leaders.

Before Chuan, the Thai military set the tone of relations with the kingdom's neighbors. The army maintained a cooperative relationship with Burma's Slorc junta and, in Cambodia, worked closely with border-based armies, including the genocidal Pol Pot and the Khmer Rouge, as they fought the Hanoi-backed Hun Sen regime. Strategically, these relationships didn't serve the Thais particularly well, but from them the Thai generals reaped millions of dollars from logging, gems, and other businesses shared with Slorc and the Khmer Rouge.

When Chuan came to power, the policy on both borders was reversed. His government fell into line with international support for Aung San Suu Kyi's fight for democracy against Slorc. With growing pressure to bring Pol Pot to justice, the government also ordered the Thai military to cut off the Khmer Rouge. The United Nations was preparing general democratic elections in Cambodia, and the Khmer Rouge had threatened to sabotage the polls.

The Thai army refused to change in both cases. Business deals with the Rangoon junta went on uninterrupted. In the run-up to the Cambodia elections, the Khmer Rouge ran a campaign of terror from camps on the Thai border. Numerous journalists and UN rapporteurs pointed out that this was only possible with Thai support. Chuan's government was embarrassed when, at the beginning of August 1993, UN peacekeepers who had been seized momentarily by the Khmer Rouge watched the Thai army share meals and medical treatment with the outlaw group. This brought sweeping international condemnation of Thailand.

While Chuan's officials denied this was official policy, King Bhumibol defended the army. He didn't accept that Slorc was a bad government. Nor did he seem to understand the problem of the Khmer Rouge. A few weeks after the Khmer

Rouge incident, in a speech to Thai diplomats, he said Thailand should cooperate with its neighbors and not pay heed to the global "police," meaning the United States.[17] "[Burma] is being treated like an undesirable. If we befriend such a person, the police are obliged to arrest us. So when we help Burma, or have contacts with Burma, the world community treats us like a pariah as well. . . . If we follow the western perception and jump on the bandwagon, saying that Burma is the bad guy, then we will have a neighboring country like Bosnia-Herzegovina." As for Cambodia, he said the Khmer Rouge should be allowed to share power, also to avoid the conflict the Europeans had created in Bosnia. He added, bizarrely, "The least we want to see is for UN forces to use Thai soil in their military intervention in Burma."

With the king's encouragement, the Thai army continued to work with Slorc and Pol Pot's army. In March 1994 the American ambassador to Bangkok raised the issue publicly. When that was rebuffed by the Thai military, at the end of May the retired former U.S. ambassador to Thailand, Morton Abramovitz, invoked King Bhumibol in a strongly worded criticism in the *Washington Post*.[18] "The only tools remaining are moral and diplomatic persuasion—continually reminding the Thais that they are undermining a neighbor and the costly work of the world community. Bangkok will resist having the issue raised, but doing so multilaterally can put greater pressure on the military and perhaps induce Thailand's top figures, including its respected monarch, to weigh in."

The reference to Bhumibol seemed innocuous, but it was clearly there to provoke the king himself. Some Thais reacted with outrage, accusing Abramovitz of lèse-majesté and demanding he be branded persona non grata.[19] The Supreme Command denied helping the Khmer Rouge but focused on the issue of the king, saying: "Ambassador Abramovitz's reference to the Thai monarchy . . . clearly indicates that [he] has no idea whatsoever of the role that his majesty the king plays as constitutional head of state. His majesty is in no way involved with politics, either domestic or foreign."[20] In contrast was the mild statement on the issue from the Thai Foreign Ministry, which agreed with the Americans. The pressure seemed to have an impact. Over the next year, the Thais mostly disengaged with the Khmer Rouge, cutting a crucial lifeline that underpinned the group's existence.

Another type of intervention in this period is worth noting, insomuch as it suggests the king's declining patience with Thai society. After years of essentially blocking it, in the mid-1990s Bhumibol effectively reactivated the death penalty.

Thailand had always had the death penalty, which the courts applied to the most egregious cases, such as killing a policeman or large-volume narcotics distribution. Each condemned person had the right to appeal to the king and could be executed only if the king rejected the appeal and returned it to the government. For much of his reign King Bhumibol hesitated to sign off. Instead he sat on the appeals, consciously staying the executions. Usually after five or ten years he commuted the sentences officially. Only extremely rarely did he allow an execution by returning the appeal without comment. With hundreds of people on Thailand's death row, from the mid-1980s he didn't permit any executions. This protected Bhumibol's image as merciful and kind.

Even so, Thailand had a serious violent crime problem, often involving police and soldiers, which Bhumibol never seemed to address.[21] The king seemed to view such problems in a Buddhist sense, that criminal behavior was unmeritorious conduct and up to the criminal to correct lest he suffer bad karma. But in the mid-1990s, with no announcement or explanation, Bhumibol began permitting executions, the first in 1995.[22] Some said the condemned man's appeal was stifled by corrections officials and the king never saw it. But it wasn't likely that the king's prerogative would be ignored. When over the next few years more executions took place, of murderers and methamphetamine dealers, it became clear that Bhumibol was actively rejecting appeals.

Some Thais said he had just become impatient with society as his reign neared its end, while others supposed that he had decided pragmatically that the death penalty was a utilitarian means of keeping order. Either way, it shifted the king's image from compassionate and forgiving to one of tough justice, making him someone to fear as much to love. It set an example for justice generally, for subsequently summary executions of suspected criminals by the police grew frequent. It harked back to the eras of Sarit and Tanin, when the law was seen as a barrier to public order.

Blustering interventions on policy were not enough to sustain royal prestige in a new environment, Bhumibol knew from experience. With all the changes taking place in the 1990s, the palace had to renew and revise its connections with the country's elite to sustain their support. The economic boom had left the palace farther away from the heart of economic power than before, for example. Parvenu capitalists cut through the turf boundaries of the old plutocracy, scores of new dollar millionaires who had no link to the old ruling class but drove the same Mercedes-Benzes and bought the same luxury goods. Their start-up businesses thrived in the face of venerable family companies, and sometimes brought the old houses down, as in the scandalous collapse of the palace-associated Bangkok Bank of Commerce. It was owned by the Pramojs, Devakuls, and other Chakri families, and many palace officials, including the royal family, banked there.

Traditionally, the monarchy harnessed the loyalty of the kingdom's wealthiest families via intermarriage and joint ventures. King Bhumibol lacked the luxury of a large pool of offspring he could share. So his team adroitly established alliances with the new tycoons. For instance, at the beginning of the decade, the palace had minimal relations with two of the country's wealthiest new Sino-Thai tycoons, liquor czar Charoen Siriwatanapakdi and Dhanin Chiaravanont, head of the Charoen Pokphand (CP) agribusiness, retailing, and telecommunications conglomerate.[23] Having skillfully found their ways into the pockets of every politician, general, and bureaucrat, both had built fortunes of over a billion dollars each, completely independent of the throne. The king was linked, in fact, to their rivals: to the small farmers whom Dhanin's corporate farm system threatened, and to the aristocratic Bhirombhakdi family, whose beer market dominance with their Singha brand was threatened by Charoen. Singha's virtual monopoly was granted by Rama VII, and the royal family privately held lucrative stakes in it.[24]

As the 1990s opened, Charoen and Dhanin were rapidly expanding and diversifying into key national industries. In arrangements that suggested mutual benefit, both took agents of the crown into their management ranks, most importantly Prem. Prem joined the CP group's executive board, while privy councilor Siddhi Savetsila was named to the boards of several CP group subsidiaries. The positions were all paid. With Charoen, the relationship was even more intimate, even as he slashed into the business of the Bhirombhakdis—or perhaps because of it. After Charoen took over the failing Imperial Hotels group, Prem became honorary chairman of the company, and the queen's cousin M.R. Saritikhun Kitiyakara was named president. Around the same time, Charoen appointed Queen Sirikit's elder brother and privy councilor M.R. Adulyakit Kitiyakara as chairman of his new brewery, Beer Chang. In the same period Charoen and his wife earned high royal decorations.

More important was the melding of capital. Charoen was the controlling shareholder of First Bangkok City Bank, but 15 percent was owned by the government. In what was a controversially preferential deal in 1996, the Crown Property Bureau was permitted to buy the 15 percent block, becoming Charoen's banking partner.

The palace took the same approach to renewing old relationships. The reins of control at Bangkok Bank, the country's largest, owned by the Sophonpanich family, were passing to a new generation, relative youngsters not spliced into the longtime connection between Bhumibol and the older Chin and Chatri Sophon-panich. To reinforce the bond, Prem became Bangkok Bank's paid honorary chairman. Always viewed as the king's agent, Prem was honorary chairman of the powerful housing developer Krisda Mahanakorn, and later also of the Bhirom-bhakdis' new airline, PB Air. The other privy councilors took their places at other companies. These were all well-paid positions, but they had another use. Prem's presence made sure each of the businesses paid a certain amount of obeisance, keeping the king's charity coffers filled.

In a different approach, the CPB took on a number of upstart tycoons as business partners. With piles of cash for investment and a huge land bank for development, the palace took part in numerous real estate projects, also involving the financial power of CPB-controlled Siam Commercial Bank. The developments included luxury condominiums, office towers, and five-star hotels and shopping complexes, done with winners in the economic boom like the Srivikorn family's President-Golden Land group, Pin Chakkaphak of Finance One, the Sansiri property group of the Lamsam and Chutrakul families, and Anant Asavabhokin of Land & Houses and Siam Sindhorn.

Another type of business brought together for the palace the money and the social ambitions of the new wealthy. In the 1990s the palace circle invested in several new private institutes in partnership with exclusive foreign schools: England's Harrow (attended by the king's father, Prince Mahidol) and Dulwich College, and Australia's Geelong Grammar. The latter, in direct partnership with the Mahidol family, launched a boarding school for rich Thais at Doi Tung, the princess mother's northern Thailand estate. It was managed by her personal secretary, M.R. Disnadda Diskul.[25] These schools didn't only promise to bring the cash of the new rich into palace hands; they guaranteed their children would be taught the palace worldview and grow up loyal to the Chakri Dynasty ideal.

The most important effort to keep the throne's popularity current was massive, constant media promotion. Tens if not hundreds of millions of dollars were spent in the 1990s in a saturation campaign advertising and celebrating the Chakri monarchy. It was designed to counterbalance the new media atmosphere, in which royal and official activities were downplayed or ignored for entertainment. It was also aimed at grabbing the attention of the under-30 generation of urban Thais, the yuppie salariat and MTV-influenced youth, who found the Mahidols old-fashioned.

Marketing the monarchy with a slicker Madison Avenue-style approach fell to a number of figures with experience in modern media techniques. They were led by

Piya Malakul, whose Pacific Communications media group included the leading women's magazine *Dichan* and the talk-and-traffic radio station Jor Sor 100, and provided programming for television stations, mainly the army-controlled Channel 5 (run by Piya's brother General Paeng Malakul). Supporting the effort were the financially flush and accomplished marketing teams of the Tourism Authority of Thailand and Thai Airways, and new courtiers like the ambitious young royalist, law professor, and TV presenter Thongthong Chandrangsu.

Their promotions were marked not by any new interpretation but simply by better presentation and packaging. They replaced the ancient grainy footage and scratchy recordings of the royal anthem that preceded every film showing in the country's movie theaters with a Hollywood high-tech computerized montage of color photos of the royal family backed by a luxuriant arrangement of the anthem. Their slick documentaries on the royal family were broadcast as television series, while a film on the king's musical hobby, *Kitarajan*, was shown in theaters to busloads of schoolchildren. New arrangers and performers turned the tired old recordings of the king's music into excessively lush chorale and orchestral pieces. Several public multimedia dramas were made on the royals. Thongthong wrote one performed by the navy, *Phaendin Ni Mi Kamlang*, or This Land Has Strength, which celebrated the kings of early Bangkok.

Productions like this required substantial money. Aside from the state budget, big Thai companies, especially those of upstart tycoons who had recently moved into the royal circle, were willing to pay. *Kitarajan*, for instance, was funded by Charoen Siriwatanapakdi. The palace's investments in mass media suggested that it wanted to be certain of the media campaign's impact. The CPB-owned United Cinema bought a printing house, Siam Press, and formed online and television new businesses together with other large media groups. In 1994 United Cinema took over *Siam Rath*, the once vibrant daily newspaper of Kukrit Pramoj, and around the same time invested in a new Thai financial newspaper, *Sue Turakij*, and Bangkok's third English daily, *Business Day*. Also pushing into publishing was Tridhosyuth Devakul, one of Prem's closest cronies and a royal-family investment partner. He took over a foundering Thai newspaper, *Siam Post*, whose audience was better-educated Bangkokians. When *Siam Post* still foundered, Piya Malakul rescued it. The most aggressive palace move was to invest in a new television station. After May 1992 exposed the military's abusive dominance of television news, the Chuan government moved to expand broadcast diversity by issuing a fifth television station license, which became ITV. The winner of the license in April 1995 was a group led by Siam Commercial Bank and the Crown Property Bureau, together with Piya's Pacific Communications and the print news group Nation Publishing.

None of these media outlets became overtly royalist, and CPB head Chirayut insisted they were purely financial investments.[26] But there was widespread suspicion that the palace was keeping its hand close to the controls just in case. Another indicator was Banharn's May 1996 appointment of a new board for the Mass Communications Organization of Thailand, which managed two television stations and a number of radio frequencies, and distributed all official government news. The chairman was General Mongkol Ampornpisit, a longtime Prem aide, and another new board member was palace insider Thongthong.

The centerpiece of the ongoing publicity effort, already being planned in 1992, was a 24-month celebration of King Bhumibol's golden jubilee, the 50th year of his reign, in 1996. The celebration would dwarf his 60th birthday fete in 1987, not only in the breadth of activities but in the heights to which Bhumibol was elevated.

The glorification began early with several unscheduled events, the first when Princess Mother Sangwal was hospitalized at Siriraj Hospital in December 1994. She was said to have "minor" heart and stomach problems, but at the age of 94, nothing was minor, and many citizen and government associations organized pray-ins and merit-making for her. Then, on March 6, King Bhumibol himself nearly collapsed while exercising. He was admitted to Siriraj for significant coronary blockage, and there was real worry in well-informed circles that he might not survive.[27] Still hospitalized in the weeks following his angioplasty, he was nevertheless seen on television daily visiting his mother and instructing officials on traffic management. It suggested the dhammaraja's superhuman persistence, in work and life.

It also reminded Thais that the Mahidols, cornerstone of the kingdom's fate, were not immortal. Some 2,000 people joined a mass pray-in at Sanam Luang to give thanks for their survival, while the supreme patriarch led 999 monks in chanting for the king. They credited the king's recovery to Siam Dhevathirat, the country's patron saint, and to his own great merit. The royal family made its own offerings to the monument of Prince Mahidol at Siriraj.

Three weeks after leaving the hospital, Bhumibol appeared on television with most of his family to explain his illness and demonstrate his fitness. On camera the king walked around a large room as doctors tested his heart. Viewers were told pulse and blood-pressure statistics and that he did seven full circuits, one kilometer, in 11 minutes 48 seconds: just as in the royal news, which reported the precise minute of the day of official royal activities, meaningless figures were given talismanic significance.

Bhumibol then sat down with a whiteboard and explained what had happened to him. He related his condition to his 1982 infection, to smoking, which he quit in 1987, and to drinking alcohol, which he now moderated—behavior most Thais never associated with him. He also said it was because he worked five or six hours at a time without break, exercised too little, and experienced great tension: his illness was the virtuous burden of being king. Even so, Bhumibol said, his doctors assured him that he could go on another 25 years, long enough to complete his royal development projects. Otherwise, he implied, there could be no progress.

Sangwal, on the other hand, deteriorated until she finally died on July 18. In her death, with the help of the palace promotion machine, she became more alive and consequential than ever before. Although well known by Thais, Sangwal never played much of a direct role in their lives. She lived in Switzerland through the 1980s, and after she returned permanently she was rarely seen outside her Doi Tung estate. But magazines frequently showed her growing flowers and doing needle-point, and published her thoughts on Buddhism.

Upon her death the palace set out to canonize her as the equivalent of a blue-blooded queen and a figure of bodhisattva status. It served both to expand the pantheon of modern royals for the public to venerate, and also to reassert that, her common birth notwithstanding, her blood was pure and virtuous as any Chakri. When she died, the king set a normal 100-day mourning period, and government employees were asked to wear black for 15 days. The supreme patriarch led mass merit-making at Sanam Luang. Her body underwent Brahman bathing obsequies in an inner Grand Palace hall, where the king and queen sprinkled lustral water on her, and Bhumibol placed on her head a *chada,* the traditional spiring Siamese crown. Her jewel-studded funerary urn was emplaced in a throne hall for paying respects. There visitors saw the urn set beneath a seven-tiered royal umbrella, reserved for the very highest royals but the king, who had nine tiers.

A massive campaign glorifying Sangwal's life was launched. Government of-fices organized commemorations, and police stations were ordered to hold formal merit-making rites on the seventh, fiftieth, and hundredth days after her death. The police posthumously promoted her to the rank of general, and the Border Patrol Police planned to build statues of her at each BPP camp.[28]

When the throne hall was opened to public mourning, each day hundreds of people, mostly elderly women, came to offer prayers and witness, late each afternoon, the king and queen themselves sitting while monks chanted. In keeping with tradition, various people and groups close to Sangwal and the royal family would sponsor a day of mourning, providing the alms for monks and leading prayers. Before the number of condolers tapered off, the palace and government prodded other groups to sponsor prayers in the palace, and to accommodate them the mourning period was extended indefinitely. Government offices, corporations, and civic associations each sponsored a mourning session, their hundreds of employees and members compelled to sit in front of the urn in meditation. It gave people the rare opportunity to witness their own king and queen up close, likewise praying, or the king working hard on traffic plans.

This went on for the rest of the year, with the royal news portraying it as a spontaneous outpouring for the princess mother. The sponsored mourning grew on itself, understood as a very meritorious practice. It took on the air of something more transmundane as auspicious signs and stories were noted. Although it was the rainy season anyway, the *Bangkok Post* reported that on July 19, just before the bathing rites, "the overcast sky broke and the rain poured down, as if to suggest that the almighty had acknowledged the passing of the princess mother and shared the grief of the people."[29]

A supernatural story was related about her death by a famous monk, Phra Pipit Thammasunthorn of Wat Suthas, who said he was told it by the king. Five years before she actually died, Sangwal said she felt tired and was ready to leave the world. Her words made Bhumibol think of the Lord Buddha, who himself told a disciple that he would die within three months. The disciple could have asked the Buddha to remain on earth, but he didn't, and so the Buddha died. So Bhumibol begged Sangwal to remain alive for the sake of her children and the Thai people. She stayed on for five more years. When she died, the king had also related, he and Galyani were holding her hands. The electrocardiograph no longer showed a pulse. But as he thought of the things he hadn't said to her, the machine miraculously showed her heart beating again. When Galyani's daughter entered and grasped her hands, Sangwal's pulse came alive again. They understood she was finally saying goodbye. The graph of the machine proved the miracle, Bhumibol told Phra Pipit.[30]

For months on radio and television, meanwhile, there was such an intense and unprecedented bombardment of programs commemorating Sangwal that even some in royal circles openly criticized the excess. On his birthday that December, Bhumibol said that it was because Thais could uniquely recognize her goodness that the kingdom remained at peace, while war raged in the Balkans. "We were glad to have a mother who was loved by everyone. They all considered her 'Grand-mother.' . . . All those who call her 'Grandmother' are thus our nephews and nieces. . . . Even in her demise, she has contributed to the country. . . . When people from all lands and all tongues, even those who dislike Thailand, see this unique situation, this deep respect for the one who deserves it, they cannot help liking this country."[31]

Sangwal's cremation was set for March 10, 1996, based on auspicious signs: palace astronomers said the comet Hyakutake would be visible in the Libra constellation, the sign under which Sangwal was born.[32] The religious affairs department recruited 34,604 men to ordain in her honor, for the number of days she lived. The youngest of the crown prince's sons ordained too. For the cremation, the palace and government issued lengthy brochures explaining the cosmic and dynastic significance of every uniform, decoration, position, and motion. Broadcast media would carry the entire event by pool, each step narrated in hushed tones by Thongthong Chandrangsu. Besides the official palace cameramen, no media were allowed near except BBC television, which received special access for filming a documentary that the palace expected would glorify Sangwal to world audiences.

The day after the cremation confirmed her magical elevation to queen status, when her relics were installed by the king in the Grand Palace's Chakri Throne Hall and in Wat Phra Kaew, housing the Emerald Buddha, honors reserved only for top royals. The funeral was also an occasion to raise money for the royal charities. Some $12 million was collected over the eight months her body lay in state, to build a hospital in her name. The government minted coins with her visage, well promoted in the funeral broadcast, to raise a target $6 million. On the day of the cremation, boxes placed around Sanam Luang collected over $160,000. The Ministry of Education also collected an unreported amount, which it said would be used to construct statues of Sangwal around the country. For the next few years, books, documentaries, CD-ROMs, and cassette tapes were produced, marketed, and shown exalting her life. The palace was determined to establish not just her royal rank but her spiritual achievement as no less than the king's own.

The consecration of Sangwal quickly folded into the celebration of the reign's 50th year. Nearly every event over 24 months was declared "in honor of the king's golden jubilee." Prince Vajiralongkorn oversaw a project to carve a gigantic Buddha image into a Chonburi hillside in the king's honor. Princess Sirindhorn presided over an international conference on vetiver grass, which the king had promoted (palace publicity often said discovered) as useful in conservation. Supreme Patriarch Yanasangworn led a project to plant sacred bho trees in the king's honor at the king-dom's 30,000 temples.

Huge sums were spent, in government budgets and from businesses. Not all of it was straightforward. Businessmen raided shareholder funds to demonstrate their own loyalty. One report said that senators had 500 baht a month deducted from salaries, to a total of 8.7 million baht, for the celebrations and royal projects.[33] Another later showed that Premier Banharn, in raising 999 million baht for the king's flood-control projects, actually borrowed much of it from the state-owned Krung Thai Bank.[34]

The hubris of the economic boom and the stock market peaking at the begin-ning of 1996 supported some lavish gifts to the king. A prominent jeweler acquired a gigantic 6.3-kilogram blue topaz to have cut with 950 facets (symbolizing the 9th reign, 50th year) and presented to the throne. The Thai military, using public funds, produced a new royal mace made with 700 grams of gold and 518 diamonds and other gems. The most extravagant gift came from the most wealthy Sino-Thai businessmen, led by Bangkok Bank's Chatri Sophonpanich and coordinated by Prem. They bought for an unknown price the world's largest cut diamond, a 546-carat yellow-brown gem from South Africa that Thais noted proudly was bigger by 15.4 carats than the Cullinan Star of Africa in Britain's crown jewels. Underscoring their view of the king's sacrality, the businessmen reportedly had the diamond consecrated by the Thai supreme patriarch, the Thai Muslim patriarch, and Pope John Paul II in Rome.

Two other lavish expenditures were noteworthy. Some $8 million in govern-ment and donated funds was used to commission new gem-studded gold vest-ments for the Emerald Buddha. And later in 1996 the government presented the king with a 2.5-kilogram gold and jeweled naga image, while naming him the Father of Water Resource Management. Several thousand books heralding his achievements in hydrology were distributed to schools around the country.[35]

The week of the jubilee was jam-packed with events honoring the Ninth Reign. Television was filled with documentaries, talk shows, and even game shows built around the monarchy. On June 7 all stations broadcast live a fund-raiser for royal charities, with Banharn and his wife kicking off the donations with 10 million baht, or $400,000.[36] Finally, on the morning of June 9, 25 caparisoned elephants carried 50 men to a royal temple to be ordained in the king's honor. The king performed private rituals to honor his ancestors and his brother Ananda, whose death 50 years earlier that morning remained an unspoken, unsolved mystery. Around the nation many merit-making rituals were undertaken, and that evening, before fireworks were launched, one million candles blessed by the supreme patriarch were lit together at the astrologer-designated auspicious time of 19:19.

The celebrations continued sporadically through the rest of the year, and all seemed to go off without a hitch, though not without a vigilant palace staff ensuring it. Officials complained, even to foreign news offices, when stories or photographs didn't put the royal family in the best light. When the *Nation* published an article on Chitrlada Palace that described the lushly planted compound as an "island of green in an ocean of gray . . . a world apart from the teeming streets of Bangkok," the palace berated the editors for making the king sound isolated in luxury from his suffering subjects.[37] More seriously, early in 1996 the leading political and social affairs show on television, *Mong Tang Moom,* was canceled for addressing controversial topics. The show's host said Prem had ordered it off the air so that it didn't embarrass any of those in power.[38]

Still tireless in her busy schedule of charity operations, rural visits, society galas, and pleasure travel, Queen Sirikit wasn't left out in all the royal promotion. The government garnered numerous honors for her from both Thai and foreign institutions. Each August at her birthday there were grand balls and demonstrations of adoration countrywide. Thousands of schoolgirls would be brought to the Royal Plaza to meditate as a group for her, dressed in white like nuns and holding candles. Buddhist amulets and statues were cast in her name and sold to raise money for charities.

For her 1992 birthday the tycoons in her regular retinue—banker Banyong Lamsam, industrialist Prayuth Mahagitsiri, Charoen Siriwatanapakdi, Dhanin Chiaravanont, and Thaksin Shinawatra—donated millions to build a Queen Sirikit wing at Chulalongkorn Hospital, to stand equally with the Bhumibol wing. For the same occasion, the Siam Society raised $1 million to fabricate, using 30 kilograms of pure gold, a massive Buddha's footprint, an extremely sacral icon of Buddhism, in Sirikit's honor. The project was inaugurated by Prince Vajiralongkorn, and the king and the supreme patriarch consecrated the completed footprint in June 1994, installing it in Wat Phra Kaew. One hundred small replicas were also cast for distribution to members of the royal family and to temples around the country in the queen's name.[39]

But Queen Sirikit aspired to be not just a complement to her husband but her own heroic figure. She wanted to be known as a modern incarnation of ancient Siam's official first heroine, the 16th-century Ayutthaya queen Suriyothai. In legend Suriyothai was the beautiful consort of the embattled King Chakkrabhat who, in 1549, dressed up as a man to go forth on elephant-back to fight Burmese invaders.

She died in the battle but saved her husband. There is little historical evidence for the story but, revived by palace historians in the Fifth and Sixth reigns, the Suriyothai tale had become standard history-book fare.

Sirikit was said to imagine herself an avatar of the ancient queen, and Bhumibol went along with it, in 1989 naming his Ayutthaya water conservation and flood-prevention project the Sri Suriyothai Park. For Sirikit's 60th birthday, the king had the park bestowed to Sirikit as her own. The army paid special homage to Suriyothai's beauty and heroism in a son-et-lumière drama for Sirikit's brand-new Ayutthaya palace; the government commissioned a Buddha image named after Suriyothai; and a new Hua Hin army base was likewise named for the legendary queen. The Suriyothai myth grew, propelled by Sirikit's visits to the supposed battle site to make offerings. In his 1995 birthday speech, Bhumibol credited the legendary queen for the success of the Ayutthaya flood-prevention project. The next year, a massive statue of Queen Suriyothai on elephant-back was erected in the park and inaugurated by Sirikit.

The mid-1990s saw new benchmark interpretations of the monarchy, each an attempt to bridge the gap between the new forces of society and the traditional Chakri throne. Each advanced the idea of the king's unknowable wisdom and unmatchable virtue, and that he embodied whatever democracy the country needed.

The first new interpreter was royal-projects aide Sumet Tantivejakul. Speaking on several occasions on the king's rural development efforts, Sumet described how the king follows the Buddhist principles of industriousness, sacrifice, and selflessness in seeking to end poverty. This came across especially in a large-format book, *Thailand's Guiding Light,* published for the 1996 anniversary. It describes Bhumibol as working hard to overcome the "forces of greed represented by the collaboration of unscrupulous private investors, politicians and public officials." In a chapter identifying the king as "Environmental Activist," Sumet explains the king's environmentalism as a superior ability to balance the needs of the people and the environment. The king is more effective than the one-dimensional, insensitive bureaucracy because he uniquely "looks at problems in a holistic manner . . . [and] never lets costs or academic correctness get in the way of his determination to help poor villagers. He does not think people's lives and happiness can or should be measured in terms of money or academic principles."[40]

Acknowledging the validity of some opposition to large-scale dams, Sumet insisted the king was well ahead of environmental activists. His projects are usually small-scale, and it is only because people have ignored his solutions to drought and flooding for years that problems continue. After the large floods in 1983, Sumet said, the king proposed solutions, but "no one paid heed."

One demand of environmental and social activists of the 1990s was that major projects be reviewed in public hearings, which the bureaucracy and politicians strongly opposed. Sumet argued that the king already fulfilled this role, so that formal hearings were unnecessary. In his visits to rural villages, Sumet said, "His Majesty has been holding public hearings for the last 30 years. . . . He urges people to say what they really feel."[41] Such informal consultations, Sumet had said earlier, justified the Pasak and Tha Dan dams. In *Thailand's Guiding Light,* Sumet further explained that the king spent hours and hours talking to villagers. "It's an untainted process of public hearing, unorganized and natural." For Sumet, this was democracy.

Erstwhile premier Anand Panyarachun was an interpreter of a different sort—necessarily so, because some of his personal views were at odds with the king's. In a newspaper interview and in a speech published in *Thailand's Guiding Light,* Anand reiterated the 800-year-old basis of the king's benevolent, paternalistic rule in the Sukhothai dhammaraja tradition.[42] The kings knew their subjects well, Anand noted, and the Chakri kings, and Rama IX specifically, protected the nation while fostering progressive change. "Thailand is now a constitutional monarchy and a country aspiring to become a newly developed society, but the traditional principles of righteous Buddhist kingship and kingly virtues remain of paramount importance to the present monarchy. His majesty has displayed, and continues to display, a profound understanding of constitutional kingship as well as the traditional sources and symbols of Thai monarchical tradition."

Even the deeply rationalist Anand found something uncanny in this. Bhumibol, he noted, "was not born to be king. As such, he had little time to be groomed to be one." In politically treacherous postwar Thailand, he traveled the entire country to get to know his land and people. "He would know every river, every stream, every creek, every mountain and every pass. He is a good map reader," said Anand. This astuteness launched Thailand to development. "After a state visit to a foreign country, his majesty inspired the then government to embark on the first national economic and social development plan."[43]

Although less enthusiastic at the mystical sources of Bhumibol's brilliance, Anand still seemed to acknowledge the king's attainment of enlightenment. "The king is a man of tremendous self-discipline. When he went into the monkhood, he studied religion very religiously and now he is a man of self-discipline. He understands reality of life. He knows that certain things cannot be changed. And he has . . . no 'atta,' he has no 'ego.' He has no sense of self-importance. . . . He is completely detached. . . . [T]o be a really good Buddhist, you must dispossess yourself of all these attachments. . . . You only do it for the good of the community, for the public good. That is how he conducts his daily life."

Among monarchs perhaps only Japan's emperor is more revered by his people, Anand said. But unlike the palace-bound Japanese emperor, King Bhumibol gets close to his people. That explains why "even without publicity, people would know that here we have a king, we have a monarch who just does not sit on the throne and idle his time away. . . . I think these are his personal characteristics that have endeared him to the nation. . . . You know, there is a dictum that the king can do no wrong. In our case, the king really can do no wrong."

Anand said that King Bhumibol's continuous political experience leads him to frequently intervene in politics. Moreover, the prime minister briefs the king once a week on policies and trends. "His indirect influence on governments' policies and measures cannot, therefore, be underestimated," said Anand. While no one else had ever dared disclose this, Anand clearly felt that making such revelations let people know that the king was well informed and put his knowledge to good use. This intervention had a constitutional foundation, Anand said. But he didn't cite the Thai constitution; he cited Walter Bagehot: "As a constitutional monarch, he only has three duties. The first one, he has the right to be consulted, so he has the right to be consulted by the prime minister or by the government. The second right, he has the right to warn; and then he has the right to encourage. He keeps strictly to the three rights." While Bagehot's distillation was convenient for constitutional kings and queens worldwide, Anand repeated it so many times that people assumed it did come from the Thai constitution.

Anand added that in Thai tradition certain powers were bestowed upon the king by the popular will of the people. Bhumibol has earned these powers, Anand said, citing the king's interventions in 1973 and 1992 (and skipping over 1976), which Anand said were "at the behest of his own people." "He knows the time is right and the nation cannot tolerate such a situation any longer. Then he would 'come down.' . . . And that automatically within a second, the whole crisis would disappear."

Somewhat defensively, Anand added that the king cannot wield his powers freely, but must follow the principles of modern civil society: "He is also accountable. What he does is seen by the public. Not accountable in the legal sense of the word . . . but there is transparency." Anand was striving to update the monarchy's image for modern intellectuals.[44] But, like Sumet, he ultimately fell back on tradition and hyperbole. "These activities do not normally fall within the domain of a constitutional monarch. But [because] he has persevered in these activities for the long-lasting benefit of the Thai people ... Thais, in general, willingly and unreservedly accord him the confidence that no other monarch in our history, or for that matter any other monarch in the world, had ever enjoyed.... He acts as a kind of guiding light, for people who occasionally have to grope in the darkness or in a mystical condition."

The third source of interpretations was King Bhumibol himself. He made several different explications of his reign, revealing, or reburnishing, different facets for different audiences. His effort for doubtful intellectuals came in publishing his own translations of two foreign biographies, William Stevenson's *A Man Called Intrepid* and Phyllis Auty's *Tito*.

Stevenson's book is a portrait of Sir William Stephenson, the little-known Canadian master of intelligence for the Allies in World War II.[45] He is shown as a self-effacing hero who shunned recognition for his supremely important behind-the-scenes war effort. Bhumibol entitled his Thai translation *Nai In: Phu Thi Pit Thong Lang Phra,* or Mr. In(-trepid): The Man Who Sticks Gold onto the Back of the Buddha Image. The king wanted his readers to see a man who worked hard without seeking reward or recognition, just how Bhumibol saw himself.

The book also recounts that in both the United States and England, wiser leaders, Roosevelt in Washington and Churchill and King George VI in London, were forced to secretly override elected politicians who resisted taking up the fight with the Nazis. Noting that Churchill lacked parliamentary authority, the author wrote: "[His] support came from the king, that higher authority whose intervention was permissible in times of crisis although it could be challenged. This traditional arrangement, by which the monarchy and the funds set aside for royal function could be used to protect those acting secretly to defend national interests, was ... to prove vital in the secret wars to come."[46]

Also pronounced were the themes of the monarch's position as a potent symbol inspiring bravery and resolve (like the Danish king during the war); of the need to keep things secret from the people; and of the need to have a higher leader beyond the elected leader, who might not be a selfless actor. When political problems developed, "The conflict was resolved by the fact that directors of British intelligence are confirmed in their appointment by the Crown. . . . This untidy British arrangement ... [has] proved relevant to today's ideological warfare with its confusions of loyalty."[47]

Bhumibol said nothing particular about what inspired him to translate Stevenson's book, but he clearly thought it was an important story. When his translation was published in 1993, 100,000 copies were printed, making it, at the time, the biggest-selling book in Thailand ever. A year later King Bhumibol published his translation of *Tito*, a biography of the late Yugoslav president. Royal aide Keokhwan Vajarodaya explained that the king recognized that Tito worked tirelessly for growth, peace, and a higher standard of living for his people.[48] In addition, remarks in several 1990s speeches on the horrific collapse into war of Yugoslavia and the Balkan states suggested that Bhumibol appreciated Tito for keeping his country united and independent for 35 years. Yet it raised the question of what Bhumibol may have thought about the fragility of that achievement, dissolving into war after Tito died.

Two other efforts by King Bhumibol to define himself were addressed to a much broader audience, everyday Thai Buddhists, from peasant farmers to civil servants to the less cynical segment of the upper class. The first came with his December 1995 birthday speech. No longer agitated or weak from surgery, he did a public stocktaking of his own leadership, over more than two hours unapologetically asserting his mastery of water resources management, economic development, and other practical subjects. It was a justification not only of his criticisms of governments but of his utter right to rule and reign, as a master scientist and engineer, a selfless, efficient administrator, and a wise dhammaraja.

After receiving lavish praise and a gold Buddha from Prime Minister Banharn, he started by saying that people should appreciate water, not curse it when there are floods, and then pray for it in the dry season.[49] He held up as a good example the Suriyothai project in Ayutthaya, citing from memory a lengthy list of statistics on water volumes, flows, and levels, which made him sound deeply expert.

He then turned to something he had introduced briefly in 1994, his "New Theory" of development. This was Bhumibol's distillation of all he had learned of the economy, farming, and sustainability over his reign. The New Theory, he explained, was at its core a system of integrated, self-sufficient small-farm management. In the ideal, a "typical" 15-rai (6-acre) family farm would produce enough, by ecologically sound methods, that the farmer could live independent of cash markets to sell his crops and buy fertilizers, seeds, and pesticides.

Honed on the king's own demonstration farms, the idea rolled into one his ideas of hard work, self-reliance, cooperative economics, water conservation, and the bucolic peasant life of the idealized dhammaraja's kingdom. Behind the concept, said his aide M.L. Birabongs Kasemsri, was that the people should develop the "right mentality" as taught by Buddha, understanding the consequences of our actions.

In fact, Bhumibol had already established the New Theory as national policy, having it inserted into the government's five-year economic development plan in early 1995.[50] At his birthday speech, a booklet explaining the theory was distributed to the audience. The king ordered: "The contents of this booklet must be studied and carefully pursued, because the application of the New Theory is not a simple thing. . . . The people at large are now aware of the existence of the New Theory and everyone wants to benefit from it. . . . The New Theory must be implemented in places where it is suitable."

All that was prologue to the core of his speech, to prove to the audience—the officials in front of him and his subjects listening on the radio and television—that his knowledge on developing Thailand's water resources was perfect and unassailable, and qualified him for kingship. On one hand, he established his credentials through his mastery of science and statistics. He started with an anecdote, of his accurate prediction of the course of a typhoon that hadn't hit Thailand as many feared it would. It showed he was better at forecasting the weather than the meteorologists of the Thai government, CNN, and the BBC. But how did he do that? the head of the meteorological department had asked him. Bhumibol turned to traditional mythology, explaining that he had consulted the "Mani Mekhala Office," "a weather forecast office which has its headquarters on Mount Sumeru." He said: "I asked Mani Mekhala to go and make arrangements [regarding the typhoon] and it yielded good results. . . . If it had not been for the auspicious things that helped us and protected us, by now, we would still be under water," he said.

Not many had known that the king had named his office for rainmaking and water-resource management after a folklore goddess. The hundreds of officials sitting in front of him knew he was being playful, but would the millions of Thais listening on the radio? Toward them the throne had always expressed itself in traditional mythological terms. For those ready to believe, the king not only could forecast the weather better than CNN but could manipulate it too.

Returning to the mundane, Bhumibol mapped out a grand approach of building pocket reservoirs all over the country to curtail flooding and drought, based on his Ayutthaya project. He called the plan *kaem ling*, or monkey cheeks. He got the idea when he was just five years old, from watching monkeys store bananas in their cheeks before eating them.

To prove that there was solid scientific basis for all of his ideas, Bhumibol recited a huge amount of national hydrological statistics, river volumes and rainfall rates and flood levels. He used the figures to "prove" that the Pasak dam was necessary. "It will help to lighten the miseries because 800 million cubic meters will be kept in that dam," he explained. He called on specific provincial governors from northern Thailand to report on flooding in their provinces. Using maps and diagrams and statistics from memory, he demonstrated that he knew the local situation better than each. As if they were his own administrators, he instructed them to report their specific problems to the prime minister—though, he sighed, the government was poor at coordinating.

Downstream again, Bhumibol gave an impressively detailed assessment of the situation in the Bangkok suburbs, in order to prove the value of his Monkey Cheeks idea. He suggested even building up the flood-prone communities on artificial mounds, on which the New Theory could be implemented. "If it is successfully carried out, it will be a profit because . . . there will be no one who will lose. Everyone will be able to work for the benefit of the community. Everybody will have enough money to subsist. The community will be self-reliant. . . . Thailand will show considerable progress."

In all its rambling and frequent humorous asides, it was a masterful presentation of royal virtue and wisdom, through science and magic. Each of his subjects, from the struggling farmer to the urban dweller, the superstitious to the defiantly rational, could find cause to believe in their king. Afterward bureaucrats rushed to launch New Theory projects, or to put New Theory signs on existing projects, even those crafted and funded by foreign development agencies that had never heard of the idea.

To make his message even more clear, Bhumibol published a third book, in which he adroitly employed a mythological dhammaraja to draw parallels with his own reign. The book was *Mahajanaka,* Bhumibol's recension of an allegorical fable from the *Jataka* stories of the Buddha's life. It was published in the form of a children's story, illustrated by the country's leading artists in the traditional temple mural form. The Mahajanaka came from the last ten Jataka tales, the *Totsachati Jataka,* known among Thais as *Phra Chao Sip Chat.* These stories had a particular place in Siamese culture as fables of the final ten incarnations of the Buddha. Each illustrated a particular virtue that corresponded to the thotsaphit rachatham.

Bhumibol chose to revise the penultimate Jataka, which tells of Prince Mahajanaka, who grows up to learn that the throne of Mithila was taken from his father by an evil uncle. Vowing to reclaim the throne, Mahajanaka embarks on a trading venture to raise funds for an army. When his ship founders, by his strength and wisdom he survives while all others perish. After floating for seven days, he is rescued by the goddess Mani Mekhala and dropped back in an orchard in Mithila.

Mahajanaka's uncle, the king of Mithila, had died. So Mahajanaka takes the uncle's daughter as a wife and becomes king, ruling wisely, according to the thotsaphit rachatham, for seven thousand years, until he achieves enlightenment. This occurred when one day King Mahajanaka came across two mango trees. One was barren of fruit but green and healthy. The other had borne delicious fruit, but had been torn apart and uprooted by the people who desired its fruit. From this the king observed that having wealth and possessions only brought sorrow; having nothing brought happiness. So he gave up his kingdom and his wife, shaved his head, and became an ascetic, never to be seen again.

Bhumibol's version of the tale is generally the same, but the differences say a lot about himself. While Mahajanaka floats on the sea, he has a long discussion with Mani Mekhala—the name Bhumibol used for his own office—about perseverance. The discussion concludes: "Any individual who practices perseverance, even in the face of death, will not be in any debt to relatives of gods or father or mother. Furthermore, any individual who does his duty like a man, will enjoy Ultimate Peace in the future." This was Bhumibol's favorite maxim: success without perseverance is empty; failure with perseverance is glorious; lack of perseverance is condemnable. Perseverance, physical or moral, was an ingredient of dhammic pure practice. Once Mahajanaka became king ("the Great Being"), "He reflected that perseverance is an essential thing: had we not persevered in the ocean, we would not be on this throne. . . . From that time on, the Great Being practiced the Ten Rules of Kingship. He reigned with righteousness. He supported all the hermit buddhas."

Bhumibol also abridged the story of the mango trees. Rather than react by becoming a recluse, Mahajanaka taps his mastery of farm technologies to save the damaged tree. Meanwhile he endeavors to change the destructive behavior of the people through education. Everyone, "from the viceroy down to the elephant mahouts and the horse handlers . . . and especially the courtiers are all ignorant. They lack . . . common sense: they do not even know what is good for them." The illustration for this episode shows the mango tree being pulled down by modern machinery. All around are the ills of modern Thai society: corruption, lasciviousness, gambling, prostitution, and drunkenness, all witnessed by innocent children.

In addition, Bhumibol's Mahajanaka builds a university to share his wisdom. In the accompanying illustration, the king is bringing life and green to a treeless, devastated landscape, resembling heavily deforested modern Thailand. It took little leap of imagination to place Bhumibol in the role of King Mahajanaka. Bhumibol too refused to retire because he still hadn't achieved his goals, as he said in the book's preface, dated on the reign's 50th anniversary: "King Mahajanaka practiced ultimate perseverance without the desire for reward which resulted in his gaining the throne and bringing prosperity and wealth to the city of Mithila. . . . [However, the author felt that] King Mahajanaka's desire to leave the city on a quest for supreme tranquility was not yet opportune nor timely because Mithila's prosperity had not yet reached an appropriate peak. . . . King Mahajanaka also had to advance his thoughts on how to revive the mango tree. . . . King Mahajanaka would have been able to achieve supreme tranquility more readily if he had completely fulfilled his worldly duties first."

The format and launch of Mahajanaka showed how seriously the palace institution took it. It was published in both Thai and English and introduced in a rare palace media briefing, foreign reporters invited alongside Thai. The first release was a large-format, hardbound collector's edition sold for charity purposes at $2,000 and $200 for different versions, inclusive of gold and silver medallions consecrated by the king and the supreme patriarch. When sales weren't feverish, as with many other palace promotions, the 15 state and commercial banks were pressed by the central bank to sell 15 million baht ($600,000) worth of the book.[51] Some ended up giving them to favored customers, ultimately costing their shareholders.

A year later the book was released in a 250-baht full-color paperback edition, and then after another year as a cheap cartoon book for children. By then the publicity had made people more aware of Mahajanaka's significance, and companies and organizations bought it in bulk to pass out—earning both merit and tax deductions. Some gave them to temples to redistribute. It became part of the magic circle of merit.

20   *Another Family Annus Horribilis*   ∾

FOR ALL ITS INTENSITY, the sweeping intervention and exaltation during 1992–96 couldn't completely seal King Bhumibol's legacy. As much as it was a climax of the Ninth Reign, 1996 was also, thanks to his children, Bhumibol's *annus horribilis.* The principal difference with Queen Elizabeth's miserable 1992 was that Bhumibol's bad news stayed out of the media, just barely.

The problem had been building for years. None of King Bhumibol's children were particularly happy, caught between what they were expected to be and what they were and wanted. First daughter Ubolrat was bored with raising her three children in southern California and craved reinstatement as the family's senior and most glamorous princess, as well as the attendant financial resources that would make her daughter Ploypailin an internationally recognized concert pianist.

Ubolrat visited Bangkok more frequently in the early 1990s, to be honored at parties with the matrons of high society and join the queen at charity balls. Although officially she was only a thanpuying, or lady, in English she was called princess and many people treated her as such. Sirikit helped her to launch an eponymous charity with a fund-raising ball on Sirikit's birthday in 1992. The Ubolrat Foundation took in a reported 5 million baht ($200,000) in its first year; the next year it raised 20 million baht, with its leading contributors the state-owned

Petroleum Authority and Tourism Authority, and Sirikit herself. The foundation was meant to establish Ubolrat's image as a public-service-minded Chakri. But the first recipient of the foundation's funds was Ploypailin, who gave a piano recital at the 1993 ball. After the news of this embarrassed the family, the foundation quickly announced the award of 3 million baht to truly needy projects, in the names of Ploypailin, Ubolrat, and her husband, Peter Jensen.

Ploypailin was an undeniably skilled pianist and a competent singer, but nowhere near world-class. To advance her career, her mother had a cassette made of the two of them singing mostly Western pop hits. More ambitiously and expensively, she hired orchestras in Bangkok, Prague, Madrid, Rotterdam, Vienna, and Osaka for her daughter to perform with. The funding appeared to come from the government, state enterprises, royal charities, and Thai businessmen. Equally deserving Thai musicians never received the same support, and Ploypailin didn't even have Thai citizenship. The implied justification was that she had Thai royal blood.

Ubolrat put herself in the public eye as well. Still very attractive at 40 in 1991, she graced numerous Thai magazines wearing smart French fashions, photographed at society parties and exclusive fashion shoots. In September 1994 she was the subject of a 36-page photo essay in *Dichan* shocking for its vulgarity. She posed provocatively in the risqué couture of Thierry Mugler in Paris's Ritz Hotel. In one photo she appeared as a call girl waiting for a client in hotpants, thigh-high leather boots, and a transparent top with a black push-up bra. As revealing were the behind-the-scenes photographs showing the magazine staff prostrated at her feet and crawling to provide her shoes, as if Ubolrat was a full princess.

The impact of such acts was mixed. The public sense of her as a real princess was revived, but she was also criticized for her crude grasping. In 1996, Ubolrat and her family made a big effort to join the two grand rituals, and it was thought she would recover her original title. But stubborn Bhumibol still refused.

Princess Chulabhorn in the 1990s created another type of problem. As the official Mahidol family scientist, she opened exhibits and presented papers at congresses. Her Chulabhorn Research Institute sponsored research and scientific colloquia, funded by corporate donations, the government budget, and international endowments. To Thais she appeared as an international force in science.

Yet she disliked the role and craved other things, friends and followers, and love and respect. But she wasn't pretty like Ubolrat, was haughty and petulant, and lacked the natural graciousness by which her parents charmed their subjects. Instead she constantly demanded first-class treatment in every venue and her taste for finery generated many ugly rumors, including that she received jewelry stolen from a Saudi prince in a notorious case. True or not, many Thais believed it.

There were many rumors about her health. She had an irregularly occurring affliction said to be lupus, and her emaciated look led people to believe she suffered bouts of anorexia. In addition, she was unhappy or just bored with her husband, Virayuth, whose main job was to accompany and serve her. To escape the court, in 1994 Chulabhorn arranged for Virayuth's assignment to the Thai embassy in Washington, D.C., as defense attaché. This was opposed by the Defense Ministry, which kept the plum job for rising stars, and the Foreign Ministry, which didn't have a budget for accommodations at the princess's standard. But she got her way. After they settled in, stories seeped back to Bangkok of serious marital problems, and around the end of 1994 one of their fights resulted in Chulabhorn accusing Virayuth of beating her. She returned to Bangkok alone and, when she didn't appear in public for months, rumors spread that she was dead or dying.

When she finally surfaced in April, her condition went unexplained, but her split with Virayuth was clear by the absence of her daughters, who reportedly preferred to stay with their father. Embarrassingly, she transferred her insistent affections to one of her father's cardiac surgeons, a married man who looked similar to Virayuth. His avoidance made her, it was said, more depressed.

None of this was comparable to the problem of Crown Prince Vajiralongkorn. At the beginning of the 1990s he seemed to shape up to his role as a king-to-be. People hopefully linked the decline in reports of his misbehavior to Sucharinee's tentative acceptance in the palace. For his 39th birthday, in 1991, Vajiralongkorn invited the Thai press into his Nonthaburi Palace. Carrying herself like a full royal wife, Sucharinee greeted the reporters saying, "The Crown Prince wants this to be very informal, very casual, nothing serious. You see, not-very-nice rumors come out now and then, probably because the press hasn't had a chance to get to know the crown prince personally. So we thought this could be a good opportunity for all of us."[1]

This affable presentation did much to gain palace and public acceptance of the couple. Combined with the demotion of Vajiralongkorn's wife, Somsawali, from "royal consort" to "mother of the king's grandchildren," the two events established that Sucharinee's four sons were the core of the next Chakri generation.

In 1992 the prince dutifully took on numerous of the official state and religious duties of the king, such as a trip to India to pay homage to Buddhist holy sites. Meanwhile, he courted his mother's favor, taking her on regular outings to swank restaurants and nightclubs in Bangkok. He had his elder sons ordain at Wat Bovornives just before her birthday. Together with the army, he built her luxurious teakwood Siriyalai Palace on the riverside in Ayutthaya. He also presided over the consecration of the gold Buddha's footprint made for the queen.

In July 1992 the prince gave another audience to reporters ahead of his birthday.[2] Neither Sucharinee nor their children were present, but he readily discussed them while not mentioning Somsawali and his daughter by her, Princess Bhajarakitiyabha. His reflection on life and karma was taken as a rare display of budding dhammaraja wisdom. "No one's life goes smoothly all the time. But it is important to remember that it is never too late to work for good things. It is never too late to start working or searching for responsibility. There is a Buddhist saying that no karma is more important than present action."[3]

Anyone unsuccessful in life, he added, can still correct their problems. If they do, "The rest of their life will see some hope and beneficial contributions." He was saying that, at 40, he was no longer a rash young man and intended to do good in the future. It didn't completely clear his reputation, and at the very end of 1992, the prince abruptly came out to defend himself in another audience with Thai journalists.[4] After general talk about the prince's work, the reporter for *Thai Rath*, the country's largest newspaper, whose owner had a close relationship to the prince, ventured a question clearly prearranged: did the prince have businesses of his own? "I have waited for this question for a long time. . . . It is something which has been very upsetting to me. . . . For some time some people have said too much that the crown prince has businesses like pubs, bars, discotheques, whatever—this is the prince's, that is the prince's, and that is the prince's. . . . The prince is a chao poh [mafia-like godfather] in trust companies and finance companies, and chit funds . . . [or] a great tycoon with billions."

To the contrary, he said, his parents never taught him anything but to serve the country. "I don't have any experience in these things. If I really did it, the business would lose millions and millions, probably lose it all. . . . I never studied business management. . . . [I only learned] to do what would bring good for the nation, and to not do anything that would bring harm to the nation, or violate the law, or be immoral . . . or anything that would damage the quality and future of the youth." The latter referred to talk that nightclubs he allegedly owned allowed in minors and stayed open beyond legal hours. He denied this, and also denied being behind the rigging of the national lottery a few years earlier. If he had, he said, he would have been rich already. "Let me say this is all untrue. Anyone who does something wrong should be taken care of by the police or authorities. And anyone who uses my name, or claims my protection or says I am involved in something for their own benefit can be reported and charged. . . . Even if it is my aides."

He noted that his father the king provides him with enough funds for his needs, adding, "The money I spend is acquired honestly. I don't want to touch money earned illegally and through the suffering of others." His denial was essentially founded on the concept of a Chakri's inborn purity and inviolateness: it wasn't possible that he could do anything but follow his father's example.

The next day all of the newspapers reported the prince's statement with large headlines. The impact was marginally more positive than negative. For some, it stirred up bad memories and raised suspicions. Others gave him the benefit of the doubt, perhaps because he was the future king. The next day, though, the story disappeared completely from the media.

The prince hadn't changed. In the same period he took in large sums of money from businessmen in exchange for inaugurating their grand projects, including the Bangkok skytrain and a large real estate development. Within military circles, he was known for having abused or roughed up some two dozen officers since the late 1980s, most of them respected men who somehow displeased the prince.[5] In March 1993 he summarily dismissed the chief of his security detachment, a highly respected major general. The prince put out word that the general had abused his name, but few believed it. Senior army officers boldly let their anger over the incident be known.

Nevertheless, the prince's efforts to spruce up his image had an impact on his parents. By late 1992 he was allowed to sue Somsawali for divorce, taking a major step toward marrying Sucharinee. It had been a long effort. Somsawali had refused a divorce for many years, as the prince lacked both legal grounds and his father's accord. In 1990, the Thai divorce code was changed, some say driven by the prince's case. The new code allowed as grounds for divorce a husband and wife living apart voluntarily for three years or more because they cannot cohabit peacefully.

At the time, it was said, Somsawali still rejected an offer of several million dollars to separate. Backed by her mother and a wing of the court determined that she become queen, Somsawali challenged that three years hadn't passed since the new law came into effect. Her side also argued that there were never formal divorces in the royal family. Even monarchs like Chulalongkorn with his prodigious harem, they insisted, always protected the status of official queens.

In 1992 the insidious senior judge Pramarn Chansue was brought in to force a settlement while avoiding a public courtroom battle. With the three-year living-apart threshold approaching, in January 1993 the prince filed his divorce suit in family court, where Pramarn's own wife was a powerful senior judge. The prince's allegations against Somsawali were brutally contrived, branding her as completely at fault for the failed relationship.[6] The prince twisted the facts of real incidents to show how Somsawali allegedly hurt the monarchy, from quarrels to borrowed jewelry that had gone missing to a car accident that took place during the prince's American stay in 1980. In most of the cases, like the missing jewelry, it was the prince who was really at fault.

The divorce hearings were closed, but the case documents were well spread around Bangkok. When Somsawali's turn in the courtroom came, she could do nothing. She couldn't call the prince a liar, for even spoken in court that would be lèse-majesté. With Bhumibol nowhere to be seen in the fray, the defense fell back on the fact that the king had not agreed. But Pramarn fixed that by ruling that although ancient law required the king to sign off on royal marriages, it said nothing specifically about divorce. Somsawali was beaten. She could appeal, but the appeal judge would be Pramarn.

The divorce became final in July 1993. It was rumored that Queen Sirikit also paid Somsawali a few million dollars as settlement. She continued to reside in the palace, though, and to demonstrate their solidarity her supporters in the court staged a ball for her third-cycle birthday the same month. The prince marked his victory by casting holy images, of the Buddha and of the popular Chinese goddess Kuan Yin, to be installed at Wat Bovornives. The images were unveiled not by Bovornives abbot Yanasangworn but by Sucharinee.

This was apparently okay with Bhumibol, for the prince and Sucharinee then scheduled a wedding for the end of February 1994 inside the palace. In the traditional fashion, monks chanted prayers while, according to royal sources, the king, Princess Mother Sangwal, and other elders blessed the union by pouring lustral water on their heads. Apparently embarrassed to turn against her own niece, Sirikit stayed upcountry. The union came with its own auspicious sign, a rainfall during the dry season. Rumors spread that the Royal Rain operations seeded the clouds for the occasion.

Nothing was said officially, and people learned through word of mouth that Vajiralongkorn and Sucharinee had married. She gained no new title but could use the family name, going by Mom Sucharinee Mahidol Na Ayutthaya, adding the suffix allowed fourth-generation descendants of Chakri kings. Under this name she was commissioned as a major in the army and given the opportunity to pass judgment in court, the traditional symbol of royal dispensation of justice. But it was a military court, not a civilian one, suggesting that her new status was still in the balance.

The official coming-out occasion was the prince's 42nd birthday on July 28. As shown widely in the media, he, Sucharinee, and their children made merit by releasing captured animals to their freedom and giving alms to monks. In a luncheon for the press, Sucharinee and children were treated as full-status royals.[7] The couple was shown speaking warmly and intimately, and the prince announced that he would soon launch a number of charity projects and make several diplomatic trips. He was also going to help build a $20 million hospital cardiac center in the queen's honor, the funding for it from the government, charity balls, a special cull of the national lottery take, and, he proposed, a special added tax on automobile fuel. It was a change from the voluntary donations that supported the king's projects.

Somsawali's palace faction counterattacked with a lengthy unsigned letter assailing the prince as well as Queen Sirikit. It called the prince a sex maniac and branded Sucharinee as a prostitute who controlled him through sexual magic. They alleged that the prince caused people to disappear and abused his charity funds, using them to build the queen's Ayutthaya palace. It said he joined hands with powerful businessmen to expand his fortune. "Don't they realize that they cannot become king and queen without the respect and support of the Thai people?" the letter asked. "What can we do to prevent The Idiot and The Harlot from attaining such exalted position?" As for the queen, whom the letter called "our own Thai Suzie Wong," it said: "My beloved fellow Thais: August 12 . . . is generally referred to as the birthday of the mother of the Thai nation. But just ask yourself, should this old courtesan really be honored as the mother of the Thai nation? . . . She dresses like an actress on stage. . . . How embarrassing! . . . The lack of moral principles demonstrated by this evil creature knows no limits."

The letter called Sirikit's behavior a family trait, noting that her sister Busba and brother Adulyakit had abandoned their own mates for other partners. "You can see how evil they all are, brother and sisters alike. . . . Are we going to donate money only to see it wasted on sexual debauchery? . . . We must resist this evil old courtesan. May she burn in hell and her children never reappear." The letter concluded: "If you were born a Thai, you must continue to endure this misfortune. We are a poor country, and must remain poor. . . . [T]he old prophecy will come true: the dynasty will have only nine kings. If there is a tenth, it will be a disaster of filth, indecency and evil. . . . I call on all the people to resist." It was signed "a citizen of Thailand." But the writer was no normal citizen. The details pointed to the palace itself, and many believed the author was none other than Somsawali's mother and Adulyakit's wife, Princess Bhandhusawali.

The letter also confirmed the rumors that Vajiralongkorn and Sucharinee's relationship was stormy. It referred to her walking out on the prince in late 1993 because he let another consort live in the Nonthaburi Palace. Sucharinee had long shared him with other women, but they couldn't move in. In this case it was said she flew to England with her five children and threatened to kill them and herself if the prince didn't get rid of the woman. The key implication of this story was that Sucharinee was fundamentally unsuitable for royal position. In taking the king's grandchildren away, she didn't put the dynasty ahead of her own interests.

Such stories fed into a new battle for prestige between Somsawali and Sucharinee. Having never made efforts to appear as a virtuous working royal, suddenly Somsawali appeared at public events, often with her daughter Bhajarakitiyabha and Princess Sirindhorn. Fighting back, Vajiralongkorn and Sucharinee themselves led important state and charity ceremonies, their children with them. Tapping traditional symbolism, he took them into the countryside to demonstrate a symbolic solidarity with rice farmers and the land. On one occasion, in front of scores of top officials and hundreds of local people and television cameras, Vajiralongkorn's three eldest sons plunged into a muddy paddy clad in farmers' outfits, plowing it behind a water buffalo and then sowing rice seeds. Several months later, they returned to the field to take part in the harvest. Such efforts had notable success, and Prince Vajiralongkorn and his family began 1995 confidently. He told interviewers that he and Sucharinee shared their work as a "legally married couple," helping the people in the manner of "a father and mother looking after their children."[8]

But then things seemed to go wrong. Two apocryphal stories, spread widely in early 1995, suggested their future together was doomed. In the first, the prince was told in so many words by Thailand's most popular country monk, Luang Phor Koon, that he would not become sovereign, but that Sirindhorn would. Incensed, the prince was said to have insulted or hit the monk and walked out. The second story had it that the prince approached King Bhumibol to request that he and Sucharinee be recognized as the future king and queen. Before he could ask, the king interrupted and said he would grant anything if the prince first did one thing for him: ordain as a monk, and remain in the monkhood forever. It was the trick of a sagacious guru.

True or not, the stories took weight with the king's hospitalization in March 1995. Except for one early occasion, the prince was never seen visiting the hospital.

Sucharinee also never appeared, but Somsawali did. The whole country took notice and sensed something was wrong. When the princess mother was rehospitalized in June, and then died, Vajiralongkorn was again visible, but Sucharinee and the children only barely so. As mourning continued over the rest of 1995, Sucharinee was no longer very visible while the prince performed a regular schedule of royal duties. Somsawali, meanwhile, gained both visibility and credibility. When floods inundated Bangkok in November, she was seen venturing out to deliver packages of goods and drinking water to victims.[9]

These Mahidol family problems reached a climax just as Sangwal's cremation and the king's golden jubilee approached in 1996. With the media saturated with promotion of the monarchy, none imagined anything could spoil the celebrations. The concurrent news of the messy public divorce fight between Britain's Crown Prince Charles and Princess Diana seemed to put the Mahidols in a good light. But then the royal grapevine spread damning new stories about Sucharinee and her children. Gossip circulated that the prince's sons had been caught with drugs at school in England. Then it was said that Sucharinee herself, traveling under Thai diplomatic cover, was nabbed in a London airport smuggling narcotics.[10] As usual, true or not, the rumors had a great impact in shaping public opinions about the royal family. Sucharinee's reputation plummeted, and she disappeared from sight.

The prince, meanwhile, reminded the informed elite of how dangerous he could be. On March 1–2, Thailand hosted the leaders of Asian and European nations for an inaugural summit meeting. It was a great status-booster for Thailand, and the king put on a grand reception for the visiting presidents and premiers. The prince gave Japanese prime minister Ryutaro Hashimoto another kind of welcome. When Hashimoto's Boeing 747 landed at Don Muang airport on February 28, before it reached the red carpet for disembarkation, the jet was blocked very publicly by three F-5 fighter jets led by the crown prince himself. Photographers at the arrival point were forced to put down their cameras as the prince held the Japanese delegation hostage on the tarmac for twenty minutes before breaking away.[11] The prince was apparently avenging his alleged mistreatment on his Japan visit in 1987. As then, the Thai and Japanese governments were both hugely embarrassed, and the Japanese diplomatically let the incident stand without protest or comment.

Meanwhile Vajiralongkorn took up the cause of his sister Princess Chulabhorn, according to palace community stories. Shortly before the princess mother's cremation, the prince summoned Chulabhorn's estranged consort Virayuth to his Nonthaburi Palace. There Virayuth was confronted by the prince, together with privy council head Prem and the top military brass. On the prince's desk, the stories had it, were a pistol and divorce papers offering Virayuth a paltry sum of money. Just as when he had been compelled to marry the princess 16 years before, he gave in and disappeared from the public eye, returning to the United States.

Sangwal's cremation served to confirm the family turmoil to the public. Chulabhorn appeared without Virayuth but with her two daughters at her side, both looking very uncomfortable. Television narrator Thongthong offered no explanation, although he detailed virtually every other appearance, explaining personal histories and relationships. When Sucharinee appeared at the pyre together with her children, Thongthong was also emphatically silent, refusing to identify them. The omission was widely noticed, but no one was certain what it meant until a few weeks later. On May 26, the televised royal news showed the grim-faced prince stepping down from a commercial flight at Don Muang airport accompanied by his daughter by Sucharinee, Busyanampetch, a girl he had never paid particular attention to. The next day photographs of the event were splashed portentously through the newspapers without explanation.

Then on May 28, the prince made a very public show of expelling Sucharinee from his palace. His aides posted and freely distributed documents alleging that she had had an affair with the prince's aide-de-camp, Air Chief Marshal Anan Rodsamkhan. One of the documents, signed by Prime Minister Banharn, dismissed Anan from the military. A second, topped with passport photos of Anan and Sucharinee, declared that they had defrauded the monarchy, engaged in adultery, and mistreated a princess, understood as Busyanampetch. "If they are seen in public, help to chase them away and condemn their actions," it read. Appended was a warning from the prince that Anan would face stronger action if he fought the charges, and that he should leave the country forever. Another document was an order by the prince to the Ministry of Foreign Affairs, dated May 24, to strip Sucharinee and Anan of their diplomatic passports. While these documents spread through Bangkok, digital photographs of Sucharinee in the nude were sent by diskette to embassies and newspapers and posted on the Internet.

Bangkok was stunned. The nation was not only in the middle of preparations for the king's jubilee but also at the height of a confidence crisis in Prime Minister Banharn's scandal-wracked government. Only two newspapers dared report the affair, both linked to Prem's close companion M.R. Tridhosyuth Devakul.[12]

Slowly an explanation seeped out. The palace believed that Sucharinee, staying in England with her children, was abusing the little princess, whose birth had spoiled the prediction that Sucharinee would become queen if she had five sons. Around May 23, the prince flew to England and grabbed the girl, taking her straight to the airport to fly back to Bangkok, where he demanded that Banharn arrange the denunciation and expulsion of Anan and Sucharinee. Banharn reportedly had several meetings with the prince and the king on the matter. Meanwhile Sucharinee apparently reported her daughter's disappearance to the British police as a kidnapping, but if she did, the Bangkok and British palaces cooperated to hush up the affair.

The true story behind the episode was unclear. Perhaps it related to Busyanampetch's mistreatment, though the prince never cared for her. As for Sucharinee's affair with Anan, Vajiralongkorn's aide and flying partner for years, according to a knowledgeable foreign defense attaché in Bangkok, it had been going on for at least three years with the prince's approval. But the real reasons weren't important. However brash the prince was, the Thai public readily accepted that Sucharinee and Anan had betrayed him, and that she had mistreated an innocent young princess. The palace concluded that she was not fit to be a Mahidol. Vajiralongkorn came out of the affair the honorable one.

To emphasize his virtue in the affair, amid the turmoil on May 28 the prince undertook a high religious ceremony in the Grand Palace to cast gold Buddha images. In the days following, he presided at funerals in his father's place, and two weeks later he joined the 50th-jubilee festivities. Constantly at his side were his first wife Somsawali and both of his daughters. On July 13, he attended Somsawali's birthday party, again with the two princesses. And Somsawali attended Vajiralongkorn's own birthday on July 28.

For many Thais, this was a long saga's fairy-tale ending. The errant husband-prince was going back to patient Somsawali, his true wife, a deserving, blue-blooded princess. To explain it all, palace officials invoked royal alchemy. They insisted privately that he and Sucharinee never had more than a morganatic union, and that the Somsawali betrothal still stood. With no sense of irony, an aide to the king explained that the divorce from Somsawali didn't stand because it was handled in a civil court and not in a palace ritual presided by the king. As for the marriage to Sucharinee, it was never official because it was done only in the palace and never registered under civil law![13]

But by the end of the year the fairy tale again faded. The prince was no longer seen with Somsawali and he passed his time with choice selections from Bangkok's legion of for-hire party girls. He still lived in his suburban Nonthaburi residence and schemed to evict Somsawali from the in-town palace. Nothing in his behavior had really changed. He was said to be behind the sacking of the national police chief Pochana Boonyachinda, because Pochana and his wife, a lady-in-waiting in the prince's palace, allegedly helped Sucharinee flee the country with all her jewelry. It was another sign that the man who would become Rama X remained, at 44, brutal and uncontrollable.

Some thought the king could take solace in the impeccable behavior of his other daughter, Sirindhorn. But even she let him down to an extent. In the early 1990s she dutifully performed her responsibilities, but she showed little readiness to lead the palace. She still seemed excessively girlish and sentimental, publishing cute books about her frequent trips abroad, pursuing her interests in history and archaeology. Meanwhile she avoided her brother and the court's pressure to be a viable alternative by frequently traveling abroad.

As she neared her 40th birthday in 1995, Sirindhorn showed signs of maturity and assuming the power of her position. She more readily commanded the people around her and confidently expressed opinions in private, even on political issues. She assumed responsibility for the upbringing of the prince's daughter Bhajarakiti-yabha, who after Sucharinee's expulsion became the leading next-generation candidate for succession. Sirindhorn also helped Somsawali to project herself better.

Even so, it was said that she still frustrated her father, who saw her as the heir to his development works. He expected Sirindhorn to show herself as knowledgeable as himself on geography, hydrology, communications, and farming. Even she admitted she disappointed him, as her weight and lack of fitness made it difficult to stride through paddies and up hills to reach remote villages.[14] This posed a real dilemma for the king. His son could command but had bad judgment and didn't care for the people. His daughter cared and had good judgment, but couldn't really command.

In the bright lights of the golden jubilee, none of this appeared to rattle Bhumibol, at least publicly. On his birthday at the end of 1996, rather than dwell like Queen Elizabeth on the horrible side of the year, he waxed grandfatherly about life, his kingdom, and his reign's success. Philosophizing randomly, he exhibited a strange preoccupation with numbers, the date the anniversary was celebrated, the average age of those listening to his speech, and other things. After noting that people wanted him to rule another 50 years, the king reflected, in the manner of a Buddhist guru, on how the country had improved.

It cannot be said that in those days, it was better than nowadays, or that nowadays is better than those past days. In these present days, what we have is what we have in the present; what we had in the past is already gone; what we will have in the future will depend on what we will be able to build up together. If we cooperate constructively, it will be good; if we don't cooperate, I am sorry to say that we will reap bad consequences. . . .

The problem is what is "good." . . . Everybody seems to understand goodness, but to say exactly what it is, is difficult. Goodness is something that makes us serene and content; it is magnificent. Those who are not good are evil. . . . Evil people are also difficult to define. A good person can make another person good. . . . Evil will make a steadfast good person bad only with great difficulty; however, it is not impossible.

He continued to suggest that, guided by dhamma, the nation would continue to progress as it had in his first 50 years. When he finished and emerged to the sunlit gardens outside, there waiting were several thousand Thais, workers and peasants and housewives who eagerly thrust banknotes into his hands as he strolled along the path, the poorest giving money to the richest, in hopes that it would improve their fate.

In his New Year's Eve speech King Bhumibol repeated his thanks to the people for the huge celebration. He noted great events of the year: a Thai boxer winning an Olympic gold medal, the visits of Queen Elizabeth and President Bill Clinton, and Thailand hosting two important international summits. It all linked somehow to the reign's success.

21 The Economic Crash and Bhumibol's New Theory ∽

IN 1996, KING BHUMIBOL TURNED 69, a time when most men slow down, when Thai civil servants are already retired nine years, and when many sovereign kings and queens rest on their laurels, comfortable in the enduring strength of their prestige. His birthday talk, coming at the end of his jubilee, seemed valedictory. But his *Mahajanaka* sent a different message, that his work wasn't done. He was rightly concerned that, without a final push, his pet dam and traffic projects would be stalled by the bureaucracy or activists. Both the Bangkok city government and a group of the city's social leaders, for instance, were resisting his proposal for a new bridge across the Chaophraya River, a bridge the king had already named after his brother, Rama VIII. It took all the force of his prestige to get it through.

The king wanted his economic ideas better accepted. There had been quiet criticism of his New Theory of farming, especially from economists, and he was frustrated that not everyone was convinced. He also took closer notice of the problem of corruption, which he had always shrugged off as a necessary evil of government and market capitalism. But certain cases had brought it too close to the throne in 1996. First was the final closure, for a loss to the state of a stunning $3 billion, of the collapsed Bangkok Bank of Commerce, once proudly a bank of the royals, aristocracy, and military. Another case erupted around Prime Minister Banharn, whose construction company received a generous $110 million government contract for the king's Pak Panang dam, putting a cloud over the entire project.[1] The king also got caught in the middle of competing corrupt factions in the judiciary, one led by Supreme Court head Pramarn Chansue, an erstwhile palace favorite. And when Chavalit Yongchaiyut finally scaled his way to the premiership in late 1996, replacing Banharn, it highlighted the fact that the most corrupt politicians were winning the battles.

The king couldn't do much on specific cases. But he appeared to become more selective about the people he allowed to enjoy palace favor, and more scrupulous on the bureaucratic promotions he approved. He also decided to give constitutional reform another hearing. Grudgingly, he lent his support to reformers who convinced him that some of these problems, and the unspoken problem of his son's eventual succession, could be better managed with a strong democratic charter. But his support was fleeting. When the effusive Thai economic bubble finally popped, Bhumibol saw one last chance for the comeback of his dhammaraja democracy. The bust exposed, however, how his own throne had been caught in the freewheeling hubris of the boom decade.

In 1993, while the Chuan government's constitutional amendments were being stymied by right-wing interests, a group of academics and social leaders outside the government organized to press for a full constitutional rewrite. Generally they wanted society and government to work more fairly and systematically, not based on the personal relationships that favored a self-perpetuating elite and self-serving politicians. They were also thinking about the dangers of a less law-based system after the eventual succession of Prince Vajiralongkorn. One leading legal scholar explained at the time: "The Thai constitution has never been a social contract, never a set of rules for those with power to service the people. It has been a set of rules between those with power."[2] The king's patronage stabilized this system as constitutions came and went, he said, but that was hardly a dependable mechanism for the future.

Other takes on reform invoked issues of the king's own interest. The *Nation*'s columnist Chang Noi cited the anger of environmentalists and villagers over the Kaeng Sua Ten dam as an example of something the constitution should address: "Kaeng Sua Ten is not such a big dam. But it is a very big issue. . . . [It] raises big questions about what sort of society we want to build: equitable, sustainable and participatory. Or urban-biased, short-term, and authoritarian."[3]

Anand Panyarachun, meanwhile, explained that a key goal of the new movement was cutting the army's political power. "It is the fault of the entire system in Thailand that somehow inadvertently we have either given or we have acquiesced to the acquisition of this very high-profile role of the army. I think we need time to think, to ponder seriously whether certain roles they have been given or they have acquired on their own are really the roles that should belong to them."[4]

With views like this coming from Anand and longtime royal intimate Prawase Wasi, the king had to pay heed. To hook him, Prawase enumerated their goals using Bhumibol's own litany of complaints: the dominance of money in politics, government unaccountability, official corruption, parliamentary indiscipline, and congenital instability. Prawase also described their work as practical steps toward achieving unity under the nation-religion-king triune, and his group cited as their guiding principles the thotsaphit rachatham.[5]

The parliament finally gave the reformers a mandate to redraft the constitution in late 1996. A constitutional drafting assembly was formed under Prawase, Anand, and a number of royalist reformers, including Kramol Thongthammachart, an architect of the royal-national government philosophy of the Prem period. With their involvement, Bhumibol was said to take a measured interest, even studying up on foreign constitutions and parliamentary systems. On January 18, 1997, the king gave the drafting assembly his benediction at the palace. His instructions, however, suggested he still was dubious. He told them to make the constitution short, because a long one would be more restrictive with less room for interpretation.[6]

By that time, things were happening in the Thai economy that would soon have Bhumibol rethinking his endorsement. Ten years of heady growth had left bureaucrats, businessmen, and politicians complacent in the idea of a Thai economic miracle. But by the end of 1996, the economy had begun to melt down, obliterating all $40 billion of national reserves and, by July 1997, forcing a massive devaluation. The entire country, including the palace, went into shock as the economy imploded over the following year. At one point the dollar value of the baht was halved, all but wiping out the country's banks and leaving thousands of Thai companies insolvent.

The collapse laid bare many of the systemic faults of governance, the sheer mismanagement and deeply corrupt cronyism that had underpinned the boom years. For several years, it became known, the Thais had proudly rejected warnings from respected economists and the International Monetary Fund. Blame for the crash could be pinned not on politicians so much as on the elite closed circle of top bureaucrats and bankers who had, in the name of tradition and culture, rigged the system for themselves.

Nearly all of the country's tycoons and large business groups, and a large portion of top bureaucrats, politicians, and high-society Thais, were devastated by the devaluation. This included members of the extended royal family, palace staff, and the businesses of the Crown Property Bureau. The Siam Cement Group was the country's largest offshore borrower, with nearly $5 billion in U.S.-dollar debts when the crisis hit. After the devaluation it was technically insolvent. Worse off was the CPB-controlled Siam Commercial Bank. The bank was heavily leveraged on funds raised abroad, as were most of its biggest customers. Their loan collateral, mostly real estate, was grossly overvalued and, with the real estate market in collapse, didn't cover even half the value of the loans.[7] While Siam Cement had productive assets to sell to cover its debts, Siam Commercial Bank (and indeed all the Thai banks) had little. This wiped out palace income, which had topped $100 million a year in the mid-1990s. Dividends stopped flowing and many tenants stopped paying rent. Even if the palace wanted to, it didn't have the funds to shore up its major holdings, much less fund its charities.

The crisis evoked extreme pressure to reconstruct the system in a more tenable, fair, and open way. The IMF offered an emergency loan of over $15 billion, tied to strict conditions for cleanup and the reform of laws, the financial system, and economic management. The plan would allow Thailand to emerge from the crisis stronger, but required allowing overindebted businessmen to fail, and punishment for the greatest wrongdoers. This threatened bankruptcy for many of the kingdom's elite, by holding them responsible for their debts.

Bhumibol was expected to support the implementation of the IMF-prescribed reforms. Instead, he interfered, by attempting to circumvent the normal political process to revive his 1980s royal government with Prem again in charge. After the devaluation, Prime Minister Chavalit came under severe pressure from the threatened Thai elite to reject the IMF plan. But the longer he resisted the IMF, the deeper the baht and the economy sank. In parliament, the pro-IMF Democrats attacked the government for incompetence and inaction, hoping they could oust Chavalit, take power, and then implement both economic reforms and the new constitution.

But when Chavalit looked likely to fall, a group of high-powered industrialists asked Prem to intervene and protect the government. After meeting with Prem, Chavalit bought more time by agreeing to the IMF's terms, while naming Prem's personal economic adviser Virabongsa Ramangkura as his crisis manager. Chavalit and his economic ministers then met with the king, and afterward made public appearances with the three military service commanders. It was a 1980s-like show of palace-military-government solidarity with king's agent Prem in the middle.

The problem was that this palace intervention wasn't made to resolve a parliamentary stalemate, but instead to interrupt the still-functioning parliamentary process. There was little justification for it, since Chuan's Democrats had already proven that they could run the country responsibly. Predictably, Chavalit stalled on implementing the IMF's painful prescriptions, and the economy spun further out of control. When the Democrats resumed their attacks, Prem stepped in more openly as Chavalit's guarantor. On his August 25 birthday, surrounded by military and political well-wishers including Chavalit, he called for cooperation and unity. "We cannot afford to be divided, particularly government leaders and the opposition . . . if we wish to see our country restored to its former prosperous state soon," he said, sounding much like Bhumibol.

But the Democrats were no longer intimidated. Sukhumbhand Paripatra, now a Democratic member of parliament, branded Prem's intervention a "silent coup," citing the constitution's stipulation that privy councilors had to refrain from politics. Another Democrat, Surin Pitsuwan, said that, again, "It looks like the top brass are in charge of the country. It doesn't augur well for the process of democracy." The criticism was directed at Prem, but it implied King Bhumibol as well.[8]

The fight wasn't only over the economy. The draft constitution was finalized at the end of August, in the middle of the crisis. Against the king's advice, it was very long and detailed, codifying the aspirations of thousands of Thais polled for what they expected a constitution to do for them. Chavalit's party fought to kill the draft, hoping the economic crisis would provide an excuse. They argued, for one, that the draft diminished royal prerogatives and military power. With the support of the powerful conservatives in the senate and the military, Chavalit tried to force a rewrite.

Now the economic crisis worked in the reformers' favor. Apparently to avoid worsening an already bad situation, Bhumibol communicated through Sumet Tantivejakul that the throne had no problem with the draft.[9] "There is no law or any powerful legal clause which could sway the people's loyalty to the king," Sumet said, adding that any problems could be amended later. With that message, Chavalit endorsed the charter and sent it to the king on October 11.

It wasn't clear whether the king intervened because he liked the draft or to avoid another confrontation like 1992. But it didn't save Chavalit. At the beginning of October the baht was still falling and the IMF deal was faltering. Across the country there was a feeling of cosmic crisis. People made merit in hopes of reversing the bad karma, and the supreme patriarch organized more than 100 monks to pray together at the chapel of the Emerald Buddha, joined by cabinet ministers and palace officials. Many people openly called on the king to save the country.

In response, Prem proposed outright a return to the idea of an unelected king's government. On October 6 he summoned the country's top newspaper editors to his home and told them that the parliamentary opposition should agree to form a nonpartisan, unified "national government," staffed by nonpoliticians, under an independent leader, understood as Prem or his agent.[10] Disingenuously, Prem insisted that the ideas were his personal view, not that of a privy councilor— meaning not from the king. "They can be considered the views of a statesman during this time of abnormality, when an economy is in crisis," he said. But like the king, he suggested the parliament had no use. "When people talk about a national government they misunderstand: they think of the 393 persons in the House of Representatives without division into government and opposition. In my private opinion, I say a national government is getting all the best people in the country to become government, not only the 393; only then can it be a national government. If you are Thai citizen No. 1, you have to be brought in as prime minister; others, numbers 2, 3, 4, 5, have to be brought into the cabinet."

Showing how far along his thinking was, he named three men, all from his own circle, who he said were the best doctors for the economy.[11] Supporting them was patriotic, he argued. Prem was proposing to turn back the clock to the 1980s, entirely contrary to the ideals expressed in the constitution just being readied for the king's signature. As ever, it was impossible to say with certainty that this was the king's proposal and not Prem's alone. But Prem was the chief privy councilor, and had always acted fully aware of and protective of the king's interests and prestige. It was hard to imagine he had not consulted Bhumibol.

The move stopped the democratic reform movement cold. It fell again to royal-blooded Sukhumbhand to fight back. The idea of a national government, he responded in the *Bangkok Post*, "can be interpreted to be less than democratic in spirit."[12] He called it an idealization of the 1991–92 technocrat administration of Anand Panyarachun, which he noted existed only in the absence of a functioning constitution and parliament. Now that the country had both, Sukhumbhand said, Prem was out of line. "As a member of the privy council, Gen. Prem is, of course, bound strictly by both constitution and etiquette not to engage in either politics, political partisanship or political advocacy. Therefore, [his interview with the newspaper editors] by definition cannot be political. But what the former premier said is perhaps the most politically significant non-political statement of this troubled year." Moreover, Sukhumbhand suggested, Prem was setting himself up to return as premier. "If some people could have their way, the privy councilor may yet be transformed from being the most politically powerful non-political person in the country to being an immensely powerful political leader once more."

Sukhumbhand avoided mentioning the king, emphasizing only that there was no reason to believe that the national government could solve the economic crisis better than any other. But at the end of his piece, he brashly sent a message to Bhumibol. He recounted the British monarchy's establishment of a national government in 1931 in response to the global economic crisis. This royal intervention only came about, Sukhumbhand pointed out, after the national government idea was proposed and agreed inside the parliament. The message was to let the Thai parliament exhaust its own processes before intervening—something neither Bhumibol nor Prem had ever had the patience for.

The choices caught King Bhumibol, like his uncle King Prajadhipok in 1932, in a complex antinomial bind. Prajadhipok faced a global depression neither he nor his princes really understood, over which his advisers disagreed. Outside the government, pressure was for sweeping reforms that would address the economic challenges, but would also devolve power from the monarchy and slash the economic entitlements of the royals and aristocracy. Prajadhipok's fateful decision was to listen to his princes' advice to reject the reforms and protect the elite, essentially themselves. Six weeks afterward, the absolute monarchy was overthrown.

In 1997 Bhumibol faced a similarly complex, partly foreign-derived economic crisis that neither he nor his advisers really understood. He could open the way for Chuan, the new constitution, and the tough IMF reforms. It might save the economy, but the cost would be heavy: the throne, and much of the elite surrounding it, would lose fortunes, and the power of the monarchy could be diluted. Or he could put Prem in charge, stall the constitution, and water down the IMF's directives. It would protect the fortunes of the aristocracy, and keep in place the hierarchy that guaranteed the throne's power. Whether or not Bhumibol realized it, it would be at considerable risk to the economy and, as in 1932, the whole system could collapse.

Because everything took place behind the scenes, it isn't possible to know exactly what Bhumibol said. But it appears he learned from Prajadhipok's record and took the path of reform. In the midst of the standoff between the Democrats and Prem, on November 3, Chavalit suddenly resigned. Simultaneously the calls for a Prem-led crisis government disappeared, opening the way for Chuan to take power. It would prove to be Bhumibol's last attempt at hijacking government.

But it hardly meant the king was ready to cede prestige to another Chuan government. The crisis snowballed through Asia, and the economic problems became too deep and intractable for any speedy solution. As the government struggled and stumbled, unencumbered King Bhumibol took ample opportunity to criticize while setting himself out as the repository of wisdom and virtue.

This followed the familiar pattern of the early 1990s. When southern Thailand was hit by extensive flooding in August 1997, as usual the royal family's foundations claimed the most credit for providing relief, even though the government did more. When urban industries began to lay off large numbers of workers, the palace announced that the king's Chai Pattana foundation would coordinate government agencies and the private sector to help find new jobs. Such grandstanding had little impact, for there weren't any jobs, and the real issue for the unemployed was the absence of a social security net of any kind. Even so, the palace appeared more concerned for the jobless than the government.

Only one month into the Chuan administration, Bhumibol used his birthday speech to say, in essence, "I told you so."[13] He attacked political leaders for having taken Thailand along the path of unbridled capitalism and consumerism. Had people embraced his own ideas of a simpler society, he suggested, the crisis would have been avoided. He began by again contrasting the great efficiencies of his own projects while denigrating the government's efforts. Then, moving to the economic crash, he hit out at the kind of modern global market capitalism that had overwhelmed his ideal of a humble, dhamma-guided kingdom.

Through several personalized parables, he said people had been overly desirous of material things and didn't think out the results of their actions, for instance borrowing money to spend without the means to repay. "The lesson should be that borrowed money must bring a profit, and not for just playing around doing useless things." He also scorned the excess ambition of people, like those who built massive factories when small ones would have sufficed. It was this greed, which Bhumibol suggested came with the orthodox capitalism preached by the IMF, that was the root of the crisis. The crash could have been avoided if the country practiced his own economic philosophy. "I have often said . . . that to become a tiger [economy] is not important. The important thing for us is to have a self-supporting economy. A self-supporting economy means to have enough to survive. . . . Each village or each district must have relative self-sufficiency. Things that are produced in surplus can be sold, but should be sold in the same region."

He acknowledged that distinguished economists considered his view old-fashioned and unsophisticated. But Bhumibol argued that chasing world markets with surplus production doesn't benefit the producers, and only leads to suffering. "Placing too much emphasis on the production of industrial goods will not succeed, as the local market has declined because the people now have a lower purchasing power... [and other] countries also have their own difficulties and will not buy our products. If there are industrial products and there are no buyers, the efforts will be of no avail. . . . A careful step backwards must be taken; a return to less sophisticated methods."

The step backward was to his New Theory. "If the situation can change back to an economy that is self-sufficient—it does not have to be a hundred percent, or even fifty percent, but perhaps only twenty-five percent—it will be bearable. The remedy will take time; it will not be easy. Usually one is impatient because one suffers, but if it is done from this moment on, the recovery is possible."

The king's argument was at best pseudo-economics. It was centuries too late for Thailand to withdraw from the global economy: ancient Ayutthaya was a rice exporter. Foreign trade and investment were key tenets of the 1959 economic plan that the palace claimed Bhumibol had inspired, and had underpinned Thai economic growth ever since.

Even so, King Bhumibol hit a bulls-eye in terms of the national mood. Confused by the government's complicated explanations, Thais readily turned to the king for inspiration and introspection. They understood the king's words as fundamental criticism, of themselves for having been greedy; of the politicians who led them into this situation; and of the global capitalists who preyed on Thailand. Like King Mahajanaka, Bhumibol's lesson was both practically and spiritually perfect: if people had followed his thinking, they wouldn't be suffering now.

Over the next year the concepts of self-sufficiency and the New Theory became the subject of endless commentary in the mass media, in temple sermons and political speeches. Foes of globalization, foreign capital, and consumerism cited Bhumibol. Students studied his ideas and the army sought ways to implement them, like growing their own vegetables (which had the effect of increasing supply and depressing the income of full-time farmers). There was a new trend of eating cheaply and healthily inspired by Bhumibol's declaring that, like the poorest peasants, he preferred to eat the coarse unmilled rice, *khao klong*. "I eat khao klong every day because it is healthy. . . . Some say it is the poor man's rice. I am also a poor man."[14]

Meanwhile, the palace as an institution was hardly returning to the simple life. Hidden from public view, the king's men were undertaking a massive rescue of the throne's collapsed billion-dollar business empire.[15] The rescue drew significantly on the stretched resources of the government.

Like many other business groups, the Crown Property Bureau and privy purse investments were in need of substantial new capital to remain solvent. The bureau had a pool of investment reserves, but hardly the several billion dollars necessary for Siam Cement and Siam Commercial Bank to survive under the throne's control. The palace pulled in the country's best talent to work on its problems, former bank heads Tarrin Nimmanhaeminda, Vichit Suraphongchai, and Yos Uachukiat. They were pragmatic, tough, and focused on keeping the throne out of the very public fights that erupted between other Thai business groups and their creditors.

The palace was determined to hold on to its 37-percent share of Siam Cement Group. Without new capital from CPB, the only choice for reducing the group's debt was to sell off subsidiaries, many of which were once seen as pioneer industries for Thailand, automobile parts and electronics manufacturing. But Siam Commercial Bank could not be broken up to raise new capital because the bank and almost all of its subsidiaries had deeply negative net worths. The other Thai banks had only one option, to offer themselves to be taken over by stronger foreign institutions. But CPB chief Chirayut said this was impossible for Siam Commercial, because "the bank is the inherited asset of his majesty King Rama V. The Crown Property Bureau will do everything it can to maintain it. Although eventually all other banks would be taken over by foreigners, Siam Commercial Bank would remain the only Thai bank in this country even if it costs us everything."[16]

This was an interesting view, since Siam Commercial Bank had served Thai national interests no better (or worse) than the other banks. Nevertheless, to save it the Finance Ministry was forced to inject some one billion dollars into the bank. The terms of this bailout were clearly disadvantageous to the state, but they managed to leave the palace with a 26-percent share, by Thai law just enough to hold veto power over key board decisions. Now the bank's controlling shareholder, the Finance Ministry ceded managerial power to the palace, and committed to selling its shares back to the CPB several years later.

As for the rest of CPB holdings, those firms that couldn't survive were shut down, and those that would survive with new capital were left to find foreign investors. According to several private accounts in the financial industry, the bureau played extremely tough even with longtime partners, forcing some essentially to recompense the palace for loss of asset value.

On the other hand, the bureau insisted on saving its insolvent construction firm Christiani & Nielsen. The company had no real strategic value, and it faced a building market that would yield little business over the next several years. But Christiani had one important asset: a contract worth hundreds of millions of dollars to build a gigantic pagoda. As with so many things in the economic crisis, this caught the king in starkly contradictory interests, on political, financial, and spiritual levels.[17] The pagoda was at Thailand's richest and most controversial temple, Wat Thammakay, whose monks were being accused of heretical Buddhist teachings and illicit investment operations. The temple's Rolls-Royce-driving abbot was under threat of being arrested and defrocked.

The impact of the crash taught both the palace and the military that they lacked the knowledge and capabilities to handle complex modern economic and social issues in such a crisis environment. The king stopped pushing for his own men to run the government. Yet, true to his Mahajanaka theme of perseverance, King Bhumibol and the palace organization insistently reminded the people of the monarchy's inherent virtue. This was institutional and cultural habit, certainly; and there was need to sustain the magic circle of merit for the royal charities. And the palace wanted people to embrace the king's wisdom on governance and economic development.

That was evident in the intensity of the promotions from his sixth-cycle, 72nd birthday in 1999. Despite the continuing financial straitjackets on the government, a lavish panoply of activities more directly than ever consecrated Bhumibol as a bodhisattva-king. Beginning in mid-1998, there was an endless run of commemorative books and slickly crafted documentaries on the king. Scandal-ridden Wat Thammakay announced it would have 100,000 men ordained in the king's honor. The army announced that it would construct a giant pagoda for the king in the poorest part of the northeast; Thai Airways, although financially deep in the red, built a grand temple named for Bhumibol in Chiangrai. When in December 1997 the palace revealed that the king had set a world record for university degrees, afterward Kasetsart University tossed off all restraint and awarded him ten honorary doctorates at once, in subjects from biology and geology to linguistics and business administration.[18]

Meanwhile, pressed by the palace, the country's leading economic think tank, the Thailand Development Research Institute, made the New Theory and self-sufficient economy the topic of its 1999 annual conference. There, speaker after speaker found great virtue in Bhumibol's economics, citing serious research and statistical bases. Shortly afterward, Bhumibol expressed appreciation that distinguished economists and professors were now taking the "King's Sufficiency Economy" seriously. Noting that they still had questions on implementing it, he chastened them for not having read the New Theory pamphlet he prepared years before. But, he added proudly, "It is a great honor when they say that the Sufficiency Economy does not exist in the textbooks, because it means that here is a novel idea."

A focal point of the celebration was King Bhumibol's role in water development. He was extolled in the language and symbols of a Hindu life-giving devaraja, like a fertility god. His cloud-seeding was made out as miraculous original technology, and he was ascribed an uncanny ability to divine weather patterns. Thai Airways passengers saw a 20-minute documentary that credited Bhumibol for most of the rain that fed the kingdom's waterways and crops. All of that paled next to a dramatic, heavily repeated television advertisement. In it, a farmer is seen standing miserably on his stark, drought-cracked fields. From the heavens above, the king's empathetic tears turn surreally into rainfall, and the farmer jumps in joy and praise as his fields are soaked. For Bhumibol personally, the high point was his inauguration of the Pasak dam, a victory more over the environmental movement than over nature. To emphasize the point, the government redesigned the 1,000-baht banknote to feature Pasak along with the king.

Perhaps the most outrageous act of reverence and myth-making came with the biweekly national lottery draw just before the December 5 birthday. The anniversary had already generated much attention to numerology, the focus on the number nine. This was the year 1999 (although on the Thai calendar it was 2542), the ninth Chakri reign, Bhumibol's 72nd birthday ($7 + 2 = 9$), and so on.

As usual, the December 1 draw offered one six-digit grand prize and prizes for four three-digit numbers. The grand prize number wasn't significant. But in an immense statistical improbability, two of the three-digit numbers came up 999. Since the number selection was televised and supposedly immune to manipulation, no one dared suggest it was rigged. The only other explanation, then, was that it was some sort of celestial event, revealing the king's deity. In huge headlines, newspapers called it a miracle. There were no questions, and no information on just how many people had won on the number. Two years later, though, a group of insiders was exposed for rigging the lottery, although police said they had only done it in recent weeks.

This excess was not all the palace's fault. The king usually permitted people to honor him however they wanted. What was noteworthy was how far the king's most sober agents went. In a formal lecture to foreigners, his close aide M.R. Butrie Viravaidhya portrayed the king as a Hindu god.[19] In a global tour of Thai communities abroad to collect funds for the royal charities, aide Sumet Tantivejakul suggested to audiences that the king alone helped the Thai people after the economic collapse, and said little about what the government did.[20] Upon his return he reported that people cried at his presentations and eagerly donated for the royal projects. Meanwhile, another royal intimate, Siam Cement chief Chumpol NaLamlieng, explained to a foreign reporter the superiority of the king's operations to the government's. "Whenever disaster strikes, the King doesn't have to check whether there is a budget or if there are IMF restrictions."[21]

As in 1996, Queen Sirikit wasn't left out of the glorification. The palace, or Sirikit herself, commissioned the leading Thai filmmaker Prince Chatri Chalerm Yugala to produce an epic movie on the legendary queen Suriyothai. The unprecedented budget, in Thai industry terms, of $8 million came from the palace at first. The movie was intensely important to Sirikit, who saw herself as Suriyothai's incarnation. She personally chose for the lead role M.L. Piyapas Bhirombhakdi, daughter of her closest aide of decades. Although Piyapas had no experience acting, Sirikit chose her so that a commoner didn't play the queen.

The original release date was the king's birthday in 1999, but the film fell behind schedule and went over budget, eventually topping $10 million, some five times the previous most expensive Thai movie. By its release finally in August 2001, the palace pulled in top Thai corporations to underwrite the costs. To ensure success, *Suriyothai* played for weeks on every theater screen and movie hall in Thailand, including Bangkok screens normally reserved for English films for foreign audiences. Ticket prices were higher than for any other Thai film, but they sold well enough for the backers to claim their investment was recovered. Artistically, it wasn't so successful, at nearly four hours overly long and confusing, to Thais as well as foreigners. Reviewers respectfully reserved their comments to the elegant costumes and scenery. Nonetheless, the palace then sought worldwide distribution with Hollywood backing.

Yet it was a sign of the social changes that had taken place that the palace experienced an increasing amount of resistance to its views and interests. In addition to the stubborn opposition to the king's proposed Rama VIII bridge across the Chaophraya River, critics boldly attacked the CPB's efforts to rebuild its income. People openly fought the CPB's plan for a huge piece of land on Sathorn Road, the city's banking hub, which had several elegant teakwood mansions dating to the Fifth Reign. When the bureau leased the plot to a developer who intended to tear down the mansions and build a new shopping center, architects and the Ministry of Education's fine arts department argued to preserve the buildings, while others demanded the land be made a park. Some even criticized the palace's support of another shopping center when many existing developments struggled to survive.

There were more challenges to the king's dam projects. The coalition of villagers, environmentalists, and scientists fighting the Kaeng Sua Ten dam found powerful support in the studies of enviro-economist Suthawal Sathirathai, the daughter of Queen Sirikit's sister. She argued with impressive detail that there was little economic rationale for the dam, helping to stall the project. At a royally proposed dam in Chumpol province, there was open resistance from the people of the area themselves. After they forced the government to stop sending surveyors to the site, two officials from the king's royal projects went anyway, and were seized by the villagers for several days. After that, Bhumibol opted for an alternative dam site, only to find the royal forestry department demanded a reduction in the dam's size to limit the flooding of protected forest.

Politicians also daringly challenged the royal will, though not always with laudable motives. In late 1999, the king's leading aide on water projects, Pramote Maiklad, was sacked as head of the royal irrigation department by the minister in charge. Such actions weren't uncommon in the government, and it was clearly a political move related to corruption and kickbacks, though just whose wasn't clear. What was significant was that it involved the once untouchable Pramote.

There were other insults to royal veracity. In 1999 the BBC finally released the documentary for which it had been given exclusive access to the funeral of Princess Mother Sangwal. The palace had presumed that Sangwal would be portrayed as a Mother Teresa-type figure. The end product was something different, examining the monarchy itself. Although respectful and positive, it boldly asked questions about the throne's role, and the filmmakers interviewed Sulak Sivaraks, a longtime critic of the Bhumibol throne.

Then there was Fox Films' feature *Anna and the King*, a costume drama based on the exaggerated diaries of Fourth Reign palace tutor Anna Leonowens (also the source of the musical *The King and I*). For many decades the palace had dismissed her writings as utter fiction, because Leonowens did not paint King Mongkut in a completely positive light. Fox wanted to film the movie in the Grand Palace in Bangkok. But, working through the government's film board, the palace could not bring itself to give permission. The script was not exactly to the official view of Mongkut, the director wasn't Thai, and Fox had recruited Hong Kong star Chow Yun Fat to play King Mongkut (against Jodie Foster as Anna), which was unacceptable: a Thai would have to play Mongkut. Filmed in Malaysia, when it was released at the end of 1999 the movie was banned in Thailand, for niggling and specious reasons.

The final film was inoffensive and middling in quality, but it evoked a lot of challenging commentary on the real issue, just whose version of Thai history was the right one: the palace's or others'? One academic, the U.S.-based Thongchai Winichakul, wrote that the government's own version of history was no more rooted in reality than Hollywood's. Pointing out that *Anna*'s Mongkut was handsome, in sharp contrast to his real-life unattractiveness, Thongchai asked: "Should the film board ban the film because it makes King Mongkut look too majestic and good looking, thus historically inaccurate? . . . If we are so concerned with historical accuracy, the entire Ministry of Education and its production of history textbooks for schools should go first. . . . The whole controversy is about which fiction is preferable, to be allowable to be consumed by Thai people." Thongchai, a 1970s student leader, was one of a number of academics who had been poking around the edges of the monarchy for years, challenging its hold on culture and history. Slowly they were getting closer to the real issues, and couldn't be stopped.

In 2000 an entire generation of middle-aged academics, activists, and progressive politicians made a consciously subversive challenge to the palace's control of Ninth Reign history. The year marked the centennial of Pridi Bhanomyong, and his supporters wanted to use the occasion to revive his name and reputation. But the year was also the centennial of the king's mother, Sangwal, and the palace wanted all the attention on her. What ensued was a battle over superior virtue, and over who could decide just who the people's heroes are. Pridi's supporters pushed first as early as 1997, prodding the government to plan commemorations, to issue a stamp or even a banknote featuring Pridi, and to nominate him to the UNESCO millennium list of great personalities of the 20th century. When palace officials caught wind of this, they responded by planning a big year for sanctifying Sangwal. They nominated her to UNESCO, despite her being virtually unknown outside of Thailand. But the palace viewed this as almost a right. The previous Thai nomination to the UNESCO list, in 1992, was the even less known Prince Mahidol, the king's father.

The battle was fought through new books, academic conferences, and media articles on Pridi challenging the official view that he betrayed the country. They exposed the manipulation and perjury that led to his being condemned for King Ananda's murder, and highlighted his advocacy of democracy and leadership of the Free Thai movement. The palace could only counter by saturating radio and television with expensive promotion of the princess mother.

The result was a draw. Events to honor Pridi were not blocked, but also not acknowledged by the palace. Both Pridi and Sangwal were named to the UNESCO list, but the palace publicized only Sangwal. Pridi was kept off stamps, banknotes, and television and radio, and out of school materials, while Sangwal surfaced in all those venues. This limited Pridi's corrected reputation to the urban educated middle and upper classes who read the Bangkok print media. The people who mattered for the palace, grade-school students and peasants in the countryside, would still only know of royal heroes.

There was a fin de siècle air in all of this: on the palace side, a rush to score more deeply into the Thai people, especially a generation of teenagers ignorant of the past, a veneration for the throne that would sustain it into the future; on another side, long-stifled Thais starting to take advantage of the throne's weakening clutch on its own image by asserting their own, contrary views. By his age, the longevity of his reign, and his genuine efforts to help his people, Bhumibol's own stature was invulnerable. But clearly, the next generation of Chakris faced more difficulties in proving themselves.

The palace establishment began to prepare for the eventual succession. Acutely conscious of how the crown prince's disrepute might lead to conflict, officials reinforced palace control over the process, to ensure that dissident bureaucratic and military cliques, politicians, and above all the public had no ability to interfere. The presumed successor was still Prince Vajiralongkorn, despite the continuing popular support for Princess Sirindhorn. The constitution gave the prince priority over his sister, but it also gave the king's own choice precedence; Bhumibol could designate any successor he chose to.

This left room for intrigue, were he to pass away and his instruction be manipulated, as was almost the case at the end of both the Third and Fourth reigns. To make sure his instruction, or the law in lieu, was followed faithfully, Bhumibol built up his privy council around Prem. Prem recruited several councilors from his own clique of bureaucrats and national security experts. The king also named to the council in the 1990s two senior judges whom he trusted, and some senior royals. But by 2000 Prem's men dominated the body, showing Bhumibol's complete trust in him. Prem's other main task was to keep his hand in the military, ensuring people he trusted were promoted. This was crucial because the military was believed divided between pro-Sirindhorn and pro-prince factions, which had dangerous overtones for the eventual succession.

To guarantee a smooth passage, the palace also had to create closer ties with a new generation of political and business leaders. It had to elevate the crown prince's image to be more kingly, while keeping him happy and out of trouble. And it started a campaign to promote in a modern way the following generation of Mahidols, the granddaughters of the king and queen.

None of this was easy, and as ever required some unseemly compromises. The military connections for all key royals were kept up: the crown prince increasingly took part in military ceremonies and still commanded the palace guards. Princess Sirindhorn regularly lectured at the Chulachomklao Military Academy and presided over its commencements. The activities of Princess Bhajarakitiyabha, the seniormost royal of the next generation, were undertaken with the military even when civilian alternatives were available. She also found a boyfriend from the army. Meanwhile the prince and Queen Sirikit more actively courted the Village Scouts in ceremonies and rallies around the country, raising the scouts' political importance again after years of laying dormant. The palace made efforts to keep its agents and supporters in positions of power besides the military. Privy councilors and other king's favorites took positions on the boards of big corporations and state enterprises. After he was sidelined from the royal irrigation department, Pramote Maiklad was elected in March 2000 to the senate, where he took a leadership position.

The palace also rebuilt its income in the wake of the economic crash. Although the crown properties were decisively cleaned up by 2000, with the economy still languishing, the profits and dividends accruing to the throne remained weak. The CPB sought to lease out more of its vacant properties and raise the rents in existing ones, a challenge since the real estate market was hugely oversupplied in all sectors. But the bureau was reported in 2000 to have mapped out a plan to increase its rental income from 300 million baht a year ($7.5 million) to 1,000 million baht within five years.[22] CPB chief Chirayut Isarangkul later explained this as correcting the distortion effect on the market of lower CPB rents.[23] The action involved raising the rent on the government, even though the government had been operating at a large deficit since the crisis broke. Chirayut insisted that the palace was still cheaper than other landlords, though he didn't explain why the throne was raising its burden on the state.

In addition to its commercial interests, the palace had to strengthen its charities by renewing the idea of the magic circle of merit. Almost nightly on the royal news, there were film clips of individuals and business and social groups ritualistically presenting their charity collections to the king, the queen, Prince Vajiralongkorn, or Princess Sirindhorn. The palace stepped up efforts to attract funds from Thais overseas, stressing that the country was in an emergency. The donations were not to the government but to royal charities.

And there was a renewed effort to raise funds through the sale of commemorative medals, amulets, statues, and books. In 1998 the king awarded the royal symbol, the Garuda, to several large corporations that made substantial contributions to his charities. It hadn't been awarded in a decade. In May 2000 the central bank auctioned commemorative banknotes for the king and queen's 50th wedding anniversary, the receipts from which would go not to the government but to the royal charities. Prominent business tycoons often seen courting the queen paid up to 5 million baht for special uncirculated 500,000-baht banknotes.[24]

Few Thais, most of whom had never lived under any king but Bhumibol, could imagine the next reign, whoever the monarch. But at least one person was planning for it, and he showed just how ready some people were to abuse the royal image, and at the same time how risk-laden the prince's elevation might be. That was telecommunications tycoon and politician Thaksin Shinawatra. Thaksin had parlayed his multibillion-dollar fortune into building a large political party and capturing the premiership in January 2001. He also insinuated himself into military and palace politics, getting dangerously close to Prince Vajiralongkorn.

Thaksin worried many as having the ambition of Phibun Songkhram, who had competed with the king to be the country's paramount leader. Thaksin's new Thai Rak Thai (Thais Love Thais) political party projected itself as a mass-based movement by signing up 11 million members, making it the country's single largest organization. Thaksin had paintings in his home that were copies of the most famous, iconic photographs of King Bhumibol, pictures that projected the king's hard work and compassion toward his people. But Thaksin's versions had himself in the place of the king.

Unlike Phibun, Thaksin used his money to buy off the palace. Early in the 1990s, his generous donations reaped him entry into Queen Sirikit's circle and closeness to Ubolrat, reportedly funding some of her daughter Ploypailin's piano recitals. Rumors spread that he and Ubolrat were lovers. More calculatingly, Thaksin used his wealth to get close to the crown prince. At the end of the 1990s many well-informed Bangkokians talked of Thaksin having taken on many of the prince's larger expenditures, including the refurbishment of the old palace of Rama VII, which the prince wanted to move into. Until then it had been entrusted to Princess Sirindhorn, but in giving it up to her brother she received instead the Srapathum Palace of Queen Sawang. That too was refurbished with Thaksin's money, it was said.[25]

Thaksin also bailed out the CPB while buying himself media control. The only independent television station was the all-news cable channel ITV. ITV's biggest financier and a key shareholder was Siam Commercial Bank, and palace public relations adviser Piya Malakul's Pacific Communications also had a significant shareholding. The other major shareholder was the decidedly non-royalist Nation media group. After the devaluation and economic crash, ITV became insolvent. The Nation group offered to take it over completely, assuming the debts. Instead, in 2000, Siam Commercial Bank insisted on selling to Thaksin. At the time all Thai TV stations were losing money, and ITV had little intrinsic value beyond its equipment. Thaksin could have launched his own new cable-based station for a small sum. Instead, he paid Siam Commercial Bank $60 million for the ITV shares. With little likelihood of ever recovering the investment, Thaksin was effectively bailing out the bank and the palace.

As expected, Thaksin used ITV to support his run for the premiership, leading to embarrassing criticisms that the palace supported his candidacy through the ITV sale. When Piya too criticized Thaksin's abuse of ownership in the station, Thaksin forced Piya and other palace allies to resign.

The ITV episode showed Thaksin's true colors, though it was clear only after a few more years: he would serve palace needs as long as it served his own, but if their interests did not coincide, he felt no obligation to gratify the palace. Moreover, he was willing to publicly snub the throne, as well as play royal family members off against each other—particularly the prince and the queen against the king and Sirindhorn.

After winning the premiership, Thaksin ingratiated himself with the palace in symbolic ways. Declaring his economic policy, he echoed the king in accusing foreign investors of exploiting Thailand—even though he himself had partnerships with foreign investors—and said that the country should be more self-sufficient and independent of the global economy.[26] He announced a program to help develop village-based handicraft industries and other self-sufficiency programs.

He named a tough interior minister whose campaign for public morality, though excessive, echoed palace complaints that Thai society had become overly permissive. Thaksin's government also increased the application of the death sentence to narcotics traffickers and in certain murder cases, and it accelerated executions. By expediting this himself, with the palace's nod, Thaksin protected the king's reputation while doing his bidding. Meanwhile, at first, Thaksin left a number of the palace's agents in the government while promoting his own cronies. He made the modern monarchist Thongthong Chandrangsu a top official in the Justice Ministry.

This had an early payoff for Thaksin, many political observers believe. Within months of taking office in 2001, he was challenged for violating a clause of the new constitution banning from office anyone who held shares in a state-granted concession business, in this case his Shinawatra telecommunications business. The case went to the supreme court, where evidence overwhelmingly showed the prime minister in violation. It was widely believed that Prem's intervention was responsible for swinging the court in support of Thaksin, by one judge's vote. The key judge was believed to be former Prem aide and constitution drafter Kramol Thongthammachart, who, it was reported, changed his vote at the last minute. After the vote, the majority judges couldn't even decide on the legal basis for letting Thaksin off.

But if Prem and the palace thought this would expand to a new era of cooperation between the throne and the civilian leader, they were wrong. Going beyond earlier throne-independent premiers Kriengsak and Chatichai, Thaksin stifled political opposition, left the palace to its rites and symbols, and actively excluded it from his political and social programs. Thaksin demonstrated moreover a cynical willingness to exploit the monarchy when it served him. With the king semi-retired and Prem no longer dominating the bureaucracy and the army, he did pretty much as he pleased. Despite being castigated by the king on several occasions during his first four years in office, and despite his government proving nearly as corrupt as many before it, his overwhelming reelection in 2005 suggested he was succeeding in an epochal challenge to Ninth Reign power.

Eventually, like the similarly-named King Taksin who preceded the Chakri Dynasty, Thaksin was undermined by his own ego. In late 2005 a popular urban movement began pressing the king to oust him. A direct result of the throne's well-advertised historical interventions on the people's behalf, it nevertheless left the palace flummoxed. They did not at all like Thaksin, but he was legitimately elected and retained strong support in the countryside, traditionally the king's base. Moreover, this new city-based monarchist league, wearing royal-yellow t-shirts proclaiming loyalty to the crown, was led by two fickle men the palace would have no business with, publisher Sondhi Limthongkul and May 1992 leader Chamlong Srimuang.

When pressure grew overwhelming in early 2006, Thaksin called a snap election to demonstrate that he still retained rural voter support. But one day after declaring victory, he went to see the king and emerged to announce tearfully that he would not be renewed as prime minister. What had transpired was unclear, but the distinct impression was that Bhumibol had weighed in again. Although the move was popular, it also validated the act of petitioning the king from the streets to step into politics before the democratic process is exhausted.

22 Going into Seclusion ~
Can the Monarchy Survive Bhumibol?

IN 2000, BHUMIBOL REMOVED HIMSELF FROM THE CAPITAL and went into semi-seclusion at his Hua Hin beachside palace. Like King Mahajanaka (in the original story) withdrawing from society to follow the last stage of enlightenment, he seemed to be letting go of his struggle to transform his kingdom.

Yet like his own mythical King of Mithila, Bhumibol couldn't relinquish his duties completely, as if his work wasn't finished. At times he emerged to swear in new cabinet members, to meet prominent guests, and to receive charity donors or the occasional group of civil servants, like the military officers' corps for their annual promotions.[1] He also returned to Bangkok for his annual birthday chats, delivered as ever with homespun morality tales, self-effacing jokes, and barbs for the politicians. But mostly he stayed secluded. His main endeavor, it appeared, was writing *The Story of Tongdaeng*, the biography of a stray dog he had adopted four years earlier.[2] Tongdaeng was well known as Bhumibol's favorite dog, and the book, published in 2002, had many pictures of the king hugging and playing with her, even, in several, broadly smiling.

At first glance, 84 pages in English and Thai on a mongrel might be dismissed as an indulgence of the king, reminding his people that stray dogs are not inferior to the newly popular luxury purebreds. But the book is much more: it is an exemplary tale for his subjects. He describes Tongdaeng as "a common dog who is uncommon," a creature who had an innate sense of respect for the king. Just days old when she was offered to him, Tongdaeng had whimpered the whole day, but "strangely enough, once she had been presented to his majesty, she stopped crying and crawled to nestle on his lap, as if entrusting her life to his care, and fell fast asleep, free from all worries, loneliness and fear."

Tongdaeng is quick, clever, and attentive, following the king's instructions without question. She protects him from other dogs without command or reward. Remarkably, for a street mutt, she has a perfect walk, perfect poise, no bad odor, doesn't bark, and, despite the king's favor, is humble. Most important, she knows how to behave when with the king. She approaches him only when summoned, always acting with "proper manners" and, by official protocol, never placing herself higher than he is. "Other dogs, even Tongdaeng's own children, would show their delight when they meet the king by jumping onto his lap and lick[ing] his face. Tongdaeng would never do that. Even if he pulls her up to embrace her, Tongdaeng would quickly crouch on the floor, her ears down in a respectful manner. . . . One royal attendant mentioned that, if one wanted to know how to sit properly when one had an audience with the king, one should look at Tongdaeng."

Some Thais were offended at such a naked reminder to adore the king, with a dog set out as a model of behavior. But mostly, Thais loved the book. They bought more than half a million copies of *Tongdaeng*, making it Thailand's biggest-selling book ever. A similar number of Tongdaeng t-shirts were snapped up, with proceeds going to the king's charities. In that way, the Tongdaeng book reflected Bhumibol's reign. Despite his questionable interventionism, his stifling of critics, and his often embarrassing family, Bhumibol remains adored and virtually worshipped by the majority of his subjects. In his unique way he has successfully protected the Chakri franchise from being overrun by modern liberal democratic practice.

In the wake of the October 6 massacre at Thammasat University, Benedict Anderson described this success as essentially impeding the country's transition from kingdom to modern nation-state. "Unlike the monarchies of Libya and Ethiopia, the Thai monarchy has survived; but it has never made the full modern transition to the Japanese or European 20th-century monarchical style. 'Royalism,' in the sense of an active quest for real power in the political system by the royal family—i.e., the role of political 'subject'—persists in a curiously antique form in contemporary Siam. . . . This is all the odder since the present ruler's accession to the throne was a product purely of formal lineage and accident and should therefore have made him an ideal political 'object.' "[3]

More than a quarter century since Anderson wrote that, Bhumibol's monarchy has continued to hold the line against full constitutional government and democratization. As a purely political achievement, this resistance to change is unremarkable: a number of contemporary monarchies, including those of Brunei, Nepal, and the Middle East, have also stalled the modernization of government. The Thai difference is that, rather than maintaining the monarchy's stature through mass coercion and repression, Bhumibol has employed language and more importantly visual statement to persuade his subjects that Thailand is culturally and corporeally dependent on a strong monarchy, and that Thais are better off for it. This achievement was not something that just happened, but the result of a plodding and often brilliant effort to make the king bigger than the institutions of modern democracy. As the political scientist Michael Connors wrote, "The God-like status of Bhumibol was not part of the family treasure, but something that he and hundreds of officials in the palace and other agencies have contrived to create."[4]

Two factors made this effort work so well. The first was that Bhumibol was an ideal apprentice to revive the monarchy and carry it forward. After Ananda's tragic death, he unconditionally accepted his duty to the throne. He had a great capacity to learn, didn't question his teachers—themselves extremely able and politically canny—and wasn't given to greed, indifference, or excessive pleasure and luxury. The second factor was the profoundly Buddhist nature of Thai society. Decades after the 1932 revolution, Thais continued to see themselves "as belonging to a Thai nation whose roots are based in the dominant Buddhist tradition and as united in their loyalty to the institution of the monarchy," Charles Keyes wrote in his book *Thailand: Buddhist Kingdom as Modern Nation-State.*[5]

The 1932 revolutionists, and Phibun especially, tried hard to disconnect Buddhism and the monarchy so they could retire the beautiful idea of dhammaraja monarchism. In the postwar revival, the monarchists recognized that it was crucial to rejoin the two and reestablish the king's sacral identity. To do so, Bhumibol's teachers Prince Dhani and Prince Rangsit stressed above all ritual as a sign of dhammic pure practice. By undertaking the most important rites like the royal kathin, and attending the most important temples housing the holiest icons like the Emerald Buddha with the most respected monks at his side, Bhumibol could never be surpassed in his virtue.

Meanwhile, Bhumibol's teachers protected him from being seen by the public as deigning to play politics. From the very beginning of his reign until the 1990s, his interventions were always conducted behind an opaque curtain of absolutely loyal princes, privy councilors, and other palace officials. They whispered his desires only to those they could trust, and couched his letters of command and inquiry in the most officious language, as if these were troublesome duties the king had to undertake, rather than his volition.

This approach differentiated him from Thai politicians, who in their desire to steer politics revealed ambition, who normally talked more than acted, and who were deficient in ritual and in association with sacral people and objects. An uncrossable chasm was established between the virtuous throne and virtueless politicians. Bhumibol would associate with bureaucrats and soldiers, but he stead-fastly avoided being seen with politicians, even those in high leadership positions, unless they wore the uniforms of army generals, like Sarit and Prem.

The result of this calculated differentiation was that the king's efforts on behalf of the people were seen as selfless acts of *dana* (generosity) and *paricakka* (sacri-fice), tenets of the thotsaphit rachatham. When politicians, or businessmen for that matter, undertook the very same acts, they were understood as seeking gain. The palace reminded the people of this dichotomy constantly. Further evidence of Bhumibol's unsurpassable pure practice of the dhamma came in the 1990s when the palace began to receive large donations directly from wealthy temples. With the merit chain now running vertically upward from the people through temples to the palace, and not from the palace to temples, the implication of the royal deity was ever greater. (To the king's critics, it suggested that the magic circle of merit had become broken.)

Having demonstrated his superiority to human rivals, Bhumibol had to do the same with democracy, an autonomous force not covered by nation-religion-king. Because calls for democratic reform could be wielded by anyone, including com-petitors with the throne, the king had to assume the idea of democracy into the dhammaraja kingship.

From early on, democracy was popularly understood as having an elected government which represents and advances the aspirations of a free people. With the king absent from that construction, it wasn't enough to simply declare the monarchy and democracy married, as was done in 1977 when the government defined Thailand as a "democracy with a king as head of state." Bhumibol had to demonstrate that the ancient monarchy was innately democratic, and so bigger and more encompassing than the narrower, Western-imported democracy the people had heard about.

Therein lay the importance of calling the Sukhothai-dated Ramkhamhaeng inscription a democratic manifesto; the insistence that all Chakri kings were men of the people; and the firm enforcement of the narrative that King Prajadhipok alone had fathered modern constitutional democracy in Thailand in 1932. Indeed, the royalists of the Ninth Reign convinced themselves of this narrative. In 1992 Bhumibol himself told two Western writers that King Mongkut first introduced democratic ideals to the kingdom, and after him, Prajadhipok, by his own volition, finished the task by delivering full democracy.[6]

Repeated often in scholarly writings, school textbooks, and television dramas, these arguments gained credibility because it was understood from Buddhist teachings that a person of pure practice, such as a dhammaraja, necessarily works for others. The king's selflessness and sacrifice make him by nature democratic, serving all of his people rather than himself or a limited constituency. (And because he is king, he has the information, or inborn omniscience, to know what the people want.) In essence, the Buddhist ruler who was once the critical element of the old feudal warrior kingdoms was established as the critical element in a modern free democracy. In contrast, members of parliament were not deemed critical to this structure. By the late 1960s, Bhumibol openly disparaged politicians as serving only themselves and narrow interest groups. He would not directly claim he was better, but by highlighting the results of his own projects, he let his actions supply the interpretation.

Still, efforts to depict the monarchy as innately democratic faced an important challenge: Thais understood democracy to involve elections of the people's representatives, a qualification that eluded the king. In response, the palace simply maintained that all Chakri kings were popular kings, who would not have stayed on the throne had they not maintained the people's support or been guilty of misrule. By that logic, Bhumibol and his predecessors on the throne were essentially elected. As he told an interviewer, "I am really an elected king. If the people do not want me, they can throw me out."

If that was true, then elections, as most commonly understood, were not really useful for choosing representative leaders, and Bhumibol's record of nonsupport for elected governments reflected that belief. He was content without any elections during the Sarit and Thanom eras, and he endorsed proposals for an unelected (and often royal-appointed) senate, which could dominate the lower house of parliament. He also supported prime ministers like Prem who could prevail over both houses. The king's stance primed the Thai public to embrace the same view of Western-style elections when elected governments failed.

Subsuming democracy into the virtue of the dhammaraja was only a partial step. Both democracy and the popular practice of dhamma were too individualistic, distracting citizens from the monarchy-centered nation. As the kingdom's most spiritually advanced, virtuous individual, Bhumibol was qualified to reconstruct both concepts.

His elemental change was to stress unity as both a civic and religious virtue, making it the keystone of both democracy and dhamma. Democracy, his argument went, was a system designed to benefit the entire community, so it could not be achieved by individuals striving and competing for their own benefits. Rather, it required everyone working together with the same goal. Hence unity—something not characteristic of the Western-conceived competitive political party and elections system—was the true path of democracy. Within the dhamma, Bhumibol's problem was that his subjects understood karma and fate as circumstances of the individual. In his reinterpretation, the destiny of every Thai was bound up with the community, and a person's actions had to be considered for their effect on everyone else. He wanted each individual Thai to understand that his or her fate was tied up with the state, and that the state's fate was tied to the monarchy.

Unity and loyalty weren't enough to solve all problems of the state, however. The king concluded that national development was constrained, for one, by the torpor of the peasantry. This could have been an issue of simple laziness, which he suspected, or the effect of the Buddhist virtue of non-desire, or both. (Bhumibol didn't attribute the matter to lack of opportunity, education, or information.) Whatever the case, the peasants did not work hard enough for the nation. So Bhumibol added industriousness to the dhammic catalogue of values, stressing communal rather than individual work. He chided people for not working hard, suggesting that they were retarding their spiritual advancement and hurting the nation. "Children must know that happiness and amenities in life are not readily available. Instead they normally transpire through continual good works and good conduct. People with bad conduct who do not work industriously can never find happiness," he said.[7]

On the other hand, he also branded the extreme desire characteristic of capitalism as a barrier to unity and progress. Capitalists were selfish, divisive, and exploitative. "Those who aim only for personal gain are not to be praised," he said in 1980. "We should endeavor to cooperate in work so the benefit that everyone aims for would turn out for the country's good." By the end of the 1990s, after the economic crash, he concluded that the capitalist overemphasis on desire was in fact the core fault of the Thai system. In its place he offered his New Theory and his self-sufficiency economy concept, which would harness the very things that Buddhism seeks to overcome: cravings and greed. "Sufficiency is moderation," Bhumibol said.

"If one is moderate in one's desires, one will have less craving. If one has less craving, one will take less advantage of others. If all nations hold this concept . . . without being extreme or insatiable in one's desires, the world will be a happier place."[8]

The most formidable barrier to advancing this vision of the dhammaraja's democracy—what some Thai political scientists called "dhammocracy"—was the free-standing constitution with its modern principle of the rule of law. A constitution was widely understood as a vital feature of democracy. That principle was reinforced, ironically, by the throne's own celebration of the myth of King Prajadhipok, bequeathing his people their first constitution, thus expressly making the kingdom democratic. Despite that claim, the palace could never own or control the constitution. When Phibun added it to the pillars of state as "nation-religion-king-constitution," he highlighted the charter, and the laws it embodied, as an institutional rival to monarchic power and discretion. Any Thai could cite the constitution in claiming his rights and his freedom, and the throne could not contradict it. (And on the rare occasion, the king himself cited the constitution to defend his prerogatives.)

During the 1945–57 period, the royalists tried to make the charter's existence work for the throne. Since then, however, Bhumibol has preferred to impair the charter, if not eliminate it completely. In the 1970s, he felt its secular freedoms were the source of the country's disunity and disorder, a door by which communists could seize power. To persuade the people of his own way, Bhumibol assigned to constitutionalism the Buddhist concept of anicca, or impermanence. The record of promulgation, alteration, and abrogation of so many charters during the Ninth Reign, he suggested, offered proof that the constitution was too mutable to serve as a pillar of the state. That Thailand had survived through so many constitutions demonstrated that a charter was not essential. Only dhamma, the perfect law that underpinned Bhumibol's own pure practice, was certain and permanent, and so fundamental to the Thai nation. "When a constitution is abrogated or a parliament abolished . . . the people's mandate reverts to me," Bhumibol said. He included in this view the entire body of civil and criminal law. He frequently pointed out how the law was used unjustly to benefit a powerful few and harm the weak, while his own actions were just and fair. The harsh and final application of civil laws didn't weigh motivation or good intentions. Nor did it consider the results of an act—for instance, if something that violated the law actually helped the community at large. As such, secular laws and the constitution were virtueless tools that could destroy unity and pit people against one another.

This belief underpinned Bhumibol's advice to the constitution drafters in 1997 to keep the new charter short and simple. As his aide Tongnoi Tongyai wrote in the 1980s, the only constitution needed was one that promoted togetherness under the king's umbrella.

The success of Bhumibol's advocacy of a throne-centered state, then, was rooted to a large extent in Thai Theravada Buddhism, and the palace's superior ability to exploit and manipulate it. There were times, in the 1930s, the early 1970s, and around 1990, when secular voices became louder and pulled the kingdom in another direction. But as the aftermath of the 1997 economic crash evidenced, his way has always exerted a very strong draw on the people, because he was and still is understood as the leading Buddhist practitioner. Like King Mongkut in the official histories, he appears to uniquely combine the wisdom of the traditional dhammaraja with modern knowledge.

Arguably, there was something much bolder in Bhumibol's effort than simply holding the reins of politics in his own hands. What emerges in the aggregate of a lifetime of verbal and ritual expression, and especially in his 1990s speeches and publications, is a vision for a sort of modern Buddhist theocratic state and society, one that presumes the king's sacredness and regulates the people's behavior by the dhammic and karmic principles he espouses. Bhumibol's vision is the idealized, exemplary Sukhothai kingdom of the Trai Phum Phra Ruang, in which a sacred leader governs according to religious law, the principles of dhamma, and personally practices dhamma at the highest level. He assumes the role of both political and spiritual leader, and rules according to his own interpretations of religious principle. His knowledge of what is best for the people arises not from his experience in modern administration but from his pure practice of the ten precepts for a king.

Certainly this religion-based state differs strikingly from the common understanding of a theocracy as an exceedingly strict and fundamentalist regime, like Iran in the 1980s under the Islamic clerics. Theocratic Iran enforced correct behavior through a systematic, legalistic court system dominated by religious judges. Hierarchy there was tied to religious training and practice.

In the Buddhist paradigm, the leader steers his people not by harsh laws and punishments but by the suasive power of example, the sheer force of his virtue. Karma governs the cosmos, not constitutional law and secular judges. If people do wrong, they will eventually suffer their deserved consequences naturally. Hierarchy, moreover, is tied to merit from pure practice. The exemplary monarch exists as living proof of how dhammic behavior is the path to greater contentedness and enlightenment.

The key to understanding this scheme as a theology-based political system, and not simply as the dream of a secular practitioner, is the calculated projection of the Chakri king, and Bhumibol specifically, as simultaneously a dhammaraja and devaraja, residing at the junction of the heavens and earth. The projections of this image have been unceasing throughout the Ninth Reign. Although he is officially a modern, limited king and the country's top civil servant, innumerable official publications and textbooks, royal ceremonies and religious rituals, and appreciations penned by other respected men, especially high monks, depict Bhumibol as a sacral leader with blood-born magical powers and transcendent vision. Added to that are the king's own sublime projections of his transcendence of the mundane world: his numerology, his unreformed practice of mystical Hindu and Brahman palace rites, his patronizing of magic monks, his dismissiveness of the people and apparatus of modern secular government, and his trust mainly in monks and devout Buddhists to promote his vision.

Admittedly, this projection is not always readily cognizable. In Thai culture and conventions the king cannot be directly identified as a god, or even said directly to have achieved enlightenment, or nirvana. (Chakri predecessor King Taksin was executed in part for having claimed this for himself.) No person presumes to have the qualification, the necessary spiritual insight, to perceive the precise level of the king's sacrality. One can know someone else has greater merit than them, but not how much greater. As Christine Gray wrote, "Mere mortals cannot 'know for sure' about the karmic heritage of kings or deities, and their 'proper duties' or codes for conduct do not include guessing about the same."[9] As a linguistic convention, Thais refer to the king as a *sommutthithep,* a "supposed angel." To outsiders this comes across as a somewhat cute characterization. But it has serious meaning. Like the Buddha in his life, a sommutthithep occupies the highest position on earth and the lowest rungs of heaven, mediating between the two, purposely ambiguous as to whether he occupies the same level as an arhat or bodhisattva, incipient Buddha forms.

The king's sommutthithep status is revealed by indexical signs: one can't directly recognize a god, but one can recognize the acts of one. Like a landscape littered with billboards, Ninth Reign Thailand is replete with such indicators. The highest monks bow down to the king; he alone conducts the most important religious rituals; he can make rain and solve insoluble problems like the people's poverty; he can tame wrongheaded and evil men, who though very powerful bow at his feet; he possesses unmatched wealth and grace; people from all over the world seek out his wisdom, as seen on television almost daily; and foreign Buddhists recognize his veracity.[10]

Equally revealing of the dhammaraja-devaraja identity are things like Bhumibol's herd of white elephants and his golden Rolls-Royce limousines; his amulets which protect men in battle; the coincidence of his 10,000th-day anniversary in 1977 with the birthday of Rama V and Rama VIII, during which the high monk Phra Yanasangworn praised his unerring adherence to the thotsaphit rachatham; the thousands of people who have ordained on the king's various anniversaries; the consecration of his own mother as a virtual saint; and the selection twice of the number 999 in the lottery on the ninth Chakri king's birthday in 1999. Reinforcing all of this is the incessant repetition of the momentous and miraculous events of his Buddha-like life story, and the wealth of the magic circle of merit.

Bhumibol directly projects this image of a sommutthithep in his annual birthday speeches. In his stories he exhibits a monklike insight into the preternatural occurrences and miraculous events that have surrounded him and his reign. More than just a wise old patriarch's homiletic ramblings, these tales display the unfathomable merit and wisdom of a demigod.

This identity is also asserted by those around the king. In a lecture on kingship to a mostly foreign audience at the Siam Society in 1999, one of Bhumibol's closest aides, M.R. Butrie Viravaidhya, explained plainly that Bhumibol is a sommutthithep. "The king is not a divine being. He is only an imaginary divine being," she explained vaguely and cautiously, aware that normally one doesn't speak of such things.[11] Even so, she proceeded to describe the monarchy through representations of its divine attributes. She noted the importance of key royal symbols and regalia that represent the Hindu gods Shiva, Vishnu, and Brahma. The palace, she said, strives to make sure Bhumibol walks on carpets so that his feet never touch the ground, like Shiva; and when he travels, the royal standard with a symbol of Vishnu is always set out by his car or helicopter.

Butrie then told a story in all seriousness in reference to the king's representation as Brahma, who rides a mythical swan, the hamsa. When the king undertakes the royal barge procession for the annual kathin to Wat Arun, he is supposed to ride the barge with a golden hamsa figurehead. In the 1996 procession, he instead mounted a vessel styled with a garuda, newly built for him by the navy. The result of this departure from the habit of Brahma, Butrie said, was a big rainstorm that doused the procession. But when the king's barge reached Wat Arun, the rain suddenly stopped, because, Butrie told the audience, the king is also Shiva, and so can't be rained upon. "So we always say that there is something up there," she said. "Even though he is an imaginary god."

It would be easy to credit this image to tradition, playfulness, and overzealous supporters, but for the king's own books published in the 1990s. The first two, his translations of *A Man Called Intrepid* and *Tito,* hold to the theme of a brilliant, selfless leader. The third was *Mahajanaka,* which very clearly cast Bhumibol as King Mahajanaka, who operated as a bridge between the earth and the gods, like a sommutthithep.

There was a fourth book, an English-language biography of Bhumibol, *The Revolutionary King,* commissioned by the king himself and published in London in 1999. Ten years earlier, Bhumibol had invited William Stevenson, the author of the original *Intrepid,* to write the book. Stevenson lodged in the princess mother's Srapathum Palace and was provided research support and unprecedented interviews with court staff and the king himself, though he didn't have access to internal documents or archives.

The result was a book that presents Bhumibol as truly inviolate, magical, and godly. *The Revolutionary King* tells of the brilliant but underappreciated king single-handedly rebuilding his country after the war and navigating with innate skill through infinite evil forces. He tries to lead his people to reject greed and ambition for Buddhist values that would deliver the kingdom to peaceful bliss. The countryside peasantry understands the king's efforts, but politicians, Chinese businessmen, unthinking bureaucrats, and ambitious generals and palace courtiers do not. Remarkably, *The Revolutionary King* hardly differs from the many Thai-language hagiographies on the Mahidol family and the Ninth Reign. Weaving together historical anecdotes and quotes from the king, his family, and his aides, the book is chock-full of the standard Ninth Reign mythology, matching the view of the palace and royal family projected in Thai publications, broadcast programs, and publicity.[12]

As in these Thai-language works, in Stevenson's book the numerous landmarks of Bhumibol's life all have an air of mystery and miracle. It starts with the story of an orphan girl, Sangwal, who against all odds becomes mother to two kings. As a boy, Bhumibol shows a preternatural predilection for hydraulics, forestry, and engineering, and is capable of translating poetry through five European languages. Ananda's mysterious death and Bhumibol's accession to the throne are depicted as heavenly events, foreshadowed by omens seen in the court. Bhumibol, beset with fear that Ananda's soul would wander in eternity, becomes one with his brother's spirit to carry out Ananda's dream of "Buddhist democracy." In the book, Bhumibol recounts meeting an apparition of Ananda in the palace several weeks after his brother's death: "I heard following footsteps as I left the urn. In royal ceremonies, I always had to walk behind my brother. In this moment I forgot he was dead, and I told him, 'It is for me to walk behind you. That is the proper way.' My brother replied, 'From now on, I walk behind you.'"

As he settled into the throne in the 1950s, Bhumibol rose speedily to a higher spiritual level in his discovery of the Siamese metaphysical world, the book reveals. He spoke with uncommon wisdom and clarity. "A growing number of older generals remembered that Buddha had spoken with the same kind of apparent simplicity," Stevenson wrote. Palace insider Thongthong Chandrangsu told Stevenson that Bhumibol was already recognized "as being the early incarnation of Buddha, wrestling demons and resisting seduction." By the 1960s, Bhumibol's wisdom spanned the breadth of the sacral and secular. He now expressed recondite concepts that Western counterparts could not understand, taught his already-wise adviser Vasit Dejkunchorn meditation, and uncannily corrected a design fault in the American M-16 rifle. In the 1970s the king had more paranormal experiences, Stevenson wrote. He constantly felt the spirit of his brother. When Princess Vibhavadi Rangsit died in 1977, her helicopter shot down by the CPT, the king claimed that her apparition had appeared to him to warn of the deep danger present.

Through the decades, Bhumibol promoted strongly his Buddhist society ideal as superior to Western culture. It required detachment, concentration, and pure practice. The king explained this, according to Stevenson: "Buddhism is very complex. It has many grades. The highest level is to attain absolute purity in yourself.... [T]o attain this purity you must do everything that is not selfish ... , to discard everything that one thinks is one's own." Loathe to claim this purity for himself, Bhumibol allowed it to be understood. In explaining how he prevailed in May 1992, for instance, he said the key was knowing that anyone who destroyed someone of great virtue destroyed themselves.

Others were more willing to attest to his mystical virtues. Stevenson quotes the supreme patriarch as saying: "The king is a special being in our Buddhist belief, who has extraordinary power and knowledge to see you not only in this life but in previous lives. He is the Bodhisattva of Compassion whose unwavering gaze pierces you to your eternal being." Stevenson was also told that Bhumibol predicted the 1997 crisis months before it broke, and when the people ignored his warnings, he finally decided himself on the devaluation. Afterward, he consoled his people with advice on how to start anew, promoting his New Theory, described in the book as the most innovative economic and political thinking since World War II. Ultimately the author describes Bhumibol as Mahajanaka in the ocean, constantly swimming to survive, his dream of a society governed by Buddhist principles always just out of reach. Like Mahajanaka, he perseveres, feeling that "I cannot afford to die."

When it came out, the book proved a misadventure. Stevenson was liberal with style and careless with facts to the point of embarrassing the palace. His errors were legion. The book opened with a map that showed Thailand in possession of significant portions of Laos and Burma, and put the king's Hua Hin palace 300 kilometers and a sea away from where it should be. It ended with a genealogical chart naming Rama VII as the son of his brother Rama VI. In between, Stevenson offended the palace community with passing references to Sirikit's fixation on herself as Queen Suriyothai incarnate, to the tension between Vajiralongkorn and Sirindhorn over the throne, and to the king's calling the ladies of the court bar-racudas. Most important, the author used unacceptable referents for the royal family, calling the king by his childhood nickname Lek; his brother, 'Nand; and Sangwal, Mama. As a rule, anything not written by the royal family itself requires consistent use of formal addresses such as "His Majesty King Bhumibol."

Such problems gave the palace cause to have the book proscribed from sale in Thailand and from discussion in the media. (It couldn't be officially banned for lèse-majesté, because as Stevenson's sponsor, the king would be culpable!)[13] This only encouraged English-fluent Thais—the rationalist nonbelievers in dhammaraja-devaraja mythology—to seek out the book in foreign markets. Thousands of copies circulated in Thailand, and the general reaction was to castigate the author's failings while not questioning the essence of his story, the magical and sacral monarchy of Bhumibol Adulyadej. That was the intended message of the Stevenson book, for foreigners, but more for Thailand's educated cynics.

Such affirmations of Bhumibol's semi-divinity went a long way toward convincing many Thais of the error in adopting a European-style constitutional and capital-ist society. Practically, though, the profound impact of this achievement was to beget two fundamental conflicts that remain the source of much of the tension in Thai society.

The first concerns the system of governance. Comfortable with managing on an ad hoc basis through his privy councilors and generals, Bhumibol made no concrete effort to arrange the political system for the long term. On the contrary, he encouraged a general cynicism that obstructed the pursuit of any kind of political reform. To the reformers' great frustration, as the millennium turned, Thais continued to place their faith in their septuagenarian sovereign and condemn democratic politics. Typical were the comments heard in the run-up to the national election in late 2000 from a shopkeeper in central Bangkok. Although she lived in a district where the leading candidate (and eventual winner) was a respected, upright doctor, she insisted that "all politicians are self-serving and corrupt. Only the king can help us."

The other main conflict ascribable to Bhumibol's reign, over which rules should govern men's behavior, is far more deleterious. By advocating a broad, flexible, and ultimately self-enforced dhamma-based moral system, Bhumibol has helped undermine the rule of law. Violent crime, vice, and corruption are widespread in Thailand, as is a highly casual view of law among both offenders and enforcers. While such problems are common in developing countries, Thailand's collective indifference toward law stands out as boldly as its open sex industry, narcotics networks, and murder-for-hire rackets.

Modern laws designed to prevent such activity are ineffective, Charles Keyes suggests, because neither the statutes nor the royal and sangha leadership establish a link between modern and dhammic law. By ignoring or condemning the modern statutes, advocates of the dhamma-based system abet the many wrongdoers who are unafraid of karmic retribution. In the realm of the dhammaraja, Keyes explained, "A Buddhist-based secular tolerance of what are considered to be matters of individual moral choice has contributed to the development of plural value-systems. . . . Such tolerance extends to an unwillingness on the part of the state to enforce some particular version of Buddhist morality through law."[14] The lack of law enforcement, and the resultant massive criminality in the country, vexes the Thai people. Often, the powerless turn to the king's morality system of dhammic fate and suffering and karmic retribution; others take the law into their own hands, adding to the problem.

It is clear that Bhumibol himself is deeply frustrated by crime. But while he has spoken out against criminality, and especially against corruption, he has rarely defended or promoted the law itself, preferring instead to criticize its inconsistencies, unfairness, and mutability. He apparently doesn't recognize his own role in sustaining the tension between the dhammic and secular approaches. This became evident in the mid-1990s when he began to approve executions after a hiatus of many years. No explanation was given for the link between certain crimes and the death penalty, so the punishments failed to serve as a deterrent to future crime. Instead, like so many other things involving the throne, the executions simply took place and were reported after the fact, as if an uncontrollable karmic force was involved. Moreover, Bhumibol appeared to give a nod to the Thaksin Shinawatra government's anti-drug campaign in early 2003, in which some 2,300 alleged criminals, most of them petty drug users at worst, were extrajudicially executed by "mysterious killers," known to human rights activists as disguised police hit squads.[15]

Instead of helping to strengthen the law with his public endorsement, Bhumibol intervenes on crime secretively, the details of each case kept inside the palace. In 1999, for instance, the palace let it be known that Bhumibol had rejected the promotion of three senior judges. Newspapers were permitted to report the incident as the king's reaction to the judges' corrupt reputations. Everyone assumed that Bhumibol's intervention was well-founded and that the judiciary would be less corrupt because of it. Yet, ironically, he wasn't willing to invoke the process of the law or offer any evidence against the three. The act demanded blind acceptance of Bhumibol as the supreme arbiter of justice. Yet it provided no example for others because the judges' alleged crimes were not made public.

The conflict between Bhumibol's way and modern constitutionalism has clearly affected Thai governance. It delayed efforts to address the economic collapse in 1997, as palace-backed figures shunned IMF support—which required systematic approaches and disciplined, transparent laws—in favor of a more elastic and invisible "Thai" fix, one that started and ended behind the scenes. This conflict was also manifest in the palace's intervention in the supreme court challenge to newly elected prime minister Thaksin Shinawatra in 2001. The episode embarrassed the court and palpably eroded public respect for the courts and the law.

But Bhumibol's most fundamental failing is the Achilles heel of every monarchy: he has been unable to guarantee an orderly succession to a wise, selfless, and munificent king like himself. This shortcoming leaves a dark cloud over the nation as Bhumibol advances in age. Although it is generally presumed that he will bequeath the throne to Prince Vajiralongkorn, the prince's succession is not guaranteed. The constitution gives him clear priority as the king's son, but it allows the king to make his own choice. Indeed, by claiming that the throne is democratic, Bhumibol has long encouraged people to think they can influence succession. "The people . . . will decide," he said in a 1992 interview. "I do not myself think that gender is so important."[16]

Such consciously ambiguous statements allow hopeful Thais to believe that Princess Sirindhorn, as the first alternate to her brother for the throne, could be named the next Chakri ruler. Sirindhorn's strength lies in her perceived great virtue. She is given to performing good deeds, fosters charity, and is genuinely interested in the people's welfare. She is linked to the arts, education, and religion, and to Thai culture generally, while her brother is not. She has also been given control of the king's wealthy charity foundations. Her stock of merit is high, and, besides her large popular constituency, she is supported by the cadets and officers from the Chulachomklao Military Academy where she teaches, as well as from within the bureaucracy.

Even so, most signs indicate that the crown will pass to Vajiralongkorn. Turning 53 in 2005, the prince has behaved well enough in recent years to appear more responsible and committed to the monarchy. With his parents' overt blessing he married for the third time, in 2001, and seemed to settle down in his private life. His attractive new commoner wife, Srirasmi Mahidol Na Ayutthaya, was introduced to the public to seeming acceptance. More socially adept than her predecessor Sucharinee, she had been close to the prince since 1992, newspapers reported, even before he married Sucharinee.[17]

When Bhumibol retired to Hua Hin, the division of his duties between Vajiralongkorn and his sisters gave the prince most of the primary state functions. He has assumed his father's icon, being seen on television poring over maps and checking out dams as he traverses the countryside. He is also shown accompanying his mother, a bond of support Sirindhorn seems to lack. Their regular appearances at Village Scout gatherings, in which the prince usually stands in military uniform with a pistol on his belt, constitute an important positioning that relates directly to succession.

Nevertheless, the prince's capacity to lead gives rise to great worries. Neither at the level of the traditional Buddhist dhammaraja kingship nor as a modern head of state has Vajiralongkorn displayed proficiency. In Buddhist kingship, power essentially derives from the king's own spiritual achievements, which are personal and ultimately transitory. Though Bhumibol can bequeath his son some of his aura, ultimately the prince must demonstrate his own virtue in the traditional framework of the thotsaphit rachatham. In the Hindu devaraja worldview, Vajiralongkorn does inherit his father's deific attributes. But this is offset by his deficiency of the accumulated merit needed to propel the kingdom forward along a dhammic path. His performance of rituals is sparing and perfunctory. He isn't believed to have explored the mysteries of the dhamma and his own soul. Instead he is seen as still caught in the world of desire and pleasure, seeking out young women to entertain him. And he remains given to violent outbursts.

On the level of modern monarchism, Vajiralongkorn also lacks the stature and skills needed to fill Bhumibol's role as a potent political actor, much less to begin the necessary task of modernizing the throne. He hasn't developed a smart-thinking support team like his father's. Instead, he flirts with ambitious and untrustworthy men, the most obvious example being Thaksin. His power rests on a narrow base of his mother, a limited sector of the military, plus the Village Scouts. This is a foundation for power and intervention by force and fear, not by royal prestige.

This inadequacy is not completely the prince's fault. Stuck in his father's shadow, he is much like Prince Charles in England, unable after 50 years to even experiment in leadership and administration. Bagehot, writing in the 19th century, observed of a king coming to the throne at middle age: "He is then unfit to work. He will then have spent the whole of youth and the first part of manhood in idleness, and it is unnatural to expect him to labor. . . . The only fit material for a constitutional king is a prince who begins early to reign—who in his youth is superior to pleasure—who in his youth is willing to labor—who has by nature a genius for discretion. Such kings are among God's greatest gifts, but they are also among his rarest."[18]

Thais recognize these weaknesses in the prince's kingly credentials. No one puts Vajiralongkorn's picture on their wall, and few seek out his amulets or want to donate to his charities. Some even interpreted the death of the prince's personal spiritual mentor in a car crash in 1999 as a sign of the dead-end of his spiritual progress.

The prince's shortcomings and Bhumibol's ambiguousness leave open the chance that the succession could be turbulent. If Bhumibol doesn't first abdicate to control the process, the succession will fall first into the hands of the privy council. With the very loyal Prem leading the council, and men handpicked by Prem filling much of it, the council theoretically would carry out the king's instructions or, in their absence, adhere to the constitution and 1924 succession law. The problem with this scenario is that Prem, seven years older than the king, might not outlive Bhumibol. No other privy councilor has Prem's standing to surmount both internal and external political pressures that could come in the succession.

Without a commanding figure like the king or Prem, Thais fear that pro-prince and pro-princess factions in the armed forces could erupt into violent conflict over the succession. Many took to heart the massacre of Nepal's king and his family by their own crown prince in 2001. They also talk of the murky two-centuries-old prediction, made perhaps by Rama I himself, that the Chakri Dynasty will have only nine kings.[19] The story's multiple versions all suggest that a substantial change could come with the death of the ninth Chakri king: a destructive regime resulting in a revolution; a peaceful turn to a republic; or even, some hopefully interpret, a regnant queen. The rumor finds further significance in the events of 1932, when anxiety built around another early prediction that the Chakri monarchy would last only 150 years. Deliberately popularized, the prediction eased the way for the coup that ended the absolute throne, becoming a self-fulfilled prophecy.[20]

This situation made all the more important Prime Minister Thaksin's climb to power. Following his 2001 election, the palace appeared sympathetic to Thaksin's tendency to snub both law and government procedure to get things done. Using his multibillion-dollar fortune the way Prem relied on the military, Thaksin gave short shrift to the constitution and jettisoned civil rights to pursue his agenda. But while Prem honored and credited the king, Thaksin governed as a rival to the throne who promoted secular government for his own purposes.[21] Thaksin's modus operandi was to draw on the palace's support when the two sides agreed, and ignore it when their interests diverged. But he also exploited differences between the king and Prem, on one side, and the queen and the prince on another. During 2004–5, Thaksin appeared to reject criticism from the king and Prem over the government's brutal crackdown on Muslim dissent in southern Thailand, where hundreds of people were killed by soldiers and police. Some observers believed the prince and the queen endorsed the heavy-handedness and gave Thaksin political support to continue.[22]

The palace could only wait until Thaksin became so reckless, and a popular movement to oust him gained enough support from his own former backers in the political, military, and business elite, that he had to step down in early 2006. It appeared that the king forced Thaksin to quit only a day after his party won a snap election, effectively leaving the country in a vacuum without a political leader to maintain stability. And it left King Bhumibol, who had no good alternatives to fill Thaksin's shoes, responsible for the vacuum.

While Thaksin's autocratic government was problematic in the context of democracy and good governance, his concentration of power around himself as the country's self-styled "chief executive" could be seen as a move to neutralize the palace in politics. This would have been a positive development in the case of a difficult succession, as well as if, as king, Vajiralongkorn embarks on a course of damaging political intervention, such as the government's bloody approach to southern Thailand problems.

In any case, Thaksin's disregard for the king and Prem, and his apparently partly successful efforts to buy off the prince, clearly highlight the need for a new palace approach to politics. Thaksin's rule showed that Thais need more institutions than the throne to turn to against a bad leader—they need to be able to rely on a more effective elected parliament, cleaner courts, and a freer media.

Beyond succession, Vajiralongkorn himself faces challenges in managing the next Chakri generation. With the birth of a boy to Srirasmi in April 2005, the prince has now had children by all three of his wives: five sons and two daughters. The leader of the next-generation Chakris is also the only fully royal-blooded of King Bhumibol's grandchildren, Princess Bhajarakitiyabha, or Ong Bha, Vajiralongkorn's daughter by his first wife, Princess Somsawali. Until Srirasmi's son was born, Bhajarakitiyabha's education and ritual participation, and Princess Sirindhorn's attention to her, indicated that she was the presumed successor of her father. A law graduate of Cornell University, she carries herself with the confidence of Sirikit, and the haughtiness of Chulabhorn.

But her place in the royal ranking is no longer as clear. Vajiralongkorn was determined to have a boy with Srirasmi to designate as his heir, and undertook a long and determined effort toward that end assisted by doctors, according to palace sources. Their son, Prince Tipangkara Rasmichote, was blessed in a holy water ceremony by the king and queen in June 2005, confirming his acceptance into the Mahidol family line.

Moreover, despite having been sent into exile and living in the United States, having claimed political asylum, Sucharinee and her four sons by the prince are said to have recovered some status in the palace, with the way possibly open for at least some of the boys to participate as titled royals. Indeed, their sister, whose name was changed from Busyanampetch to Siriwanwaree, remained in Thailand after 1996 and has been treated as an important rising palace figure. In 2001 she was given a high royal decoration, paving the way for her eventual elevation to official princess status. That suggests that Vajiralongkorn and Sucharinee's son Chudhavajra, who, at 26 in 2005, is the eldest grandson of the king, could have a fair claim to the throne.[23] Indeed, in a dynasty with a male-focused tradition but only a minute number of men in its newest generations, Sucharinee's sons are necessary to keep the royal family's numbers healthy. In part for that reason, their return is likely, say royal and political observers.[24]

To clear up questions of the future and avoid turmoil in the following generation, Vajiralongkorn will be pressed to establish a ladder of seniority for succession covering his three wives and all their children, as King Vajiravudh did in the 1924 succession law.

If it happens that Sucharinee's sons are not rehabilitated back into the palace, the institution faces another type of challenge: the dominance of women in the newest generation of Chakris. Besides Princesses Bhajarakitiyabha and Siriwanwaree, the only others of Bhumibol's grandchildren who have been raised as innerpalace royals are the two daughters of Princess Chulabhorn, Siribha Chudhabhorn and Adithayadhorn Kittikhun. They have also taken part in royal duties and rituals, partly under Princess Sirindhorn's direction.

Possibly joining them will be the daughters of Ubolrat, Ploypailin, and Sirikitya. In 1999 Ubolrat broke with husband Peter Jensen and brought their three children back to Thailand, where they received Thai citizenship. The girls are treated as royals by the public, the government, and even the palace to an extent, despite being commoners and given more to the habits of American culture. On the day they received Thai citizenship, they handed out commencement certificates at an elementary school, just like their grandfather did at universities. (Ubolrat's autistic son Poomi, the only other male of his generation, died in the December 2004 tsunami.)

Whatever happens with their status and marriages, these young women represent a momentous change for the court and the monarchy. Rather than be at the back of the palace, they will be at the center of power, where Thai women have rarely stood. Yet none of this generation, male or female, has had the royal training and indoctrination that King Bhumibol and his children had. They have grown up in a modern, well-off urban culture of discos and shopping centers, MTV and Japanese fashions, tattoos and piercings, fast cars and global culture. None are deeply schooled in the dhammaraja tradition as Bhumibol was, and this cannot help but affect how the throne is handled.

Protecting royal prestige against an aggressive media, bolder academics, and a dismissive public will also pose a huge challenge to the post-Bhumibol court, especially given the prince's personal history. The growth of such uncontrollable global media as cable television and the Internet have already made it difficult to maintain the royal family's inviolateness.

The media's potential impact on the monarchy can be understood through the British example. In June 1977, the year of Queen Elizabeth's jubilee, the unknown punk music group the Sex Pistols rocketed to fame in England with its iconoclastic anthem: "God save the queen, her fascist regime, it made you a moron . . . There is no future in England's dreaming." "God Save the Queen" was immediately banned from airplay, but to no avail. It caught the mood of an entire generation of disaffected youth and became the top-selling record in the country. British society was never the same. The freer media coverage and criticism of the royal family that the Sex Pistols inspired peaked in Elizabeth's 1992 annus horribilis, when the royal family's deep personal conflicts and mismanagement of family and state assets became daily fodder for the tabloid newspapers and cable television. The monarchy could never again assume full protection from public scrutiny.

In Thailand, all that truly stands between royal virtue and London-tabloid-style media treatment is the lèse-majesté statute—and that showed signs of frailty in the more open atmosphere of the 1990s. One such sign emerged during the second trial of Sulak Sivaraks, a social activist who had previously been arrested in the early 1980s for lèse-majesté. (At that time, international criticism forced the palace to quietly intervene and have Sulak let off.) Just after the 1991 coup, strongman General Suchinda charged Sulak with lèse-majesté for attacking the junta, because, Suchinda maintained, the king himself had approved it. The absurdity was underlined by the fact that Sulak had called Suchinda guilty of the same charge for overthrowing a government installed by the king.

Surprisingly, after Suchinda was overthrown and granted amnesty by the king, Sulak's case did not disappear. The palace wanted him chastised again. As the case proceeded in 1993, Sulak recruited the country's feisty human rights lawyer Thongbai Thongbao, who, when jailed by Sarit Thanarat three decades before, declared notably that "they don't charge people with being communists anymore—they use the lèse majesté charge."[25] This time, local and international attention to the case was greater than in the 1980s, and Sulak was again let off, the palace apparently having decided to avoid a showdown.

A year later, the lèse-majesté statute came under fire in a separate and more problematic incident involving a foreigner and the foreign press. A week before Christmas in December 1994, a French businessman, Lech Kisielwicz, was flying first-class on a Thai Airways flight from Paris to Bangkok, where he planned to transfer to a flight to Tokyo. Also in first class was Princess Somsawali, along with some other prominent Thais. At one point she apparently complained about Kisielwicz, who, in response, swore back at the princess. When the plane landed in Bangkok, Thai police arrested Kisielwicz for lèse-majesté, even though the Thai constitution stipulated that only the king, queen, regent, and heir-apparent were protected as inviolate. It didn't take long for Thai Airways' management and the palace to understand that the case had the potential to cause great embarrassment for the country. But officials couldn't withdraw the charge because, for one, the Frenchman might sue, and second, other Thais might accuse them of not defending royal dignity—a lèse-majesté offense as well.

Thai Airways sought in vain to obtain a guilty plea from Kisielwicz, after which he would be set free, saving face for the airline. With its European headquarters in Paris, Thai Airways was worried about the fallout to its business and the potential for foreign attacks on the Thai monarchy after the French press caught on to the story. It took several weeks to work out a deal under the eyes of palace officials, during which the Thai media were prevented from reporting on the case. Finally, the Frenchman sent an apology to the king—duly reported by the Thai press—and pleaded guilty in court. Then, bizarrely, the judge threw out the charge for lack of evidence. Kisielwicz was free, but because he pleaded guilty, he couldn't sue Thai Airways. Because he was found innocent, no one could condemn the Thais for their old-fashioned law.

Nevertheless, the law still has some potency. In late 2001 the American-owned *Far Eastern Economic Review* referred briefly to the unseemly financial connections between the crown prince and Prime Minister Thaksin. The government and palace threatened to charge the magazine's reporters and editors with lèse-majesté, and only after several weeks of attacks did they let the case die down in a cloud of obfuscation. The palace and government could claim victory, as the magazine became significantly less aggressive in its reporting. But because Thailand has become a center for travel, diplomacy, and media in Southeast Asia, the incident is likely to be repeated, drawing uncomfortable attention to the monarchy.

The battle to oust Thaksin in 2005–6 reduced the lèse-majesté charge to absurdity, with he and his critics constantly leveling it at each other. Though clearly politically motivated, the charges could not easily be dismissed. They also hindered palace-linked efforts to apply the charge to serious direct criticisms.

Regardless of the changes that come to the throne, the revelations that emerge from the past, or the behavior of his children and grandchildren, King Bhumibol Adulyadej has sealed his own reputation, and it is unlikely to be undone. His prestige has survived unscathed, by the virtue of his sheer longevity and his personality— earnest, hardworking, gentle, with an impeccably simple lifestyle. Having portrayed himself as the Buddha-like King Mahajanaka, Bhumibol will very possibly become a cult figure of worship, like his grandfather King Chulalongkorn.

But with Bhumibol's eventual passing, the monarchy's desacralization will probably begin. His heirs are not conditioned to act as incipient Buddhas, nor do their personalities fit the mold. They must evolve and remake the throne themselves before they are forced to do so by the media and a generation of better-educated Thais—a generation that never experienced the Cold War that was so crucial to Bhumibol's restoration. This challenge is little different from what many Western monarchies faced during the 19th and 20th centuries: how to cede responsibility for the daily management of the state to politicians, bureaucrats, and businessmen not selected by the king. "Once . . . it had become accepted that the prime minister owed his or her position, not only to royal favor but also to parliamentary approval, the sovereign's role came inevitably to be limited," wrote Vernon Bogdanor.[26]

The Chakri throne does have the alternative of retreating into its implicit sacrality, omniscience, and infallibility, but this option mandates that it mostly disappear from public view, like the Japanese throne after World War II, and become wholly symbolic, abstract, and remote from modern life. It is a situation Bhumibol is aware of, telling visitors in 1992 that Emperor Akihito of Japan frets over being only a symbol confined to ceremonial duties, lacking a political role, even a consultative one.[27]

So far there is no sign that Bhumibol's heirs will share Akihito's fate. Instead, the throne is moving in the opposite direction, thanks to Thailand's all-important tourism industry, the country's largest source of foreign income. The Grand Palace in Bangkok has long been the capital's leading attraction, and the royal rituals are well advertised by the Tourism Authority of Thailand. In 1998–99 the royal family's palace homes in Hua Hin and Doi Tung were opened for tourist visits, and luxury hotels were added to Princess Mother Sangwal's estate in the north. The king's development project at Doi Angkhang was also turned into a tourist attraction with a resort hotel.

But to prevent its princes and princesses from being relegated as actors in an ongoing period costume drama, the monarchy has to better connect with contemporary Thai society, especially by asserting a role in the urban culture of the present and the future. The basis for this already exists, in the king's royal projects, the royal charity operations, and the Mahidol family's social works. Bhumibol's children have long been assigned modern missions to help people: Princess Sirindhorn has her foundations that aid the poor and underprivileged, and she now oversees the king's foundations; the prince has, in name, his chain of rural hospitals; and Princess Chulabhorn is the national patron of scientific research. The king's grandchildren, too, have been introduced to charity work. It must become central to their lives after they move into adulthood.

The palace's approach to social work requires an overhaul, however. The mystical ways in which the king and queen raise and distribute funds must be replaced with transparency and discipline to avoid troubling questions. The charities have to become more open and cautious of their image, and not contradict positive social trends. In the 1990s, for instance, Chulabhorn's institute accepted money from the tobacco industry to perform research that was at odds with the government's campaign to discourage smoking.[28] An only slightly more aggressive media will begin raising such issues.

More broadly, the social efforts of the royal family and the charities themselves need to stop competing with the government and other charity and social operations, including public and private NGOs. This antagonism undermines the throne's unifying role. Instead, the royal family must become a partner with these organizations, not claiming to be the sole source of compassion within the country but simply an exemplary one that can make things happen. The late Princess Diana set the standard by lending her presence to the work of other prominent organizations on very current issues like AIDS and land mines.

This acknowledgment should also extend to the throne's award of royal honors and medals. During the entire Ninth Reign, the palace has refused to recognize prominent contributors to Thailand's development and unity who do not also contribute to royal power. The great men of Thai history are all kings and princes, and the great men of modern Thailand all dedicated royalists. Excluded from this list are non-royalists like Pridi Bhanomyong, the late world-renowned monk Buddhadasa, and many widely respected social workers outside the royal umbrella who have been implicitly regarded as rivals.

This stance is unnecessary and counterproductive. The monarchy can and must broaden its support base by recognizing achievement and honesty rather than simple loyalty, or risk being left behind by modern culture. The British throne grants knighthoods to artists, musicians, and social workers, among others, people without any traditional connection to Buckingham Palace who nonetheless help shape and define modern Britain in positive ways. In turn, the monarchy appears modern and virtuous, able to recognize selflessness and goodness outside its own elite circles. Expanding its recognition of achieving Thais would enable the modern Chakri throne to maintain its reputation for generosity and wisdom in a way that the secular government cannot. The throne can remain a moral leader.

Some of this change is already happening, and some will be forced on the next generation in the court. Ultimately, members of the royal family will have to make use of one of the monarchy's greatest unspoken prerogatives: the alchemic ability and right to remake itself before others do it. That is the key to its survival.

Notes ॐ

Introduction

1. E. Bruce Reynolds, *Thailand and Japan's Southern Advance, 1940–1945* (New York: St. Martin's, 1994), 25.
2. The deep involvement in the narcotics trade of Generals Phao Sriyanond and Sarit Thanarat, both palace allies during the 1940s and 1950s, is detailed in Alfred McCoy, *The Politics of Heroin in Southeast Asia* (Singapore: Harper and Row, 1972), 135–45. Respectively chief of police and army chief, both also controlled key commercial and industrial businesses during the 1950s.
3. Bhumibol's taut face does not give up smiles easily, or frowns for that matter. But the existence of only a few official photographs of him grinning, amid thousands released, suggests deliberateness on the part of the palace. In contrast are the many official photographs of his family with beaming smiles. According to members of the Thai media, this is the result of long-standing palace image-management efforts.

1 A Dhammaraja from America

Epigraph: *The Chakri Dynasty and Thai Politics, 1782–1982: The Monarchy Through Two Centuries of Change and Challenge* (Bangkok: privately circulated paper, 1983, the author understood to be M.R. Sukhumbhand Paripatra, Chulalongkorn University), 69.

1. Much of the Mahidol family history in this section relies on the accounts in Galyani Vadhana, *Chao Nai Lek Lek Yuvakastriya* (Chiangmai: Suriwongs Book Center, 1996), and Galyani Vadhana, *Mae Lao Hai Fang* (Chiangmai: Suriwongs Book Center, 1995).
2. Francis Bowes Sayre, *Glad Adventure* (New York: Macmillan, 1957), 99.

3. John Girling, *Thailand: Society and Politics* (Ithaca: Cornell University Press, 1981), 22.

4. David K. Wyatt, *Thailand: A Short History* (New Haven: Yale University Press, 1982), 54. Some scholars argue that the Ramkhamhaeng inscription is a 19th-century counterfeit, created to legitimize Chakri royal power by its alleged ancient roots. See James F. Chamberlain, ed., *The Ramkhamhaeng Controversy: Selected Papers* (Bangkok: The Siam Society, 1991). Yet without any conclusive evidence one way or the other, the inscription still carries much weight in modern Thai self-identity and in the modern throne's self-justification.

5. Prince Dhani Nivas, one of the architects of the Ninth Reign revival, called the Thai absolute throne "no less of a democracy than some of the modern democracies of the world, with the exception that it frankly called itself an absolute monarchy." *Journal of the Siam Society* 48 (1960): 118.

6. Frank E. Reynolds and Mani B. Reynolds, *Three Worlds According to King Ruang* (Berkeley: University of California Press, 1982), 146–47.

7. Christine Gray, *Thailand: The Soteriological State in the 1970s* (Ph.D. dissertation: University of Chicago, 1986), 162.

8. David K. Wyatt, *The Politics of Reform in Thailand* (New Haven: Yale University Press, 1969), 7–8.

2 From Pure Blood to Dynastic Failure

1. National Identity Board, *Thailand into the '80s* (Bangkok: Office of the Prime Minister, 1979), 21.

2. National Identity Board, *Thailand in the '90s* (Bangkok: Office of the Prime Minister, 1995), 53.

3. B. J. Terwiel, *A History of Modern Thailand, 1767–1942* (St. Lucia: University of Queensland Press, 1983), 121.

4. Gray, *The Soteriological State*, 223.

5. See, for instance, Chula Chakrabongs, *Lords of Life* (London: Alvin Redman, 1960), 145–47.

6. Gray, *The Soteriological State*, 267.

7. This has become part of palace mythology. However, the dating of Mongkut's birth is disputed by some, by both day and year.

8. Pasuk Phongpaichit and Chris Baker, *Thailand: Economy and Politics* (Kuala Lumpur: Oxford, 1995), 217.

9. Chula Chakrabongs, *Lords of Life*, 262.

10. Gray, *The Soteriological State*, 289.

11. Thak Chaloemtiarana, "The Evolution of the Monarchy and Government: Institutional Conflicts and Change," *Asia Bulletin* Supplement 2, 1976, 43.

12. Chula Chakrabongs, *Lords of Life*, 268.

13. Wyatt, *A Short History*, 225.

14. On the other hand, he didn't end the palace's elaborate royal funerals and cremations, all heavily colored by Hindu cosmology. They grew grander in the 1920s as a large number of celestial-ranked royals died.

15. Benjamin Batson, *The End of Absolute Monarchy in Siam* (Singapore: Oxford University Press, 1984), 26.

16. Ibid., 65.

17. Prajadhipok was referring to the recent royal assertion that the king is "elected by the people" when a succession council votes on the successor.

18. As published in Batson, *The End*, 284–97.

19. Chula Chakrabongs, *Lords of Life*, 307.

20. Batson, *The End*, 205.

21. Lae Dilokvidhyarat, *Transformation and Persistence of Kinship in Thailand* (M.A. thesis: Institute of Social Studies, The Hague, 1982), 122.

3 1932: Revolution and Exile

1. As translated in Pasuk Phongpaichit and Chris Baker, eds., *Pridi by Pridi* (Bangkok: Silkworm, 2000), 70–72.

2. Translations from Sombat Chantornvong, "To Address the Dust of the Dust Under the Soles of the Royal Feet: A Reflection on the Political Dimension of Thai Court Language," *Asian Review* 6 (1992): 146.

3. Much of this section draws on Vernon Bogdanor, *The Monarchy and the Constitution* (Oxford: Clarendon, 1995).

4. Bogdanor, *The Monarchy*, 302.

5. Walter Bagehot, *The English Constitution* (1867; reprint, Glasgow: Fontana/Collins, 1963), 111.

6. The memoir of Queen Rambhai in Thak Chaloemtiarana, ed., *Thai Politics, 1932–1957* (Bangkok: Social Science Association of Thailand, 1978), 25.

7. Scott Barmé, *Luang Wichit Wathakan and the Creation of a Thai Identity* (Singapore: Institute of Southeast Asian Studies, 1993), 72.

8. Thak, ed., *Thai Politics*, 96.

9. Appeasing the throne, the drafters included in the constitution that in 20 years, the king would be able to choose half the members of the assembly.

10. Thak, ed., *Thai Politics*, 11–13; Thawatt Mokarapong, *History of the Thai Revolution* (Bangkok: Thawatt Mokarapong, 1972), 110.

11. Barmé, *Luang Wichit*, 73.

12. Thak, ed., *Thai Politics*, 193.

13. Thawatt, *History*, 188.

14. Some historians argue that proroguing the assembly was Manopakorn's decision in concert with dissenters in the People's Party, and was opposed by Prajadhipok. But proroguing was a specific prerogative of the king, and he readily signed off on it, indicating no opposition. See Judith Stowe, *Siam Becomes Thailand* (Honolulu: University of Hawaii Press, 1991).

15. Barmé, *Luang Wichit*, 82.

16. *New York Times*, January 22, 1935. The *Times* reported that the king's property yielded an income in excess of 500,000 pounds sterling annually.

17. This section relies largely on the family accounts in Galyani, *Chao Nai*, and Galyani, *Mae*.

18. See Pridi's comments in Pasuk and Baker, eds., *Pridi*, 212–14.

19. To match Prajadhipok's abdication, Ananda's accession was backdated to February 3, 1935.

20. These and other letters referred to are reproduced in Galyani, *Chao Nai.*

21. Galyani, *Chao Nai,* 242.

22. See for instance *New York Times,* March 4, 1935.

23. In mid-1934, a battle erupted in the assembly over who would control the building of 122 new temples. See Gray, *The Soteriological State,* 357.

24. Some of the alleged attempts on Phibun's life in the 1930s were likely at least exaggerated, if not conjured up completely, by Phibun himself. Moreover, it is probable that not all were royalist plots. Phibun had rivals in the military and the People's Party, in particular Col. Song Suradej.

25. Stowe, *Siam Becomes Thailand,* 106.

26. Charivat Santaputra, *Thai Foreign Policy, 1931–1946* (Bangkok: Thammasat University, 1985), 170–71.

27. How advanced the plot was, how broad its support, and whether it was specifically monarchist or generally anti-Phibun in nature are all disputed points. Rangsit's involvement remains unclear, and Stowe argues that Song Suradej's rivalry with Phibun was the main motive for the plot. Song went into exile following the roundup. Prince Subhasvasti, brother-in-law and close aide of King Prajadhipok, also suspected of involvement in the plot, argued later that Rangsit was innocent while even Pridi had secretly endorsed a move against Phibun. See Subhasvasti Wongsanit Svastivat, *Noeng Sotwarot Subhasvasti* (Bangkok: Family of M.C. Subhasvasti Wongsanit Svastivat, 1999).

28. Sombat, "To Address," 154.

29. Ibid.

30. This explanation of Phibun's grand plan was used to undermine him, and there may have been some truth to it. But others understood Phibun to be hedging his bets by turning Petchabun into a strategic redoubt in preparation for Thailand's officially joining the allied war against the Japanese. The move would also allow the government to avoid the expected Allied bombing of Bangkok. See, for instance, Subhasvasti, *Noeng Sotwarot Subhasvasti,* 107; and Reynolds, *Thailand,* 169–71.

4 Restoration to Regicide

1. Information on the family's life in Lausanne in this section draws heavily from Galyani, *Chao Nai,* and Galyani, *Mae.*

2. Barbara Crossette, "King Bhumibol's Reign," *New York Times Sunday Magazine,* May 21, 1989.

3. *Journal of the Siam Society* 36, no. 2 (1947): 91–106.

4. Galyani, *Mae,* 432.

5. Alexander Macdonald, *Bangkok Editor* (New York: Macmillan, 1949), 52.

6. *Bangkok Post,* January 25, 1949.

7. *Bangkok Post,* May 2, 1950.

8. Subhasvasti, *Noeng Sotwarot Subhasvasti,* 48.

9. Ibid., 69.

10. Sulak Sivaraksa, *Powers That Be: Pridi Bhanomyong Through the Rise and Fall of Thai Democracy* (Bangkok: Runkaew, 1999), 18–19.

11. Created by Rama VI, Siam Commercial Bank was the palace's bank. When Phibun took power in the 1930s, King Prajadhipok's men were forced out of the bank and Sixth Reign

courtier Ram Raghob was installed to run it. (Ram was son-in-law of Phraya Yommaraj, who the People's Party installed on the Ananda regent council in 1935.) Just after Prince Rangsit and the other royals were released from prison in 1944, Ram left Siam Commercial to join Chaleo in launching Bangkok Bank. Siam Commercial Bank was returned to royal hands, its assets and customer base apparently severely depleted. Several other Pridi and Free Thai associates joined Bangkok Bank as well—Luang Banakorn Kovit (Pao Chakkaphak), Sawat Sotthitada, Chittasen Bancha, Fuen Suphansam, and Sino-Thai businessman Chin Sophonpanich. Following Pridi's exile and Chaleo's arrest, the bank faltered. Switching his allegiance to a new backer, police chief Phao Sriyanond, Chin took control and, over time, turned it into Southeast Asia's largest bank.

12. Subhasvasti, *Noeng Sotwarot Subhasvasti*, 497, 501.
13. Elliot Kulick and Dick Wilson, *Thailand's Turn* (London: Macmillan, 1992), xviii.
14. William Stevenson, *The Revolutionary King* (London: Constable, 1999). The way the book was shunned by the palace after publication suggested that, among many other things, the king himself rejected this theory.
15. Macdonald, *Bangkok Editor*, 50.
16. See "A Memorandum on a Certain Aspect of Siamese Politics," letter to King Bhumibol of June 20, 1947, in Subhasvasti, *Noeng Sotwarot Subhasvasti*.
17. Biographer Stevenson says Bhumibol had intended to annul the death sentences, but police chief Phao Sriyanond carried them out secretly and hurriedly after the conviction. Yet four months had elapsed between final conviction and the executions, and more than seven years since the three were first charged.
18. Bhumibol was quoted in *Life* magazine just after Ananda's death as being certain his brother was assassinated, saying, "I will destroy the murderer." *Life*, July 15, 1946. But if he said that—nowhere else is it recorded, and the magazine's source for the quote isn't revealed—he never later repeated the sentiment.

5 Revenge of the Monarchists, 1946–49

1. Subhasvasti, *Noeng Sotwarot Subhasvasti*, 82.
2. Sulak, *Powers That Be*, 18–19.
3. Rayne Kruger, *The Devil's Discus* (London: Cassell, 1964), 103.
4. Ibid., 98.
5. Dhani Nivas, "The Old Siamese Conception of the Monarchy," in *Chum Num Phra Nipond* (funeral volume of Dhani Nivas, Bangkok, 1974).
6. Ibid.
7. Dhani Nivas, "Monarchical Protection of the Buddhist Church in Siam," in ibid.
8. Pasuk and Baker, *Thailand*, 267.
9. *Bangkok Post*, April 5, 1948.
10. Kobkua Suwannathat-Pian, *Thailand's Durable Premier* (Kuala Lumpur: Oxford University Press, 1995), 39.
11. Translation from Thak, *Thai Politics*, 524.
12. Kobkua, *Thailand's Durable Premier*, 39.
13. Frank C. Darling, "American Influence on the Evolution of Constitutional Government in Thailand" (Unpublished thesis, Washington: American University, 1960), 185.
14. *Bangkok Post*, January 18, 1949.

15. Thak, *Thai Politics*, 592.

16. *New York Times*, April 12, 1948.

17. Kobkua, *Thailand's Durable Premier*, 24.

18. *Bangkok Post*, February 5, 1949.

19. *Bangkok Post*, September 25, 1948.

20. Born M.R. Chuen Noppawongse, and later elevated to the prince rank of krom luang.

21. Peter A. Jackson, *Buddhism, Legitimation, and Conflict* (Singapore: Institute of Southeast Asian Studies, 1989), 75.

22. Juan had effectively been sanghanayok for three years, however, since Phuttakosajan's stroke in 1948.

23. *Bangkok Post*, June 22, 1949.

24. This is more significant when considered against the widespread belief that the rite was only revived by Bhumibol at the end of the 1950s, encouraged by Field Marshal Sarit Thanarat.

25. Pasuk and Baker, *Thailand*, 282.

26. *Bangkok Post*, June 8, 1948.

6 Romance in Lausanne: Bhumibol Prepares to Reign

1. *Nation*, April 28, 2000.

2. Subhasvasti, *Noeng Sotwarot Subhasvasti*, 554–56.

3. Vichitvong Na Pombhejara, *Pridi Bhanomyong and the Making of Thailand's Modern History* (Bangkok: Siriyod, 1980), 270.

4. *Life*, February 20, 1950.

5. *Bangkok Post*, September 14, 1948.

6. *Time*, April 3, 1950.

7. *Soul of a Nation: The Royal Family of Thailand*, television documentary by the British Broadcasting Corporation, 1980.

8. Joseph Wright, *The Balancing Act* (Oakland: Pacific Rim, 1991), 192.

9. *New York Times*, March 14, 1950.

10. *New York Times*, May 1, 1950; *New Yorker*, May 27, 1950.

11. See *Bangkok Post*, May 5, 1950, June 7, 1950, and July 14, 1950.

12. *Bangkok Post*, April 7, 1950.

13. Despite the presence of communist-inspired insurgencies in neighboring states, in Thailand there was minimal evidence of a domestic communist threat at this time. The left-leaning American magazine *The Nation*, December 25, 1948, reported that Phibun was claiming a communist threat simply to strengthen his own position. Pressed by *The Nation*'s reporter, Phibun reportedly conceded that, in fact, there were no communists in Thailand. The *New Republic*, October 31, 1949, wrote on the exaggerated threat that in Bangkok, "Red flags abound, to be sure, but they indicate government liquor stores." The magazine said the main political problem in Thailand was Bhumibol's reticence to return. At the same time, on the other hand, the Thais were accused by the French of supporting Ho Chi Minh's Viet Minh anticolonial insurgency, which the Thai government called a struggle for independence. See *New York Times*, April 8, 1950.

7 The Cold War, 1952–57

1. Kobkua, *Thailand's Durable Premier*, 98n.95.
2. *New York Times*, December 4, 1951.
3. *New York Times*, December 8, 1951.
4. Kobkua, *Thailand's Durable Premier*, 76, 98n.96.
5. *Bangkok Post*, January 17, 1952.
6. *Bangkok Post*, January 26, 1952.
7. U. Alexis Johnson, *The Right Hand of Power* (New Jersey: Prentice-Hall, 1984), 280.
8. The first issue of June 17, 1954, featured the king on the front and three pages of photographs of the royal family.
9. Thomas Lobe and David Morell, "Thailand's Border Patrol Police: Paramilitary Political Power," in *Supplementary Military Forces: Reserves, Militias, Auxiliaries,* ed. Louis Surcher and Gwyn Harries-Jenkins (Beverly Hills: Sage, 1978), 157.
10. Kobkua, *Thailand's Durable Premier*, 77, 98n.101.
11. Stevenson, *The Revolutionary King*, 111–18.
12. See Kobkua, *Thailand's Durable Premier*, 79; *Bangkok Post*, November 30, 1954; Thailand Development Research Institute, *Policy on Agricultural Land Reform in Thailand* (Bangkok: Thailand Development Research Institute Foundation, 1990).
13. Kobkua, *Thailand's Durable Premier*, 99n.108.
14. *Bangkok Post*, January 16, 1956.
15. Thak, *Thai Politics*, 716.
16. Gray, *The Soteriological State*, 394.
17. Ibid., 399.
18. That Ananda had never ordained before he died was seen as a blemish on his kingship and was said to have dismayed his mother.
19. The principal source for details on Bhumibol's ordination is the official publication *Phrarachapiti Lae Phrarachakij Nai Kaan Song Phonwej* (Royal Ceremonies and Activities for the Royal Ordination, Bangkok, 1957).
20. According to Prince Dhani, the king should have been ordained together with only Thammayut novices, but Bhumibol requested that Mahanikay monks be included. So a special "sort of confirmation ceremony" was added for only the Thammayut group. *Journal of the Siam Society* 59, no. 1 (1971): 279.
21. A later name. At the time he was called by his ecclesiastical title Sophonkhanaporn, and his monkhood name Charoen Suwattano.
22. *New York Times*, August 24, 1989.
23. *Sayam Nikorn*, February 11, 1956.
24. *Siam Rath*, February 12, 1956.
25. Phraya Srivisarn Vacha, "Kingship in Siam," *Journal of the Siam Society* 42, no. 1 (1954): 1–10.
26. Kobkua, *Thailand's Durable Premier*, 30.
27. *Bangkok Post*, January 2, 1957.
28. Thak Chaloemtiarana, *Thailand: The Politics of Despotic Paternalism* (Bangkok: Social Science Association of Thailand, 1979), 98.
29. Thak, *Thailand*, 99.
30. Kobkua, *Thailand's Durable Premier*, 100n.114.

31. Ibid., 99n.113.

32. *Bangkok Post,* June 20, 1957. The palace recognized that Phibun's move copied the method by which British kings had protected themselves before the 20th century, increasing the membership of the House of Lords to surmount challenges from the elected lower body.

33. Gray, *The Soteriological State,* 414. The term *chao,* or lord, was used to denote "royalty."

34. The accusation went unproven, but it carried plausibility because of Seni and Kukrit Pramoj's closeness to the palace.

35. Kobkua, *Thailand's Durable Premier,* 30.

36. Chula Chakrabongs, *Lords of Life,* 337.

37. Kobkua, *Thailand's Durable Premier,* 30. In attacking Phao, Sarit had criticized his closeness to the United States, and Kukrit and Seni had likewise attacked the U.S. for supporting the generals. With Washington concerned that Sarit might be anti-American, immediately after the coup the U.S. ambassador sought meetings with the king and Sarit. Both confirmed their pro-U.S., anti-communist stance.

8 Field Marshal Sarit: The Palace Finds Its Strongman

1. *Pho-khun,* in Thai: see Thak, *The Politics,* xii–xiv.

2. Surachart Bamrungsuk, *United States Foreign Policy and Thai Military Rule, 1947–1977* (Bangkok: Duangkamol, 1988), 80.

3. Thak, *The Politics,* 150n.65: "It is likely that the king was informed of Sarit's coup and gave his approval, for very soon a law giving amnesty to those engaged in the October 20, 1958, affair was signed by the king."

4. Ibid., 150.

5. Wyatt, *A Short History,* 280.

6. Thak, *The Politics,* 317.

7. *Journal of the Siam Society* 61, no. 1 (1973): 251–52.

8. Thak, *The Politics,* 320–21.

9. *Bangkok Post,* April 29, 1958.

10. Thak, *The Politics,* 331.

11. Johnson, *The Right Hand,* 279–81.

12. The trips were not all perfectly smooth. In Australia several small protests greeted the royal couple, as did uncomplimentary media coverage of Sirikit's ostentatious jewelry and clothing collection. There was also turmoil surrounding Canberra's plan to have Australia National University award Bhumibol an honorary doctorate. The university refused because Bhumibol had never earned an undergraduate degree from a college or university. Finally the government persuaded a lesser institution, the University of Melbourne, to give the king an honorary doctorate of laws. See *Nation* (Australia), August 11, 1962; *Sydney Morning Herald,* August 14, August 15, 1962.

13. Eric Wakin, *Anthropology Goes to War* (Madison: University of Wisconsin, 1992), 124.

14. Thak, *The Politics,* 325.

15. *Nation,* November 11, 1995.

16. Much is owed in this discussion of rajasap to Sombat, "To Address," and Gray, *The Soteriological State.* The translations are mostly Sombat's.

17. Sombat, "To Address," 149.

18. Jackson, *Buddhism,* 96.

19. For a review of lèse-majesté in Thailand, see David Streckfuss, "Kings in the Age of Nations: The Paradox of Lèse-Majesté as Political Crime in Thailand," *Comparative Studies in Society and History* 37, no. 3 (July 1995), and David Streckfuss, *The Poetics of Subversion: Civil Liberty and Lèse Majesté in the Modern Thai State* (Ph.D. thesis, University of Wisconsin, Madison, 1998).

20. Thongthong Chandrangsu, *A Constitutional Legal Aspect of the King's Prerogatives* (M.A. thesis, Chulalongkorn University, 1986), 160.

9 *Bhumibol in the 1960s: A Dhammaraja's Brilliance Unfolds*

1. *Nation,* August 14, 1994.

2. John Hoskin, "The King as Artist," in *Sawasdee,* republished in *The King of Thailand in World Focus* (Bangkok: Foreign Correspondents Club of Thailand, 1988), 141–42.

3. Confidential interview with an American academic, 1994.

4. Confidential interview with a Thai political figure, 1995.

5. From various confidential interviews. See also the description of a 1965 concert at Thammasat University in William L. Bradley, "The Evolution of Education and Society," *Asia,* Supplement No. 2, Spring 1976.

6. *Saturday Review,* January 1, 1957.

7. *Jack Teagarden at the Roundtable,* recorded July 1, 1959 (Roulette, 1959).

8. *Look,* June 27, 1967.

9. From confidential interviews with musicians in Bangkok.

10. Clips from the film are often seen in documentaries on the king, but never in full and never with the original music; the music is always overlaid with professional recordings by other musicians. I was able to see and hear the original from a collection in the National Library.

11. Col. C. C. Jacobs, quoted in *Nation,* commemorative supplement, n.d.

12. Palace and palace-endorsed literature frequently recounts that Bhumibol and Ananda uniquely liked to play at building dikes and dams and canals for water at the beach and after rainstorms.

13. *Bangkok Post,* May 7, 1953.

14. *Bangkok Post,* April 10, 1953.

15. From confidential interviews, 1994.

16. Other large dams are named after the queen, princess mother, crown prince, and the royal daughters.

17. This was seen by some as a political move. The controversial Mahanikay leader Phra Phimontham, after study with Burmese monks (in the tradition of King Mongkut) had in the 1950s become a leading promoter of vipassana and was seen as the conveyor of the tradition from renowned meditation masters. The royal Thammayut school had no such reputation in the capital. To compete with this, vipassana practitioner Yanasangworn organized in Wat Bovornives a meditation teaching center, and established associations with respected meditation masters in forest temples deep in the countryside. This would secure the sangha royalists leadership of an ostensibly more pure and so superior religious movement. See Stanley J. Tambiah, *The Buddhist Saints of the Forest and the Cult of Amulets* (Cambridge: Cambridge University Press, 1984), 155.

18. Ibid.
19. See Gray, *The Soteriological State*, 314–17.
20. *Supreme Artist* (Bangkok: Ministry of Education, 1987), 90–97.
21. "Khwam ben Thai" here has the literal meaning "[what it is] to be Thai." It can also be translated as "to be free," the word "Thai" meaning both a member of the Thai nation and free. For foreign consumption, official publications usually use the latter translation. But for most Thais, the former concept is transmitted.
22. *Supreme Artist*, 97.
23. This discussion of the royal kathin and Bangkok Bank's involvement owes much to Gray, *The Soteriological State*.
24. Ibid., 611.
25. David K. Wyatt, "The Student Prince Who Saved a Monarchy," *The Asia-Pacific Magazine*, June 1996.
26. Gray, *The Soteriological State*, 510.
27. *Look*, June 27, 1967.

10 Going to War

1. Louis Kraar, E. Hughes, and James Linen, "A Monarchy Fights for Freedom," *Time*, May 27, 1966.
2. See Craig J. Reynolds, *Thai Radical Discourse: The Real Face of Thai Feudalism Today* (Ithaca: Cornell University, 1987), and Pasuk and Baker, *Thailand*, 305–6.
3. See, for instance, *Foreign Relations of the United States, 1964–1968*, vol. 27, *Mainland Southeast Asia* (Washington, D.C.: U.S. Department of State), Documents 303–14, in which various figures spoke of the communist ability to take power through elections, and of the conduct of a reign of terror by communist infiltrators. In contrast, Document 316, the National Intelligence Estimate of June 1, 1966, strongly downplayed the insurgent threat, branding it merely an "expensive nuisance."
4. E. Thadeus Flood, *The United States and the Military Coup in Thailand* (Washington, D.C.: Indochina Resource Center, 1976), 2.
5. David Morell and Chai-anan Samudavanija, *Political Conflict in Thailand* (Cambridge, Mass.: Oelgeschlager, Gunn & Hain, 1981), 82.
6. Louis Lomax, *Thailand: The War That Is. The War That Will Be* (New York: Vintage, 1967), 138–40.
7. *Look*, June 27, 1967.
8. Thak, *The Politics*, 331.
9. In Bardwell Smith, ed., *Religion and Legitimization of Power* (Chambersburg, Pa.: Anima, 1978), 105.
10. Charles Keyes, *Thailand: Buddhist Kingdom as Modern Nation State* (Bangkok: Duang Kamol, 1989), 1–5.
11. Humphrey's report to President Johnson, *Foreign Relations of the United States*, Doc. 309.
12. His visits to aircraft producers, especially Britain's Beagle Aircraft Works, were also in search of planes for the cloud-seeding program and for the official royal transport.
13. *Far Eastern Economic Review*, October 13, 1966.

14. *Foreign Relations of the United States, 1964–1968,* Doc. 314.

15. *New York Times,* June 14, 1967.

16. *The Pentagon Papers: The Defense Department History of United States Decisionmaking on Vietnam* (Boston: Beacon, 1971–72), 4:523–24.

17. *Foreign Relations of the United States, 1964–1968,* Doc. 362, Doc. 372.

18. Thomas Lobe, *United States Security Policy and Aid to the Thailand National Police* (University of Denver, Colorado, 1977), 93–95.

11 Reborn Democrat?

1. Abroad, there were still questions about Bhumibol's and Thailand's commitment to fighting communism. In a November 1967 article, *Newsweek* went so far as to paint the monarch as gutless. While describing a grim picture of the insurgency's progress, the magazine noted that on an October visit to army bases southwest of Bangkok, Bhumibol had been afraid to descend from his helicopter to meet the troops. "The king's appearances may not have done much good," *Newsweek* added parenthetically, for "at each stop he cautiously elected to remain inside his helicopter while aides handed out mementos attesting to his visit." The government took extreme offense, issuing categorical denials as Prime Minister Thanom lodged accusations of lèse-majesté. *Newsweek* apologized, probably under U.S. State Department pressure, but didn't back off its claim. The incident remained problematic. Thanom insisted the king had come out of his aircraft, but the Thai ambassador to Washington wrote to *Newsweek* that the king had remained inside to prevent the necessity of pulling soldiers back from the front to protect him. *Newsweek,* November 6, 1967, and December 4, 1967.

2. A much later account of the U.S. meetings is found in Stevenson's hagiographical *The Revolutionary King,* 165. Citing the king, Stevenson describes the main topic of the meetings as Bhumibol's request for several aircraft for use in his rural support programs. This, the king allegedly said, was all that was needed to defeat the communists. The request was granted by Johnson, this version went, but McNamara never followed through.

3. *Far Eastern Economic Review,* December 28, 1967.

4. See *Foreign Relations of the United States, 1964–1968,* Doc. 381, for a discussion between U.S. officials and unnamed senior Thais on how the United States might deploy funds to influence the elections; and Doc. 304, dating from 1965, which further indicates American readiness to provide money to favored politicians and parties.

5. Saiyudh Kerdphol, *The Struggle for Thailand* (Bangkok: S. Research Center, 1986), 86.

6. *Far Eastern Economic Review,* April 25, 1968.

7. Jeffrey Race, "The War in Northern Thailand," *Modern Asian Studies* 8, no. 1 (1974): 85–112.

8. *Far Eastern Economic Review,* May 13, 1972.

9. Despite claims that the king originated this effort, it was launched in the wake of much larger operations by U.S. government agencies and the UN Development Program doing the same thing. Because of the persuasiveness of his image, the king was made the nominal head of all such efforts.

10. This effort amounted to granting hill tribes medallions with a portrait of the king and a serial number inscribed on the back. Because this brought few real privileges, to many

hill tribes these were shamanist tokens. The movements of the "new citizens" remained restricted, and their newborn weren't recognized as Thai.

11. See, for instance, Race, "The War in Northern Thailand," 105.

12. Speech at Chulalongkorn University, March 13, 1969, cited in Gray, *The Soteriological State*, 686–88.

13. June 1969 speech in Chonburi, cited in ibid., 692.

14. Speech of March 15, 1969, cited in Morell and Chai-anan, *Political Conflict*, 69.

15. Gray, *The Soteriological State*, 688.

16. Cited in Kevin Hewison, ed., *Political Change in Thailand* (London: Routledge, 1997), 66.

17. Bhumibol Adulyadej, *Royal Addresses and Speeches* (Bangkok: Office of the Prime Minister, 1976), 26.

18. Gray, *The Soteriological State*, 694.

19. Cited in ibid., 696.

20. Ibid., 697.

21. Ibid., 690.

22. Ibid., 685–88.

23. Ibid.

24. Ibid., 695.

25. Bhumibol Adulyadej, speech to Bangkok Rotary, February 27, 1969, *Ruam Phrarachadamras Khong Phrabat Somdej Phrachao Yu Hua* (Bangkok: Boriphat Bophit, 1970).

26. See Gray, *The Soteriological State*, 694–96.

27. Ibid., 695–96.

28. Ibid., 697.

29. Cited in *Far Eastern Economic Review*, January 2, 1971.

30. *Bangkok World*, March 8, 1970.

31. *Bangkok Post*, September 21, 1971.

32. Benedict Anderson, "Withdrawal Symptoms: Social and Cultural Aspects of the October 6 Coup," *Bulletin of Concerned Asian Scholars*, July–September 1990, 30.

33. Morell and Chai-anan, *Political Conflict*, 144–45.

34. Gray, *The Soteriological State*, 708.

35. Bhumibol, *Royal Addresses*, 72–74.

36. *Bangkok Post*, October 9, 1973.

37. Vasit Dejkunchorn, a personal aide to the king involved in the talks, later recalled it as much longer, 18 months. *Nation*, April 28, 1982.

38. Ibid. In a lecture about the king, Vasit recalled that the violence occurred because the students refused the king's recommendation to accept the government's offer to amend the constitution over the next year. "The king patiently pointed out to the student leaders that the government had already agreed to give more than it was asked. . . . Realizing that the situation was practically a polarization between the government consisting mostly of old people, and the students who were young, the king suggested that the students should try to benefit from the experience of the older. . . . Obviously, the mobs were out to create chaos as a retaliation. And they were successful."

39. *Far Eastern Economic Review*, October 18, 1974.

40. Wright, *Balancing Act*, 211.

41. William Bradley, David Morell, David Szanton, Stephen Young, *Thailand, Domino By Default?* (Athens, Ohio: Ohio University, 1978), 21.

42. Gray, *The Soteriological State*, 717.

12 Royal Vigilantism and Massacre, 1974–76

1. Morell and Chai-anan, *Political Conflict*, 68.

2. *Far Eastern Economic Review*, December 17, 1973.

3. Quoted in ibid.

4. Morell and Chai-anan, *Political Conflict*, 99.

5. Jackson, *Buddhism*, 104. Jackson translates *duang chataa* as fate, not stars. But the idea embraces not simply fate but a horoscopic destiny, involving harmonization of the stars. Phimontham's horoscope, as well as his politics, dangerously conflicted with the king's.

6. *Far Eastern Economic Review*, December 6, 1974.

7. Pasuk and Baker, *Thailand*, 294.

8. *Far Eastern Economic Review*, August 23, 1974.

9. *Nation*, May 14, 1974.

10. Thomas Marks, *Making Revolution* (Bangkok: White Lotus, 1994), 83.

11. This and later discussions of the Village Scouts owe much to Katherine Bowie, *Rituals of National Loyalty* (New York: Columbia University Press, 1997).

12. Ibid., 287, quoting Village Scout publications, slightly modified by the author.

13. Ibid., 199.

14. Ibid., 82.

15. Gray, *The Soteriological State*, 711.

16. Bowie, *Rituals*, 109.

17. *Far Eastern Economic Review*, July 18, 1975.

18. *Far Eastern Economic Review*, July 25, 1975.

19. See, for instance, *Far Eastern Economic Review*, January 17, 1975.

20. Morell and Chai-anan, *Political Conflict*, 130.

21. Significantly, Pramarn was brother-in-law of Phao Sriyanond, the corrupt and brutal police chief of the 1950s.

22. See comments by former ISOC intelligence chief General Pinyo Vacharadej and Thanom Kittikachorn in Samran Bhaetyakul, *Life and Accomplishments* (Funeral volume, 1986), 295, 314. Also, E. Thadeus Flood, "The Vietnamese Refugees in Thailand," *Bulletin of Concerned Asian Scholars* 9, no. 3 (1977): 46n.78.

23. Confidential interview, 1995.

24. See Thongchai Winichakul, "Thai Democracy in Public Memory: Monuments and Their Narratives," Seventh International Conference on Thai Studies, Amsterdam, July 1999.

25. *Bangkok Post*, February 4, 1976.

26. Surachart, *United States Foreign Policy*, 185, quoting the 1983 memoirs of Bunchana Attakor.

27. Tanin Kraivixien, *The Thai Monarchy Under the Democratic System* [Phramahakasatriya Thai Nai Rabob Phrachathipathai] (Bangkok: Ministry of Education, 1977).

28. *Far Eastern Economic Review*, February 27, 1976.

29. See Bhumibol, *Royal Addresses and Speeches* (1976).

30. Speech to Village Scouts in Khon Kaen, February 19, 1976, in ibid.

31. Speech to Village Scouts at Chittipawan College in Chonburi, May 23, 1976, in ibid.

32. Speech to Village Scouts in Singburi, July 29, 1976, in ibid.

33. Morell and Chai-anan, *Political Conflict*, 247.

34. *Sadet Saharat '80* [The Royal Visit to the U.S., 1980] (Bangkok, 1980), 54.

35. Norman Peagam in *Far Eastern Economic Review,* July 9, 1976.

36. Tambiah, *Buddhist Saints,* 158.

37. Morell and Chai-anan, *Political Conflict,* 271.

38. Ibid., 273.

39. William Shawcross, *New York Review of Books,* December 9, 1976, 59–62.

40. As McCargo points out, this lineup of forces without army troops appeared to exonerate the army and the Supreme Command while putting the blame on the police. However, he notes, the BPP were operationally controlled by the Supreme Command, which also had numerous intelligence and provocateur teams active at the scenes of violence. Duncan McCargo, *Chamlong Srimuang and the New Thai Politics* (London: Hurst, 1997), 35–38.

41. Bowie, *Rituals,* 329n.24; Benedict Anderson, "Withdrawal Symptoms," *Bulletin of Concerned Asian Scholars* 9, no. 3 (1977): 30n.100.

42. Puey Ungphakorn, "Violence and the Military Coup in Thailand," *Bulletin of Concerned Asian Scholars* 9, no. 3 (1977): 12.

43. Marks, *Making Revolution,* 147.

13 What Went Wrong: Cosmic Panic, Business Failure, Midcareer Crisis

1. Anderson, "Withdrawal Symptoms," 30.

2. Roger Kershaw, "A Little Question of Dynastic Survival: King Bhumibol Adulyadej of Thailand," *Contemporary Review* 234, no. 5 (1979): 256.

3. Bhumibol, speech of June 27, 1973, in *Royal Addresses and Speeches, December 1972–November 1973* (Bangkok: Royal Secretariat, 1974), 199.

4. Bhumibol, speech of May 11, 1983, in *Royal Remarks on Various Occasions* (Bangkok: Amarin Printing, 1997).

5. Denis Gray, "Thailand's Working Royals," *Sawasdee,* January 1987.

6. See United Nations Environment Program, *Sustainable Development of Natural Resources* (United Nations Environment Program, 1988), especially pages 96–97: "Unfortunately, [the strategy to drain the swamps] has not proved successful with the phru. Drainage has caused the upper layer of peat soil to dry out substantially in the dry season, which in turn has made it more susceptible to fire damage. This . . . has resulted in a high rate of compaction of the soil. . . . At the same time, in the dry season the low water table has had the effect of exposing to the atmosphere the pyrite pan which lies beneath the muck-peat soil and which when exposed to oxidation is transformed to a form of ferrous sulphate and releases a strong sulphuric acid . . . which in turn brings about an increase in the acidity of the soil and the flood water which drains from the phru during the rainy season, exacerbating the existing flood problem in the bordering rice lands. . . . the compaction of the peat layers has also had the effect of increasing flood levels in the area adjacent to the phru rendering it impossible to grow rice in the

wet season. Moreover . . . drainage has meant that the phru forest has become more susceptible to fire damage.

"The process of draining the phru in Narathiwat province has thus had little success in its objective of reducing flooding in the immediately adjoining areas. Nor has the second objective [of] the creation of new lands for settlement . . . been any more successful." The report then exculpates the king by stating that it was not in his original plans to make the drained land available for settlement. However, statements at the time of launching the Bachoh drainage project suggest this was, along with flood prevention, a primary objective.

7. Originally called Firestone Tyre and Rubber (Thailand), it later became Siam Tyre and Rubber, a unit of the Siam Cement Group.
8. Sukhumbhand's paternal grandmother, the second wife of Prince Paripatra, also was a commoner.
9. *Dichan*, August 15, 1986, 227, and October 15, 1987, 255.
10. The choice of Australia came about apparently because of his middling school performance. Both West Point in the United States and Britain's Sandhurst heavily emphasized academics, and West Point was especially demanding in engineering. That left Duntroon.
11. She eventually graduated with a bachelor of science degree in biochemistry in 1973.
12. Confidential interview with an American academic, 1994.
13. Confidential interview with a former Australian army officer and Duntroon graduate, 1998.
14. *Economist*, May 17, 1975.
15. According to police general Vasit Dejkunchorn, *Nation*, April 28, 1982.
16. See, for instance, his speech to provincial governors on November 17, 1976, in Bhumibol, *Royal Addresses and Speeches* (1976).
17. Gray, *The Soteriological State*, 718.
18. Yanasangworn (Nanasamvara), *Ten Thousand Days on the Throne* (Bangkok: Thai Watana Panich, 1977).
19. Gray, *The Soteriological State*, 685.
20. Anderson, "Withdrawal Symptoms," 23.
21. Gray, *The Soteriological State*, 810–11.
22. Keyes, *Thailand: Buddhist Kingdom*, 210.

14 Who's the Enemy?

1. *The Chakri Dynasty and Thai Politics, 1782–1982*, 62, 64.
2. Tanin Kraivixien, *Phramahakasat Thai Nai Rabob Phrachatipatai* [The Thai Monarchy in the Democratic System] (Bangkok: Ministry of Education, 1977); analyzed in Roger Kershaw, "Modernizing the Thai Monarchy? Theory and Practice of Two Intellectuals Turned Prime Minister," from the Thai-European Seminar on Social Change in Contemporary Thailand, May 28–30, 1980, University of Amsterdam.
3. *Bangkok Post*, November 19, 1976.
4. *Annual Reports of the Royal Thai Police Department*, 1950–79.
5. *Far Eastern Economic Review*, June 3, 1977.

6. Andrew Turton, Jonathan Fast, and Malcolm Caldwell, eds. *Thailand: Roots of Conflict* (Nottingham: Spokesman, 1978), 91.

7. John L. S. Girling, *Thailand: Society and Politics* (Ithaca, N.Y.: Cornell University Press, 1981), 215.

8. Information on the history and political manipulation of the Democracy and Rama VII monuments comes from Thongchai Winichakul, "Thai Democracy in Public Memory: Monuments and Their Narratives," presented at the Seventh International Conference on Thai Studies, Amsterdam, July 1999.

9. Batson, *The End*, 252.

10. Communist Party of Thailand broadcast quotes are from Marks, *Making Revolution*, 176–78.

11. Thomas Marks, "The Thai Monarchy Under Siege," *Asia Quarterly* 2 (1978): 135.

12. *Far Eastern Economic Review*, November 4, 1977.

13. Ibid.

14. Roger Kershaw, "Three Kings of Orient: The Changing Face of Monarchy in Southeast Asia," *Contemporary Review*, May 1979, 259–60.

15. Michael Connors extensively covers this recrafting of national ideology in *Democracy and National Identity in Thailand* (London: Routledge, 2003).

16. Gray, *The Soteriological State*, 525.

17. With a heavy Asian presence and a base in Shanghai, Eisenberg's group mainly traded in farm and heavy equipment, entire plants, chemicals, and arms-related equipment, as well as consumer goods.

18. Without ignoring the original context and meanings, interview segments have been altered in sequence in order to develop certain themes. This is something the original makers of the documentary clearly did as well.

19. *National Geographic*, October 1982.

15 In the King's Image: The Perfect General Prem

1. Serm's politics were regarded as the principal reason for the palace's preference for Prem. But rumors had it that it was also his family blood and history: the Na Nakhon family had descended from King Taksin, who had been killed by Rama I. Allegedly, the palace didn't trust that Serm might want to avenge history.

2. The planned trip accompanying the royals to the United States showed Prem at his most obsequious. Critics asked publicly how the commander of the army, the most important military post, could spend three months abroad when Vietnamese troops sat threateningly just across the Thai border inside Cambodia.

3. Confidential interview, Bangkok, 1997.

4. *Bangkok Post*, December 2, 1983.

5. *Far Eastern Economic Review*, December 12, 1980.

6. Bhumibol, *The Royal Speeches and Addresses of His Majesty King Bhumibol of Thailand. The Royal Blue Book Part II*, 1987, 62–63.

7. Wright, *Balancing Act*, 264.

8. Supamit Pitipat, *The Evolution of the Thai Monarchy in the Constitutional Period, 1932–Present* (M.A. thesis, American University, Washington, D.C., 1990), 112.

9. Wright, *Balancing Act,* 265.

10. United Press International, April 2, 1981, reproduced in *The King of Thailand in World Focus,* 94.

11. *Time,* April 13, 1981.

12. *Far Eastern Economic Review,* February 17, 1983.

13. *Far Eastern Economic Review,* June 2, 1983.

14. *Bangkok Post,* December 5, 1983.

15. Wright, *Balancing Act,* 186.

16. See Jackson, *Buddhism,* 109.

17. "Concensus" (understood to be Tongnoi Tongyai), "Entering the Thai Heart," *Bangkok Post,* August 22, 1983.

18. *Asiaweek,* April 23, 1982.

19. *National Geographic,* October 1982.

20. *Bangkok World,* July 31, 1982.

21. See, for instance, Sumet Tantivejakul in *Nation,* July 25, 1993.

22. Bhumibol, "Royal Address, February 26, 1981" (Bangkok: Amarin Printing, 1987).

23. *Nation,* July 25, 1993.

24. See Streckfuss, "Kings in the Age of Nations."

25. *Asian Wall Street Journal,* December 23, 1981.

26. *Nation,* April 28, 1982.

27. See Connors, *Democracy and National Identity,* for an extended discussion of this topic, especially 129–90.

28. Pasuk and Baker, *Thailand,* 316.

29. Connors, *Democracy and National Identity,* 145.

30. These articles were subsequently reprinted as a booklet, *Entering the Thai Heart* (Bangkok: Bangkok Post, 1983). Tongnoi's authorship was confirmed when he adapted the articles into a formal paper published as "The Role of the Monarch in Modern Thailand," in *Development, Modernization, and Tradition in Southeast Asia: Lessons from Thailand,* ed. Pinit Ratanakul and U Kyaw Than (Bangkok: Mahidol University, 1990).

31. *Leaders,* April–June 1982.

32. *Asian Wall Street Journal,* December 23, 1981.

33. Even so, they made clear that they didn't regret the action. Weeks later a palace official toured Australia and in closed meetings with academics insisted fervently that Sulak and the others had to be arrested because they posed a great danger to society. "We had to teach him a lesson" was the message, recalled political scientist Kevin Hewison, one of the organizers of the petition.

34. *The Chakri Dynasty and Thai Politics, 1782–1982.*

16 Family Headaches

1. *Parade,* October 16, 1977.

2. *Bangkok Post,* December 2, 1983.

3. Sirikit was awarded the Ceres Medal from the UN Food and Agriculture Organization in 1979; an honorary doctorate from Tufts University's Fletcher School of Law and

Diplomacy in 1980; the Asia Society's Humanitarian Awards, also in 1980; and the Distinguished Service Award from Save the Children in 1981.

4. Associated Press, May 22, 1979, reproduced in *The King of Thailand in World Focus*, 118–19.

5. *Bangkok Post,* December 2, 1983.

6. Confidential interview with a Thai academic, 1996.

7. This group was evidently organized in the wake of the 1981 coup attempt as a special unit to defend the throne.

8. Confidential interview with a foreign military attaché, 1994.

9. *Sadet Saharat '80* [The Royal Visit to the U.S., 1980] (Bangkok: 1980).

10. Sucharinee had several aliases. Her original name was Yuwathida Pholprasert. She also was called Yuwathida Surasawasdee, and later, Sucharinee Vivatcharavong. When her relationship with the prince became more open, she was permitted the modern Chakri pedigree name Sucharinee Mahidol Na Ayutthaya. She also was known by the nickname Mom Ben, "Mom" suggesting her royal status, Ben, some said, for a penchant for Mercedes-Benz autos.

11. There have always been rumors that the prince was not the boy's father, but he always treated Chudhavajra as his own.

12. Confidential interview with a U.S. official who was at Fort Bragg at the time.

13. *Far Eastern Economic Review,* December 18, 1981.

14. *Los Angeles Times,* February 5, 1982.

15. Arthit's challenge to replace Prem while he was ill was met with a well-timed statement by the U.S. ambassador that Washington would look very critically at any such act.

16. *Nation,* December 5, 1984.

17. *Nation,* January 27, 1987.

18. Wright, *Balancing Act,* 300.

19. *Bangkok Post,* May 7, 1984.

20. In or around 1983, Ubolrat's husband, Peter Jensen, joined with California financier Richard Silberman to invest in Yuba Natural Resources, which intended to mine gold out of tailings on California's Yuba River. The financing from Siam Commercial Bank to Jensen was to be invested in the very speculative operation. The mining produced no gold, and apparently the loan went into default within two or three years. By the end of the decade the company was sold to another firm, having produced no gold. See *San Diego Reader,* May 20, 1999; R. Behar, "Fear and Loding on the Yuba River," *Forbes,* October 7, 1985.

21. Broadcast on Thai Channel 3 on August 12, 1986. But a transcript was published earlier, in *Nation,* August 8, 1986.

22. *Bangkok Post,* August 19, 1986.

23. *Far Eastern Economic Review,* August 7, 1986.

24. *Dichan,* August 15, 1986, 227. Some parts of the interview have been transposed here, to make more sense from the wandering nature of the original.

25. *Far Eastern Economic Review,* December 10, 1987.

26. Interview by a delegation of the Foreign Correspondents' Club of Thailand, June 10, 1987, from the unpublished transcript.

27. *Dichan,* October 15, 1987, 255. Parts of the interview have been transposed.

28. Galyani, *Chao Nai,* 1996.

29. Coordinating Committee for Royal Development Projects, *His Majesty King Bhumibol Adulyadej and His Development Work* (Bangkok: Bangkok Printing, 1987), 25.

30. Further bolstering the Mahidol family aura, just a few months later Princess Sirindhorn was named the Supreme Patroness of Thai Cultural Heritage.

31. Tongnoi (as "Concensus"), *Entering the Thai Heart*.

32. Speech to the Foreign Correspondents Club of Thailand, June 22, 1988, reprinted in "Rachamangklapisek, The Longest Reign Celebrations," supplement in *Nation*, n.d. (July 1988).

33. Crossette, "King Bhumibol's Reign."

34. *Bangkok Post*, August 16, 1999; *Far Eastern Economic Review*, March 26, 1987.

35. *Far Eastern Economic Review*, July 23, 1987.

36. *Far Eastern Economic Review*, February 19, 1987.

37. This was even taught as political philosophy at Chulachomklao Military Academy. The military popularized its view through media slogans like "Only the army has never abandoned the people and is sincere towards the people," and "Only the army promises hope for the people." See *Far Eastern Economic Review*, November 28, 1985.

38. *Far Eastern Economic Review*, August 13, 1987.

39. *Far Eastern Economic Review*, June 4, 1987.

40. Her name was later changed to Siriwanwaree Mahidol.

41. Thailand proved to be the only buyer ever of Stingray tanks, which performed worse than critics anticipated.

42. "Cracks in the Kingdom," no author, n.d., 1988, 4.

43. *Far Eastern Economic Review*, December 24, 1987.

44. *Far Eastern Economic Review*, January 21, 1988.

45. Ibid.

46. In an investigation and trial lasting into 1994—evidence that the court system wasn't too determined to pursue the case—most of the accused were let off for lack of evidence. A handful, though, received uncommonly stiff jail terms, up to ten years, because they had damaged the monarchy.

47. *Far Eastern Economic Review*, February 4, 1988.

48. *Far Eastern Economic Review*, June 16, 1988.

49. Chalongphob Sussangkarn, *Income Distribution and Long Term Development: A Summary* (Bangkok: Thailand Development Research Institute, 1989).

50. *Policy on Agricultural Land Reform in Thailand* (Bangkok: Thailand Development Research Institute, 1990), 16–18.

17 *Another Coup for the Throne*

1. For numerous reasons, including financial problems and bureaucratic interference, the Hopewell project was eventually canceled.

2. Confidential interview with a British embassy official, 1995.

3. See *Nation*, December 15, 1990.

4. Author's interview with Chirayut, September 11, 1992.

5. *Nation*, July 4, 1992.

6. *Bangkok Post*, December 5, 1989; *Nation*, December 5, 1989.

7. Confidential interview.

8. In the late 1980s, Chavalit made some lengthy, perplexing statements about the Thai political system, advocating a "revolution by the people," and suggesting he favored a government with a "presidium" (using the English word) and a "president." To some, the two terms evoked, respectively, communism (Chavalit had an adviser who was a former CPT leader), and a republic. Such statements were said to raise strong concerns in the palace.

9. From reports in *Nation, Bangkok Post,* and Associated Press, all December 5, 1989.

10. Kulick and Wilson, *Thailand's Turn,* xxii.

11. If anything, Chatichai's was a dictatorship by the cabinet, as he and his ministers increasingly bypassed the parliament in decision making. But afterward, "parliamentary dictatorship" became a widely brandished epithet against elected politicians, especially among supporters of a Prem-style regime.

12. One of the leaders of the corruption investigation told me in a confidential interview that the evidence was clear and substantial, while acknowledging that the investigation and the choice of targets were entirely driven by politics.

13. See *Far Eastern Economic Review,* October 31, 1991.

14. *Nation,* September 17, 1991.

15. One view is that this was done actually to lessen the prince's independent power. In 1978 he was assigned to the palace guard, the King's Own Bodyguard Regiment, and in 1984 promoted to commanding officer. In that position he was still under the regional army commander. In 1988, General Chavalit made a change to the regiment's command structure to allow the prince to be promoted to general and remain directly in charge of the regiment. This effectively gave the prince his own independent command, which, one foreign military expert observed, was potentially dangerous, given the prince's personality. When the NPKC promoted the prince in January 1992 to Commanding General of the Royalty Security Command, he came directly under the Supreme Commander, who by then was General Suchinda.

16. *Bangkok Post,* February 1, 1992.

17. My translation, based on the text in "Royal Speech Given to the Audience of Well-Wishers on the Occasion of the Royal Birthday Anniversary Wednesday, 4 December 1991" (Bangkok: Amarin Printing, 1992).

18. This sentence was excised from the palace's official version of the speech.

18 May 1992: October 1976 Redux

1. *Bangkok Post,* April 4, 1992.

2. Cited in *Far Eastern Economic Review,* April 2, 1992.

3. *Far Eastern Economic Review,* June 19, 1986; *Bangkok Post,* April 17, 1992.

4. Chamlong's move also threatened the unity of the opposition. He hadn't coordinated his move with the CPD leaders or other opposition political parties, and they weren't fully trustful of his motives, which some suspected as selfish. See McCargo, *Chamlong Srimuang,* 250–53.

5. *Nation,* May 6, 1992.

6. Prawase was the very first recipient of the king's Ananda Mahidol scholarship, and had treated Bhumibol on occasion as a doctor.

7. *Bangkok Post,* May 7, 1992.

8. See *Bangkok Post* and *Nation* of May 30–31, 2000, and June 26–July 1, 2000, for details of the Pichit Kullavanich report on May 1992. See also *Far Eastern Economic Review,* various issues, April–June 1992.

9. See *Bangkok Post,* May 9, 1992.

10. The description of the events of this period come from my own on-the-scene observations, as well as those of many other journalists and observers present, media reports, and later comprehensive reports and reviews by various organizations.

11. Confidential interview with a Confederation for Democracy leader, 1995.

12. *Bangkok Post,* May 20, 1992.

13. Interview with the author, May 20, 1992.

14. Bhumibol, *Royal Remarks,* 1997.

15. Although Anand wasn't elected, his appointment was legal because the king hadn't promulgated the constitutional amendments, which he did only several days later.

16. *Far Eastern Economic Review,* July 16, 1992.

17. *Bangkok Post,* May 24, 1992.

18. For a discussion of a sovereign's rarely used powers and issues surrounding a royal order to dissolve parliament, see Bogdanor, *The Monarchy.*

19. *Far Eastern Economic Review,* June 25, 1992.

20. Confidential interview with an adviser to the prince, 1992.

21. *Bangkok Post,* August 31, 1992.

22. *Far Eastern Economic Review,* June 25, 1992.

23. *Nation,* October 30, 1992.

24. Bhumibol, *Royal Speech, December 4, 1992* (Bangkok: Krungthep Printing, n.d.).

25. From several confidential interviews.

19 *Sanctifying Royalty and Stonewalling Democracy in the 1990s*

1. *Nation,* November 11, 1992.

2. Confidential interview with a Thai environmentalist, 1995.

3. *Bangkok Post,* September 5, 1993.

4. In fact, the projects had been stalled mainly by the politicians of three governments who, with the support of government researchers, argued the projects weren't cost-effective.

5. *Nation,* December 5, 1993.

6. This quote from Pichai Chuensuksawadi, ed., *Thailand's Guiding Light* (Bangkok: Post Publishing, 1996), 108.

7. *Nation,* December 9, 1993.

8. *Nation,* February 24, 1994.

9. *Nation,* October 14, 1993.

10. See *Nation, Bangkok Post, Matichon,* and *Thai Rath,* August 18–22, 1995.

11. *Nation,* August 23, 1995.

12. *Matichon,* August 27, 1995.

13. *Far Eastern Economic Review,* October 26, 1995.

14. It was clear that the vote was a pointed rebuff to Chuan by the military. Many if not most of the military senators never attended parliamentary proceedings, maintaining their status by simply signing in when necessary and then leaving. On the day of the

vote, March 30, and a subsequent vote to reject the other Chuan amendments on April 30, they attended en masse and remained throughout the session.

15. *Bangkok Post,* February 3, 1994, and *Nation,* May 1, 1994.

16. *Nation,* May 3, 1994.

17. *Nation,* August 30, 1993, and *Bangkok Post,* September 5, 1993.

18. *Washington Post,* May 29, 1994.

19. *Bangkok Post,* June 8, June 30, July 1, July 2, 1994, and *Nation,* July 1, 1994.

20. *Bangkok Post,* July 2, 1994.

21. See for instance Pasuk Phongpaichit and Sungsidh Piriyarangsan, *Corruption and Democracy in Thailand* (Bangkok: Chulalongkorn University, 1994), and Pasuk Phong-paichit and Sungsidh Piriyarangsan, *Guns, Girls, Gambling, Ganja: Thailand's Illegal Economy and Public Policy* (Bangkok: Silkworm, 1999). In April 1996, one of Bhumibol's favorite officials was assassinated, Saengchai Sunthornwat, head of the government office that supervised mass media.

22. See *Bangkok Post,* April 14, 1994; *Nation,* September 24, 1995.

23. The initials CP stand for Charoen Pokphand; they are used to avoid potential confusion with Charoen Siriwatanapakdi.

24. According to confidential sources, members of the royal family are shareholders or beneficiaries in the tightly held Boonrawd Company, producer of Singha. Members of the Bhirombhakdi family have also served as aides and advisers to the king and queen and have married members of the royal family.

25. The Geelong Doi Tung venture drew private criticism. Formerly settled by hill tribes, the land used was fertile, flat lowland, a rare commodity in northern Thailand where hundreds of thousands of peasants were landless.

26. In several incidences, though, *Siam Post* was alone in reporting controversial news regarding the royal family, especially the crown prince.

27. After the operation, the palace provided details of the illness. But the public was never told whether the king's life was much in danger or not. Rumors among the Bangkok elite suggested it was more serious than the palace allowed, but at the same time, there was no information released on whether the king had designated a regent or a successor before undergoing surgery, and if so who was designated.

28. *Nation,* July 20, 1995; *Bangkok Post,* July 20, 1995.

29. *Bangkok Post,* July 20, 1995.

30. *Bangkok Post,* March 11, 1996.

31. Bhumibol, speech of December 4, 1995, http://www.kanchanapisek.or.th/speeches/1995/.

32. *Nation,* March 2, 1996.

33. *Nation,* March 16, 1996.

34. See *Bangkok Post,* July 9, 1996; *Nation,* July 30, 1996.

35. *Nation,* November 15 and November 22, 1996.

36. *Bangkok Post,* May 16, 1996; *Nation,* June 10, 1996.

37. *Nation,* April 28, 1996.

38. Hewison, ed., *Political Change,* 57.

39. *Nation,* June 26, 1994, and Siam Society brochures, n.d.

40. Pichai, ed., *Thailand's Guiding Light.*

41. *Nation*, December 14, 1993.

42. The interview with Malaysia's *New Straits Times* was reproduced in the *Bangkok Post*, March 12, 1995. Some of the comments have been transposed from the original sequence.

43. Anand is apparently referring to the first National Five-Year Development Plan of 1961, actually crafted under the guidance of World Bank and U.S. advisers, before the king made his first foreign state visit.

44. Anand sometimes went too far. Quoted in the *Nation*, June 9, 1996, Anand said: "His majesty is the longest-practicing monarch, the longest-practicing politician. Governments come and go, army chiefs come and go." Calling King Bhumibol a politician probably took the palace aback, since they had spent two generations condemning politicians as selfish and corrupt.

45. Several historians have discredited author Stevenson's history as potted and hyperbolic, and full of errors. See, for instance, Hugh Trevor-Roper's piece in the *Sunday Telegraph*, February 19, 1989.

46. William Stevenson, *A Man Called Intrepid* (New York: Harcourt Brace Jovanovich, 1976), 28.

47. Ibid., 43.

48. *Bangkok Post*, June 9, 1996.

49. Bhumibol, speech of December 4, 1995, http://www.kanchanapisek.or.th/speeches/1995.

50. *Business Day*, March 4–5, 1995.

51. Confidential interview with a Thai commercial bank official, 1996. Banks were not the only underwriters or distribution network for the book, but they became the main ones outside the palace itself.

20 *Another Family Annus Horribilis*

1. *Bangkok Post*, July 27, 1991.

2. *Bangkok Post*, July 21, 1992; *Nation*, July 21, 1992.

3. *Patjuban karma*, or karma of the present.

4. See *Thai Rath, Matichon, Bangkok Post*, and *Nation*, all December 31, 1992; *Nation*, January 5, 1993; and *Far Eastern Economic Review*, January 14, 1993.

5. Confidential interview with a senior foreign military official posted to Thailand, 1994.

6. Nonthaburi Family Court, Documents of Case #79/2536, January 27, 1993.

7. *Nation*, August 1, 1994; *Bangkok Post*, July 30, 1994; *Matichon Weekly*, August 5, 1994.

8. *Nation*, January 3, 1995.

9. Royal News, various channels, November 10–11, 1995; *Nation*, November 11, 1995; *Bangkok Post*, November 13, 1995, and January 19, 1996.

10. There is no evidence in the public domain to support this story, but it is believed by some Thais in high circles.

11. Confidential interview with an eyewitness, 1996.

12. These were *Bangkok Post* and its sister *Siam Post*.

13. Confidential interview; the source was given this explanation by the king's personal private secretary, M.L. Birabongse Kasemsri.

14. See *Bangkok Post*, February 4, 1994, and January 18, 1995.

21 *The Economic Crash and Bhumibol's New Theory*

1. See *Bangkok Post,* September 13 and September 28, 1996.

2. Confidential interview.

3. *Nation,* December 10, 1996. Chang Noi is a pseudonym for academics Pasuk Phong-paichit and Chris Baker.

4. *Bangkok Post* supplement, August 1, 1996.

5. Connors, *Democracy and National Identity,* 154–76.

6. *Nation,* January 19, 1997.

7. Typically, the problems at SCB fed on themselves. The bank would finance private com-panies developing Crown Property Bureau land into office towers or luxury condomini-ums, in a joint venture with the bureau. The developer would use a contractor also financed by Siam Commercial Bank (sometimes, in the case of builder Christiani Nielsen Thailand, one owned by SCB and the CPB), buying materials from the SCB-financed Siam Cement group, and selling to customers whose mortgages were held by Siam Commercial Bank or its subsidiaries. When the crash came, all flows of money around an unfinished project halted, at each stage causing a new default. The bank was left with nothing to grab. It was a recipe for disaster repeated by most Thai banks, but Siam Commercial appeared to have gone farther than others.

8. *Far Eastern Economic Review,* September 4, 1997; *Nation,* August 26, 1997.

9. *Nation,* September 4, 1997.

10. *Nation,* October 7, 1997, and *Bangkok Post,* October 11, 1997.

11. These were the recently appointed deputy prime minister Virabongsa and finance min-ister Tanong Bidaya, and central bank governor Chaiyawat Wibulsawat. Chaiyawat, it would later be revealed, was most responsible for the amazing loss of nearly the entirety of the country's $40 billion in reserves through foreign exchange market intervention.

12. *Bangkok Post,* October 11, 1997.

13. Text from http://www.kanchanapisek.or.th/speeches/. In cited passages, I have made slight adjustments of awkward phrasing of the translation.

14. *Bangkok Post,* November 19, 1998; *Nation,* November 19, 1998.

15. In 1997, *Forbes* magazine estimated the king's fortune at $1.8 billion. *Forbes,* July 28, 1997, 168.

16. *Nation,* April 2, 1999.

17. The king's awareness of these issues was clear. Chirayut later said that the king must sign off on even the smallest sale of royal property. See *Corporate Thailand,* December 2003.

18. By the end of 1997 the king had 136 honorary degrees, compared with the 131 of Father Theodore Hesburgh, president of Notre Dame University. *Bangkok Post,* December 3, 1997; Reuters, December 3, 1997; *Nation,* October 17, 1999.

19. From a Siam Society recording of a lecture by M.R. Butrie Viravaidhya at the Siam Society, Bangkok, February 11, 1999.

20. *Kinnaree,* December 1999.

21. *Business Week* (international edition), March 26, 1998.

22. *Bangkok Post,* April 12 and October 6, 2000; *Nation,* October 6 and October 9, 2000.

23. *Corporate Thailand,* December 2003.

24. *Nation,* May 4 and May 9, 2000.

25. Also involved, according to palace gossip, was Mohamed al-Fayed, owner of London's

Harrods department store and father of Dodi, who died with Princess Diana in a car wreck. Thaksin had at least once taken al-Fayed to meet the prince, and Harrods had participated in furnishing the Rama VII palace.

26. Thaksin's own businesses, of course, depended heavily on foreign equipment, services, media content, and financing.

22 Going into Seclusion: Can the Monarchy Survive Bhumibol?

1. In September 2000, the king appeared on television with an audience of Bangkok planners, giving them lengthy instructions on managing Bangkok traffic. When floods hit the southern city of Haadyai a few weeks later, he made another long, televised lecture to an audience of relief workers. Televised royal news, various channels, November 28, 2000.

2. Bhumibol Adulyadej, *The Story of Tongdaeng* (Bangkok: Amarin Printing, 2002).

3. Benedict Anderson, "Studies of the Thai State: The State of Thai Studies," in *The Study of Thailand*, ed. Eliezer B. Ayal (Athens, Ohio: Ohio University, 1978), 209.

4. Connors, *Democracy and National Identity*, 128.

5. Keyes, *Thailand: Buddhist Kingdom*, 203.

6. Kulick and Wilson, *Thailand's Turn*, xvi.

7. Bhumibol, *The Royal Blue Book Part II* (Bangkok: Working Committee of the Royal Initiation Projects, 1987), 96.

8. Some observers privately argued that this was actually an attempt by the king to forestall possible public disturbances or broader upheaval that might have erupted out of the crash.

9. Gray, *The Soteriological State*, 107.

10. In the 1990s, the king's global dhammaraja identity was revealed when the ritual performance of the royal kathin was expanded to China, Cambodia, Laos, Burma, and Sri Lanka; and when the Indian and Chinese governments sent relics of the original Buddha to Thailand to honor him.

11. Butrie, Siam Society lecture, February 11, 1999.

12. Stevenson's one main innovation was to interject his own unique theory of Ananda's murder, pinning it on Japanese "master spy" Tsuji Masanobu, a notorious wartime commander in Southeast Asia. Most other historians and Tsuji experts repudiate Stevenson's theory.

13. Stevenson told a foreign reporter that he understood the king liked the book, and had checked part of the manuscript for accuracy, but that schemers around him opposed it. "The king had made it clear from the beginning that he did not want the book published inside Thailand," he said. *International Herald Tribune*, August 27, 1999.

14. Keyes, *Thailand: Buddhist Kingdom*, 207.

15. Bhumibol called for an investigation into the murders, but only several months after the campaign had receded. Human rights groups had called attention to it within two weeks of the first killings. Moreover, Bhumibol accepted without criticism Thaksin's announcement that the anti-drug campaign was carried out in the king's name to honor him.

16. Kulick and Wilson, *Thailand's Turn*, xxi.

17. After the prince's expulsion of Sucharinee in 1996, a palace official explained that the

two were never formally married, under civil law, so that a divorce was not necessary. At the same time, the official suggested that the prince remained married to first wife Somsawali, because their divorce in a civil court was not matched by the king's sanction. At least publicly, then, Somsawali's status remained unclear as the prince married in the palace in 2001.

18. Bagehot, *The English Constitution*, 119.

19. Another version, cited in Morell and Chai-anan, *Political Conflict*, 309, has a ten-king dynasty as predicted by Rama I. However, the prophecy most widely understood is of nine kings. Even so, Morell and Chai-anan conclude similarly that the Tenth Reign could "perhaps" result in a republic, ending the dynasty.

20. Batson, *The End*, 264n.2.

21. See Pasuk Phongpaichit and Chris Baker, *Thaksin: The Business of Politics in Thailand* (Chiangmai: Silkworm, 2005).

22. See Duncan McCargo, "Network Monarchy and Legitimacy Crises in Thailand," *Pacific Review* 18, no. 4 (December 2005). Also see articles regarding Thaksin's military promotions and the palace's response, *Nation*, August 22, August 31, and September 9, 2005.

23. The first son of Sucharinee, though, is rumored to have had a DNA test that found the prince is not his father. That could put the second son, Vajaresra, born in 1981, high in the succession line.

24. Confidential interviews with a senior politician and a minor royal family member.

25. *Far Eastern Economic Review*, April 29, 1993.

26. Bogdanor, *The Monarchy*, 13, 27.

27. Kulick and Wilson, *Thailand's Turn*, xxiii.

28. Documents detailing Philip Morris's support for the Chulabhorn Research Institute, http://www.pmdocs.com.

Index ∾